KU-190-749

INSIDE FLASH MX

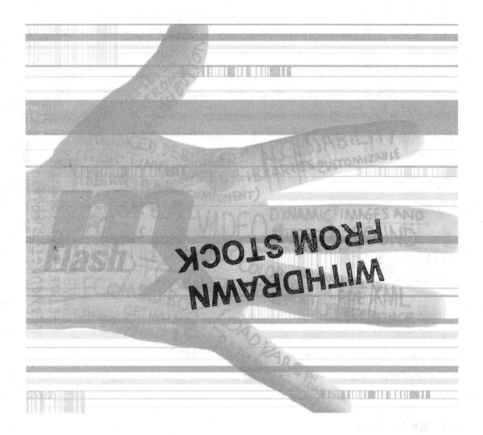

WITHDRAWN FROM STOCK

BY
Jody Keating
Fig Leaf Software

New Riders

201 West 103rd Street, Indianapolis, Indiana 46290

Inside Flash MX

Copyright © 2002 by New Riders Publishing

All rights reserved. No part of this book shall be reproduced, stored in a retrieval system, or transmitted by any means—electronic, mechanical, photocopying, recording, or otherwise—without written permission from the publisher. No patent liability is assumed with respect to the use of the information contained herein. Although every precaution has been taken in the preparation of this book, the publisher and author(s) assume no responsibility for errors or omissions. Neither is any liability assumed for damages resulting from the use of the information contained herein.

International Standard Book Number: 0-7357-1254-9

Library of Congress Catalog Card Number: 2001098239

Printed in the United States of America

First Printing: June 2002

06 05 04 03 02   7 6 5 4 3 2 1

Colaiste
Mhuire Gan Smal
Luimneach
Class No. 006.78
Suffix KEA
Acc. No. 01709040
Ord. No. M/01002186

Interpretation of the printing code: The rightmost double-digit number is the year of the book's printing; the rightmost single-digit number is the number of the book's printing. For example, the printing code 02-1 shows that the first printing of the book occurred in 2002.

Trademarks

All terms mentioned in this book that are known to be trademarks or service marks have been appropriately capitalized. New Riders Publishing cannot attest to the accuracy of this information. Use of a term in this book should not be regarded as affecting the validity of any trademark or service mark. Flash MX is a trademark of Macromedia Corporation.

Warning and Disclaimer

Every effort has been made to make this book as complete and as accurate as possible, but no warranty or fitness is implied. The information provided is on an "as is" basis. The authors and the publisher shall have neither liability nor responsibility to any person or entity with respect to any loss or damages arising from the information contained in this book or from the use of the CD or programs accompanying it.

Publisher
David Dwyer

Associate Publisher
Stephanie Wall

Executive Editor
Steve Weiss

Managing Editor
Sarah Kearns

Acquisitions Editor
Deborah Hittel-Shoaf

Development Editor
Linda Laflamme

Project Editor
Jake McFarland

Copy Editors
Jill Batistick
Krista Hansing

Product Marketing Manager
Kathy Malmloff

Publicity Manager
Susan Nixon

Technical Editors
Christian Buchholz
Sally Cruikshank
John Davey
Larry Drolet

Cover Designer
Aren Howell

Compositor
Amy Parker

Proofreader
Jessica McCarty

Indexer
Angie Bess

Media Developer
Jay Payne

Contents at a Glance

Table of Contents

20 Server-Side Communication   567

About the Authors

About Fig Leaf Software

Fig Leaf's Creative Media Department has designed and developed engaging web-based media for some of the most recognized companies and organizations in the country. Fig Leaf offers creative services from a talented team of award winning graphic artists, programmers, writers, and instructional technologists who consistently build next-generation solutions for our clients. Using a blend of creative talent, experience and technical know-how, we are able to take our client's web media to a new level that balances form, flow and function.

Members of the Creative Media team speak regularly at tradeshows, user groups, and design conferences to inform others about the tools, technologies, and processes that they successfully employ.

Fig Leaf Contributors

Jody Keating is the Assistant Director of Interactive Media at Fig Leaf, where she makes the Interactive Media programmers and designers play nice together. Jody is a Macromedia Certified Professional (MCP) and has taught Macromedia Authorized classes for Flash, Generator, UltraDev, Dreamweaver, Fireworks, and CourseBuilder. In addition to her duties at Fig Leaf, Jody is the Program Coordinator for the Washington Area Macromedia Organization (WAMMO). Jody is also a Cold Fusion developer and is having way too much fun playing with integrating Flash and ColdFusion. She has an undergraduate degree in Anthropology from the George Washington University and has done graduate work in Geobiology. When Jody's not writing or managing, she's racing sailboats, kayaking, or rowing on the Chesapeake Bay.

Tom Pizer is a partner and the Vice President of Creative Media for Fig Leaf Software. He is responsible for Fig Leaf's creative vision and the success of the client web sites and interactives that Fig Leaf creates. During his career, he has written course material on computer-based design and collaborated on industry-related books. His work has been featured in leading industry magazines and been written up in online trade sites. Tom is the current president of the Washington, DC area Macromedia User's Group (WAMMO). During his tenure as president, he has forged strong ties with Macromedia and their Product Directors, programmers, sales staff, and training managers for the full suite of Macromedia's web tools.

When **Branden Hall** is not working with computers (rarely), he enjoys the great outdoors: camping, hiking, biking, and climbing. As an Eagle Scout, these playtime pursuits come as naturally to him as programming, which is what Branden is doing much of the rest of the time. Branden is known for developing cutting edge ActionScript techniques. At Fig Leaf Software, he is the Senior Interactive Developer and a Macromedia Instructor. His work at Fig Leaf, combined with Branden's prominence on his Flash ActionScript mailing list, FlashCoders, and his participation in many other lists, conferences, and user groups have spawned speculation that Branden Hall cannot possibly be just one man. Amusing though the thought of a host of Branden clones running around may be, his wife Patricia Hall guarantees us all that there is, indeed, only one.

Tracey Sheeley is the Assistant Director of Creative Services at Fig Leaf, and is one of the original "Figs". While creating many online presences for clients, she has eagerly watched Flash evolve into the indispensable program it is today. Tracey has a BA in Studio Art earned at the University of Maryland. Spanning three states throughout her life, she grew up in Maryland, works in Washington, DC, and now lives in Virginia.

Chris Smith is an instructor and designer at Fig Leaf. He also teaches Flash, Dreamweaver, and Fireworks at the Corcoran School of Fine Arts in Washington, DC. Chris graduated in 1995 with a BFA from the University of Southern California. While earning his degree, he worked at Activision, Inc. and contracted an incurable interest in computer game graphics and animation that has dominated his creative pursuits ever since. Thirty years before the mast, he lives in Alexandria, VA.

Additional Contributors

Kevin Towes is a Co-Founder and Chief Technical Officer of Pangaea NewMedia Inc. in Toronto, Canada. His experience ranges from traditional film, photography, and sound to 3D animation and database and software development, culminating in the integration of all of these disciplines. Kevin's rich mix of visual and technical knowledge has been a leading force in Pangaea's success. A leader in the ColdFusion community for the past three years, Kevin is the founder of the Toronto Cold Fusion Users Group, one of the largest CF groups in the world. He is a certified ColdFusion Developer and has led his team at Pangaea to achieve much success with Macromedia Products.

Matthew David has been developing Internet solutions for over seven years and has serviced many Fortune 500 companies. His books include *Flash MX Magic* (New Riders) and contributions to *Flash 5 Magic, Flash 5: Visual Design, Web Development Bible, Inside Dreamweaver 4*, and the *Dreamweaver Bible*. He is currently working on chapters for three new books. Matthew also contributes regularly to *Devx.com, Element K Journal's Macromedia Solution,* and *Inside Project Management* magazines, as well as web sites such as Macromedia.com, SitePoint.com, and UDZone.com. His own web site is www.matthewdavid.ws.

Guy Rish is an independent consultant. He carries developer and instructor certifications from Macromedia and Rational, and in the last few years he has concentrated on applying object-oriented methodologies to web development. When not consulting or training, he does technical writing and editing for various publishers. In recent years he has taken up a traveling habit with his wife, with the end goal of seeing it all.

Patricia Lee Hall is both a ColdFusion developer and Allaire Certified Instructor. Patti has degrees in English and French. She has also pursued higher education in Public Relations. She has a cat named Reese.

Doug Clarke has a background in illustration, 3D motion graphics, and sound design, and he likes to use his multi-disciplinary background to push the envelope of interactive animation. "I'm never ever really satisfied with my work, but I do enjoy the process of creating and combining different mediums within Flash. Drawing is the foundation for all my work, which in turn is based on keen observation." His work has been featured in various publications including *USAToday, Richmond Times Dispatch,* and the *Virginian Pilot.* When he's not working in Flash, Doug enjoys illustration and painting. Doug is also an avid surfer and spends his off time with his family and friends in Virginia Beach. He holds a Bachelor of Fine Arts degree, graduating Magna Cum Laude of Virginia Commonwealth University. You can find Doug's current work at www.liquidmethod.com.

Christopher Hayes has been using Flash since Flash 3 and enjoys creating bleeding-edge design. Chris received his Master's degree in Computer Art from Savannah College of Art and Design and his Bachelor's degree in Fine Arts from Xavier University of Louisiana. Chris (aka P the Wicked) is also an emcee/music producer and enjoys the true hip hop culture. Chris believes that his best work ever is the next one.

About the Tech Editors

Initially enjoying a successful career as a fashion photographer, **Christian Buchholz** was seduced by the Web in 1997 and freelanced as a web designer. In the next few years, Christian developed and worked on over 100 sites for Australian and international companies, building his expertise in high-end Flash and Flash Generator development, Streaming Media/Broadband, and project management of backend solutions for rich media sites. His work as Head of Spike multimedia team received several awards for outstanding Flash work for sites such as `www.elle.com.au` and the youth site of Commonwealth Bank and Lemon Ruski. He is recognized worldwide as a technical author for the *Flash Bible 5*. He is now Managing Director for Bromide73 Network.

For many years, **Sally Cruikshank** has been known as one of the top independent animators in the country; in fact, she was awarded the first Maya Deren Award by the A.F.I for her body of work: imaginative, bizarre, constantly moving, inspired by Betty Boop. If you're a parent, you've probably seen some of her animated songs on *Sesame Street*. "Above It All" sound familiar? Lately her focus of interest is interactive animation, and ActionScript code is her obsession. Her interactive website, `www.funonmars.com`, features a Starbucks satire and a leading Chatterbot—Whinsey—created in Flash 5 with a JavaScript engine.

John Davey does high-end Flash, Actionscript, and Generator work—in fact, strike that—he does anything that involves Flash and back-end. His portfolio includes Robbie Williams, Disney, The BBC, The Science Museum, Kelloggs, and being technical editor and author on many books, chapters, and articles. Married to Jo and daddy to 3 1/2 year old Amy, he's also a skier who knows that extreme skiing is cooler than snowboarding all day, every day.

Larry Drolet, co-founder of Answer Studios Inc., is an idea machine. Coming out of college, he was computer illiterate, but with a promotion he decided a PC could be a good thing. That was just the beginning! Today he is a contributing author to various Flash pieces, a Macromedia trainer for Generator, Flash, and ActionScript, and certified as a Flash Developer. With a background in ASP, he has become well versed in server-side integration and Flash. You can hear his latest "off the wall" idea at the San Diego Server-side and Flash user groups each month.

Dedication

For my husband Wick Keating and my fellow Figs. Rock the Fig!

Acknowledgments

If you've never written a book before, let's just say it's kind of like giving birth. You forget how painful it was—eventually. All kidding aside, I think the only thing that keeps any of us coming back are the terrific people we get to work with throughout the process—the folks at New Riders, my fellow authors and tech editors, and my fellow Figs.

An enormous debt of gratitude goes out to Deborah Hittel-Shoaf, Linda Laflamme, and Theresa Gheen at New Riders. You guys got me through another one. I couldn't have gotten through this without your patience and help. Thanks also goes out to David Dwyer and Steve Weiss who had enough faith in Fig Leaf to let us do this.

To all of the tech editors and reviewers—Larry Drolet, Sally Cruikshank, John Davey, and Christian Buchholz—thank you from the bottom of my heart. Your hard work, edits, and thoughtful comments really added to the final product.

To the non-Fig authors—Kevin Towes, Matthew David, Guy Rish, and Patti Hall (former Fig!)—thank you guys so much for everything. You accomplished a lot under a tremendous amount of pressure and helped take some of the pressure off me. You'll never know how much that means to me.

To my fellow Figs—you are still the most talented and amazing group of people I've ever been lucky enough to work with. To the Big Figs, Steve Drucker, Tom Pizer, Dave Gallerizo, Dave Watts, and Ed Southerland—thank you (I think) for giving me the time to organize this effort. To all of the writers and artists who participated in the development of the book, I am, once again, eternally grateful that you didn't try to pelt me to death with cans of Red Bull, even when I know you really wanted to. Even those of you who didn't contribute directly to the book effort certainly helped the rest of us maintain some semblance of mental health.

Once again, thanks to my husband Wick. Happy 20th Anniversary dear! Even when we were both insanely busy, he helped me find some sense of balance. I think without him the house would have collapsed under the weight of the dust bunnies and I would have starved to death. It's been two years—I think we've finally earned that vacation.

And as a special treat for those of you who actually read the acknowledgements—there's an Easter Egg in Flash MX! From the main menu, choose Help > About Flash. Click on the bottom of the X where the lines connect. There's a single pixel spot you have to hit. If you find it you'll get access to six video games. Woo Hoo! Say goodbye to productivity. Hint: if you normally have your monitor at high resolution (mine's at 1600 X 1200), you'll probably have to bump the resolution down to make the spot easier to hit.

Last, but by no means least, thanks goes out to Macromedia for creating such a great product. You guys rock!

A Message from New Riders

As the reader of this book, you are our most important critic and commentator. We value your opinion and want to know what we're doing right, what we could do better, in what areas you'd like to see us publish, and any other words of wisdom you're willing to pass our way.

As Executive Editor at New Riders, I welcome your comments. You can fax, email, or write me directly to let me know what you did or didn't like about this book—as well as what we can do to make our books better. When you write, please be sure to include this book's title, ISBN, and author, as well as your name and phone or fax number. I will carefully review your comments and share them with the authors and editors who worked on the book.

Please note that I cannot help you with technical problems related to the topic of this book, and that due to the high volume of email I receive, I might not be able to reply to every message. Thanks.

Email: steve.weiss@newriders.com

Mail: Steve Weiss
Executive Editor
New Riders Publishing
201 West 103rd Street
Indianapolis, IN 46290 USA

Visit Our Web Site: www.newriders.com

On our Web site, you'll find information about our other books, the authors we partner with, book updates and file downloads, promotions, discussion boards for online interaction with other users and with technology experts, and a calendar of trade shows and other professional events with which we'll be involved. We hope to see you around.

Email Us from Our Web Site

Go to www.newriders.com and click on the Contact link if you

- Have comments or questions about this book.
- Want to report errors that you have found in this book.
- Have a book proposal or are interested in writing for New Riders.
- Would like us to send you one of our author kits.

- Are an expert in a computer topic or technology and are interested in being a reviewer or technical editor.

- Want to find a distributor for our titles in your area.

- Are an educator/instructor who wants to preview New Riders books for classroom use. In the body/comments area, include your name, school, department, address, phone number, office days/hours, text currently in use, and enrollment in your department, along with your request for either desk/examination copies or additional information.

Introduction

With the release of Flash MX, Macromedia has firmly established Flash as a tool not just for creating interactive and engaging animated web sites, but also for using high-end web applications. So, what can you do with Flash MX? The answer is, anything you want to.

With Flash MX, you have the capability to do the following:

- Set up your movie so that a user can navigate using the browser Back and Forward buttons. You can also create pages that can be bookmarked.
- Share Libraries at both run time and author time.
- Dynamically import JPEGs and MP3s.
- Embed video directly in Flash.
- Recognize when a sound has completed playing.
- Use the greatly improved XML parser.
- Take advantage of support for Unicode and vertical text.
- Turn buttons on and off.
- Turn the hand cursor on and off.
- Set global variables.
- Treat movie clips, buttons, and text fields as objects.
- Debug your code with the new debugger.
- And more....

The high penetration of Flash into the browser market means that, as designers and developers, we finally have a viable alternative to the standard HTML/DHTML site.

Additionally, many of the features that we've become accustomed to in the HTML world, such as being able to use the browser Back button to navigate, being able to load images and sounds dynamically, and being able to set bookmarks, are now available in Flash.

From its March 2002 survey, Macromedia reports that 98% of all users browsing the web now have a version of the Flash player installed. A breakdown based on player version shows the percentage of users who can view the content of the different player versions:

- Flash 2: 97.1–98.6%
- Flash 3: 95.5–98.2%
- Flash 4: 94.7–97.8%
- Flash 5: 90.7–94.8%
- Flash 6: 3.2–8.1%

The next survey is scheduled for June 2002. To check the current statistics, visit www.macromedia.com/software/player_census/flashplayer/.

Who Is This Book For?

This book is aimed at two very different audiences: artists and developers. We know that not all artists will want to become hard-core developers, nor will most developers make the leap to becoming gifted artists, but we hope that we can bring about a meeting of the minds. The more each group understands how the other thinks, the better chance each has of leveraging the true power of Flash MX. Development in Flash has truly become a collaborative effort, more so in Flash MX than before.

What's on the CD

The CD that comes with this book includes all the asset files you'll need to complete the exercises in each chapter. You'll also find trial software from some of the vendors mentioned in the book that you can use in conjunction with Flash to speed up your development process. Additionally, you'll find a few extra goodies (such as sounds) tucked in that you can use in your own files.

System and Setup Considerations

The minimum system requirements for authoring Flash files, as posted on the Macromedia site, are shown in the accompanying table.

Minimum System Requirements

	Windows	Macintosh
System software	200MHz Intel 10.1 or later 98 SE, Me, NT 4, 2000 Professional, XP, or later	System 9.1 or Pentium Processor; Microsoft Windows or later, Mac OS X
Available RAM	32MB (64MB recommended)	32MB
Available disk space	40MB	40MB
Resolution	1024 × 768; 16-bit color	1024 × 768; 16-bit color

Yes, you can get away with the minimum requirements, but you really want more power than that. Personally, I prefer working on a machine with at least 500MB of RAM.

That being said, I keep my old 133MHz, 32MB system around just to keep me honest—although, after this release, I think I might have to retire it. Flash files can become very CPU-intensive if you're not careful; remember that you're depending on your user's computer to perform the calculations to play back your file. Although it would be nice if everyone had a spiffy 1–2GHz system with 1GB of RAM and a 21-inch monitor on which to play your creations, that just isn't how things work in the real world.

People often ask what kind of a setup we use here at Fig Leaf for development. It varies from person to person, but all the programmers work off Windows laptops—some with attached monitors, some not. We're all currently running 750MHz and 500MB of RAM.

The artists are split; some use Macintosh computers, some use Windows. And, yes, we all rib each other about that. The Macintosh desktops all run with 512MB of RAM.

Personally, I really like having a 21-inch monitor with the resolution set at 1600×1200 pixels when I work in Flash. I get positively claustrophobic on anything else because of all those panels. I do a lot of scripting, so I like to have my Actions panel open and expanded at all times. In fact, my Actions panel and the Flash work area are usually side by side and opened up to about the same size.

If you're lucky enough to be set up for dual monitors, that's even better. I'm not, but if it were an option, that's the route I'd take: panels on one monitor and the Stage and Timeline on another. As an added bonus, if you have the right graphics card, this is a snap to set up.

A graphics tablet is great to work with, and I also use a wireless mouse and keyboard. Flash FLA files can be on the large size, especially if you're working with sound, so having a Zip drive also is useful. The Iomega 250MB Zip drive is our choice.

Going Forward

So where do you go after you've finished the book? The best thing to do is practice, practice, and more practice. Come up with a problem and see if you can solve it. One of the things we've learned at Fig Leaf is that just because it hasn't been documented doesn't mean it can't be done. In fact, we break the rules every day—that's half the fun.

A lot of tutorial and resource sites are available to you on the web. You'll find a number of these listed in Appendix D, "Flash Resources." Most of them have tutorials and downloadable FLA files. Download them. Pick them apart. That's how you'll learn.

Another good thing to do is find the closest Macromedia Users Group (MMUG) and start attending meetings. That way, you can share ideas and network with other designers and developers. If you happen to be in the Washington, D.C., area on the second Tuesday of the month, come visit the Washington Area Macromedia User's Group (WAMMO); we'd love to see you. If Washington is too far away for you, you can find the nearest MMUG by visiting Macromedia's web site at `www.macromedia.com/support/programs/usergroups/worldwide.html`.

You can subscribe to a number of mailing lists for additional support. At Fig Leaf, we run two different mailing lists: Flashnewbie for new Flash 5 users, and Flashcoders for Flash 5 programming (high volume). To sign up for either of these mailing lists, point your browser toward `http://chattyfig.figleaf.com/`.

Pick the list you want, and follow the directions; lots of good folks from all over the world will help you answer your questions.

You can also take advantage of a number of forums on the web. Three well-known Flash forums are located at `http://webforums.macromedia.com/flash`, `www.were-here.com`, and `www.flashkit.com`. All of these sites run a series of Flash forums broken down by topic. You can read posted questions and answers and even register to be able to ask and answer questions yourself.

If you're willing to spend the time to really learn Flash, you'll discover that it is an incredibly powerful addition to your tool chest. In fact, when clients are asking you for solutions to complex problems, you might frequently find yourself saying, "Well, I could do that in Flash."

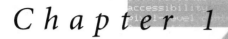

Chapter 1

Changes in the
Flash Workflow

I suppose the first question is, "What's new

in Flash MX?" And the answer is, "A lot."

Certainly much more is new than you can

write about in one chapter. What you'll

take a look at here are the features in Flash MX that will change how most of you work with Flash.

Specifically, you'll get an overview of the following:

- Changes to the Timeline
- The Drawing toolbar and the Properties Inspector
- Changes in the panels
- Changes to the Color Mixer
- Changes in the Actions panel
- A brief overview of components
- The Distribute to Layers option

More advanced topics, such as the new objects that have been added to Flash, the Event Model, and other topics that don't directly influence the workspace, are covered in later chapters. You'll begin with taking a look at the changes to the Timeline.

Changes in the Timeline

At first glance, the Flash MX Timeline doesn't appear to be that different from the Flash 5 Timeline, but there are some significant changes that you need to be aware of.

First and foremost, you can now collapse the Timeline without removing it from the Stage altogether. This is particularly handy when you have a lot of layers. To collapse or expand the Timeline, just click the white triangle to the left of the word *Timeline*. Figure 1.1 shows both a closed and an expanded version of the Timeline.

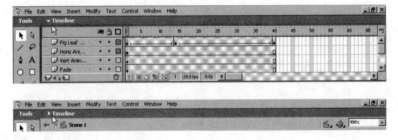

Figure 1.1   The Timeline can now be expanded or collapsed with the click of a button.

Next, you'll notice that the icons at the bottom of the Timeline have changed. The Delete Layer icon is still in position on the right, but on the left you now have icons for Insert Layer, Insert Motion Guide, and Insert Layer Folder (see Figure 1.2).

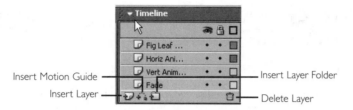

Insert Motion Guide
Insert Layer
Insert Layer Folder
Delete Layer

Figure 1.2 The icons below the Timeline have changed. You can now insert a layer, insert a motion guide, or insert a layer folder.

Of these three, Insert Layer Folder is the most significant. Yes, you can now organize your layers into folders. This is a huge step forward in organization.

To insert a layer folder, select the layer that you want to insert the folder above and click the Insert Layer Folder icon.

To add a layer to a folder, you can either drag a layer to the folder or select a layer that is already in the folder and then click the Insert Layer icon. Layer folders are illustrated in Figure 1.3.

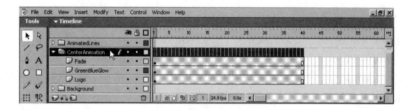

Figure 1.3 Layer folders are a great organizational tool.

You can also choose, through the Preferences panel (Edit > Preferences), whether to turn on span-based selection for the Timeline. By default, this option is not selected and you will be using frame-based selection.

Using frame-based selection, when you click a frame in the Timeline, you select only that frame (see Figure 1.4).

With span-based selection enabled, when you click a frame in the Timeline, you select an entire frame sequence (see Figure 1.5). For example, clicking inside a tween selects the entire tween. Clicking between two keyframes or on a keyframe at the beginning of a sequence selects all frames from the beginning keyframe to the next keyframe. Clicking a keyframe in a series of keyframes selects only that keyframe.

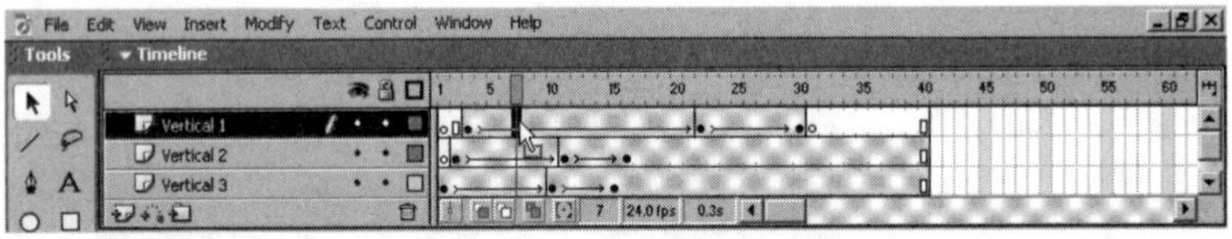

Figure 1.4   With span-based selection disabled, you select only one frame at a time when you click the Timeline.

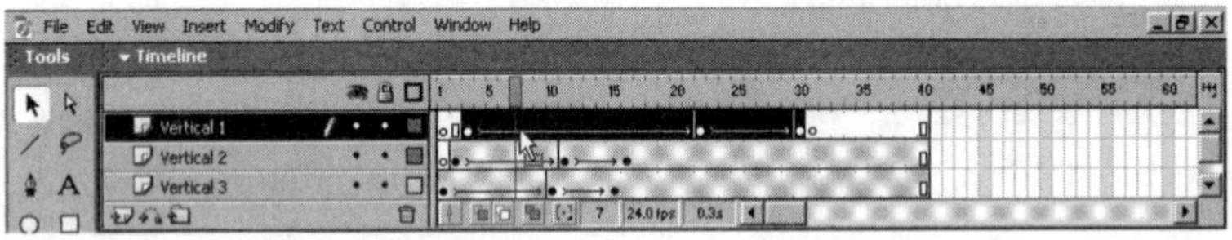

Figure 1.5   Span-based selection is useful when you want to be able to easily select frame sequences.

When you right-click (Windows) or Control-click (Macintosh) a frame, you get a context menu. You should be aware of a couple of additions to the Flash MX context menu for frames:

- **Convert to Keyframes.** Selecting this option converts any selected frames or frame sequences into keyframes. The keyframes selected do not have to be contiguous. To select keyframes that aren't contiguous, Control-click (Windows) or Command-click (Macintosh) each frame that you want to convert to a keyframe, and then select the Convert to Keyframes option. Make sure that Span-Based Selection in the Preferences dialog box (Edit > Preferences) is turned off when you do this.

- **Convert to Blank Keyframes.** This is similar to the preceding option, but instead of converting frames to keyframes, this converts them to blank keyframes.

- **Properties.** Selecting this opens the Properties Inspector, if it isn't already open. The Properties Inspector is discussed in the next section.

- **Actions.** This one isn't new to Flash MX, but it is still worth mentioning. You can launch the Actions panel directly from the frame context menu.

If you are working with span-based selection, you might notice a moderately annoying new feature. When you roll over a keyframe, you'll see a selection symbol <-> appear. I find that this makes clicking the keyframe awkward. To get around this, either use the Preferences dialog box to disable span-based selection or hold down the Control key (Windows) or the Command key (Macintosh) while you click.

After the Timeline, the part of the interface used the most is the Drawing toolbar. A few changes have been made to the toolbar, and it's now tied to the new Properties Inspector.

The Drawing Toolbar and the Properties Inspector

The Drawing toolbar and the Properties Inspector work in tandem and deserve to be mentioned together. The Properties Inspector is a context-sensitive panel that allows you to set the properties for whichever tool on the Drawing toolbar, object on the Stage, or frame in the Timeline you have selected. For tools that don't have properties to set, the Properties Inspector defaults to the document properties. If the Properties Inspector is not currently open, you can open it by choosing Window > Properties.

One thing to note is that not all options for a particular tool are available via the Properties Inspector. In fact, most of them still have their main options in the Drawing toolbar, and Fill Transform requires opening the Color Mixer to customize.

This combo of the Properties Inspector and the Drawing toolbar is most useful when you are using the Text tool and the Properties Inspector together (see Figure 1.6). You now have an Uber-panel for working with text that has all of the options from the old Character, Paragraph, and Text Options panels in one place.

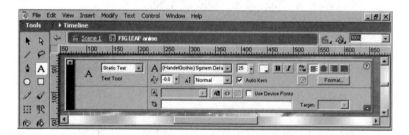

Figure 1.6   Using the Text tool on the Drawing toolbar in conjunction with the Properties Inspector gives you all the options you'll need for working with text.

You will want to know about a couple of additions to the Drawing toolbar—specifically, the Fill Transform tool and the Free Transform tool.

The Fill Transform tool isn't really new. It has just been moved from being a Paint Bucket option to being its own tool. Just as in the past, you use this to transform gradient fills.

You use the Free Transform tool, along with its options, to rotate and skew, scale, distort, or transform an object. You can also reset the transform point of an object so that you can transform it around a specific point.

Figure 1.7 shows an object that has been selected with the Free Transform tool on and no options selected. You'll notice that the object is surrounded by a bounding box with eight handles. It also has a transformation point. If you mouse around the edges of the bounding box or over the transformation point, your cursor changes to reflect what operation you can perform.

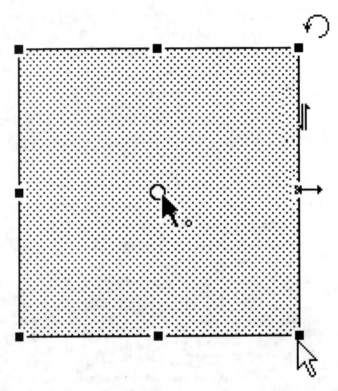

Figure 1.7   When you are using the Free Transform tool, your cursor changes to reflect what functions you can perform.

By default, the transformation point is always equivalent to the registration point of an object. If you change the transformation point by moving it, you can transform your object around that new point. For example, you can choose to rotate a square around one of its corners rather than the center. You can always choose to reset the transformation point back to the registration point by double-clicking it.

You have four options when using the Free Transform tool. All these options can be used with ungrouped shapes. Rotate and Scale can also be used with symbols:

- **Rotate and Skew.** With this option selected, you can use the corner handles to rotate and you can use the side handles to skew an object. You also have the option of moving the transformation point so that you can rotate the object around a new point.

- **Scale.** With this option selected, you can use the corner handles to scale proportionally or you can use the side handles to scale in a particular direction.

- **Distort.** With the Distort option selected, you can quickly create perspective distortions. Distort works only with ungrouped shapes; you can't use it with symbols. You can click the side handles to drag the edge in any direction. You can also click the corner handles to drag a corner in any direction. By holding down the Shift key and dragging a corner, you drag the handle and its opposing corner in opposite directions (see Figure 1.8).

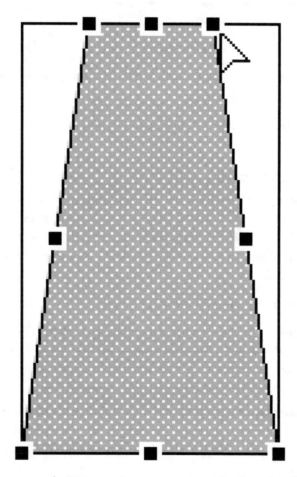

Figure 1.8   You can use the Distort option to create perspective distortions. By clicking a corner handle and holding down the Shift key, you can drag the handle and its opposing corner in opposite directions.

- **Envelope.** Using this option, you can completely reshape your selected shape or shapes. Unfortunately, the Envelope option can't be used with symbols or grouped text. When you select this option, you'll see the usual corner and side handles, but you'll also see a series of circles. In this case, the squares are anchor points and the circles are the tangent handles (think Bezier curves). Figure 1.9 illustrates using the Envelope option. This one is the most fun of all. Play with it.

Figure 1.9   You can use the Envelope option to completely reshape an object or group of objects.

The next biggest change you'll notice is what has become of the panels.

Changes in the Panels

One of the first things you'll notice is that the old tabbed panels are gone. The panels can still be docked together, but in a little different way. Panels can also be docked to the Flash interface. Some preconfigured panel layouts are available (Window > Panel Sets), and you can save custom layouts as well (Window > Save Panel Layout). Figure 1.10 shows the default panel set.

You can work with panels in several ways:

- **Undock a panel.** To undock a panel from the Flash interface or a particular panel set, grab it by the textured area on the left side of the title bar. You'll know you're in the right place because the cursor will change from a pointer to a four-way arrow symbol. When that happens, just click and drag.

- **Dock panels together.** To dock panels together, drag the panel that you want to move by the title bar and release it on the title bar of the panel that you want to dock it to. Panels in Flash MX dock in a vertical stack, as illustrated in Figure 1.11.

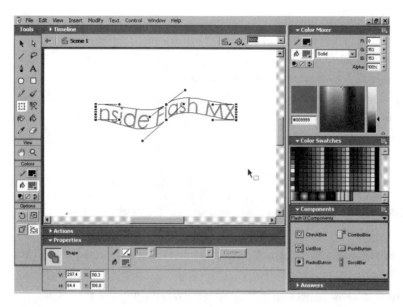

Figure 1.10   The default panel layout has the Timeline docked to the top of the Flash interface, the Properties and Actions panels docked to the bottom of the interface, and the Color
Mixer, Color Swatches, Components, and Answers panels docked on the right side.

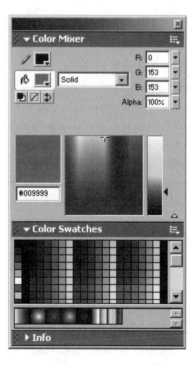

Figure 1.11   Panels can be docked together in a vertical stack.

- **Dock panels to the interface.** Panels can be docked to the top, bottom, right, or left of the Flash interface. Forewarned is forearmed: You can get some unexpected results when you play around with docking panels to the interface. As you drag panels around the interface, the panel being dragged dims; when you drag it over an area that it can dock to, that area displays a darkened outline. Panels automatically expand to fit the space available, and they stay that size when undocked. It's annoying.

Tip

I find that docking the panels to the interface takes up too much real estate. The only panels that I consistently leave docked are the Timeline, the Tools panel, and Properties Inspector. I then create detached panel sets for everything else I need.

- **Expand and collapse panels.** Panels can be expanded or collapsed by clicking the white triangle in the title bar.
- **Hide or show panels.** To hide all panels, press the Tab key. Press Tab again to reveal the panels.
- **Close all panels.** You can collapse but not close all panels at once by choosing Window > Close All Panels.
- **Use panel options.** All the panels have additional options that you can access through their Options menus. To access the Options menu for a panel, click the symbol on the far right side of the title bar.
- **Create and delete panel sets.** You can create your own panel sets to suit the way you work. All you have to do is rearrange the panels to your liking—either docked to the interface or floating—and choose Window > Save Panel Layout. Assign your panel set a name, and it will be there for you under Default Panel Sets to select anytime you need it. You can also delete a panel set by browsing to the application directory and opening the First Run and then Panel Sets folders. Just delete whichever panel sets you no longer want to keep.

That covers most of the issues for dealing with the new panels and the main Flash interface. You're going to want to take a closer look at a couple more panels because of significant changes in their functionality.

Changes to the Color Mixer

The Color Mixer panel is much improved in Flash MX. The first thing you want to do when you open the Color Mixer is make sure that it's expanded (see Figure 1.12). If you can see a downward-pointing white triangle in the lower-right corner of the mixer, you need to click that to expand the panel.

Figure 1.12   The expanded Color Mixer panel showing the Stroke, Fill, Fill Type, and color-manipulation tools.

The upper part of the panel is much the same as what you had in the old mixer. All of the Fill Type information is included here as well. If you choose Radial or Linear from the Fill Type menu, you'll see the familiar gradient-editing controls.

In the bottom part of the panel are much improved color-manipulation tools. To select a color, click in the color space and use the Brightness control to the right to darken or lighten your color. To the left of the color space is a split color swatch that lets you see before and after colors when you are working with solid colors.

In the Hex box below the split color swatch, you can see the hex value for the currently selected color. You can also enter hex values directly.

Another panel that is significantly improved is the Actions panel.

Changes in the Actions Panel

This book assumes that you'll be working in Expert mode, so I won't touch on changes in the Normal mode. If you're not accustomed to working in Expert mode, don't panic. Trust me, you'll learn much faster and become more adept at using Flash by sticking with Expert mode. The most significant changes in the Expert mode for the Actions panel (Figure 1.13) are listed here:

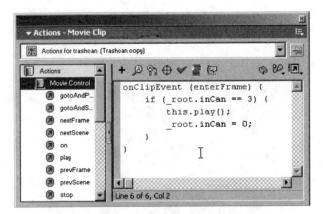

Figure 1.13   The Actions panel.

- **Launching the Actions panel.** You now have a shortcut for launching the Actions panel: All you have to do is press F2.
- **Navigating to other scripts.** This drop-down menu at the top of the Actions panel (see Figure 1.14) is a very handy feature. The list displays the symbols and frames in your current Timeline where ActionScript can be applied. You can choose any item in the list, and Flash will select the frame or symbol on the Stage and display any current actions. You can add or edit actions directly.

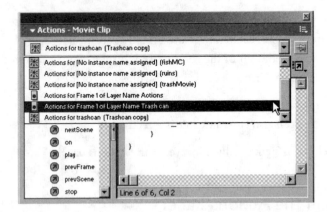

Figure 1.14   Use the Navigate to Other Scripts option to find the symbols in the current Timeline that actions can be applied to.

- **Organizing the Toolbox list.** With the addition of a number of new objects in Flash MX, the Toolbox list has been reorganized a bit. The categories can be a bit confusing, but you do have the option of reorganizing the list—it's all based on an XML file (ActionsPanel.XML in the application folder).

- **Using Find and Replace.** These icons are the second and third icons just above the Actions list. They do exactly what you would expect: They enable you to search for and replace pieces of code in the Actions list.

- **Inserting a target path.** It's easy to forget how all of your symbols relate to one another. In Relative mode, this pop-up window shows the symbol hierarchy for your current clip. If you want to see the complete hierarchy of symbols for your entire movie, you can switch to Absolute mode (see Figure 1.15). I recommend that you leave the notation as dots. Slash syntax is deprecated.

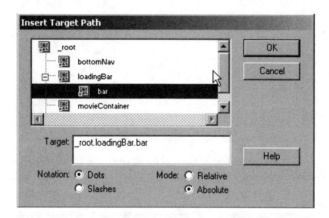

Figure 1.15   You can use the Insert a Target Path option to figure out where a symbol is in the movie hierarchy.

- **Checking Syntax.** Always check your syntax before you test your movie. It'll save you a lot of heartache—and headache.

- **Using Auto Format.** Auto Format applies formatting rules to your ActionScript based on the preferences that you have set up under Auto Format Options in the Action panel options (see Figure 1.16).

- **Showing code hints.** When you work in Expert mode, you don't have the luxury of being able to see the parameters available for methods and objects. Show Code Hints (see Figure 1.17) takes care of that problem for you by giving you a list of available parameters. The code hints pop up as soon as you type an opening parenthesis. You just have to scroll down the list and double-click the one you want.

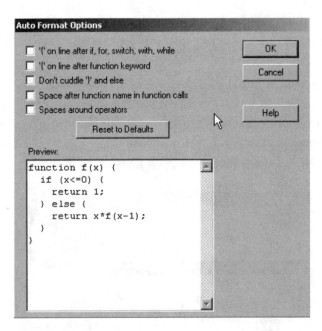

Figure 1.16   You can change how Auto Format formats your ActionScript by changing your preferences in Auto Format Options.

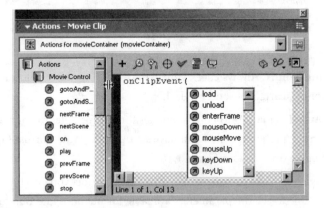

Figure 1.17   Code hints let you quickly see what parameters are available for the method or object you are working with.

- **Using the Reference Icon.** This is an excellent feature: It's a built-in context-sensitive ActionScript dictionary, as illustrated in Figure 1.18. Just select the item in the ActionScript that you are unsure of and click the Reference button (which looks like a book with a question mark) to get more information. You must click the Reference button each time you want to look up another element. Alternatively, you can choose from the list on the left.

Figure 1.18   The Reference icon gives you access to a context-sensitive ActionScript dictionary.

- **Using Debug Options.** Use Debug Options to set and remove breakpoints in your script. Breakpoints are lines in your code where you want the program to stop during debugging. When you reach a breakpoint, you can advance your code line by line to see exactly what is happening.

- **Viewing line numbers.** The View Line Numbers option is available under the Actions panel option list. It allows you to turn on line numbering (see Figure 1.19) in the Actions panel, which is very helpful.

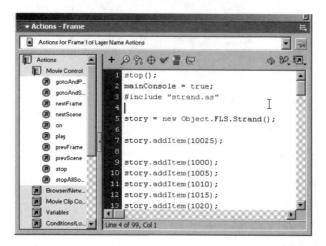

Figure 1.19   Being able to see the line numbers in the Actions list helps immensely when you are trying to debug your code.

Additionally, moving lines of code around is much easier to do in Flash MX. You can just highlight a line of code and then drag it to a new location. That's even easier than cutting and pasting!

That's a long list of improvements to the Actions panel. The good news is that you'll find yourself less reliant on external editors. It's much easier to get your work done inside of Flash now.

A Components panel has replaced the old Smart Clips Library. It's worth taking a quick look at what the components are—you'll be examining these in detail in a later chapter.

A Brief Overview of Components

Components, like smart clips, are complex, reusable movie clips that you can use to quickly add common user interface elements to your project. You can drop these components directly into your movie, change a few parameters, and change their color and appearance to fit into your project. (See Figure 1.20.)

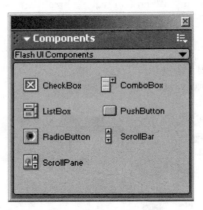

Figure 1.20   The Components panel.

Currently there are seven components:

- **CheckBox.** You use the CheckBox when you want your users to make a single choice.
- **ComboBox.** If you need to display a list of choices in a drop-down menu, use the ComboBox.
- **ListBox.** If you need to display a list of choices in a scrollable list, use the ListBox.
- **PushButton.** A PushButton executes a command when pressed.
- **RadioButton.** You use RadioButtons to set up a list of mutually exclusive choices in response to a question. Only one button can be selected.

- **ScrollBar.** This lets you add a scrollbar to a Text field.
- **ScrollPane.** This lets you add a scrollbar to an Image field.

These components can be used individually or together to create complex applications.

Next you'll step away from the panels and take a quick look at a new option in Flash MX that you should know about.

The Distribute to Layers Option

This feature is so handy that it deserves mention here. Have you ever started a project with multiple objects on one layer and decided that they really all needed to be on their own layers? That makes for a lot of cutting and pasting, which is time-consuming. Flash MX has a new quick fix for this problem.

All you have to do in Flash MX is select the objects that you want to place on different layers and choose Modify > Distribute to Layers. If your objects are named symbols, the layer names will reflect the symbol names, making it easy to keep track of what's where.

This also works with text, simplifying the process of creating text effects. Add some text to the Stage, and break it into individual letters using Modify > Break Apart. With all the letters selected, choose Modify > Distribute to Layers. Each letter will be on its own layer, and each layer will be named according to the letter that it contains (see Figure 1.21). This one is truly a great timesaver!

Figure 1.21   When you distribute text to layers, each letter is placed on its own layer and the layer is named according to the text that's on it.

Summary

Flash MX has some truly great features that help streamline your workflow. The list here is only the tip of the iceberg, but these are the features that you are most likely to encounter in your day-to-day work.

Chapter 2

Finding Your Way with the Movie Explorer

Prior to the introduction of the Movie

Explorer in Flash 5, inheriting a complex

Flash project from another designer or

programmer could be nothing short of a

nightmare. Teasing apart a large file, particularly one with lots of nested symbols, named instances, and ActionScript, could take hours. In some cases, it could take days. Flash 5 came to the rescue with the introduction of the Movie Explorer. Although the Movie Explorer is essentially unchanged since Flash 5, it still is a very powerful tool. You might find that the Movie Explorer doesn't always show all the movie assets, which can be a little frustrating from time to time, but it still gives you a wealth of information about your file that you wouldn't have otherwise.

The Movie Explorer gives you a quick snapshot of your Flash movie in the form of a hierarchical tree (see Figure 2.1). It displays the contents of your movie scene-by-scene, layer-by-layer, and frame-by-frame. You usually can find every symbol, every instance name, and every line of ActionScript in your movie. Better yet, you can even print a copy of your movie's structure so that you can keep a record of its evolution over time.

- **Using the filters in the Movie Explorer.** By using the Filter buttons, you can set up the Movie Explorer to show specific types of elements. You can also set up a custom filter.

- **Searching your movie using the Find Text input field.** You can search for specific elements in a Flash Movie by using the Find Text input field. This is great for finding all the instances of a symbol in a movie.

- **Using the Options menu.** The Options menu in the Movie Explorer gives you an alternative method for working with your hierarchical movie tree.

- **Finding and replacing fonts using the Movie Explorer.** If you've ever had one of those miserable days when the boss decided that she wanted to change every single font in your Flash project, you'll appreciate this feature. You can change not only your fonts, but also the actual text, without ever leaving the Movie Explorer.

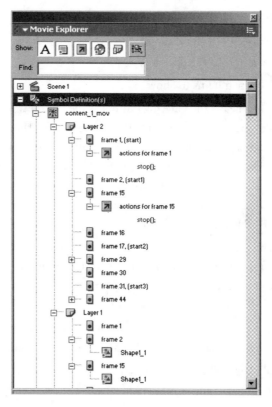

Figure 2.1   The Movie Explorer enables you to quickly find the elements in your movie.

The Movie Explorer Interface

As you saw in Chapter 1, "Changes in the Flash Workflow," the Movie Explorer is no longer docked to the Actions panel. In fact, all the panels are independent of one another. You can open the Movie Explorer by using the new shortcut key—F4. Alternatively, you can choose Window > Movie Explorer from the Main menu. The Movie Explorer has remained essentially unchanged since Flash 5.

There are four main parts to the Movie Explorer window:

- **Filtering buttons.** This is the row of buttons at the very top of the Movie Explorer window. These buttons enable you to choose what you want to see in the Display list. From the left, they are as follows:
  - Show Text
  - Show Buttons, Movie Clips, and Graphics

101709040

- Show ActionScripts
- Show Video, Sounds, and Bitmaps
- Show Frames and Layers
- Customize Which Items to Show

- **Find text box.** Just below the Filtering buttons is the Find text box. You can search for any element of the movie by name by typing a string into the text box. You can search for a symbol name, an instance name, a font name, a string of ActionScript code, or a frame number. The Find function acts as a filter for the items currently shown in the Display list. The filtering takes effect as soon as you begin typing. To restore the complete Display list, you have to clear all information from the Find text box.

- **Display list.** The main body of the Movie Explorer window is the Display list. The Display list shows the hierarchical listing of the movie contents based on which filters you have selected using the Filtering buttons or a custom filter (more on these to come).

- **Status bar.** The Status bar is the gray bar just below the Display list. After you select an item in the Display list, the full path to that item is shown in the Status bar. For example, this path:

  Scene 1 > tank body > frame 1 > tankBody_mc

  tells you that the item you selected is in Scene 1 on frame 1 of a layer named "tank body." The item you selected is tankBody_mc. It's just another useful data point when you're trying to orient yourself in your movie.

In the next section, you take a look at how you can use some of the features of the Movie Explorer to make working with your Flash movie easier and more efficient.

Searching for Elements

As mentioned, you can use the Movie Explorer to display elements that appear in your Flash movie. In addition to using the standard filters, you have the option of using a custom filter. The Customize Which Items to Show button opens the Movie Explorer Settings dialog box (see Figure 2.2).

Any item checked in the Show section of the Movie Explorer Settings dialog box is shown in the Display list. This list is where you can pick and choose specific items, rather than relying on the preset filters.

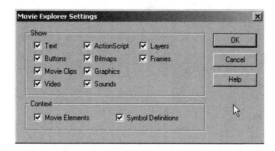

Figure 2.2   The Movie Explorer Settings dialog box enables you to specify the types of elements for which you are looking.

You can choose to view Movie Elements, Symbol Definitions, or both. Movie Elements includes scenes, layers, and frames. Symbol Definitions displays all the symbols in a movie.

To get used to how all the filters work together, you need to practice using the Movie Explorer in Exercise 2.1.

Exercise 2.1   Using the Show Text Filter

In this exercise, you open a moderately complex file and take a look at how you can use the Movie Explorer to find specific elements of the movie.

1. Open MovieExplorer.fla in the Examples/Chapter02 folder.

2. Test the movie so that you can see the different interactions. Don't be afraid; click all the buttons!

3. Open the Movie Explorer (Window > Movie Explorer), and click any Filter button that is currently selected to deselect it. Unselected buttons appear to be raised, and selected buttons appear to be depressed. Your Movie Explorer Display list should look like Figure 2.3.

4. Click the Show Text button (the first button).

    Because you are showing only text, and not frames or layers, the only Movie Element to display is Scene 1. Everything else you see is a symbol definition.

5. Four Movie Clips and two buttons contain text elements. Click the + next to each symbol to expand that branch and see the text it contains. Figure 2.4 shows the Display list with the branches expanded.

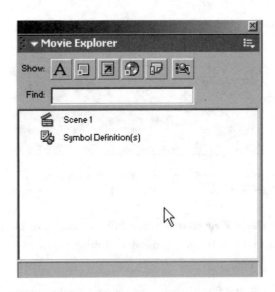

Figure 2.3   The Movie Explorer Display list with all the Filter buttons unselected.

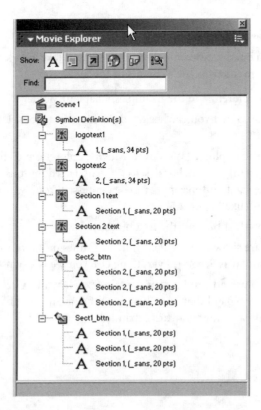

Figure 2.4   The Display list with the branches expanded. Every time you see a + next to a branch, you can expand that branch to get more information. To collapse a branch, click the –.

Note

Whenever you see a + in the Display list, that tells you that you can expand the branch and get more information. Click the + to expand a branch. Click the – to collapse a branch.

6. Double-click the Text symbol (the A) under the logotext1 Movie Clip. Two things should happen. Your Flash movie opens up the text you've selected in Symbol Editing mode, and the text becomes editable inside the Movie Explorer.

   Editing text without leaving the Movie Explorer is an extraordinarily useful feature in Flash. Not only can you edit the body of the text, but also you can make changes in the Properties inspector (font size, font color, and so on) and watch the changes happen on the Stage in real time (see Figure 2.5).

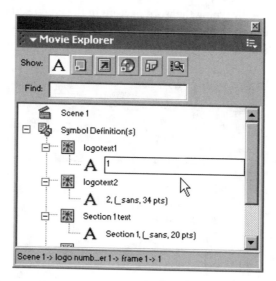

Figure 2.5   You can edit text in the movie directly from the Movie Explorer.

7. Change the 1 in the editable field in the Movie Explorer to **3** and press Return or Enter on the keyboard. The 1 in the Movie Explorer and on the Stage changes to a 3. You can edit text in your movie directly from the Movie Explorer.

Tip

Is editing text through the Movie Explorer not working for you? Make sure that the layer the text is on isn't locked. You probably locked that layer for a reason. Flash is just protecting you from yourself. Unlock the layer and you're good to go.

Using the Movie Explorer also simplifies finding a particular instance of a symbol on the Stage. In Exercise 2.2, you use the Show Buttons, Movie Clips, and Graphics Filter to locate and edit a symbol in your movie.

Exercise 2.2   Using the Show Buttons, Movie Clips, and Graphics Filter

In this exercise, you learn how to quickly locate and edit any symbol in your movie.

1. Select the second filter by clicking the Show Buttons, Movie Clips, and Graphics button.
2. You suddenly have a lot more information about the movie available to you. Double-click any symbol. You either open the symbol in Symbol Editing mode or advance to the proper frame and layer on the main Timeline.
3. Refine your filter by typing the word **Section** in the Find text box. Now you should see only movie elements and symbol definitions that include the word "Section" either as text or as part of the symbol name (see Figure 2.6).

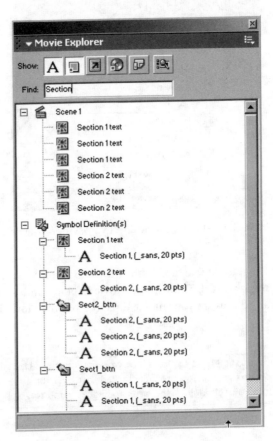

Figure 2.6   You can use the Find text box to refine your selected filter(s).

> **Note**
>
> In Flash 5, typing a single letter in the Find text box would find all elements *beginning* with that letter. Typing a single letter in the Find text box in Flash MX will find all elements that *contain* that letter.

4. Delete the word "Section" from the Find text box to see the rest of your symbols.

What about ActionScript? To view ActionScript in the Movie Explorer panel, click the third filter button. In Flash MX, you can use the Movie Explorer to find ActionScript, but you no longer can edit ActionScript directly from the Explorer panel, nor does double-clicking ActionScript in the Explorer panel open the ActionScript panel. However, if you already have the ActionScript panel open, you can click any line of ActionScript in the Movie Explorer and it will appear in the ActionScript panel, ready for editing—at least for actions in frames.

If the actions are inside or attached to a Movie Clip or attached to a button, you need to double-click the line with the ActionScript symbol—not the ActionScript itself. Another caveat: This works only for the symbols under Movie Elements, not for those under Symbol Definitions.

The fourth filter displays videos, sounds, and bitmaps, none of which are present in this file, so you won't see additional information if you select this filter.

You can turn on the Show Frames and Layers filter in the same way you did the previous filters. This time, you click the fifth filter to see every layer, keyframe, and symbol on each layer (see Figure 2.7).

The filters and the Find text box are not the only tools you can use in the Movie Explorer. There are more tools available on the Movie Explorer Options menu as well.

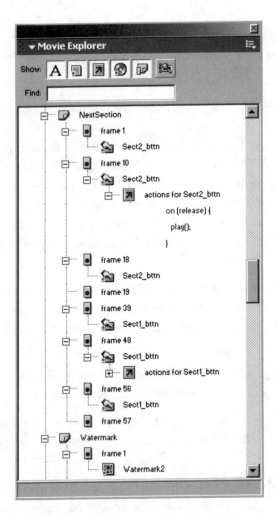

Figure 2.7   With the Show Frames and Layers filter selected, you can see each layer of your movie and the keyframes, symbols, and actions on that layer.

Using the Movie Explorer Options to Edit Your Flash Files

You access the Options menu by clicking the white check mark over the small white symbol in the upper-right corner of the Movie Explorer window. You can also access the Options menu (shown in Figure 2.8) by right-clicking (Windows) or Control-clicking (Macintosh) any item in the Display list.

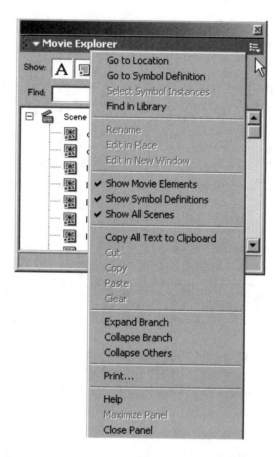

Figure 2.8   The Movie Explorer Options menu.

From the Options menu, you can do the following:

- **Go to Location.** You can select any item in the Display list and use this option to go directly to the appropriate layer, scene, and frame in your movie where the item exists. Make sure your layers are unlocked when you do this.

- **Go to Symbol Definition.** You can select a symbol instance in the Movie Elements area and then choose Go to Symbol Definition to locate the symbol definition for the instance. The symbol definition lists all the other symbols, text, and actions associated with the symbol you selected.

- **Select Symbol Instances.** Use this option to find all instances of the symbol selected in the Symbol Definitions area of the Display list. The instances of the selected symbol are highlighted in the Movie Elements area. You might need to scroll up in the Movie Explorer to see the selected instances. If you have the Timeline in which the symbol exists open, this also selects the first occurrence of that instance on the Stage.

- **Find in Library.** You can select any symbol in the Display list and use this option to find the symbol in the movie's Library. The Library opens if it's currently closed.

- **Rename.** This option enables you to rename a selected element. It works just like the Rename feature in the Movie Library and will rename all instances of that symbol in the Movie Explorer. The name change is automatically reflected in the Library.

- **Edit in Place.** This has the same effect as double-clicking an item on the stage. It enables you to edit a symbol and still see other items on the stage in context.

Tip

Edit in Place is a nice feature, but you can do the same thing by double-clicking an element in the Movie Explorer.

- **Edit in New Window.** This has the same effect as double-clicking an item in the library. It opens the symbol in a separate window for editing.

- **Show Movie Elements.** This option displays the elements in your movie, organized by scenes, layers, and frames. You can have both Show Movie Elements and Show Symbol Definitions open, or you can switch between the two.

- **Show Symbol Definitions.** This option displays all the elements associated with a symbol. You can have both Show Movie Elements and Show Symbol Definitions open, or you can switch between the two.

- **Show All Scenes.** Selecting this option lists all the scenes and all the items that are contained in them.

- **Copy All Text to Clipboard.** In theory, this option copies the selected text (including the ActionScript) that you have listed in your Movie Explorer to the Clipboard so that you can use the text in other applications or paste it into a word-processing program and spell check it. In practice, it doesn't work. What you really get is all the text, including symbol names, layer names, and so on that can be displayed in the Movie Explorer. In other words, you get a completely expanded version of the tree. Fortunately, you do have another option when it comes to ActionScript—you can always export your ActionScript to an .as file and then reimport it after you make your changes.

Tip

Okay. Copy All Text to Clipboard still doesn't work. Don't waste your time unless what you are looking for is a completely expanded printout of the hierarchical tree.

- **Cut, Copy, Paste, Clear.** These options enable you to cut, copy, paste, and clear items in the Display list. In case you are unfamiliar with the Clear option, Clear removes an item from the Stage without placing it on the Clipboard. Editing an item in the Display list modifies the corresponding item in the movie. Be *very* careful here—cutting or clearing an item in the Display list deletes it from the Stage.

- **Expand Branch, Collapse Branch.** Use these options to expand or collapse the branch that you have selected.

Note

You can completely expand a scene in the Movie Explorer by first collapsing the scene in the Display list and then choosing Expand Branch from the Options menu. You can do the same thing for the symbol definitions. However, with the symbol definitions, this gives you some quirky behaviors when you start working with the individual symbols. Double-clicking any one symbol causes all or most of the branches to collapse when you've expanded the definitions using Expand Branch—including the branch on which you've double-clicked. Forewarned is forearmed! Individually expanding the branches in the symbol definitions causes them to stay open. Another odd bit of behavior you might encounter is that when you use this method to expand the whole tree with all elements selected in the filter list, the tree might collapse when you click or right-click a branch. Again, this doesn't happen if you have expanded the branches individually.

- **Collapse Others.** Use this option to minimize all branches not containing the item you have selected.

- **Print.** The Print option enables you to print a snapshot of all the elements currently displayed in the Movie Explorer. To get a complete look at your movie's structure, expand all the branches and then print. There is no better way to get a thorough overview of your movie.

Tip

The Print option is hands-down my favorite option. This is a great way to learn how a movie is structured.

The only way to become really familiar with the Movie Explorer Options is to work with them on a regular basis. Use the preceding listing as a reference to remind you of what each option does.

Replacing Fonts

One issue that does come up repeatedly in Flash development is how to find and change all occurrences of a particular font inside a Flash movie. You can take advantage of the Movie Explorer's Find feature and just type the name of the font you are looking for in the Find text box. You then can change each instance of the font at one sitting. Although you can't do a global change, you can at least find them all.

In Exercise2.3, you can practice replacing fonts using the Movie Explorer.

Exercise 2.3   Using the Movie Explorer to Replace Fonts

In this exercise, you change all instances of the device_sans font to Arial (or Helvetica).

   1. Open MovieExplorer.fla from the Examples/Chapter02 folder.
   2. In the Find text box, type **_sans** to see all the symbol definitions where text with a font type of _sans is located. Make sure that you have selected Symbol Definitions in the Options panel. (See Figure 2.9.)

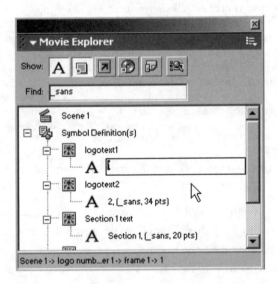

Figure 2.9   Use the Find text box to filter the Display list based on font type.

   3. Make sure you have the Properties Inspector open (Window > Properties) and double-click the text symbol beneath the logotext1 Movie Clip on the Display list.
   4. Select a new font type (Arial or Helvetica) from the Properties Inspector.
      Two things should happen. First, you should notice that the font type of the text on the Stage changed. Second, the Movie Clip containing the font you just

changed is no longer available in the Display list. It's not available because you're filtering on _sans.

5. Repeat Steps 4 and 5 for any other occurrence of the _sans font that you want to change.

You don't need to save any of the changes you made to this movie. This was just for practice.

Although it would be nice to be able to globally change fonts in a Flash movie, that capability just isn't available yet. However, being able to find all occurrences of a font so that you can change each one is a powerful tool that was unavailable before the introduction of the Movie Explorer.

Summary

The Movie Explorer is a great addition to Flash. Being able to quickly locate the elements of a movie is useful. The ability to edit text and modify fonts also is quite useful. Best of all is the ability to print a complete hierarchical tree of the movie structure.

Spend some time experimenting with the Movie Explorer. Remember: Just because something isn't documented doesn't mean it can't be done. After you have the features and quirks of the Movie Explorer mastered, you'll find that using it significantly increases your productivity and reduces your reliance on over-the-counter headache remedies.

Now that you've taken a look at the overall structure of your movie, we dig in a little deeper and look at the structure of the movie library in Chapter 3, "Tips for Using the Library and Shared Libraries."

Tips for Using the Library and Shared Libraries

If you've been using Flash for any amount

of time, you are familiar with the Library.

Most people look at the Library as just a

storage cabinet for the symbols in a Flash

movie. In this chapter, you take a look at some of the Library's lesser-known functions and some of the features that are new to Flash MX. In particular, you look at the following:

- **Using counts and getting rid of unused items.** Use this feature to keep track of how many times each item is used. Get rid of unused items to keep your FLA file organized and as compact as possible.

- **Creating new symbols by dragging elements to the Library.** Yes, good old F8 could become a thing of the past. Now you can drag a shape to the Library to convert it into any type of symbol.

- **Dragging folders between Libraries and resolving naming conflicts.** You now can drag entire folders from Library to Library and keep the folder structure. Mercifully, Flash no longer ignores you when you try to drag an item into a Library that already has an item with that name—it actually helps you resolve the situation.

- **Using the Update feature.** You can use the Update feature to update a bitmap or sound that has been modified in an external editor.

- **Working with runtime shared Libraries and author-time sharing.** Shared Libraries enable you to link to and use items in external Flash movies or FLA files. You can even put fonts in a shared Library to help keep your file size down. There are, however, a couple of issues you need to be aware of when using shared Libraries; you'll learn about them here.

- **Creating custom permanent Libraries.** If you find yourself using the same elements over and over in your movies, why not just put them in a Library that is available to you directly from the Flash application interface? You'll be surprised how easy it is to do.

Using the Use Counts

When you create files, you often end up having several assets in your Library that you don't use in your final Flash movie. You might import several sounds and use only one, or you might create a particular symbol and then change your mind and never use it. When your file starts getting large, it gets harder and harder to keep track of all your assets. Why confuse things by having unused assets in your file?

Flash gives you the ability to track which symbols are being used in your presentation and how many times each symbol is being used. You do this by using the Keep Use Counts Updated option located on the Library Options pop-up menu (see Figure 3.1).

When the Keep Use Counts Updated option is selected, Flash updates your use count automatically every time you use an item from the Library.

After your use counts are updated, you can see which items aren't currently being used and then delete them. One caveat is that any objects that are being attached to your movie through ActionScript using methods such as attachMovie or attachSound show a use count of 0 if you haven't physically placed them on the Stage. However, their Linkage properties do display, so you should know they are in use—you just won't know how many times they are used.

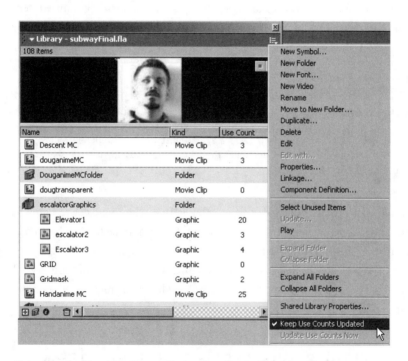

Figure 3.1   Use the Keep Use Counts Updated option in the Library Options pop-up menu to keep track of how many times a symbol is being used in your Flash file.

 Note

Make sure you select Keep Use Counts Updated rather than Update Counts Now. Update Counts Now doesn't keep a continuous count of the items on the Stage that are currently in use. It just takes a snapshot of the Stage at the time at which you select it.

Note

Don't casually delete items that are not listed as being used on the Stage. After you delete a symbol, it's gone. If you think there is any chance you might need an unused symbol later, don't delete it! You can always make a folder in your Library, name the folder Junk, and place questionable items in there until your project is finished and you're sure you won't need the items anymore.

If you aren't using ActionScript to attach objects to the Stage and if you are absolutely certain that your unused items really are unused, you can use the Select Unused Items option in the Library Options menu to quickly select all currently unused items. That way, you can delete all your unused items at one time. Do be careful—when you delete an object from the Library, it's gone.

Tip

If you do decide to delete a symbol that is in use, you have a new option in Flash MX: Delete Symbol Instances. You can delete all the instances of that symbol in the movie. In previous versions of Flash, the instance would remain as an empty square on the Stage. Now, all you need to do is select "Delete Symbol Instances" in the Delete dialog box and Flash deletes not only the symbol in the Library, but also any references to that symbol on the Stage.

One thing that might make you a little crazy is that when you delete items from the Library and save your file, your file size doesn't decrease; in fact, it might even increase. To get around this quirk in Flash, choose File > Save As and give your file a new name (project1.fla, project2.fla, and so on). Keeping incremental files while you're working on a project is a good idea anyway. You never know when you might need a previous version of the file.

Creating New Symbols, Using Folders, and Resolving Name Conflicts

One really nice little enhancement to Flash MX is that you can create a new symbol just by dragging an item to the Library. You can either drag a shape to the Library or nest a symbol by dragging an existing symbol to the Library.

When you drag an item to the Library, the Convert to Symbol dialog box will automatically pop up (see Figure 3.2). You can go ahead and name the symbol, select its behavior, and set the Registration point.

Pay special attention to the Registration point. In Flash 5, you had two options. You could have the Registration point in the center of the object or in the upper-left corner.

Now you can set the Registration point at the center, at any of the corners, and at the top, the bottom, or either side. You'll have to make the decision based on the intended use of the object. You'll probably stick with the upper-left corner or center, but sometimes those aren't the best choices. Say, for example, you were creating a slider to adjust another movie clip or value on the Stage. For a vertical slider, you might want to make the gutter that the slider moves on have its Registration point at the bottom to make your calculations easier (the top would work, too!)

Figure 3.2   When you drag an item to the Library, the Convert to Symbol dialog box pops up, making creating symbols easy and fast.

Another enhancement comes in how Flash handles folders in the Library. In earlier versions of Flash, if you dragged a folder from one Library to another, all the contents would transfer but they wouldn't stay organized in folders. In fact, they wouldn't stay in folders at all, but would come across as individual files. That was a real annoyance and it's been fixed. In Flash MX, you can cheerfully drag a folder from one Library to another and keep the folder structure, including nested folders, completely intact.

If you try to drag a folder into a Library that already has a folder of the same name, you get this warning: One or more Library items already exists in the document. You then have the option of overwriting the existing items or not. If you really want to replace the items in the existing folder, you can choose to overwrite. If the two folders have differing content, you end up with one folder with all the items from both. If the folders had files with the same names, the symbols being dragged in will replace the existing symbols. If you choose not to overwrite the files, nothing happens.

Previously in Flash, if you tried to drag an item into a Library and the Library already contained an item with that name, Flash would just ignore you. Now it at least acknowledges your presence and gives you the option of replacing the existing component with the new one (see Figure 3.3).

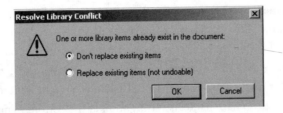

Figure 3.3   When you drag an item to the Library and the Library already has a symbol with the same name, Flash asks you if you want to use the existing component or replace it with the new one that you're dragging in.

Updating Library Items

Swapping symbols and updating files, such as bitmaps or sounds, that were imported from an external editor used to be handled through the Library and Instance panel. Things are a little bit different in Flash MX. Swapping symbols is now handled by either right-clicking (Windows) or Control-clicking (Macintosh), and then choosing Swap Symbol, or by clicking the Swap button on the Properties Inspector. However, you can still choose to update or edit bitmaps or sounds from the Library.

So, when would you use the Update feature? Well, say the graphics artist on your project isn't done with a particular piece of artwork that you need. Instead of waiting for a final image, you can start your work from a comp or dummy version of the image. If you plan to use the Update feature, the original piece of artwork needs to be in a directory on the network to which you have access.

All you need to do to use the Update feature in the Library is the following:

1. Right-click (Windows) or Control-click (Macintosh) the image in the Library and choose Update from the context menu. You can also select the item and choose Update from the Options menu. Alternatively, you can select the image and click the Properties icon (the little blue circle with an "i" in it at the bottom of the Library panel).

2. If you choose Update from the context menu or Library options, the Update Library Items dialog box opens (see Figure 3.4). If the bitmap (or bitmaps) you selected have changed since you did the import, the check box next to it will have a check mark.

3. If you selected more than one item and don't want to update all the items that have changed, just deselect the check boxes for the items you don't want to update.

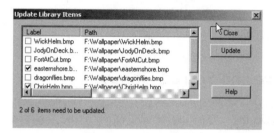

Figure 3.4   You can select a series of bitmap images and check whether any of them have been updated by right-clicking or Command-clicking, and then selecting Update.

4. If you clicked the Properties icon, you'll see the Bitmap Properties dialog box (see Figure 3.5). In this dialog box, you have a Preview window that shows the current image.

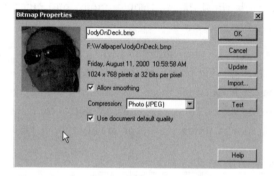

Figure 3.5   If you use the Properties icon to update your bitmaps or sounds, you get a Preview window that lets you check the current image.

5. In either case, all you have to do to update the image is click Update.

If you're really organized and you keep all your media files in their own folders, you can quickly tell which original files have been updated. To do so, Shift-click to select all the media elements in which you're interested, and then select Update from either the context menu or the Options menu. In the Update Library Items dialog box, any media element that has a more recent version will have a check mark next to it, as illustrated in Figure 3.4.

To update all selected images at one time, click Update. A message appears at the bottom of the Update Library Items dialog box, telling you how many elements were updated. Close the dialog box and you're ready to get back to work. Notice that the elements in the Library and all instances on the Stage have been updated.

Now that you know some of the tricks for working with an internal Library, it's time to take a look at using linkage and shared Libraries.

Using Linkage and Shared Libraries

Any time you create a new symbol, you have the option to set up linkage for that symbol. With the linkage, the symbol can be used either in the movie on which you're working (without actually placing the symbol on the Stage) or by another movie as a shared-Library item. The concepts of linkage and shared Libraries first appeared in Flash 5 but have been modified, streamlined, and expanded in Flash MX.

In Flash 5, you could set up linkage for symbols so that they could be used in a movie without being placed on the Stage. You could do this through attachMovie, for example. You could also create external SWF files, or shared Libraries, with symbols (such as sounds, fonts, and movie clips) that you could import into other Flash movies. The importing would keep files sizes small.

Shared Libraries have taken a bit of an interesting twist in Flash MX. In Flash MX, you have the option to create linkages and both runtime and author-time shared Libraries. Yes, I know, that sounds clever. What does it mean? Well, *runtime shared Libraries* are the equivalent of the old shared Libraries. They are external SWFs that contain symbols that can be shared across multiple movies. Runtime elements are incorporated when an SWF is called.

Tip

It's a good idea to keep your runtime shared Libraries small. When you use a symbol from a runtime shared Library, you have to download the entire Library, not just the single symbol you want to use.

Author-time sharing is a little different. Author-time sharing takes place before you publish your files and while you're still in the authoring environment. In other words, rather than draw symbols from SWFs, author-time sharing enables you to draw multiple symbols from multiple FLA files to create one composite file. Author-time elements are incorporated when you publish your movie.

If you select a symbol in the Library and bring up the Linkage Properties dialog box (see Figure 3.6), you'll notice that you now have four linkage options:

- Export for ActionScript
- Export for Runtime Sharing
- Import for Runtime Sharing
- Export in First Frame

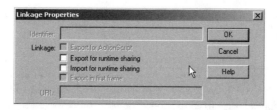

Figure 3.6   When you bring up the Linkage Properties dialog box, you now have four options.

You'll also notice that the options for Identifier and URL are grayed out. Before you can assign either of these options, you need to choose one of the Linkage options. The Identifier is equivalent to an instance name. The URL is the URL where that file is going to exist on the server, if you end up importing the file. This can be an absolute or relative URL.

One of the issues you have to deal with in Flash, and this is a good thing, is that when you publish a movie, only the symbols that exist somewhere on the Stage are exported with the SWF, unless you set up Linkage properties for them. Unused Library elements don't get to go along for the ride. This helps keep file sizes small.

Setting up Linkage Properties is the only way to export, and make available, any symbol that you access only through ActionScript for methods such as attachMovie() and attachVideo(). In Flash MX, you do this by selecting Export for ActionScript from the Linkage Properties dialog box. Then, just as in Flash 5, you assign a unique Identifier. You'll notice that when you do this, the Export in First Frame check box becomes available. Select this check box if the symbol doesn't actually exist in your movie somewhere.

Shared Library symbols download before the first frame loads. This can cause a pause when your movie loads. You can choose to have Library symbols load in the first frame by selecting the Export in First Frame option. You can use this option only for internal Libraries. You cannot attach items from a shared Library.

Export for Runtime Sharing and Import for Runtime Sharing are analogous to the Export This Symbol and Import this Symbol from URL Flash 5 options.

The simplest way to work with runtime shared Libraries is to build the Library you want to share first. You will create a shared Library in Exercise 3.1.

Exercise 3.1   Creating a Runtime Shared Library

The best way to approach this is to keep things simple. You'll build a very simple runtime shared Library from an existing file.

1. Open the logo.fla file from the Examples/Chapter03 folder on the CD and save it to your hard drive.

2. Open the Library. This Library contains only one symbol, the figLogo_mc movie clip, and the bitmap of the logo in the Bitmaps folder.

Tip

With Flash, there's always more than one way to do things. You can open the Linkage panel by right-clicking (Windows) or Control-clicking (Macintosh) on an item in the Library and selecting Linkage from the context menu. You can also select an item and then choose Linkage from the Library options menu. Last, you can set the Linkage properties when you first create a symbol by pressing the Advanced button on the Convert to Symbol dialog box.

3. Select the figLogo_mc movie clip in the Library and select Linkage from the Options menu to open the Linkage Properties dialog box.

4. Select the check box next to Export for Runtime Sharing. Now the Identifier text box and the Export in First Frame option are available. Export in First Frame is automatically selected. The Identifier is the same as the symbol name.

Tip

The Identifier name for a symbol must be unique and cannot have spaces in it. That doesn't mean that you can't use the same name for the movie clip and the Identifier. It just means that two different objects cannot have the same Identifier.

5. In the URL text box, you need to enter the URL where the published file will be located. This can be either an absolute URL or a relative one. Your shared Library and the file with which you're sharing symbols do not need to reside on the same server. They don't even have to be in the same domain (this wasn't always the case). In this case, all your files are going to be in the same directory, so just type **logo.swf**, and then click OK (see Figure 3.7).

6. Save and publish your file.

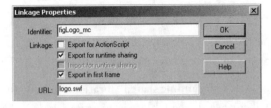

Figure 3.7 You use the Linkage Properties dialog box to select how you want a symbol to be shared and to assign a unique Identifier.

Now that you've created a runtime shared Library, it's time to use it in Exercise 3.2.

Exercise 3.2   Using a Runtime Shared Library

Using a Shared Library is extremely simple.

1. Close logo.fla if you still have it open.

2. Create a new file and save it as sharing.fla to your hard drive.

3. From inside sharing.fla, open logo.fla as a Library (File > Open as Library).

4. Drag a copy of the figLogo_mc movie clip onto the Stage. Both figLogo_mc and the bitmap on which it was based appear in your new file's Library. (You can also drag it to the Library of your current movie.)

Tip

You can drag a shared Library symbol onto the Stage of your new movie or drag it directly to the Library.

5. Select figLogo_mc in your new Library (sharing.fla) and open the Linkage Properties dialog box by right-clicking (Windows) or Control-clicking (Macintosh) and selecting Linkage from the context menu.

    All the Linkage properties are already set up for you. The things you need to take note of are the following:

    • The Identifier name is the same as the Identifier name you established in the shared Library. This is always the case. The shared symbol and the symbol sharing it must have the same Identifier.

    • Import for runtime sharing is selected. This must be selected for any symbol based on a shared symbol.

    • The URL is the URL where you stored the published SWF of your shared Library.

6. Save and publish your movie.

See? It wasn't a big deal. After all, you just dragged items from a Library into another file. The power of shared Libraries, however, is in how you update them. Which you will do in Exercise 3.3.

Exercise 3.3   Updating Symbols Using Shared Libraries

By making changes to and republishing your runtime shared Library, you automatically update all movies that depend on it.

1. Close sharing.fla if it is still open, and open the copy of logo.fla that you saved to your hard drive.

2. Open newLogo.fla as a Library (File > Open as Library) from the Examples/Chapter03 folder on the CD. You're going to update the Fig Leaf logo.

3. Double-click the existing figLogo_mc to open it in Symbol Editing mode.

4. Delete the existing logo on the Stage.

5. Drag a copy of newLogo_mc from the newLogo.fla Library onto the Stage and center it.

6. Save and publish your file.

7. Double-click sharing.swf on your hard drive. This is the file that still contains the old logo. The old logo was updated as soon as you launched the SWF file.

8. Open sharing.fla from your hard drive. The old logo is still there, but because it is linked to the logo.swf file, it reflects the contents of that file whenever it is published.

   You might find it irksome that you can't see the changes to the logo in your FLA file. There is a simple way to get around that, however.

9. Select figLogo_mc in the Library and launch the Symbol Properties panel.

Tip

You can launch the Symbol Properties panel by right-clicking (Windows) or Control-clicking (Macintosh) an item and selecting Properties from the context menu. You can also select the item and choose Properties from the Library Options menu. Another method of launching the Properties panel is to select the respective item and click the Properties icon (the blue circle with an "i" in it) at the bottom of the Library panel.

10. Make sure the Advanced button is selected. Note that this button toggles back and forth between Advanced and Basic; if it says Basic, you're in Advanced. Under Source, select the check box next to Always Update Before Publishing, and then click OK.

11. Publish sharing.fla (File > Publish).

12. Now your file will show the correct logo. Save your file.

You'll use the Always Update Before Publishing option again when you work with author-time sharing.

Runtime shared Libraries sound like a pretty cool concept, but there are some issues you need to be aware of if you plan on using shared Libraries:

- If a shared Library is corrupted or missing, then your movie that is depending on using the shared symbols does not function. It simply stops dead in the water.

- Shared Libraries should be kept small. When you link to a shared Library, you download the entire Library, even if you are trying to use only one of the symbols in the shared Library. Thus, if the shared Library contains 100 symbols and you want to link to one of them, you have to download all 100 symbols.

Author-time sharing is a little different from working with runtime shared Libraries. Author-time sharing enables you to update your file with any symbol in any FLA file that is accessible on your internal network. This is particularly useful when you have multiple people working on parts of your final file. Unlike runtime Libraries, with author-time sharing, the files cannot be on separate domains.

When you use this option, the symbol in your current Library retains its name and properties, including any actions that are attached to that symbol. Note that this does not include actions inside the symbol. You can practice using author-time sharing in Exercise 3.4.

Exercise 3.4   Using Author-Time Sharing

In this short exercise, you get a chance to experiment with author-time sharing.

1. Open tankGame.fla from the Examples/Chapter03 folder and save it to your hard drive.

2. Copy tankGameArt.fla to the same directory in which you saved tankGame.fla.

   The file tankGameArt.fla contains some rudimentary "sketches" of objects for use in a tank game. You as the programmer need to start coding while your artist works on the final artwork. All you need to do is give the artist an outline of the artwork you need and its basic dimensions. He or she then can go to work.

   To update your artwork with the most current version of the artist's work, you need only link to the file he or she created.

3. Open the Library for tankGame.fla.

4. Select the island_mc movie clip and choose Properties from the Library Options menu.

5. In the Source section of the Symbol Properties panel, click Browse and select the copy of tankGameArt.fla that you copied to your hard drive. Click Open.

 Tip

If you don't have the same fonts on your system that were used in building a file, Flash pops up this warning: One or more fonts used by this movie are not available. Substitute fonts will be used for display and export. They will not be saved to the Macromedia Flash authoring document.

If you don't want to mess with the fonts that your artist used, just choose Use Default. Flash picks a font that's close, and if you ship the file back to your artist, it will open for him or her with the correct fonts.

If you want to permanently change the fonts, select Choose Substitute.

6. In the Island items folder, select Island, and then click OK.

7. Select the Always Update Before Publishing check box.

8. Click OK. Your file now should show the updated symbols.

9. Repeat this process for tankTurret_mc, tankBody_mc, player_1_mc, player_2_mc, and fire_btn.

10. Save your file.

Now, every time you publish your file, it will reflect the most recent artwork, enabling your artists and programmers to work together more efficiently.

Creating and Using Font Symbols

Using fonts can add a lot to the size of a Flash movie. Before Flash 5, if you used the same font in multiple movies, that font information was included in each movie you created. That's a lot of redundant download time. Now Flash enables you to place fonts in a shared Library for reuse. Information about the font doesn't get embedded in each Flash file. These fonts, called Font Symbols, can be used in multiple movies, but need be downloaded only once.

"That's great," you say. "I can finally format all my input and dynamic text to look just like I want without embedding the fonts." Not so fast. At this writing, there's an issue with the current Flash player. It doesn't enable you to use Font Symbols for dynamic text or input text. Sorry. Don't worry, though. Macromedia is well aware of this issue and is working on it. In the meantime, you can use Font Symbols for static text. That's still a file-size saver.

Note

One of the great things about Macromedia is that it is very responsive to its users, and it does its best to keep us informed about what's happening with Flash. If you're having any problems with a Flash feature, visit the Macromedia Flash Support Center at www.macromedia.com/support/flash. You can search the TechNotes there for more information.

Exercise 3.5   Creating a Font Symbol

Before you can share a Font symbol, you have to create it.

1. Create a new Flash file and save it as shared_fonts.fla.

2. With the Library open, click the Options button at the top-right of the Library window, and then choose Options > New Font.

3. In the Font Symbol Properties dialog box, name the font **FontA**. In the Font pull-down menu, select the font you want to use as a shared font (see Figure 3.8). If you would like to be able to italicize or bold your font, make sure you check the appropriate check boxes. Click OK.

The font named FontA now appears in your Library. Notice that the letter A appears to the left of the name to represent an included font (see Figure 3.9). Now it's time to turn this into a shared Library.

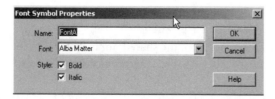

Figure 3.8   You use the New Font option and the Font Symbol Properties dialog box to create Font symbols that you can share with multiple files.

Figure 3.9   Font symbols are indicated by the letter A preceding them in the Library.

4. Select FontA in the Library. Right-click (Windows) or Control-click (Macintosh), and then choose Linkage.

5. In the Linkage dialog box, select Export for runtime sharing. The Identifier is automatically filled in with the name FontA. Yes, this is the same name as the Font symbol. I mean really, how many different names do you want to come up with for this one font?

6. Because this will be a shared Library, you need to enter a location for the file in the URL text field. Type **shared_fonts.swf** and click OK.

7. Save and publish your file. Close the file.

Now that you have your Font symbol set up in a shared Library, it's easy to use it in your files. You can practice using a shared font in Exercise 3.6.

Exercise 3.6   Using a Shared Font

Now that you've created a shared font, using it is easy.

1. Open a new file and save it as font_test.fla in the same directory where you saved shared_fonts.swf.

2. Open shared_fonts.fla as a shared Library.

3. Select the FontA symbol from the shared_fonts.fla Library and drag it into the font_test.fla Library. Alternatively, you can just drag the FontA symbol onto the Stage.

4. Select the Text tool. In the Properties inspector (Window > Properties), select FontA* (see Figure 3.10) from the Font drop-down list. The * indicates a shared font.

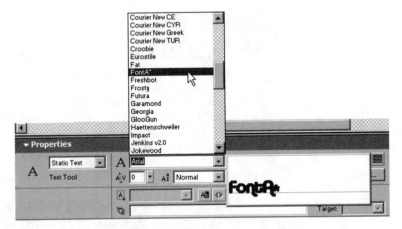

Figure 3.10   Shared fonts are easy to recognize in the Character panel—just look for the fonts that have asterisks after the font name.

5. Place some text on the Stage using the myFontA* font.

6. Save your file. Choose Control > Test Movie to display the shared font.

If you want to prove to yourself that you're saving file size by using a Font symbol in a shared Library, all you have to do is create another file using the same font and text but without using a Font symbol and shared Library. Make sure the Bandwidth Profiler is on and test away. You will see a reduction in file size for the file using the shared font.

Avoiding Shared Library Headaches

You already know that if a shared Library is corrupted or missing, all the Flash movies depending on it for shared elements stop playing. That's why it's important to keep the size of your shared Libraries as small as possible and use shared Libraries only when it's really necessary.

There are a couple of other not-so-well documented issues surrounding shared Libraries that can cause you some serious aggravation. If you know what they are ahead of time, however, you can work around them.

- You cannot attach ActionScript to a button on the Stage if that button was brought in from a shared Library. You can, however, attach ActionScript to the button in the shared Library and import that button, ActionScript and all, into your movie. That'll work just fine.

- The attachMovie action, with which you become acquainted in later chapters, enables you to retrieve a copy of a movie clip from the Library and load it into another movie clip. However, it does not work with a shared Library item. If you are planning to use the attachMovie action in your file, the movie clip you want to use must be in your internal Library.

Now you know how to create shared Libraries. You also know some of the caveats about using them. In addition, you have the option of creating custom permanent Libraries that can become part of your Flash application.

Creating Custom Permanent Libraries

Flash 5 has a built-in set of Libraries that includes buttons, graphics, learning interactions, movie clips, smart clips, and sounds (Window > Common Libraries). In addition to these Libraries, you can create your own custom Libraries.

If you have a set of graphics that you use all the time, it might be helpful for you to place them in a custom permanent Library. A custom permanent Library is added to the list of common Libraries and accessed the same way. In addition, it becomes part of your local Flash installation.

Creating a custom permanent Library couldn't be easier. All you have to do is the following:

1. Create a Flash movie with all the symbols you want to have available in a permanent Library.

2. Copy the FLA file into the Libraries folder in your Flash application folder.

The next time you select Window > Common Libraries, you'll see your new Library listed.

To get rid of a custom Library, browse to the Libraries folder in your application folder and delete the FLA you no longer want to use as a custom Library.

Obviously, because custom Libraries are really just Flash files, they can be shared among members of your team.

Summary

You've had a chance to look at some of the Library's special features. You've also learned about how and when you can use the shared Library features. As long as you understand the possible pitfalls of using shared Libraries and plan accordingly, you can use this feature that was introduced in Flash 5 and refined in Flash MX to help you manage your file sizes and maintain version control.

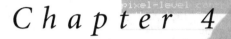

Chapter 4

Importing, Using, and Optimizing Graphics

You aren't limited to using only the graphics you create in Flash in your movies; you can also import a wide variety of graphics formats. Table 4.1 lists the standard file types you can import for both the Windows and Macintosh platforms.

Table 4.1   Standard File Types of Flash MX Imports

Format	File Extension	Platform
Adobe Illustrator 8.0 or earlier	.eps, .ai	Both
AutoCAD DXF	.dxf	Both
FreeHand	.fh7–.fh10	Both
FutureSplash	.spl	Both
GIF and animated GIF	.gif	Both
JPEG	.jpg	Both
PNG	.png	Both
Flash Player	.swf	Both
Bitmap	.bmp	Windows
Enhanced Windows Metafile	.mf	Windows
Windows Metafile	.wmf	Windows
PICT	.pct, pic	Macintosh
Toon Boom Studio	.tbp	Both

If you have QuickTime 4 (www.quicktime.com/) or later installed, you can also import the formats in Table 4.2 for either platform.

Table 4.2   Formats That Flash MX Imports with QuickTime Installed

Format	File Extension	Platform
MacPaint	.pntg	Both
Photoshop	.psd	Both
PICT (for Windows as bitmap)	.pct, pic	Both
QuickTime Image	.qtif	Both
QuickTime Movie	.mov	Both
Silicon Graphics	.sai	Both
TGA	.tfg	Both
TIFF	.tiff, .tif	Both

That's a lot of potential formats to work with. No matter what type of graphics you use in a Flash movie, you need to understand how to optimize your graphics to keep your file size low and your playback fast.

In this chapter, you'll take a look at the following:

- **Optimizing bitmaps for use in Flash.** You learn the tips and tricks that help you make the best use of bitmaps in Flash.
- **Converting bitmaps to vector graphics.** Sometimes, you can keep your file size small by converting bitmaps to vector graphics. You learn what types of bitmaps lend themselves to this type of treatment.

- **Monitoring memory and CPU usage.** When you start combining bitmap and vector graphics, you need to pay special attention to how your movie is affecting memory and CPU usage. You learn how to monitor your CPU usage and modify your files to improve performance.

- **Importing vector graphics.** Learn how to import SWF files that are created either in Flash or by other programs.

- **Importing artwork created in other programs.** Flash MX can import files created by a number of other programs. Among the file types you can import directly into Flash are EPS and AI (Adobe Illustrator), PSD (Adobe Photoshop—this works only if you have QuickTime 4 or higher installed), FH* (Macromedia FreeHand), PNG (Macromedia Fireworks), TBP (Toon Boom Studio), and DFX (AutoCAD programs). You learn the ins and outs of importing these types of graphics.

- **Using the Bandwidth Profiler and Size Report.** Learn how the Bandwidth Profiler and Size Report can help you pin down potential trouble spots in the playback of your movie.

You begin by taking a look at how you can optimize bitmaps for use in Flash.

Optimizing Bitmaps for Use in Flash

Even though Flash MX is a vector-based graphics program, you can still use bitmapped (raster) graphics inside it. You just need to be aware that if you use many or large bitmaps, you're going to increase the size of your Flash movie and decrease its efficiency. After all, Flash is most efficient when it's used for its original intent—generating vector-based graphics. That being said, you can get some very interesting effects by using bitmapped art in Flash.

Importing bitmapped or raster graphics as either individual elements or as a series of images is simple. For a single image, all you have to do is select File > Import and browse to the image you want to use. When you click OK, the image is placed on the Stage. Note that images that have been exported as a series of images from a QuickTime movie or animated GIF or that have been imported from a digital camera, for example, usually have a numbering scheme that Flash recognizes as being sequential. For a series of images, you'll get this pop-up message: "This file appears to be part of a sequence of images. Do you want to import all of the images in the sequence?" When you click Yes, each image in the sequence is imported onto its own keyframe.

Before you go crazy and start importing every bitmap in sight, however, there are a number of issues you need to consider:

Tip

A new feature of Flash MX is that you have the option of not just importing graphics and files directly onto the Stage, but also importing them directly into the Library by choosing File > Import to Library.

- **Do you really need it?** This is the first question you should ask yourself. If the bitmap isn't essential to the overall movie, don't use it. Remember that bitmaps are not processed as efficiently as vector graphics.

- **Can it be converted to a vector graphic?** If you absolutely need the bitmap to get a particular effect, that's fine. If it doesn't need to be photo-realistic, however, you might be able to optimize it by converting it to a vector image. You take a more detailed look at this option a little later in this chapter.

- **Let Flash handle the image compression for you**. Flash does a very good job of compression. When you are importing bitmaps, you want to start with a relatively uncompressed file and let Flash compress it for you. You learn more about global versus individual image compression schemes later in this chapter.

- **Crop your image before you import it**. Before you even think about importing a bitmap into Flash, do all your scaling and cropping in your image editing software of choice. The goal is to import the image into Flash at the same size you plan to use it in your movie. If you import a large image and crop or scale it inside Flash, you pay a hefty price in file size.

Theory is fine, but seeing is believing. To see how the size of an imported file and the export quality affects a final movie's file, work through Exercise 4.1.

Exercise 4.1   How Imported Bitmaps Affect File Size

The file you'll be working with already has two different versions of a photo of Times Square imported into it. You can use these images to create Flash player movies and observe the differences in file size.

1. Open nyc.fla in the Examples/Chapter04 folder.

2. Open the Library and drag a copy of the nyc.jpg file onto the Stage.

3. Before you do anything else, test your movie. You can test it with Control > Test Movie, or you can use the keyboard shortcuts—Control + Enter (Windows) or Command + Enter (Macintosh). Make sure the Bandwidth Profiler is open (View > Bandwidth Profiler) and use the Profiler to check your file size. (See Figure 4.1.)

The file size should be about 61KB.

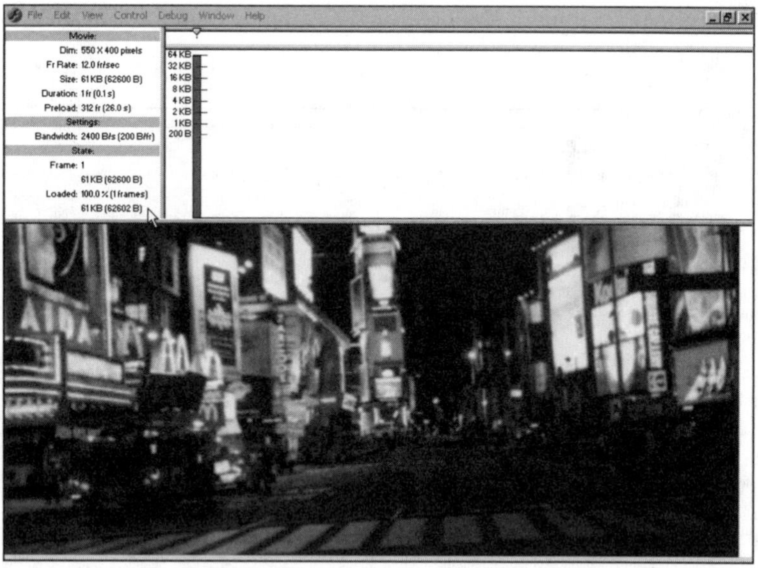

Figure 4.1   When you test your movie, you can use the Bandwidth Profiler to check the size of the SWF file. This saves you from having to browse to the file directory to check file size every time you make a change. Here, nyc.swf is about 61KB.

4. Back in your movie, select the image on the Stage and use the Free Transform tool with the Scale option selected to scale the image to just fit the Stage. Test your movie again and check the file size.

   There is no change in file size, even though the image is smaller.

5. Change the instance on the Stage again by breaking it apart (Modify > Break Apart), and use the Arrow tool to crop the image so that it focuses on the central street scene. Test your movie (see Figure 4.2).

   There still is no change in file size. No matter what you do to resize that image, you are not saving any file size.

6. Delete the instance of nyc.jpg from the Stage and drag a copy of nyc_cropped.jpg onto the Stage. This is the same image of Times Square, but it was cropped and reduced inside Macromedia's FreeHand before it was imported into Flash.

7. Test the movie and check the file size.

The file should have dropped to about 17KB—that's a savings of 44KB. Despite the fact that this looks just like the movie you created in Step 5, you're saving a substantial amount in file size because the cropping was done outside Flash. Lesson learned?

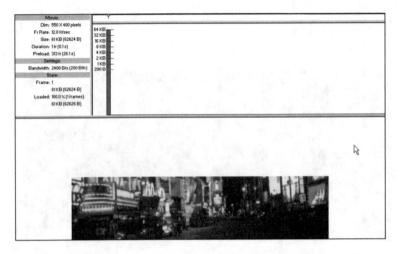

Figure 4.2   Even cropping out portions of the image so that just the central street scene shows won't save you anything in file size.

8. Up until now, you've been using the default compression setting for JPEGs, which, in Flash, is 80%. Override that setting by double-clicking nyc_cropped.jpg in the Library.

9. Clear the Use Document Default Quality check box in the Bitmap Properties dialog box. Change the Compression Quality setting to 30. (See Figure 4.3.) Click OK.

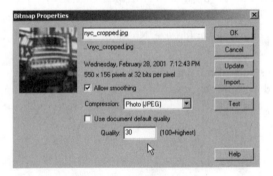

Figure 4.3   You can control the compression rate for each individual bitmap in your Flash file by using the Bitmap Properties dialog box. Just double-click a bitmap in the Library to access this dialog box.

10. Test the movie and check the file size.

You now have a movie with a file size of about 8KB. The background image is a little blurry, but that's okay—it's only a background.

Now that you've seen how to import bitmaps and the impact of handling the cropping and transformations outside Flash before importing, take a look at how and when you can convert imported bitmaps to vector graphics.

Converting Bitmaps to Vector Graphics

One of the most reliable ways of keeping the download time of your Flash movie quick is to use vector-based graphics in the place of bitmaps whenever possible. Because vector-based graphics use mathematics to describe objects, as opposed to using the pixel-by-pixel storage of bitmaps, vector graphics usually, but not always, are the optimal choice.

What kind of bitmapped images are suitable for conversion to vector graphics? It depends on the effect you are trying to achieve. If you try to convert a highly detailed image to a vector graphic, but still try to keep it as photorealistic as possible, you'll end up with a vector image that produces a much larger file than you would have gotten by just using the original bitmap. However, if you don't need or want the bitmap to be photorealistic, you might find that you can actually save file size and get interesting effects by converting it to a vector graphic.

Tip

You can use Macromedia's FreeHand or Adobe's Streamline to convert bitmaps to vector art. You actually have a higher degree of control over the final product by using one of these, but the Flash conversion process is very serviceable.

When you import a bitmap into Flash, you have the option of using Flash's Trace Bitmap command (Modify > Trace Bitmap) to convert it to vector art. (See Figure 4.4.)

Tip

If you find that the File > Import option isn't available, make sure that the layer you currently have selected isn't locked or hidden! The same holds true for using the shortcut keys.

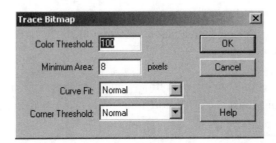

Figure 4.4   You can control the appearance of your traced bitmap by changing the Color Threshold, Minimum Area, Curve Fit, and Corner Threshold settings in the Trace Bitmap dialog box.

There are four settings you can change when you're using Trace Bitmap:

- **Color Threshold.** Enter a value between 0 and 500. When Flash converts a bitmap graphic to a vector graphic, it does so by comparing adjacent pixels. If the RGB values of two adjacent pixels have a difference of less than the Color Threshold value, they are considered to be the same color. The resulting color is a mix of the original colors. The higher the Color Threshold value you use, the fewer colors and shapes there will be in the final vector-based image. In this case, 0 would be considered a high setting, and 500 would be considered a low setting. In other words, with a setting of 0, you get a near photorealistic vector image (and a huge file size). With a setting of 500, you most likely have an unrecognizable image with just one or a few colors (and a small file size).

Tip

You can achieve an interesting two-toned effect by setting your Color Threshold high. You can see an example of this at www.egomedia.com. Fair warning—they'll take over your entire screen—which I find highly annoying. The Exit button is in the upper-right corner.

- **Minimum Area.** Enter a value between 1 and 1000. Flash uses this setting to determine how many adjacent pixels to consider when converting the image to vectors. In this case, 1 is a high setting and 1000 is a low setting.

Tip

Where to start with these settings? It depends a lot on the image you're tracing, but I usually start with the Color Threshold at 50 and the Minimum Area at 10 pixels. Then it's test, test, test.

The file size effects of both the Curve Fit and Corner Threshold are more subtle than the effects of the Color Threshold and Minimum area. Generally speaking, you see a file size increase if you choose Many Pixels for Curve Fit or Many Corners for Corner Threshold. Choosing Very Smooth for Curve Fit or Few Corners for Corner Threshold usually yields a slightly smaller file.

- **Curve Fit.** This dictates how smoothly the resulting curves are drawn. There are six possible choices: Pixels, Very Tight, Tight, Normal, Smooth, and Very Smooth. The smoother the curve, the more complex it is to calculate. Very Smooth gives you longer curve segments while Pixels gives you multiple short curves. The fewer curves you have in your object, the faster it renders.

- **Corner Threshold.** This determines how far a curve can bend before it is broken into two separate curves that are connected by corner points. The choices are Many Corners, Normal, and Few Corners.

By having all the settings, particularly Color Threshold and Minimum Area, at their highest values, you can easily end up with a vector image with a larger file size than the original bitmap. In addition, choosing high settings is very CPU intensive. If you have a complex bitmap and you choose a setting of 0 for the Color Threshold and 1 for the Minimum Area, you might as well click OK and then go out to lunch. If your computer doesn't crash, it might be done with the conversion by the time you come back.

Conversely, if the image you are starting with is relatively simple, you can make this work. Take, for example, the Marilyn Monroe print by Andy Warhol. You could scan that in at high settings and just change the individual fill colors, which would give you some interesting effects.

After you've traced your bitmap, you can reduce the size even more by selecting the traced image and choosing Modify > Optimize from the main menu. Figure 4.5 shows the difference between an unoptimized trace and an optimized one.

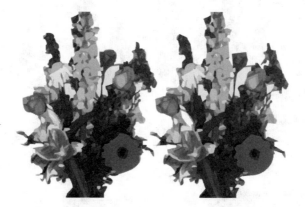

Figure 4.5   The image on the left was traced with a Color Threshold of 50 and a Minimum Area of 10. The image on the right is the same image optimized, with smoothing set to maximum. If you look closely, you'll see that the image on the right has more sharp angles and merged curves than the image on the left. The optimization reduced the number of curves by about 41%.

> **Note**
>
> Just as a test, I traced the bitmap for the next exercise with a Color Threshold of 0 and a Minimum Area of 1. I left both the Curve Fit and the Corner Threshold set to Normal. My CPU usage immediately spiked to 100% and stayed there for eight minutes. It took another eight minutes at 100% CPU to deselect the traced bitmap after it was complete. The final SWF file size was 332KB, as opposed to the 8KB file I got when I used the unaltered bitmap. That's a great example of how *not* to use Trace Bitmap.

Exercise 4.2 demonstrates how these settings can affect your final file size.

Exercise 4.2   Converting a Bitmap Graphic to a Vector Graphic

The settings that you choose when using Trace Bitmap to convert a bitmap to a vector graphic have a significant impact on the final file size.

1. Open vase.fla from the Examples/Chapter04 folder.

    This is a moderately complex image with a lot of colors, so you'll have a tough time getting the file size really small, but with it, you'll get a good introduction on how to use Trace Bitmap. The image on the Stage is a photo of a vase of flowers that was saved as a JPEG with a quality setting of 100% and no blur.

2. Before you convert this bitmapped image to vectors, test your file (Control > Test Movie). Open the Bandwidth Profiler (View > Bandwidth Profiler) and check your file size. You should have a file that is about 8KB, assuming the default JPEG compression of 80%. (See Figure 4.6.)

Figure 4.6   The image on the left still is in bitmap format and weighs in at about 8KB. The image on the right has been converted to a vector graphic, but is actually larger—about 22KB—than the original bitmap.

3. Back in your movie, select the image on the Stage and choose Modify > Trace Bitmap. Start with the following settings:

Color Threshold: **50**
Minimum Area: **10**
Curve Fit: **Normal**
Corner Threshold: **Normal**

You get an interesting painterly effect. Test your file and check the SWF size in the Bandwidth Profiler. The size comes in at about 22KB, so by tracing the image, you've actually increased your file size.

4. Go back into your file and choose Edit > Undo (or Ctrl + Z or Command + Z) until you're back to your original JPEG. This time, choose Modify > Trace Bitmap and change your settings to these:

Color Threshold: **100**
Minimum Area: **20**
Curve Fit: **Normal**
Corner Threshold: **Normal**

The file size drops to about 10KB, but the quality loss is significant. Depending on what you plan to use it for, that might or might not be okay.

You might find that bringing in bitmaps that are already compressed will result in a larger file than when you use uncompressed bitmaps. What's happening here? Compressed JPEGs always have artifacts created by the compression process. Those artifacts can add to the file size when you are trying to use Trace Bitmap. As a rule, bring in the cleanest, most uncompressed file you have. Then let Flash work its magic.

Note

How else could you approach this file? How about tracing the image and then separating out some of the flowers? Then you could convert the traced flowers to symbols and create your own bouquet. Alternatively, you could skip using the Trace Bitmap feature and hand trace the elements of the bouquet you want to use, but that's quite a bit more time consuming.

So, for your own work, how are you going to know what settings to choose? It's going to take a little "guestimation" on your part. You might have to convert the image several times before you get the look and file size that you're after. In addition, you might find that you need to rethink your approach altogether. If you're unhappy with the look of the traced image, just choose Edit > Undo until you have your original bitmap back. You then can change your settings and run the Trace Bitmap command again.

You've imported bitmaps. You've converted bitmaps to vector graphics. What else can you do? You can also import SWF files that were created by Flash or a third-party vendor.

Importing Vector Graphics

Many graphics programs are capable of exporting in the SWF format, either natively or with the help of a plug-in. For a list of third-party programs that can export in the SWF format, see Appendix D, "Flash Resources." You can import those SWF files just like you would any other graphic. After an SWF is imported, it can be left as is or broken apart and further modified inside Flash.

There are a few things you need to know about importing SWF files that might not be intuitively obvious. Because of the way SWF files are compressed, not all elements of the original file can be extracted from an SWF. This holds true for SWF files created both in Flash and in other programs. Some of the issues you need to be aware of include the following:

- When you import an SWF file, you lose all the layers of the original FLA file—everything is reduced to one layer.
- Any symbols in the movie are converted to graphics symbols and you lose all the symbol names. The symbols are named Symbol 1, Symbol 2, and so on.
- The tweens from the original FLA files are converted to frame-by-frame animations when the files are compressed as SWFs. That means that you lose any motion paths you originally set up; the frame-by-frame animation follows the original motion path, but the path itself is gone.
- You lose any sounds that were in the SWF file.
- Any graphics symbol animations, tweened or otherwise, are converted to frame-by-frame animations.
- Only the first frame of any movie clip placed on the main Timeline appears. The rest of the movie clip Timeline is ignored; hence, you lose any animation or interactivity that was internal to the movie clip.
- You *can* break apart and modify any of the graphics in the imported SWF.

Now that you know what will be preserved and what won't, try importing an SWF file and modifying it inside Flash in Exercise 4.3.

Exercise 4.3   Importing an SWF File

The file you are going to import was created in Swift 3D and exported as an SWF without shading.

1. Create a new movie. Choose File > Import and browse to the Examples/ Chapter04 folder. Select camero.swf from the file list and click Open.

2. Flash imports the SWF and creates a series of keyframes for each frame in the SWF file.

3. To break up one of the images so that it can be modified in Flash, select the image and choose Modify > Break Apart.

4. To break apart all the images, select Onion All in the Modify Onion Markers menu list (the icon just to the left of the frame number in the Timeline panel). Then select the Edit Multiple Frames icon (just to the left of the Modify Onion Markers icon). Either drag a marquee around all the shapes or choose Edit > Select All to select all the shapes in all the frames. Finally, choose Modify > Break Apart. (See Figure 4.7.)

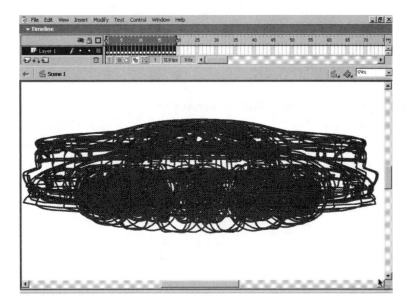

Figure 4.7   You can break apart all your frames at one time by using the Modify Onion Markers and Edit Multiple Frames options. Just make sure to select Onion All under Modify Onion Markers.

If you want to take a look at importing a more complex file that was created natively in Flash, try importing subculture.fla from the Examples/Chapter04 folder. You'll be taking a very close look at that file later in this chapter and you can get a good feel for what is lost and what is preserved.

You can import vector artwork that's been created in other programs but not converted into the SWF format. We discuss that next.

Importing Files Created in Other Programs

You might find yourself starting your design work in a program other than Flash and then having to repurpose it. Sometimes, the simplest way to import art from other programs is to drag and drop between the application windows. However, that doesn't work for all programs, and for more complex artwork, you usually are better off importing the artwork into Flash. In this section, you take a look at importing files created in Adobe Illustrator, Adobe PhotoShop, Macromedia FreeHand, Macromedia Fireworks, and Toon Boom Studio. Several of these programs are available in trial version on the CD.

Regardless of the type of file you're importing, the basic import process is the same:

1. Choose File > Import.

2. Browse to the file you'd like to import, and then click OK.

Each type of file that can be imported will have its own Import dialog box with options specific to importing that file type.

Importing Files Created in Adobe Illustrator

Importing from Adobe Illustrator (Illustrator 8 or earlier) is very straightforward. You have only a few options from which to choose. The Illustrator Import dialog box is shown in Figure 4.8.

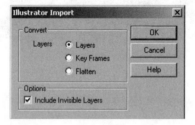

Figure 4.8   The Illustrator Import dialog box lets you control how you import an Illustrator file into Flash.

In the Convert Layers section of the Import dialog box, you have three options for converting your Illustrator layers:

- **Layers.** Each layer of the Illustrator file is converted into a Flash layer. The original, named layer structure is maintained. All the elements are imported as grouped objects.

- **Key Frames.** Each layer of the Illustrator file is converted into a Flash keyframe. Each keyframe is labeled with the original layer name.

- **Flatten.** The entire Illustrator file is compressed onto one layer and one keyframe. Flash imports all the elements of the Illustrator file as graphic symbols. These symbols appear in the Library as Symbol 1, Symbol 2, and so on.

The only other option you have in the Illustrator Import dialog box is whether you want to import all layers of the Illustrator file or only the visible ones. If you want to import all layers, make sure that the Include Invisible Layers check box is selected under Options.

Depending on how the Illustrator file was set up, you might or might not be able to see the imported images in your Flash workspace. To reposition the elements if you imported them either as layers or as flattened, choose Edit > Select All and use the Info panel to reposition the selected elements with both X and Y at 0. If you imported the file as Key Frames, you'll need to choose Onion All from the Modify Onion Markers icon. Then choose the Edit Multiple Frames icon. Choose Edit > Select All and use the Info panel to reposition the elements.

Be patient. Depending on the complexity of the file, this process might take several seconds. All the imported objects come in as grouped objects. You'll have to ungroup them to work with them (Modify > Ungroup).

Next you take a look at importing files from Adobe Photoshop.

Importing Files Created in Adobe Photoshop

You can import Photoshop PSD files only if you have QuickTime 4+ installed. The import for Photoshop files is fairly primitive, which shouldn't come as a surprise. After all, Photoshop is used for working exclusively with bitmapped images.

When you initiate the import of a PSD file, you'll first get an error message that states the following: "The import didn't finish because an unknown error occurred."

If you click OK and you have QuickTime installed, you'll get a second pop-up message that says the following: "Flash doesn't recognize the file format of 'yourfile.psd.' Would you like to try importing via QuickTime?"

To continue the import, click Yes. Figure 4.9 shows the dialog box that pops up.

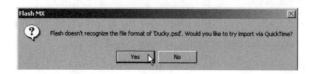

Figure 4.9   There is no Import dialog box for Photoshop files. Instead, you get an error message and then an option to import using QuickTime.

What will import is a flattened bitmap of the visible layers in the Photoshop file. No invisible layers will import.

Because Macromedia products are designed to integrate very closely, you have more control when you import a FreeHand or Fireworks file. You'll take a look at these options next.

Importing Files Created in Macromedia FreeHand

When you import a FreeHand file, you'll get the FreeHand Import dialog box with a series of options. (See Figure 4.10.) You can choose which pages you want to import and how to map the pages and layers.

The FreeHand Import dialog box is divided into three sections: Mapping, Pages, and Options.

In the Mapping section, you have two options for importing pages from the FreeHand file:

- **Scenes.** Each page of the FreeHand file is placed in its own scene. Because pages in FreeHand are not named, the scenes are numbered with the first page corresponding to Scene 1.

- **Keyframes.** Each page is placed in its own keyframe on the main Timeline.

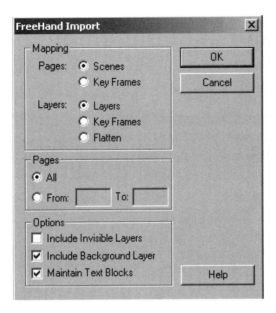

Figure 4.10   The Import dialog box lets you control how you import a FreeHand file into Flash.

   Tip

Because I almost never work with scenes (I prefer using movie clips), I always import my FreeHand pages as keyframes.

A fair question here is why not scenes? Scenes are just extensions of the main Timeline—unlike movie clips, which are objects. You have a fair amount of control over movie clips using ActionScript. You can control their positioning, change their visibility, load variables into them, and so on. You can even create movies that exist only in your library and use `attachMovie()` to attach them to the Stage as needed. Because movie clips are objects, you can give them instance names, which makes it easy to communicate between movies. You're probably starting to get the picture. Whenever someone sends me something that's been broken out into scenes, the first thing I usually do is reorganize it into a series of movie clips.

You also have three options for importing the FreeHand file's layers:

- **Layers.** If you choose to have the FreeHand layers imported as layers into Flash, the FreeHand layers and layer names are preserved.

- **Keyframes.** If you choose to import the layers as keyframes, each layer is imported as a labeled keyframe in Flash with the keyframe label being the same as the old layer name.

- **Flatten.** All the layers are collapsed and placed in Layer 1 of the Timeline.

In the Pages section, you can choose to either import all the Pages of the FreeHand file or a contiguous sequence of pages.

You have three other options you can set under the Options section:

- **Include Invisible Layers.** If you select this option, any layers marked as hidden still are imported. If you don't select this option, hidden layers are not imported.

- **Include Background Layer.** The Background layer in FreeHand is a nonprinting layer that is somewhat equivalent to a Guide layer in Flash. With this option selected, the Background layer, with all its elements, is imported.

- **Maintain Text Blocks.** Select this if you want any text blocks you import to be editable as text blocks in Flash. If you don't select this option, the text still is imported, but it won't be editable as text.

Any symbols in the FreeHand Symbols panel will be imported as graphic symbols into the Flash Library. The symbols retain their original names. Any elements that were not symbols in FreeHand also are imported into the Flash Library as graphic symbols. These symbols are organized by type (Clipping Paths, Lenses, and so on) in a Folder called "FreeHand Objects" and are named Symbol 1, Symbol 2, and so on.

So far, so good, but how do combinations of these selections affect the file import? The combinations that follow assume that all three options in the Options section are selected. Pay special attention to the note about including or not including invisible layers.

- **Pages as Scenes/Layers as Layers.** Each FreeHand page is imported as a numbered scene in Flash. Each layer is imported to a Flash layer with the appropriate layer name. The entire content of the layer is in one keyframe. Locked layers still are locked, and hidden layers still are hidden, but their contents are imported. Any layers in the current Flash movie remain unchanged. The new layers are added below existing layers in the layer stack.

Note

As a general rule, I usually include invisible layers when importing from a FreeHand file, especially if the FreeHand file has multiple pages. Why? Every scene in Flash can have its own set of layers. This is not so for pages in FreeHand. In FreeHand, the layers defined for the file carry through all the pages. If you've hidden a layer on any particular page, that layer does not import for any of the pages. It's easy to get rid of any imported material you don't need in Flash.

- **Pages as Scenes/Layers as Keyframes.** Each FreeHand page is imported as a numbered scene in Flash. Each layer is imported as a Flash keyframe with a keyframe label that is the same as the FreeHand layer name. Layers that were empty in the FreeHand file still are labeled, but they are imported as blank keyframes. The contents of hidden layers are imported. Any layers in the current Flash movie remain unchanged. The new layers are added below existing layers in the layer stack.

- **Pages as Scenes/Layers as Flattened.** Each FreeHand page is imported as a numbered scene in Flash. All the layers are compressed into one layer with all content in frame 1. The individual elements of the page still are grouped and editable.

- **Pages as Keyframes/Layers as Layers.** All pages are imported into the Timeline in which you are currently working; it can be the main Timeline, a movie clip, a graphic symbol, or a scene. All layers and layer names are preserved and are inserted at the bottom of the layer stack.

- **Pages as Keyframes/Layers as Keyframes.** All pages and layers are imported onto one layer in a continuous series of labeled keyframes.

- **Pages as Keyframes/Layers as Flattened.** All pages and layers are imported into a single keyframe. All elements are grouped and remain editable.

In addition to FreeHand files, you can import the PNG files that are created using Macromedia Fireworks.

Importing Files Created in Macromedia Fireworks

One of two things will happen when you import a PNG file created with Fireworks. If the only element in the file is a bitmap, Flash imports the bitmap directly with no additional dialog boxes. Otherwise, when you import a Fireworks file, you get the Fireworks PNG Import Settings dialog box with a series of options. (See Figure 4.11.)

By default, the Import as a Single Flattened Bitmap option is selected and all other options are grayed out. If you keep this as your selection, all the artwork in the Fireworks file—including any vector graphics—is imported as a single bitmap. Even if you import the artwork as a flattened bitmap, you still can launch Fireworks from inside Flash and use it to update the original artwork by selecting the item in the Library and right-clicking (Windows) or Control-clicking (Macintosh) and choosing Edit with Fireworks 4 from the context menu.

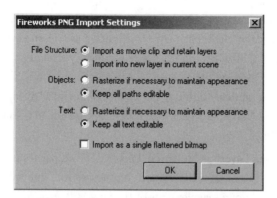

Figure 4.11   The Fireworks PNG Import Settings dialog box lets you control how you import a Fireworks file into Flash.

Except for extremely simple files, I don't recommend choosing Import as a Single Flattened Bitmap. You tend to lose a lot of flexibility and information this way. If you deselect the Import as a Single Flattened Bitmap option, you suddenly have a lot more with which to work. However, you lose the option of making continued edits inside Fireworks and having them reflected in your file.

Under File Structure, you have two options:

- **Import as Movie Clip and Retain Layers.** If you choose this option, the entire PNG file is imported into a movie clip with all its layers and frames intact.

- **Import into New Layer in Current Scene.** This option enables you to import the Fireworks file directly into your current scene as a single, flattened layer. Using this option, the frames are preserved. The new layer appears at the top of your layer stacking order.

Under Objects, you can choose the following:

- **Rasterize If Necessary to Maintain Appearance.** Selecting this option enables you to keep any fills, strokes, or effects that were created inside Fireworks.

- **Keep All Paths Editable.** Selecting this option keeps all vector graphics editable as vectors, but you might lose some fills, strokes, and effects.

Finally, under Text, you have two more options:

- **Rasterize If Necessary to Maintain Appearance.** As with objects, choosing this option maintains the appearance of any fills, strokes, or effects.

- **Keep All Text Editable.** Selecting this option keeps all text editable, but you might lose any fills, strokes, or effects.

You also have the option of importing files that were created in Toon Boom Studio.

Importing Files Created in Toon Boom Studio

You can import SWF files created by using Toon Boom Studio in the same way that you would any other SWF file. However, in Flash MX, you can import the uncompiled Toon Boom (.tbp) files. This means that you can use some of Toon Boom's features during your initial work, and then add the interactivity you need in Flash MX.

The Toon Boom Studio Importer dialog box has six sections: Scenes, Elements, Frames, Soundtracks, Layers, and Global Templates, as shown in Figure 4.12.

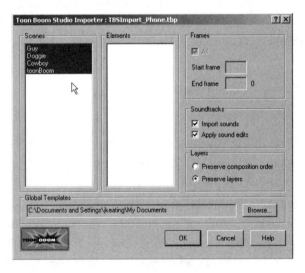

Figure 4.12   The Toon Boom Studio Importer dialog box lets you control how you import a Toon Boom Studio file into Flash.

You should begin your work with the Scenes and Elements panes:

- When you start the import of a Toon Boom project, you see all the scenes in the Toon Boom file highlighted in the Scenes pane. If your goal is to import the entire project, leave all the scenes highlighted. If you are importing more than one scene, you must import all the elements and frames of all selected scenes. You won't see any elements listed in the Elements pane.

- Use Control-click (Windows) to select or deselect individual scenes that are not next to each other in the stacking order. To select a sequence of contiguous scenes, click the first scene you want to import, and then Shift-click the last scene.

- If you want to import only one scene, or even just a few elements from a particular scene, you need to click the scene from which you want to import. When you do that, you see all the scene elements highlighted in the Elements pane. Each element is marked as either a vector or a sound.

- Just as in the Scenes pane, use Control-click or Shift-click to select the element or elements you want to import.

If you are importing from one scene only, you have the option in the Frames section of choosing to import all frames, or you can specify a series of frames to import. This option is grayed out if you have more than one scene selected. To import a specific sequence of frames, deselect the All check box and enter the Start and End frame numbers.

Regardless of whether you are importing one scene or many, you have options to choose in both the Soundtracks and Layers sections.

In the Soundtracks section, you have two options:

- **Import Sounds.** Select this check box if you want to import any sounds that were added to the Toon Boom file. If you select this option, the Apply Sound Edits option becomes available.

- **Apply Sound Edits.** If you select this option, Toon Boom exports a new sound file that contains any edits that were added inside Toon Boom—including fades and start and stop envelopes. The sound file is in stereo and is exported (and incorporated in your Flash movie) in .aif format. If you don't select this option (but do select Import Sounds), Toon Boom exports the original unedited sound file.

In the Layers section, you have the option either to preserve the composition order or to preserve the elements on individual layers:

- **Preserve Composition Order.** This option compresses all the elements in a scene into one layer. It preserves the positioning of each element relative to the others during the animation.

- **Preserve Layers.** This option separates the individual elements onto their own layers. It also creates a keyframe for every element and every frame where that element occurs.

Which of these options should you select? It really depends on what you want to accomplish. If your primary concern is preserving animation sequences, you'll want to preserve the composition order. If you're more concerned with extracting the individual elements of the file, you'll want to opt to preserve layers.

If you have used a Global Template in your Toon Boom file, you need to browse to that template so that its elements are included in your file. In Toon Boom, templates are repositories of reusable objects.

The Toon Boom animation imports after the current scene in your Flash movie. Thus, if you've opened a new movie and imported a Toon Boom file, your Scene 1 will remain blank. All the scenes you imported from Toon Boom will follow Scene 1.

You've looked at importing different types of bitmap and vector artwork into Flash; now it's time to look at how you can combine vector and bitmap art to create interesting effects.

Combining Bitmaps and Vector Art

Whenever you plan to use bitmaps and vectors together in Flash, you need to be aware of a few issues. Combining bitmaps and vectors almost always has an impact on file size, but increased file size isn't the only issue with which you have to deal. Whenever a Flash movie plays, it's using the computer on which it's playing to run the calculations necessary to render the vector art. Let me tell you—having some types of vector art animating over the top of a bitmap can turn your file into a real resource hog.

If you're depending on other people's computers to do some work, the issue becomes how much work you are expecting them to do. You won't make friends by crashing their computers and consuming all their system resources!

To understand the issues involved in combining bitmaps and vectors, take a look at an example of how *not* to do it. Why start from there? Because if you know how to spot the problems, it'll make it easier for you to avoid making them as you start to build your own files.

Bitmap/Vector Combinations Gone Bad

Sometimes, the best-laid plans go astray. That's what happened with the next file. At this time, open FigSubCulture.swf from the Examples/Chapter04 folder.

This file originally was created as a background screen, something that would be left open and running on the desktop as a backdrop for presentations. It doesn't have to actually do anything other than sit there and look pretty. It does that part fairly well, so what's the problem? The problem is performance.

You might find that when you create a Flash file, your primary concern is with keeping the file size within certain limits. After all, file size dictates download time. That was the case with this project. The final size of the Flash Player movie was about 60KB, which is acceptable, especially for a file that was intended for internal use. However, there are issues other than file size that you have to take into consideration.

For instance, the problem with this file is that when we left it open and running in the background at Fig Leaf, we noticed some significant system performance problems. After a little checking around, we discovered that the file, even when idle, was causing the CPU usage to average about 75%, with frequent peaks to 100%. That is not a good thing.

So what is it in this file that is causing such a huge performance hit? It's not any individual element of the file that is causing the problem, but a combination of several elements.

Think about the operations in Flash that are processor intensive. The big CPU killers are the following:

- Shape tweening
- Multiple tweens in the same frame
- Alpha animations
- Masking
- Gradients
- Any of the preceding items over a bitmap

This file has them all. So, how do you avoid making this mistake? How do you tell when you have too much of a good thing? You can tell by monitoring the effect of your SWF file on your CPU usage as you build the file.

Monitoring Your CPU Usage

Monitoring your CPU usage is easy if you are running Windows NT or Windows 2000. If you're using Macintosh OS X, you also have access to a CPU monitor—just look under Applications > Utilities. (Note to Macintosh 9 and earlier users: There is no equivalent utility for you. Sorry! You'll have to pester your Windows or OS X friends.)

Just open the Task Manager (see Figure 4.13) by right-clicking the taskbar and choosing Task Manager or by pressing Ctrl+Alt+Delete and selecting Task Manager from the pop-up window. To see overall system performance as a graph, select the Performance tab. If you want to watch just the Flash player performance, choose the Processes tab and look for FlashPla.exe.

Tip

I use a third-party tool, TaskInfo2000 by Iarsn, to monitor my CPU usage because it also gives me a long-time average of the CPU usage. I find that that gives me a better feel for the performance of my file. TaskInfo2000 is available for Windows 95/98/ME/NT/XP/2000 and can be found at `www.iarsn.com/index.html`.

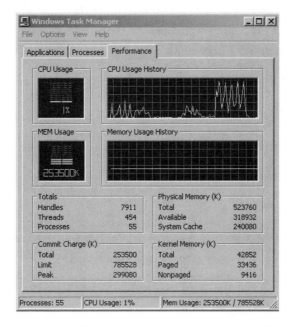

Figure 4.13   On the Windows NT or 2000 platforms, you can use the Task Manager to monitor the effect of your SWF file on the CPU usage.

When you are monitoring the CPU usage for a movie, you need to make sure that you are monitoring the usage outside the Flash authoring environment. If you use just Test > Movie, you get an incorrect reading because of the internal Flash processes that are taking place. You always want to launch the actual SWF file outside Flash.

Obviously, different computers are going to vary in processor speed. However, you should be able to get a good feel for what is acceptable and what is not. A spike in CPU usage at the beginning of a file—while it's still loading—is okay, but only if it immediately drops down to 30% or lower. It's always a good idea to test on as many different types of machines as possible.

Can This File Be Saved?

How drastically would you have to alter the construction of this file to make it perform better? Well, it's definitely worth taking a look at.

On the CD in the Examples/Chapter04 folder, there is a series of FLA files (subculture_ build and subculture_build_a through subculture_build_f) that reconstructs this file, layer by layer. By building the file in this fashion, you can find and tweak the problem areas as you go. In all cases in the following sections of this chapter, the SWF was tested at the size at which it was built (800 pixels wide × 400 pixels high). If you increase the SWF to full screen, it consumes more resources. I'm showing you the results I got on my computer; your mileage might vary, but this should give you a good base from which to work.

Tip

You might notice a slight and unexpected shift in your bitmap image when you have an alpha tween over a bitmap. Before you panic, make sure you test it using the player (use F12 to launch it in a browser). If the shift still happens, there are several potential fixes:

- If your alpha tween is set at 100% or 0% at any point, try changing the setting to 99% or 1%.

- You can also try resizing your bitmap slightly or setting the alpha of your bitmap to 99%.

- Make sure your bitmaps are aligned exactly on a pixel, not on a subpixel. In other words, make sure that the X and Y are even numbers. For example, 4.0 is good, but 4.3 is bad.

- Use your Align tool to align the bitmap to the top-left corner of the Stage.

- Open the Bitmap Properties dialog box in the Library and deselect Allow Smoothing.

File: subculture_build.fla

Content: Background bitmap

File (SWF) size: 59KB

CPU usage: Minimal, drops to 0 almost immediately

Change: In Publish Settings, change the JPEG compression from 80% to 30%

New (SWF) size: 23KB

New CPU usage: No change

File: subculture_build_a.fla

Added content: BlueGreenGlow

File (SWF) size: 26KB

CPU usage: Spikes to 6%, but averages 4%

Change: No changes

New (SWF) size: 26KB

New CPU usage: No change

File: subculture_build_b.fla

Added content: Animated logo, with mask and alpha

File (SWF) size: 28KB

CPU usage: Spikes to 48%, but averages 22%

Change: Remove all unnecessary content, trim logo vector to size of mask, and remove masking layer

New (SWF) size: 27KB (subculture_build_c.fla)

New CPU usage: Spikes to 20%, but averages 11%

File: subculture_build_d.fla

Added content: Black gradient fade over logo tween

File (SWF) size: 27KB

CPU usage: Spikes to 35%, but averages 15%

Change: Trim unnecessary part of gradient fade

New (SWF) size: 27KB

New CPU usage: Spikes to 30%, but averages 13%

File: subculture_build_e.fla

Added content: Horizontal and vertical tweening lines

File (SWF) size: 29KB

CPU usage: Spikes to 35%, but averages 21%

Change: Trim unnecessary parts of horizontal and vertical lines

New (SWF) size: 27KB

New CPU usage: Spikes to 30%, but averages 19%

File: subculture_build_e.fla

Added content: Animation of Fig Leaf name

File (SWF) size: 32KB

CPU usage: Spikes to 40%, but averages 24%

Change: No additional changes

New (SWF) size: 32KB

New CPU usage: Spikes to 40%, but averages 24%

Original file: subculture.fla

File (SWF) size: 59KB

CPU usage: Spikes to 100%, but averages 75%

By making just a few changes, you are able to dramatically improve the performance of this file. Keep that in mind as you build your own files. Test early, test often!

Not only can you monitor your CPU usage to isolate problem areas, but you also can use the Bandwidth Profiler, which you briefly looked at earlier in this chapter, to check for potential playback problems.

Bandwidth Profiler

Flash movies play frame-by-frame. A frame cannot play until all the information it needs has downloaded; the playback of the movie pauses until all the information is available. The Bandwidth Profiler gives you a graphical view of how your file is downloading.

You can use the Bandwidth Profiler to answer these important questions:

- Are there sections of the file where there is going to be too much information for Flash to stream effectively?
- How does the file stream at different connection speeds?
- How much of the file needs to load before it plays back smoothly?

As you saw earlier, to use the Bandwidth Profiler, just test your movie (Control > Test Movie) and then choose View > Bandwidth Profiler. (See Figure 4.14.) The Bandwidth Profiler is displayed above your Flash movie.

When you use the Bandwidth Profiler, you can simulate how your file would perform at different download speeds. All you have to do is choose Debug from the main menu and then select 14.4KB, 28.8KB, or 56KB. Alternatively, you can customize the download settings by choosing Debug > Customize. You then can enter the speeds at which you want to test.

After you choose a download speed at which to test, you have several options for viewing your file's performance. By default, the Bandwidth Profiler displays a Streaming Graph of your movie. The left side of the Bandwidth Profiler displays information about your movie. The information includes the following:

- **Dimensions (Dim).** This gives the height and width of the movie.
- **Frame Rate (Fr Rate).** This gives the frame rate at which the movie is set.
- **Size.** This is the total file size in KB.
- **Duration.** This is the total number of frames and playback time on the main Timeline.

- **Preload.** This doesn't seem to be documented anywhere. It appears to be the total number of frames (including all movie clips) that need to preload to ensure smooth playback and how many seconds those frames will take to download.

- **Bandwidth.** This is the bandwidth rate at which you are testing.

- **Frame.** This is the frame number on which the Playback head is currently located.

- **Loaded.** This is the total number of frames currently loaded (main Timeline).

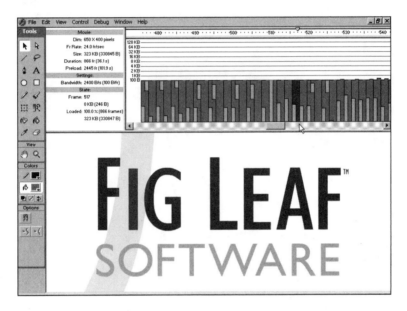

Figure 4.14   The Bandwidth Profiler gives you a lot of information about your movie's playback at different download rates. The default display is the Streaming Graph.

On the right side of the Bandwidth Profiler is the Streaming Graph. The Streaming Graph is interesting because it gives you immediate visual clues about where the slowdowns in your movie are. Frames are represented by alternating dark gray and light gray bars. The height of the bar indicates how many kilobytes of information have to be downloaded for that frame. That means that frames with only small amounts of information are stacked on top of each other, giving a striped effect.

You'll notice something else interesting here. See that red line? That's the red line of death. If the bar for a frame extends above the red line, that indicates that you might see a pause in your movie at that point. Simply put, there's too much information in that frame to ensure uninterrupted playback. Click one of the frame bars, and the movie moves to that point.

The Streaming Graph isn't the only view you have of the Bandwidth Profiler; it's just the default view. You can also view a Frame-by-Frame Graph, or, if you really want to share your viewers' experience, you can set the view to Show Streaming.

The Frame-by-Frame Graph is similar to the Streaming Graph. Instead of showing you how the file streams, it shows you exactly how much information is in each frame. (See Figure 4.15.) Thus, you can quickly isolate your problem frames.

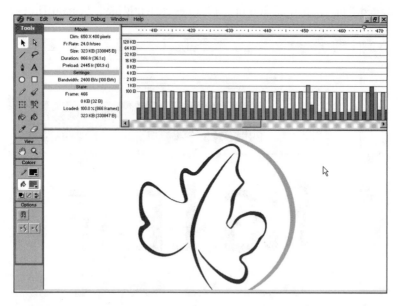

Figure 4.15   You can choose to view how your file streams frame-by-frame. This is particularly useful when you are trying to isolate problem areas in your file.

Show Streaming can be a real eye-opening experience. At whatever bandwidth you choose to test, you can see how your movie actually loads at Internet speed. (See Figure 4.16.) Remember that the entire frame has to load before it can play, so if you have a lot of information in the first frame, a lot of nothing might happen for a while. Fortunately, depending on how you set your layers to load, bottom up or top down, you have a little bit of control over what your viewer sees.

In the next exercise, you look at a movie that has some download problems. You use the Bandwidth Profiler to isolate and help you remedy those problems.

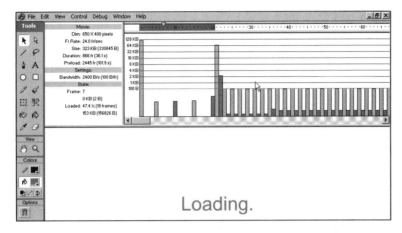

Figure 4.16   The Show Streaming view of the Bandwidth Profiler lets you see what your viewers see as your file downloads. This can be a real eye-opening experience. Use it.

Exercise 4.4   Using the Bandwidth Profiler

You're going to use the Bandwidth Profiler to find the problems in this movie and to come up with a strategy to fix them.

1. Open the magnatec.fla file from the Examples/Chapter04 folder on the CD. Choose Control > Test Movie and open the Bandwidth Profiler if it isn't already open.

2. Set the bandwidth to 56KB by choosing Debug > 56 KB.

    You should be able to tell right away that there is a problem here. You have five frames that are spiking substantially above the red line.

3. Switch to Show Streaming (View > Show Streaming) if you want a real indicator of how long your viewers are going to have to wait to see anything. Note that it's a good 24 seconds before the entire frame loads. That's too long.

4. Choose View > Frame by Frame Graph. There should be no question about where the problems are: frames 1, 30, 31, 32, and 33 are all problems. Of these, frame 1 is the most problematic.

 Note

Although 28.8 modems theoretically have a download rate of 3.5KBps, Flash simulates the download at 2.3KBps because this more accurately reflects the average performance on the Internet. Your mileage might vary.

OK, so you've tested your file and you found some potential download problems. How do you go about solving them? Well, for starters, there are a few questions you can ask:

- Can some of the information that is currently loaded in the problematic frames be moved to another frame?

- Can some of the movie clips that are used be changed to external SWF files that are loaded on demand?

- Do you need to preload the information in your file?

- Did you use `attachMovie()` or `attachSound()`? If so, unless you selected not to export in the first frame, it loads everything before the movie starts playing. If you do choose not to export in the first frame, you must include the movie or sound you want to attach somewhere in your movie. It can't just exist in the Library.

- For your text fields, did you embed the entire font library or just the parts of the font you needed?

Before you start rearranging, take a moment to look at another tool you can use to give you more information about what is going on in your file. That tool is the Size Report.

Creating a Size Report

Another useful troubleshooting feature built into Flash is the Size Report. (See Figure 4.17.) The Size Report is a text file that lists the size (in bytes) of every frame and every element in your Flash file.

The report is broken into different sections:

- **Movie Report.** This tells you how much information has to download for each individual frame.

- **Page.** This gives the size of all items on the stage that are not symbols. Text, grouped items, and drawn graphics are listed here.

- **Symbol.** This lists the name and the size of each symbol, as well as the size of any text used in the symbol, for your movie.

- **Bitmap.** This lists the imported bitmapped images. This section is particularly useful because it shows the uncompressed size, along with the compressed size, for each element. Thus, you can get a quick visual check of how compressed each element is.

- **Sound.** This lists all the sounds, their sizes, and the compression ratios.

- **Font.** This lists all the fonts that you use in your movie. Notice that Flash imports only the characters actually used in your movie.

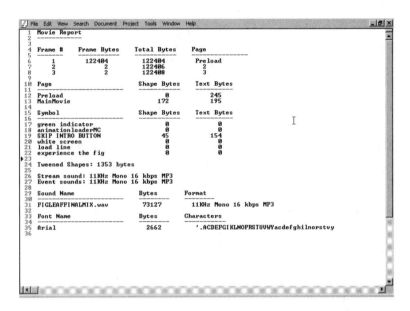

Figure 4.17   The Size Report gives you additional information that is not available by using just the Bandwidth Profiler. You can see the information that needs to be downloaded for each frame and for each movie element.

In Exercise 4.5, you create a Size Report that you can use in conjunction with the Bandwidth Profiler to help you optimize your movie.

Exercise 4.5   Creating a Size Report for Your File

The Size Report gives you additional information that you can use when you are trying to optimize your movie.

1. If you don't have the magnatec.fla file open, open it now.

2. Choose File > Publish Settings. Select the Flash tab and under Options, choose Generate Size Report.

3. If you click Publish now, the Size Report is created in the same directory as the magnatec.fla file. The Size Report is generated every time you test your movie.

4. Browse to the directory where the magnatec.fla file is located and find the text file named Magnatec Report. Open the file in your text editor of choice.

A quick look at the Size Report confirms what you already know from using the Bandwidth Profiler—frame 1 is a problem. You could set up a preloader to enable all the information in the file to download before playing. A preloader just pauses the movie until the assets that you specify have downloaded. Before you decide you need to use a preloader, however, take some time to explore your other options. In the next exercise, use the information you have available to you from the Bandwidth Profiler, the Size Report, and the Movie Explorer to optimize your file.

Using the Diagnostic Tools to Pinpoint Problems

You already know that frame 1 is a problem. Take a look at what is currently being loaded in that frame by opening the Movie Explorer and filtering for Frames, Layers, Movie Clips, Graphics, and Bitmaps. You'll find that the following information is loaded in frame 1:

- **Nav Bar MC.** This contains the navigational elements, including these movie clips: innovationMC, technologyMC, and performanceMC.
- **StaticMC.** This contains all the moving lines and flashes that overlay the street scene.
- **Frame.** This contains the upper and lower horizontal graphics that frame the street scene.
- **NewWorldTransMC.** This contains the semitransparent words that move over the street scene.
- **Next Button.** This contains the tweened button that appears above the upper part of the frame.
- **Streetscene.jpg.** This contains the background street scene.

Now you see why you need to use the Bandwidth Profiler, Size Report, and Movie Explorer together to make sense of the situation. The Nav Bar MC shows up in the Size Report as having 41 shape bytes and 542 text bytes. However, the innovationMC inside the Nav Bar MC has 52 shape bytes, and the Innovation text graphic inside that has 1148 text bytes. It gets frustrating real fast.

In the Movie Explorer, completely expand the node for the Nav Bar MC. You'll notice that you can find the innovationMC movie clip there, but not all the information embedded in the innovationMC movie clip. To find that, you have to drill down through the Symbol Definitions. After you have a list of all the elements in the original movie clip, you can use the Size Report to determine how much information has to be downloaded for that movie clip—or you can cheat. For the lazy person's approach to this problem, read Exercise 4.6.

Exercise 4.6   Using the Information from Bandwidth Profiler and Size Report to Pinpoint Problems

Although the Size Report and Movie Explorer help you pin down the general problem areas, you should use the Bandwidth Profiler to help make this information more meaningful.

1. Open magnatec.fla if it isn't already open.

2. Try staggering the introduction of the content in each layer. In other words, leave the keyframe on the Border layer in frame 1, but drag the keyframe from the first frame of the Logo layer to frame 2.

3. Continue staggering the introduction of the first frame of the layers as follows:

    Next Button: Move to frame 3
    Nav Bar: Move to frame 4
    StaticMC: Move to frame 5
    GraphicMC: Move to frame 6
    Mask: Move to frame 7
    NewWorldTransMC: Move to frame 8
    Streetscene: Move to frame 9

4. Test your movie and switch the view for the Bandwidth Profiler to Frame-by-Frame Graph. Now you can see exactly where the worst of the problems are.

The first major hit is in frame 4—that's where you introduce the Nav Bar movie clip. If you check the Size Report now, you'll see that, in that one frame, you are introducing 98306 bytes of information.

If you open the Nav Bar movie clip, you'll see that the problem is that you have not only the navigational bar and buttons in this movie clip, but also the movie clips with information that is presented whenever you press a button.

You have a couple of options for approaching this. You can move the movie clips that are currently embedded in the Nav Bar movie clip to the main Timeline. Alternatively, you could have each movie clip be independent movies that are loaded only as needed using the LoadMovie function.

By moving that information into separate movies, you not only help optimize your file, but also you get the benefit of reducing the download time for the file.

The next significant problem is in frame 9, which is where streetscene.jpg resides.

Because this is a bitmap, you're going to take a penalty for file size, but you can minimize it as much as possible. Try changing the compression for the bitmap, and see how much file size you can save. Remember: Test early, test often.

To see how else you can optimize your file, from rearranging frames and layers to splitting some of the other movie clips into separate movies, examine magnatec_final.fla in the Examples/Chapter04 folder.

If you decide to break your FLA file into several movies, you'll have to dive into ActionScript to load those movies as they're needed. It's not at all difficult to do.

Breaking a Large Movie into Several Smaller Ones

Obviously, you'd prefer to plan ahead and know you are going to want to have several smaller movies rather than one really large one. Sometimes, however, projects take on a life of their own and expand way beyond what you originally had in mind. When that happens, you have to take the situation in hand and decide what to do.

Breaking a movie into several individual movies involves copying frames from the current movie into a new blank movie or duplicating the movie you have and eliminating the frames you don't need. That's easy enough; just highlight the frames you want to move to a new movie and choose Edit > Cut Frames. In your new movie, select frame 1 and choose Edit > Paste Frames. All the necessary assets are imported with their original library names intact. Unfortunately, you lose your layer names.

If you're pasting your frames into an existing movie, be a little careful. Unless you paste them into the same number of frames that they occupied in the original movie, results might not be what you expect. If you try to paste your frames into a single frame, Flash inserts new layers to accommodate the frames and layers you're pasting. If, however, you highlight a series of frames and layers into which to paste, Flash happily pastes your new frames without adding additional layers to your movie—as long as you highlight the same number of frames (or more) that you cut or copied from the first movie.

Okay, that part is easy—just break your big movie into a series of smaller movies. However, how do you get your new smaller movies to load? You have a couple of options. You can load the movies based on a specific event, such as entering a particular frame, or you can load them based on user demand. The second method, loading on demand, is especially effective on large sites where users might be looking for specific information. You are giving them just what they want.

If you're going to let users choose when to load extra movies, you need to attach actions to the appropriate buttons to let them make that choice. The actions you need are quite simple; all you need to do is tell Flash what button event it should react to (press, release, and so on) and then add a `loadMovie()` or `loadMovieNum()` action.

The `loadMovie()` and `loadMovieNum()` actions can take the following parameters:

- **URL.** This is the required URL of the movie being loaded.
- **Target or Level.** This is required. You can target a movie to replace by specifying a path, or you can load your movie into a new level (see the Note after this bulleted list). If you specify 0 for the level, the `loadMovie` action replaces the base movie in level 0. Any movies loaded into other levels are unloaded.
- **Variables.** This is optional. Your choices are GET or POST, and you can use this option if you are sending variables with the movie to load. GET attaches any variables to the URL string. This is fine for short strings. POST sends the variables in a separate HTTP header. This method is better suited to longer strings.

Note

The loadMovie() action is used to load an SWF to a target, and loadMovieNum() is used to load an SWF to a level. When you're working in Normal mode in the Actions panel, Flash chooses the appropriate function for you. If you're working in Expert mode, you need to make that choice for yourself.

If you load a movie into a level that already contains a movie, the new movie replaces the old movie. If you load your movie into unique levels, you need to unload them using the `unloadMovie` action. If you don't unload the movies, you end up with layered movies, which might or might not be what you intended.

For `loadMovie()`, the syntax is the following:

```
on (release) {
      loadMovie("newmovie.swf", "_root.placeHolder");
}
```

For `loadMovieNum()`, the syntax is the following:

```
on (release) {
      loadMovie("newmovie.swf", 1);}
```

That's really all there is to loading new movies into an existing Flash movie. Just remember that if you don't target a movie or don't load into a level that already has a movie in it, you have to use `unloadMovie()` and `unloadMovieNum()` to clear any existing movies.

Summary

In this chapter, you've explored a wide range of techniques, including importing and optimizing bitmaps, converting bitmaps to vector graphics, and importing files created in other programs. You've also looked at a number of ways to monitor how well your file has been optimized. You've learned how to monitor CPU and memory usage and how to organize files to reduce download waits and overall download times. Keep this information in mind as you build your own applications. Remember: Test early, test often, and remember to check not only download times, but also CPU usage. Doing so keeps your viewers coming back for more.

Coláiste Oideachais Mhuire Gan Smál
Luimneach

Chapter 5

Using Sound in Flash

Where would *Star Trek* be without the
sound of the sliding doors as the captain
enters the bridge? Where would folk music
be without a guitar? Face it—we associate
sound with events.

Sound can be a potent memory trigger. It conveys mood, sets tone, and elicits an emotional response. It's another layer of description about the world in which we live. Used properly, sound can enhance and add to your Flash project.

When you're working with sound in Flash, there are two topics that you'll come up against on a regular basis: bandwidth issues and sound synchronization. To help you understand these subjects as thoroughly as possible, this chapter covers the following:

- **The basic theory behind sound.** The ways in which you see and hear details are significantly different, and those differences have a direct impact on the size of files that use motion and sound. You learn how you can manipulate sampling rate and bit depth to keep your file sizes as small as possible.

- **Layering and synchronizing sound tracks.** You can use short loops of different sounds to create soundtracks inside Flash. Learn how to get the different sounds to synchronize with each other.

- **The limits of editing a sound file in Flash.** Flash is not an ideal sound-editing environment. You learn some workarounds to add variety to your files.

- **Synchronizing simple animation and sound.** Synchronizing animation and sound can be a challenge. The tricks you learn here help you pull it off. You also learn how to preload all your movie elements to ensure proper playback.

- **Turning off the music.** If you're going to have sound on your site, you really should give your audience the option of turning the off sound. Not doing so is rude. You learn how to add the necessary user controls.

Before you jump into manipulating and working with sounds in Flash, you need to get some basic sound theory under your belt. The more you understand about how sound data is handled, the more efficient you can make your Flash files.

Sound Basics

You live in an analog world. The data you receive from the world around you is presented as a continuous stream of information that your eyes, ears, and brain interpret. When sound or video is recorded for use on a computer, it has to be captured in discrete units or bits.

A sound is usually thought of as a wave; however, when we deal with sounds in the computer world, that same wave must be represented by several smaller pieces. Everything comes down to a one or a zero; sound is not any different. By its very nature, digital information cannot be continuous. That presents some challenges.

Note

Think about the differences between an analog watch and a digital watch. An analog watch has hands that are in continuous motion and that can represent every possible increment of time. A digital watch, on the other hand, can display time only in very specific increments—you go from one number to the next without ever seeing any of the values between the two numbers.

Vibrations traveling through the air in the form of sound waves are what you perceive as sound. The sound waves reach your eardrum, which in turn begins to vibrate. Sound waves have both frequency and amplitude.

Frequency is how many waves of a sound pass a given point in one second; it is measured in hertz (Hz). The higher the frequency, the higher you perceive the *pitch* of that sound to be. Lower frequency sounds are heard as lower pitches. The distance from the peak of one wave to the peak of the next wave is known as the *wavelength* (see Figure 5.1).

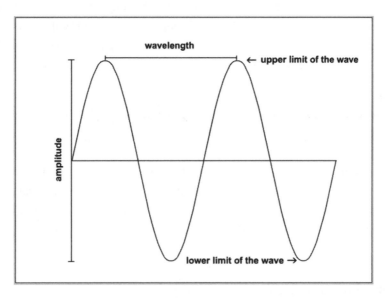

Figure 5.1   One complete cycle for a sound wave has both an upper limit and a lower limit. The greater the height or amplitude of the wave, the louder the sound. The length between the peaks is known as the wavelength.

The height of the sound wave, its *amplitude*, determines its *loudness*. Loudness is expressed in terms of decibels. Human speech is typically at about 60 decibels. Music is generally played at 30 to 100 decibels. (Of course, if you're younger than 20 years old, 100 decibels is probably the lower range.)

Sound versus Vision

Think for a moment about the differences in the way you perceive motion and the way you perceive sound. Your eye and brain retain a visual impression for a fraction of a second—depending on the brightness of the image. How many times have you looked at a bright light, closed your eyes, and still were able to "see" the image? You could see it because the retinas in your eyes hold on to some of the information with which they were stimulated.

The ability to retain an image is known as *persistence of vision*. Because of this, your eyes have a relatively slow response to change. In fact, your eye/brain combination can't really register pulses that come at you any faster than 50 or 60 times a second. You can take advantage of this fact when producing visual content.

Persistence of vision helps make the visual sample rate of 24 frames per second that is used in motion pictures work. In fact, you can use a lower visual sampling rate and still get satisfactory results. However, you can't do that with sound. The lowest frequency that most humans can hear is about 20Hz, and the highest is about 20,000Hz. What all this means is that your ear is reacting to a stimulus that is changing between 20 and 20,000 times per *second*. Unlike your eyes, your ears have a rapid response to change.

Note

You can recognize sounds below the 20Hz range, but rather than hear them, you feel them as vibrations.

That's why sound adds so much weight to a file. To retain fidelity, you have to sample sound at a much higher rate than you would sample images. You can't fake out the human ear in the same way you can the eye. The sound has to be exactly right. The quality of a sound is controlled by both the sampling rate and the bit depth at which it is recorded.

Sampling Rates and Bit Depth in Sound

The quality of a sound is determined by a combination of the rate at which it is sampled and how many bits are used to store information about the sound. The *sampling rate* is how many times per second the sound was sampled during recording; it is measured in Hz.

In Flash, the sampling rates you'll see range from 5kHz (5,000 samples per second) to 44.1kHz (44,100 samples per second). The *bit depth* is how many bits of information you are using to store your data. The higher the bit depth, the more detailed your sound will be. The lower the bit depth, the more noise you can expect in your file. Bit depths in Flash range from 4 bits to 16 bits.

Bit depth and the quality of a sound have a direct correlation, as shown in Table 5.1. The higher the bit depth, the more information you can save about a sound. The more information you can save, the higher the quality of the sound.

Table 5.1 The Correlation of Bit Depth to Sound

Bit Depth	Pieces of Information Stored per Sample	Quality
16	65,536	CD quality
12	4,096	Near-CD quality
8	256	FM-radio quality
4	16	Acceptable-for-music quality

If humans can hear sounds only between 20 and 20,000Hz, why do you see sampling rates that are so much higher than that? According to the Nyquist theory of signal processing, your audio sampling rate must be at least twice the highest frequency (think Hz) of the sound you are trying to capture to get the full dynamic range.

Don't sweat the theory too much. In English, it just means that sound waves have an upper limit and a lower limit (see Figure 5.1), and you need to sample each sound wave twice to capture both. Thus, to capture all the sounds that a human can hear (with the highest frequency being 20,000Hz), you need to sample at a frequency of at least 40,000Hz.

Table 5.2 lists the five standard sampling rates that are recognized by most audio cards. The higher the sampling rate, the higher the quality of the sound.

Table 5.2 Standard Sampling Rates and Related Quality

Sampling Rate	Quality
48kHz	Digital Audio Tape (DAT) quality
44.1kHz	CD quality
22.050kHz	FM-radio quality
11.025kHz	Quality sufficient for voice and music clips
5kHz	Quality sufficient for simple, short sounds

Now that you've been introduced to bit depths and sampling rates, the next logical step is to look at how you can manipulate those two aspects of sounds to keep your Flash file sizes as small as possible.

Keeping File Size Small: Voice versus Music

Your speaking voice has far less variation in pitch than does a piece of music. In general, you can assume an upper frequency range for speech of 4,000–5,000Hz. What kind of sampling rate would you need if you wanted to capture the full tonal range of the human voice? Referring again to Nyquist's theory, a rate greater than 8,000–10,000Hz accurately reproduces the sound you are recording. Thus, you should get good voice quality at a standard, 11kHz sampling rate.

Whenever you speak, you naturally have pauses between words and gaps between sentences. These pauses and gaps are where any noise or hissing would show up in your audio file. To reduce noise, you need to record spoken sound at a relatively high bit depth.

Music, on the other hand, has a far greater range in pitch than does the spoken voice. Because the range of frequency is much greater than the spoken voice, music needs a higher sampling rate. Music, however, usually doesn't have gaps between the sounds, and it plays along smoothly. Because you don't have to be worried as much about noise in a recording of music—some of the noise is masked naturally—you can record music at a lower bit depth.

To recap, for human speech, you need a low-to-moderate sampling rate and a relatively high bit depth. For music, you need a high sampling rate and a relatively low bit depth. These tradeoffs are important because you can use them to help keep your file size down.

For both music and voice, you can cut file size in half by cutting the sampling rate *or* the bit depth in half. Another way to cut the size of your sound file in half is to use mono sound instead of stereo sound.

In fact, you can calculate the size of a sound file with a simple formula that takes into account all the issues discussed so far in this chapter:

file size = number of seconds × number of channels × sample rate × number of bits ÷ 8

Thus, if you have a 30-second sound clip that was recorded in stereo at a sampling rate of 44kHz and at a bit depth of 16, your file size is as follows:

5,280KB = 30 seconds × 2 channels × 44kHz × 16 bits ÷ 8

Wow. You can see that high quality sound files get really big.

If you convert the sound from 2 channels to 1, the file size drops to 2,640KB. Go even further—if it's a voice recording, you're probably safe dropping the sampling rate to

11kHz. That saves you even more in file size. Now you're down to 660KB. That's a huge file size savings and a relatively small loss in quality.

Now take a look at the types of sound you can bring into Flash and how you add these sounds to your movie.

Importing and Adding Sound to Your Movie

Now that you've been through the theory, what kinds of sounds can you bring into Flash? Flash supports three main audio file formats:

- Waveform Audio File format for Windows (WAV)

- Audio Interchange File Format for Macintosh (AIFF)

- MPEG-1 Audio Level 3 for Macintosh and Windows (MP3)

Note

Sound Forge is a good program for converting sounds between AIFF and WAV file formats.

Note

If you have QuickTime 4 or greater installed, you can import several other types of audio file formats, including System 7 Sounds (Macintosh only), Sound Designer II (Macintosh only), SunAU (Windows/Macintosh), and Sound Only QuickTime Movies (Windows/Macintosh). In addition, with QuickTime 4 or greater installed, you can import AIFF and WAV files regardless of the platform you use.

Supporting the import of MP3s was introduced in Flash 5. MP3s are much smaller in file size than either WAV or AIFF files. However, most MP3s already have been substantially compressed before you import them. Carefully check the quality so that you don't get any nasty surprises, such as hissing, silence, crackling, hiccups, or just lower-than-expected quality. As a general rule, always bring in sounds uncompressed and let Flash handle the compression for you.

Note

Flash 5 supported only the import of MP3s recorded at a constant bit rate (CBR), as opposed to the newer variable bit rate (VBR). Flash MX enables you to import both CBR and VBR MP3s. Occasionally, you'll still run into issues. If you're having problems importing an MP3 file, try opening it in a program such as MusicMatch Jukebox. Then, convert it to a CBR.

Before you can add sound to a Flash movie, you have to import it into the Library. You import sound the same way you import artwork. You just select File > Import from the main menu and take it from there. You can also open an existing file as a Library (File > Open As Library). You then can drag a sound into your current Library or drop the sound onto the Stage. At this point, you can also select whether you want this sound to stream in. See the "Streaming Versus Event Sounds" section of this chapter for more details.

After a sound has been imported into your movie, it can be used as many times as needed. You can also share sounds among Flash movies by including the sounds in shared libraries (for more information about shared libraries, see Chapter 3, "Tips for Using the Library and Shared Libraries").

After you import your sound, you actually have to add it to the movie. Sounds get dropped onto the Stage, not into the Timeline. However, sounds show up in the Timeline and not on the Stage. By extending the Timeline to the length (in time) of the sound, you can see the sound wave inside the Timeline for as long as it lasts. (See Figure 5.2.) Weird, huh? It makes sense, however, because you can't "see" sound.

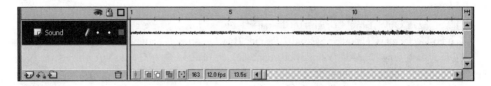

Figure 5.2   When you add sound to the Stage, the waveform is visible in the Timeline.

Tip

As a standard practice, I usually keep all the layers containing sounds at the bottom of the layer stack. Conversely, I keep my actions and labels at the top of the stack. This just makes it easier to find everything during edits. New to MX is the concept of folders; you can place several layers into a folder and then minimize it. When using many layers with unique sounds, using this new concept will make authoring and layer management a lot easier.

Note

Sounds can be added to the main Timeline, a movie clip, or buttons. You can drop a sound into a graphic symbol, but it won't play. You can also use sounds in conjunction with the Sound object in ActionScript. You'll be visiting that topic later.

Adding sound to buttons is pretty much the same as adding sound to any other Timeline. You can place a keyframe and sound in each of the three active states of a button: Up, Over, and Down. Because the sounds are stored within the button symbol, the sounds work for all instances of that button within the Flash movie.

Now that you know how to add sounds to a Flash movie, it's time to take a look at how Flash handles sound.

Streaming versus Event Sounds

Sounds in Flash can be either *streaming sounds* or *event sounds*. When you stream a sound, you lock it to the Timeline. That means that the sound plays frame by frame and forces any animations to keep up with it. If the animation can't render fast enough, frames of the animation are skipped. The downside of this is that your presentation can get jumpy. The upside is that you can use streaming to synchronize your animation and sound.

A general rule of thumb to keep in mind is this: If you're going to stream your sound, keep your animations simple and your movie clip usage to a minimum.

Streaming sounds begin to play as soon as enough frames of the sound have downloaded. If a streamed sound is longer than the Timeline it's in, the sound is cut off. In terms of behavior in the Timeline, streamed sounds are like graphic symbols—they are tied to the Timeline.

Event sounds are more like movie clips. They're independent of the Timeline in which they exist. They can play continuously, regardless of the length of the Timeline. Event sounds don't begin to play until the entire sound is downloaded. Therefore, unless you are going to preload your sounds, event sounds are best for buttons, short sounds, and "ear candy" in your movie. Event sounds can be looped without affecting the final file size.

After you import an event sound into Flash, you can use it over and over again without increasing your file size. You don't get that benefit with streamed sounds. When you set a sound to stream, Flash breaks up that sound into a series of frames, forcing it to play at a constant pace. If you loop a streamed sound, Flash adds additional frames to the Timeline, increasing your file size.

If you're working with animations that have specific sounds triggered by specific events, you're in luck. You can use event sounds keyed to a specific keyframe of the animation. It's when you're trying to synchronize animation to a continuous audio track that things become more difficult. They are more difficult because your sounds and animations won't necessarily play back at the same rate.

Streaming is the only way you can effectively synchronize long-playing sounds and animation in Flash. Thus, the question becomes this: How do you deliver the smallest possible file size and still have the ability to synchronize it with animation? The answer is that you have to get creative. There are a couple neat tricks you can use to get the results you want.

Tip

In general, you don't want to loop a streamed sound. If a streamed sound is set to loop, additional frames are added to the final movie and the file size increases according to the number of frames added for the looped sound.

Flash is not particularly good at delivering long audio presentations. Sound is, by its very nature, data-intensive and the file sizes quickly get out of hand. What you can do in Flash is use short event sounds that loop. After the sound is downloaded, it can be used as many times as you need it. Looping doesn't have to be boring. If you get creative, you can use Flash to mix your sounds and create an interesting audio track.

Layering Sounds in Flash

You can layer looped event sounds in Flash and apply effects to different segments of the looped sounds to get a fair amount of variety for relatively little overhead. If you're just synchronizing sounds, you can divide your sounds into tracks or layers and loop each sound all the way across the Timeline. You then can fade in, fade out, and otherwise manipulate the loops using Flash's custom sound-editing controls. If you choose to bring the sounds in at different frames, or if you're trying to synchronize a long-playing sound and animation, you'll have to resort to streaming your sound.

In either case, the first thing you want to do is make sure that all the sounds that you want to synchronize are recorded at the same tempo. (A tempo is a specific number of beats per minute.) If you don't do this, you're never going to have happy results. There are a number of sound-editing programs out there that let you import a sound, set a tempo for it, and export it as a WAV or AIFF file. If you are unsure of the tempo of the sound you are importing, it's a good idea to check it and reset it in one of these programs. Sonic Foundry's Acid Pro for Windows or Macromedia's Sound Edit 16 for the Macintosh are popular choices.

Now that you know the basics for creating a layered soundtrack, let's give it a try.

Exercise 5.1   Creating a Layered Soundtrack

Creating a layered soundtrack in Flash isn't difficult, as long as you start with good building blocks. Make sure all the sounds that you are trying to synchronize are recorded at the same number of beats per minute.

1. Create a new movie and import the following sounds from the Examples/ Chapter05 folder on the CD (Windows users, use the WAV files; Macintosh users, use the AIFF files):

    - claps
    - highhats
    - guitar

2. Create a layer for each sound (name your layers appropriately) and drag an instance of each sound onto the Stage. Don't make me say it—put them in the appropriate layers.

3. Save your file as **sound.fla**, publish your movie, and take a quick look at the file size of the SWF file. Assuming you haven't changed the sound compression from the default in Publish Settings, your file should be about 26KB.

4. Use the guitar sound as your base sound. Click frame 1 of the layer to which you added your guitar sound. Make sure the Properties Inspector is open (Window > Properties) and set the guitar.wav sound to loop four times. Extend the frames in all layers until you can see the entire waveform for the guitar sound (about 210 frames at 12fps). If you're not streaming the sound, you don't actually have to do this, but it does enable you to see your waveform.

5. Loop the rest of your sounds until they also extend the entire length of the Timeline (see Figure 5.3).

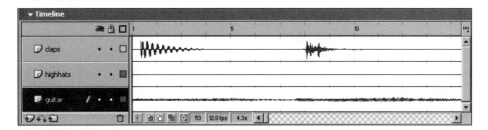

Figure 5.3   After you've imported sounds into your Library, you have to place them onto the Stage in the appropriate layers. If you extend your Timeline, you can see the complete waveforms.

6. Save your file and test your movie. Check your file size again. You should see only a miniscule, if any, increase in file size and that's due to adding extra frames, not looping the sound.

You've layered your sound and depending on your processor, it might sound acceptable or it might sound out of synchronization. Don't worry about that; it's a continuous annoying loop. You'll be fixing that shortly. First, you set up the layered sound you already have so that it plays back more predictably.

Synchronizing Layered Sounds

Even though all your sounds start on the same frame, playback is not always predictable. Logically, you'd expect the sounds to play back in perfect synchronization; after all, that's how you placed them on the Stage. That's not always what happens, however. Depending on the capabilities of the computer on which the sound is being played back, some of the sounds might not begin playback at precisely the same rate or time. This gives your soundtrack an "off" sound. Staggering the introduction of sounds, even sounds recorded at exactly the same rate, is even more problematic. Remember that an event sound has to download completely before it can start to play, so unless you've preloaded your sounds, there will be a lag before the sound starts to play.

There are a variety of ways you can approach this problem. You could set one of the sounds to stream. That would lock the rate at which the movie plays back. However, you'll most likely hear degradation in the quality of whichever track you stream. You'll definitely get an increase in your file size. If you're going to take a hit in file size for streaming, why not do it in such a way that your overall sound quality doesn't suffer?

Fortunately, there's a handy little trick you can use to accomplish this. All you need is a very short, low-quality sound that has been recorded at the same tempo as the rest of your sounds. It doesn't particularly matter what the sound is; you're going to mute it anyway. After you have the sound, you're going to do exactly what you were told not to do a few sections ago—you're going to loop the sound and set the synchronization to stream. Yes, this increases your file size. However, because you never actually hear the additional sound, you don't have to worry about the quality of the sound degrading while streaming. In addition, it serves to lock down your Timeline so that all the music plays back in synchronization.

Exercise 5.2   Synchronizing Sounds in Layers

To get predictable playback of sound, you need to lock your Timeline. You do that by inserting a streaming layer.

  1. Open sound.fla, if it isn't already open, or if you're starting the exercises at this point, open sound1.fla from the Examples/Chapter05 folder on the CD.

2. Add a new layer at the top of the stack, and name it **Streaming**.

3. From the Examples/Chapter05 folder, import the Click sound (WAV for PC users; AIFF for Mac users).

4. With the Streaming layer selected, drag the Click sound onto the Stage.

5. With the Click sound selected, press the Edit button on the Properties Inspector.

6. For both channels, drag the envelope handles to the bottom of the Channel window to mute the sound, and then click OK. (See Figure 5.4.)

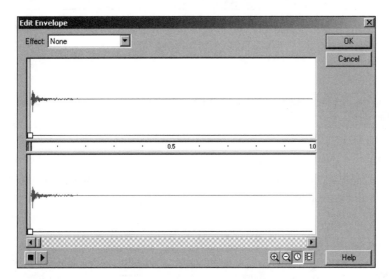

Figure 5.4   To mute a sound, open the Edit Envelope window and drag the Envelope handles for both channels to the bottom of their respective windows.

7. Back on the Properties Inspector, set Sync to Stream. Set Loop to 4.

8. To ensure that the synchronization is properly set, select frame 1 of each sound layer (except for Streaming), and drag the starting frame to frame 3. (See Figure 5.5.) This gives your movie a brief period of time to lock down the Timeline before the music begins to play.

9. Save and test your movie. Now your movie should play back predictably on any computer.

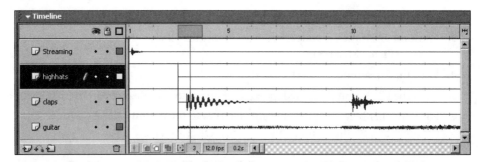

Figure 5.5   It's usually a good idea to start your streaming sound a couple frames before your nonstreaming sounds.

Tip

Starting the streaming sound a few frames before the rest of your sounds helps to lock the Timeline.

You get another chance to practice using a streaming track a little later when you learn how to synchronize a spoken soundtrack to animation. Before you do that, however, take some time and learn how to customize the soundtrack you have.

Note

On a PC, you can create a layered track in Flash and export it as a WAV file. You then can import and work with the single sound rather than with layers (File > Export Movie > WAV Audio). Unfortunately, there isn't an equivalent export on a Macintosh.

Editing Sound in Flash

Flash gives you some rudimentary control over your sounds. You can add simple effects, as well as control the sound type, by using the Properties Inspector.

You'll find the available canned effects in the Effect pop-up menu on the Properties Inspector. The effects are pretty self-explanatory, but here's a quick recap:

- **None.** Indicates that there are no effects applied to the sound. You can select this option to clear any previously selected effects.

- **Left Channel/Right Channel.** Enables you to control the playback of the sound in either the left or right channel.

- **Fade Left to Right/Fade Right to Left.** Enables the sound to be shifted from one channel to the other, simulating a pan effect.

- **Fade In/Fade Out.** Gradually increases or decreases the volume of the sound.

- **Custom.** Enables you to customize your effects using the Edit Envelope dialog box.

You've already been introduced to stream and event sound synchronization. There are two additional settings you can choose from the Sync drop-down menu:

- **Start is similar to Event.** The main difference between the two is that each time a Start sound is introduced, it plays to the end before it can play again. This is useful if you have a series of buttons that all have the same sound—no icky overlap effects.

- **Stop mutes the specified sound.** To use this option, you need to create a new layer, insert a keyframe where you want the specified sound to end, insert the sound you wish to end, and set the Sync option to Stop.

Note

To fine-tune your buttons, choose Start from the Sync pop-up menu within the Sound panel for each sound of each button state. That way, the sound plays only once, and you avoid any unwanted sound stutters or overlap.

Tip

The largest number of times you can loop a sound is 99,999,999. That really ought to be sufficient!

Adding Custom Effects

Generally speaking, you want to do as much of your sound editing as possible before you import a sound into Flash. However, within Flash, you can modify your existing sounds to a certain extent.

In the Properties Inspector, you'll notice an Edit button. This button is active if you have a sound selected. Click this button to open the Edit Envelope dialog box. You use the Edit Envelope dialog box to control the volume of the sound.

The Edit Envelope dialog box consists of three windows:

- The top window is for the left channel.

- The narrow middle window shows the Timeline for the sound. The Timeline can be set to either seconds or frames.

- The bottom window is for the right channel.

Each channel has an Envelope line that appears at the top of the Channel window. The open square on the Envelope line is an Envelope handle and enables you to control the volume of the sound. If you drag an Envelope handle down, it brings the volume down. Dragging the handle up increases the volume. The top of the window is full volume and the bottom of the window is no volume.

You can add up to seven additional (for a total of eight) Envelope handles by simply clicking anywhere on the Envelope line. When you add an Envelope handle in one channel, a handle is automatically inserted in the other channel. To remove a handle, drag it out of the window. You can use the Envelope handles to create custom fade-ins and fade-outs. As you saw earlier, dragging both the left and right channel handles to the bottom of their respective windows completely mutes a sound.

Tip

When you're trying to remove an Envelope handle, you can drag it out of the Channel window in any direction. Dragging it to the top or bottom of the window usually is the fastest way to delete a handle.

The Timeline window has two controls: Time In and Time Out. You use these controls to establish the starting and stopping points of the sound. You can use the In and Out controls to extract unnecessary dead areas at the beginning or end of a sound clip. You can also use it to remove parts of the sound you don't want to use.

Tip

Be careful when you use the Time In and Time Out controls—especially when you're trying to synchronize loops that have been recorded at a specific number of beats per minute. You can easily mess up your synchronization this way.

In the upper-left corner, above the left Channel window, you'll see the familiar Effect drop-down menu (see Figure 5.6). The effects in this menu are the same effects to which you have access on the Properties Inspector.

In the lower-left corner, below the Right Channel window, are the Play (triangle) and Stop (square) buttons. As you use the Envelope handles to manipulate your sound, it's always a good idea to test and make sure you're getting the effect you want.

In the lower-right corner are the Zoom In, Zoom Out, Seconds, and Frames buttons. Use the Zoom In and Zoom Out buttons to change the view of the sound. Use the Seconds and Frames buttons to switch the view of the Timeline back and forth between seconds and frames.

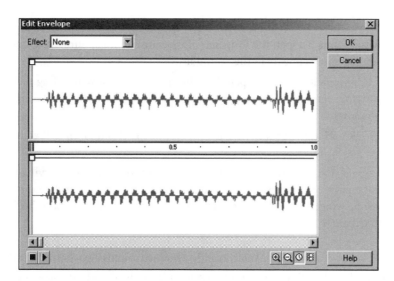

Figure 5.6 This is the window layout for controlling a sound within Flash.

Tip

When you are working on modifying effects in the Edit Envelope dialog box, it's usually easier to precisely place effects when you view the Timeline in terms of seconds.

That's it. That's the extent to which you can modify sounds inside Flash. It's not a lot with which to work, but you can get some interesting effects this way. Take a few minutes to work through the next exercise. Be creative! Make this sound clip your own.

Exercise 5.3 Customizing a Layered Sound Track

Rule number one: There is no such thing as a bad sound clip, only a bad sound clip editor. Okay, rule number one isn't true. Sometimes, however, you just have to work with what you're given, so you might as well learn how to make the best of it. Remember that all these sounds are recorded at the same number of beats per minute. To determine the in and out points of the sounds, it'll be easier if you view them in terms of seconds rather than in terms of frames.

1. Open sound.fla, if it isn't still open. If you're starting the exercises at this point, open sound2.fla from the CD. Test it to refresh your memory.

2. The guitar.wav sound forms the base of this file. Why not start the music with the guitar piece? You can build the file from there. Mute all the sounds except the guitar.

For each sound, except the guitar:

- Select frame 3. Open the Properties Inspector and make sure the sound you want to mute appears in the Sound list.
- Click the Edit button to open the Edit Envelope window and drag the Envelope handles for both channels to the bottom of their respective windows.

3. Click OK and test your movie. The only sound you should hear is the guitar loop.

4. The guitar doesn't really need to be played at full volume. You're trying to set a mood, not re-create a rock concert. Select guitar.wav and open the Edit Envelope window again and drag the Envelope handles down about halfway in both channels.

From here on out, it's up to you. You can add or remove sounds anywhere along the track by using Envelope handles. You can choose to fade loops in and out or you can bring them in abruptly. Just remember that you have only eight handles to work with and bringing in a sound abruptly costs you two of those handles.

Here's one possible scenario for adding in the additional sounds:

- Let the guitar play for two full loops.
- Just before the start of the second loop, begin to fade in the highhats. Bring the highhats all the way up to full volume.
- Have the claps indicate the end of the clip. Abruptly bring them up to half volume just before the end of the last loop.

When you're happy with your sound track, save it.

Next, you take a look at how compression affects your sound and file size on export.

Sound Compression

As mentioned, sound is data intensive. To help you minimize file size, Flash offers two approaches to compression. You can either create individual compression settings for each sound or you can use Publish Settings to apply a global compression scheme. You're generally much better off setting up compression for each sound individually than letting Flash use one overall compression scheme.

By default, Flash uses MP3, 16-bit mono compression. You can change this default by specifying a different compression scheme in Publish Settings. Although MP3 compression does a terrific job with keeping file sizes small, it does have some limitations of which you should be aware. The higher frequency sounds tend to get lost during heavy compression. In fact, if you've been testing your movie by publishing it, you've probably noticed that the highhats sound is kind of muddy. That's MP3 compression kicking in.

To compress a single sound, you use the Sound Properties dialog box. To open it, double-click the sound icon next to the sound you want to compress in the Library. (See Figure 5.7.)

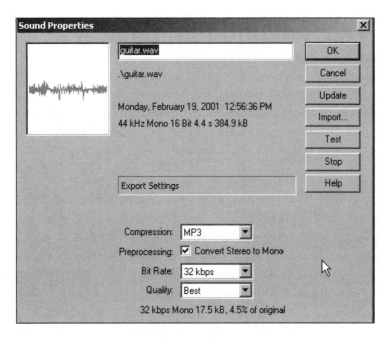

Figure 5.7   Use the Sound Properties dialog box to set the compression for each sound in your movie.

The upper half of the Sound Properties dialog box contains information about the sound:

- A view of the waveform (one waveform for mono sound and two for stereo)
- The name of the file in the Library
- The name and path of the original sound file
- The last date the sound was updated
- The sampling rate, bit depth, time in seconds, and size of the original file

Take a glance to the right side of the window. You'll see a series of buttons. In addition to the usual OK, Cancel, and Help buttons, there are the following buttons:

- **Update.** If you've updated the original sound file and you want those changes to be incorporated into your Flash movie, click Update.

- **Import.** You might change your mind about using a particular sound. Want to swap in a new sound without removing the existing sound from your file? No problem—just use the Import button.

- **Test.** When you start adjusting the compression for your sound, you need to test it to make sure the new compression setting is acceptable.

- **Stop.** Stop the sound you're testing.

At the bottom of the Sound Properties dialog box are the current export settings for the sound. Depending on the type of compression selected, the options vary. You can choose from five compression options: Default, ADPCM, MP3, Raw, or Speech.

Unless you have a compelling reason not to, use MP3 compression to get the highest quality and the lowest file size—especially for delivery of sound over the Internet. What would constitute a compelling reason not to use MP3? One reason would be if you knew your target audience was using the Flash 3 or earlier player. The earlier players don't support the playback of the MP3 format. If you're targeting those players, you need to use ADPCM compression. Unless you're not concerned about file size, you should avoid Raw compression—which is no compression at all.

 Tip

Using stereo versus mono sound doubles your file size and few people notice the quality difference. Thus, for preprocessing, it's usually a good idea to check the Convert Stereo to Mono check box.

If you are using MP3 compression, keep in mind that sounds with low frequencies can be compressed more than sounds with high frequencies can be compressed. Higher frequencies are what tend to get dropped during compression. Thus, if you've got a sound with higher frequencies, you might want to up the bit rate for that sound.

Exercise 5.4   Compressing the Sounds in Your Soundtrack

To keep your final file size as small as possible, you need to compress your sounds as much as you can without losing too much quality. To do this, you need to compress and test, compress and test.

1. Open sound.fla, if it isn't still open. If you're starting the exercises at this point, open sound3.fla.

2. Double-click guitar.wav in the Library to open the Sound Properties window. Right now, the compression should be set to the default.

3. Switch the compression to MP3. The preselected bit rate is 16Kbps. Test the sound. The rates you can choose range from 8Kbps–160Kbps. The only rate lower than 16Kbps is 8Kbps. Select 8Kbps. Test again. There is definitely some loss of quality at 8Kbps, but it isn't too bad. Because you've set the volume for this sound to 50%, it'll probably be acceptable.

4. Do the same for each sound in the file, picking the lowest bit rate at which the quality is acceptable. For some sounds, you might want to increase the bit rate slightly for better quality.

5. When you're done, check your final file (SWF) size. Depending on the compression settings you've chosen, your file size has either increased or decreased. By using MP3 compression, however, it's sure to be smaller than it would have been by using any other method.

You've mixed your sound in Flash. It's obviously not a perfect editing environment, but you do have rudimentary control over your sounds. Next, take a look at how you can synchronize a spoken sound track to a simple animation.

Synchronizing Simple Animation and Sound

Synchronizing animation and sound is more of an art than a science, but there are a couple tricks you can use.

Some sounds and animations are relatively easy to synchronize. If you have a series of short sounds, you can add them to the appropriate frames to match the animation. It's when you have longer sounds that the trouble begins. You've already seen how you can use a small, streamed sound looped over the length of the movie clip to synchronize different musical tracks. You can do the same thing to synchronize longer soundtracks and animation.

When you're using this method, you also can temporarily set your primary sound to stream to help you synchronize your sound and animation. Why do this? When Stream is selected for the Sync type, you can drag the playhead through the Timeline and hear the sound play frame by frame. It sounds awful, but it can be really helpful when you're trying to precisely place an animation.

Remember that long drawn-out explanation of the differences in our perceptions of sound and motion? Keep those concepts in mind as you synchronize sound and animation. In the next exercise, you'll be synchronizing typed words to a spoken soundtrack. It takes your eye/brain combo longer to register what they see than it does for the ear to process the sound. The trick is to actually have the words appear slightly before they are spoken—which enables your eyes the time to process the words and keep up with what your ear is hearing. The animation you're going to set up in the next exercise is pretty simple. You shouldn't have any problems with the frames not rendering fast enough to keep up with the sound.

Exercise 5.5   Synchronizing Simple Animation and Sound

You're going to be working with a movie that's already been started. In fact, for now, you'll be working with just one of the movie clips in that movie.

1. Open the NewYork.fla file in the Examples/Chapter05 folder. Test the movie to see with what you'll be working. You're going to synchronize typed words to the voice-over.

2. Open the Library and double-click the Voiceover movie clip in the Audio folder to open it in Symbol-Editing mode. You'll notice that you currently have five layers:

   - **Actions/Labels.** Has a frame labeled "Restart" just before the audio track begins. You'll use this label in a later exercise.

   - **Streaming.** This is the layer with a small, streamed sound that is used to lock down the Timeline.

   - **Audio: WWW.** Contains the first instance of the World Wide Web soundtrack.

   - **Audio: WWW2.** Contains the second instance of the World Wide Web soundtrack.

   - **Audio: News.** Contains the News soundtrack.

3. Add a new layer above the Audio: WWW layer and name it **Text: WWW**.

4. Set the sound in the Audio: WWW layer so that it streams. Drag the playhead across the Timeline to hear the sound play out frame by frame. Insert a keyframe in the Text: WWW layer where you first hear the word "The" being played in the Audio: WWW layer.

Tip

Didn't I say earlier that streaming can cause your sound to degrade? Yes, I did. Particularly in this clip, you'll notice a distinct loss of quality when you stream it. However, if the sound is streamed, you can drag the playhead through the Timeline and hear the sound play frame by frame. Don't worry—you'll unstream it later!

Tip

Unless you actively detest your office mates, do sound synchronization with your head-phones on. You're going to have to listen to this over and over again. Don't take your buddies down that path with you.

5. Select the Text tool and open the Properties Inspector. Change to the following settings:

    Font: **Arial or Helvetica**
    Size: **16**
    Color: **#0066CC**

6. Type the word **The** on the Stage. Switch to the Arrow tool and use the Align panel to center the text on the Stage. (See Figure 5.8.)

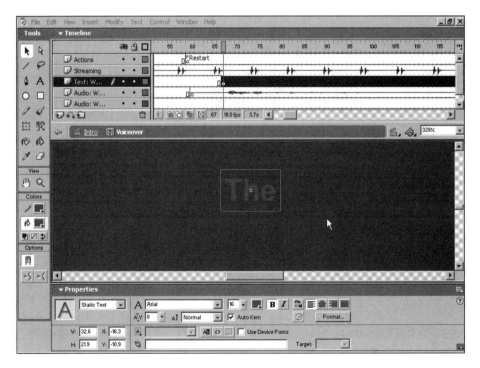

Figure 5.8   The animation for this movie clip will be printed words appearing as they are spoken.

7. Make sure the Controller toolbar (Window > Toolbars > Controller) is showing. Rewind the movie clip and press Play. If "The" is in the right position, you can go on to the next step. If not, shift the keyframe to the right or the left as necessary and test the movie clip again until "The" appears as you hear the word.

Tip

You might find it easier to test your synchronization if you undock the Controller toolbar and drag it onto the Stage. It'll be just a little closer at hand.

You're going to repeat Steps 4–7 for each word in this sound clip. For some of the words, you will be able to judge their approximate position based on the waveform. Others won't be so easy. See Figure 5.8 if you need some help on placement.

I'll cut you a little slack here. You really need to complete this only to the word "about." Because you're working with a series of layered audio tracks, you'll synchronize only the words to the important sections for each track. Thus, you'll need keyframes for each word of this text: The World Wide Web is at a revolutionary point right now. It's about....

8. When you're done setting up your animation, set the Sync option for the sound back to Event.

Note

Why can you see where some of the words are spoken on the waveform in the Timeline, but you cannot see the others? The waveform in the Timeline is showing the amplitude, or loudness, of the sound on the Y-axis. The X-axis is obviously time. The softer words barely register on the amplitude scale at the resolution that you can see in your Timeline.

9. Add a new layer above the Audio: WWW2 layer and name it **Text: WWW2**.

In the next few steps, you're going to repeat the animation sequence you set up for the first WWW Voiceover layer. If you play back your file, you'll hear the phrase "The World Wide Web is at a revolutionary point right now. It's about..." repeat. You want the words to show up for the repeat of the phrase. Lucky for you, you've already synchronized this phrase. All you have to do is copy the work you've already done.

10. In the Text: WWW layer, select the first frame above the beginning of the Audio: WWW soundtrack. Hold down the Shift key and select the last keyframe in the same layer.

11. Right-click (Command-click) and choose Copy Frames from the pop-up menu.

12. In the Text: WWW2 layer, select the frame just above the beginning of the Audio: WWW2 soundtrack. Right-click (Command-click) and choose Paste Frames from the pop-up menu.

13. Rewind the movie clip and press the Play button. You'll need to insert a blank keyframe in the Text: WWW layer after the last keyframe and before the word "The" appears in the Text: WWW2 layer. If you don't do this, the word "about" won't go away, and that will mess up the rest of your animation.

14. Save your file.

That was pretty easy. Now you can use what you just learned to synchronize the rest of the animation. (You might want to go out and get another cup of coffee first.)

To synchronize the phrase "In other news, United Nations declares New York City the new world city for international trade and one united currency. Other…," you follow the exact same process you used in Exercise 5.4 to synchronize the first phrase. Just as you did there, you'll need to add a blank keyframe after the last word in the Text: WWW2 layer. Now it's up to you. Happy synchronizing. Don't forget to set the Sync option for the sound back to Event when you're through.

After you are finished synchronizing the News audio, you need to add one more layer. Because the voice-over is in its own movie clip, you need to add an action at the end to force it to stop. Otherwise, it'll loop endlessly.

1. Add a layer and name it **Actions**. Drag the Actions layer to the top of the stack. Insert a keyframe in the last frame of the Actions layer. Open the Actions panel. With the keyframe selected, add a Stop action.

2. Save your file, and you've done it.

You've synchronized a simple animation to a soundtrack. It wasn't a difficult task, just a tedious one! Now that you've got a voice-over with synchronized animation, give your audience the chance to turn the noise off.

Turn Down That Noise

Whenever you plan to use sound in a presentation, please give your audience a way to turn off the sound. Nothing drives people away as fast as a booming audio track with no off button—especially if they're in the office within earshot of the boss.

What do you want to accomplish here? You want to press a button, and then have the sound go off. You want to press another button, and then have the sound come back on. How hard can that be? Put on your ActionScripting shoes for this one (it won't be too bad, I promise). You haven't gotten into object-oriented programming and the Flash objects yet, so you'll be doing this the old-fashioned way.

Turning the sound off is the easy part. In Flash ActionScript, there is an action that stops all sounds (stopAllSounds). Using this action stops every sound that is currently playing. You should be forewarned that if any of your sounds are in movie clips that loop, the sound restarts as soon as the movie or movie clip begins to play again. You can get around that by setting up some variables to capture information about whether a button has been pressed.

Note

Just in case you need a refresher, a variable is just a placeholder for information. In this case, the variable is "music" and the value of "music" can be true or false.

Exercise 5.6   Turning Off the Sound

Start by turning off just the music.

1. Open the NewYork.fla file, if it isn't already open, or open NewYork1.fla from the CD.

2. Select the Music On | Off button in the Sound Toggle layer. Launch the Actions panel (F2). For now, set the Actions panel to Normal mode by using the Options pop-up menu.

3. Click the Actions category in the Toolbox list to expand it, and then click Movie Control. Scroll down until you see the stopAllSounds action. Double-click stopAllSounds to add it to the Actions list.

    Because you're in Normal mode, Flash was smart enough to recognize that you're adding an action to a button, so it added the mouse event, which is called on (release), for you. (See Figure 5.9.)

4. Save your file and test it. Try clicking the Sound On | Off button to see what happens.

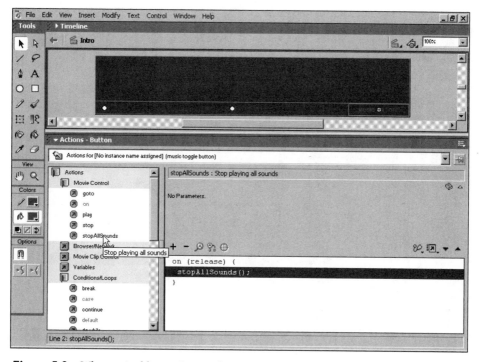

Figure 5.9   When you add an action to a button in Normal mode, Flash automatically adds an on (release) mouse event.

You can turn the sound off, but you can't turn it back on. There is no "start all sounds" option. To restart the sound, you have to get a little creative.

Exercise 5.7   Restarting a Sound

When the movie starts to play for the first time, the sound is on. Why not set a variable in the main Timeline that reflects that? You'll set a variable called "music" and give it a value of true. Then, when the On | Off button is clicked, you can change the value to false.

1. Select frame 1 of the Actions/Labels layer in the main Timeline. Launch the Actions panel (F2). Under the Actions category, click the Variables category to expand it, and then double-click to set the variable in the Toolbox list.

2. In the Parameters pane (see Figure 5.10), fill in the following:

   Variable: **music**
   Value: **true** (make sure that Expression is checked)

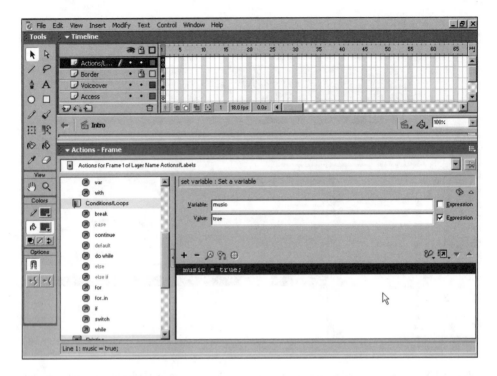

Figure 5.10   In Normal mode, you can fill in the necessary parameters in the Parameters pane.

3. Select the On | Off button on the Stage. In the Actions panel, select the line that begins on (release).

   When the button is clicked, you want to check whether the current value of music is true. If it is, you want to stop all sounds and you want to change the value of music to false. That means that the sound is on.

4. In the Toolbox list, expand the Conditions/Loops category under Actions, and then double-click if. In the Parameters pane, type **music==true**. (See Figure 5.11.)

 Note

What does the == mean? Well, that's the equality operator. It tests whether the expressions on either side are equal to one another. If they are, it returns true. If not, it returns false. What's the difference between == and =? Using the operator == tests for equality; using = sets the value of a variable.

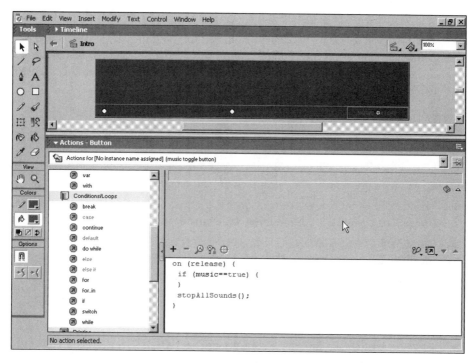

Figure 5.11   Use an if statement to test whether the `music` variable has been set to `true`.

5. With the first line of the if statement selected, double-click set variable again and change the settings in the Parameters pane to the following:

> Variable: **music**
>
> Value: **false** (make sure that Expression is checked)

6. Right now, the `stopAllSounds` action is outside the if statement. Move it inside the if statement by clicking `stopAllSounds` and dragging it inside the if. Your ActionScript should look like the following:

```
on (release) {
    if (music==true) {
        music = false;
        stopAllSounds ();
    }
}
```

So far, so good. But what are you going to do if the value of the variable `music` is equal to `false`? You need to test for that and figure out how to restart your sounds.

7. Highlight the `stopAllSounds` line. Double-click else if in the Toolbox list under Conditions/Loops. In the Parameters pane for Condition, type **music=false**.

If the variable `music` is `false`, that means that the sound is currently turned off.

You next need to restart two separate movie clips: Soundtrack and Voiceover. Before you can restart the two movie clips, you need to assign their instances on the Stage unique names so that you can use ActionScript to "talk" to them. These two movie clips are the open circles on the Stage.

8. Select the Voiceover layer. The Voiceover movie clip on the Stage is now selected. Open the Instance panel and give the movie clip the name **Voiceover**.

9. Select the Soundtrack layer to highlight the Soundtrack movie clip on the Stage. Open the Instance panel and give the movie clip the name **Soundtrack**.

10. Open the Actions panel and select the On | Off button again.

11. Select the line that reads `stopAllSounds();` and double-click `else if` under Conditions/Loops. For the condition, type **music==false**.

12. Select the line that reads `else if (music == false)`. If you reach this part of the script during processing, the sound is already off; you want to turn the sound back on and set the value of the music variable back to true. Double-click Set Variable in the Toolbox list and change the settings in the Parameters pane to the following:

    Variable: **music**
    Value: **true** (make sure that Expression is checked)

    Your code at this point should look like the following:

```
on (release) {
    if (music == true) {
        music = false;
        stopAllSounds ();
    } else if (music == false) {
        music = true;
    }
}
```

13. Use the Options pop-up menu to switch to Expert mode. (See Figure 5.12.)

    For the next three lines of code, you'll find it easier to set up the proper dot syntax if you're in Expert mode. In Normal mode, it's a little tricky to get the syntax correct for the movie clips you're targeting.

Note

If you're ever unsure of the path to a particular movie clip, you can use the Insert a Target Path button on the lower-left side of the Parameters pane. It's the icon that looks like a target with crosshairs. Whenever it's shaded dark blue, you can click it to launch the Insert Target Path dialog box. You'll see a hierarchical tree of the named movie clips in your movie. Notation can be either dot or slash syntax. Use dot syntax; slash syntax is deprecated. You also can choose whether the path should be relative to the movie clip you're currently in or whether it should be absolute, that is, based from the root. I usually use absolute paths when I'm working on complex movies, but using relative paths is fine for simple movies.

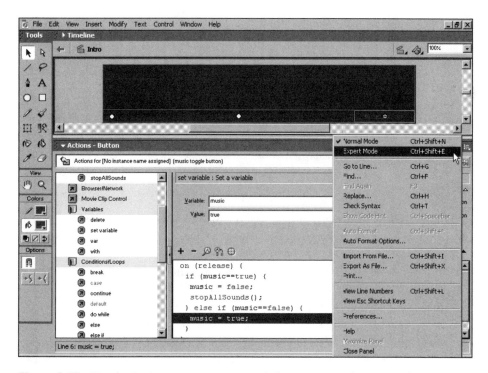

Figure 5.12 Use the Options pop-up menu to switch to Expert mode.

14. Position your cursor at the end of the line you just added (`music = true;`) and add a new line by pressing the Return or Enter key. Tab twice and type the following:

```
Voiceover.gotoAndPlay("Restart");
```

What does that do? You are telling Flash to go the movie clip named Voiceover and play the frame labeled Restart. If you open the Voiceover movie clip, you'll see that there is a frame labeled Restart right where the voice-over and animation start.

15. You are going to do something similar for the Soundtrack movie clip, but instead of going to a labeled frame, you'll just go to frame number 1. Add a new blank line, tab twice, and type the following:

```
Soundtrack.gotoAndPlay(1);
```

16. It would be nice to restart the background animation when you restart the sound. The respective movie clip already has an instance name of NewYork. It also has a frame labeled Restart. Add a new blank line, tab twice, and type the following:

```
Soundtrack.gotoAndPlay(1);
```

Now your code looks like the following:

```
on (release) {
    if (music == true) {
        music = false;
        stopAllSounds ();
    } else if (music == false) {
        music = true;
        voiceover.gotoAndPlay("Restart");
        soundtrack.gotoAndPlay(1);
        NewYork.gotoAndPlay("Restart");
    }
}
```

Before you test your movie, you'll need to add a couple more lines of code. What happens if you've made a mistake and the variable music isn't set to either true or false? You'd like to know that. You can set a Trace action to pop up an error message for you in the Output window.

17. You can switch back to Normal mode now. Select the line that starts with NewYork.gotoAndPlay. In the Toolbox list, double-click else. Flash adds a line that looks like this: } else {. (The line does not include the period.)

With that line still selected, double-click trace in the Toolbox list, and in the Parameters pane, type the following: **"This is not working"**. (Do not type the period.) Remember to surround this piece of text with quotes; you need to tell MX to display this text string if music is neither true nor false. The quotes will do that for you.

Do not select Expression. Your final code should look like this:

```
on (release) {
    if (music == true) {
        music = false;
        stopAllSounds ();
    } else if (music == false) {
        music = true;
        voiceover.gotoAndPlay("Restart");
        soundtrack.gotoAndPlay(1);
        NewYork.gotoAndPlay("Restart");
    } else {
        trace ("This is not working");
    }
}
```

 Note

Trace is one way to debug your ActionScript code while in development. See Chapter 15, "Introduction to Object-Oriented Programming," for more on debugging your code.

18. Save and test your file.

If all is well, you should be able to turn the sound for the file off and on. If there are any problems, the message "This is not working" should appear in the Output window.

Whenever you are using both sound and animation in a movie, it's a good idea to pre-load all the elements in your movie to make sure everything runs smoothly. You'll take a look at how to add a simple preloader next. Preloaders are discussed in more detail in a later chapter.

Preloading Your Sound and Animation

Because sound files are by their nature large, whenever you're adding sound, particularly sound that has been synchronized to animation, it's a good idea to make sure that all the sounds have loaded before the movie begins to play. You can do that by adding in a pre-loader.

Preloaders can be simple or complex. You'll add in a very simple one here. You'll take a look at preloaders in more detail in a later chapter.

Exercise 5.8   Adding a Preloader

Okay, this is an easy one. You deserve a break about now. So far, you've been working with just one frame in your main movie. Now you're going to add some extra frames and set up a check to see whether the whole movie has loaded.

1. You still should have NewYork.fla open, or you can open NewYork2.fla from the CD.
2. Make sure you are working on the main Timeline. Select frame 20 in all layers and press F5 to extend the Timeline.
3. Select frame 1 of all layers except the Actions/Labels layer, and drag those keyframes to frame 20.
4. Add a new layer just below the Actions/Labels layer and name it **Load**.
5. Select the Text tool. Open the Character panel (Window > Panels > Character) and change the following settings:

   Font: **Arial** or **Helvetica**
   Size: **16**
   Color: **White (#FFFFFF)**
6. With the Load layer selected, type **Load** in the lower-left corner of the Stage.
7. Still in the Load layer, insert a keyframe (F6) in frame 5. With the Text tool, click the word Load and add a single period at the end of the word.

8. Repeat Step 7 for frames 10 and 15, adding an additional period to the end of the Load phrase each time. Insert a blank keyframe (F7) in frame 20. (See Figure 5.13.)

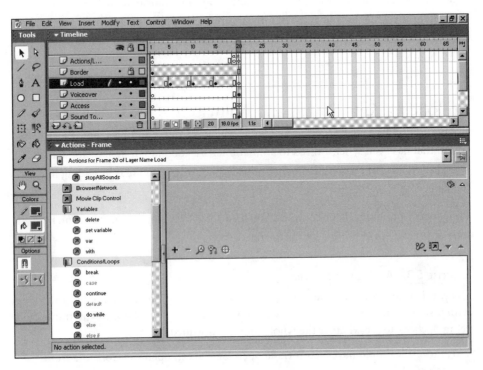

Figure 5.13   The Load layer has a four-keyframe loading sequence with a blank keyframe in frame 20.

9. Save your file.

When the movie starts, it'll play the new loading sequence you just created, but you don't want the rest of the movie to play until all the assets have loaded. You'll need to build what's called a "gate" to handle that.

Exercise 5.9   Building a Gate

On the first frame of the Actions/Labels layer, you'll test whether everything has loaded. If it has, you'll jump straight to the frame where the rest of the movie starts. If it hasn't, you'll play through the loading sequence. At the end of the loading sequence, you'll send the movie back to frame 1 again to test if everything has finished loading.

1. You should still be in sound.fla. Select frame 20 of the Actions/Labels layer and open the Frames panel (Window > Panels > Frame). Assign frame 20 a label of **Begin**.

2. Still in the Actions/Labels layer, select frame 1 and launch the Actions panel. Frame 1 currently has one action, the one where you set the value of the variable music to true. In Expert mode, add a new blank line after the line with the music variable. You're going to set a new variable called Percent here.

You're going to do something a little different for the value of the variable this time. Movie clips are objects in Flash 5. You can apply certain methods to movie clip objects. Don't stress about this—you're going to cover object-oriented programming in Chapter 15. All you really need to know right now is that there are two methods that you can use to figure out whether a movie has completely loaded:

- getBytesLoaded() checks how many bytes of information have already loaded.

- getBytesTotal() checks how many bytes are in the entire movie, including any movie clips in that movie.

3. In the Actions list, type the following:

```
percent = getBytesLoaded() / getBytesTotal();
```

Spelling and capitalization count, so check them twice.

As long as the number of bytes loaded is less than the total number of bytes, the value of percent is less than 1. As soon as all the bytes are loaded, percent is equal to 1. You can check that with a simple if statement. If percent is equal to 1, it's okay to go ahead and jump to the frame you labeled Begin.

4. Add a new line after the line you just entered, and type the following:

```
if (percent == 1)   {
    gotoAndStop("Begin");
}
```

Your completed code should look like the following:

```
music=true;
percent = getBytesLoaded() / getBytesTotal();
if (percent == 1)   {
    gotoAndStop("Begin");
}
```

5. You have only one more thing to do to finish your preloader. In the Actions/Labels layer, insert a keyframe in frame 19. Open the Actions panel and type the following:

```
gotoAndPlay(1);
```

6. Save and test your movie.

That's all you have to do. Now when the movie starts, it checks whether percent is equal to 1. If it's not, the movie continues to play through to frame 19, which sends it back to the beginning. If percent is equal to 1, the movie jumps past frame 19 to frame 20, which is labeled Begin.

Now you have a movie with synchronized sound and animation—all of which is pre-loaded. You can turn the sound off and on. Life is good.

Summary

You've covered a lot of territory in this chapter. You've been introduced to basic sound theory. You've learned how to layer and synchronize sounds. You've also had a look at how you synchronize simple animation with long-playing sounds. As an added bonus, you've learned how to turn sound off and on and how to preload your entire movie. In Chapter 18, "Components," you'll further refine your sound-editing skills by using the Sound object.

Now that you understand the basics of using sound in Flash, you can apply the techniques you've learned to all your projects. To aid you in future efforts, you'll find a list of sound resources in Appendix D, "Flash Resources."

Chapter 6

Introduction to ActionScripting

This chapter is designed to be an introduction to programming for designers and developers who are new to coding in ActionScript. If you are already a programmer, you still might want to skim it to refresh yourself on a few ActionScripting concepts.

Even if you have a programmer on staff and your job is only to do the design work, it doesn't hurt to know a little bit about basic ActionScripting. If you're a one-person team, it's absolutely essential that you understand at least the basic concepts because you'll soon discover that it's very tough to create compelling presentations or applications without using at least a little bit of coding. This chapter is intended to give you a gentle, but thorough, introduction to basic programming concepts, along with examples of when and how you use some of the concepts to which you'll be introduced.

If you've never programmed before, you'll need a quick introduction to the concept of variables. In this chapter, you learn all about using variables, including:

- The naming and setting of variables
- The use of variables in ActionScript
- Dot syntax and the variable hierarchy
- Variable scope
- Method syntax and variable types

Begin by taking a look at some of the fundamentals of programming.

Basic Programming

ActionScript in Flash is a full-blown, object-oriented programming (OOP) language. You aren't going to get an explicit introduction to OOP here—that comes in Chapter 15, "Introduction to Object-Oriented Programming." Besides, there's a lot you can accomplish without completely understanding the ActionScript language. In this chapter, you're going to get an introduction to programming concepts that are fundamental to all programming languages. You'll also get an introduction to the portions of ActionScript that will help you get started.

Variables

Variables shouldn't alarm you; they are nothing more than placeholders for information. You can put information in and take information out of a variable.

Creating variables in Flash is simple. All you need to do is decide on a variable name and pass a value to it. For example, the line of code below creates a variable called firstName and assigns it the value of Jody.

```
firstName = "Jody";
```

Note

The use of a variable called `firstName` follows the convention for naming variables. Spaces are not allowed, so when two words are needed to accurately describe a name—such as "first name"—you combine them and capitalize the first character of the second word, as in `firstName`.

Notice that the value for the variable is in quotes. It's in quotes because you're passing in a string of information. If you are passing in a number, you don't need the quotes, as in the following example:

```
age = 29;
```

You do not have to declare the type of variable. (Declaring a variable is also known as typing a variable.) In other words, you don't have to let Flash know, explicitly, that you're passing in a number or a string. Flash is smart enough to evaluate the variable type (text or number).

Note

One other item worth mentioning here is the use of a semicolon at the end of a line of code. Get into the habit of ending each line with a semicolon; this tells Flash that this line is terminated, done, complete, and finished and that it is time to go to the next line of code.

When naming variables, you need to keep the following in mind:

- Variable names can't have any spaces.

- In variables, you can use any combination of letters, numbers, and underscores, but no other special characters. Keep in mind that the hyphen is an illegal character within a variable name. I know it's tempting to use, but be careful and use an underscore instead.

- A number by itself cannot be used as a variable name. For example, 3 is not an acceptable name.

- Don't use any of the reserved Flash keywords. Keywords have special meaning in the ActionScript language. Common keywords are this, var, for, and in.

Note

When you are entering ActionScript, if you use a reserved word for a variable name, the color of that word will change. This signifies that the word is not available for a variable name.

- Give your variables meaningful names so that you can remember their purpose. It is okay to have long variable names such as myFirstVariableName.

- Pick a convention for your variable names and stick to it. The most commonly used convention is to start the variable with a lowercase letter and then capitalize the first letter of each additional word. For example, this convention would produce firstName or lastButtonPressed.

In the first exercise, you get a chance to work with setting variables inside a Flash movie.

Exercise 6.1   Working with variables

If you've never worked with variables before, the best way to get used to how they work is to practice. This exercise gives you a chance to learn how to set and retrieve variables using input and dynamic text fields. In this exercise, you work with variables that exist on the main Timeline.

1. Open the file variables.fla from the Examples/Chapter06 folder on the CD and save it to your hard drive.

    You have a file with four panels. Each panel has a series of input or dynamic text fields already set up for you. You can test the movie and enter information in the fields, but you can't do anything with it yet. You start by working with the top two panels.

    The Enter Info panel has three input text fields. You are going to use the Properties Inspector to assign variable names to those fields.

2. Select the input text field under First Name.

3. Open the Properties panel and assign a variable name by typing **firstName** in the Var field (see Figure 6.1).

4. Repeat Steps 2 and 3 for the other two input fields in the Enter Info panel, changing the variable names to **lastName** and **email**, respectively.

    So now you have variables set up in your input fields. What are you going to do with them? Well, as soon as you enter a value in an input field to which you've assigned a variable name, the value is available for use in your movie. In the next step, you change the input boxes in the Variables in Same Timeline panel to dynamic text fields and then assign them variable names. After you do that, any information you enter in the input fields will be reflected in the dynamic text fields.

Note

You use input text fields to enter information. Dynamic text fields are used to display information.

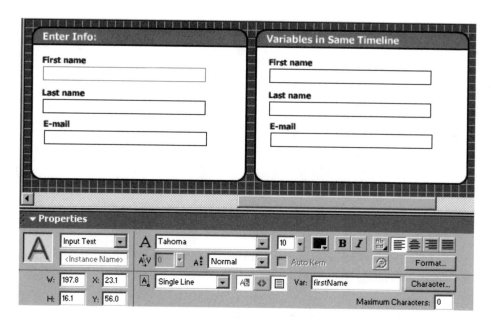

Figure 6.1   You use the Properties Inspector to assign variable names to input dynamic text fields.

5. For each input text field in the Variables in Same Timeline panel, change the text type to Dynamic Text and assign the following variable names: **firstName, lastName,** and **email.**

6. You'll notice that these are the same variable names you assigned to the input text fields in the first panel. Save and test your movie.

7. Fill out the information in the Enter Info panel and observe what happens in the Variables in Same Timeline panel. As you fill out the information in the input text fields, the information appears in the dynamic text fields (see Figure 6.2). That happens because they both have the same variable name and they both exist on the main Timeline.

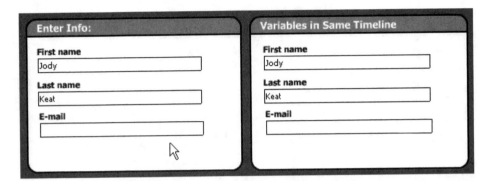

Figure 6.2   When you enter text in the input text fields, the same text immediately shows up in the dynamic text fields because both sets of fields have the same variable names.

This isn't the only way you can enter information into variables. You can also initialize variables elsewhere and change the value of a variable at any time.

Exercise 6.2   Initializing and Changing Variables

The Setting Variables panel has three dynamic text fields already set up for you with variable names of myColor, myAnimal, and myNumber. Rather than set the values for these variables from input fields, you'll initialize them on the main Timeline.

1. You should still be working in variables.fla.
2. Select frame 1 from the Actions layer and launch the Actions panel (Window > Actions).
3. Make sure you are set to Expert mode (check the Options menu by clicking the icon on the right side of the title bar). You'll be using Expert mode throughout this book because it forces you to learn correct syntax, which is a good thing.
4. Enter the following lines of code in the Actions panel:

```
myColor = "Purple";
myAnimal = "Crocodile";
firstNumber = 6;
secondNumber = 8;
myNumber = firstNumber + secondNumber;
```

   In the first four lines, you set variables directly. In the last line, you set a variable by adding together the values of two other variables.
5. Save and test your movie. The values in the dynamic text boxes of the Setting Variables panel should be filled in with the values you set in frame 1 of the main Timeline.

   You can also change the values of variables at any time. For example, you can set up the buttons at the bottom of the Setting Variables panel to change the variables when a button is pressed.

6. Select the blue button next to the word Red. In the Actions panel, enter the following code (don't worry about the curly braces; we'll discuss them in a moment):

```
on (release) {
        myColor = "red";
}
```

The code that you just entered is called an event handler. The event occurs when you release the mouse button. Thus, on release, you are setting the value of myColor to red.

7. Repeat Step 6 for each button, changing the variable names and values as appropriate. The code for the nine buttons is as follows:

```
on (release) {
    myColor = "red";
}
on (release) {
    myAnimal = "Dog";
}
on (release) {
    myNumber = 6;
}
on (release) {
    myColor = "blue";
}
on (release) {
    myAnimal = "Cat";
}
on (release) {
    myNumber = 356;
}
on (release) {
    myColor = "green";
}
on (release) {
    myAnimal = "Horse";
}
on (release) {
    myNumber = 95;
}
```

8. Save and test your movie. When the movie first loads, the fields are populated with the values you set on the main Timeline. You can change the values by pressing the buttons (see Figure 6.3).

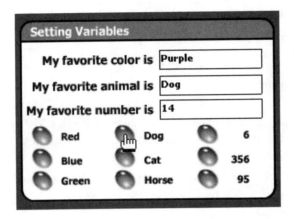

Figure 6.3   One way you can populate variables is by setting their values on the main Timeline. You can change them by setting new values when you press a button.

You now have one more item to test. You can set up variables and calculations and have them change dynamically.

Exercise 6.3   Using Variables to Perform Calculations

The final panel—Calculating Using Variables—has three rows of dynamic text boxes, one row of input boxes, and a Calculate button.

You are going to give all the text boxes in the first column the same variable name.

1. Shift-click the first three text boxes in the first column and change the variable name in the Properties Inspector to **columnA**.

2. Select the fourth box and name it **columnA**.

 Note

You can't select all four text boxes at the same time because three are dynamic text boxes and one is an input text box.

3. Repeat Steps 2 and 3 for the second column, changing the variable name to **columnB**.

4. The three boxes for the totals have to be set up a little differently because each will contain a unique value. Give each text box in the third column these variable names:

First box: **addition**

Second box: **multiplication**

Third box: **subtraction**

5. Select the blue button next to Calculate. This is where you'll set up your calculations.

6. With the blue button selected, enter the following code:

```
on (release) {
        addition = columnA + columnB;
        multiplication = columnA * columnB;
        subtraction = columnA - columnB;
}
```

7. Save and test your movie. Enter numeric values in the two fields under Enter Values. When you click the Calculate button, all the calculations are performed (see Figure 6.4).

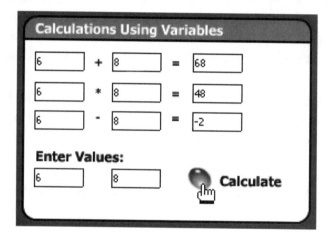

Figure 6.4   You use the Properties Inspector to assign variable names to input and dynamic text fields.

You might ask yourself what would happen if you entered non-numeric values in the input text fields. Well, go ahead and try it! The results might surprise you. The addition calculation will concatenate, or join, the two strings. The other two calculations will return NaN (not a number).

So far, you've been working with variables on only one Timeline, which has been the main Timeline. Note, however, that variables can go other places as well. In the next section, you're going to address the issue of variable scope.

Variable Scope

Variables have what is called *scope*. The scope of a variable is where it exists in the movie or the time at which it is actually available for you to use. There are three types of variable scopes in Flash MX:

- **Timeline.** Each Timeline can have its own variables that are independent of variables in other Timelines. Just as in Flash 5, you cannot have actions, and hence variables, inside buttons or graphic symbols. Flash MX won't let you apply actions in a button. If you try to add ActionScript inside a button, the Actions panel displays this message: "Current selection cannot have actions applied to it." It will, however, let you add actions in a graphic symbol, which won't work. Unlike Flash 5, you can now treat buttons and text fields as objects. You take a look at this option a little later in this chapter.

- **Local.** Not all variables need to be available at all times. In fact, sometimes it's preferable for variables to expire. For example, "i" is frequently used in programming as a counter. You don't need that counter to be available in memory after you're done with it. All you have to do is use the var action and create the variable inside a function.

- **Global.** Global variables are new to Flash MX. The information held in a global variable is available for you to use no matter where you are in a Flash movie. Global variables are set by using the _global prefix.

Before you dive into real world examples of how these variables work, you need to understand a little bit about syntax in ActionScript, particularly about how you use dot syntax.

Dot Syntax

If you want to communicate with an object in your movie, or if you want your objects to communicate with each other, you need to become familiar with how you use *dot syntax* in Flash. Later, as you become more familiar with the concepts behind object-oriented programming, this will become even more important.

Using dot syntax is like giving directions to your Flash movie about how to get to the code you want it to run next. Think of it as giving a person directions. For example, if you want someone to retrieve a package from your office desk and he or she doesn't know where your desk is, you might give him or her the following directions:

1. Enter the building.
2. Go to the fifth floor.
3. Go to my desk.
4. Pick up the package.

In dot syntax, the same directions would look like this:

```
building.5thFloor.myDesk.pickUpPackage();
```

Without the directions, the person would not know where to get the package, and therefore, would be unable to perform the task. The same holds true in programming. If your program doesn't know where to get the code, it is unable to run that code. Thus, by using dot syntax, you're giving your program the information it needs to run the code you requested.

> **Note**
>
> In Flash MX, ActionScript can be attached to either frames in a Timeline or to objects themselves. Depending on which you have selected, the Actions panel displays either "Frame Actions" or "Object Actions." It's important to pay attention to what the Actions panel says because it's very easy to accidentally attach code in the wrong place. If that happens, you'll be sitting there scratching your head and wondering why your movie isn't playing properly.

Dot Syntax and Timeline Variables

Let's say you have a movie clip on the Stage and inside that movie clip is some code that sets the value of a variable that you want to use on the main Timeline. In other words, you have a movie clip on the main Timeline (the _root) and then another movie clip inside the first one. This is called a *child* or *nested* movie clip because it is within another object. Within the nested movie clip, you have some ActionScript that sets a variable value to the main Timeline, or the _root.

Now you actually have a couple options. You could create the variable directly on the main Timeline by entering

```
_root.valueA = "Branden";
```

or

```
_parent.valueA = "Branden"'
```

This example uses the parent/child concept where the variable is set with the object that contains the movie clip.

If you had entered

```
valueA = "Branden";
```

this would be a useable variable only in the Timeline in which you created it, *unless* you have assigned your movie clip an instance name.

If you assigned your movie clip an instance name in the Properties Inspector, any movie clip, including the main Timeline, has access to this variable. You need only enter the *path* to the variable, as shown in the following code:

```
_root.movieA.valueA = "Branden";
```

Now you get to venture into the world of paths and hierarchical movie structures, which is not anywhere near as bad as it sounds. You already know that you can embed movie clips inside movie clips, embed buttons and text fields inside movie clips, and so on. What this does is create a branching or tree structure. As long as the elements in the tree have instance or id names, you can navigate to them using ActionScript.

Figure 6.5 shows the hierarchical structure of a single Flash movie. This movie consists of the main Timeline and 10 embedded movie clips. The instance name for each movie clip is shown. The clips movieA and movieB are on the main Timeline. The clips movieC, movieD, and movieE are embedded inside movieA. Additionally, movieG and movieH are embedded inside movieD. The clip movieF is embedded inside movieB, and movieI and movieJ are embedded in movieF.

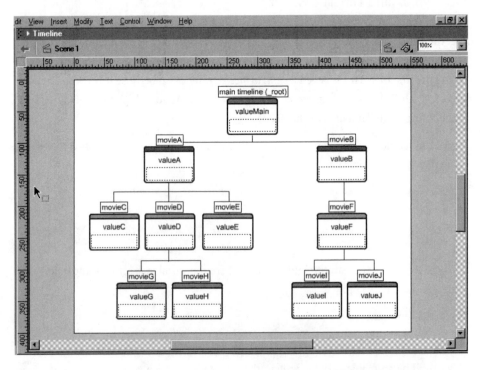

Figure 6.5   When you embed movie clips, buttons, or text fields inside other movie clips, you create a hierarchical tree.

How are you going to get these movies to communicate with each other? You already know the hierarchy of the movie and the instance names of the individual movie clips. The rest is actually easy after you get the hang of it.

Let's say there is a variable on the main Timeline called elapsedTime. You can access that variable from anywhere in your movie by using this path:

`_root.elapsedTime`

`_root` always refers to the main Timeline of the main movie.

This is not the only way to access the variable. The movie clips in your movie all have what are known as parent/child relationships. The main Timeline is the parent clip for movieA and movieB. movieA and movieB are children of the main Timeline. movieA is also the parent of movieC, movieD, movieE, and so on and so forth. Thus, from movieA, you can access the elapsedTime variable by using the following path:

`_parent.elapsedTime`

To reference the same variable from movieC, movieD, or movieE, you would have to use the following code:

`_parent._parent.elapsedTime`

From movieG or movieH, you would need to use this code:

`_parent._parent._parent.elapsedTime`

You might be asking why you would ever want to use _parent instead of directly referring to _root; that's actually a good question to ask. Frequently, you will find yourself embedding movies inside movies, and you might even find yourself loading external movies into existing movie clips. If you load an external movie into a movie clip and you have paths inside the external movie clip that refer to _root, you might find yourself in trouble. The trouble occurs because _root in the external movie used to refer to the main Timeline of that movie. Now it refers to the main Timeline of the movie into which you loaded it. The exception to this is when you load movies onto levels instead of loading them onto the main Timeline.

Another way to think about _parent and _root is direction. In Figure 6.5, the main Timeline is at the top, and the child movie clips are below. When referencing a variable from the _root, it is as if you are moving from the top down; conversely, when using the _parent method, you are moving *up* from your current location.

What if the variable in which you are interested is not on the main Timeline, but in another movie clip? Inside movieA there is a variable called valueA. To reference that variable from the main Timeline, all you need to enter is this:

```
movieA.valueA
```

Remember that movieA is the instance name of the clip on the Stage.

Now look at how you would reference that variable from the other movie clips in your movie:

- **From movieA.** valueA or _root.movieA.valueA
- **From movieC, movieD, or movieE.** _root.movieA.valueA or _parent.valueA
- **From movieG or movieH.** _root.movieA.valueA or _parent._parent.valueA
- **From movieB.** _root.movieA.valueA or _parent.movieA.valueA
- **From movieF.** _root.movieA.valueA or _parent._parent.movieA.valueA
- **From movieI or movieJ.** _root.movieA.valueA or _parent._parent._parent.movieA.valueA

What if you have a variable in movieJ that is named valueJ? Using the same pattern as above, the possible paths to yourName would look like the following:

- **From movieA.** _root.movieB.movieF.movieJ.valueJ or _parent.movieB.movieF.movieJ.valueJ
- **From movieC, movieD or movieE.** _root.movieB.movieF.movieJ.valueJ or _parent._parent.movieB.movieF.movieJ.valueJ
- **From movieG or movieH.** _root.movieB.movieF.movieJ.valueJ or _parent._parent._parent.movieB.movieF.movieJ.valueJ
- **From movieB.** movieF.movieJ.valueJ, _root.movieB.movieF.movieJ.valueJ, or _parent.movieB.movieF.movieJ.valueJ
- **From movieF.** movieJ.valueJ, _root.movieB.movieF.movieJ.valueJ, or _parent._parent.movieB.movieF.movieJ.valueJ
- **From movieI.** movieJ.valueJ, _root.movieB.movieF.movieJ.valueJ, or _parent._parent._parent.movieB.movieF.movieJ.valueJ
- **From movieJ.** valueJ, _root.movieB.movieF.movieJ.valueJ, or _parent._parent._parent.movieB.movieF.movieJ.valueJ

It's all about learning to climb a tree. You just have to know which branch you're on and which branch you want to get to.

You can probably guess what's coming next—practice, practice, practice. In the next exercise, you practice setting variables from different Timelines.

Exercise 6.4   Setting Variables in Multiple Timelines

In this exercise, you work with a movie that has already been started. In fact, this movie should look pretty familiar. It's the reference for Figure 6.5.

1. Open tree.fla from the Examples/Chapter06 folder on the CD and save it to your hard drive.

2. Start by setting variables from the main Timeline. Select frame 1 in the Actions layer and open the Actions panel (Window > Actions).

3. You are going to set the values for valueMain, valueA, and valueJ. Enter the following code:

```
valueMain = "timeline";
movieA.valueA = "this is A";
movieB.movieF.movieJ.valueJ = "this is J";
```

4. Save and test your movie. Your movie should look like Figure 6.6.

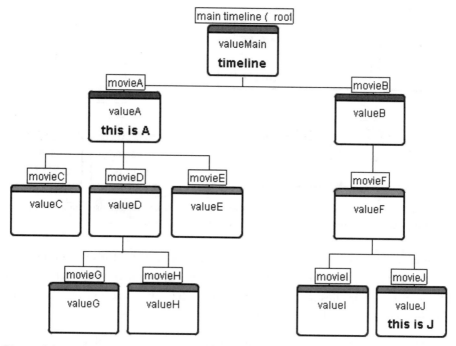

Figure 6.6   As long as you use the correct path, you can set variables for any movie clip from your main Timeline.

Before you move on to the next step, try setting some of the other values on your own. For example, see if you can figure out how to set values for valueG and valueF. Now that you're comfortable setting values from the main Timeline, try setting some variables across different movie clips.

5. Double-click movieB to open it in Symbol-Editing mode.

6. Select frame 1 of the Actions layer. From here, you are going to set the values for valueB, valueE, and valueI. Enter the following code:

```
valueB = "this is B";
_parent.movieA.movieE.valueE = "this is E";
movieF.movieI.valueI = "this is I";
```

7. Save and test your movie. Your movie should look like Figure 6.7.

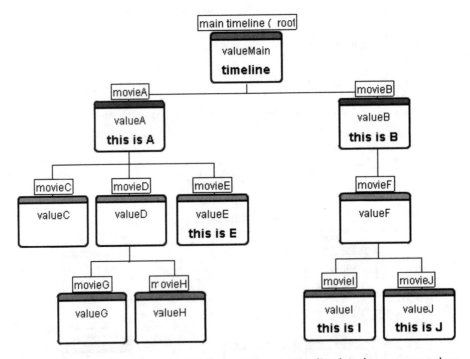

Figure 6.7   Not only can you set variables from the main Timeline, but also you can set them from any place in your movie, as long as you know the correct path.

A legitimate question to ask here is the following: What if I set a value in the main Timeline and in one of the movie clips? The actions in the main Timeline occur first; the actions in the movie clips take place as they load. Thus, any value you set on the main Timeline will be overridden by a value that is set in a movie clip.

As if that isn't enough to absorb, there's yet another way to set values for objects in Flash MX.

Addressing Objects Directly

In Flash MX, movie clips are objects, and buttons and text fields are objects as well. What does that mean for you? It means that you have more control over the behavior of buttons and text than you ever did before. The instance name or identifier is set using the Properties Inspector. For an example, see Figure 6.8.

Figure 6.8   You can set the instance name for an object in the Properties Inspector.

Dynamic or input text boxes, when used with an instance name, have a property called text. They also have a host of other properties with which you can work; you'll learn more about them in Chapter 9, "Working with Text Effects." By using the text property, you can set the value of the text field.

Using the same file structure you worked with in the last exercise, you could set the value of valueE by entering the following code on the main Timeline:

```
movieA.movieE.valueE.text = "object E";
```

The big difference is that you assign an instance name rather than a variable name in the Properties Inspector; then you reference the text property.

Global Variables

Rather than having to use paths to get to all your variables, it would be nice if you could just say, "Make this variable available all the time no matter where I am in the movie structure." Well, in Flash MX, you can. After you've declared a variable as being global, you can access it from anywhere in your movie without using a path.

How do you work this magic? All you have to do is precede the variable with _global. There is one caveat here, however. This doesn't work with input or dynamic text boxes that have variable names assigned to them. You can still use global variables with input and dynamic text boxes; you just have to take one extra step and assign the global variable in each Timeline or on the main Timeline itself.

You can test this very easily for yourself in the next exercise.

Exercise 6.5   Using Global Variables

The file with which you'll be working should look familiar; it's the hierarchical tree you worked with in the earlier exercises.

1. Open global.fla from the Examples/Chapter06 folder on the CD and save it to your hard drive.

2. On the main Timeline, you are going to set up a series of global variables to populate the dynamic text boxes in the different movies. Select frame 1 of the Actions layer on the main Timeline and enter the following variable assignments:

```
_global.valueMain = "Main Timeline";
_global.valueA = "Timeline A";
_global.valueB = "Timeline B";
_global.valueC = "Timeline C";
_global.valueD = "Timeline D";
_global.valueE = "Timeline E";
_global.valueF = "Timeline F";
_global.valueG = "Timeline G";
_global.valueH = "Timeline H";
_global.valueI = "Timeline I";
_global.valueJ = "Timeline J";
```

3. Go ahead and save and test your file. Nothing happened, did it?

4. Double-click movieA to open it in Symbol-Editing mode.

5. On frame 1 of the Actions layer, enter the following code:

```
valueA = valueA;
```

6. Save and test your movie again. This time, you can see the value of the global variable you set. The global variable is available, but for input and dynamic text fields, you need to explicitly assign the variable.

   You can also set this variable directly from the main Timeline by entering the following:

```
movieA.valueA = valueA;
```

7. Go ahead and experiment with assigning the values of the global variables to your dynamic text boxes. Try making the assignment from both the main Timeline and from within the individual movies.

One of the real values in using global variables is in setting constants to which you can easily refer.

Note

Be careful while naming variables. Duplicating variable names will present problems. Try differentiating global variables with a naming scheme. For instance, begin the name with an initial g, as in _global.gValueA.

Local Variables

As mentioned, not all variables need to be available at all times. In fact, sometimes it's preferable for variables to expire. For example, "i" is frequently used in programming as a counter. You don't need that counter to be available in memory after you're done with it. All you have to do is use the var action and create the variable inside a function. Note that the software documentation suggests that you can create local variables inside any block of code, but that's not how it works.

Note

Functions are blocks of code that execute an action. The curly braces "{ }" denote a function, and whatever is inside these curly braces will be processed.

For example, the following bit of code:

```
function myfunction() {
      phrase = "My first function";
      var question = "What for?";
}
myfunction();
trace(phrase);
trace(question);
```

will produce the following results in the Output window:

```
My first function
undefined
```

Because question was declared as a local value inside the function, it exists inside that function only. After you exit the function, it expires. That is why you see the undefined result.

So why use local variables? The best answer is so that you can use variables many times without creating them over and over again. If you have a movie that has many child movie clips, you might want to reuse the same set of variables for similar functions. By using a local variable (signified by the keyword var), you can copy and paste your code without fear of resetting other variables.

Now that you've looked at how to set variables and variable scope, it's time to take a look at some other programming concepts.

Method Syntax

You've probably noticed that a lot of the actions and objects in Flash have a set of closed parentheses following the name. For example, you might see `loadMovie()` or `attachMovie()`. You use the parentheses to pass information, usually referred to as parameters or arguments, into and out of the action or object being used. For example, the `attachMovie()` method takes three pieces of information: the name of the movie to be attached, the new name for the instance of the movie on the Stage, and the level number on which the movie should exist. The syntax for `attachMovie()` looks like this:

```
attachMovie("movieName","newName",1);
```

Each ActionScript method has its own requirements for what information, if any, it needs. You'll quickly become familiar with these, but if you get stuck, just position the cursor on the method with which you're having trouble. Then, launch the Reference panel by clicking the book icon in the upper-right corner of the Actions panel. The Reference panel is context sensitive, so you get the information you need quickly. You can also check the contents of Appendix A, "ActionScript Objects Quick Reference," for more information.

Other Keys to Programming

Now that you understand variables and syntax, it's time to explore some of the other programming concepts that will help move you on your way. You'll start with arrays, check out some loops, and then look at a few of the key actions and objects you'll use in Flash MX.

Arrays

The fastest way to clear a group of nonprogrammers out of a room is to start talking about arrays. You don't need to fear arrays, however; they're actually easy to work with.

Arrays are used to hold lists of information, such as the following types of sports: soccer, football, basketball, baseball, and hockey. You reference a specific item (element) in an array by referring to its index. The name of the array would be sports, and the five kinds of activities would be the elements of the array. The index tells you the item's place in line.

Creating an array is easy; all you need to do is type the following:

```
sports = new Array();
```

or

```
fruit = new Array();
```

Either line of code creates a new empty array object called fruit. You can also populate the array at the same time you create it by passing to it the list of information you want it to hold. For example:

```
fruit = new Array("apples","oranges","bananas");
```

creates a new array with three elements:

```
fruit[0] == apples;
fruit[1] == oranges;
fruit[2] == bananas;
```

Notice that arrays begin their numbering system with 0. You just have to cope with that in programming. Get used to the idea of an array; you'll be using them a great deal.

Note

The square brackets [] are important to mention here. These brackets are symbolic for arrays. When you see these brackets, you should know that you are dealing with an array.

Curly Braces

Curly braces are the bane of new programmers. Don't worry—you can tame the curly brace beast, or at least come to terms with it.

Curly braces are used to group sections of code. That is their sole purpose in life. They always come in pairs, so whenever you need to enclose a block of code in curly braces, type both braces at the same time and then separate them with a return. For example, when you call an onClipEvent() method, you want to perform a series of actions that are triggered by the clip event. Those actions need to be grouped like this:

```
onClipEvent(enterFrame) {
    first do this;
    next do this;
}
```

Do the curly braces have to be positioned in the manner shown? No, they don't, but after you get used to curly braces, it actually does make reading your code easier. Open your curly brace on the same line as the event or statement under which your code is being grouped. Then close the curly braces after the last line of grouped code.

Notice that the code inside the curly braces is indented. Indentation is a nicety, nothing more. You use it to make your code more readable. This becomes important as your code becomes more complex.

Loops

When you are coding, there are times when you'll want to run a certain block of code multiple times. For instance, you might want to output the numbers 1–20. One option would be to write 20 trace statements to print the numbers 1–20 in the Output window:

```
trace(1);
trace(2);
trace(3);
trace(4);
    .
    .
    .
trace(20);
```

Although that is doable, there's an easier way. You can use something known as a *loop*. Loops are used to run the same code a set number of times. You tell the loop how many times you would like the code to run, and it loops through the code that many times (hence the name).

Loops are particularly useful when you need to run the same code more than once. Loops are even more useful when the number of times you wish to run the code is variable or based on a changing condition. For example, you might want to output the numbers 1–*x*, where *x* is calculated earlier in your script. In this instance, you can't write a series of trace statements because you don't know in advance how many you need to write. This is a perfect time to use a loop.

Loops are a simple and effective way to repeat code. There are two types of loops of which you need to be aware. The first type is a *conditional loop*. A conditional loop repeats a chunk of code until a certain condition is met—hence the name. For instance, suppose you want to run a piece of code until a variable, myNumber, is less than 10. This situation is perfect for one type of conditional loop—the *while loop*. A while loop is a conditional loop in which the condition is checked before entering the loop and before every iteration of the loop.

It's always a good idea to initialize your variables so that you know the value with which you're starting. In this case, myNumber has an initial value of 0. The while loop would look like this:

```
myNumber = 0;
while ( myNumber < 10 ) {
    trace(myNumber);
    myNumber++;
}
```

This block of code essentially says, "For as long as myNumber is less than 10, run my code." The actual code that's being processed prints the current value of myNumber in the Output window and increments myNumber by 1 on each pass through the loop. You can test this for yourself. Just open a new Flash movie, select frame 1, and in the Actions panel, enter the code in the previous code block. When you test your movie, Flash prints the numbers 0–9.

The other type of conditional loop is the *do…while loop*. This loop is very similar to the while loop in that it also runs code until a certain condition is met. The difference between the while and do…while loops is that the do…while loop checks the condition *after* the code is run; the while loop checks the condition *before* the code is run. This means that a do…while loop always runs its code at least one time.

You can write the previous loop as a do…while loop, and it would look like this:

```
myNumber = 0;
do {
    trace(myNumber);
    myNumber++;
} while ( myNumber < 10 );
```

This loop does essentially the same thing as the previous loop. However, it checks the state of myNumber at the end of the loop instead of at the beginning. This type of loop is very helpful in situations in which you know that you want the code to run at least once.

The second type of loop is an *iterative loop*. These loops are simply counting loops. Iterative loops repeat a block of code a certain number of times. For instance, if you wanted to repeat a piece of code five times, and if there is no condition as there would be in a conditional loop, you would set up an iterative loop to handle the situation.

The most commonly used iterative loop is the *for loop*. In the for loop, you specify the starting point, the ending point, and an increment factor. The increment factor specifies how you want to step through the loop.

When you work with the code this time, you'll do something a little different. Say that myNumber already has a value of 10 and that you want to loop through a piece of code that many times. You can use a counter—"i" commonly is used—to monitor how many times the loop has processed, as shown in the following code:

```
myNumber = 10;
for (i=1; i<=myNumber; ++i) {
    trace(i);
}
```

There are three parts to the opening statement of the for loop. The first part, i=1, simply initializes the variable to 1. The second part, i<=myNumber, is a conditional expression that the loop uses to determine if it is done. After every pass through the loop, this condition is checked to see if i is still less than or equal to myNumber. When i is greater than myNumber, the loop is exited. The last part, ++i, increments i by 1 every time the loop is processed.

As you can see, working with loops is fairly simple. As an added bonus, using loops makes your code more efficient, readable, reusable, and modular. Practice with loops on your own until you're comfortable with them. You'll be seeing them again in subsequent chapters.

Commenting Your Code

One practice I'd strongly suggest you get accustomed to is commenting your code. You can think of comments as being pseudo-code; they clearly explain what you are doing in each section of your script. This might not seem important to you now, but when you start creating long complex projects or revise a project that you last looked at three months ago, you'll be grateful for those comments.

During testing, you might want to comment out some of your code so that it won't run. You can put anything you like on a commented line, and Flash will ignore it.

There are two ways to comment your code. For a single line of comments, you just start the line with two forward slashes:

```
// This is a comment
```

To comment out several lines of code at one time, you bracket the code between a forward slash and asterisk, and an asterisk and a forward slash:

```
/*     this is my first line
       this is my second line
       this is my last line
*/
```

Now you're ready to think about debugging the code you write.

Simple Debugging

As you start to write code using ActionScript, you're going to make mistakes. We all do. What you need to learn to do is debug your code. Flash MX has a built-in debugger, but you still can do quite a lot of debugging by just using the Output window and trace statements.

The first thing is to set the debug level of the Output window to Verbose (see Figure 6.9). This setting will give you the most information about what is going on in your movie.

Figure 6.9   Setting the Output window to Verbose gives you the most information about what is happening in your movie and helps you debug.

To set the debug setting for the Output window, all you need to do is this:

1. Open the Output window (Shift+F9).
2. Open the Options menu by clicking Options in the upper-right corner of the Output window.
3. Select Debug Level > Verbose.

Whenever you write some new code or edit some existing code, check it for syntax errors before you run it. You can check it by pressing the blue check mark icon in the Actions panel. In response, you'll see one of two messages, as shown in Figures 6.10 and 6.11.

Figure 6.10   This is the message you'll get if your code is free of syntax errors.

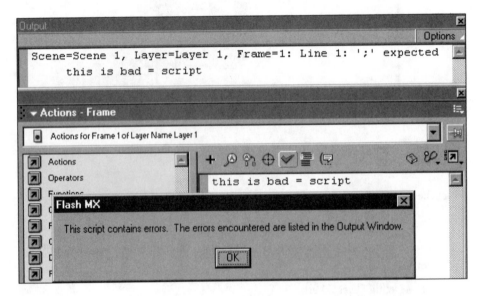

Figure 6.11   If there are syntax errors in your code, Flash MX will pop up both a warning window and your Output window.

If you get the latter message, just check the Output window. It will tell you where it encountered a problem so that you can go back into the code and fix it. Besides simple spelling errors, the most common mistake you will make is leaving out a closing quote, a parenthesis, or a curly brace.

Sometimes, you'll run into the situation where your syntax is fine, but the code just isn't doing what you expect it to. When that happens, it's time for the trace statement.

You use the trace statement in Flash to send messages to the Output window. The message can be as simple as a string of text that says, "I reached this section of the code," or it can be a more complex combination of text strings and variables. The trace statement works only when you are in test movie mode; it doesn't work if you preview your movie in a browser.

In its simplest form, a trace statement looks like this:

```
trace("This is my first trace statement.");
```

Figure 6.12 shows the result of this trace.

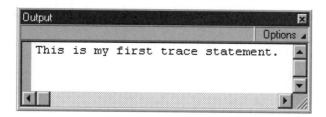

Figure 6.12   The Output window will look like this for a simple trace statement.

Sometimes just being able to output a message that lets you know that a certain portion of your code ran is all you need. However, you'll find that there are times when you need more information than that. In such situations, you can choose to output the value of a variable by putting the variable name in the trace statement without the quotes:

```
trace(thisValue);
```

You can concatenate variables and strings in your trace statement using the + operator (see Figure 6.13). The figure was produced with the following code:

```
trace("The value of X is: " + thisValue);
```

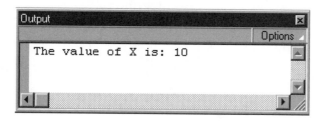

Figure 6.13   When you concatenate strings and variable values, you can format the content of the Output window.

Even though trace statements don't appear when you run your movie in a browser, they still add weight to your file. You can tell Flash to omit the trace statements from the final movie by selecting Omit Trace Actions in the Flash tab in the Publish Settings panel (File > Publish Settings).

Summary

Now you understand the basics of ActionScripting. Obviously, there's a lot more to it than what we've covered here, but this should give you a good start. You've been introduced to the different types of variables, syntax, arrays, and loops. You've even learned the basics of debugging. Now you've got some additional tools in your Flash toolkit. Don't be afraid to use them.

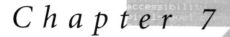

Chapter 7

Working with Named Anchors

Even though Flash is a plug-in and is relatively free of browser-based limitations, it still works within a browser environment— and people expect browser windows to behave in certain ways.

In particular, people are very accustomed to using the Back button to return to the page they were previously on. They also want to be able to bookmark pages that they find interesting. As you know, that can present a real problem for Flash movies. If you hit the Back button, the page that you were on before the Flash page simply reloads. That can be really annoying, not only to people who aren't accustomed to Flash, but also to Flash-savvy people. You can kind of get around the Back button issue by having your pages load as new Flash movies in individual HTML pages, but then you have to deal with page-refresh issues. Flash MX addresses these problems, with varying degrees of success, by using Named Anchors.

Specifically, this chapter covers these topics:

- **How to add Named Anchors to your movie.** To work with Named Anchors, you need to add special frame labels to your movie.

- **How to correctly publish your movie.** Publishing movies with Named Anchors is a little different than publishing a normal movie. Learn what you need to do here.

- **What's going on behind the scenes.** Take a look at what makes this feature work.

- **What happens if a user jumps past scripts that need to execute.** You might find that you need to address maintaining state for your application. (Here, *state* refers to the process of saving information about you and your browser travels.) You'll look at one of the ways you can do that.

- **Where it does and doesn't work—and why.** Unfortunately, Named Anchors don't work on all platforms or browsers. Learn where the problems are.

At the simplest level, Named Anchors works very well. But with more complex movies, you can run into some potential issues. They're solvable issues, but you must be prepared to address them.

Adding Named Anchors to Your Movie

When you add a Named Anchor to your movie, you are adding a reference point that your user can return to, either by using the Forward and Back buttons on the browser or by bookmarking the "page." So, anchor points belong at logical breaks in your movie—midtween is probably not a good choice. You can place Named Anchors only in the main timeline.

Only a few steps are involved in adding a Named Anchor:

1. Insert a keyframe.

2. Use the Properties Inspector to label the keyframe.

3. Select the Named Anchor check box in the Properties Inspector.

4. Change your publish settings.

5. Publish your movie.

That really is all there is to it—at least, on the most basic level. As you'll see a little later, you'll need to address some difficult issues for complex movies.

The issue of browser compatibility also arises. For example, Exercise 7.1 works in Netscape 4+ but not Netscape 6. It works for any flavor of IE as long as you're not on a Macintosh. You'll see the explanation for this in the next section.

That being said, it's time to give it a try. In the following exercise, you'll set up a very simple, linear Flash movie to take advantage of the browser Forward and Back keys, along with bookmarking.

Exercise 7.1   Adding Named Anchors to a Flash Movie

You start this exercise with an existing file.

1. Open namedAnchor.fla from the Examples/Chapter07 folder on the CD and save it to your hard drive.

    This file has four layers: Images, Button, Named Anchors, and Actions. There are keyframes in frames 1, 2, 3, 4, and 5 in all layers except the Button layer. The Images layer contains a series of different colored shapes and numbers. The Button layer contains a button with the following actions attached:

    ```
    on(release) {
        play();
    }
    ```

2. In the Named Anchor layer, select frame 1 and use the Properties Inspector (Window > Properties) to give it a label name of **one**.

3. Make sure that you select the Name Anchor check box just below the label name.

    Notice that the frame now sports an icon that you haven't seen (see Figure 7.1). Appropriately, it looks like a brown ship's anchor.

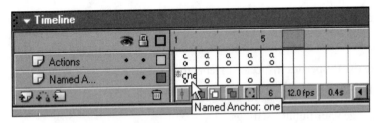

Figure 7.1   Frames that have Named Anchors show an anchor symbol rather than the flag you're accustomed to for labeled frames.

4. Repeat Steps 2 and 3 for the remaining keyframes in the Named Anchor layer, naming them two, three, four, and five, respectively.

   If you save and test your file now, it won't work. You need to make a change to the Publish Settings.

5. Choose File > Publish Settings.

6. On the HTML tab, select Flash with Named Anchors as the Template (see Figure 7.2).

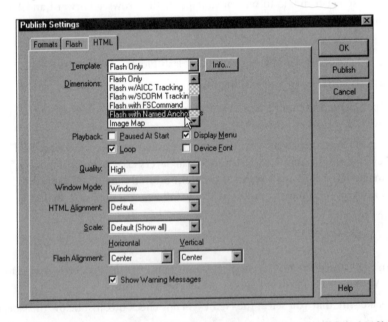

Figure 7.2   You have to use the Flash with Named Anchors template to publish this file and actually have it work.

7. Publish your file.

8. Preview the file that you just created in a browser (Ctrl+F12 for Windows, or Command+F12 for Macintosh).

Now it's time to have a little fun. Click the button to advance to frame 2. Notice that when you do that, the Back button on the browser undims. That wouldn't happen in a regular Flash movie. Now click the button again to advance to frame 3. Press the browser Back button once to go back to frame 2; press it twice to go back to frame 1. You can also use the browser Forward button to advance up to frame 3.

What about bookmarking? Try it. Select any frame (other than the first one—you want to test and see if you can bookmark an internal frame) and bookmark it in your browser. Advance off the frame that you bookmarked, and then select that bookmark from your browser. Pretty cool, huh? Take a moment and look at the URL string. Your named anchor is being passed as follows:

```
#nameAnchorName
```

But what about that browser compatibility issue? That has to do with how Flash is working its magic.

What's Happening Behind the Scenes?

The first question that you should have is, "How do Named Anchors work?" That's a good question to have because, if you understand how this is being accomplished, you'll be better prepared to handle the problems that arise.

The best place to look to get an inkling of what is happening is in the HTML code that you generated from Publish Settings. You know that you used a special template, and that template can give you some information. Listing 7.1 shows the code generated by the Flash with Named Anchors template.

Listing 7.1   Named Anchor Published JavaScript

```
<HTML>
<HEAD>
<TITLE>namedAnchors_final</TITLE>
<script language="JavaScript">
    // This is needed only for Netscape browsers.
function flashGetHref() { return location.href; }
function flashPutHref(href) { location.href = href; }
    function flashGetTitle() { return document.title; }
    function flashPutTitle(title) { location.title = title; }
</script>
</HEAD>
<BODY bgcolor="#FFFFFF">
<!-- URLs used in the movie-->
<!-- text used in the movie-->
<OBJECT classid="clsid:D27CDB6E-AE6D-11cf-96B8-444553540000"
```

continues ▶

<u>Listing 7.1   Continued</u>

```
codebase="http://download.macromedia.com/pub/shockwave/cabs/flash/swflas
h.cab#version=6,0,0,0"
 WIDTH="550" HEIGHT="400" id="namedAnchors_final" ALIGN="">
 <PARAM NAME=movie VALUE="namedAnchors_final.swf"> <PARAM NAME=quality
⮩VALUE=high> <PARAM NAME=bgcolor VALUE=#FFFFFF> <EMBED
src="namedAnchors_final.swf" quality=high bgcolor=#FFFFFF WIDTH="550"
⮩HEIGHT="400" NAME="namedAnchors_final" ALIGN="" swLiveConnect=true
⮩TYPE="application/x-shockwave-flash" PLUGINSPAGE="http://www.
⮩macromedia.com/go/getflashplayer"></EMBED>
</OBJECT>
<!-- Bookmarks used in the movie-->
<A NAME=one></A>
<A NAME=two></A>
<A NAME=three></A>
<A NAME=four></A>
<A NAME=five></A>
</BODY>
</HTML>
```

You should notice two things about this code right away. Four functions appear at the top between the script tags (needed only for Netscape browsers), and at the bottom of the listing are a series of <A NAME> tags.

The <A NAME> tags are the easiest to figure out—there's one for each frame label that you set up and marked as a Named Anchor. What about those functions, though, and why do you need them only for Netscape?

Using the Back and Forward buttons works really well. Bookmarking pages is great. But what if you have calculations that control your movie behavior from frame to frame? Or a movie that creates variables in earlier frames? A bookmark bypasses the code where those variables were set. Using the Forward and Back buttons runs all the code in that frame every time the frame is accessed. So now you have a new problem on your hands.

What Do You Do About Nonlinear Access to Movies?

One of the problems you'll run into is how to tell if someone got to a certain frame by working through the movie or by jumping to it directly from a bookmark. If your movie is set up so that one frame isn't dependent on information from any other frame, this won't pose a problem for you. However, if you are performing calculations or gathering information, it's a different situation.

Take the example you were just working with. What if a value is set in frame 1 that is needed to make something work in frame 3? If your user jumps directly to frame 3, you're in trouble.

In fact, every time the user presses Back or Forward or jumps to a bookmark, you have an issue. The code in that frame will run each time the frame is entered. The newer and more efficient way to do this is to use sharedObject(), which is new to Flash MX. This sharedObject() method is not quite as easy as using the Named Anchors, but it is the better way to use the browser Forward and Back buttons with your Flash movie.

Using *SharedObject()*

So what is SharedObject()? SharedObject() works like cookies in the HTML world: It stores persistent data or information on the user's machine. You can set a number of properties for a SharedObject() object, but we won't go there just yet.

Note

This section is a little out of place because you have to deal with some advanced topics to make it work. However, you really need to see some of the possibilities for bookmarking and enabling the browser buttons. You might want to work through Chapter 6, "Introduction to ActionScripting," and Chapter 15, "Introduction to Object-Oriented Programming" before diving into this section.

Because this chapter falls before the more advanced chapters, I'm not going to walk you through building the file. Instead, I'll walk you through the concepts behind building the file. The source code is available on the CD in the Examples/Chapter07 folder as bookmark.fla.

Exercise 7.2   Exploring the File

You use another existing file from the CD for this exercise.

1. Open bookmark.fla from the Examples/Chapter07 folder on the CD, and save it to your hard drive. You first should make sure that the movie is published correctly for use with Named Anchors.

2. Select File > Publish Settings, and select HTML and Flash on the Formats tab.

3. Select the HTML tab, and make sure that you are using the Flash with Named Anchors Template.

4. Publish your movie.

5. In a browser (or by using File > Publish Preview), open the HTML page that you just created (see Figure 7.3).

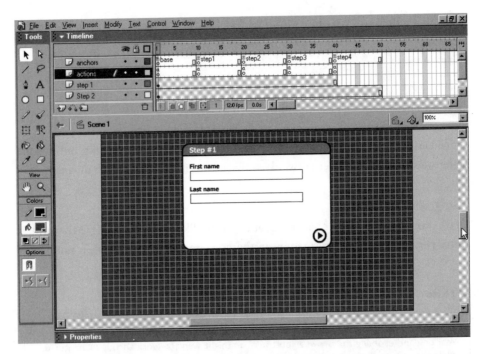

Figure 7.3   After you open this file in a browser, you can see the first of the four steps.

This is actually a fairly simple movie to construct, but it has lots of potential for modification and expansion.

6. Enter your information on each of the four pages. Notice that as soon as you advance off the first page, your browser's Back button is enabled, just like what you saw in Exercise 7.1.

7. Bookmark one of the pages.

8. Close your browser and reopen it.

9. Jump to the page that you bookmarked. All the data that you entered is still there! In fact, you can open this page in another browser entirely, and your information still will be there—it's stored on your computer.

So, how did that happen? Let's take a peek under the hood at the ActionScript that controls this file.

Dissecting the File

To see the ActionScript that controls your file, open the copy of bookmark.fla that you saved on your hard drive, if it's not still open. You have four movie clips, one for each of the steps. No code is attached to any of these movie clips or to any of the buttons inside them. Every single bit of code is in the frames on the Actions layer of the main Timeline.

Select frame 10 of the Actions layer, and open your Actions panel. You'll see two lines of code:

```
anchor = "step1";
gotoAndStop("base");
```

The first line sets a variable named anchor to step1. The second line tells the movie to go to a frame labeled base, which happens to be the first frame of the movie. Each of the subsequent frames (20, 30, and 40) has exactly the same code, except that the step number changes. All the action takes place in frame 1.

Select the frame 1 Actions layer and look at the code in the Actions panel. You'll see the code in Listing 7.2. It might look a little daunting at first, but it's mostly the same code repeated for each of the four movie clips.

Listing 7.2   The Complete Listing of Code from Frame 1 of the Actions Layer

```
stop();

// if we didn't come from an anchor, set step1 as the anchor
if (anchor == null){
    gotoAndStop("step1");
}else{

    // if we haven't initialized our form yet...
    if (!initialized){
        // get a shared object
        personalInfo = SharedObject.getLocal("personalInfo");

        // place that data into the text fields
        step1_mc.firstName_txt.text = personalInfo.data.firstName;
        step1_mc.lastName_txt.text = personalInfo.data.lastName;
        step2_mc.email_txt.text = personalInfo.data.email;
        step2_mc.homepage_txt.text = personalInfo.data.homepage;
        step3_mc.color_txt.text = personalInfo.data.color;
        step3_mc.animal_txt.text = personalInfo.data.animal;
        step4_mc.password1_txt.text = personalInfo.data.password1;
        step4_mc.password2_txt.text = personalInfo.data.password2;

        // place code in each step's buttons

        // step 1
        step1_mc.next_btn.onRelease = function(){
            var info = this._parent._parent.personalInfo;
            info.data.firstName = this._parent.firstName_txt.text;
            info.data.lastName = this._parent.lastName_txt.text;
            info.flush();
            this._parent._parent.gotoAndStop("step2");
        }
```

continues ▶

Listing 7.2   Continued

```
// step 2
step2_mc.next_btn.onRelease = function(){
    var info = this._parent._parent.personalInfo;
    info.data.email = this._parent.email_txt.text;
    info.data.homepage = this._parent.homepage_txt.text;
    info.flush();
    this._parent._parent.gotoAndStop("step3");
}

step2_mc.prev_btn.onRelease = function(){
    var info = this._parent._parent.personalInfo;
    info.data.email = this._parent.email_txt.text;
    info.data.homepage = this._parent.homepage_txt.text;
    info.flush();
    this._parent._parent.gotoAndStop("step1");
}

// step 3
step3_mc.next_btn.onRelease = function(){
    var info = this._parent._parent.personalInfo;
    info.data.color = this._parent.color_txt.text;
    info.data.animal = this._parent.animal_txt.text;
    info.flush();
    this._parent._parent.gotoAndStop("step4");
}

step3_mc.prev_btn.onRelease = function(){
    var info = this._parent._parent.personalInfo;
    info.data.color = this._parent.color_txt.text;
    info.data.animal = this._parent.animal_txt.text;
    info.flush();
    this._parent._parent.gotoAndStop("step2");
}

//step 4
step4_mc.prev_btn.onRelease = function(){
    var info = this._parent._parent.personalInfo;
    info.data.password1 = this._parent.password1_txt.text;
    info.data.password2 = this._parent.password2_txt.text;
    info.flush();
    this._parent._parent.gotoAndStop("step3");
}
step4_mc.done_btn.onRelease = function(){
    var info = this._parent._parent.personalInfo;
    info.data.password1 = this._parent.password1_txt.text;
    info.data.password2 = this._parent.password2_txt.text;
    info.flush();
    this._parent._visible = false;
}
initialized = true;
```

```
    }

    // hide all of the steps
    step1_mc._visible = false;
    step2_mc._visible = false;
    step3_mc._visible = false;
    step4_mc._visible = false;

    // show only the one specified by the current anchor
this[anchor+"_mc"]._visible = true;

}
```

So what's going on in this code? Everything is nested inside a big if statement. That if statement just tests to see whether you are coming from one of the anchor pages or whether you've just opened the page directly. If no value is set for the variable anchor, you are redirected to the Step 1 screen, which is then set as the anchor.

Now, remember, on the Step 1 frame, the actions send you back to the base frame (this one) and you execute this code again. This time you drop into the else statement.

This line is particularly interesting here:

```
personalInfo = SharedObject.getLocal("personalInfo");
```

If the shared object already exists, this line retrieves it. If the object doesn't exist, this line creates it.

The next chunk of code initializes all the variables for the four movie clips with the values from the shared object (if it exists).

```
// place that data into the text fields
step1_mc.firstName_txt.text = personalInfo.data.firstName;
step1_mc.lastName_txt.text = personalInfo.data.lastName;
step2_mc.email_txt.text = personalInfo.data.email;
step2_mc.homepage_txt.text = personalInfo.data.homepage;
step3_mc.color_txt.text = personalInfo.data.color;
step3_mc.animal_txt.text = personalInfo.data.animal;
step4_mc.password1_txt.text = personalInfo.data.password1;
step4_mc.password2_txt.text = personalInfo.data.password2;
```

You can see the use of targeting nested movie clip variables with that code. Each line sets the variable to equal the value from the sharedObject()'s data.

The bulk of the rest of the code controls what happens when you click a button.

If you're familiar with Flash 5, you know that movie clips are objects that you can talk to. In Flash MX, buttons and text fields are also objects, so you can address them directly from anywhere in the movie—you don't have to attach code to them.

This application has three buttons:

- The Next button (next_btn)
- The Previous button (prev_btn)
- The Done button (done_btn)

The Next and Previous buttons do essentially the same thing: They collect the information that you enter in the text fields and save it in the shared object when you reach the info.flush() line. Then you're redirected to the next step or the previous step. That's really all that's happening.

The other interesting thing happens at the bottom of the code: All the Step movie clips are set to be invisible (_visible=false). Only the selected step is set to visible, with this code:

```
this[anchor+"_mc"]._visible = true;
```

The most important part here is that you have the capability to save existing values. So, using the SharedObject object in conjunction with the Named Anchors gives you a lot of flexibility that you would otherwise lose.

But you still have to deal with the browser compatibility issue, and there isn't a workaround for that.

What About Browser Compatibility?

Because of the way Named Anchors work, you can't use them if your target audience is using IE on the Macintosh or Netscape 6+ on either platform. It's a limitation that you need to be aware of.

Flash can communicate with a browser in two ways: It can use FSCommands or JavaScript methods to communicate with browsers that support Netscape's LiveConnect technology or Microsoft's ActiveX technology. Netscape 6, unlike previous versions of the browser, does not use LiveConnect, and we don't know whether or when LiveConnect will be supported again. The Macintosh version of Internet Explorer doesn't support ActiveX technology. So, you can rest assured that any files that you create using Named Anchors will not work on these browsers/platforms. It's unfortunate, but it's a fact of life.

Summary

Named Anchors introduce a new functionality to Flash. MX has made it possible to use the browser Forward and Back buttons with Flash and without the headache of programming. Using Named Anchors, you can easily set up your Flash movie to work with browser navigation, as well as bookmark specific locations within your movie. sharedObject is another new feature of MX that takes you to the next level of managing browser navigation within Flash. Hopefully, this brief introduction to the sharedObject will open the doors of opportunity for you to do more with your Flash movies and provide unique information for each viewer.

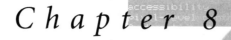

Chapter 8

Printing in Flash

Printing information from web sites is generally something of a pain. Go to a page, print. Go to a page, print. Wouldn't you rather allow your users to print all the applicable information in one print job?

Better yet, how about letting them print additional information that isn't even on the screen? What tends to surprise people is that, when done correctly, Flash can actually make this a simple process.

In this chapter, you look at the following:

- **What happens if you ignore the printing issue.** You always have the option of ignoring this issue altogether. Many developers do. But if you choose to ignore it, you should understand what the implications are.

- **How printing in Flash works.** Take a look at the different ways you can print a Flash movie, along with the special markup you have to include.

- **How to disable printing in the Flash Player context menu.** If you're going to use internal commands to control printing, or if you just don't want people printing your movie, you might want to disable printing in the Flash Player context menu.

- **Using ActionScript to control printing.** Controlling printing using ActionScript is by far the most flexible approach. Take a look at how the different print commands affect your final product.

- **Printing hidden content.** When you control your printing with ActionScript, you have the option of downloading and printing extra materials on demand.

Start by taking a brief look at what happens if you choose to ignore the printing issue.

What Happens If You Ignore the Printing Issue

You can choose to ignore the printing issue altogether, but if that's your choice, you still should understand what will happen when someone tries to print your Flash movie. Unless you've disabled printing from the Flash Player context menu (you'll learn how to do that a little later), anyone viewing your movie can choose to print it. So the question is, what will print?

If you choose Print from the context menu, Flash brings up your standard Print dialog box. If you choose to print all pages, you'll get every single frame in the movie's main Timeline. If you have an animation that is 800 frames long, you'll be printing 800 pages. Not good.

You can limit the number of frames that print by selecting a page range—pages translate to frames. But someone visiting your site isn't going to have any idea how many frames to print. Forcing a user to use the print screen button repeatedly is kind of cruel.

So, ignoring the problem is not an optimal solution. Fortunately, the potential solutions are pretty painless.

How Printing in Flash Works

When you want to print Flash content (other than one screen at a time from the browser), you have two options:

- You can use the Flash Player command.

- You can control printing from within your movie using ActionScript.

In either case, you will want to designate what content should be printed and what should not. If you don't specifically designate certain frames as being printable, all frames will print. All you have to do is give your printable frames special labels.

To label a frame to be printable, follow these steps:

1. Insert a keyframe at the frame you want to print.

2. In the Properties Inspector, give the keyframe a label of #p (see Figure 8.1).

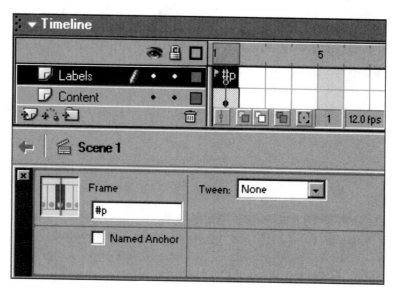

Figure 8.1   To designate a frame as being printable, you just insert a keyframe and give it a label name of #p.

That's it, in its simplest form. In Exercise 8.1, you'll get a chance to designate certain frames as being printable and test the output using the Flash Player context menu.

Exercise 8.1   Designating Frames as Printable

You'll begin by working with an existing file.

1. Open bounce.fla from the Examples/Chapter08 folder on the CD, and save it to your hard drive.

   This file is a simple 20-frame tweened animation of a bouncing ball (see Figure 8.2). If you publish this file as is and print it using the Flash Player context menu, you'll get 20 pages, each showing the ball at a different place in the tween.

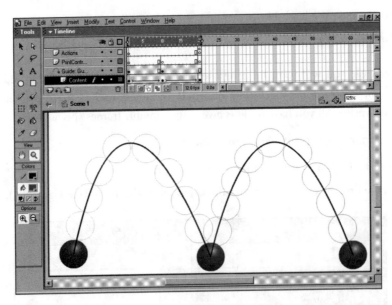

Figure 8.2   The file you'll be working with is a simple tweened animation. Currently no frames are labeled as being printable.

Rather than show all the positions of the ball, you're going to select a few key positions to print.

2. Open the Properties Inspector, if it isn't already open.

3. Insert a new layer and name it Print Actions.

4. Select frame 1 and, in the Properties Inspector, give it a frame label of #p.

5. Insert a new keyframe in frame 5 of the Print Actions layer.

6. Give your new keyframe a frame label of #p in the Properties Inspector.

7. Repeat Steps 5 and 6 for frames 10, 15, and 20 (see Figure 8.3).

8. Save your file and choose File > Publish Preview > Default HTML.

9. Right-click (Windows) or Control-click (Macintosh) the Flash animation and choose Print from the Flash Player context menu. Print all pages.

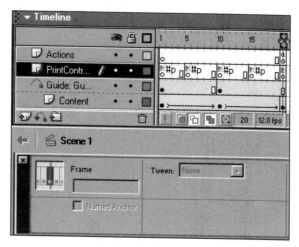

Figure 8.3   Add print labels to the major frame changes in the movie.

You probably noticed that you got an ugly warning message in the Output window when you published your file ("WARNING: Duplicate label, Scene=Scene 1, Layer=Print Actions, Frame=5, Label=#p"). Don't worry about it. In any other case, having duplicate label names is a bad idea, but it's perfectly okay when you are setting up frames to print.

When you pick up your job at the printer, you should have five pages. Notice that the movie scaled to fit the paper you printed on—that's because Flash prints as vectors.

That worked pretty well, but there are some issues you should be aware of when allowing people to print your Flash Movie using the Flash Player context menu.

- First and foremost, most people won't even realize that printing from the context menu is an option unless you explicitly explain that to them.
- You can print only frames that are in the main Timeline when you allow printing from the context menu.
- You can't specify a particular area to print—the entire frame prints instead, including any elements that are in the work area off the stage.
- You can't print color effects such as alpha transparency.

As it turns out, you can control all these issues by using ActionScript to print from within the Flash Movie. But first, if you want a finer level of control over what prints, you might want to disable the Print option in the context menu.

Disabling Printing in the Flash Player Context Menu

To disable the Print option in the Flash Player context menu, follow these steps:

1. Add a new layer to your movie.

2. Select frame 1 of your new layer and use the Properties Inspector to give it a label name of !#p.

That's all it takes. Now if you choose File > Publish Preview > Default HTML and try to use the context menu, you'll see that the Print option is dimmed out (see Figure 8.4).

If you're going to disable printing of your movie from the Flash Player context menu (and you could just stop here with printing completely disabled), you might want to consider adding print functionality from within the movie itself. The next section takes a look at using ActionScript to control printing.

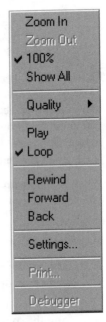

Figure 8.4 You always have the option of disabling the Print option in the Flash Player context menu.

> **Note**
>
> You can disable the Flash Player's Print command by disabling the whole Flash Player context menu in Publish Settings (File > Publish Settings). This removes not only the Print command but also the other pop-up menu commands, such as Zoom In, Zoom Out, and Quality. All you need to do to disable the context menu altogether is select the HTML tab in Publish Settings and deselect the Display Menu option.

Using ActionScript to Control Printing

When you use the print() action to control your printing, you not only restrict which pages will print, but you also can control how the pages that you want to print will print. You can even control the area of the page to print, as well as what content will print—even if that content isn't visible.

Your first decision is whether the movie should print as vectors or as a bitmap. You need to keep in mind a few considerations before you make this decision:

- **Color effects.** If you want your color effects (transparency, tint, brightness, and so on) to appear in the printed movie, you have to print as a bitmap.

- **Print quality.** Printing the movie as vectors usually results in a higher-quality printout. Although the highest available resolution of the printer is used when printing as a bitmap, this usually results in a lower-quality printout than printing as vectors will. If print quality is important, stay with vectors.

- **Scalability.** If you want your movie to scale to fit a certain size, you should print as vectors. Otherwise, your bitmaps are likely to pixelate.

When you've decided whether to print as bitmap or vectors, you can start working with the print() action.

The syntax for the print() action can take a number of forms, each requiring slightly different parameters. The three possible parameters are listed here:

- **level.** You use the level parameter to specify which Timeline (levels 0, 1, 2, and so on) to print from. The default is level 0, which is the root or main Timeline.

- **target.** Rather than print from a specific level, you can to choose to print from the Timeline of a named movie clip instance.

- **Bounding box.** You can set up bounding boxes to set the print area for the entire movie or for specific frames. The bounding box options are as follows:

  - **bmovie.** You can use the dimensions of the movie as the print area. You can force this option to use the dimensions of a specific frame in the targeted movie, labeled #b, to specify the bounding box.

  - **bmax.** This uses the composite bounding box of all printable frames in the targeted Timeline as the bounding box for the printed content. That means that if you have only one frame labeled #p in the targeted Timeline, the bounding box of that frame is the bounding box for the printed content. If you have two frames labeled #p, the composite bounding box of both frames becomes the bounding box for the printed content.

  - **bframe.** This prints the content of each frame, using the bounding box of each individual frame. That means that the print area for each frame can change and that the objects in each frame are scaled to fit the full printed page.

So, now you know what the parameters are. What about the syntax for the action itself? There are six combinations of print actions and parameters:

- **print(level, "Bounding box").** Both level and Bounding box are required. This prints any vector artwork as vectors. Any bitmaps print as bitmaps.

- **`print("target", "Bounding box")`**. Both `target` and `Bounding box` are required. This prints any vector artwork as vectors. Any bitmaps print as bitmaps.

- **`printAsBitmap(level, "Bounding box")`**. Both `level` and `Bounding box` are required. This prints both vector artwork and bitmaps as bitmaps. Any transparency or color effects are preserved.

- **`printAsBitmap("target", "Bounding box")`**. Both `target` and `Bounding box` are required. `target` is the instance name of a movie clip on the Stage you want to print from. This prints as a bitmap.

- **`printNum(level, "Bounding box")`**. Both `level` and `Bounding box` are required. This prints any vector artwork as vectors. Any bitmaps print as bitmaps.

- **`printAsBitmapNum(level, "Bounding box")`**. Both `level` and `Bounding box` are required. This prints both the vector artwork and the bitmaps as a bitmap. Any transparency or color effects is preserved.

A couple of caveats here: All the printable elements of the movie must be loaded to print. If you haven't specifically marked any frames as being printable, all of the frames of the movie will print.

Enough talk already. Time to practice. In the next exercise, you'll use a Print button with the `print` action attached to it.

Exercise 8.2   Using the *print()* Action to Print the Main Timeline

In this exercise, you'll use a button in conjunction with the `print()` action to print a movie. You'll just be working with one frame this time, but you'll use the actions on the button to change the level and the target that you're printing from. You'll also make some changes to the bounding box. So get yourself a fresh cup of coffee and get ready to work!

1. Open printFun.fla and level1.fla from the Examples/Chapter08 folder on the CD, and save them to your hard drive. You'll need to publish level1.fla. It will load as a watermark in printFun.fla.

   This file has only one frame, so you don't need to label any keyframes as printable. All the layers are locked except for the button layer.

2. Select the button and open the Actions panel (F2), if it isn't already open. Make sure you're working in Expert mode.

3. Add the following code to the button:

```
on (release) {
        printNum(0, "bmovie");
}
```

This prints all frames on the main Timeline and uses the movie size as the bounding box (see Figure 8.5).

Figure 8.5   You can attach the `print()` action to a button to trigger printing on a button event.

4. Save and test your movie. Press the Print button.

The vector artwork will be nice and crisp, and the bitmap banner will be slightly fuzzy. Notice that the watermark didn't print. That's because levels don't composite when you print from Flash.

5. Change `printNum` to `printAsBitmap`, and test the movie again.

The printed file will look much the same, but you'll lose some of the sharpness because the vector graphics are printed as a bitmap.

Next you'll use the `print()` action to target a level.

Exercise 8.3   Using the *print* Action to Print a Level

The large Fig Leaf logo watermark (see Figure 8.6) is loaded into level 1. It has an alpha transparency of 10%. In this exercise, you'll learn not only how to print from levels, but also how vector versus bitmap printing affects the output of images that have effects applied.

1. You should still have printFun.fla open. If not, open it now.

2. Select the Print button.

3. Open the Actions panel (F2) and change the code on the button to this:

```
on (release) {
     printNum(1, "bmovie");
}
```

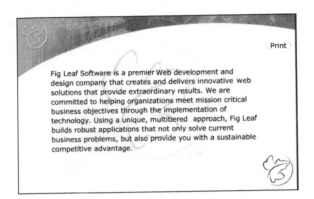

Figure 8.6   The watermark in the center is loaded into Level 1. It has an alpha transparency of 10%.

4. Save and test your movie. Press the Print button.

   Notice that the faded watermark printed without preserving the transparency. That's because you printed it as a vector.

5. Change printNum to printAsBitmapNum, and test your movie again. This time when you print, you'll lose the crispness of the vector art, but you'll preserve the transparency.

So you can see the trade-offs you have to make when printing: preserve special effects or make sure that your graphics print in vector format. Sometimes it's a tough choice, but it's one you'll have to make.

You can also print any movie on the Stage that has been assigned an instance name.

Exercise 8.4   Using the *print* Action to Print a Target

This time you are going to print a target movie clip, the small Fig Leaf logo in the lower-right corner.

1. You should still have printFun.fla open. If not, open it now.

2. Select the Print button.

3. Open the Actions panel (F2) and change the code on the button to this:

```
on (release) {
        print("figLogo", "bframe");
}
```

4. Save and test your movie. Press the Print button.

   This time you got the Fig Leaf logo from the lower-right corner, but it scaled to fit the page you printed it on—that's because you used the frame, not the movie, as the bounding box. Because you used print instead of printAsBitmap, it printed as vector artwork.

You can also use a custom bounding box to control the output of the print action.

Exercise 8.5   Using the *print* Action with a Custom Bounding Box

Until now, you have been using `bmovie` and `bframe` to control the printable area. Because you didn't set a #b frame, bmovie uses the Stage size as the default bounding box. You can change that.

1. You should still have printFun.fla open. If not, open it now.

2. Insert a keyframe in frame 2 of the Actions layer on the main Timeline.

3. Extend the Timeline for the rest of frames out to frame 2 as well—just regular frames.

4. Add a new layer just beneath the Actions layer and name it Bounding Box.

5. Insert a keyframe in frame 2 of your new layer.

6. Select the Rectangle tool and draw a rectangle on the Stage (color doesn't matter). Use the Info panel to resize it to 300 W × 185 H. Center it on the page (see Figure 8.7).

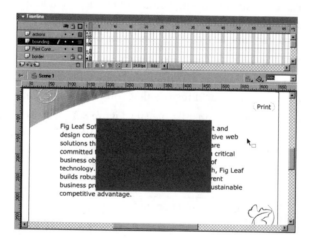

Figure 8.7   You always have the option of setting up a custom bounding box. In this case, the bounding box will constrain the movie's printed size to roughly half its size on the screen.

7. Select frame 2 of the Actions layer and give it a Frame Label of #b.

8. Select the Print button and change the actions to this:

```
on (release) {
        printNum(0, "bmovie");
}
```

9. Save and test your movie. Press the Print button.

   This time the entire contents of the main Timeline print, properly scaled, at half the size of the original.

There's one more situation you haven't looked at yet—printing content from a hidden frame or target.

Printing Hidden Content

Printing hidden content takes a few extra steps but is well worth the effort because you can defer the download of information until the user makes a conscious choice that he wants that information. This is particularly useful for printing coupons, printing additional product information, and such.

You could approach setting this up in dozens of ways. I find it easiest—and this is just a personal preference—to break it down into discreet chunks and then use one off-Stage movie clip to control the loading of the new data and a second off-Stage clip to load the data into. Your mileage might vary.

Exercise 8.6   Printing Hidden Content

You'll begin this exercise with an existing banner ad movie, and add the additional print functionality to it. This one will take a little while to work through, so make sure that you have some uninterrupted time ahead of you and your caffeinated beverage of choice.

1. Open figBanner.fla from the Examples/Chapter08 folder on the CD, and save it to your hard drive. You'll also need to copy both wammoAd.fla and wammmofla.swf to the same directory that you saved the figBanner.fla file to.

    Go ahead and test the figBanner.fla file (see Figure 8.8). It's just a simple banner ad that at the end displays a button that says Learn More! You're going to set it up so that the Learn More! button prints additional information about the WAMMO organization.

Figure 8.8   Right now, this is just a simple banner ad with a Learn More! button. You'll set it up to print content that's currently hidden.

In the figBanner.fla, you'll notice that on the container layer there is a single empty movie clip just above and to the right of the main Stage (see Figure 8.9) with an instance name of bannerAd. All the interesting things that take place are on the Learn More! button and on the bannerAd movie clip.

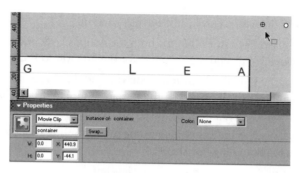

Figure 8.9   The two important parts of this movie are the Learn More! button and the empty bannerAd movie clip.

You're going to start by setting up the actions on the Learn More! button.

2. Select the Learn More! button and open the Actions panel (F2).

   All you need to do here is load wammoAd.swf into the bannerAd movie clip. Just add the following code:

```
on (release) {
     _root.bannerAd.loadMovie("wammoAd.swf");
}
```

 Tip

You can't print a movie clip that hasn't completely loaded. Anytime you are using the `print()` action, you have to make sure that you've put in a check to make sure that all the data has loaded before you try to print it. If you're loading into an empty movie clip, you can use the `onClipEvent(data)` handler.

3. Select the bannerAd movie clip on the Stage. All you need to do is attach the `onClipEvent` handler that fires when all the data is loaded. Enter the following code:

```
onClipEvent(data) {
     print(_root.bannerAd, "bmovie");
}
```

   There's only one thing left to do, and that's designate which frames of the wammoAd file should be printable.

4. Earlier in this exercise, you saved the wammoAd.fla file to your hard drive. Open it now.

   If you publish the file as is and try to print it, you will not get the results you want; you need to set up a bounding box for this movie.

5. Add two new layers to this movie. Name them Actions and Bounding Box, respectively.

6. In frame 1 of the Actions layer, add a `stop()` action.

7. At frame 2, insert keyframes (F6) for both the Actions layer and the Bounding Box layer. Use F5 to extend the Timeline for the Ad layer to frame 3.

8. In frame 2 of the Bounding Box layer, you will add the shape that controls the size at which this file will print. Use the Rectangle tool to drag a shape that completely covers all the text and graphics in the Ad layer.

   Now you just need to indicate which frame is the printing frame and which frame holds the bounding box shape.

9. Give frame 1 of the Actions layer a frame label of #p.

10. Give frame 2 of the Actions layer a frame label of #b.

11. Save and publish your file.

12. You should still have figBanner.fla open. If not, open it now.

13. Choose File > Publish Preview > Default HTML to test your banner ad in a browser.

14. When the Learn More! button becomes visible, go ahead and press it. Your printer dialog box should pop up, and you can print the information from the unseen movie clip. If you have any problems, take a look at the FigBanner_Final.fla on the CD.

That's actually pretty cool. If you think about it a bit, you can probably come up with a lot of uses for this—coupons, catalogs, and so on. And the best part is that this information doesn't have to be downloaded unless someone really wants it.

Summary

Very few users will know that they can right-click on a Flash movie to get a context menu. Expecting them to know how to print your site this way is unrealistic and not very user-friendly. Additionally, the Flash Player command is rather limited—it prints frames in the main movie's Timeline only and does not allow you to print any color effects. If you don't intend for users to print your site, you might want to consider disabling the Flash Player context menu.

If, however, you want to give users a way to print your site or print additional information on demand, using the `print()` action in Flash is the way to go.

Chapter 9

Working with Text Effects

How many times have you been faced with

a project without any photos, images, or

any type of support files? Text becomes

your only means of expressing an idea.

If that's the case, you had better be sure that you can face the music and that your typographic skills are on point. When used properly, text effects can be just as intriguing, if not better, than imagery and photos.

That being said, you want to make sure that you use text effects judiciously. Some effects grab everyone's attention and get imitated on every other web site—and then quickly become passé. Do you really want people to look at your site and say, "That's so 10 minutes ago"? I don't think so. Sometimes restraint with a technique is more effective than overkill. Don't confine yourself to what everyone else is doing—stretch!

In this chapter, you'll take a look at several different types of effects that you can create with text. You will learn about the following:

- **Simple changes to text.** Using nothing more than the Properties Inspector and the Color Mixer, you can make interesting changes to your text.

- **Alpha transparency and brightness.** You can use alpha transparency to make your text appear to be translucent, or you can use it to make your text fade out completely. On the right background, you can use brightness, which is less CPU-intensive, to achieve a similar effect.

- **Tweening text on paths.** You can combine tweening text on motion paths with other effects to simulate motion in 3D space.

- **Text and masking.** You can use text, both static and animated, as a mask for an underlying graphic.

- **Third-party text tools.** To speed up the development process, you can use third-party tools to create text effects and import them into Flash.

- **ActionScript, for creating an effect.** So you want to know how those third-party tools actually create those effects. Can't leave well enough alone, can you? Even if you don't like the idea of getting your hands dirty with code, you can use the code here and just modify a simple animation. You'll also get a chance to look at a couple properties of the new TextField object, a good addition.

Now it's time to start looking at how you can use text to create effective files.

Simple Text Changes

Sometimes an effect can be as simple as a color change or a change in the kerning. You don't always have to hit people over the head to get their attention. Just using the Text tool and the Properties Inspector settings, you can make some interesting changes.

It's always a little surprising that people don't realize that you can apply different effects within a single text block. You don't have to break your text out into individual letters just to change the font, color, size, or tracking (kerning). However, you should be aware that breaking your text into individual letters is incredibly simple in Flash MX—and you'll be taking a look at that a little later. One of the cool things about using multiple effects in a single text block is that it's so easy to go back in and edit later.

The new Properties Inspector is now an Uber-panel for any text changes you want to make.

The best way to see what you can do with simple text effects is to try it.

Exercise 9.1   Creating Simple Text Effects

You'll start by working with a file that already has some text on the Stage.

1. Open simpletext.fla from the Examples/Chapter09 folder on the CD. For this exercise. you'll be using the Properties Inspector (Window > Properties, or Ctrl+F3 [Windows] or Command+F3 [Macintosh]) and the Color Mixer panel (Window > Color Mixer, or Shift+F2), so go ahead and open those now.

2. On the Stage is the phrase "all men are created equal" (see Figure 9.1).

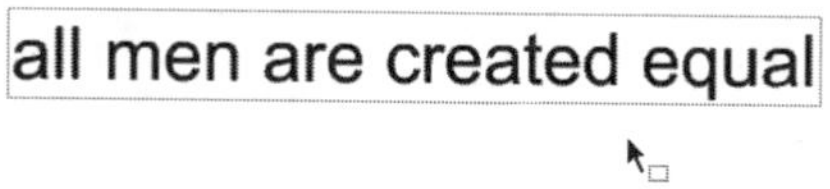

all men are created equal

Figure 9.1   The basic text "all men are created equal" might ring true, but the current presentation doesn't have a lot of impact.

3. Double-click the phrase to edit it. Select a single character by highlighting it. Choose a new color by selecting the Text (fill) color box on the Properties Inspector. Alternately, you can choose the Fill Color box on the Mixer panel or click a color in the Color bar at the bottom of the Mixer panel. The color change is applied immediately. Make as many color changes as you like.

    You're not stuck with just using one font type or font size in a text block. In fact, you could make every single letter a different font type or size, although I wouldn't recommend that unless you're writing a ransom note.

Tip

In the previous exercise, you worked with static text; Flash enables you to manipulate it easily, but not with other text fields. So, these techniques only work with static text. Flash will cheerfully let you apply different effects to individual letters in Input and Dynamic text fields, but they won't be reflected in your published file.

4. Select another character. This time, make an alpha transparency change using the Color Mixer. To do so, you need to change the alpha setting by clicking the down arrow next to Alpha and then moving the slider that opens to the desired setting. You can also type a number directly into the input box next to Alpha (see Figure 9.2).

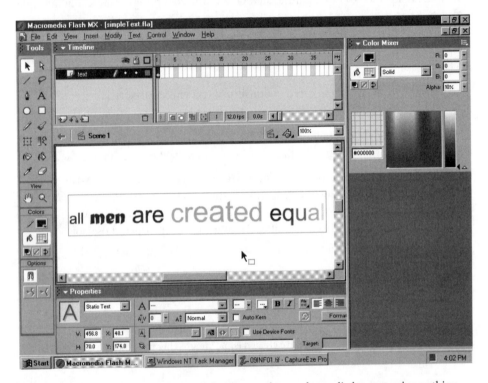

Figure 9.2 Now you can see some of the changes that can be applied to text using nothing more than the options available on the Properties Inspector and the Color Mixer.

5. Click once outside the text box to exit Text-Editing mode. Click once on the text block with the Arrow (V) tool to select it. (Don't double-click—if you do, you'll find yourself back in Text-Editing mode.) One of the simplest changes that you can make is to change the character spacing. If you look at the Properties Inspector, you'll notice both Character Spacing and Auto Kern settings just below the Font setting. These concepts are related. Character Spacing alone puts a uniform amount of space between each character. With Auto Kern selected, the characters are compared as pairs and are spaced appropriately if kerning information is built in for the font.

Note

See Figure 9.3 for an example of how Character Spacing and Auto Kern affect font spacing. On the Properties Inspector (Window > Properties), select the down arrow next to Character Spacing (the Character Spacing icon is the A\V right below the A symbol for the font). On the Character Spacing pop-up slider, drag the pointer in the slider bar up and down to see the character spacing change.

If you want to create an animation using changes in character spacing, you'll have to do it the old-fashioned way—frame by frame.

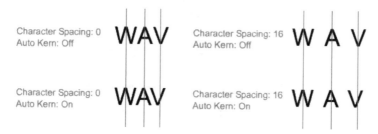

Figure 9.3   The effects of Character Spacing and Auto Kern are easy to see if you draw a vertical line through kerned and unkerned samples.

Now that you have your text set up, you might decide to animate the individual letters. If you will use tweening, you'll want to have each letter on its own layer. Breaking apart the text and placing each letter on its own layer used to be horribly time-consuming. In Flash MX, it's a snap.

6. Select the text box on the Stage. Break the text apart by choosing Modify > Break Apart or using Ctrl+B (Windows) or Command+B (Macintosh).

7. If you want each letter on its own layer, make sure that all the letters are still selected and choose Modify > Distribute to Layers or press Ctrl+Shift+B (Windows) or Command+Shift+B (Macintosh).

If you want only certain letters distributed to certain layers, just select the ones that you want and choose Modify > Distribute to Layers (see Figure 9.4).

Each letter that you choose to distribute will be placed on its own layer, and the layer name will be the same as the letter.

Figure 9.4   Flash MX has a new feature that enables you to quickly distribute selected items onto their own layers.

By now you should be getting the idea. You can change the color, alpha, font, font size, and character spacing on a character-by-character basis for static text. You also know how to break apart text and distribute it to layers. That gives you a lot of options for formatting easily editable text.

Next, take a look at some of the ways that you can use alpha transparency and brightness with text.

Alpha Transparency and Brightness

You can use alpha transparency and brightness to create interesting effects. Changes in the alpha transparency can be used to make text fade in or fade out. At intermediate settings, you can use alpha transparency to complement other elements in a movie.

Brightness adjusts the relative lightness or darkness of the image from black to white. On a black or white background, you can use brightness as an alternative to changing the alpha transparency. The bonus is that brightness changes are far less CPU-intensive than alpha changes.

A very effective, if potentially CPU-intensive, effect is to use alpha transparency and tweening over a bitmap.

Exercise 9.2   Using Alpha Transparency to Create a Text Effect

The base for this file has already been created for you.

1. Open alpha.fla from the Examples/Chapter09 folder on the CD, and save it to your hard drive. In this exercise, you'll still be using the Properties Inspector (Window > Properties) and the Color Mixer (Window > Color Mixer). At the lower part of the image is a cropped version of the phrase "In God We Trust." You can overlay that phrase fragment with the complete phrase and animate it for an interesting and organic effect.

2. Select the Text tool, and use the Properties Inspector to select the font Garamond Book or some other font similar to the one in the graphic image. Set the height of the font to roughly match the height of the font on the Stage. If you are using Garamond Book, the height should be about 170.

3. Use the Color Mixer to set the font to light gray, with an Alpha setting of 50%.

4. Add a new layer named Text above the Background layer. With the new layer selected, type the phrase **In God We Trust** on the Stage. Position the text so that it almost—but not quite—matches the text in the background graphic; offset it slightly (see Figure 9.5).

5. Make this more interesting by adding a little motion. Remember, a little goes a long way.

6. To start setting up your tweens, insert a keyframe (F6) in frame 4 of the Text layer. These movements will be subtle—nothing too overt. Make sure that you extend the Background layer by inserting a frame (F5) in frame 4.

7. Select the text block in frame 4, and use the left arrow on your keyboard to nudge the text about 10 pixels to the left.

   Add a motion tween by selecting any frame between your two keyframes and then either right- or Control-clicking and choosing Create Motion Tween. Alternately, you can create the tween from the Properties Inspector (Window > Properties) and choose Motion from the Tween drop-down list.

 Tip

You can use the arrow keys on the keyboard to move selected items on the Stage by 1 pixel at a time. If you hold down the Shift key and press one of the arrow keys, you can move the item by 8 pixels at a time. One caveat here: You will always move by either 1 or 8 screen pixels, regardless of the magnification. That means that if you have the object highly magnified, the movement that you get by using the arrow keys might be more subtle than you intended.

Figure 9.5 By adding text with an alpha transparency setting of 50% over the background, along with some tweening, you can create an interesting effect.

8. Add another keyframe in frame 10 of the Text layer (and a regular frame [F5] in the Background layer), and move the text block back to its original position (move it 10 pixels to the right). Add a motion tween the same way you did in Step 7.

9. Add a keyframe in frame 16 (and extend your Background layer), and move the text block another 10 pixels to the right. Add your tween.

10. Add one more keyframe in frame 25 (extend your Background layer again), and move the text block 10 pixels back to the left. Don't forget your motion tween.

11. Test your file. The translucent letters shifting back and forth over the static text give an interesting feel to the piece.

Because this movie has a patterned background, using brightness to simulate an Alpha effect doesn't work. But in the next section, you'll take a look at tweening text on a path and using brightness to fade it in and out on a white background.

Tweening Text on Paths

Obviously, you can use motion tweens to move text around the Stage. You can also use tweening on paths and scaling to create the illusion of text moving in three-dimensional space.

When you are simulating three-dimensional space in Flash, you need to remember two rules:

- Objects that are closer to you appear larger than objects that are farther away.
- Objects that are closer to you appear to move faster than objects that are farther away.

To see how you can use these types of effects, take a look at a couple files. First, look at an example of how you can use tweening on a curved path with scaling and brightness changes.

Open tweening.fla from the Examples/Chapter09 folder on the CD, and then test the file to see what it does.

The main part of the animation is the tween of the letters of the word *one*. Each letter is converted to a graphic symbol. Why? Because you can tween a text block, but you can't apply an effect to it. To use the brightness effect, the letters must be embedded in symbols.

In the first frame, each letter is scaled and a brightness of 100% is applied. The scaling is proportioned so that the *e* always appears to be closer and the *o* appears farthest away until they reach their final positions. The tweens are staggered so that the *e* moves the fastest and the *o* moves the slowest (see Figure 9.6). That's an important concept to remember, and you'll see it again in later chapters: Objects that are closer to you appear to be moving faster than objects that are farther away.

Just to add a little more interest, as soon as the *o* is in place, another tween is started. This time, each letter is scaled to 150% and brightness is set back to 100%, in effect making the letters expand, fade out, and disappear.

At the same time that the final tween is taking place, the letters for "one nation" are being spelled out on the Stage. See how these remain in place for a number of frames and then appear to blink in and out, again using changes in the brightness rather than the alpha transparency. In the next exercise, you use tweening on a motion path to create a text effect.

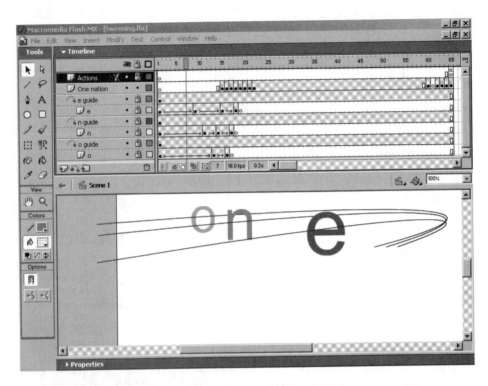

Figure 9.6   By staggering the motion tweens, you can make the letters move at different speeds. In this case, the foreground letters move faster than the background letters.

Exercise 9.3   Creating a 3D Text Effect

In this exercise, you use alpha transparency, scaling, and tweening on an elliptical path to mimic 3D motion.

1. Create a new movie and rename Layer 1 to **Freedom Text**.

2. Select the Text tool and open the Properties Inspector (Window > Properties). Make the following changes to the Properties Inspector:

   > Font: **Arial or Helvetica (or your choice)**
   > Color: **Pick one**
   > Size: **9**

3. Type the word **FREEDOM** (in all caps) on the Stage.

4. Embed the text field in a movie clip (F8), and name the movie clip **Freedom Text**.

   You'll need to set up a motion path on a Guide layer to control the movement of your text movie clip.

5. Add a Guide layer above the current layer (click the Add Motion Guide icon next to the Insert Layer icon).

6. With the Guide layer selected, use the Oval tool to draw an unfilled ellipse on the Stage.

Tip

When you are using an ellipse, a circle, or any closed outline as a motion guide, you can set up your tweens in two ways. You can remove a small segment of the outline to create discrete stopping and starting points, or you can space the contents of your keyframes in such a way that the distance to the next keyframe is always shorter than the distance to the previous keyframe.

Flash is very economical: It always takes the shortest route to the next point on a closed path. This means that you might get objects moving in predictable but undesired directions. For this exercise, you practice removing a line segment.

7. For now, you need to remove a small segment of the ellipse so that Flash knows where the starting and stopping points on the tween are. Use the Magnifier tool, and zoom in on the right side of the ellipse. Use the Eraser tool to remove a small segment of the line (see Figure 9.7).

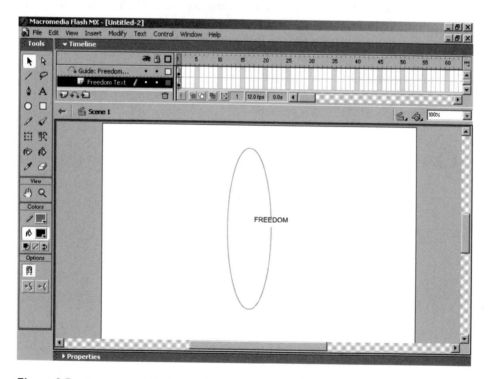

Figure 9.7   Create an elliptical shape for your motion guide. You can put a break in the oval to more easily set your start and end points.

8. Make sure that you have Snap to Objects selected (View > Snap to Objects).

9. Click the Freedom Text movie clip to select it, and then click its registration point and drag it to the ellipse. Snap it to the upper end of the line where you cut the ellipse.

10. Insert keyframes (F6) in frames 10, 20, 30, and 40 of the Freedom Text layer. Extend the Guide layer to frame 40 as well (F5).

11. Reposition the movie clip in the new frames (you might find this easier to do if you lock the Guide layer):

    Frame 10: Top of the ellipse
    Frame 20: Left side of the ellipse
    Frame 30: Bottom of the ellipse
    Frame 40: The other endpoint of the ellipse

12. To create all the motion tweens at once, click the Freedom Text layer name to highlight the entire layer, and then right-click any frame and select Create Motion Tween from the context menu. Test your tween to make sure that you have everything snapped into place.

    Next you'll make changes to the scaling and transparency to make it feel more 3D.

13. Use the Properties Inspector and the Transform panel (Ctrl+T, Command+T) to make the following changes. (See Figure 9.8.) Notice that you increase the scale and the alpha settings for the text that is "closer" to you:

    Frame 1: Alpha 50%
    Frame 10: Alpha 75%/Scale 300%
    Frame 20: Alpha 100%/Scale 600%
    Frame 30: Alpha 75%/Scale 300%
    Frame 40: Alpha 50%

14. Test your file again. By changing the scale and transparency, you get a more 3D–like effect.

Figure 9.8   If you turn on Onion All and Edit Multiple Frames, you can see the five different instances of the Freedom Text movie clip with the scaling applied.

In the next section, you take a look at how you can use text as a mask to create interesting effects.

Text and Masking

Masking can be used to produce some of the more interesting effects that you see (see Figure 9.9). Whenever you are working with masks, you are working with at least two separate layers: the layer being masked and the layer doing the masking. You can have anything that you like on the layer that is being masked. What you place on the masking layer acts as a window to the layer below. You can use static text as a mask, use text as a mask with tweening, or use a static text mask and tween the masked layer. You get a more advanced look at masking in Chapter 10, "Masking Effects."

The best way to get a handle on this concept is to just try it.

Exercise 9.4   Using Masking to Create Text Effects

If you are already comfortable with masking, go ahead and skip to the next section. If you haven't used masking, this is just a quick exercise to introduce you to the concept.

1. Open masking.fla in the Examples/Chapter09 folder on the CD.
2. Right now, all you have is a Background layer. Add a new layer and name it **Mask**.
3. Select the Text tool and then choose any font from the Properties Inspector. Set a font height of about 50. With the Mask layer selected, type the phrase **One Nation** on the Stage.
4. Right- or Control-click the Mask layer and select Mask from the Options menu.

Now you can see the effect of masking. The letters that you typed on the Stage create a window that you can look through to the graphic on the layer below. Note that both the masking and masked layers are locked. If you unlock either layer, you won't be able to see the masking effect again until you relock it or right- or Command-click and choose Show Masking (see Figure 9.9).

Figure 9.9   With both the mask and the masked layers locked, you can see the effect of the text mask.

You can also choose to tween your mask or to leave your mask stationary and tween the graphic or graphics beneath it. Again, you explore masking techniques in more detail in Chapter 10.

Sometimes it's easier to let someone else do the work for you. Take a quick look at how you can use text effects created in a third-party program.

Using Third-Party Text Tools

Sometimes it just makes more sense to use a third-party tool rather than beat your head against the wall trying to create a text effect that someone else has already figured out and packaged up for you. A number of tools available now let you quickly create text effects that would otherwise be very time-intensive to develop on your own. SWfX from Wildform Internet Media Software and Swish from swishzone.com are two of the better known of these, and both do a good job of creating a wide variety of effects. (See Figures 9.10 and 9.11.)

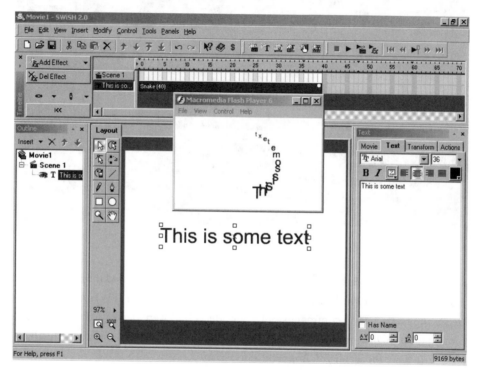

Figure 9.10   The Swish interface.

Figure 9.11   The SWfX interface.

Some of the SWFs created by these programs can be directly imported into your current movie; others have to be loaded as movies. You can directly import SWFs that were created using Flash 3–level commands only. For effects that were developed using Flash 4 commands or higher, you need to load the SWF as a movie. Why? Because of what happens to an SWF file when you import it into Flash:

- Everything in the SWF is flattened into one layer.

- Animated graphic symbols are converted to frame-by-frame animations rather than tweens. The content of the frames is converted to new graphic symbols named Symbol 1, Symbol 2, and so on.

- Only the first frame of any movie clip is imported. The rest of the movie clip Timeline is ignored. Hence, any animation in the movie clip is ignored.

If you look at the source files for the SWfX effects, you'll see that many of the effects rely on using movie clips, which, of course, won't import as movie clips after they've been compressed into an SWF file. That's why you have to use the `loadMovie()` command. This is true for any SWF, whether created by a third-party tool or created natively in Flash.

How can you tell which files can be imported? Swish files don't contain embedded movie clips (at least, not in version 2.0), so you can directly import any of the Swish-created SWFs. When you create SWfX files, the effects that are Flash 3–level only are not highlighted in the effects list. If you use one of the highlighted effects, you'll need to load the final SWF file using `loadMovie()`. You're almost always better off using `loadMovie()` rather than importing files directly into Flash anyway because you have lots more control that way.

If you do choose to import SWFs into your movie, it's a good idea to import them into movie clips rather than onto the main Timeline. They'll be much easier to reposition, and you'll find that this gives you much more flexibility.

Exercise 9.5   Importing and Loading Third-Party Effects

This exercise doesn't teach you how to use third-party software, but it does show you the options that you have for importing third-party SWFs into your movie. The lessons that you learn here will work for importing any SWF into your movie.

1. Create a new blank movie.

2. Because you know that if you are going to import SWFs into your Flash movie, you should always import them into movie clips. Start by creating a new movie clip (Ctrl+F8 or Command+F8), and name it **Explode**.

3. While inside the Explode movie clip, choose File > Import and browse to explode.swf in the Examples/Chapter09 folder. Click Open.

   You'll see that you now have a frame-by-frame animation inside your movie clip (see Figure 9.12). You can drag this movie clip from your Library and use it anywhere in your movie.

4. Now do the same thing with an SWF that was created using Flash 4 commands. Create a new movie clip, and name it **bigWave**.

5. While inside the bigWave movie clip, choose File > Import, and browse to bigWave.swf in the Examples/Chapter09 folder on the companion CD. Click Open.

   Whoa, there. Nothing but blank frames. That's no fun. You're going to have to use `loadMovie()` to get this one to work.

6. Create a new blank movie clip, and name it **Placeholder**.

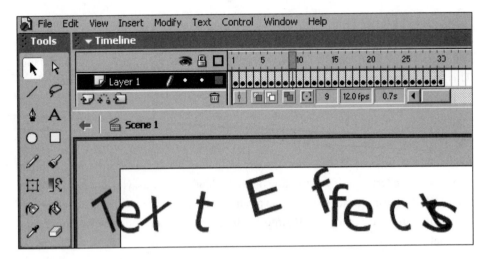

Figure 9.12   When you import the Swish-generated file, you get a frame-by-frame animation.

7. Drag a copy of the Placeholder movie clip onto the Stage. In the Properties Inspector, give it an instance name of **placeholder**.

8. Add a new layer on the main Timeline, and name it **Actions**. Select frame 1 of the Actions layer, and open the Actions panel (F2).

    You need to tell Flash which movie clip you want to load into (target), how to do it (loadMovie()), and what movie to load (bigWave.swf).

9. In the Actions panel (set to Expert mode, Ctrl+Shift+E or Command+Shift+E), enter the following:

```
placeholder.loadMovie("bigWave.swf");
```

    Alternately, you can enter this:

```
loadMovie("bigWave.swf", placeholder);
```

10. Now test your movie (see Figure 9.13). With your SWF file imported into the movie clip, you can move it wherever you need it on the Stage. Flexibility is the key here.

Note

Make sure that your files are located in the same folder. Because the loadMovie() action was made with a relative reference, Flash looks only in the current folder.

Figure 9.13   You won't actually be able to see the movie that you're loading until you test your movie.

As mentioned earlier, some of you will want to know how to create this type of effect yourself. You won't be happy using a third-party tool, and that's fine. But you'll have to play with ActionScript to make it work. The good news is that you can just steal the code here and modify a single movie clip to make changes.

Building Your Own Effects

So how can you build effects like that yourself? Well, one way is to use `onClipEvent()` handlers and the `attachMovie()` method. If the idea of working with ActionScript gives you the willies, you can skip to the section "Using This Movie as a Template for Your Own Effects."

You can hand-build a frame-by-frame or tweened animation to duplicate these effects, but what if you actually want to reuse the effect that you come up with using different text?

You've looked at `loadMovie()` already. You can use another method built into Flash, called `loadVariables()`,to load information into your file.

What you want to do here is be able to pass the text from a text file into a Flash movie and then use Flash to dynamically generate a nifty little text effect. Simple, huh? Yeah, right. Actually, it's not that bad—it's just a new way of thinking.

This will not be a complete description of how this works. If you are already into scripting, you'll be able to figure it out. If you've never scripted, you'll still be able to use this information to modify the movie to suit your needs. When you have a little more scripting experience under your belt, you can revisit the code and modify it at will.

Exercise 9.6   Setting Up the Basic Animation

You can create your own effect fairly easily—all you need to do is embed a dynamic text field in a movie clip symbol and animate that symbol inside another movie clip. You'll be taking advantage of the fact that dynamic text fields can be treated as objects in Flash MX.

1. Create a new movie and save it as **effect.fla**.

2. Select the Text tool and open the Properties Inspector (Window > Properties). Pick the font, size, and color settings that you want to use, and type a capital **M** on the Stage.

   Why *M?* It doesn't really matter what letter you choose. In fact, you don't need to put any letter in there—it just makes it easier to see what you're doing.

3. With your new text field selected, make the following changes in the Properties Inspector:

   Text Type: **Dynamic Text**
   Line Type: **Single Line**
   Instance Name: `letterContainer`
   Selectable: **Not selected**
   HTML: **Not selected**
   Border/Bg: **Not selected**

Note

The Selectable option enables a user to click inside this text field and play with the contents, much like a form text input. The HTML option allows HTML tags to be placed inside the text field—be careful what you enter, though, because Flash can handle only certain tags. The last option, Border/Bg, simply draws a border line around the text field selected.

4. Make sure that you embed your font! With the text field selected, press the Character button in the Properties Inspector. For now, select the All Characters radio button.

5. With the text field on the Stage selected, choose F8 to embed it in a movie clip symbol. Name the symbol letter_mc, and make the upper-left corner the registration point.

   Now that you have a container for your letter, you'll embed it inside another movie clip so that you can animate it. Why not just animate the text box in the movie you're in? Because it limits the effects that you can apply.

6. With the letter graphic selected, use F8 again to embed it in a movie clip named **letter_anime_mc**.

7. Double-click letter_anime_mc in the Library to open it in Symbol-Editing mode.

8. This is when you get to have some fun: You get to set up the animation for your text.

   I suggest starting with something simple and then working from there. If you need an idea, open effects_final.fla in the Examples/Chapter09 folder and examine the letter_anime_mc in the Library. It's a simple motion tween with rotation. The movie clip in the first frame is skewed and has an alpha change.

9. Make sure that you add an Actions layer and put a `stop` action in the final keyframe of your animation. Otherwise, it will loop endlessly.

After your animation is set up, you have a little more to take care of. So far, you've animated the letter *M*—what next? The next step is to create a text file that will hold the actual string of characters that you want to animate.

Exercise 9.7   Creating a File to Hold Your Text and Loading the Data into Your Movie

You can pass in whatever text you want to animate in your Flash movie from a text file. This means that the file you are creating is completely reusable for any string of text—without you having to go in and make any modifications to the Flash movie itself.

1. Open your text editor of choice. You will set up a name/value pair, a variable that will hold all the text that you want to use in your movie.

2. All you need to put in the text file is the variable name and the text that you want that variable to hold—this is the text that you'll be animating. For example, on the CD there's a file called data.txt that has the following name/value pair already set up:

   `dataString=Fig Leaf`

   In this case, the text string "Fig Leaf" is passed into the variable `dataString`. For your animation, you can change "Fig Leaf" to whatever text string you want to animate, but the variable name `dataString` must stay the same. So, if you think of it as a name/value pair, the name is `dataString` and the value is `Fig Leaf`.

3. Set up your name/value pair and save your file as data.txt in the same directory as your Flash file.

   You need to load this data into your Flash movie; make sure that it has been loaded before you try to use it. You do that by loading it into an empty movie clip so that you can use an `onClipEvent()` handler to see if it's loaded.

4. Choose Insert > New Symbol. Create a blank movie clip and name it **container_mc**.

5. Return to the main Timeline and drag a copy of the Container movie clip from the Library onto the Stage (it will be a small open circle). You can delete the letter_anime_mc from the Stage; you'll be attaching it dynamically.

The rest of the Actions for your movie are attached to the container movie clip.

The ActionScript for Movie Control

This is where those of you who haven't coded might get a little lost. Don't panic—I'll explain the code line by line. Alternately, you can forget the code altogether and just skip to the next section to see how to use the finished file (dynamic.fla) as a template for your own effects.

You're going to be working with three different onClipEvent() handlers. These handlers can be attached to only movie clips. You'll be using the following:

- **onClipEvent(load).** Any code inside a load event is executed only the first time that the movie clip loads. This is a good place to initialize any values that you'll be using later.

- **onClipEvent(data).** The code inside the data event doesn't run until all the data being sent to the movie clip has been received.

- **onClipEvent(enterFrame).** The code inside an enterFrame event runs repeatedly—as long as the movie clip exists.

You'll also be working with arrays, variables, and loops, so get ready to get your hands dirty!

Exercise 9.8   Adding the ActionScript

You can either continue working in the previous file or open effect1.fla from the Examples/Chapter09 file on the CD.

1. The first thing you need to do is set up the letter_anime_mc so that it can be used by the attachMovie() method. All you need to do is select the letter_anime_mc in the Library, right- or Command-click, and choose Linkage.

2. In the Linkage Properties dialog box, select Export for ActionScript and give it an Identifier name of letter. Leave Export in the first frame selected. (If you need a refresher on what these mean, refer back to Chapter 3, "Tips for Using the Library and Shared Libraries.")

   You'll be adding the rest of your code directly to the container movie clip.

3. Select the container movie clip on the Stage and open the Actions panel (F2).

4. The first thing to do is set up the event handler that tells Flash what to do when the container movie clip first loads. In the Actions panel, enter this code:

```
onClipEvent(load) {
}
```

5. Use `loadVariables` to load the data into the text file that you created. Position your cursor between the curly braces and enter this:

```
this.loadVariables("data.txt");
```

6. Next you'll add two variables, `startXpos` and `startYpos`. These are used to tell Flash where to begin attaching movie clips to the movie—in this case, 100 pixels in from the left and the top of the movie. Add a blank line after the line that you entered in Step 5, and add the following:

```
startXpos = 100;
startYpos = 100;
```

7. You need to keep track of the position where each subsequent movie clip gets attached; that value goes in the variable `nextX`. The variables `elapsedTime` and `enterTime` keep track of the amount of time since the last movie clip was attached; this enables you to set up a delay. Finally, `i` is just a counting variable. Add a blank line after the lines that you entered in Step 6, and add the following:

```
nextX = 0;
elapsedTime = 0;
enterTime = 0;
i=0;
```

Your completed `onClipEvent(load)` should look like this:

```
onClipEvent(load) {
    this.loadVariables("data.txt");
    startXpos = 100;
    startYpos = 100;
    nextX = 0;
    elapsedTime = 0;
    enterTime = 0;
    i=0;
}
```

8. The next event handler fires after all the data from data.txt file has loaded. First, you create a new array; then you use the `split` method of the String object in Flash to break apart the string and place each character in its own element in the array. Just for good measure, throw in a `trace` statement to see how many items your new array contains. Add a new line after the last curly brace in your current code, and add this:

```
onClipEvent(data) {
    newLetters = new Array();
    newLetters = dataString.split("");
    trace("length: "+this.newLetters.length);
}
```

Note

You advanced ActionScripters out there might want to use the String Split Prototype with MX because it is be faster. This script can be found at `http://chattyfig.figleaf.com/~bhall/code/string.as`.

Now the real work begins. You'll use an `enterFrame` event to actually place your movie clips on the Stage. Here is the pseudocode (English) for what you want to do:

> If elapsedTime is greater than 100 milliseconds (ms), store the current time in the enterFrame variable and check to see if the value of the variable i is less than the length of the array that you created. If it is, start attaching movies. Position each movie on its own level, and move it so that it doesn't overlap with the previous movie. Add 1 to the counter variable, and reset elapsedTime to 0. If elapsedTime is less than 100ms, check the timer again and update elapsedTime.

Sound a little overwhelming? It's really not that bad. Here's the actual code:

```
onClipEvent(enterFrame) {
     if (elapsedTime > 100) {
          enterTime = getTimer();
          if (i < this.newLetters.length) {
_root.attachMovie("letter", "letter"+i, i);
               _root["letter"+i].letterContainer.text = newLetters[i];
               trace(_root["letter"+i].letterContainer.textWidth);
               _root["letter"+i]._x = nextX;
               _root["letter"+i]._y = startYpos;
               nextX = _root["letter"+i]._X +
               ➥_root["letter"+i].letterContainer.textWidth;

               ++i;
               elapsedTime = 0;

          }
     }else{
          elapsedTime = getTimer() - enterTime;
     }
}
```

Take a look at a line-by-line breakdown:

```
if (elapsedTime > 100) {
```

When the movie first loads, the `elapsedTime` variable is equal to 0. On the first pass through the code, Flash skips everything inside this `if` statement and drops down to the

else clause, where elapsedTime gets updated. As soon as 100ms have elapsed, the code
inside the if statement gets processed.

```
enterTime = getTimer();
```

This line makes a call to the getTimer() function in Flash. That function returns, in milliseconds, how long it has been since the movie started. You're saving that value in the
variable enterTime.

```
if (i < this.newLetters.length) {
```

The first time you enter this event, i is equal to 0—you initialized in
onClipEvent(load). So, if 0 is less than the number of letters in your text file, you'll
continue.

```
_root.attachMovie("letter", "letter"+i, i);
```

This is the line that actually attaches new movies. You are attaching an instance of the
movie letter—remember, that's the identifier name that you have the letter_anime_mc
movie clip set to in the Linkage Properties in the Library. Because you're going to be
attaching multiple instances of this movie clip to the movie, each one must have a unique
instance name. The easiest way to do that is to concatenate the counter variable i to a
string of letters. In this case, the first instance will have an instance name of letter0, the
second will be letter1, and so on. You also need to attach each movie to a unique level, so
again use the counter variable. The first movie attaches to level 0, the second to level 1,
and so on.

```
_root["letter"+i].letterContainer.text = newLetters[i];
```

This is something a little new. Rather than assign the value of the letter to a variable,
you'll be using the text property of the TextField object. Back in the beginning of this
exercise, you gave the dynamic text box an instance name of letterContainer; this is
where that comes into play. On the first pass, you're telling Flash that you want to give
the TextField object letterContainer inside the movie clip named letter0 whatever is
in position 0 inside the newLetters array.

```
_root["letter"+i]._x = nextX;
_root["letter"+i]._y = startYpos;
nextX = _root["letter"+i]._x +
➥_root["letter"+i].letterContainer.textWidth;
```

These three lines position the new movie instance in the main movie. The y position
doesn't change; it takes whatever value you assigned it in the load event. The x position
does change. You need to know the current x position of the movie clip (_x), which is the
center of the movie clip. Add to that width of the current letter to move it over. Notice

that again you're taking advantage of the `TextField` object to get the actual width of the letter using the `textWidth` property.

```
++i;
elapsedTime = 0;
```

After everything else in the `if` statement is done, increment your counter variable and reset the `elapsedTime` variable to `0`.

The complete code that gets attached to the container movie clip is shown in Listing 9.1.

Listing 9.1   The Completed ActionScript for Attaching Your New Text Effects Movie Clips to Your Movie

```
onClipEvent(load) {
    this.loadVariables("data.txt");
    startXpos = 100;
    startYpos = 100;
    nextX = 0;
    elapsedTime = 0;
    enterTime = 0;
    i=0;
}

onClipEvent(data) {

trace("I'm here");
    newLetters = new Array();
    newLetters = dataString.split("");
    trace("length: "+this.newLetters.length);
}

onClipEvent(enterFrame) {

    if (elapsedTime > 100) {
        enterTime = getTimer();
        if (i < this.newLetters.length) {

            _root.attachMovie("letter", "letter"+i, i);
            _root["letter"+i].letterContainer.text = newLetters[i];
            trace(_root["letter"+i].letterContainer.textWidth);
            _root["letter"+i]._x = nextX;
            _root["letter"+i]._y = startYpos;
            nextX = _root["letter"+i]._x +
            ➥_root["letter"+i].letterContainer.textWidth;

            ++i;
            elapsedTime = 0;

        }
    }else{
        elapsedTime = getTimer() - enterTime;
    }
}
```

You don't actually have to enter this code yourself if you are uncomfortable doing that. You can use this file as a template and modify it to suit your needs.

Using This Movie as a Template for Your Own Effects

So you've waded through the previous section and you've decided that you just don't want to mess with all that ActionScript. Not to worry—you can just use the file as is and modify it to suit your needs.

You need to make only a few changes to the existing file. You already know how to change the text being loaded into the file—just change whatever is in data.txt. The other things that you might want to change are the actual animation itself and the font type, size, and color. To change the font attributes, just open the letter symbol and use the Properties Inspector to make any changes you want.

You can also add to the data.txt file and have your `startx` and `starty` variables come from this text instead of being hard-coded into your ActionScript.

Changing the actual animation is just as easy as changing the font. Double-click the letter_anime_mc movie clip and modify the animation to suit your needs. Add a motion guide, play with the effects, and do whatever you want. You don't need to touch the code at all.

Summary

Never discount text effects as an effective means of communication. You don't have to go into mind-bending mathematical manipulations of text to create great effects. All you need to do is understand the different methods that you can use to give life to your text, from the simplest of changes on the individual letters of a text block to the most complex changes involving ActionScript. Just remember, you're limited only by your imagination.

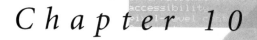

Chapter 10

Masking Effects

Masking is one of those concepts with
which people sometimes have a little trouble. However, after you get past the concep-
tual hurdle, masking is a great addition to
your Flash skill set. So what is a mask?

I think my favorite analogy is that a mask is like a stencil. You probably used stencils in your early school years to create posters and signs with neat, concise lettering. To do so, you lay the stencil on top of a piece of paper and paint in the holes. The stencil protects the underlying paper except where the holes are. When you peel off the stencil, you can see nice, neat painted letters. That's pretty much what a mask does in Flash—it screens off the underlying layer so that you see only the part where the holes are.

In this chapter, you learn how to do the following:

- **Create various types of masking effects.** Masking can be used in many ways. You can use it to create interesting motion and text effects. You also can use it to quickly and easily apply static effects to objects on the Stage.

- **Soften mask edges.** Masks in Flash don't work with gradients, but you can use a little trickery to give your masked effect a nice, soft edge.

- **Dynamic masking with the `setMask()` method.** One of the complaints we've always had with masks in Flash is that you couldn't use movie clips as masks. Good news—now you can.

- **Using functions and `setMask()` to control a mask inside a movie clip.** One of the joys of Flash MX is the ability to set up event handlers on the main Timeline to handle actions for objects in your movie. Now you can easily create a drag-gable magnifying glass and keep all of your code in one frame on the main Timeline.

Just in case masking is new to you, and even if it isn't, it's a good idea to review the basics of masking so that you know what works and what doesn't.

A Quick Overview of Masking

Masking in Flash is a two-layer (or more) process. You have a masking layer and you have the layer—or layers—being masked.

When you're creating a mask, you can use the following:

- Simple shapes.
- Static text.
- Single-layer graphic symbols that contain only simple shapes.
- A new feature in Flash MX is the ability to use complex movie clips as masks.

You can't, however, use the following:

- Lines (strokes)
- Gradients
- Bitmaps

So now you know what you can and can't use as a mask. Are there rules about what can be masked? Yes, there are.

In Flash MX, you could use graphic symbols as masks. But now you can also effectively use movie clips. However, you do need to understand how graphic and movie clips behave when they are in a masking layer. It's not intuitively obvious, and it might not be what you expect. Additionally, movie clips no longer have to be in masking layers to act as masks.

Movie Clips and Graphic Symbols as Masks

Trying to use a movie clip as a mask previously was a frustrating experience. Flash 5 used only the first frame of the bottom layer of a movie clip as the masking element. Not only that, but if you had nested movie clips, Flash 5 used only the first frame of the bottom layer of the most deeply nested clip. All that has changed. You can now use movie clips with multiple layers and frames in a masking layer. As you might anticipate, objects in the movie on higher levels take precedence over those on lower levels. In fact, movie clips don't have to be in a masking layer. As you'll see later, you can use ActionScript to tell a movie clip to become a mask for another movie clip.

Graphic symbols, on the other hand, are more limited than movie clips when you are creating a mask. Flash recognizes only the bottom layer of a graphic symbol. Like a movie clip, Flash does recognize multiple frames when you use a graphic symbol as a mask. This means that as long as your animation is contained in one layer, you can use an animated graphic as a mask. Of course, this works only if your main Timeline is long enough to accommodate the tween in your graphic symbol. Unlike Flash 5, in Flash MX you can create a motion tween inside a graphic, and it will work as a mask. Also, if each frame contains shapes only, you can animate. Thus, you can have shape tweens inside a graphic symbol. You also can do frame-by-frame animations using either simple shapes or graphic symbols inside your graphic symbol. Again, make sure that you extend your Timeline to accommodate the Timeline of the graphic.

On the masking layer itself, you can animate whatever you're using as a mask as either a shape or a motion tween. However, you can't use a motion guide to control the path of the tween. It won't work—don't waste your time trying. But you can control the path of your mask using ActionScript. You also can have more than one layer under a single mask—but only if you're using masking layers, not if you're creating the mask with ActionScript. A movie clip that is set as a mask using the setMask() method can mask only the movie clip that it's set as the mask for.

Tip

Frankly, with the new masking capabilities of movie clips, I don't advise wasting time with graphic clips as masks anymore.

New to Flash MX, you can finally control a masking layer with ActionScript. You can also control the layer being masked with ActionScript, so you have some interesting options with which to work.

The layer being masked isn't governed by the same set of rules as the masking layer, with the exception that you still can't use a motion guide. However, you can use either movie clips or graphic symbols in all their glory, and you can control a named movie clip in the layer being masked with ActionScript.

Tip

One of the guidelines you'll see on the Macromedia web site is to use masks sparingly in your movies—and with good reason. Masks are CPU-intensive. If you use a lot of animated masking in your movie, you run the risk of grinding your viewer's computer to a halt. That won't make you very popular. When in doubt, refer back to the "Monitoring Your CPU Usage" section in Chapter 4, "Importing, Using, and Optimizing Graphics."

Now that you've had a review of the basics, why not create a mask? The next section guides you through the process of working with masks.

A Simple Spotlight Mask

The spotlight effect is the classic effect that people show when they are trying to demonstrate masking. Creating a spotlight effect involves nothing more than doing the following:

- Placing the graphic that you want to affect on a layer
- Creating a spotlight by tweening a shape on the layer above the graphic
- Making the layer with the tween a mask layer

If you've never used a mask, this is your chance to give it a try.

Exercise 10.1   Creating a Spotlight Mask

This file already has been started for you.

1. Open spotlight.fla in the Examples/Chapter10 folder on the CD.

   The file currently has one layer named Tulips with a copy of the tulip movie clip on it.

2. Add a new layer above the Tulips layer and name it **Mask**.

3. With the first frame of the Mask layer selected, draw a filled circle in the work area to the left of the Stage (see Figure 10.1). The color of the circle is irrelevant.

4. Convert the circle to a movie clip (F8) and name it **circle_mc**.

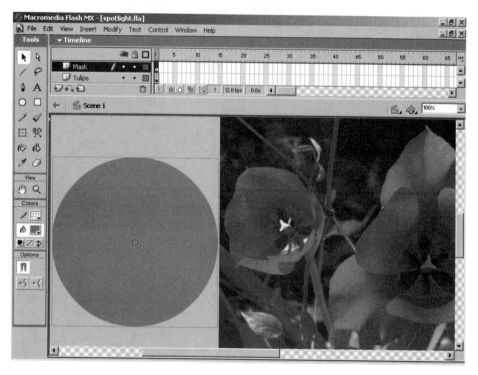

Figure 10.1   Draw a filled circle and place it to the left of the Stage. Convert the circle to a movie clip so that you can tween it.

5. Extend the Timeline (F5) out to frame 30 in both layers.

6. Insert a keyframe (F6) in frame 30 of the Mask layer, and drag the circle in frame 30 until it is off the Stage in the work area to the right.

7. Select any frame between 1 and 30 on the Mask layer; right- or Control-click and choose Create Motion Tween.

8. Select the Mask layer. Right- or Control-click and select Mask from the menu.

Notice how the layer icons change when you do this. The icon on the masking layer is an oval with a checkerboard pattern; the masked layer has a rectangle with a checkerboard pattern and is indented under the masking layer. (See Figure 10.2.)

Now you see only the tulip image where the mask is. That's an interesting effect, but why not add a simple twist?

Figure 10.2   After you turn on masking for the Mask layer, you see only the portion of the tulip graphic that is beneath the circle. The layer icons change as well, indicating which layer is the mask and which layer is masked.

9. Add a new layer named **Dark Tulips**, and drag it to the bottom of the stack. Make sure it's not indented under the Mask layer. If it is indented, just select Modify > Layer and select Normal to toggle it back to a normal layer, or double-click it and check Normal. (No, the old Flash 5 Alt+Click trick doesn't work anymore.)

   Drag a copy of the Tulips movie clip from the Library onto the Stage and align it with the Stage, top left corner.

10. With the Tulips movie clip selected, use the Properties Inspector (Window > Properties) to set the Brightness to –50%.

11. Test your movie again. Now you have a real spotlight effect. (See Figure 10.3.)

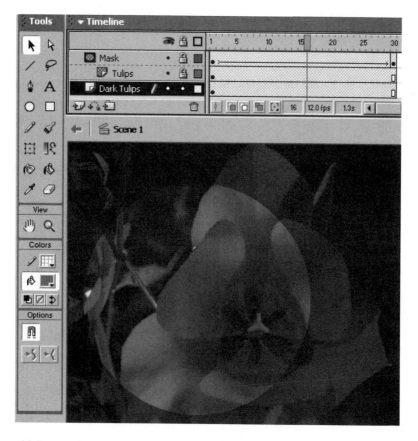

Figure 10.3   By adding another instance of the Tulips movie clip to the Stage and changing its Brightness settings, you can give an interesting twist to your spotlight effect.

You already know that you can't use a gradient as a mask in Flash. You might be wondering, however, if there is a way to soften the edges of your mask. The answer is, you can—but you need to use a little trickery.

Softening the Mask for Simple Shapes

Masks in Flash can't use gradients. By default, they are opaque. If you want a soft edge around your masked image, you have to fake it. You fake it by using a gradient in the shape of your mask either above the masking layer or in the stack of layers being masked. You'll stick to simple layer masks for this section.

The most effective gradient to apply is the one that meets the following criteria:

- Has a single color
- Matches the background color
- Has an alpha transparency of 0% at the center
- Has an alpha transparency of 100% at the outer edge

You'll probably want most of the gradient to be transparent. This is easy to accomplish when you have three gradient pointers that are set to the background color. The two left-most pointers will have an alpha transparency of 0%, and the rightmost pointer will have an alpha transparency of 100%.

You can have up to eight gradient pointers, but you must have a minimum of two. To add a pointer, click beneath the Gradient Definition bar. To remove a pointer, click it and drag it away from the bar.

If you want to experiment with this technique, the next exercise walks you through the process.

Exercise 10.2   Creating Soft Edges with a Gradient

1. Open softmask.fla from the Examples/Chapter10 folder on the CD. The mask for this file has already been set up; you just need to add the gradient for a softening effect.

2. Add a new layer between the Tulips and Mask layers, and name it **Gradient**.

3. Open the Library and make a duplicate of the circle movie clip (right- or Control-click the Circle symbol and choose Duplicate), and name it **Gradient**.

4. Double-click the new symbol that you just created to open it in Symbol-Editing mode. Click the Stage to deselect the shape.

5. Select the Color Mixer (Window > Color Mixer) and choose Radial from the drop-down menu.

   In this case, you'll want an all-white gradient that has an alpha transparency of 0% at the center and an alpha transparency of 100% at the outer edge.

6. Set up three white gradient pointers. The first one should be to the far left of the Gradient Definition bar, the second should be about three quarters of the way to the right, and the third should be on the far right. To add a pointer, just click beneath the gradient bar. To remove a pointer, just drag it away from the gradient bar. To change the color of a pointer, select it and then choose white from the color well.

7. To change the transparency for the gradient pointers, click the pointer and make the appropriate changes using the Alpha slider. (See Figure 10.4.) Change the transparencies to these settings:

   Left: **0%**
   Middle: **0%**
   Right: **100%**

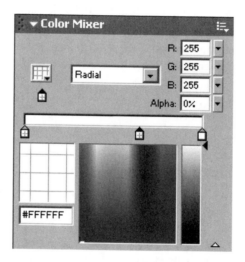

Figure 10.4   When you set up your gradient, you want the center of the circle to have an alpha transparency of 0% and the outer edge to have an alpha transparency of 100%.

8. Switch to the Paint Bucket tool, and click the center of the circle shape on the Stage to fill it with the new gradient. Switch back to the main Timeline. You'll need to temporarily switch your background color to see your gradient.

9. Unlock the Mask layer and copy the circle graphic. Switch to the Gradient layer and choose Edit > Paste in Place. Lock the Mask layer.

10. With the circle graphic in the Gradient layer selected, open the Properties Inspector and click the Swap button. (See Figure 10.5.)

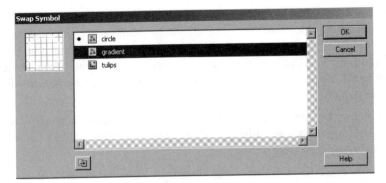

Figure 10.5   Use the Swap button on the Properties Inspector to swap in the Gradient symbol.

11. Select the Gradient symbol in the Swap Symbol dialog and click OK.

12. Lock all your layers; you should be able to see your mask with a softened edge. You can adjust your gradient to get the look and feel you want. You also could have placed the Gradient layer above the Mask layer for the same effect.

Gradients work fine for simple shapes, such as ovals and rectangles, but what about irregular shapes?

Softening the Mask for Complex Shapes

Irregular shapes present a bit more of a challenge when you are trying to soften the mask edge. In most cases, a simple gradient overlay won't really work. However, there's another way to fake a soft edge. You can use the Soften Fill Edges option under Modify > Shape.

This time, you use the mask shape to create a hole in a second shape on the Gradient layer. Sounds a little strange, doesn't it? However, after you have a hole in the shape of your mask, you can use Soften Fill Edges (Modify > Shape > Soften Fill Edges) to expand a gradiated fill into the masked area.

The Soften Edges dialog box has three settings:

- **Distance.** Number of pixels over which the edge will be softened. The minimum setting is 1px, and the maximum is 144px. Your setting is dependent on the effect you are trying to achieve.

- **Steps.** Number of curves created for the softened edge. The more curves there are, the softer the edge will be. Be careful, however: The more curves you add, the longer the shape takes to draw. The minimum setting is 1, and the maximum setting is 50.

- **Direction.** Can be Expand or Inset. Expand creates the curves starting at the outside edge, moving outward. This enlarges the shape. Inset creates the curves starting at the outside edge, moving inward. This does not change the overall shape size.

The next exercise demonstrates how this method works.

Exercise 10.3   Creating Soft Edges for Irregular Shapes

This file already has been started for you. The mask has been set up and a blank Gradient layer has been added.

1. Open irregularMask.fla in the Examples/Chapter10 folder on the CD.
2. Select the Gradient layer and use the Rectangle tool to draw a white rectangle with no stroke that completely covers the green mask over the large red tulip (see Figure 10.6).

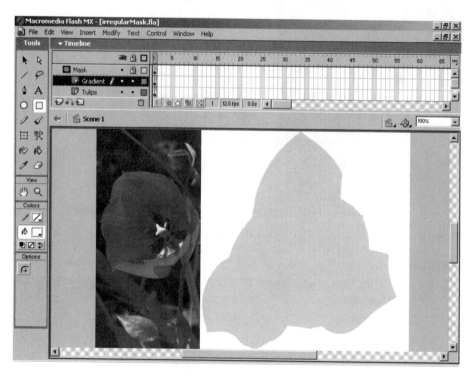

Figure 10.6   To soften the edges on an irregular shape, you start by creating a screening layer between the mask and the shape that you want to mask.

3. Unlock the Mask layer and copy the green mask (tulip shape).

4. Lock and hide the Mask layer.

5. Select the Gradient layer and select Edit > Paste in Place. Click the work area to deselect everything on the Stage.

6. Select the green shape on the Gradient layer and delete it. You now should have a tulip-shaped hole in the white rectangle (see Figure 10.7).

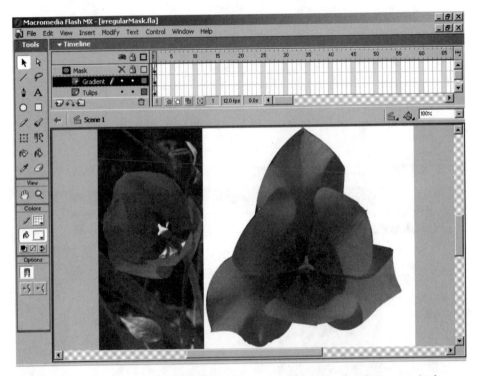

Figure 10.7   Use the shape from the Mask layer to punch a hole in the white screen in the Gradient layer.

7. Select the white shape and choose Modify > Shape > Soften Fill Edges. In the Soften Edges dialog box, make the following changes:

    Distance: **20 px**
    Number of Steps: **10**
    Direction: **Expand**

Tip

> When you are creating an irregular mask that you'll be using to punch out space in another layer, be absolutely sure that your mask is solid. If there are any empty pixels in the mask, those will cause problems when you try to soften the edges. If you have problems with the entire center of the hole filling when you choose Soften Fill Edges, empty pixels are the first thing to look for.

8. Click the work area to deselect the white shape.

9. Make the Mask layer visible and lock all layers. You now can see the effect that you created (see Figure 10.8).

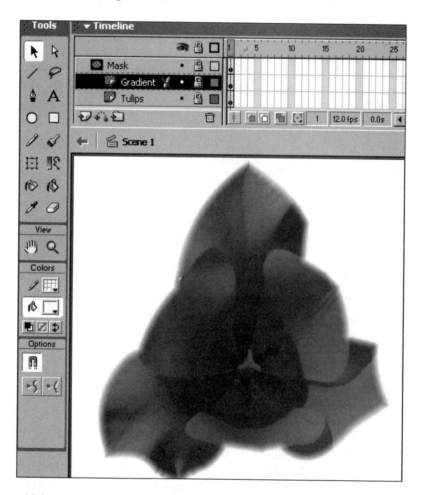

Figure 10.8   You can see your completed gradient when you lock both the masked and masking layers.

The previous steps take you through the classic way of creating a masking effect. But doing it that way isn't your only option. Instead of manually creating the tween on the masking layer, you can do exactly the same thing using ActionScript. You'll take a look at that option next.

Exercise 10.4   Moving a Mask with ActionScript

This file already has been started for you. The basic mask has already been set up.

1. Open cheetahs.fla from the Examples/Chapter10 folder on the CD and save it to your hard drive.

   One of the curious things about movie clip masks that have multiple graphic symbols embedded in the same frame is that they show only the first graphic symbol—or sometimes nothing—while you're in authoring mode (if masking and masked layers are locked). But if you test your movie, you'll see that everything is there.

2. Select the mask movie clip on the Stage.

3. Open the Actions panel (Window > Actions) and enter the following code:

```
onClipEvent(enterFrame) {
      this._x += 3;
}
```

   For as long as this movie clip exists, this event will continue to fire—but be aware that in a real-world example, you would want to stop the enterFrame event when you no longer needed it.

4. Go ahead and test your movie. Wow, a mask tween without tweening!

You can start to have some real fun with masking effects when you start applying Actions to the masking movie clips and the movie clips being masked.

ActionScript and Masking

It used to be that you couldn't move a mask with ActionScript. Your only options were to control the movie clip that the mask was in or to control a movie clip that was being masked. But Flash MX introduced scriptable masks. You can control any movie clip that is behaving as a mask with ActionScript, which means that you can apply all the potential movie clip functionality to it, including the events formerly associated only with buttons. Even a text mask can be scripted to interesting effect, as you will see next.

When you want to apply a gradient or bitmap fill to a block of text, you might want to consider using masking instead of breaking apart the text to modify it. The benefit of using text as a mask instead of breaking the text apart is that the mask still is always editable as text.

Text masks are applied in exactly the same way as any other mask. You just have to type the text that you want to use as a mask on the masking layer. You can take advantage of the capability to animate either the masking or the masked layer to create some interesting effects that would be difficult to create in any other way.

Exercise 10.5 Setting and Controlling a Mask with ActionScript

This file already has been started for you.

1. Open the gorillas.fla file from the Examples/Chapter10 folder on the CD and save it to your hard drive.

   You could easily do this the old-fashioned way, using a masking layer, but why not have some fun and play with Flash MX's new capabilities? This time you'll both set and remove a mask using ActionScript.

2. Select the gorillas_mc movie clip on the Stage and use the Properties panel to give it an instance name of **gorillas**.

3. This image is a little dark for our purposes, so use the Properties Inspector to change the Brightness to +14. (See Figure 10.9.)

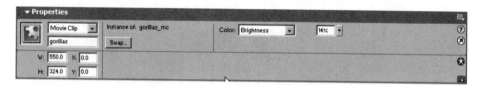

Figure 10.9 Use the Properties Inspector to both assign an instance name and change the brightness of the movie clip.

4. Add a new layer and name it **Mask**.

5. With the Mask layer selected, select the Text tool and use the Properties Inspector to pick a fairly heavy font. If you have Haettenschweiler installed, that's a good choice. The color doesn't matter.

6. Make sure that your text type is static, and type the phrase **Gorillas in the Mist** on the Stage, with line breaks after *Gorillas* and *the*. Select Center Justify in the Properties Inspector.

7. Center the text on the Stage and increase the font size until the text block is nearly the same height as the movie.

8. With the text still selected, embed it in a movie clip (F8) and name the movie clip **mask_mc** (see Figure 10.10). Make sure the registration point is set to the center of the movie.

9. Give your new movie clip an instance name of **mask** in the Properties Inspector.

10. Now you need to use ActionScript to assign the mask. Add a new layer named **Actions**; select frame 1 of the Actions layer and open the Actions panel (Window > Actions).

11. To set the mask, enter the following code:

```
gorillas.setMask(mask);
```

This is the setMask() method of the movie clip object. You tell it which movie clip to mask (gorillas) and which movie clip to use as a mask (mask). You can't see the masking effect until you test your movie.

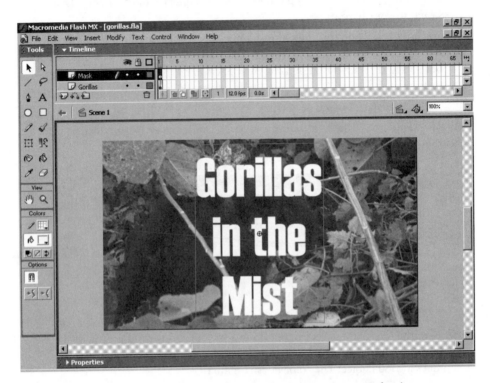

Figure 10.10   You have to embed the text in a movie clip to set it as a mask using ActionScript.

12. Save and test your movie. So far, so good. You should see the phrase that you entered acting as a mask for the gorilla movie clip (see Figure 10.11).

    This would be a little more fun if the text scaled and then the mask disappeared at a certain point so that you could see the image below.

13. Select the mask movie clip and open the Actions panel (Window > Actions). Limit the scale of the clip to 300%, or it'll just keep growing. To scale the clip, enter the following code:

```
onClipEvent(enterFrame) {
      if (this._xscale < 300) {
            this._xscale += 4;

      }
}
```

Figure 10.11   The text that you entered is now masking the movie clip beneath it.

14. Save and test your movie again.

15. Now you make the mask disappear. Select the mask movie clip again. Change your code so that it looks like this:

```
onClipEvent(enterFrame) {
    if (this._xscale < 300) {
        this._xscale += 4;

    }else{
        this._visible = false;
        _root.gorillas.setMask(null);
    }
}
```

All you're doing here is adding an `else` statement that tells the movie clip what to do when it's finished scaling. The important part is `_root.gorillas.setMask(null)`. Anytime you want to get rid of a mask that you created with `setMask`, you just set it to `null`. After you set the mask to `null`, the movie clip is just a plain old movie clip, and the text will show up on the Stage. Just make the movie clip invisible, and all is well.

16. Save and test your movie. If you're having any trouble, check gorillas_final.fla on the CD. If you don't have the Hattenschweiler font installed, you'll be prompted to substitute fonts—just accept the default.

Okay, admit it, that's a pretty cool concept. Now take it a step further and work with a more complex action.

The one big difference between using masking layers and using Actions alone to set a mask is that you can mask multiple layers at one time using a mask layer. A mask created using ActionScript can mask only the layer that set it as a mask using setMask();.

Now you're ready to tackle something a bit more challenging. Take a look at draggable_final.swf in the Examples/Chapter10 folder. Try dragging the circle around the Stage. Not impressed? Position the circle over the fighter's head and then drag the slider in the lower-right corner. It acts like a magnifying glass, with the degree of magnification changing depending on position of the slider. That's all done with masking and ActionScript. And because movie clip objects can now react to button events (except for masks), every bit of code that controls this movie is in frame 1 on the main Timeline. No additional code is embedded inside nested movie clips or buttons; that makes maintenance and setup so much easier than it used to be.

Believe it or not, this effect is not difficult to create; it's just a little time-consuming. So where do you start with a project like this?

Your goal is to create a mask that you can drag around the Stage. You already know that you can't attach button actions to your mask, so that isn't an option. To create a draggable mask, you're going to have to embed the mask in a movie clip. You can assign button events to the movie that your mask is embedded in. So what inventory of elements do you need for your movie clip? You'll need the following:

- The image to be masked
- The mask itself
- A frame for the mask (if needed)

You already know that this is going to be embedded in a movie clip, so that's a good place to start.

Exercise 10.6   Setting Up the Draggable Movie Clip

A few elements of this file already have been created for you, but you have to do all the assembly and coding.

1. Open draggable.fla from the Examples/Chapter10 folder.

2. Open the Library. The elements you're interested in for now are the following:

   - The maskFrame_mc movie clip

   - The smackdown_mc movie clip

3. Create a new movie clip symbol (Insert > New Symbol) and name it **draggableMask_mc**. You'll be working inside this movie clip for a while.

4. Still in draggableMask_mc, drag a copy of the Smackdown_mc movie clip from the Library onto the Stage.

5. Use the Properties Inspector to set the X and Y positions of the movie clip to 0.

6. Still in the Properties Inspector, assign the Smackdown_mc movie clip an Instance name of **Steve**. (In case you're wondering, this is a cartoon of Fig Leaf's CEO Steve Drucker).

7. Rename Layer 1 **Steve**.

8. Add a new layer above the Steve layer and name it **Mask**.

9. You'll do something a little different this time; you'll use a frame for your mask to dress it up a little. Add a new layer above the mask layer and name it **Mask Frame**.

10. With the Mask Frame layer selected, drag a copy of the maskFrame_mc movie clip onto the Stage. Center the maskFrame_mc so that its registration point, which is in the center of the movie clip, is centered on the upper-left corner of the Stage, right over the registration point for the steve_mc movie clip. This makes the calculations that you have to set up later in this exercise simpler to deal with (see Figure 10.12).

11. Select the Mask layer. Use the Oval tool to draw a filled circle that is the same size as maskFrame_mc.

12. Position the circle that you just created directly under Mask Frame.

13. Select the circle and convert it to a movie clip named **mask_mc**, with a center registration point.

14. Give mask_mc an instance name of **mask** in the Properties Inspector.

15. Add a new layer above the Steve layer, and name it **Mask Back**.

16. Draw another circle to fit under maskFrame_mc, but make it invisible by setting the alpha to 0% with the Color Mixer.

17. Save your movie.

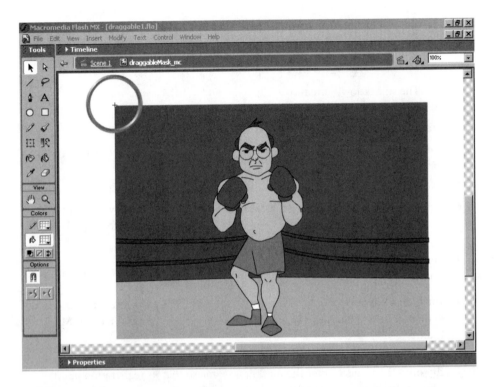

Figure 10.12   Align the maskFrame_mc so that it is centered on the upper-left corner of the steve_mc movie clip.

That's all you need to do inside this movie clip. In the next exercise, you'll start writing the code that will control this movie.

Adding Actions

This is where the real fun begins. You'll start building up your code using functions, which are nothing more than reusable bits of code. You'll also get to work with the setMask method and a number of different properties of the movie clip object.

In Flash 5, if you wanted to drag an object around in your movie, that object had to have a button embedded inside it (you had to use complicated scripting workarounds). Why? Because buttons used to be the only things that could react simply to mouse events, such as press, release, rollover, and so on. In Flash MX, you can make any movie clip (except a mask) react to button events. Say goodbye to the invisible button.

The best part of this is that it allows you to keep all your code in one place—you don't have to attach code to buttons embedded inside movie clips. Time to do some coding!

Exercise 10.7   Setting Up the Mask

You still should be working in draggable.fla, or you can open draggable1.fla from the Examples/Chapter10 folder on the CD. The first thing you need to do is add `draggableMask` to the Stage and activate the mask inside it.

1. Return to the main Timeline and drag a copy of the draggableMask_mc movie clip from the Library onto the Stage. Don't worry too much about positioning because it doesn't matter. You'll be controlling its movement with ActionScript.

2. Give the draggableMask_mc movie clip an instance name of **draggableMask**.

3. Rename Layer 1 to Draggable Mask. While you're there, add a new layer and name it **Actions**.

4. You need to add an action to convert the mask movie clip in the draggableMask movie clip into a functioning mask. The movie clip that gets masked is Steve. Select frame 1 of the Actions layer and enter the following code in the Actions panel:

```
draggableMask.steve.setMask(draggableMask.mask);
```

So now the movie clip named Steve will be masked by the movie clip mask. Because both are embedded in draggableMask, you have to be specific about the path.

5. Go ahead and test your movie. All you should see is the mask frame with the upper corner of the Steve movie clip visible (see Figure 10.13).

Figure 10.13   At this stage in the game, all you will see is the mask frame with the upper-left corner of the Steve movie clip visible.

You want to be able to drag the draggableMask clip around the Stage. The logical time to start the dragging action is when you click (press) the movie clip. When you release the movie clip, it should drop or stop moving on the Stage. Fortunately, Flash has two functions tailor-made to handle these events: `startDrag()` and `stopDrag()`.

Instead of using the `onClipEvent` to which you're accustomed, you're going to use the `onPress` event handler, which you can assign to a movie clip. Say goodbye to the old invisible button trick. Now movie clips can recognize button actions.

6. Adding a drag action is easy. You'll use the onPress event handler and the startDrag method of the movie clip object. Whenever you use an event handler, you have to create a function that executes when the event occurs. In this case, you want to start dragging the movie clip when you click or press it.

   Add the following code after the line where you set up your mask (frame 1 in the Actions layer):

```
draggableMask.onPress = function() {
      this.startDrag();
}
```

   First you declare which object and which handler you want to use. Then you pass to it the function that you want it to perform.

7. Go ahead and add the code for dropping the clip. This time you'll use the onRelease event handler. Add the following code to your actions list:

```
draggableMask.onRelease = function() {
      this.stopDrag();
}
```

8. Save and test your movie. You should be able to drag the masked clip around the Stage.

Okay, your movie clip is draggable, but you see only the bit of the movie that's under the mask. That's no fun. You'll fix that next.

Controlling a Masked Movie with ActionScript

You need to be able to control the movie clip (Steve) that's under the mask inside the draggableMask clip.

When you drag the draggableMask movie clip, the Steve movie clip just moves in synch with it, so the picture under the mask never changes. What you want the Steve movie clip to do is move in the opposite direction that the draggableMask movie clip is moving. What? Well, think about it for a minute. If both movie clips are moving in the same direction, the picture never will change. However, if they're moving in opposite directions, you'll see the changing scenery. (See Figure 10.14.)

This might sound like a complex interaction, but it's really not. The relative positions of the two movie clips need to be continuously updated, and you can do that with the onEnterFrame event handler. This is just like using onClipEvent(enterFrame), but you don't have to attach it directly to the movie clip. The onEnterFrame event handler fires continuously at the frame rate of your movie. So how are you going to make the two movie clips move in opposite directions? You can do the following:

- Check the current X and Y positions of the draggableMask movie clip.

- Set the X and Y positions of the Steve movie clip based on the current position of the draggableMask clip, multiplied by −1. That's all it takes.

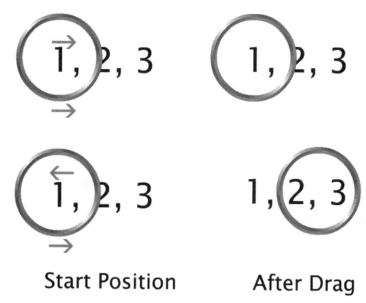

Start Position   After Drag

Figure 10.14   When you are working with one movie clip that's being masked inside of another draggable movie clip, you have to take into account that the movie being masked is moving with your draggable clip. In other words, the two clips are moving together at the same pace–the picture never changes. To have your mask reveal different portions of the movie underneath it, the copy of the movie clip being masked inside of the draggable movie clip must move in the opposite direction.

How do you check the X and Y positions? Every object on the Stage has certain properties that you have access to using ActionScript. The properties that you use to get to the X and Y positions are _x and _y. To get the X and Y positions of specific movie clips, you just need to give Flash directions through dot syntax.

In the next exercise, you create another function using the onEnterFrame event handler.

Exercise 10.8   Controlling the Masked Movie Clip

You still should be working in draggable.fla, or you can use draggable2.fla from the Examples/Chapter10 folder. You know what you want to do: You need to set up an action that will continually update the position of the Steve movie clip in response to the position of the draggableMask movie clip.

1. Select frame 1 of the Actions layer and open the Actions panel (Window > Actions) if it isn't already open.

2. You want the onEnterFrame event handler to be triggered for the draggableMask movie clip, so add the following code to your actions list:

```
draggableMask.onEnterFrame = function () {


}
```

3. The movie clip that you want to make the updates to is the Steve movie clip inside the draggableMask, so all you need to add between the curly braces is this:

```
this.steve._x = this._x*-1;
this.steve._y = this._y*-1;
```

4. Save and test your movie. As you drag the draggableMask around the Stage, you'll see different portions of the underlying movie exposed.

   Your code in the actions panel up to this point should look like this:

```
draggableMask.steve.setMask(draggableMask.mask);
draggableMask.onPress = function() {
    this.startDrag();
}
draggableMask.onRelease = function() {
    this.stopDrag();
}
draggableMask.onEnterFrame = function () {
    this.steve._x = this._x*-1;
    this.steve._y = this._y*-1;
}
```

Tip

You might notice that this is not optimal code. You don't really want an onEnterFrame action running all the time—it's very CPU-intensive. You'll fix that later. First you want to get your code working.

You could just stop here. After all, you have your draggable mask working. But with just a little more effort, you can add the magnification that you saw when you opened the SWF file at the beginning of this section.

Exercise 10.9   Adding a Background and Slider Control

In this exercise, you'll add both a background layer and a slider that will be used to control magnification—and a little more code, of course.

You still should be working in draggable.fla, or you can use draggable3.fla from the Examples/Chapter10 folder.

1. Make sure that you're on the main Timeline, and add a new layer named **Background**. Drag the background layer to the bottom of the layer stack.

2. Drag a copy of the smackdown_mc movie clip from the Library onto the Background layer, and use the Properties Inspector to set its X and Y positions at 0.

3. Do a quick test of your movie. Now you can drag the movie clip around, but you also can see the rest of the Smackdown_mc movie clip. (See Figure 10.15.)

Figure 10.15   With a new instance of the Smackdown_mc movie clip on the Stage, the mask frame appears to be just a window to the background image. In reality, the background image is stationary and the smackdown_mc clip inside the draggable movie is in motion.

4. Add a new layer named **Slider** above the Draggable Mask layer, and drag a copy of the sliderControl_mc movie clip from the Library onto the Stage; position it in the lower-right corner.

5. Notice that the sliderButton_mc movie clip has an instance name of slider, and the gutter_mc movie clip has an instance name of gutter.

6. Return to the main Timeline, and give the sliderControl movie clip an instance name of **sliderControl**.

7. The first thing you need to do is make the slider movie clip draggable—and you want to constrain the drag to just be vertical and be just the length of the gutter movie clip. You also need to keep track of a variable that monitors whether the mouse has been pressed. Add the following code the code already entered in frame 1 of the Actions layer:

```
//
//add in slider controls
//
sliderControl.slider.onPress = function () {
    this.startDrag(true,0,sliderControl.gutter._height*-1,0,0);
    trace(sliderControl.gutter._height);
    _root.down=true;
}
sliderControl.slider.onRelease = function () {
    this.stopDrag();
    _root.down=false;
}
```

You've got another onPress event handler, and you've constrained the movement of the slider to vertical. In addition, it can go only as high as the height of the gutter. You need to multiply the height of the gutter by –1 because up is a negative direction on the y axis. The only other thing of note is that you set a variable down on the main Timeline. The variable is true when the slider is being pressed and false when it is not.

There's no point having a slider if you're not capturing values from it. You'll take care of that now.

8. You will set up the sliderControl to return a value between 0 and 1. Why? Because it makes the returned value easily adaptable to any kind of measurement system that you want to use. In this case, you'll set it up so that the maximum magnification is 5X. You'll be capturing information as the mouse moves, so you'll be using the onMouseMove handler. Go ahead and enter the following code after the last line of code that you entered:

```
sliderControl.slider.onMouseMove = function () {
    if (_root.down) {
    _root.sliderVal = (this._y*-1)/sliderControl.gutter._height;
trace (_root.sliderVal);
    }
}
```

9. Save and test your movie. You should be able to drag the slider and see the trace values in the Output window.

You are interested only in capturing information while the slider is being dragged, so you set up the calculation inside a conditional statement. If down is true, perform the calculation.

So, how do you convert the number returned by sliderVal to a value that you can use to scale your movie clip? First, you need to understand how to scale a movie clip. Just as you can set the x and y positions of a movie clip using the _x and _y properties, you can use the _xscale and _yscale properties to scale a movie clip.

The scale for anything that you place on the Stage starts with an _xscale and _yscale of 100. Anything above 100 increases the size; anything below 100 decreases the size. You want to be able to make your movie clip anywhere from normal size (100) up to five times that size (500). To convert the value returned by the slider, you need to perform a little calculation.

We need to go back to basic math for a moment. Any number multiplied by 0 returns a value of 0. That's not an acceptable value for your purposes. The minimum value that you want to have is 100. So right off the bat, you know that you need to add 100 to whatever value is returned. Because you've already established that the maximum scale value will be 500, by what number do you multiply the number in sliderVal? Your first thought might be 500, but remember that you'll be adding 100 to the value. The answer? Just multiply sliderVal by 400 and then add 100 to that. That way, your number always is between 100 and 500. Your equation will look like this:

```
scaleFactor = (_root.sliderVal*400)+100;
```

In the next exercise, you add the code to scale the movie clip that's being masked.

Exercise 10.10   Scaling the Smackdown_mc Movie Clip Under the Mask

All you have to do is add a few lines of code to adjust the scale.

You should still have your movie open, or you can start with draggable4.fla from the Examples/Chapter10 folder on the CD.

1. Select frame 1 in the Actions layer and launch the Actions panel.

2. First you're going to add in the scaleFactor calculation, but where? It needs to be continuously calculated, so the logical place is inside the onEnterFrame handler that you already have set up. Enter the code between the asterisks:

```
draggableMask.onEnterFrame = function() {
//**********************************************
     scaleFactor = (_root.sliderVal * 400) + 100;
     this.steve._xscale = scaleFactor;
     this.steve._yscale = scaleFactor;
//**********************************************
     this.steve._x = this._x*-1;
     this.steve._y = this._y*-1;
}
```

3. Test your movie again. Whoops! That's not quite the desired result. (See Figure 10.16.)

Figure 10.16 When Flash scales this movie clip, it does so from the upper-left corner. To magnify the image in place, you need to account for that.

What's happening here? When Flash scales this movie clip, the upper-left corner, which is the 0,0 point, stays the same. The movie scales out and away from that point, essentially changing the position of the rest of the image on the Stage. You have to accommodate for that by adjusting the code where you set the x and y values of the Steve movie clip.

Exercise 10.11   Adjusting the Motion of the Scaled Movie Clip

You know that when you move the slider, the movie clip changes. At the bottom of the slider track, the movie is its original size. At the top of the slider track, the movie is five times its original size. You need to multiply the X and Y positions of the movie clip by a number between 1 and 5. You get that number by dividing the scaleFactor by 100. Why? Remember that the scaleFactor was set up to accommodate the necessary changes to _xscale and _yscale, both of which needed to start at 100 and go no higher than 500. Because the movie is changing by a factor of 5, if you want to use the scaleFactor value, you have to divide it by 100.

1. You still should have your Actions panel open. Change the code between the asterisks:

```
draggableMask.onEnterFrame = function() {
    scaleFactor = (_root.sliderVal * 400) + 100;
    this.steve._xscale = scaleFactor;
```

```
     this.steve._yscale = scaleFactor;
//****************************************************
     this.steve._x = (this._x*-1)*(scaleFactor/100);
     this.steve._y = (this._y*-1)*(scaleFactor/100);
//****************************************************
}
```

All you're doing is multiplying the calculation that you already have set up by the scaleFactor divided by 100. (See Figure 10.17.)

2. Now save and test your movie.

Figure 10.17 When you multiply the output by the scaleFactor ÷ 100, the Smackdown_mc movie clip scales properly.

Your code should look like Listing 10.1.

Listing 10.1   Full Code for the Draggable Mask

```
draggableMask.steve.setMask(draggableMask.mask);
draggableMask.onPress = function () {
     this.startDrag();
}
draggableMask.onRelease = function() {
     this.stopDrag();
}
draggableMask.onEnterFrame = function() {
     scaleFactor = (_root.sliderVal * 400) + 100;
     this.steve._xscale = scaleFactor;
     this.steve._yscale = scaleFactor;
     this.steve._x = (this._x*-1)*(scaleFactor/100);
```

continues ▶

Listing 10.1   Continued

```
        this.steve._y = (this._y*-1)*(scaleFactor/100);
}
//
//add in slider controls
//
sliderControl.slider.onPress = function () {
        this.startDrag(true,0,sliderControl.gutter._height*-1,0,0);
        trace(sliderControl.gutter._height);
        _root.down = true;
}
sliderControl.slider.onRelease = function () {
        this.stopDrag();
        _root.down = false;
}
sliderControl.slider.onMouseMove = function () {
        if (_root.down) {
                _root.sliderVal = (this._y*-1)/sliderControl.gutter._height;
                trace(_root.sliderVal);
        }
}
```

Although this code does work, it's not optimal. Right now you have onEnterFrame and onMouseMove events that fire continuously, even when you don't need them, and that's very CPU intensive. With a few changes to the code, you can make this much more efficient. You'll find as you build more complex files that your first goal is to get the file to work. After you have working code, you can focus on optimization.

The easiest piece to fix is the onMouseMove in the sliderControl. You need this event to fire only when you are actually dragging the slider movie clip. So why not embed that portion of the code inside the onPress function? After you do that, you can eliminate the _root.down variable altogether.

The onEnterFrame event handles both the scaling and the positioning of the draggableMask. But you don't need both things happening all the time. You need to reposition the draggableMask only while you're dragging it—no scaling required. You need to both reposition the draggableMask and scale it when the slider is being dragged. You can break this up into two separate functions inside the draggableMask—one to position and one to scale. Then just call them as necessary.

Anytime you no longer need the event handlers (after you release the movie clips being dragged), just set their values to undefined.

Listing 10.2 shows you a more optimal version of the code for this movie clip.

Listing 10.2   Optimized Code for This File

```
scaling=1;
draggableMask.changeScale = function () {
        scaleFactor = (_root.sliderVal * 400) + 100;
        this.steve._xscale = scaleFactor;
        this.steve._yscale = scaleFactor;
        _root.scaling = scaleFactor/100;
    }

    draggableMask.changePosition = function () {
        this.steve._x = this._x*-1*_root.scaling;
        this.steve._y = this._y*-1*_root.scaling;
    }

draggableMask.steve.setMask(draggableMask.mask);

draggableMask.onPress = function () {
        this.startDrag();
        this.onEnterFrame = this.changePosition;

}
draggableMask.onRelease = function () {
    this.stopDrag();
    this.onEnterFrame = undefined;
}

sliderControl.slider.onPress = function () {
    this.startDrag(true,0,sliderControl.gutter._height*-1,0,0);
    this.onMouseMove = function () {
        _root.sliderVal = (this._y*-1)/sliderControl.gutter._height;
        draggableMask.changeScale();
        draggableMask.changePosition();
        updateAfterEvent();
    }
}
sliderControl.slider.onRelease = function () {
    this.stopDrag();
    this.onMouseMove = undefined;
}
```

That's all there is to it. If you worked through the draggable mask exercise in *Inside Flash,* you'll notice that this one is much shorter and easier to work with. Those are some of the benefits that you get from Flash MX.

Summary

Now you know how to create and animate masks. You've played around with fooling Flash into giving your masks a softened edge. You also know how to control a masked layer inside a movie clip using ActionScript. That last technique is actually quite powerful. Knowing that you can script the behavior of both a masking layer and a masked layer gives you a lot of options.

You also had the chance to work with separating the code from the artwork, by placing all your code in frame 1 of the main Timeline and letting event handlers do your work. Keeping your code in one place makes it much easier to maintain. Finally, you took a look at optimizing a working but not perfect piece of code.

Masking is extremely useful in Flash when it's used wisely. Just remember to monitor your CPU usage carefully, especially with animated masks.

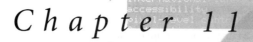

Chapter 11

Animation Techniques

When you think of animation, you might

recall Warner Brothers cartoons and full-

length Disney animated movies from your

childhood (or your adult childhood).

These relatively large-scale productions follow the same principles required to create the simplest of Flash animations. As a matter of fact, much of the illusion of movement that you see in full-motion cinematic pictures can be broken into components to reduce the amount of time and effort required to create an animated story.

When cartoons entered the television age, animators began to take greater advantage of techniques that you also can use to economize repetitive motion and reduce the amount of time required to produce a cartoon or animated piece. By breaking the animation into reusable pieces such as walking, talking, and so on, you can use these actions in more than one area of the animation on which you're working. Pattern identification is part of human nature—we're good at it, so when these techniques are overused or poorly employed, people notice. However, when you use these tricks correctly, they can be subtle, imperceptible, and, ultimately, economical to the development process.

One of the key advantages of the Flash animation environment is that it's engineered to take advantage of looping techniques by virtue of its symbol and movie clip library. Create a walking sequence for your character, turn it into a character movie clip inside Flash, and then have that movie clip walk in place as a background layer moves behind it. Then, later in the animation, you can use that same character movie clip in connection with a motion tween to make the character walk across the foreground of a motionless background. Reuse is key here. In fact, you'll see this same concept come into play as you work through some of the more programming-related chapters. Reuse is efficient.

The process of creating a rich and engaging animation involves so much more than "leading the character" around the stage. Some of the other common elements that will be discussed in this chapter are as follows:

- **Building the story.** Before you begin to develop your character, you need to flesh out your story. Planning ahead saves you a lot a time that would otherwise be wasted in revisions.
- **Creating a character.** When you have a story and a setting in place, it's time to start creating your character. From behavior to appearance, it's all up to you.
- **Using the animation capabilities of Flash to pull it all together.** When you start developing your character, you can take advantage of Flash's symbol capabilities and tweening to help speed up your development time and keep your file size low.

You'll start by learning how to build the story.

Building the Story

Usually, when you begin thinking about an animation, you already have an idea of what you'd like portions of the story to be. It really is important to flesh out these ideas before you begin putting graphics directly into Flash. Why? It gives you the opportunity to plan your ideas from beginning to end so that you don't find yourself wasting time by creating animations that end up being superfluous or incongruent to the final story. Another reason is that you can begin planning exactly what reusable assets you need to build to bring the story to life. There's that word again: *reuse*. Burn that one into your brain.

Creating an animation is like building a house. Would you just head off to a spot of land and start hammering a bunch of boards together in the rough outline of a house and then refine it as you go? Certainly not. Too many important details would be lost. A well-designed house begins with a detailed blueprint that takes into consideration all the structural integrity that will make it beautiful and functional when it is complete. The same can be said for your animation. The best way to achieve success is to plan for it.

The blueprint process in the world of animation has two parts. Because you are dealing with visual media, the story must be represented both textually and visually in the form of a script and storyboards. Although they are separate steps, they function as a whole to describe in detail how the final story plays out.

Creating the Script

In the commercial world of animation, the roles of the scriptwriter and storyboard artist tend to be split into two distinct professions. However, the world of Flash is anything but typical. Not only is it common for a single person to wear all the hats in the production process, but also the animated projects can be anything from traditional to experimental. This means that the process of writing a script for a Flash animation can be as detailed as any script that you would expect to see for an actual movie. On the other hand, if the purpose of the animation is to be eye candy for a marketing presentation, the script can do nothing more than describe the emotional aspects of the animation and provide a descriptive setting.

Script development, like many writing projects, provides structure and detail. It's always good to start in outline form to make sure you hit the high points. When you have your outline, you can flesh out the details. The areas on which you'll want to focus are these:

- **Descriptive setting.** The first thing is to describe the environment for the opening scene. This description needs to encompass the set, setting, atmosphere, and mood. It also needs to place the main character or subject matter in the scene.

Then, as your story transitions from one scene to the next, you describe these changing settings.

- **Character and subject development.** As characters or subject matter are introduced to the scene, you'll need a brief description of their characteristics, appearance, and style.

- **Transitions.** When moving the action from one scene to the next, you need to think through how the transition will be handled. You don't want to alienate your audience with inappropriate scene changes. This might be in the form of fades, camera motions (pan/zoom), refocussings, and so on. Transitions are covered in more detail in Chapter 12, "Making the Transition."

- **Character dialogue or action.** When you actually have a character or characters, you will need to detail the dialogue and actions.

- **Important action characteristics.** If there are sound effects, visual effects, or action sequences, they need to be described in context with the character, object, action, or transition with which they are associated.

Your script puts your words in order; your storyboard organizes your animation's visuals.

Storyboarding Your Action

Storyboarding has a lot in common with the world of comic books. Illustrations are provided inline with the script to provide a visual narrative for what is being described by the words themselves. However, storyboards are typically more regimented than comic book panels. Your average set of storyboards is a sequence of illustrated and numbered panels arranged in a linear fashion. Next to or below these panels is an area for the related script text that accompanies the illustration. In a rudimentary sense, when you look at the storyboards, you are looking at the animation itself, but in skeletal form. (See Figure 11.1.)

When preparing your storyboards, you'll want to set them up in roughly the same aspect ratio as you anticipate you'll use for your final animation. That way, when you're illustrating scenes, sets, and actions on your boards, you'll have a good visual sense of how the scene will play out.

The average computer monitor displays at an aspect ratio of 3 × 4. Thus, if you set up your storyboards as a series of 3-inch-by-4-inch or 6-inch-by-8-inch panels, you'll be in good shape. Blank note cards are convenient for this.

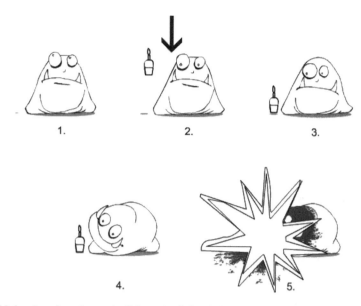

Figure 11.1   Storyboards are the "blueprints" that help build your animation.

When your storyboards are complete, you have a number of options at your disposal to aid you in the process of converting your story to reality. Hand-drawn storyboards can be scanned, placed on a background layer in Flash, and traced using the drawing tools in Flash. For artists who like to start out the process by hand sketching, this can be an appealing option.

Another option is to use Macromedia FreeHand as your storyboarding tool. In the years that Macromedia has owned FreeHand, a number of features have been added to this already-rich illustration environment. These features make it a valuable productivity tool for Flash.

FreeHand enables you to define multiple pages inside a single FreeHand document, much like a Microsoft Word document can contain hundreds of pages. Although this might seem insignificant, if you are trying to create storyboards in some other illustration packages, you'll need to create several documents to accomplish the same task.

Note

FreeHand is simply one of the best drawing tools on the market. This translates to a richer and more flexible set of illustration tools than you will find inside Flash. Because the two programs are so tightly integrated, you can copy your illustrations from FreeHand and paste them into Flash in the standard Flash format. Yes, this includes the Flash style gradients as well.

Now that you've got your storyboards in place, it's time to talk about animating your characters.

Character Animation Basics

Animation is simply the illusion of movement. However, in the world of animation, stark realism doesn't necessarily make for a successful animation. If you faithfully reproduce a photographic sequence by meticulously tracing the cycle of images, the resulting animation would likely be a little mechanical and stiff.

Professional animators take advantage of techniques that exaggerate and embellish motion to create a more interesting story. There are certainly different degrees to which you can use these techniques to affect the presentation of your story, so it really comes down to the kind of emotional response that you're trying to elicit from your audience.

Before you can dive into animation, you need to become familiar with the language of animation. As with any profession, animation has its own set of jargon that you need to know. Some of the basic concepts are outlined here:

- **Keyframes.** In the world of hand-drawn animation, *keyframes* represent critical moments in the Timeline. This same concept holds true in the Flash environment. Keyframes in the application Timeline are the points at which changes in a character or object's orientation take place.

- **Tweening.** The term *tweening* is derived from the old animation industry term of "in between," which referred to the profession or duty of creating the animation sequences "in between" the keyframes. In Flash, tweens also take place in the space between keyframes, but they can be used to automate transition effects such as scale, rotation, visibility, and so on.

- **Easing.** *Easing in* and *easing out* indicate the acceleration or deceleration of an object or character when it begins or ends a tween.

- **Action and reaction.** These refer to exaggerated qualities such as "squash and stretch." They occur when a character or object interacts with force or motion.

- **Timing.** Both a mechanical function and an aesthetic quality. You, as the animator, are required to set up an event and then give it plausible timing as it occurs.

- **Posing.** This communicates mood, emotion, and attitude. Posing helps orient the audience to a character or object's disposition.

- **Anticipation.** This is used to forecast to the viewer what is about to happen or what has the potential to happen. If a character is preparing to run, anticipation is the wind-up that he or she does before bolting.

- **Mechanics.** In the physical world, objects tend to behave in predictable ways. More often than not, animated characters follow arcing motions because they are hinged (swinging arm) or are reacting to a force such as gravity.

You've got the basics in hand; it's time to take a look at how you actually go about creating the illusion of movement.

Illusion of Movement

The principle behind animation is quite simple: Fool the viewer into believing that your creation is alive and moving. Although it's not as easy as it looks, if you plan everything and do your homework, you can do the following successfully:

- **Stop motion.** Stop-motion animation is accomplished by taking successive photographs of posed objects that are moved slightly after each shot. The classic example of stop motion is claymation, in which clay figures are posed and photographed. This leaves you with a series of sequential bitmaps that, when played back, give the illusion of movement. If you've seen the movie *Chicken Run,* you are familiar with this type of animation.

- **Rotoscope.** In rotoscoping, you import live-action footage and trace over it frame by frame to give your characters realistic movement. It should be noted that most animators look on rotoscoping as a crutch, but it can be quite useful. Examples of this kind of animation can be seen in the opening sequence of the Japanese animated movie *Ghost in the Shell.* It can also be seen in the 1980s pop video "Take on Me," from the band a-ha.

- **Cel animation.** This is the classic hand-drawn style of animation that you've come to know and love from Disney. In cel animation, the keyframes are drawn and the tween frames are added later. The good news is that Flash does both simple shape and motion tweening for you. The bad news is that most character animation is done frame by frame.

Stop-motion animations can be set up inside Flash, but because they depend on bitmaps, they can leave you with large file sizes. As an example, look at the StopMotion.swf file in the Examples/Chapter11 folder. This is a classic stop-motion sequence in which each frame of the animation was posed and photographed. When the frames are played one after another, you get the illusion of movement. You also get a file that's 188KB. Granted, you've added effects, but it's still a large file size.

Rotoscoping, on the other hand, takes advantage of what Flash does best: vector graphics. By tracing over a video sequence, you can get life-like effects and keep your file size low. The next exercise walks you through setting up a simple rotoscope animation.

Exercise 11.1   Rotoscope Animation

With rotoscoped animation, you import live-action footage and trace over it. In this simple exercise, you use a series of images that were converted to JPEGs from a movie clip. This type of animation can be fairly tedious, but it can also give you a realistic effect that would be difficult to achieve otherwise. In addition, it's a great crutch for those of us who can't draw.

1. Open handAnime.fla in the Examples/Chapter11 folder on the CD and save it to your hard drive.

2. In the Library, double-click the imagesMC movie clip to open it in Symbol Editing mode. This clip contains the sequenced JPEGs of the hand motion.

3. Obviously, tracing that itty-bitty image would be an incredible pain. Use your Magnifying tool to drag a marquee around the image to make it large enough to work with comfortably.

4. Add a new layer and name it **tracing**. Lock the images layer.

5. Select one of the smaller Paint Brush sizes. To get a sketch-like appearance, you'll want to use the Paint Brush rather than the Line tool. If you have a pressure-sensitive tablet, all the better—you'll get variations in your lines, depending on the pressure you use.

6. On the tracing layer, trace each hand image with as much detail as you want.

7. When you've finished tracing the individual hand frames, hide the bottom layer and play through your animation.

8. When you're happy with your animation, you can delete the images layer.

9. Save and test your movie.

To see an example of a completed rotoscoped animation, open handAnime_final.fla in the Examples/Chapter11 folder. (See Figure 11.2.)

Traditional or cel animation is probably the most widely used form of animation in Flash. You have the opportunity to work with this type of animation in the following sections.

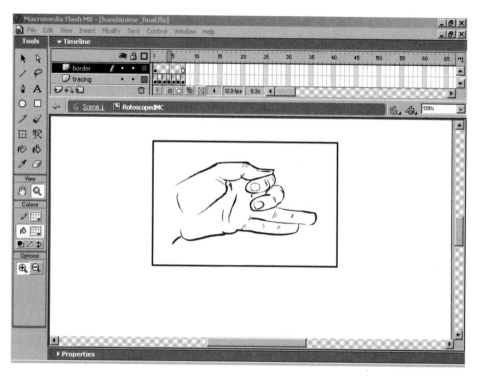

Figure 11.2   The hand sequence is traced frame by frame from video stills.

Timing and Synchronization

Timing and synchronization are two of the most crucial elements that you need to deal with when animating.

Timing can make or break a good animation, whether it is abstract or character-based. One of the most essential messages that you are trying to convey to the audience is the passage of time. The speed at which an event happens carries a tremendous amount of emotional weight. For example, a hand that is animated in a sweeping gesture can be interpreted in different ways, depending on the timing. A very fast and abrupt transition from one end state to another could be interpreted as a slap. A slower, more deliberate motion could be interpreted as a sweeping gesture. It's all in the timing.

Likewise, timing of motion can help outline the relative weight of objects on your Stage. Something that is large and heavy should be harder to place in motion and should move more slowly than a smaller, more lightweight object. In fact, if your large objects move faster than your smaller ones, chances are good that your animation will feel "off."

Synchronization occurs when things happen at the same time. For example, when your character speaks, two things should happen. The mouth should move (assuming that your character has a mouth), and you should hear a sound. Those two events have to be timed properly, or they just won't work.

Now it's time to use some of these concepts to help bring your character to life.

Adding Life to Your Character

When you create a character, you need to think about its personality and how its personality relates to its appearance. You can give personality to almost anything. A line or a dot can have character. If you've ever seen Disney's *Aladdin*, think about the magic carpet. It's just a rug—no mouth or eyes—but it has personality nonetheless. Just push your creativity to find ways to give your object its own internal life.

A good way to get started is to draw sketches of your character in different moods so that as you animate, you have a visual reference from which to work (see Figure 11.3). In the animation industry, studios will often get a reference actor to pose for the artists so that they can observe actual moods and reactions. It's the nuances that help give their characters more life. This technique was used in creating the animated feature *Shrek*. The artists clearly picked up on some of the actors' movements and expressions as they recorded their lines, and they incorporated those traits directly into the actors' animated alter egos.

Figure 11.3   By sketching your character in different moods, you have a reference from which to work during the process of animation.

Walking and Other Motion Cycles

You can give your character the appearance of self-mobility and save yourself a lot of work by animating it in a cyclical fashion. You can make your character hop, jump, crawl, swim, run, waddle, or fly at will. All you do is combine keen observation with a little bit (or a lot) of creativity.

One of the first things you have to do is to figure out "how" your character gets around. If your character has no feet, it can't walk or run. If your character has fins, your audience is going to expect it to be able to swim.

How does your character move? Are its movements slow and methodical, or jumpy and frenetic? Does your character have a limp or a particular style of walking? Just as you need to be sensitive to your character's environment, you must be sensitive to your character's physical state.

Many types of movement are cyclical. Take walking as an example. You can capture the full range of motion needed for walking in relatively few frames. When you have the basic sequence, you can loop or reuse it to give the illusion of continuous motion.

Note

These "rules" about how you approach animation aren't set in stone, and you wouldn't want them to be. Consider them as more of a guide. It can actually be quite funny and entertaining to have your character do something completely "out of character." However, you can't get there until you have a solid understanding of how your character should behave.

Tex Avery was renowned for his ability to put his characters in surreal situations. Another great animator from the Golden Age was Chuck Jones, who was well known for his ability to give his characters a wide range of expressions. Both are credited with creating Warner Brothers' most popular characters, including Bugs Bunny, Daffy Duck, Elmer Fudd, Road Runner, and Wily E. Coyote.

Looping Animations

As you've probably figured out, looping your animation is a common technique. You create a loop by having your beginning frame match up with your end frame; the movement between depicts an action. When played back to back, the looping animation gives the appearance of continuous motion.

Looping is used in many aspects of animation, whether it's constantly moving the background in one direction or having your character running. These actions are repeated until your character is ready to do something else. In Flash, it's relatively simple to make loops within loops by using embedded movie clips. Although creating detailed vector art for each frame is possible, using loops is a great way to cut down on file size and production time.

Loops are commonly used to create the illusion of walking and running. Now's the time to get out of your chair and walk down the hall. You are going to be your own model. Really pay attention to how your legs are moving.

Start from a standing position, and step forward with your right foot. Your leading leg should be only slightly bent, with your foot flat on the ground. Your trailing leg will have more of a bend, with only your toes resting on the ground.

Continue your step. Your left foot should lift off the ground, the bend in your left leg should become more pronounced, and your left leg should move forward.

Continue monitoring the sequence of your steps. If you break the pattern into five steps, it would look something like Figure 11.4 (assuming that you were a grape with legs, of course).

Figure 11.4   The walking grape demonstrates how you can capture the walking motion in relatively few frames. Put this sequence in a loop, and he'll walk forever!

You can practice breaking an animation into loops in the next exercise.

Exercise 11.2   Looping Your Animations

This animation has already been created for you; your job is to figure out which segments could be effectively converted into symbols so that you can combine and reuse them to your advantage.

  1. Open walker.fla in the Examples/Chapter11 folder on the CD.
  2. Scrub through the animation several times to see your little walking grape stand up, do a flip, and walk.

     Your next step is to isolate those individual motions into reusable movie clips.
  3. Go to the first frame of the standing-up sequence. If you advance through the animation one frame at a time, you'll see the following sequence:

     Frame 1: The little guy is just sitting there.
     Frame 2: His feet, such as they are, appear.
     Frame 3: He's in a crouch.

Frame 4: He's fully upright and ready to go.

Frame 5: This is a repeat of frame 4.

Frame 6: He begins his flip.

4. It looks like frames 1–4 can be converted into a functional standing sequence. Highlight frames 1–5 in both layers, right- or Command–click one of the highlighted frames, and then choose Copy Frames.

5. Create a new movie clip symbol (use Insert, New Symbol, or Ctrl+F8/Command+F8) and name it **standUp_mc.**

6. Right- or Control-click frame 1 and choose Paste Frames. If you were working in Flash 5 right now, you'd have two unnamed layers, but Flash MX remembers your layer names! No more tedious renaming of layers every time you cut and paste.

7. Add a new layer to the top of the stack, and name it **actions**. Insert a keyframe in the last frame of your movie clip, and use the Actions panel to give it a stop() action.

8. Now it's time to move to the next logical step: the flip. Return to the main Timeline and scrub through the animation again by dragging the playhead across it. Begin with frame 6 (you already know that this is where the flip starts).

Frame 6: He begins to crouch to get leverage for the flip.

Frame 7: He crouches a little lower; he's going for the gold.

Frame 8: He begins the release into the flip.

Frame 9: He's got some good stretch now.

Frame 10: His feet come off the ground.

Frame 11: He's completely upside down

Frame 12: The flip is almost complete.

Frame 13: He lands safely, absorbing the impact in his feet. It's a perfect 10.

Here's where it starts to get interesting. In fact, here is where you might want to rethink the first movie clip you set up. What is the logical breaking point here? Is it when the flip is nearly complete? Or is it when his feet are back on the ground?

In terms of reuse, it probably makes more sense for the flip sequence to end just before the character makes contact with the ground because, after he is in contact with the ground, the stand-up sequence begins again. If that's the case, the first frame in the standup_mc sequence should be removed from the movie clip. Then frames 6–12 should be used for the flipping sequence. Try this approach.

9. Double-click the standup_mc movie clip to open it in Symbol-Editing mode. Insert a keyframe in frame 2 of the Shadow layer so that you don't lose your first shadow. Highlight frame 1 in all three layers, right- or Control-click, and choose Remove Frames.

10. Back on the main Timeline, highlight and copy frames 6–12 in both layers. Create a new movie clip called flip_mc, and paste these frames into it. Don't highlight

these frames and choose convert to symbol. If you do, you'll just get the last frames of the sequence. You need to physically paste them into an empty movie clip.

11. Add an actions layer to the top of the Stack, and put a `stop()` action in the last keyframe.

   The next unique set of movements comes as the grape actually begins to walk (you already have the standup_mc sequence taken care of). Frame 15 ends the standing-up sequence, and, in frame 16, the grape turns and begins to walk. Frames 16–23 comprise the complete walking sequence.

12. Copy frames 16–23, create a new movie clip named **walk_mc**, and paste these frames into the new movie clip. Add an actions layer, and add a `stop()` action to the last frame.

Now you have all the pieces of your animation. How do you reassemble them? Well, you can add the appropriate symbol to the Timeline wherever you want it to play. Just remember to leave enough frames before the next movie clip so that it can play all the way through. You could alternately allow your user to control the movement with button clicks, using on (release) events to go to named frames. It's really up to you and depends on what you want to accomplish. In most cases, you'll want to control the animation of your character.

Now that you've got things moving, it's time to give your character a voice.

Speaking Vowels and Consonants

Getting your character to speak isn't really as hard as it might first appear. You just have to look at it from a simplified point of view. Many of the letters of the alphabet can be broken into phonetic groups. Your mouth opens and closes differently when pronouncing different letters. For example, the letters *A*, *O*, and *T* are pronounced differently and require different mouth positions, but the letters *A*, *H*, and *I* have similar pronunciations and only minor differences in mouth positions.

So, how does all this help you get your characters to speak? Well, first of all, it means that you don't have to animate the mouth for every letter of the alphabet! You can group the similarly pronounced letters into one drawing.

One possible breakdown of letter groupings looks like this:

- A, H, I
- B, M, N, F, T, J, K, P, V, W
- C, D, E, G, X

- L, R, S, W, Z
- O, Q, U, Y

Of course, you could break this out even further, depending on your animation needs. However, for now, instead of having to deal with 26 different mouth shapes (we're talking about the English alphabet here—your mileage may vary), you've boiled it down to 5.

These groupings of letters can be modified to fit the way your character speaks. When you have the drawings of your character grouped for each different vowel sound, you can convert each drawing into a symbol. Now all you have to do is synchronize your new mouth symbols to a voice-over (V.O.).

Synchronizing Drawings to a Voice-Over

You now have your letter patterns arranged in separate groups. Next, you need to import your V.O. and set it in a frame with its own layer. When you have done that, you can begin to piece together your talking sequence.

Figure 11.5 shows a monster named Bob the Blob. Bob has no feet and no arms. Basically, Bob's just a blob with a big mouth and a tendency to get into trouble.

Figure 11.5   Bob the Blob does the alphabet.

To see Bob in action, open BobTheBlob.swf from the Examples/Chapter11 folder on the CD. Press the Birthday button. In this V.O., Bob wants a cupcake because it's his birthday. I'm warning you—he's going to beg. Now would you give an ugly, green, big-mouthed blob of a monster *your* cupcake? I don't think so! Well, not if you like cupcakes, anyway.

Bob's voice was captured using CoolEdit Pro and then was altered to a lower pitch with a lot of bass. He's got a big mouth. He needs a big voice. It's important to make the voice "fit" the character. Imagine Fred Flintstone's voice swapped with Elmer Fudd's voice—that wouldn't sound right at all, would it? That's why animation studios take their voice talent for each character very seriously. In the next exercise, you get your chance to synchronize Bob to a V.O.

Tip

I almost always create my sound and V.O. before I begin to draw the mouth stages. It can be done the other way around, of course, although it's much more difficult to do.

Exercise 11.3 Synchronizing to a V.O.

In this exercise, you use what you know to synchronize sounds to mouth shapes.

1. Open BobPhonetics.fla from the Examples/Chapter11 folder on the CD.

    This is our old friend, Bob the Blob. Bob has already been given the basic vowel and consonant groupings; your job is to use those frames, as needed, to create a convincing animation of Bob talking. Make no mistake—it is a tedious and time-consuming project. However, when you learn how to do this well, you can make your animations much more convincing.

2. The phrase to which you're going to be synchronizing is this:

    My name is Bob. Bob the Blob. B-O-B B-L-O-B.

3. The first thing you need to do is *put your headphones on*. Otherwise, your office-mates will hate you. Even if you work alone, you'll find it easier to concentrate and hear the sounds with your headphones on.

4. Next, set the V.O. track BobVO.wav to Stream. Why? You then can scrub through the sound using the playhead. It'll sound awful, but it'll make synchronization much easier. Select the first frame of the AUDIO V.O. layer, and open the Properties Inspector.

5. Set the Synch for the sound to Stream, and leave all else as is.

6. Add a new layer named **Animation**, and extend the frames so that the Animation layer has the same number of frames as the AUDIO V.O. layer. (Highlight frame 116 and press F5.)

7. Now you're ready. You already know what the first word is—My. That's going to require the phonetic grouping with the consonant *M* and the grouping with the vowel *I*.

8. Because the *M* sound is a closed-mouth sound, copy and paste the frame from the TALK BMNFTJKP layer into frame 1 of the Animation layer. You don't need to unlock or unhide the TALK BMNFTJKP layer to do this, and keeping the existing layers hidden and locked makes your file easier to work with.

9. Scrub slowly through the Timeline, and determine where you think the *I* sound should start. When in doubt about placement, place the visual for the sound a frame earlier than you think it should go. Anticipation is half the game. Frame 3 seems like a pretty logical spot.

10. The next sound you'll hear is the *N* in *name*. Scrub through the Timeline again and listen carefully—it's a soft sound. For the *N* sound, you'll use the frame that you used for the *M* sound. I picked frame 5, but it's up to you.

Tip

It's important that you actually test your synchronization in a browser by pressing F12. If you don't, you might find that your carefully synchronized piece isn't really synchronized at all.

11. By now, you should be starting to get the picture. It's listen, pick a sound, find the frame—over and over again. Go ahead and complete the rest of the phrase for this exercise. When you're done, check it against BobPhonetic_final.fla in the Examples/Chapter11 folder on the CD.

12. When you've finished, test your file and make sure you're happy with it. Frequently, when you stream a sound, particularly music, you'll hear a loss of quality. In this case, with this sound, it's not too bad. If you encounter a case in which streaming has a significant negative impact on your sound, set the sound to Event and use a small sound, muted and streamed, to lock in the file synchronization. This technique is covered in more detail in Chapter 5, "Using Sound in Flash."

Expressions

Simple changes to your character's facial expressions can convey enormous amounts of information about your character's general state of being. The way your character reacts to situations and the range of emotions that it displays give your viewers valuable clues about what is happening in your movie.

The Double-Take

The double-take is a technique used in comedy (see Figure 11.6). A person observes something extremely unusual or bizarre, but it takes a few seconds for it to register in his or her mind, so he or she has a delayed reaction. If you watch a lot of early sitcoms from the 1950s and 1960s, you will notice this technique. The Three Stooges were famous not only for their double-takes, but also for anticipating the gag sequences.

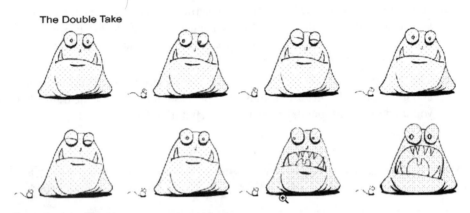

Figure 11.6   Bob the Blob does a double-take.

Anticipating the Gag

This is kind of like basketball, but instead of positioning yourself for the lay-up, you are setting up your audience to anticipate that something funny is about to happen. For example, anticipating the gag sequence might go something like this:

- Shot 1: The first person is hiding behind a corner and holding a moon-pie.
- Shot 2: The second person is running down a hall.
- Shot 3: You show the first person lifting the pie and taking aim.
- Shot 4: The second person turns the corner and is hit in the face with the moon-pie.

The audience laughs—not because they weren't expecting the action to happen, but because they were given the suggestion that something funny was going to happen. Timing does play a part in how well the anticipated gag plays out.

You'll also have to deal with how your character displays emotion.

Emotions

Every character needs emotions. Even showing no emotion is an emotion. Emotions define a character. As an example, think about Oscar the Grouch from the show many of you watched when you were kids—*Sesame Street*. (You can stop humming now—we all know it by heart!)

In the show, Oscar is a "grouch"—hence his name—and this defines his personality and who he is as a character. Your character doesn't have to always display one emotion all the time, but how his personality is defined can make a difference in how he reacts to the environment surrounding him. You could say that how you handle situations defines you as an individual. Everyone reacts in a different way to the surrounding environment and your character should do the same.

Just as actors do research on the characters that they perform in plays and movies, animation studios do research on the subjects that they animate. In fact, Disney is well known for sending its animators to distant locales to observe the actual subjects and environments that they are animating. Some argue that that's going to the extreme to capture the realism in animation, but you can't deny that this devotion to keen observation and efforts to capture all the nuances of their subjects makes for some terrific animation. It's this dedication to the smallest details that makes these films "classics" and that sets the bar for all movies to follow.

So how can you give your characters emotions? Start by looking in the mirror. What happens to your face when you're happy or angry or sad? Your expression changes. Your overall body language probably changes as well. Figure 11.7 shows Bob the Blob in a variety of emotional states.

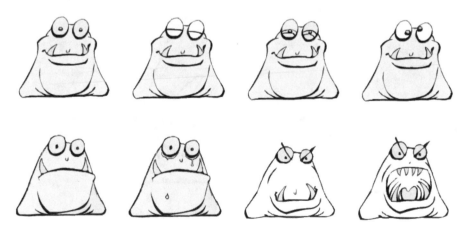

Figure 11.7   With only minor changes to the body and facial expressions, Bob the Blob can display a wide variety of emotions.

Exercise 11.4   Giving Your Character Emotions

In this exercise, see if you can give Bob more emotions.

1. Open simpleBob.fla from the Examples/Chapter11 folder on the CD.

    This version of Bob the Blob has been somewhat simplified to make him easier to work with.

    You have a happy Bob. Why not make Bob just slightly unhappy—you can significantly alter his appearance and mood by making a few simple changes to his eyes. You already saw the changes that took place in angry Bob in Figure 11.7. His eyes lowered, and he gained a pair of angry eyebrows. His cheeks deflated, and his happy smile disappeared.

    By just lowering his eyes and adding in some eyebrows, you can make Bob look like he's just itching to get into trouble. In addition, it makes a good transition frame between happy Bob and angry Bob.

2. Insert a keyframe in the Bob layer and in the Eyes layers at frame 3. Lock the Bob layer.

3. Select both eyes by dragging a marquee around them. Use the arrow keys on the keyboard to lower the eyes until they protrude just slightly above the top of Bob's head.

4. Use the Paint Brush tool with a small brush setting and the black fill color to add a pair of slanted eyebrows (see Figure 11.8).

    Bob isn't looking so happy anymore. Would you trust a face like that?

Figure 11.8   Making minor alterations to the eyes of happy Bob leaves us with a not-so-happy Bob.

5. Insert keyframes in both layers at frame 6, and take Bob one step further. When you're pouting, you usually drop your lower lip—why not try that with Bob? Unlock the Bob layer, select Bob's teeth and lips, and move them down closer to his chin. You'll probably need to hold the Shift key down to select all the parts of his lips. Using the Eyedropper tool, sample Bob's green color and fill in the holes in his face where his teeth used to be!

6. He's no longer smiling, so you might as well go ahead and reshape his cheeks as well—flatten them out a bit. Use the Arrow tool to reshape the lines.

7. Save and test your movie.

The very minor alterations that you made to your character significantly changed his demeanor. You could give Bob a bit of a saucy look by alternating between the happy Bob and the not-quite-happy Bob. I'm pretty sure that I've met a guy like Bob in a bar at some point in my life.

When you're done playing with alterations to Bob, go ahead and launch the BobAnime.html file from the Examples/Chapter11 folder on the CD. Click the different buttons and put Bob through his paces. You'll see that, for a mere blob, Bob has quite a bit of character. The source file, BobAnime.fla, is also available on the CD for you to pick apart.

Every character needs a background to operate against. Because you're dealing with animation, you'll be working with an animated background.

Animating Your Backgrounds

Backgrounds in traditional animations are created for each shot. However, there are plenty of ways to reuse (there's that word again) a background. Background artists don't get a lot of recognition, but they are just as important as the character animator. A background artist is charged with creating an environment that fits the actions that take place in each scene.

If you're creating a scary animation, your background probably won't be a field of daisies with birds chirping and rainbows in the sky, will it? It will probably be dark and intense. You're setting a mood.

So what kind of techniques can you use in animating a background? Controlling the panning of the background is critical when you are working with a looped animation such as a walking sequence. Remember that if your character stops, the background should stop at the same time. Alternately, if your character stops to take a rest and the background keeps panning, you character needs to move backward with the scenery, as if someone were driving by and filming your character as he or she went past.

This discussion can be a nearly endless topic. There's so much that you can do in Flash to add life to your background. For the sake of brevity, let's keep things simple and talk about panning the background.

When you pan a background, you are basically just tweening it across the Stage. Your background can be a single layer, or you can go for multiple layers to create the illusion of depth.

One thing to keep in mind when you're creating backgrounds that will be panned is that they need to be substantially wider than the Stage. (This might sound obvious, but it is worth mentioning.) Twice the width of your screen is a good rule of thumb.

If you're really sneaky, you can make the left side of your background match up with the right side. That way, you can actually put your background in a looping movie clip and give the impression that you are continuously panning in one direction.

With a looping background that pans in one direction, you can add a walking loop animation of your character and have him face in the opposite direction that your background is panning. Now you've created the impression that a camera is panning alongside your character, who is walking.

When you are panning a background with multiple layers, you need to think about the camera position and relative depth of your layers. Here are a few rules of thumb when working with multiple layers:

- Objects that are far away usually appear to be darker or fainter than objects that are closer to you.
- Objects in the foreground appear to move faster than objects in the background.
- The farther back in the background layer an object is, the less detail it needs.

You put these concepts to practice in the next exercise.

Exercise 11.5   Animating Your Character and Background

This file has already been started for you. You'll be setting up the animated background.

1. Open BobWalks.fla from the Examples/Chapter11 folder on the CD.

   First you'll set up your scrolling background, and then you'll animate Bob and add him to the scene. You're going to build a scrolling background with two layers.

Tip

You'll be sorely tempted to use gradients and alpha transparency when you build these backgrounds because the effects that you can get are so cool. Try not to do that, or, at least, try to be judicious in your use of these techniques. Gradients and alpha transparency, particularly when combined with animation, are very processor-intensive. Use flat, solid colors where you can. You don't want to bring your visitor's processor to its knees.

2. Rename layer 1 **Trees**, and drag a copy of the Trees graphic symbol from the Library onto the Stage.

3. Align the Trees symbol so that it is justified with the right side of the Stage. The top of the symbol should be aligned with the top of the Stage.

4. Add another layer, and name it **Grass**. Drag a copy of the Grass symbol from the Library onto the Stage. Align the right side of the Grass symbol with the right side of the Stage. The bottom of the Grass symbol should be aligned with the bottom of the Stage.

5. Notice that the two graphic symbols on the different layers are different lengths. If you tween them so that their left sides line up with the left side of the Stage at the same time, they will appear to move at different speeds.

The longest symbol moves the slowest, and the shortest symbol moves the quickest.

6. Place a keyframe in both layers at frame 50 (which marks roughly 4 seconds of play time).

7. In frame 50, align the left side of each movie clip with the left side of the Stage.

8. Apply your tween by selecting any frame between 1 and 50 (in both layers); right- or Control-click and select Create Motion Tween.

9. Save and test your movie.

If you watch closely, you'll see that the Grass symbol is moving faster than the Trees symbol. This creates an aspect change and enhances the depth effect.

You've got your background in place; now you need to get Bob moving.

10. You should still be working with BobWalks.fla. Create a new blank movie clip, and name it **Bob**.

11. Bob has four body positions:

- LegsBack
- LegsForward
- LegsRest
- LegsUp

Your mission, should you choose to accept it, is to arrange these movie clips into a good moving sequence for Bob.

12. For the moment, use just four keyframes—one for each of Bob's body positions. As an example, you could place the movie clips in the following order:

Frame 1: LegsUp
Frame 2: LegsForward
Frame 3: LegsBack
Frame 4: LegsRest

Add the four movie clips to the Stage on successive frames.

13. From the main menu, select Control>Loop Playback, and then press Enter or Return to play the movie clip. Press Enter or Return again to stop the animation.

I don't know about you, but I just don't think that Bob would move like that. At least, not unless he was being poked by a cattle prod. Bob is a big guy; his movements should probably be more deliberate. This is going to require some effort on his part.

14. Use LegsUp as the starting frame. For Bob to lift his legs probably takes some effort. I imagine that he'd drop them pretty quickly, so leave LegsForward in frame 2.

15. When Bob drops his legs, I think he'll take a short rest before pulling himself forward. Insert a regular frame after frame 2 by selecting frame 2 and pressing F5.

Frame 4 should now be LegsBack.

Frame 5 should be LegsRest.

16. After Bob makes it through one complete walk cycle, I think he'll take a rest. Select frame 10 and press F5 to extend your Timeline.

17. Press Enter or Return to test your movie clip again.

Bob's movements look a little more natural now.

18. Return to the main Timeline, and add a layer named **Mr. Bob**. Move the layer between the grass and the trees. Drag a copy of Bob from the Library onto the Stage.

19. Test your movie. Doesn't quite look right, does it? When Bob stops moving, the background keeps scrolling. Your options are either to stop the background scroll or to make Bob move with the scroll.

The simplest thing to do is to make Bob move with the scroll. When Bob stops to rest, he needs to slide back with the background tween.

20. Double-click the Bob movie clip in the Library to open it in Symbol-Editing mode. Most of your sequence is in pretty good shape. All you really need to do is to add a motion tween at the end to get Bob to slide backward while he's at rest.

21. Insert a keyframe in frame 10 of the Bob layer in the Bob movie clip. Even though you haven't moved the new instance of Bob yet, go ahead and right- or Control-click and select Create Motion Tween from the pop-up menu.

22. How far are you going to move Bob? That's easy. Just go back to your main Timeline and measure how far the Grass clip moves in five frames. It's about 130 pixels.

23. Open the Bob movie clip again. Make sure that you have your rulers turned on (View>Rulers), and drag a guide from the left ruler onto the Stage.

    Align the guide with the front of the instance of Bob on frame 5.

24. Drag a second guide onto the Stage, and position it 130 pixels to the right of the first guide.

    Select frame 10, and use your arrow keys to align the front of Bob with the second guide.

25. Save and test your movie.

Bob should take a step, stop, and move in synchronization with the background scenery. Not only do you have a character in motion, but you have your background in motion as well. Where could you go from here? You could add sound—the sound of Bob moving or the background noises. You could add additional layers with assorted forest creatures popping up. The possibilities are endless. It all depends, of course, on the story.

Summary

Now that you've covered the basics of character animation, you're ready to take off on your own. Just remember that, to make a successful animation in Flash, you have to take many factors into consideration, from personality to environment. However, with hard work and a willingness to learn and adapt, each animation that you create will get better.

As mentioned earlier, there are many sources out there to help you learn more about animation in general. Some useful books are these:

- *Cartoon Animation*, by Preston Blair (Walter Foster Publishing)
- *The Animator's Workbook*, by Tony White (WatsonGuptill Press)
- *Digital Character Animation 2: Essential Techniques*, by George Maestri (New Riders Publishing)
- *The Animation Book*, by Kit Laybourne (Three Rivers Press)
- *How to Draw Animation*, by Christopher Hart (WatsonGuptill Press)

Some web sites worth looking into include these:

- `www.precinemahistory.net/`. The complete history of the discovery of cinematography, from 1600 to 1890.

- `hotwired.lycos.com/animation/`. A Flash cartoon site, with plenty of animations to see. It includes links to get you started with creating your own original Flash Toons.

- `www.campchaos.com/`. Flash cartoons ranging from sci-fi to parody and everything in between. You can find great examples of animation here, and it's also a great source of inspiration.

- `www.wildbrain.com/`. Animated shorts and previews done in Flash, for inspiration.

- `animation.about.com/arts/animation/cs/flash/`. About.com's listing of Flash-related animation sites.

- `www.awn.com/tooninstitute/`. Larry's Toon Institute, by Larry Lauria, a former Disney Institute animator. It offers a free online animation course. `www.awn.com` is a great animation resource.

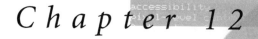

C h a p t e r 12

Making the Transition

tran·si·tion (tran-'si, shən) *n.*

1. Passage from one form, state, style, or place to another.

2. Passage from one subject to another in discourse.

Whether you're using Flash to create a web site, a cartoon, or a commercial, there will be a time when you need to let your audience know that a change in content or scenery is coming. That's what transitions are all about. Transitions can be subtle or obvious, but either way, they should give you a visual clue that something new is about to happen.

Transitions can be a part of a story as well. From watching television and movies, you're probably familiar with a variety of transition styles. Fade-ins, fade-outs, zooms, pans, swaps—you've probably seen them all, even if you didn't recognize them at the time.

The idea of using visual transitions isn't new. Storytellers have been using them since the beginning of time. Animal skins, fiber mats, and curtains all have been used to hide items on the stage until they were needed. Time has passed and the stage has changed, but the need for transition is still important to visual communication. Flash turns the web into your stage. The animal skin might be composed of bits and bytes of information now, but as always, the purpose is the same—a sense of continuity and the expression of change.

With a visually powerful program like Flash, there's always a tendency to "push the envelope." The ability to shrug off the limitations of tables and bitmapped graphics creates a feeling of creative liberation that you just don't get when you have to work with straight HTML.

Although creative liberation is a good thing, you need to know when to temper your creativity with a degree of restraint. It's easy to create incredibly complex movies that are so far over-the-top that they just don't work for their intended purpose. Simple is sometimes better. Say it again: Simple is sometimes better. Repeat this phrase to yourself several times before you start any new project. Just because you *can* make something more technically sophisticated doesn't always mean you *should.*

In this chapter, you take a look at three different types of transitions that you can build using Flash:

- **Simple transition.** Simple transitions usually involve only one or two graphical elements.

- **Combination transition.** Combination transitions are just that, combinations of different transitions to create a new transition.

- **Spatial transition.** Use spatial transitions to give your viewers the feeling that they are physically moving through an interface.

Each transition type is presented in more detail in the following sections and exercises.

Simple Transitions

A simple transition is exactly that—simple. Simple transitions rely on modifying single elements on the Stage using motion tweening, changes in scaling, and alpha transparency. Depending on how you use it, this type of transition can be just as effective as more complex transitions.

Examples of simple transitions include, but are not limited to, the following:

- **Fade-ins and fade-outs.** The most common approach is a fade to black or white and then a fade to the next scene, but you can make this work with any color.

- **Dissolves.** This involves overlaying scenes and having one scene dissolve away to reveal the next.

- **Wipes.** This uses motion to move one scene off the Stage and then bring the next scene onto the Stage.

Each transition can be used to create a different mood to help establish the rhythm of a piece. For example, abrupt cuts from one scene to the next can create a chaotic and somewhat disoriented effect. Dissolves and fade-ins/outs create a smoother transition. These transitional effects can be used in combination with one another as well.

You can affect how people browse within your site by the mood and pace of your navigation. For instance, fast transitions can get people to important information quickly.

Exercise 12.1   Fade from Black

In this exercise, you use one of the simplest and most effective transitions: fading from black to an image. This type of transition works particularly well when your base movie color is black.

1. This file has been started for you. Open FadeFromBlack.fla from the Examples/Chapter12 folder on the CD. The movie currently has the following settings:

   Frame Rate: **18fps**
   Dimensions: **650 × 250 pixels**
   Background Color: **Black**

   Additionally, there is one element in the Library, escalator.jpg.

   This image was taken inside the Dupont Circle Metro Station in Washington, D.C. You are going to convert this JPEG to a graphic symbol because you'll be applying effects to it, and effects can be applied only to symbols. (See Figure 12.1.)

2. Rename Layer 1 **Escalator**, and drag a copy of escalator.jpg from the Library onto the Stage.

3. With the image selected, press F8 (Convert to Symbol). Give it a symbol name of **Escalator** and make it a graphic symbol. Make sure to set the registration point in the upper-left corner. Click OK.

4. Use the Properties Inspector (Window > Properties) to set both the X and Y positions of the image to 0.

5. You're going to be using brightness and tweening to make this image fade in from black. To make it a gradual fade-in, you will spread the tween across 4 seconds. At 18fps, 4 seconds will be 72 frames. Insert a keyframe at frame 72.

6. Return to frame 1 and select the Escalator graphic on the Stage.

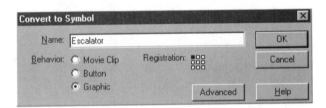

Figure 12.1   By embedding the escalator.jpg in a graphic symbol, you can apply effects such as brightness or alpha changes to it.

7. Now go back to frame 1 and click the Elevator. Open the Properties Inspector and from the Color drop-down menu, choose Brightness. Change the Brightness setting to –100%. The image should appear to be completely black.

8. Next, set up your motion tween. Select any frame between 1 and 72. In the Properties Inspector, select Motion from the Tween drop-down menu. (See Figure 12.2.)

9. Press Enter or Return to test your scene. You should have a smooth fade-in from black to your image.

10. Another trick you can use when you are using fade from black is to use white text on the screen. If any part of your image—in this case, the entrance to the Metro—is white, the text appears to dissolve as the brightness increases. Add a new layer and name it **Text**.

11. Select the Text tool and select a font in the Properties Inspector. You can use any font you like. I used Hooge 8 by mimiml (see Tip) set at a point size of 8. Set the font color to white.

Tip

Anti-aliased fonts in Flash, especially in small sizes, don't render well. If you need clear, crisp text, use aliased fonts. Miniml fonts (www.miniml.com) are specifically designed to remain crisp (aliased) in Flash. However, to make them work, you have to follow the guidelines in the guide.txt file that is in the font zip file. Specifically, you have to set these fonts at their recommended point size, and you must place them on an exact pixel (for example, at 15, not at 15.3).

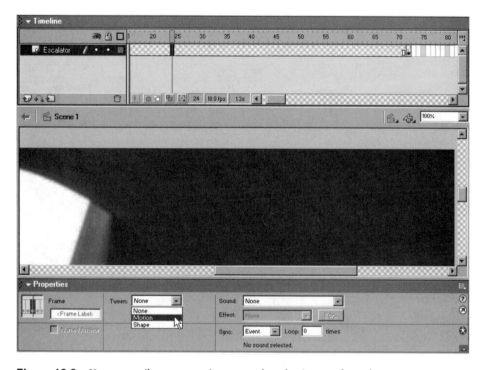

Figure 12.2   You can easily create motion tweens by selecting any frame between two keyframes and then selecting Motion from the Tween menu in the Properties Inspector.

12. On the Stage, type **I DREAM ON THE SUBWAY** (use the capitalization shown). Check that it's positioned over the white area by looking at frame 72; otherwise, the effect won't work.

13. If you are using one of the miniml fonts, you'll need to make sure your text is positioned on an exact pixel. (See Figure 12.3.) With your text still selected, use the Properties Inspector to position the text box at the following coordinates:

X: **100**
Y: **75**

14. Press Enter or Return to test your scene again. Now, as the elevator image fades in, the text appears to dissolve.

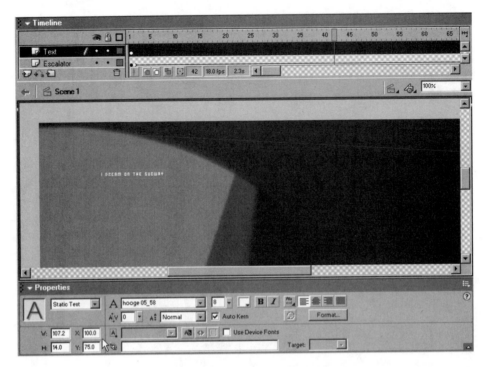

Figure 12.3   If you use one of the miniml fonts, you need to place it on an exact pixel.

Is using a brightness change the only way you could make this work? Of course not. We're talking Flash here. There's always more than one way to accomplish a task, but there's usually a good reason to choose one option over another. For instance, you could have accomplished the same thing by using an alpha transparency tween rather than a brightness tween. Instead of using the Properties Inspector to set the brightness to −100 on the first frame, you could have opted to set the alpha transparency to 0%. The effect would have been the same. The downside of using an alpha tween is that alpha tweens are notoriously processor intensive.

Brightness can be used effectively only if the background for the image is 100% black or 100% white. In this case, the background is black, so the brightness change is an effective choice.

The transition effect you just set up is a gradual fade from black to a photographic image. Subtle fades of this type usually are used in conjunction with low-key music and designs that lend themselves to smooth and soft transitions. Sites with hard edge graphics and high tempo music, on the other hand, tend to use hard and fast transitions.

Combination Transitions

Simple transitions used alone are fine and are frequently all that you need. However, there are times when you'll want to layer transitions to achieve a richer and more complicated effect.

The camera flash, for example, is a common and simple technique; it's nothing more than the act of inserting a single white frame to give the effect of a camera flash. However, by combining a flash with a fade to black, you create a more complex transition.

The next exercise expands on the techniques you learned in the previous one.

Exercise 12.2   Flash and Fade to Black

This time, you use a quick flash and fade to black to create your transition. This effect has a camera flash feel to it, and it's a good way to quickly establish your shot or scene and let its image resonate.

1. Once again, this file has been started for you. Open FlashFadeToBlack.fla from the Examples/Chapter12 folder on the CD.

    In this exercise, you start with a black screen, and rather than transition gradually to an image, you introduce a bright flash and snap immediately to the image, which then fades out.

2. Rename Layer 1 **Train**, and then insert a keyframe in frame 6.

3. With frame 6 selected, open the Library and drag a copy of the InsideTrain graphic symbol onto the Stage.

4. Use the Properties Inspector (Window > Properties) to set both the X and the Y properties of the InsideTrain graphic to 0.

5. This time, you'll fade the image partially to black instead of fading in from black. Insert a keyframe in frame 11. With the image on the Stage in frame 11 selected, use the Properties Inspector to set the Brightness to –75%.

6. To apply a tween to the image, select any frame between frame 6 and frame 11, and use the Properties Inspector to apply the Motion Tween option.

7. Insert a blank keyframe (F7) in frame 12 and extend the Timeline out to frame 20 by selecting frame 20 and then pressing F5.

8. Now if you play your movie by pressing Return or Enter, you start with a black background, flash to the image, and then see the image fade to black.

9. You can give more impact to this effect by enhancing the changeover from black to the image. Start by adding a new layer and naming it **White Flash**.

10. Insert a keyframe in frame 5 of your new layer.

11. Select the Rectangle tool and set the Fill option to White and the Stroke option to None. Draw a rectangle on the Stage.

12. With the rectangle selected, use the Properties Inspector to resize the rectangle to 650 × 250 pixels, and then set both X and Y to 0.

13. You're going to use the white flash only once in this transition, but it will be used multiple times in the next one, so convert the white rectangle to a graphic symbol (F8) and name it **whiteFlash**. The Registration point should be at the top left. Then, insert a blank keyframe in frame 6 of the White Flash layer. This ensures that the white flash will play for only one frame.

14. Press Enter or Return to test it again. Now the transition effect is heightened by the addition of the white flash just before the image becomes visible.

15. Just to add a little more visual interest, create a new layer and name it **Text**. Insert a keyframe in frame 6. (See Figure 12.4.)

16. Select the Text tool and use the Properties Inspector to set the text fill color to #FFCC33. Choose Arial, or a similar font, and set the size to 18 points.

17. Type the word **LIGHTS** in all caps on the Stage.

18. Use the Properties Inspector to reposition the text block with X at 80 and Y at 25.

19. Select the text block and use the Mixer panel (Window > Color Mixer) to set the alpha transparency to 60%.

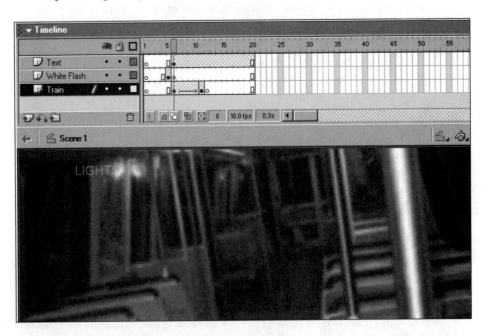

Figure 12.4   When you have completed this transition, you'll have three separate layers: the first for the train image, the second to create the camera flash, and the third to hold the text.

20. Test your movie again. Now you start with a black screen and get a bright white flash. Then you get the train image, which fades out to black while the text remains visible.

Whenever you are setting up transitions, remember that transitions are part of the story. There's actually a story behind the subway sequences you've been using.

Doug Clarke came up with the idea of trying to capture the essence of his daily commute on the Metro as a Flash movie. The complete movie is available in the Examples/Chapter12 folder on the CD. Just launch and play Transit.swf.

Doug wanted to capture the hypnotic effect of riding the Metro those many late nights and early mornings. In the next exercise, you recreate part of Doug's nightmare and capture the transition from a waking state to a subconscious state. Thus, you see, this exercise is not only about transitions, but also about how transitions impact your story.

The next exercise builds on the transition you began creating in the previous exercise.

Exercise 12.3   Using Repetition to Create a Transition

In this exercise, you combine a flashing transition with a fade to black. This is going to be a repetitive transition with a speed change.

To create the flashing sequence, you do a lot of cutting and pasting. Cutting and pasting frames on multiple layers in Flash is no big deal, as long as you know a trick or two. When you are copying frames from multiple layers, you have to make sure that you paste them into multiple layers. Although this might seem intuitively obvious, it's not. Follow the directions in the next two steps carefully and you'll be good to go.

1. You should have the file you were just working on in Exercise 12.2 open, or you can open FlashFadeToBlack_final.fla from the Examples/Chapter12 folder on the CD.

2. Hold down the Shift key and highlight frames 5–20 in all three layers. Right-click (Windows) or Control-click (Macintosh), and then select Copy Frames. (See Figure 12.5.)

3. Highlight the first empty frame (frame 21) in all three layers, right-click or Control-click, and then select Paste Frames. (See Figure 12.6.) Your frames should paste neatly into place.

4. Repeat Step 3 three more times. The frames you'll be highlighting and pasting into are 37, 53, and 69.

5. Next, you're going to change the text in the keyframes on the Text layer. Without changing the color or opacity, change the text in the following keyframes as shown:

    Frame 21: **SUBDUE**
    Frame 36: **ME**
    Frame 51: **TO**
    Frame 66: **SLEEP**

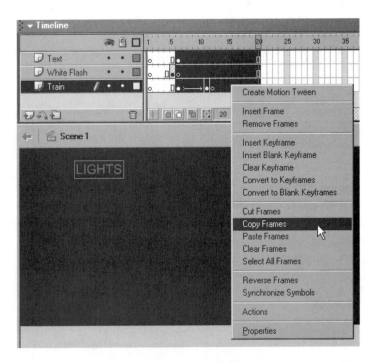

Figure 12.5   You easily can copy a group of frames by highlighting them and using the Copy Frames option on the pop-up menu that appears when you right-click or Control-click a frame.

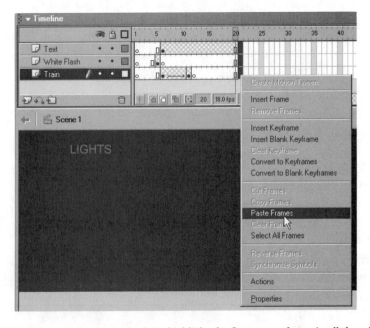

Figure 12.6   To paste the frames back in, highlight the first empty frame in all three layers, and then choose Paste Frames from the pop-up menu.

Note

Save your file as often as possible. On longer projects like this, it can be a heartbreak when you encounter a crash and have to rebuild everything.

6. Go back to frame 1 and press Enter or Return to do a quick test of your scene. You'll start with a black screen and get a slow strobing effect.

7. Next, you're going to repeat the sequence you just set up, minus the text, and shorten the individual transitions. This gives the effect of rushing toward some kind of a conclusion. Highlight frames 5 through 84 in the WhiteFlash and Train layers. Right-click or Control-click, and then select Copy Frames.

8. Highlight frame 85 in both the WhiteFlash and Train layers, right-click or Control-click, and then select Paste Frames.

9. Now you'll successively shorten the transitions. The directions here will become a little less exact because the frame numbers will change as you delete frames. However, for the last five transitions, you are going to want to shorten both the tween and the static frames following each tween.

   Beginning with the tween/static frame combo that begins on frame 84, remove one frame of the tween. Then remove one frame from the static frames that follow the tween. On the next sequence, remove two frames from the tween and static frames, and so on. Make the last three tweens the same, with the tween having three frames (two keyframes and a middle frame).

10. Next, you'll need to adjust the position of the frames in the WhiteFlash layer. You can do this easily by highlighting the frames you want to move and dragging them to their new positions. Be sure to highlight the empty frames after the flash as well; otherwise, Flash might extend the length of the white flash. The frame with the white flash should immediately precede the frame with the image on the Train layer. The frame following the white flash should always be a blank keyframe. (See Figure 12.7.)

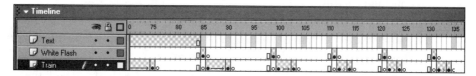

Figure 12.7   By shortening the transitions, you give the effect of rushing into a change.

11. Now you're building up to a major transition. Speed things up a bit by first repeating the last transition several times and then alternating between the white flash and the train image set at −75%.

12. In the Train and WhiteFlash layers, copy the frames that contain the white flash, the last tween, and the blank keyframe that follows the last tween. You can do the copying by highlighting the frames (a total of five frames), right-clicking or Control-clicking, and then selecting Copy Frames. (See Figure 12.8.)

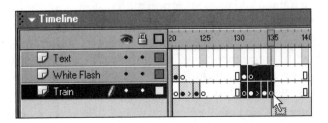

Figure 12.8   Copy one complete sequence of the shortest tween. You'll use this to build a strobing effect.

13. Paste your copied frames after the last frame of the current Timeline. Remember that you have to highlight a frame in both layers for this to work. Continue pasting the frames until you have 10 copies. Don't worry about exact numbers here; it simply doesn't matter.

14. Alter the last tween sequence so that it consists of two frames: the white flash and the train interior set at a brightness of –75%. Copy and paste this sequence several more times.

15. Now return to the Text layer. Part of this transition is a transition from a state of consciousness to unconsciousness. You currently have the words LIGHTS SUB-DUE ME TO SLEEP showing up as the movie progresses. Sleep is the important concept here, so extend the Timeline out to 100 in the Text layer by selecting frame 100 and pressing F5. This keeps the word SLEEP on the scene about twice as long as the other words.

16. Insert a blank keyframe in frame 101 of the Text layer to make SLEEP disappear, but only momentarily.

17. Wait about a second and a half (27 frames) and add SLEEP back in by copying and pasting the earlier frame (the last frame with the word "SLEEP"). This time, however, you'll change it so that it will be larger and fainter.

18. Select the text you just pasted into frame 128. Select the Text tool and with the Properties Inspector (Window > Properties), change the font size to 96.

19. Use the Color Mixer panel (Window > Color Mixer) to change the Alpha setting to 20%.

20. Extend the Timeline out to frame 164 in the Text layer so that SLEEP stays on the Stage for another 2 seconds. Then, insert a blank keyframe (F7) in frame 165.

21. You already know that the whole point of this piece is to complete the transition to the subconscious, so you'll add that in now. Insert a blank keyframe (F7) after the last frame of the Train layer.

22. Add another white flash to the last frame of the WhiteFlash layer.

23. You're going to play around with brightness again to make your text fade in. You start by inserting a keyframe (F6) in the Text layer that lines up over the last two keyframes you just added for the Train and the WhiteFlash layers.

24. Next, select your Text tool and make the following changes in the Properties Inspector (Window > Properties):

> Font: **Arial** (or similar)
> Size: **24**
> Color: **White**

25. Next, use the Color Mixer panel to set the Alpha option to 50%, and in the keyframe you added to the Text layer type **transition to the subconscious**. Then, use the Properties Inspector to set the X position to 0 and the Y position to 36.

26. Almost done! All you need to do now is extend the Timeline for the WhiteFlash and Text layers out to frame 225 by highlighting frame 225 in both layers and pressing F5.

27. Insert a keyframe in frame 225 of the WhiteFlash layer.

28. Select the WhiteFlash graphic on the Stage and use the Properties Inspector to change the brightness to –100%.

29. Select any frame between the start of this last white flash section and 225 in the WhiteFlash layer, and use the Properties Inspector to create a motion tween. (See Figure 12.9.)

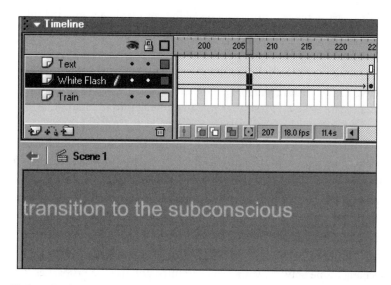

Figure 12.9   The final text is for the transition to the subconscious, which will fade in as the white flash fades to black.

30. That's it! Test away. If you're having problems, you can check yourself against the FlashFadeToBlack2_final.fla file on the CD. As you test, you'll get a slow strobing effect that eventually speeds up until it fades into the transition to the subconscious.

In the next section, you look at ways that you can immerse your viewer into your scene by using spatial transitions.

Spatial Transitions

In a spatial transition, you give your viewers the feeling that they are actually moving into your movie. You can achieve this by using a combination of tweening and scale changes. Spatial transitions are especially effective when you are trying to draw your viewer into an experience. These types of transitions create an immersive effect.

Exercise 12.4   Creating a Spatial Transition

This time, you're going to build on Exercise 12.1, the "Fade from Black" exercise. You're going to transport your viewer from the subway escalator into the subway itself and from the depths of the subway into a dream. To do so, you're going to be combining a series of techniques.

1. Open the file you created in Exercise 12.1, or you can start with FadeFromBlack_final.fla from the Examples/Chapter12 folder on the CD.

The first part of the transition will be taking your audience into the subway. You'll start by setting up a simple tween, and then you'll give it some edge by superimposing additional images over the tween.

2. Add a new layer beneath the Escalator layer and name it **Escalator Down**.

You're going to create a simple tween that takes you down the escalator and then use scaling to make it appear that you are moving into the station.

3. Insert a keyframe in frame 73 of the Escalator Down layer and open subwayImages.fla (Examples/Chapter12 folder) as a Library. Drag a copy of the escalator 2 graphic onto the Stage. Use the Properties Inspector to position the graphic with its X at 0 and its Y at –613.

4. Insert a new keyframe in frame 98 of the Escalator Down layer. Select the graphic on the Stage and reposition it with an X position of –441 and a Y position of 0.

5. Select the graphic in the Escalator Down layer in frame 73, and use the Properties Inspector to set its brightness to –100%.

6. Select any frame between your two keyframes, and use the Properties Inspector to create a motion tween.

7. Insert another keyframe (F6) in frame 115 on the same layer and use the Transform panel to scale it to 200%. Set the X position to –1460 and the Y position to –450.

8. Set the brightness for the graphic in frame 115 to −100%. Then, select any frame between your two keyframes and apply a motion tween.

If your viewer tested your work now, he or she would see the effect of moving down the escalator and into the dark confines of the station itself. (See Figure 12.10.)

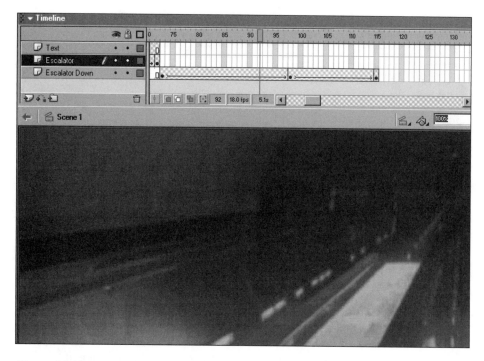

Figure 12.10 By combining a simple tween with a tween and scaling, you give your viewers the impression that they are moving into the subway station.

9. The program is okay as it stands, but you can give it a bit more of an edge by continuing the tween in the overlying layer and selectively removing frames from the tween to reveal the underlying tween.

The Escalator layer stops with a shot looking up the elevator. You can set up a tween that gives the impression that you are descending into the station while looking up the escalator. If you selectively remove frames, you can flip back and forth between the perspectives of looking up the escalator and looking down as you descend. It gives a nice surrealistic feel.

10. On the Escalator layer, insert a keyframe in frame 98 and reposition the graphic so its X position is at −260 and its Y position is at −965. Go ahead and add your motion tween.

11. You want to remove frames, but you don't want to lose your tweened positions, so select frames 73–97 and right-click or Control-click anywhere on the high-lighted frames to get the context menu. Select Convert to Keyframes.

12. Replace the odd numbered frames (73–97) with blank keyframes (F7). This will require two steps for each keyframe you want to replace. First, you have to clear the keyframe; then you have to insert a blank keyframe.

13. Now test your movie. You have the beginnings of a pretty cool transition. (See Figure 12.11.)

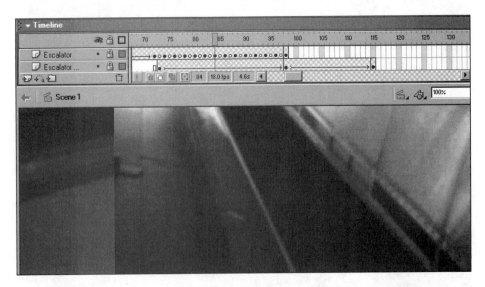

Figure 12.11 By setting up a secondary tween and selectively removing frames so that you can see the tween below, you get a much richer and more textured effect.

14. You can add one more piece to the escalator portion of the transition. If you were sinking into the subway, you might take a quick look back toward the top before you were swallowed up completely. To make this happen, add a new layer beneath the Escalator Down layer and name it **Escalator Back**. Insert a keyframe in frame 115.

15. If it's not still open, open subwayImages.fla (Examples/Chapter12 folder) as a Library and drag a copy of the Escalator3 graphic onto the Stage. Leave this Library open. You'll be using it again.

16. Use the Transform panel (Window > Transform) to scale the graphic to 400%. Position the graphic so that its left side is aligned with the right side of the Stage (see Figure 12.12) and the top is aligned to the top of Stage.

17. Insert a keyframe in frame 121 and reposition the graphic with X at 285 and Y at 0. Add a motion tween between the two keyframes.

18. Insert a new keyframe in frame 122 and set both the X and Y positions for the graphic to 0.

19. Insert another keyframe in frame 132. Reset the X to 650 and leave Y at 0.

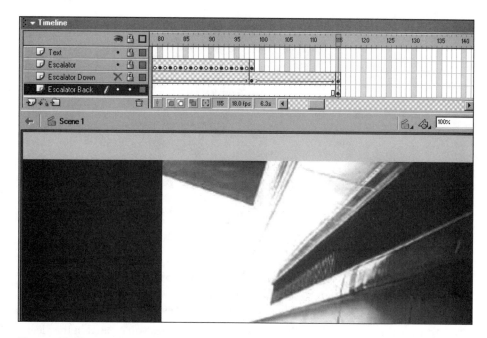

Figure 12.12   Position the graphic so that its left side lines up with the right side of the Stage.

20. Set the brightness for the graphic in frame 122 to –100% and add a motion tween between the two keyframes. Then, insert a blank keyframe in frame 133 of the Escalator Back layer.

You've created the transition into the subway, but to what are you transitioning? To sleep. To make this effective, you need to add the sleep sequence.

21. Add a new layer above the Escalator layer and name it **Sleep**.

22. Insert a keyframe in frame 133 of the Sleep layer and drag a copy of the dougSleeping graphic from the subwayImages Library onto the Stage.

The whole feel for this piece is somewhat surrealistic, and you want to maintain that. An easy way to do that would be to distort the image.

23. Select the dougSleeping image on the Stage and use the Transform panel to increase the width to 330% (make sure you deselect Constrain on the Transform panel). Reposition the image so that its left side lines up with the right side of the Stage, and then use the Properties Inspector to change the alpha to 25%. (See Figure 12.13.)

24. Insert a new keyframe in frame 142 and change the setting for the width on the Transform panel back to 100%. Reposition the graphic with X at 5 and Y at 0. Then, create a motion tween between your two keyframes.

25. Insert a keyframe in frame 151 and shift the image to an X position of 360. Leave the Y position at 0 and set up a tween.

Figure 12.13   By distorting the dougSleeping image, you add to the surrealistic feel of this transition.

26. Add one more tween. Insert a keyframe in frame 160 and use the Transform panel to stretch the X axis again. Set the width to 475% and reposition the graphic so that the right side of the graphic lines up with the left side of the Stage. Then, add a motion tween between the two keyframes.

27. Add a new layer and call it **Sleep2**. Duplicate the frames you created in the Sleep layer and paste them into the same position in the Sleep2 layer.

28. In the Sleep2 layer, move the current keyframe that's on frame 142 to frame 143. Reposition the graphic so that its X position is at 292. Leave Y at 0.

29. Move the frame that's on frame 151 to frame 152 and change its X position to 356.

30. Go ahead and test your movie. In doing so, you'll descend into the dark confines of the subway through a series of transitional steps until you merge with Doug's dream.

There's a lot more you could do with these transitions. The final Transit film has some additional elements that you didn't add here. These elements include some animated text and train lights. See if you can pick them out when you play Transit.swf. Transit.fla also is available on the CD for you to open and examine.

Summary

As you've seen, you can use single transitions or a series of transitions to make changes from one scene to the next. You've also seen how transitions can be more than just a method of moving from one scene to the next; they can be an integral part of the overall story you are trying to tell.

You saw only a few examples of transitions in this chapter, but those should be enough to get you thinking about how to make changes between scenes. Next time you watch a movie or television, pay close attention to how skilled (or not so skilled) directors use transitions to establish pace and timing. Now go out there and experiment with your own stuff and see what you can create!

Chapter 13

Flash and Video

In addition to raster and vector graphic formats, with Flash MX, you can now not only import video formats directly into Flash, but you also can play them back in the Flash Player! Nothing but Flash is required.

In the past, you could import video, but the Flash player couldn't play it back—your only options were to export the video as a QuickTime movie or to use an external program such as FLIX by Wildform to encode it in the SWF format. Now all you need is Flash. That's not to say I'm throwing FLIX out of my toolkit. FLIX 2.0 actually has some cool features—like converting video into vector format.

Tables 13.1 and 13.2 show the different types of video that can be imported into Flash. You should note that to import most of these files, you need to have QuickTime 4 or higher installed. If you are on a Windows machine with no QuickTime and no DirectX, you can still successfully import AVI files.

Table 13.1   Video Formats Flash MX Imports

Format	File Extension	Platform
Audio Video Interleaved	.avi	Both
Digital Video	.dv	Both
Motion Picture Experts Group	.mpg, mpeg	Both
QuickTime Movie	.mov	Both

Table 13.2   Video Formats Flash MX Imports if DirectX 7 or Higher Is Installed (Windows Only)

Format	File Extension	Platform
Audio Video Interleaved	.avi	Windows
Motion Picture Experts Group	.mpg, mpeg	Windows
Windows Media File	.wmv, .asf	Windows

In addition to all of the above, you can import FLV (Flash Video) files. The makers of the video codec used in Flash MX, Sorenson Spark by Sorenson Media, have another application available—Sorenson Squeeze for Flash MX. Squeeze allows for higher compression rates than the basic Spark codec. You can produce Flash-specific FLV files, as well as SWFs, with Squeeze. You'll take a look at Sorenson Squeeze later in this chapter.

In this chapter you'll learn how to

- Import linked videos into Flash and export them as QuickTime movies
- Embed videos in Flash using the Sorenson Spark codec
- Embed and manipulate videos in movie clips
- Use Sorensen Squeeze to create Flash Video files

But before you jump into all of that, take a few moments to review some video basics, such as codec.

Video Compression Basics

A *codec* is simply a method of compressing and decompressing a media file, such as a movie. Codecs are based on two fundamental approaches to encoding video: spatial (intraframe) and temporal (interframe) compression. Spatial, or intraframe, compression is applied to still images or to video images on a frame-by-frame basis. Temporal, or interframe, compression is applied to a sequence of video frames rather than on a frame-by-frame basis. This type of compression takes advantage of the fact that from one frame to the next, in most cases, relatively few pixels change. Each frame is compared to the next and only the pixels that have changed are stored. Any areas that have not changed from the previous frame are just repeated.

Video in Flash MX is encoded using the Sorenson Spark codec. If you've ever watched or created a QuickTime movie, you've already been introduced to the Sorenson codec, because it's also used for QuickTime movies. The Sorenson Spark codec is ideally suited for creating highly compressed movies with good resolution, larger window sizes, and higher frame rates than most other codecs.

The Sorenson Spark codec relies primarily on temporal or interframe compression, but like other interframe codecs, it also makes use of intraframes as keyframes. Each compressed movie begins with a keyframe that the following frames refer to. Additional keyframes are inserted whenever there are significant changes from the previous keyframe.

Another reason that the Spark codec is so effective is that it relies on the use of the YUV-12 color space. Because the human eye is more sensitive to brightness (luminance) than it is to color (chrominance), you can reduce file sizes by storing more information about brightness than you do about color. In this case, you're talking about storing 8×8 pixel blocks of color, each of which stores twice as much information about brightness as it does about color.

 Tip

Sorenson video divides images into 16×16 pixel blocks, so it is most efficient when the frame size is an even multiple of 16.

Even with a great compression codec, you still have to be sensitive to bandwidth issues. What is going to most affect the final size of your video? The height and width of your movie and its frame rate are certainly going to be determining factors.

There are some standard video sizes that you can use as a baseline for specific bandwidths:

- Modem: 160 × 120 pixels
- Dual ISDN: 192 × 144 pixels
- T1/DSL/Cable: 320 × 240 pixels

If you are unsure of the capabilities your audience will have, one option is to record videos at multiple sizes and give your viewer a choice.

Generally speaking, you'll get better quality results if you encode the video at the same rate that it was originally recorded at. Standard video on TV is recorded at 25–30 frames per second. Movies are recorded at 24 frames per second. If you are targeting lower bandwidths, you might want to consider halving the frame rate, which has the effect of dropping every other frame, but maintains relatively smooth playback.

The type of content in your video is also going to affect how it compresses. High energy, fast-moving scenes are much harder to compress due to the high number of pixel changes between frames.

Okay, now it's time to take a look at the import options for video in Flash MX.

Importing Basics

Video clips can be imported as either embedded or linked objects. Embedded videos are encoded using the Sorenson Spark codec and included in the Flash movie. Movies encoded in this fashion can be displayed by the Flash player. Linked videos are exported as QuickTime movies with a Flash track. Linked videos cannot be played back inside the Flash player.

Starting the import process for a video is no different from what you've already looked at for importing other external files. All you need to do is this:

1. Select File > Import or File > Import to Library.
2. Select the type of movie you want to import from the Files of Type list.
3. Browse to the movie you want to import and click Open.

4. The Import Video dialog box will open with two options (see Figure 13.1):

   • Embed Video in Macromedia Flash Document.

   • Link to External Video File (Video Will Only Be Visible When the Movie Is
     Published as a QuickTime Movie File).

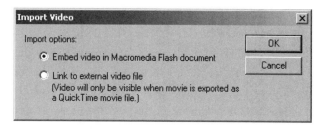

Figure 13.1   You have two options when you import video into Flash. You can embed the
video in your Flash movie, or you can link to an external file.

The first option is entirely new. The second option is essentially equivalent to the
old Export as QuickTime option. Start by looking at linking to external files.

5. After you select one of those options, if your Timeline doesn't have enough
   frames for the video to play, you'll get another dialog box (see Figure 13.2) that
   will say the following:

   "This video requires XXX frames to display its entire length. The selected
   Timeline span is not long enough. Do you want the required number of
   frames automatically inserted into the Timeline span?"

Figure 13.2   If you don't have sufficient frames in your movie to display the imported video,
Flash will warn you and give you the option of expanding your Timeline.

6. To automatically expand your Timeline, select the Yes button.

You can import videos to the main Timeline or into a movie clip in your existing movie. If you want, you can then export the video as a SWF that can be brought into another project via `loadMovie()`.

In the next section, you'll take a brief look at linking imported videos to external files.

Linking Imported Videos to External Files

It's kind of hard to get excited about publishing videos from Flash as QuickTime movies when you know you can publish them directly in Flash, but there may be times when all you really want to do is add a Flash track to an existing QuickTime movie. Why would you want to add a Flash track to a QuickTime movie? Because you can import graphics into Flash that are not directly supported by QuickTime. When you export these graphics in a QuickTime movie, they retain their native format because they export on a special Flash track. That means that you can add in vector art that you create in Flash, FreeHand, Illustrator, or AutoCad. You can also include Flash 4-level interactivity, so you can add navigational elements to a QuickTime movie.

When you import a video that you plan to link to an external file, that video must be imported on the main Timeline or directly into the Library. You cannot import a linked video into a movie clip. Okay, you can, but it won't do you any good because it won't export.

You also can't tween a linked video. Again, you may be able to get the tween to work inside of your Flash file, but the tween won't export.

Any changes you make in the video you link to will be automatically reflected when you open your Flash file—because you have linked to that file.

When you want to view the imported QuickTime movie inside of Flash, select Control > Play from the main menu. Testing the movie won't work because you can't display a QuickTime file that is linked using the Flash Player.

Another thing of note: If you are going to publish your movie as a QuickTime file with a Flash track, you must make sure you are publishing in Flash 5 or lower format—the QuickTime 5 player doesn't understand the Flash 6 player format. Additionally, you can only use Flash 4-level commands. Subsequent releases of QuickTime, depending on their release cycle, might support the Flash 6 player.

In the next section, you'll take a look at what is really new and interesting in Flash—embedding videos.

Embedding Videos Directly in Flash

This is the really fun part. The capability to embed video directly in Flash is a huge step forward. You no longer have to depend on other tools to encode video to the SWF format. You don't need to depend on people having QuickTime or RealVideo anymore.

When you import a video file type that can be embedded into Flash and you choose the Embed Video in Macromedia Flash Document option, you'll get the Sorenson Spark Import Video Settings dialog box (see Figure 13.3).

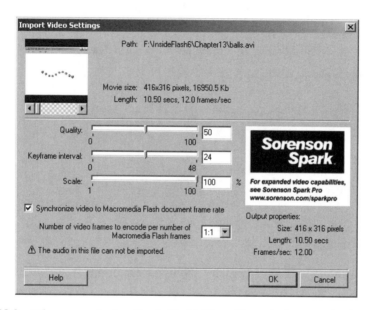

Figure 13.3   When you embed a video in Flash MX, you'll use the Sorenson Spark Import Video Settings dialog box.

There are two main parts to the Sorenson Spark Import Video Settings dialog box. The upper part of the dialog box has a preview window so that you can scrub through the video you are preparing to import. More importantly, this is where you can get basic information about the movie you are importing, including the following:

- The path to the movie
- The original video size in both pixels and Kb.
- The length of the movie in seconds
- The frame rate the movie was recorded at

This information is important because, as you'll see, it helps you make some decisions about how you are going to import the video.

The lower part of the dialog box has all of the settings you can change, along with additional information. In particular you need to take a look at these settings:

- Quality
- Keyframe Interval
- Scale
- Synchronize Video to Macromedia Flash Document Frame Rate
- Number of Video Frames to Encode per Number of Macromedia Flash Frames
- Import Audio or Audio Import Warning

You'll examine each of these settings in a series of simple exercises.

Quality

The Quality setting controls the amount of compression that will be used for the video. The values range from 0 to 100. The lower the value for the Quality setting, the more highly compressed the video will be. The default value is 50 the first time you import a video. This setting is "sticky": It will always reflect the last setting you used to encode a video.

Generally speaking, a Quality setting of 100 is lossless, or nearly so. A setting of 80 is visually lossless. Movie trailers are typically recorded at a setting of 60, which introduces some noise but is usually of acceptable quality.

To understand how this setting alone affects the final file size and quality of a video, run the simple test in Exercise 13.1.

Exercise 13.1   The Effect of the Quality Setting

The video clip, balls.avi, is available in the Examples/Chapter13 folder on the CD for you to test against. This video is an AVI capture of the Flash scripted 3D file created in Chapter 14, "Creating 3D Effects in Flash." The original file is a 416×316-pixel AVI file. It is 10.5 seconds long and was recorded at 12.0 frames per second. The size of the original AVI file is 16,950.5Kb.

1. Open a new movie in Flash.
2. Choose File > Import and navigate to the balls.avi file in the Examples/Chapter13 folder on the companion CD.

3. In the Import Video dialog box, choose Embed Video in Macromedia Flash Document and click OK.

4. In the Import Video Settings dialog box, choose the following settings:

   Quality: **100**
   Keyframe Interval: **0**
   Scale: **100**
   Synchronize Video to Macromedia Flash
   Document Frame Rate: **selected**
   Number of Video Frames to Encode per
   Number of Macromedia Flash Frames: **1:1**

5. Click OK. Click Yes when the "This video requires 126 frames..." dialog box pops up.

   With no compression, your video looks pretty good (see Figure 13.4). Save and publish your file. Your file size should be right around 243KB.

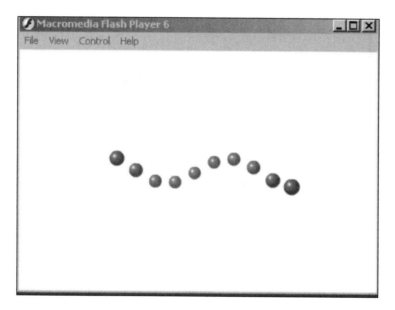

Figure 13.4   With a Quality setting of 100, the visual quality of the video is, not surprisingly, very good.

6. Delete the video from the Stage and import the balls.avi file into your file again. This time, drop the Quality setting to 80 and click OK.

7. When the Resolve Library Conflict dialog box pops up, select Replace Existing Items and click OK.

8. The quality of the video is still quite good. Save and publish your file. Your file size should be about 55KB. By dropping the Quality setting to 80, you saved about 188KB is size without appreciable loss in visual quality. That's a significant savings.

9. Delete the video from the Stage and reimport it, experimenting with Quality settings of 60 and then 10. Dropping the quality to 60 lowers your file size to about 32KB with some loss of quality. Dropping the Quality to 10 lowers your file size to about 18KB, but the quality is unacceptable (see Figure 13.5). Keep this file open—you'll need it for the next exercise.

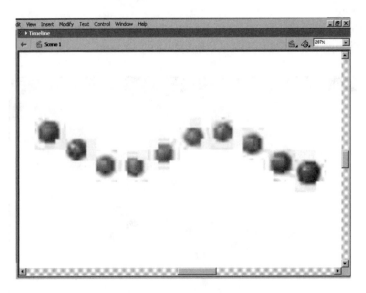

Figure 13.5   By the time you drop the Quality setting to 10, the visual quality of the video is unacceptable.

There are no magic numbers here. The appropriate setting is going to vary depending on the type of video you are importing. But this should give you a good feel for how Quality affects your final file size.

Keyframe Interval

The next setting that you can work with is *Keyframe Interval*. As mentioned earlier, the Sorenson Spark codec is an intraframe codec, but it does make use of interframes, or keyframes, as well. By default, keyframes are inserted every time there is a significant change between frames. You can choose to have keyframes inserted after a specified number of frames. The values range from 0 to 48. A value of 0 results in no keyframes being added. A value of 1 will insert a keyframe for every frame of the video. A value of 48 will insert a keyframe every 48 frames. Because keyframes store all of the information for a frame, the lower the keyframe interval setting (except for 0), the larger your file size will be.

In the series of tests in Exercise 13.2, the Quality setting is constant at 100%, and only the Keyframe Interval is varied.

Exercise 13.2   The Effect of the Keyframe Interval Setting

You should still have the file you used in the previous exercise open. If you don't, repeat Steps 1–3 of Exercise 13.1. If you are still working in the same file, just delete the existing video from the Stage and import the video once again.

1. In the Import Video Settings dialog box, change the following settings:

    Quality: **100**
    Keyframe Interval: **0**
    Scale: **100**
    Synchronize Video to Macromedia Flash Document
    Frame Rate: **selected**
    Number of Video Frames to Encode per Number of Macromedia
    Flash Frames: **1:1**

2. Click OK. Click Yes when the "This video requires 126 frames…" dialog box pops up.

3. With a Keyframe Interval of 0, your file should be about 243KB.

4. Delete the video from the Stage and import the balls.avi file into your file again. This time, change the Keyframe Interval setting to 1 and click OK.

5. When the Resolve Library Conflict dialog box pops up, select Replace Existing Items, and click OK.

6. Publish your file. You'll notice that this results in a substantial increase in your file size. That's because you're not taking advantage of interframes—every frame in the movie is a keyframe. You only want to use this setting for very small videos that have a lot of action.

7. Repeat Steps 5–7, changing the Keyframe Interval to 24 and then to 48.

As you increase Keyframe Interval, you'll see a continuing decrease in file size. The change is not as dramatic as the changes you saw when you changed the Quality settings, but they do make a difference. Again, keep this file open for the next exercise.

Scale

The next setting you can change is *Scale*. Not surprisingly, this setting will change the scale or size of the imported video. The possible values for this are 1–100% of the original video size. The default value is always 100%. In the next series of tests (Exercise 13.3), the Quality is constant at 100%, and the Keyframe Interval is constant at 0.

Exercise 13.3   The Effect of the Scale Setting

You should still have the file you were using in the previous exercise open. If not, repeat Steps 1–3 in Exercise 13.2. If you are still working in the same file, just delete the existing video from the Stage, and import the video once again.

You already know what to expect if the Quality is 100, the Keyframe Interval is 0 and the Scale is 100—243KB.

1. In the Import Video Settings dialog box, change the following settings:

   Quality: **100**
   Keyframe Interval: **0**
   Scale: **75**
   Synchronize Video to Macromedia Flash Document
   Frame Rate: **selected**
   Number of Video Frames to Encode per Number of Macromedia
   Flash Frames: **1:1**

2. Publish your file. By reducing the scale to 75%, your file size drops to about 163KB (see Figure 13.6).

3. Experiment changing the Scale to 50%, 25%, and then 1%. Each time you publish your file, you'll see a substantial reduction in file size.

The smaller the scale, the fewer the pixels that have to render. This can improve playback performance in the Flash player. Of course, you'll probably never really want to scale a video all the way down to 1%—no matter how bandwidth-friendly you want to be (see Figure 13.7).

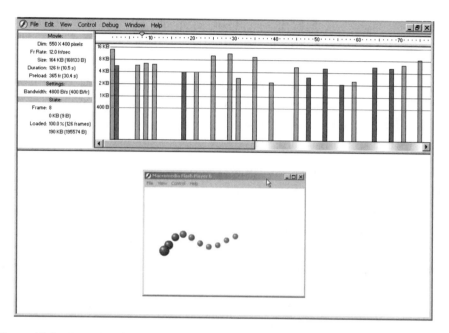

Figure 13.6   By setting the scale of the imported video to 75% of the original size, you save a substantial amount in file size.

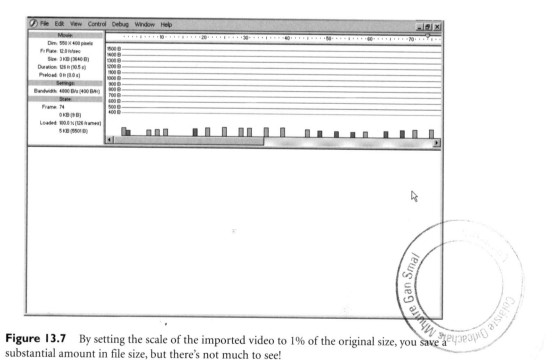

Figure 13.7   By setting the scale of the imported video to 1% of the original size, you save a substantial amount in file size, but there's not much to see!

By now, you should have the idea. You can hold all of your settings steady except for one to test how the one setting affects file size.

Synchronize Video to Flash Frame Rate

The next option is Synchronize Video to Macromedia Flash Document Frame Rate. The default is for the check box to be selected. When the check box is selected, the movie playback will synchronize to the frame rate on the main Timeline.

The AVI file you've been working with was recorded at 12fps. When you import that into a Flash movie that has the same frame rate (the default frame rate for a Flash movie is 12fps), the video needs 126 frames to play in its entirety. If you import the same video into a movie with a frame rate of 24fps, and you choose to synchronize the movie to the frame rate, Flash will need 252 frames for the entire movie. You might think that this would increase your file size, but it doesn't. Additional frames aren't added to the video. Therefore, in this case, both the 126 frame movie and the 252 frame movie would be roughly the same size. What would happen if you imported a video that was recorded at a higher frame rate than your Flash movie?

If you reset your movie frame rate to 8 frames per second and import the video again, Flash will require only 32 frames for the video. This time, you do get a slight reduction in file size (about 10KB).

If your frame per second setting in your Flash movie is lower than the frames per second your video was recorded at and you choose not to synchronize the frame rates, the video will take longer to play back.

Number of Video Frames to Encode

The next setting you can change is Number of Video Frames to Encode per Number of Macromedia Flash Frames. Your options for this setting are 1:1, 1:2, 1:3, 1:4, 1:8, 2:3, and 3:4. If you choose 1:1, Flash will play back one frame of the video for every frame on the Flash Timeline. If you choose 1:2, Flash will play back one frame of the video for every two frames on the Flash Timeline, and so on.

Import Sound

The final setting that you can work with is Import Sound. If you are importing a video into Flash, you can choose whether to import the audio as well by selecting or deselecting the Import Audio check box. If you are importing a file type that has an audio codec that isn't supported by your machine, Flash can't import the audio, and the Import

Audio check box is replaced with a message that reads "The audio in this file cannot be imported." Obviously, importing audio will greatly increase your file size, but in most cases, you're probably going to want it in there anyway.

Which Setting Is Best?

From the preceding tests, it should be clear to you that your largest file size savings come from changing the Quality and Scale settings.

There is no clear cut answer for what the best settings for your particular movie are going to be. It's going to depend on your delivery method and your content. If you are going to deliver video over the web, you need to be mindful of your audience's data rate or connection speed. The final section of this chapter, "Using Sorenson Squeeze for Flash MX to Process Video," takes a brief look at using Sorenson Squeeze to further decrease the size of your video while increasing the quality. You might want to use some of the presets described there as guides when you import into Flash.

Note

As with most other media types in Flash, you can update an embedded video if it has been altered in an external editor. You can also swap one video for another one in your Library using the Swap button in the Properties Inspector.

You know how to get a video into your Flash file, and you know what the basic compression settings are. Next, take a look at what you can do with a video if you embed it in a movie clip.

Embedding and Manipulating Videos in Movie Clips

One of the exciting things you can do with videos in Flash MX is import them directly into movie clips. After you have a video inside of a movie clip (embedded videos only), you can apply all the same effects to it that you can to any other movie clip, including controlling it with ActionScript. You can tween it, skew it, rotate it, hide it, change its tint and alpha—the possibilities are endless. You can also use ActionScript to set up playback controls for your video.

Tip

The number of frames that you can have in a video is limited by the upper frame number limit in Flash—16,000. If your video is longer than 16,000 frames, you'll need to break it up into smaller chunks. Otherwise, nothing after frame 16,000 will display.

In Exercise 13.4, you'll import a video, embed it in a movie clip, and have a little fun.

Exercise 13.4   Embedding Videos in Movie Clips

You'll import a different video in this exercise.

1. Open video.fla from the Examples/Chapter13 folder on the CD and save it to your hard drive.

2. Create a new movie clip (Insert > New Symbol) and name it **video_mc**.

3. Still in the video_mc movie clip, choose File > Import. Browse to the Examples/Chapter13 folder on the CD and select talkingBob.avi (see Figure 13.8). Click OK.

4. In the Import Video dialog box, select Embed Video in Macromedia Flash Document and click OK.

5. In the Import Video Settings dialog box, set the Quality to 80 and the Keyframe Interval to 48. Click OK.

6. Choose to automatically insert the proper number of frames (409). Click Yes.

Figure 13.8   Bob the Blob makes his video appearance.

7. Return to the main Timeline and select the Video layer. Drag a copy of the video_mc movie clip on to the Stage.

8. Go ahead and test your movie. Bob the Blob should start begging you for a cupcake.

   Notice that this is not a small file—it's about 1MB, but that's a lot better than the 54MB AVI file you started with.

In Exercise 13.5, you'll add in the ActionScript to control the Playback buttons.

Exercise 13.5   Setting Up the Playback Buttons

You'll set up the playback controls using event handlers. Each of the playback controls is a movie clip. From left to right, they have been assigned the instance names: toBeginning, rewindVideo, pauseVideo, playVideo, and toEnd.

1. Double-click on the video_mc to open it in Symbol-Editing mode. Add an Actions layer with a stop() action in the first frame.

2. Return to the main Timeline. The simplest actions are for the Play and Pause buttons, so you'll do those first.

3. Before you do anything else, you need to give the video_mc movie clip an instance name—go ahead and use the Properties Inspector to give it an instance name of **bobVideo** (see Figure 13.9).

Figure 13.9   Assigning an instance name to the movie clip on the Stage enables you to control the video embedded in it.

If each of the playback controls were buttons, you could simply attach the code to control them to the buttons, but you're going to take a different approach. All of the code that controls the playback of the video will be in the first frame of the main Timeline.

4. Select frame 1 of the Actions layer on the main Timeline and open the Actions panel.

   In Flash MX, movie clip objects can now recognize mouse events using the event handlers. Whenever you use an event handler in Flash, you also need to create a function that tells your movie clip what to do when the event fires.

5. To activate the Play button, all you need to do is add the following code to the main Timeline:

```
FplayVideo.onPress = function() {
      bobVideo.play();
}
```

6. The code that controls the Pause button is very similar. After the last curly brace, add the following code:

```
pauseVideo.onPress = function() {
      bobVideo.stop();
}
```

7. Save and test your movie. Bob should start begging when you press the playVideo button, and he should shut up when you press the pauseVideo button.

8. The toBeginning button is another easy one. On press, your movie needs to go back to frame 1 and stop. Add the following to your Actions list:

```
toBeginning.onPress = function() {
      bobVideo.gotoAndStop(1);
}
```

9. The next button you need to deal with is the toEnd button. This one is also easy—you can use the value for _totalframes to find out where the last frame is. Just enter the following code:

```
toEnd.onPress = function() {
      bobVideo.gotoAndStop(bobVideo._totalframes);
}
```

Because the last frame of the video is, in fact, the same image as the first frame of the video, you won't see any change going from the toEnd button to the toBeginning button.

The only button that presents any kind of challenge is the Rewind button. There are a couple of ways you can set this up. You can set the Rewind button so that it rewinds for as long as the button is pressed, or you can set it up so that once you press the button, it keeps rewinding. Either way, you need to have an action that is continuously updating, so you're going to be looking at an onEnterFrame event handler inside of your onPress event handler.

10. When the Rewind button is clicked, you want the bobVideo to continually move backward by one frame. That's easy enough to do—you just continually set the value of the frame to be the number of the current frame minus one. Your code will look like this:

```
rewindVideo.onPress = function() {
      bobVideo.onEnterFrame = function() {
            bobVideo.gotoAndStop(bobVideo._currentframe -1);
      }
}
```

There is one problem with this—once you fire off the onEnterFrame handler for an object, it just keeps running, which has the effect of disabling all of your other buttons. It doesn't actually disable the buttons, but since it's running continuously and the other events are only fired on press, the effect is the same. It's also not very efficient. You need to have a way to terminate the object's onEnterFrame event handler either when the Rewind button is released, or when another button is pressed. You can terminate the onEnterFrame handler by setting its value to null.

11. To keep things simple, set the onEnterFrame event to null when the rewind button is released. Enter the following code:

```
rewindVideo.onRelease = function() {
      bobVideo.onEnterFrame = null;
}
```

12. Save and test your movie. Now all of your buttons should be functional. If you don't want to terminate the onEnterFrame handler when the Rewind button is released, you can add that same line:

```
bobVideo.onEnterFrame = null;
```

This matches the first line inside of the other event handlers. For example:

```
playVideo.onPress = function() {
      bobVideo.onEnterFrame = null;
      bobVideo.play();
}
```

Adding playback controls isn't the only thing you can do with a video inside a movie clip. Because you're working with a movie clip, you can apply any of the transformations and actions that you can normally apply to a movie clip, such as skewing, tweening, rotating, scaling, alpha changes, brightness changes, or color transformations.

Play around with making some changes—use the Free Transform tool to rotate or skew the bobVideo movie clip and play it back. Try adding in some color effects, such as changing the alpha or brightness. What the heck—try tweening your video under a mask, or try masking your video with a dynamic mask. You really do have a lot of options.

Another thing you could do is create a movie in Flash, import it into another movie, and use some of Flash's built-in components to play around with it.

Using *loadMovie()* with Flash Videos

Since videos tend to be on the large size, an option you might want to consider is creating the video as its own SWF file and then using `loadMovie()` to add it to your existing project. In Exercise 13.6, you're going to create a movie, load it into another movie, and use some of the Flash components to create a movie bookmarking system.

Exercise 13.6   Creating a Movie Bookmarking System

For this movie, you can import any video you might have on your system. If you have QuickTime Pro, you can actually save video trailers from the QuickTime site and use one of those. Otherwise, you're stuck using the talkingBob.avi file that you've been working with.

1. Open a new file and save it to your hard drive as **videoDemo.fla**.
2. Import your video of choice (you can always use the talkingBob.avi file in the Examples/Chapter13 folder on the companion CD).
3. In the Import Video Settings dialog box, make sure to take note of video size (height and width) under Output Properties—you're going to resize your movie to match your video.
4. Once the import is complete, resize your movie to match the size of your video and use the Properties Inspector to reposition the video at X=0, Y=0.
5. Publish your movie. Close the videoDemo.fla—you won't need it anymore.
6. Create a new movie and name it **videoBookmark.fla**. Save it to the same directory on your hard drive where you saved videoDemo.swf.
7. The first thing you'll do is create a placeholder movie clip to import your video into. For positioning purposes, you're going to make it the same size as your video. Alternatively, you could place a blank movie clip on the Stage or use the `createEmptyMovieClip()` method.
8. Rename layer 1 to **Video** and select the Rectangle tool. Draw an unfilled rectangle on the Stage.
9. Use the Properties Inspector to resize the rectangle to the same size as the videoDemo.swf you created earlier.
10. Convert the rectangle to a movie clip (F8), set the registration point to top-left, name it **videoMovie**, and position it on the Stage at X=10, Y=10.
11. Use the Properties Inspector to give the movie an instance name of **video_mc** (see Figure 13.10).

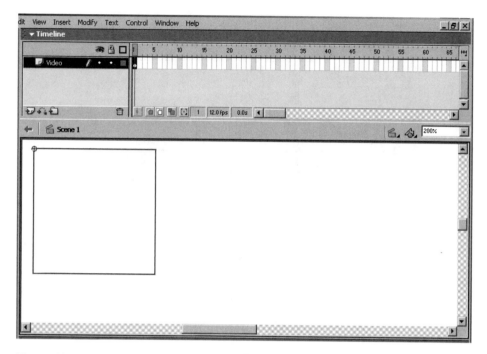

Figure 13.10   The video_mc movie clip is used to load an external file.

12. Add a new layer to your movie and name it **Actions**.

    In the Actions panel, you're going to set up the call to loadMovie().

13. To load your video, enter the following code in the Actions panel:

    ```
    video_mc.loadMovie("videoDemo.swf");
    ```

14. Save and test your movie. The video should load very nicely into the video_mc movie clip and begin playing. If the videoDemo.swf doesn't load, you probably forgot to save your file before you published it—remember that both the videoDemo.swf and videoBookmark.swf files need to reside in the same directory.

In Exercise 13.7, you'll add a button that will be context sensitive to play and pause the movie. You'll use one of Flash MX's built-in components—the pushbutton.

Exercise 13.7   Adding Play and Pause Functionality with the Pushbutton Component.

Flash MX has a bunch of nifty built-in components. Why not go ahead and make use of one to add a Play/Pause toggle for your video?

1. Add a new layer to your movie and name it **Buttons**.

2. Open the Components panel (Window > Components) and drag an instance of the pushbutton object onto the Stage. Position it beneath the video_mc movie clip (see Figure 13.11).

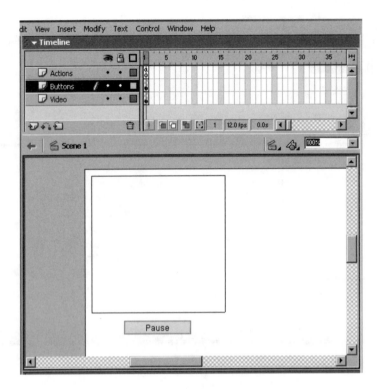

Figure 13.11   The Components panel has seven pre-built UI components for you to use.

3. Select the pushbutton you just placed on the Stage. In the Properties Inspector, make the following changes:

   Label: **Pause**
   Click Handler: **onToggle**

4. In the Properties Inspector, give your new button an instance name of **toggle_mc**.

5. Save and test your file. The videoDemo.swf should load and start playing. The button will press, but it won't work yet.

6. You need to set up a variable to track whether your movie is playing—the default value will be `true`. After the last line you added in the Actions panel, add the following:

   ```
   isPlaying = true;
   ```

   Next, you'll write a function that will toggle the Pause button between Pause and Play, and actually pause or play your video.

7. First, set up the shell for the `onToggle()` function. You should still be on frame 1 of the Actions layer. Enter the following code after the last line you entered:

```
function onToggle() {

}
```

In between the curly braces, you are going to create a conditional statement that will check to see if the `isPlaying` variable is `true`. If it is, you'll toggle it to `false`, and tell the video_mc to stop playing. Then you'll switch the label that's currently on your button from Pause to Play.

8. Add the following code between the curly braces:

```
if (isPlaying) {
// if the movie is playing, set the isPlaying value to false
    isPlaying = false;
// stop the video
    video_mc.stop();
// use the setLabel function of the pushbutton object
// to set a new label at runtime.
    toggle_mc.setLabel("Play");
}
```

So far so good, but you need to be able to handle what happens if `isPlaying` is currently set to `false`. That part is easy. Just copy the lines between the curly braces of the if statement you just entered and reverse their values.

9. To set up the else statement, modify your code to look like this:

```
if (isPlaying) {
// if the movie is playing, set the isPlaying value to false
    isPlaying = false;
// stop the video
    video_mc.stop();
// use the setLabel function of the pushbutton object
// to set a new label at runtime.
    toggle_mc.setLabel("Play");
}else{

}
```

10. Now copy the three lines of code (you don't need to carry the comments over) from your if statement, paste them between the curly brackets of your else statement, and modify them as follows:

```
isPlaying = true;
video_mc.play();
toggle_mc.setLabel("Pause");
```

Your complete code for frame 1 of the Actions layer should look like Listing 13.1.

Listing 13.1   Completed Code for Actions Layer: Frame 1

```
//load video into movie
video_mc.loadMovie("videoDemo.swf");

//track state of movie
isPlaying = true;

function onToggle() {
      if (isPlaying) {
// if the movie is playing, set the isPlaying value to false
            isPlaying = false;
// stop the video
            video_mc.stop();
// use the setLabel function of the pushbutton object
// to set a new label at runtime
            toggle_mc.setLabel("play");
      }else{
            isPlaying = true;
            video_mc.play();
            toggle_mc.setLabel("Pause");
      }
}
```

11. Save and test your movie. Now you should be able to play and pause your movie—and the button should automatically toggle states.

But why stop there? If you're using a really cool trailer, you might want to bookmark different scenes in the trailer so that you can jump right to them. It doesn't take much to add that bit of functionality, and Exercise 13.8 shows you how.

Exercise 13.8   Setting Up the Bookmarking Functionality

You can use another of Flash MX's built-in components—the listBox to store your bookmarks.

1. Add a new layer to your movie and name it **List Box**.
2. From your Library or the Components panel (Window > Components) drag a copy of the listBox component onto the Stage. Position it to the right of the video_mc clip.

Note

Once you drag one component into your movie, the whole Flash UI components folder is in your Library. Although this will increase the size of your FLA, it won't affect the size of your final SWF.

3. Scale the clip box, as shown in Figure 13.12.

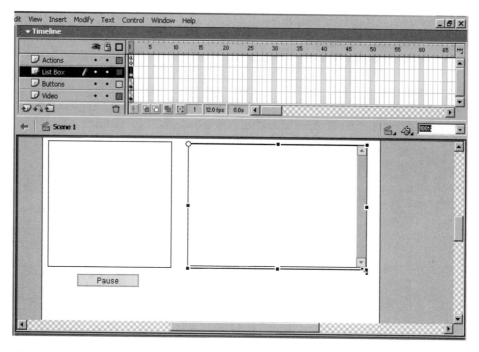

Figure 13.12   Position the listBox component to the right of your video_mc movie clip.

4. In the Properties Inspector, give the listBox an instance name of
   bookmarkList_mc.

5. Change the Change Handler in the Property Inspector to onSelectBookmark. Yes,
   you'll be writing another function.

   You're going to add and name bookmarks, so you need a text input box to capture the name.

6. Add a new layer and name it **Text Box**. Draw a text box under the listBox you
   added to the Stage. Change the properties for the text box to this:

   Input: **Text**
   Instance name: **bookmarkName_txt**

   Also, make sure your text color is different from your background (duh, I know,
   but it's a common mistake), and select Show Border Around Text.

   Next, add the button that you'll press to add your bookmark.

7. Select the Buttons layer.

8. Add another pushButton component to the Stage from the Components panel or
   from your Library. Position it under the text box you just added.

9. In the Properties Inspector, change the following (see Figure 13.13):

Label: **Add Bookmark**
Click Handler: **onAddBookmark**

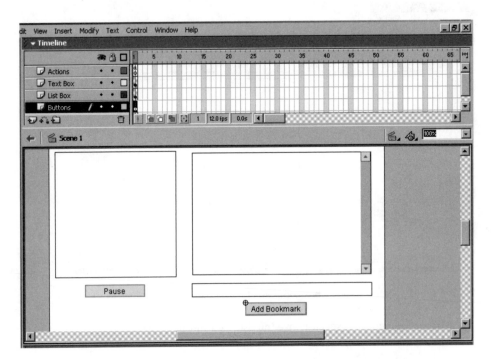

Figure 13.13   The input text and Add Bookmark buttons are positioned just beneath the listBox.

Okay, now it's back to the Actions panel to add in the two new handler functions you just referred to.

10. Select frame 1 of the Actions layer.

11. After the last line of code, add the shell for the onAddBookmark() function. Enter the following:

```
function onAddBookmark() {

}
```

12. You only want to add a bookmark if a name for the bookmark has been entered in the Input Text box, so first test to make sure the box isn't empty. You just need to check the Text property of the Text field (remember that Text fields can be treated like objects now). Within the curly braces, enter the following:

```
if (bookmarkName_txt.text != "") {

}
```

So what should happen next? You need to add the bookmark whose name you just entered into the Text Input field into the list when you click on the Add Bookmark button. The listBox has an instance name of bookmarkList_mc, so you can use the addItem() method of the listBox component to pass in the text from the Text field and the current frame of the video you are trying to bookmark.

13. Between the curly braces of the if statement, add the following code:

```
bookmarkList_mc.addItem(bookmarkName_txt.text, video_mc.
_currentframe);
```

14. The only other thing you need to do here is empty the text field after you've added your bookmark to the list. Just enter the following line immediately after the previous line:

```
BookmarkText_txt.text = "";
```

Your completed onAddBookmark function should look like this (the third and fourth lines are actually one line):

```
function onAddBookmark() {
        if (bookmarkName_txt.text != "") {
                bookmarkList_mc.addItem(bookmarkName_txt.text,
video_mc._currentframe);
                bookmarkName_txt.text = "";
        }
}
```

15. Save and test your movie.

Now you can pause and play your movie and add in bookmarks (see Figure 13.14), but the bookmarks don't actually do anything. You'll fix that in Exercise 13.9.

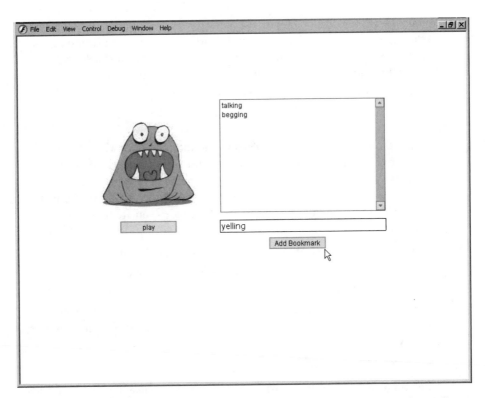

Figure 13.14   Now you can play and pause your movie and add named bookmarks to a list.

Exercise 13.9   Activating the Bookmarks

This final function you're going to create, `onSelectBookmark()`, is a little interesting—you're going to do something a little different. You need to pass a reference to the listBox component in the function call.

1. You should still be in frame 1 of the Actions layer. After the last line of code in the Actions panel, set up the shell for this function by entering this code:

```
function onSelectBookmark(obj) {

}
```

2. Now all you want to do is tell the video_mc clip to go to and play whatever the value of the selected bookmark is in the listBox. Use the `getValue()` method of the listBox component to do this. Add the following code between the curly braces:

```
video_mc.gotoAndPlay(obj.getValue());
```

Then add two more lines:

```
isPlaying=true;
toggle_mc.setLabel("Pause");
```

This will keep the label on the button up to date and the onToggle() function working properly.

3. Save and test your movie. Go ahead and let the video play out to a frame you like. You can pause the video, type in a bookmark name, and click Add Bookmark. Create several bookmarks. To reset the video to your bookmark of choice, just click on the bookmark in the list. That's it! Now you have your own bookmarking system.

Just in case you're having any problems, the completed code is shown in Listing 13.2.

Listing 13.2   The Complete Bookmarking System Code

```
//load video into movie
video_mc.loadMovie("videoDemo.swf");

//track state of movie
isPlaying = true;

function onToggle() {
        if (isPlaying) {
// if the movie is playing, set the isPlaying value to false
                isPlaying = false;
// stop the video
                video_mc.stop();
// use the setLabel function of the pushbutton object
// to set a new label at runtime
                toggle_mc.setLabel("play");
        }else{
                isPlaying = true;
                video_mc.play();
                toggle_mc.setLabel("pause");
        }
}

function onAddBookmark() {
        if (bookmarkName_txt.text != "") {
                bookmarkList_mc.addItem(bookmarkName_txt.text,
video_mc._currentframe);
                bookmarkName_txt.text = "";
        }
}

function onSelectBookmark(obj) {
        video_mc.gotoAndPlay(obj.getValue());
        isPlaying=true;
        toggle_mc.setLabel("Pause");
}
```

As mentioned earlier in this chapter, Flash MX takes advantage of the basic Sorenson Spark codec. In this next section, you'll look at how you can use Sorenson Squeeze to create even more highly compressed SWF or FLV files.

Using Sorenson Squeeze for Flash MX to Process Video

The basic version of the Sorenson Spark codec is embedded in Flash MX. To access the more advanced features of the codec, you have to purchase Sorenson Squeeze for Flash MX, which, at this writing, sells for $299. Sorenson Squeeze gives you a higher level of control over the compression process, including variable bit rate compression, so you can create the smallest files possible. You can find Sorenson Squeeze at http://www.sorenson.com.

It would be easy to write an entire chapter just on Sorenson Squeeze, but since this is an additional product, and not built directly into Flash MX, you'll just get an overview of some of its basic features (see Figure 13.15).

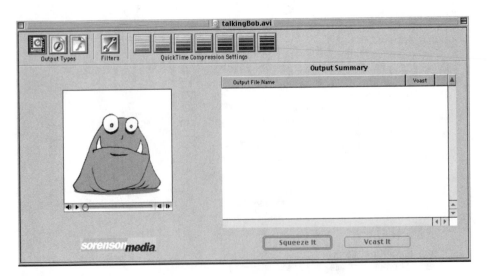

Figure 13.15   The Sorenson Squeeze interface.

One of the big differences between the basic Sorenson Spark built into Flash and Sorenson Squeeze is that Squeeze offers two-pass variable bit rate (VBR) compression, whereas Flash MX offers only basic compression. With two-pass VBR, Sorensen Squeeze analyzes the whole movie first and then compresses it. This takes about twice as long as compressing at a constant bit rate or at a single pass with variable bit rate, but results in much higher quality.

Squeeze also offers a series of preset data rate compression schemes that you can use if you are not familiar with compressing video. These compression schemes use different settings based on whether you are compressing the video as a QuickTime movie, an SWF file, or an FLV file. The default settings for both SWF and FLV files, which are optimized for bandwidth, are outlined in the following table. Even if you're not planning to use Sorenson Squeeze, these settings give you good guidelines for setting your Sorenson Spark import settings inside of Flash MX (see Figure 13.16).

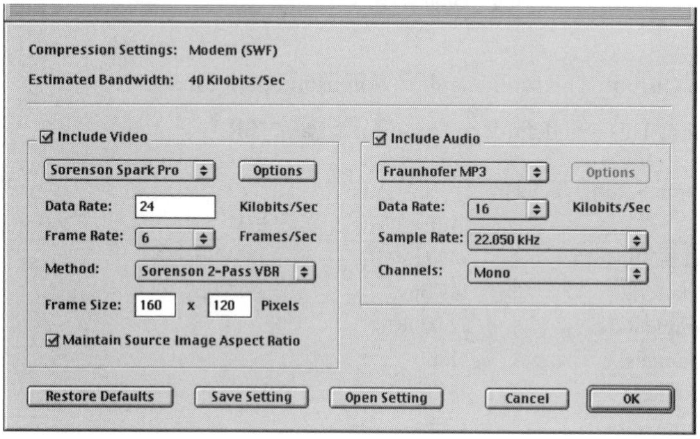

Figure 13.16   The Sorenson Squeeze default Compression Settings for exporting a SWF for viewing over a Modem connection.

Compression Setting: Modem
Estimated Bandwidth: 39Kbps
SWF & FLV

Audio Output	Fraunhofer MP3
Data Rate	8Kbps
Sample Rate	11.025Khz
Channels	Mono
Video Output	Sorenson Spark
Data Rate	31Kbps
Frame Rate	6fps
Method	Sorenson 2-pass VBR
Frame Size	160W×120H

Once you get past the Modem settings, several of the settings will change for SWF versus FLV files. The following settings don't change:

- **Audio Output.** For SWFs, the default will always be Fraunhofer MP3. For FLVs, the default will be Raw Audio.

Note

You might be wondering why FLVs default to Raw Audio, which we all know leads to huge file sizes. It's because you'll always be using FLVs inside of Flash or other products that will handle the MP3 compression for you.

- **Video Output.** This will default to Sorenson Spark for both.

- **Method.** This will default to Sorenson 2-Pass VBR.

Compression Setting: ISDN

	SWF	FLV
Estimated Bandwidth	94Kbps	430Kbps
Audio Data Rate	16Kbps	352Kbps
Audio Sample Rate	22.050Khz	
Audio Channels	Mono	
Video Data Rate	78Kbps	
Video Frame Rate	1:3fps	
Video Frame Size	240W×180H	

Compression Setting: Broadband_Low

	SWF	FLV
Estimated Bandwidth	196Kbps	869Kbps
Audio Data Rate	32Kbps	705Kpbs
Audio Sample Rate	22.050Khz	
Audio Channels	Mono	
Video Data Rate	164Kbps	
Video Frame Rate	1:2fps	
Video Frame Size	240W×180H	

Compression Setting: Broadband

	SWF	FLV
Estimated Bandwidth	298Kbps	955Kbps
Audio Data Rate	48Kbps	705Kpbs
Audio Sample Rate	44.100Khz	
Audio Channels	Stereo	
Video Data Rate	250Kbps	
Video Frame Rate	1:2fps	
Video Frame Size	320W×240H	

Compression Setting: Broadband_High

	SWF	FLV
Estimated Bandwidth	415Kbps	1762Kbps
Audio Data Rate	64Kbps	1411Kbps
Audio Sample Rate	44.100Khz	
Audio Channels	Stereo	
Video Data Rate	351Kbps	
Video Frame Rate	1:2fps	
Video Frame Size	320W×240H	

Compression Setting: LAN_CD

	SWF	FLV
Estimated Bandwidth	878Kbps	2161Kbps
Audio Data Rate	128Kbps	1411Kpbs
Audio Sample Rate	44.100Khz	
Audio Channels	Stereo	
Video Data Rate	750Kbps	
Video Frame Rate	1:1fps	
Video Frame Size	480W×360H	

Compression Setting: CD_High_Quality

	SWF	FLV
Estimated Bandwidth	1104Kbps	2387Kbps
Audio Data Rate	128Kbps	1411Kpbs
Audio Sample Rate	44.100Khz	
Audio Channels	Stereo	
Video Data Rate	976Kbps	
Video Frame Rate	1:1fps	
Video Frame Size	480W×360H	

You can also customize a number of the compression settings if none of the presets suits your needs. For several of the presets you can customize, see the following list:

- **Audio Data Rate (SWF only – Kilobits/Second).** 8Kbps–192Kbps
- **Audio Sample Rate.** 11.025Khz, 22.050Khz, 44,100Khz
- **Audio Channels.** Mono or Stereo
- **Video Data Rate (Kilobits/Second).** 48–1600
- **Video Frame Rate (Frames/Second).** 30, 29.97, 25, 24, 15, 12.5, 12, 10, 8, 7.5, 6, 5, 1, 1:1, 1:2, 1:3

- **Compression Method.** Sorenson 2-Pass VBR, Constant Bit Rate
- **Frame Size (pixels).** Width (160–640), Height (120–480)

If you are serious about delivering video in Flash and are interested in producing the smallest file sizes possible, you should consider investing in Sorenson Squeeze.

Summary

The new and long-awaited video import options in Flash MX are impressive. The ability to fine-tune settings for different bandwidths is enormously useful to developers. When you combine video with all of the other functionality in Flash MX, you have the capability to create some impressive new tools. Just remember that video is still video—it's a bandwidth hog. Keep your videos short and focused, and take advantage of the ability to create videos as separate SWF files and load them as needed. I can't wait to see all of the applications for this feature people are going to come up with—including you!

Chapter 14

Creating 3D Effects in Flash

Flash approaches 3D animation in much the same way that the program approaches other visual technologies: Flash simulates it. Even though Flash is actually a 2D program, it handles 3D very well. It possesses all the tools necessary to control the elements crucial to 3D animation, such as shading, perspective, and motion.

There are a number of ways you can approach working with 3D in Flash. You can use shading tricks to make an object appear to be three dimensional. You can use tweening and perspective to give the appearance of 3D motion. You can also use ActionScript to create complex 3D movement that would be difficult, if not impossible, to create in any other way.

Flash by itself isn't your only option. There are a number of programs that you can use to work with three-dimensional wireframe models and export directly to SWF files. The first two of these to come along were Swift 3D by Electric Rain and Vecta3D by Ideaworks3D Limited. Both Swift 3D and Vecta3D come as standalone packages or as plug-ins for the higher-end 3D modeling programs. Specifically, Vecta3D has a plug-in for 3ds max; Swift 3D has plug-ins for 3ds max, LightWave 3D, and SoftImage XSI. These plug-ins enable you to export directly into SWF format for import into your Flash project. Using these programs, you can quickly and seamlessly integrate animated wireframe models with generated light sources and use the output in your Flash movies. Whether you're working with an interface or a 3D technical illustration, the potential uses for 3D models in Flash are obvious.

Automatically generating lighting and perspective with one of these programs brings added power and flexibility to Flash. However, sometimes being able to do things the old-fashioned way is still useful and often necessary. An understanding of how to manipulate gradients based on light sources and how those relate to perspective and motion will always be indispensable tools for you to fall back on when using Flash for 3D projects.

In this chapter, you will learn about the following:

- **Using gradients to create 3D effects**. You'll take a look at how you can use gradients to create convincing 3D effects in Flash.

- **Using third-party 3D software**. You'll take a look at how you can use third-party software to create 3D movies that you can import into Flash.

- **Using scaling and motion paths for 3D motion.** You will simulate dimensional motion using scaling and motion paths.

- **Using layers, shading, and multiple speed scrolling to create perspective.** You will animate your backgrounds and props on the stage by using some creative tweening and changing the scrolling speeds of your various background elements to create a three-dimensional scene.

- **Using ActionScript to create 3D motion.** For more complex 3D movement, you can use ActionScript and a simple 3D event engine to control movement of objects on the Stage.

Using Gradient Fills to Simulate 3D

You can use Flash's capabilities to convert lines to fills and then use gradients for those fills to give your objects a very nice 3D fill. Setting this up is a multi-stage process, but it's pretty simple.

The basic steps are as follows:

1. Start with a line drawing (see Figure 14.1).

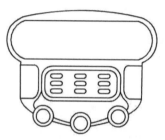

Figure 14.1   The initial design was a simple line drawing.

2. Add the basic colors (see Figure 14.2).

Figure 14.2   When the line drawing is complete, the next step is to work out the basic color scheme.

3. Add in the basic gradients (see Figure 14.3).

Figure 14.3   Use gradients to give the existing fills a more three-dimensional feel.

4. Selectively convert certain lines to fills and apply appropriate gradients (see Figure 14.4).

Figure 14.4   The final step is what really unifies this piece—selectively converting some of the lines to fills and adding gradients.

Perhaps the greatest point of interest here is that you can do away with that black-lined, cartoon look and achieve rendered-quality results by selectively converting certain lines to fills (Modify > Shape > Convert Lines to Fills) and then applying the appropriate gradients. Like everything else, if used with proper lighting in mind, it creates a very solid, tight look and 3D feel.

This is one of those cases in which practice is your best teacher. In Exercise 14.1, you get to play around with converting lines to fills and adding gradients to the fills.

Exercise 14.1   Converting Lines to Gradient Fills

By converting lines to fills and adding gradients, you give your object a much smoother and more realistic look.

1. Open linestofills.fla from the Examples/Chapter14 folder on the companion CD and save it to your hard drive. The interface has already been set up with some basic gradients.

2. Use the Zoom tool to drag a marquee around the two button slots on the lower left of the uncompleted interface.

    As you can see in Figure 14.5, the two button slots look significantly different. The one on the right uses simple solid lines. The one on the left uses a line converted to a fill with a gradient.

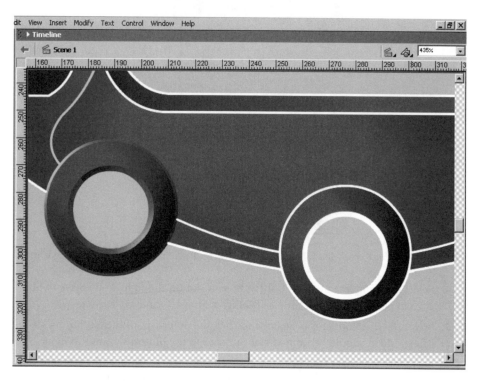

Figure 14.5   The close-up of the two lower-left buttons shows the difference between solid lines and lines that have been converted to fills with a gradient added.

Pay attention to how the gradient is set up. The light source is to the upper left. That means that the outer rim of the button will show a highlight on its upper-left edge. Conversely, the inner rim shows a highlight on its lower-right edge. In the next step, you'll set up the second button to match the first.

3. Select the Eyedropper tool and click on the gradient in the outer rim of the button on the left. Open the Color Mixer (Shift + F2) and look at the way the gradient is set up. It's a four-color linear gradient, with the leftmost gradient well being a pale pinkish-red and the rightmost gradient well being nearly black. (See Figure 14.6.) The Hex colors for the four gradient wells are as follows:

   Left: **#FFCCCC**
   Left center: **#F80000**
   Right center: **#660000**
   Right: **#2F0000**

Figure 14.6   The Color Mixer shows the setup for the gradient that you'll be working with.

4. Select the complete outer rim of the button slot on the right. You'll have to Shift-click to get all the pieces. Choose Modify > Shape > Convert Lines to Fills.

5. Select the Eyedropper tool again, and click the outer rim of the left button slot. The gradient should be immediately applied to the button slot on the right.

   Switch to the Arrow tool (V), and click on the Stage to deselect the gradient fill. You'll probably need to adjust the alignment of the gradient a bit.

6. Select the Fill Transform tool. Click the gradient that you just applied, and play around with the settings (rotate and expand) until you have the effect you want.

There's no real science to this; you just have to eyeball it. Use the first button slot as your reference point. Ensure the Lock Fill button isn't selected.

Figure 14.7 shows the rotated and expanded Transform Fill bounding box.

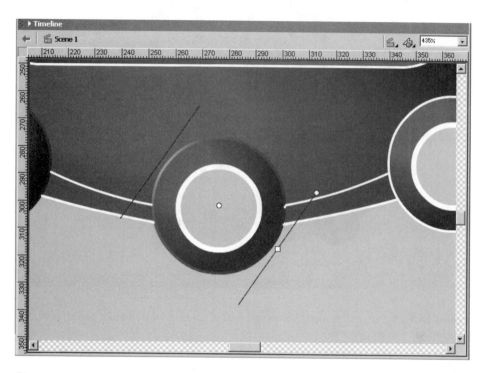

Figure 14.7   Use Transform Fill to rotate and expand the gradient for your new fill until it accurately reflects the light source.

7. Repeat Steps 4–6 for the inner rim of the button slot. This time, you'll rotate the gradient with the Transform Fill tool so that the lower right is highlighted.

8. You can continue in the same vein for the rest of the lines, not just the button slots.

When you compare the file that you started with the completed file (see Figure 14.8), you can clearly see how converting lines to gradient fills dramatically alters the look and feel of the entire piece. In fact, many people might question whether your interface was done in Flash at all.

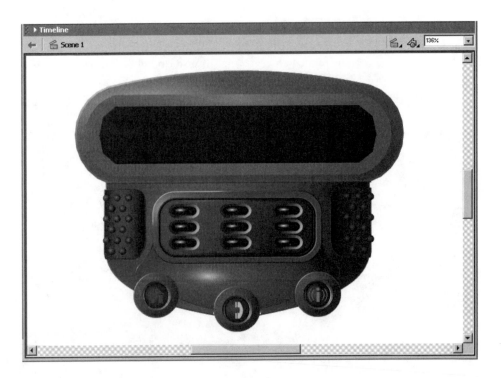

Figure 14.8   When used properly, converting lines to gradient fills can add a nearly photo-realistic feel to your Flash project.

In the next section, you'll take a look at creating a rotating panel for the interface using third-party software.

Using Third-Party 3D Software

Perhaps the most common use of 3D–generated animations is rotating text or logos in a Flash-generated user interface. Although these work as animated decorative elements, they can also be a functional part of the interface. With a little planning and forethought, any number of simple Swift 3D animations can be incorporated into menus, buttons, levers, and doors, and sliding, folding, or flipping panels. But, remember to use restraint. If you've got everything on your page madly spinning and rotating, you're just going to distract your users, not engage them. This is a case of a little going a long way. It's like a simple black dress and pearls—keep it classy and elegant, not garish.

Both Swift 3D and Vecta3D are nifty and inexpensive little programs that almost any Flash developer can afford as part of a toolkit. These packages enable you to quickly import and animate 3ds max objects, EPS or AI files, primitive shapes, or text, and then export the animation as an SWF for use in Flash.

Although both programs allow you to animate models of significant complexity, they're most effectively used for simpler, low-polygon (surface facet) shapes that work well with rotational type animations.

Aside from being fast and easy to use, one of the greatest benefits of these tools is that they automatically generate frame by frame the effect of light, color, and motion in a way that would be extremely difficult, if not impossible, to do by any other means. At the same time, after the shapes and animations are imported into Flash, they remain completely editable. For the examples in this chapter, you'll use Swift 3D, but Vecta3D would handle the project very nicely as well.

Animating a File Using Swift 3D

Because you might not have Swift 3D installed on your system, this is just an overview of how to take a static file originally created in 3ds max and quickly animate it using Swift 3D. The process would be similar for Vecta3D. If you're going to work through these steps using Swift 3D, it's a good idea to look at the finished product so that you understand what you're attempting to create. To see the rotating panel in action, double-click the plateInterface.swf file in the Examples/Chapter14 folder. When you've had a look at the file, close it and open Swift 3D. (See Figure 14.9.)

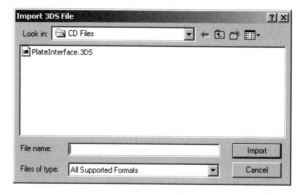

Figure 14.9   The Swift 3D interface displays the Import 3Ds File dialog box.

1. Create a new Swift 3D document from an existing 3ds file by choosing File > New from 3DS.

2. Click the Browse button, and browse to the PlateInterface.3ds file in the Examples/Chapter14 folder on the companion CD. This file was created in 3ds max. Click Import. (See Figure 14.10.)

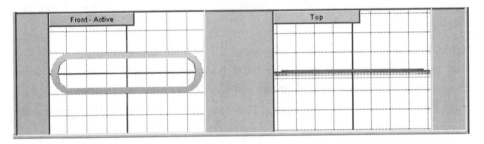

Figure 14.10   The PlateINTERFACE.3ds file has been imported into the Swift 3D editing environment.

3. Add color to the imported object by dragging one of the red color spheres onto the model on the Stage.

4. You can use a drag-and-drop behavior to get your model to rotate vertically. Select Vertical Down from the Regular Spins, and drag it onto your model. This creates a 20-frame 360° rotation.

5. Click the Play button to watch your image rotate.

6. Save your file as a T3D (Swift 3D) file.

7. Switch to the Preview and Export Editor and click the Generate Entire Animation button.

8. After the animation has rendered, click the Export Entire Animation button and save the SWF file.

At this point, you're ready to import the new SWF file into Flash.

In Exercise 14.2, you'll take the output from the Swift3D file and import it into the Flash file you created in the previous exercise as the rotating main display panel.

Exercise 14.2   Incorporating an Animated 3D SWF into Your Flash Movie

You'll use a completed version of the 3D interface you created in the exercise as the base file. Then you'll import the 3D sequence that was generated by Swift 3D and incorporate it into the interface.

1. Open rotate.fla from the Examples/Chapter14 folder on the companion CD.

You want to import the rotating panel you created in the last exercise, but you don't want it to be on the main Timeline. It should be in its own movie clip.

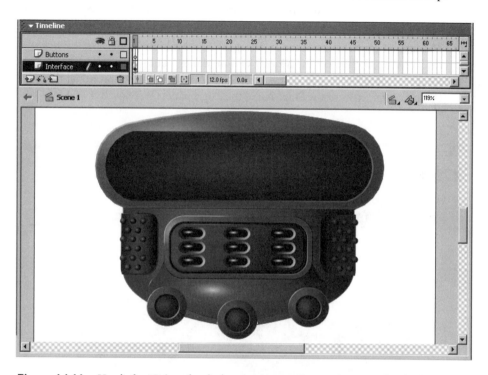

Figure 14.11   Here's the 3D interface before you import the rotating pane. (In the file, the background is blue, not white.)

2. Create a new movie clip (Insert > New Symbol) and name it **panel_mc**. Click OK.

3. Rename the current layer **Panel**. Choose File > Import and select the PlateInterface.swf you generated, or you can use the one in the Examples/Chapter14 folder on the CD.

The rotating panel imports as a frame-by-frame animation on 19 frames.

4. If the SWF was exported in Flash 5 format, you're good to go. If it was exported in Flash 4 format, there will be an extra frame with text on it in frame 1. If that is the case, delete frame 1 by selecting it, right- or Ctrl-clicking, and choosing Remove Frames.

This frame is inserted by Swift3D to get around an export issue with Swift3D and Flash 4. You can safely get rid of it.

5. Scrub through the frames. You will occasionally get one or two frames that don't render properly. Remove any bad frames.

6. You're going to need to modify this clip—you want all the frames centered on the movie clip's registration point (crosshair), and you need to break them apart so that you can fill the center with color.

   To make all your changes at once, select the Edit Multiple Frames button beneath the Timeline; then select the Modify Onion Markers button and choose Onion All. (See Figure 14.12.) Using the Arrow tool, drag a marquee around all the panels and center them to the Stage using the Align panel (Window > Panels > Align).

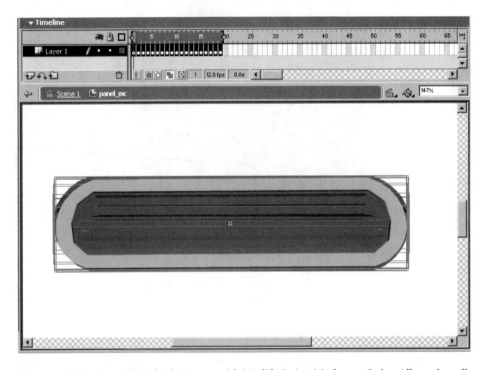

Figure 14.12   Use Edit Multiple Frames with Modify Onion Markers > Onion All to select all of the images on all of the frames.

7. Before you deselect your mass of panels, choose Modify > Break Apart. Turn off the Edit Multiple Frames button.

8. One more bit of prep work here: You need to fill the center of the panels with black. Select the Paint Bucket with a black fill, and fill the centers frame by frame. Make sure that you deselect the panel before you use your Paint Bucket. The keyboard shortcuts are useful here: V for the Selection tool, K for the Paint Bucket, and . (period key) to advance a frame at a time.

9. Go back to your main Timeline and add a new layer also called **Panel**. Drag the panel_mc movie clip from the Library onto the Stage, and center it over the open window on the Interface. (See Figure 14.13)

10. Scale the movie clip until it is the same size as the open window.

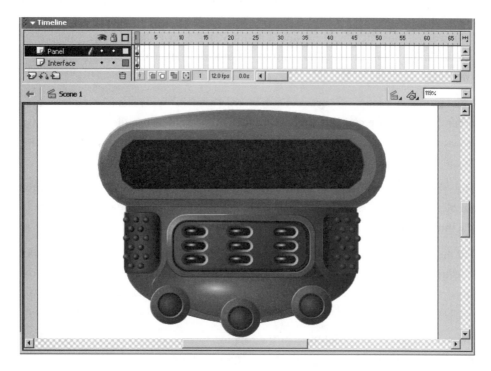

Figure 14.13   The rotating panel is in place in the 3D interface.

11. Save and test your movie. You now have a rotating 3D element inside your Flash movie.

That's all you'll be doing with this interface in these exercises, but think about what else you could do with the file. You could easily set up the buttons on the interface to control not only the motion of the rotating panel, but also any content you might want to have appear there. Go ahead—play around with this file and have some fun.

Yet another way to simulate 3D in Flash is to use a little visual trickery along with scaling and brightness changes.

Using Scaling and Paths for 3D Motion

Although light and motion are the primary ingredients of a 3D animation, you can achieve respectable results without ActionScripting or 3D models. Using the gradients, scaling, and motion path capabilities that already exist in Flash, it's a snap to put together convincing 3D animations with minimal wear and tear on your brain. In the section, "Controlling Movement with Advanced ActionScript" later in this chapter, you'll create a much more complex 3D motion using ActionScript rather than motion guides and tweening.

This lesson uses a couple of tricks in Flash to make a smaller sphere look as if it is rotating around a larger sphere. Take a moment to look at the final source file, satellite_final.fla. When you test the movie, you will notice that the two smaller satellite images rotate convincingly around the larger sphere. Now take a close look at the source file.

Hide the first layer, TopSphere, and drag your playhead across the screen. Did you see the problem? Without this layer, the small satellites cut in front of the main large sphere in the middle. Now "unhide" the layer and take a look at the Timeline.

For the first several frames, another copy of the large sphere is placed so that the smaller satellites are hidden. Then a blank keyframe is inserted to remove this sphere so that the smaller satellites appear to pass in front of the larger sphere. Finally, another copy of the large sphere is put in place to hide the smaller spheres and simulate the complete orbit.

Changing the scale and brightness of the rotating spheres adds to the 3D effect. These rules have been stated before, but they bear repeating now:

- Objects closer to you generally appear to be brighter in color than objects that are farther away.

- Objects closer to you generally appear to be larger than objects that are farther away.

- Objects closer to you generally appear to move faster than objects that are farther away.

You can use these concepts to your advantage. You'll be experimenting with these techniques in Exercise 14.3.

Exercise 14.3   Using Scaling and Motion Paths to Simulate 3D Motion

Now that you know what concepts you can use to simulate 3D motion, it's time to start applying them.

1. Open satellite.fla from the Examples/Chapter14 folder on the companion CD. Rename Layer 1 **BottomSphere**.

2. Drag a copy of the satellite movie clip onto the Stage, and use the Transform panel (Window > Transform), with Constrain selected, to resize it to 600%.

3. Add a second layer to the Stage and name it **TopSphere**. Copy the existing satellite clip and choose Edit > Paste in Place to paste it into the second layer. Now the two spheres are positioned with one directly over the other.

4. Add a layer between the top and bottom layers, and name it **Moon**. With the Moon layer selected, drag another copy of the satellite movie clip from the Library onto the Stage. Don't resize this one just yet.

5. You already know that the moon needs to orbit the larger sphere—that's the whole point of this exercise—so it's going to need a motion guide. With the Moon layer selected, click the Add Guide Layer icon beneath the layer stack.

6. On the guide layer, use the Oval tool to draw an unfilled ellipse on the Stage. The ellipse should be at least twice as wide as the large sphere. (See Figure 14.14.) You can use the Rotate tool to give the ellipse an angle.

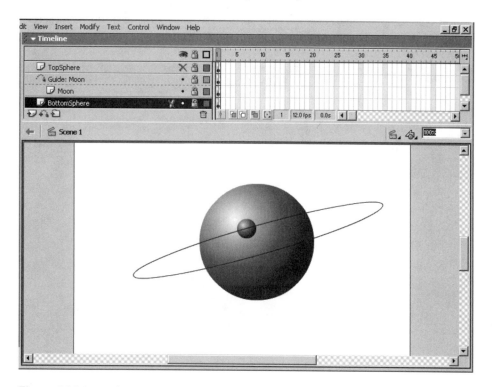

Figure 14.14   At this point in the process, you should have the two large spheres, the small moon, and a motion guide on the Stage.

7. Lock and hide the TopSphere and BottomSphere layers. Lock the Guide layer, but don't hide it.

8. Make sure that Snap to Objects is on (View > Snap to Objects), and snap the moon to the guide in the middle of the upper side of the ellipse.

9. Extend your Timeline out to frame 40 by selecting frame 40 in all four layers and pressing F5.

Tip

When you are using an ellipse or a circle as a motion guide, you have to be a little careful. Flash really likes to have beginning and ending points for its tweens. When the endpoints aren't clearly delineated, Flash will choose the shortest path possible. This can cause some interesting behavior, such as tweens suddenly reversing their motion. One way to handle this is to force a break in the ellipse by removing a line segment. Another option is to place your keyframes so that the distance to the next keyframe is shorter than the distance to the previous keyframe. This is a snap to do with three keyframes.

10. Insert keyframes (F6) at frames 20 and 40 in the Moon layer. Position the satellite clip in frame 20 so that it is on the opposite side of the ellipse from the movie clip in frame 1. Position the clip in frame 40 so that it is just to the right of the clip on frame 1. Use Onion Skinning, if you need it. (See Figure 14.15.)

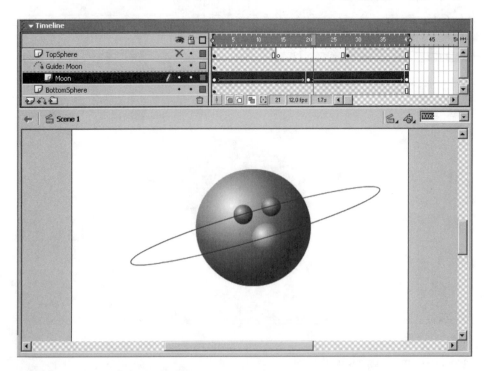

Figure 14.15 With Onion Skinning turned on, you can see the relative placement of the moon in the three keyframes. After applying a motion tween, scrub through your animation to make sure that the moon keeps moving in the proper direction.

11. Click the Moon layer label to highlight all the frames and add a motion tween. Turn off Onion Skinning and scrub the playhead through the animation to make sure that the moon keeps moving in the appropriate direction.

12. You can add a little more realism to the scene by scaling the moon and changing the brightness, depending on its position.

    Select the satellite that will appear in the foreground (frame 20), and use the Transform panel to scale it to 150%. As long as you have the satellite selected, use the Properties inspector to change its Brightness to 25%. For the two other satellites, all you need to do is change their Brightness to −10%.

    Next, you will make that top sphere disappear when the satellite is supposed to be crossing in front of it.

13. Unhide any hidden layers, and scrub slowly through the animation. You need to add a blank keyframe to the TopSphere layer just at the point when the moon should start to cross in front of it.

14. Copy frame 1 of the TopSphere layer, and paste a copy of it into the frame right after the moon passes off of the sphere again.

15. Click anywhere on the background and the Properties Inspector will show a background color box. Change the Background, Color to black.

    This gives your file a lot more impact.

16. Save and test your file.

For added fun, try copying your Moon and Guide layers into two new layers. Use Edit Multiple Frames to rotate the whole thing; then select all the frames in the second Moon layer, right-click, and choose Reverse Frames. You'll probably have to turn on Scale in the Properties Inspector for the tween before it'll work properly. You might have to move your frames slightly as well.

As you can see, adding interesting three-dimensional effects to Flash movies is not difficult—and you can do it without a lot of ActionScripting.

Cinematography and Perspective in Flash

More often than not, knowing how to simulate realistic action in Flash is the name of the game. In the 2D world of the computer screen, where there are no cameras or true 3D environments, it's necessary to create effects that mimic camera movements and perspectives. Part of Flash's versatility as a 2D animation program is that it gives you a number of ways to deal with these issues.

In a sense, Flash has a great deal in common with older forms of animation. Just like traditional cel animation, Flash relies on changing items in front of a stationary camera or stage to create the impression of movement. Layers serve the same purpose as the acetate transparencies in cel animation that are used to create the illusion of depth. By combining these techniques, you can use Flash to create convincing 3D effects.

Take a moment to play Martian_final.swf. (Use Martian_final_low.swf, if you have an older or slower machine.) Each file is in the Examples/Chapter14 folder on the companion CD. Watch it several times, paying special attention to the movement of the background scenery, especially when it falls away as the Martian Terror Machine enters the scene. (See Figure 14.16.)

Figure 14.16   The Martian Terror Machine enters the city toward the end of the final movie.

Note

The Martian Terror Machine is H.G. Wells' name, not mine, but it's cool nonetheless. I like to think he'd approve of my rendition.

The animation makes use of a formula that relies on using a large amount of descriptive visual detail that is seen over a brief period of time. The visual detail, combined with the perspective scrolling of the scenery, creates an interesting and realistic 3D effect.

On the surface, this looks like a complex animation, but actually, it's not. The entire sequence consists of four strips of scenery, two prop items, and a few lines thrown in for the "old film strip" effect. The entire animation is accomplished with simple tweening. You work on re-creating this scene in the next several exercises.

Start by examining the Library items in the base file, Martian.fla, which is found in the Examples/Chapter14 folder.

Note

If you have an older or slower machine, you might want to use the Martian_low.fla file instead. It's the same file, but with the gradients removed.

The Library has three folders:

- **Scenery.** This folder contains the three scenery graphics: Foreground, Ruins, and Backdrop. These graphics are used to create the 3D city scene. Notice that each graphic is a different length. This fact becomes important later.

- **Machine.** This folder contains the Martian Terror Machine and the Machine leg graphics.

- **Bitmaps.** This folder contains the JPEG for the sky.

The three scenery symbols are all highly detailed, single-frame movie clips. Essentially, they're graphic "strips" similar to painted and cut-out cardboard scenery pieces.

These graphic strips are going to move across the Stage from left to right. To make that work, part of the strip is always off the Stage. When you create a scrolling scene like this, it's a good idea to create graphic strips that are longer than you think you'll need. That way, you can be sure that you won't run out of scenery when you start scrolling the scenes. After you're happy with the timing of the scrolling and everything is properly in place at the end of the animation, crop the images on the Stage to eliminate any unseen portions. This substantially cuts down on the final file size.

Now that you've had a chance to acquaint yourself with the individual elements you'll be using in this movie, it's time to add them to the Stage. In the next section, you look at how you can use layers to achieve a feeling of depth. You also look at how you can tween graphic strips of different lengths to achieve the feel of moving down a 3D city street.

Note

I originally planned to have the Sky JPEG slowly scroll across the screen with the rest of the scenery, but I decided to crop it and keep it stationary to reduce processor lag. Sometimes you have to make trade-offs between art and CPU usage!

Note

It might not look like it, but when completed, this is a small file (36Kb). It's kept that way by eliminating and cropping *anything* that leaves the viewable portion of the Stage—a rule of thumb worth mentioning. The graphic strips used for this exercise were quite a bit longer than the ones you have in the current movie. They were trimmed to size after it was determined how long they needed to be. In other words, after the tween was set up, it was easy to see which portions of the graphic would never need to be on the Stage.

Simulating a Movie Camera and Dolly

Rather than thinking of the Flash Stage as a camera, think of it as an electronic puppet show stage. Although Flash graphics are 2D in nature, Flash's animation capabilities enable scenes and characters to enter and leave the Stage in a way that mimics an actual movie camera operating in a 3D environment. The only fundamental difference is that the items on the Stage do the moving and the "camera" (Stage) remains stationary.

Because there are no actual cameras to position in Flash, it's important for the artist/animator to be innovative when it comes to designing and animating the graphics that enter the viewable portion of the Stage. By thinking ahead and building distortions of perspective into the graphics, you can achieve truly dynamic camera effects with a simple motion tween.

Setting the Scene

All the scenery symbols begin the animation with their right sides flush with the right side of the Stage. When the movie starts, they begin their journey across the Stage at different speeds, according to their order on the Stage. The top layer with the Foreground strip moves the fastest, the middle layer with the Ruins graphic strip moves a little slower, and the bottom layer with the Backdrop graphic clip moves even more slowly. Why is it set up this way? It's a perspective trick. You'll take a more in-depth look at how this works after Exercise 14.4, when you have all your graphic strips on the Stage.

Tip

Look at the base file's three scenery clips closely. The farther in the background the scene is supposed to be, the darker it is. That's another visual clue that helps create the illusion of perspective.

Exercise 14.4   Preparing the Basic Scenery Setup

Enough talking about what you're going to do; let's just do it. In this exercise, you place all the scenery elements, including the sky background, on the Stage and get them aligned properly so that you can begin the city scene animation.

1. Open Martian.fla (or Martian_low.fla for slower or older systems). Double-click Layer 1 and rename it **Background**.

2. Open the Library and drag a copy of sky.jpg from the Bitmaps folder onto the Stage.

3. Scale the sky JPEG so that it covers the entire Stage.

4. Lock the Background layer.

5. Add a new layer above the Background layer and name it **Backdrop**. You're going to layer the three scenery images on top of each other. The Backdrop movie clip is the scenery clip that appears in the back (above the Background, of course), and hence at the bottom of the Timeline.

6. Drag a copy of the Backdrop movie clip from the Scenery folder onto the Stage.

   You'll notice that the movie clip you just dragged onto the Stage is substantially wider than the Stage. That's because you're going to animate it across the Stage.

7. The movie will pan from right to left, so align the movie clip on the right side of the Stage with the bottom of the movie clip aligned to the bottom of the Stage. (See Figure 14.17.)

Tip

The quickest way to align items to the Stage is to use the Align panel (Window > Align) with To Stage selected.

8. Lock the Backdrop layer.

9. Add two new layers: **Ruins** and **Foreground**. The Foreground layer should be on top of the layer stack.

10. Select the Ruins layer and drag a copy of the Ruins movie clip from the Scenery folder onto the Stage. Align it in the same way that you did the Backdrop movie clip.

11. Lock the Ruins layer.

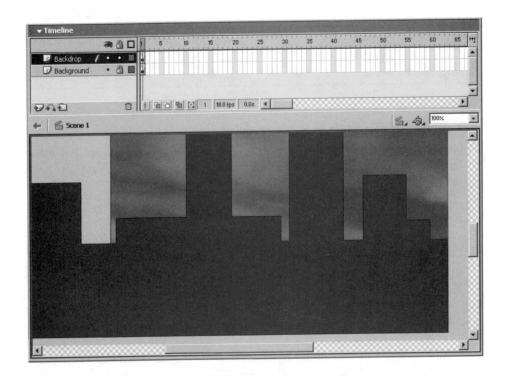

Figure 14.17   The movie will pan from right to left, so begin by aligning the scenery on the right side of the Stage.

> **Tip**
>
> You've probably noticed by now that I'm a fanatic about locking layers I'm not using. It just makes life so much easier. You don't have to worry about accidentally selecting and moving elements that you didn't mean to move.

12. Repeat Step 10 for the Foreground movie clip, but make sure that the Foreground layer is selected.

13. Lock the Foreground layer. Save your file and test your movie. (See Figure 14.18.)

Yes, it looks pretty cool, but you need some action here!

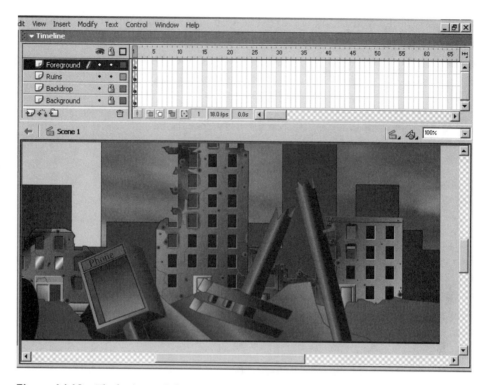

Figure 14.18   The basic movie layout is now set up with all three scenery layers and the background in place.

Relative Motion

In the final movie, the three scenes moved at different speeds. The scene closest to you moved more quickly than the scenes that were farther away. The principle here is the same as what you have undoubtedly observed when you look out a fast-moving car. Objects that are closer appear to move by faster than objects that are farther away. Don't believe it? The next time you are in a car that's moving at a good clip (excuse me, but need I say that you should be the passenger in this car?), try focusing on objects that are right by the side of the road. It's pretty hard to do. However, it's easy to focus on distant objects because they appear to move more slowly.

You animate the scenery clips across the same number of frames. The question is how to get them to scroll at different speeds. The answer is remarkably simple. The key is that each clip is a different width. When you animate different width clips across the same number of frames, you get different relative speeds. Wide clips appear to scroll faster than narrow clips. Think about it in terms of physics. Speed is equal to distance traveled divided by the time of travel. For you, distance is the number of pixels between the left and right sides of the clip. The number of frames you use to animate the clip represents time. What the heck—let's do the calculations:

Foreground: **1120px ÷ 100 frames = 11px per frame**

Ruins: **910px ÷ 100 frames = 9px per frame**

Backdrop: **818px ÷ 100 frames = 8px per frame**

The backdrop has the slowest speed and the foreground has the fastest speed. In Exercise 14.5, you put this theory into practice.

Exercise 14.5   Adding Some Motion

When adding motion to your scenery, allow for three to four seconds of animation to pan all the way across the city. For the purposes of this movie, that translates to about 65 frames. With this type of scene, especially with the combination of tweening and gradients, you want the animation to be relatively short. Otherwise, you're talking about a huge file size—not to mention maxing out the CPU.

1. Continuing in the file from Exercise 14.4, add keyframes (F6) in frame 65 of the Foreground, Ruins, and Backdrop layers.

2. Extend the Background layer to frame 65 (F5).

3. Align the left sides of the scenery elements with the left side of the Stage in frame 65. The fastest way to do this is to select frame 65 in all three layers, launch the Align panel, select the To Stage button, and align the left sides. Don't forget to unlock your layers first.

4. Select any frame between 1 and 65 in all three layers. Right-click (Windows) or Ctrl-click (Macintosh) and apply a motion tween by selecting Create Motion Tween from the pop-up menu. (See Figure 14.19.)

5. Save your file and test the movie.

Figure 14.19   After you set up your new keyframes and align the clips to the left side of the Stage, you can apply your motion tweens.

Once again, because each movie clip has a different width, you get the illusion of different speeds. The Foreground clip moves faster than the Ruins clip, and the Ruins clip moves faster than the Backdrop clip.

What else do you need to have come into this movie? You need an invasion from Mars! Think back to the completed movie. At the end of the scenery scroll, a giant mechanical leg comes down in the middle of the scene.

At around frame 65, the scrolling tweens come to a halt. This is where the disembodied Martian leg makes its brief, but dramatic, five-frame debut. This signals the arrival of its larger, fully complete sibling. Proceed to Exercise 14.6 to start the invasion.

Exercise 14.6   Introducing the Martian Terror Machine Leg

In this exercise, you bring the Martian terror machine from off-Stage into the center of the city scene by using a simple tween combined with some scaling.

   1. Continuing in the same file, lock the scenery layers, and add a new layer above the Foreground layer. Name the new layer **Leg**.

2. Insert a keyframe (F6) in frame 66. Extend all other layers to frame 66 (F5).

3. With frame 66 of the Leg layer selected, open the Library and drag a copy of the Leg movie clip from the Machine folder onto the Stage.

4. Use the Transform panel, with Constrain selected, to scale the Leg movie clip to 300%.

5. Position the leg so that it is off the top of the Stage and centered over the right edge of the Stage. (See Figure 14.20.)

Figure 14.20   The Martian leg begins its entry into the scene from off the upper part of the Stage.

6. The leg should come in quickly. Insert a keyframe in the leg layer at frame 70. Extend the entire Timeline out to frame 100 so that you can see the rest of the scene.

7. Position the instance of the leg in Frame 70 so that it is fully on the Stage with the point at the bottom of the leg between the broken wall and abandoned tire. (See Figure 14.21.)

8. Still on the Leg layer, select any frame between 66 and 70. Right-click (Windows) or Ctrll-click (Macintosh) and apply a motion tween by selecting Create Motion Tween from the pop-up menu.

9. Save your file and test your movie.

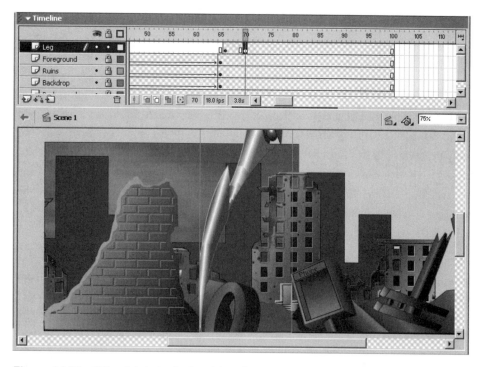

Figure 14.21   When it is in its final position, the Martian leg intrudes on the city scene.

Why just bring in the leg and not the whole Machine? Well, we do it that way to alleviate the processor lag of needlessly moving the entire Machine symbol five frames. Remember that when you work with vector graphics, you're making a lot of demands on your audience's computers. There are a lot of calculations involved both in tweening and using gradients. You have both here. The less you have to move around, the better off you are.

Okay, if you saw that big metallic leg plop down right in front of you, your first inclination would be to look up and see what it was attached to. Don't you think? Enter the complete Martian Terror Machine.

Panning Across Martian Terror

The Martian Terror Machine is actually a graphic that is specially designed to integrate with the final frame of the animation. Hand-drawn, scanned, and traced, the leg portions are depicted from a dead-on perspective, whereas the upper body portions are drawn as though you were looking up at it. Because it was drawn this way, when the Machine tweens into place at the end, it seems as though the "camera" is actually moving to look up at it.

Creating this type of effect is the art of building distortion of perspective into your graphics; it's a useful technique. It's all about creating an optical illusion of perspective. How do you do that? Start by observing the world around you. Go outside and look up at a tall building. Observe what happens to the parallel lines of the building's sides. They appear to converge. In other words, they look closer together at the top than they do at the bottom. That's a visual clue you can carry with you. When you look up, or off into the distance at something, whatever you are looking at appears to be smaller the farther away from you it is. It's not really smaller; it's an optical illusion. After you understand this concept, you can re-create it. That's how the Martian Terror Machine works—the legs, which are closer to you, appear to be proportionally larger than the body of the machine. Next, you'll take a look at how you're actually going to create the tween for the entry of the Machine onto the Stage.

After the Martian leg is in place, two things happen simultaneously. The Machine tweens into position so that its "body" occupies the Stage, and the scenery begins to exit from view to the lower left of the stage. In Exercise 14.7, you'll scale down the Machine in size a little bit to fit it on the Stage. Scaling down the Machine symbol actually increases the dramatic effect by making it appear farther away, hence, taller.

Note

As soon as the images are no longer viewable on the Stage, you should terminate their Timelines. This saves wear and tear on the processor. However, beware of accidentally resetting tween end points. To retain their desired value, add a keyframe to the point in the tween where the image is no longer visible. Then remove the frames beyond that.

Exercise 14.7   Introducing the Martian Terror Machine

In this exercise, you add the complete Martian Terror Machine to the Stage and scale it up so that it matches the size of the disembodied leg.

1. Continuing in the same file, lock the Leg layer, and add a new layer above the Leg layer. Name the new layer **Machine**.

2. Insert a keyframe (F6) in frame 71 of your new layer.

3. Drag a copy of the Martian Walker movie clip from the Machine folder onto the Stage. (See Figure 14.22.)

   You'll have to scale the Martian Walker clip so that the completed leg is the same size as the disembodied leg already on the Stage.

4. Select the Martian Walker on the Stage. You already scaled the disembodied leg to 300%. Use the Transform panel to do the same for the Martian Walker.

5. Position the Walker so that its completed leg covers the Leg symbol on the Stage. (See Figure 14.23.)

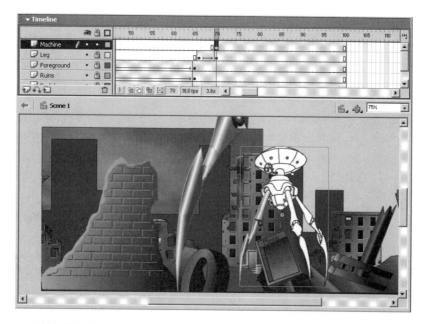

Figure 14.22   The Martian Walker when it is first brought onto the Stage is a little on the small side.

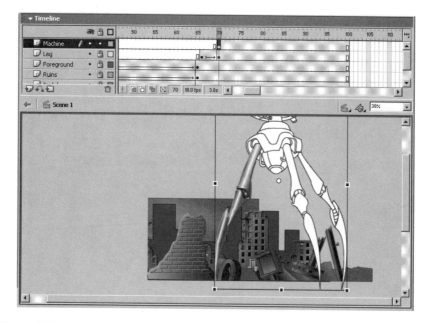

Figure 14.23   After you've scaled the Martian Walker, it should completely, or nearly completely, cover the Leg symbol.

6. Select the Leg layer and insert a blank keyframe in frame 71.

7. Save your file and test your movie.

At the end of the scrolling sequence, the Martian leg enters the scene and is replaced by the Martian Walker. In Exercise 14.8, you pan the camera up to see the rest of the machine.

Exercise 14.8   Panning Up the Martian Terror Machine

Once again, you're going to use tweening to imitate the effect of a camera panning up the Machine body. This time, you use an angled tween rather than a simple side-to-side tween.

1. Continue in the same file, but hide the four scenery layers for the time being.
2. Insert a keyframe in frame 95 of the Machine layer.
3. Use the Align panel to center the Martian Walker instance on the Stage. Right now, it's a bit too large to actually fit on the Stage.

    You want to give the impression that you are on the ground looking up at this monstrosity. You'll need to reduce the Walker's size so that its upper body fits on the Stage.
4. Select the Martian Walker in frame 95 of the Machine layer and use the Transform panel to reduce the Walker's size to 200%, still with Constrain checked.
5. Position the newly scaled Martian Walker toward the right side of the screen. (See Figure 14.24.) The right knee joint should be on the Stage.

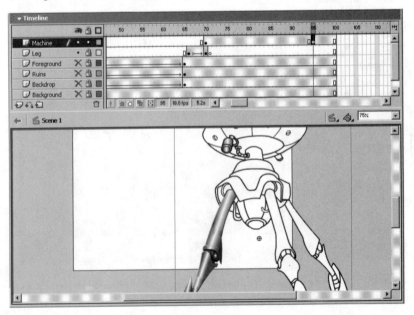

Figure 14.24   After the Martian Walker is scaled, it can be correctly positioned on the Stage.

6. Select any frame between 70 and 95 on the Machine layer and apply a motion tween.

7. Save your file and test your movie.

Okay, this just doesn't look right yet. You need to have the scenery move down and to the left during the pan to get a realistic effect. Think about what needs to happen. As the camera pans up, the scenery needs to disappear. Exercise 14.9 shows you how.

Exercise 14.9   Losing the Scenery During the Pan

The scenery shouldn't start receding until you begin to pan up the Martian Walker. You need to begin by inserting keyframes in the three scenery layers where the change in action occurs.

1. Unhide and unlock the scenery layers if necessary and insert keyframes in frame 71 of each of the three layers to mark the beginning of the scenery change.

2. The city scene should disappear before the upper part of the Martian Walker comes into complete view. Insert keyframes in frame 90 of the three scenery layers.

3. With frame 90 in all three layers selected, use the Arrow keys to move the scenery (all three layers at once) until it is below the Stage and to the left. (See Figure 14.25.)

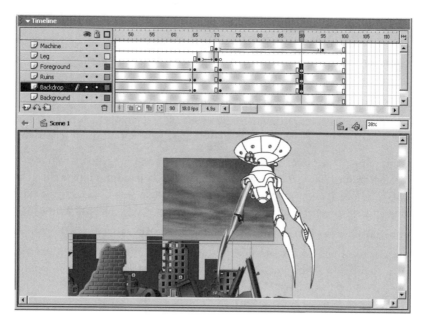

Figure 14.25   As the camera pans up the Martian Walker, the city scene recedes below. By frame 90, all three scenery instances should be off the lower-left edge of the Stage.

4. Select frame 80 of all three layers and apply a motion tween.

5. Save your file and test your movie.

Now when the Martian Walker enters the scene, the city recedes below the Stage as you pan up toward the top of the Walker.

Optimizing Your Tween

It's time to do some optimization. You need to tween the scenery layers only for as long as they are visible.

Think for a moment about the order in which each piece of scenery leaves the screen. Once again, you're going to be dealing with perspective issues:

- **Foreground.** This is the scene closest to you. As you begin to look up, these elements disappear quickly.

- **Ruins.** This is the mid-level scene. This scene is visible until you are looking up at the body of the Martian Terror Machine.

- **Backdrop.** This is the far distant scene. Because you are changing the angle at which the camera is viewing the scene, this scene disappears behind the mid-level scene.

In Exercise 14.10, you're going to have to make some adjustments to the scenery tweens based on the order in which the pieces of the scenery leave the screen.

Exercise 14.10   Optimizing the Scenery Tween

There's no real science to adjusting these tweens (well actually there is, but do you really want a two-day physics lecture here?); you just have to eyeball it until it feels right.

1. Continuing in the same file, use the period key (.) on the keyboard to move through frames 70 to 90 one frame at a time. The Foreground movie clip currently exits the Stage at about frame 85 (your mileage might vary). Speed up its exit by dragging the final keyframe to frame 80 (you'll have to eyeball this a little bit).

2. The Ruins movie clip exits the Stage at frame 90. You can leave that tween as is.

3. The Backdrop movie clip should exit the Stage sometime between when the Foreground and Ruins movie clips exit. (See Figure 14.26.) Frame 86 wouldn't be a bad choice for this layer. Drag the final keyframe to frame 86.

4. To save wear and tear on the CPU, remove all frames after the end of the new tween.

5. Save your file and test your movie.

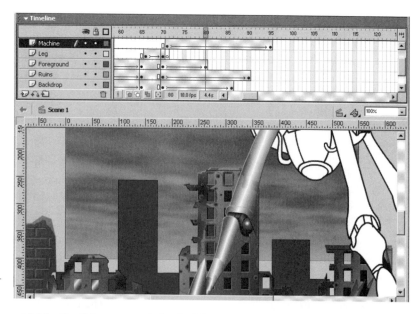

Figure 14.26   You'll have to tweak the final frames in the scenery tweens to get the city scene to recede in a realistic fashion.

Not bad. That's a pretty slick animation without too much pain. Do be aware that this type of animation—with lots of gradients and tweening—will be, by definition, processor intensive. Just remember that routinely removing frames that your tweens don't need and keeping your images cropped to their smallest possible sizes lightens the load.

You've looked at a number of techniques that you can use to simulate 3D in Flash—using gradients, motion tweens, imported files, parallax scrolling, and so on. For extremely complex or organic tweens, you'll probably find that you'll need to use ActionScript. In the next section, you'll have the opportunity to work with a simple 3D event engine to develop a complex 3D animation.

Using a 3D Event Engine

When you want to control 3D motion using ActionScript, you have to rely on a bit of math. In fact, you really need to create a 3D event engine to handle the positioning of the item or items on the Stage. Don't panic, you won't be creating the 3D event engine here—that's a little beyond the scope of this chapter—you'll look at and use an engine that has been created for you. Before you do, you need to think about some of the differences in working in 3D and 2D space.

You are already accustomed to working on a monitor in 2D space. The concept of an X-axis and a Y-axis should be familiar to you. You also should understand how this translates to Flash. In Flash, the upper-left corner of the Stage is where the X-axis and Y-axis cross (where X and Y both equal zero). To describe any point in a 2D system, you just need the X coordinate and the Y coordinate.

When you work in 3 dimensions, you add another axis: the Z-axis. The Z-axis passes through the point where X and Y cross and is perpendicular to both. Think of the Z-axis as passing from your eyes, through the (0,0) point on the screen, and out the back of your monitor. You need three numbers to describe any 3D point: the X, Y, and Z coordinates. The is in translating a 3D system into a 2D one. You can't just take away the Z-axis. If you do, you can't add depth or perspective. Think about what this means—this seems simple, but it's important. As an object moves toward you, it appears larger. As an object moves away from you, it appears smaller and fades out. That's the key! You can simulate 3 dimensions by using the Z value to scale and change the alpha settings of your object.

So now it's time to take a look at the code in the event engine. The code for the event engine is contained in an AS file that you'll include in your movie. The entire code listing is shown below, separated into Listings 14.1–14.3. The only part of the code you actually need to worry about is shown in Listing 14.1—it outlines what information you need to send to the event engine to make it work. To see the complete code, open 3d.as from the Examples/Chapter14 folder on the companion CD. If looking at the code listings leaves you squirming in your chair, just take a look at Listing 14.1 and then proceed to Exercise 14.11, which shows you how to use the event engine.

Listing 14.1   The First Section of the 3D Engine Code

```
// Library to allow placement of movieclips in 3D space
// Requires:
// MovieClip.origin_x (this is the 3D x offset)
// MovieClip.origin_y (this is the 3D y offset)
// MovieClip.fov (this is the Field of View smaller numbers = more
↪severe angles)
// MovieClip.center_x (this is the x center of the stage)
// MovieClip.center_y (this is the y center of the stage)
```

You'll notice that the first section of the code in Listing 14.1 is all comments. It simply outlines the information that is required by the event engine to function. You'll set up all of this information in the first frame of your Flash movie.

`MovieClip.origin_x` and `MovieClip.origin_y` represent where your object sits in 3D space. You can think of this as your vanishing point. `MovieClip.fov` is the field of view. This describes how wide or narrow a view you have of your 3D world. Think of it as how close or far you are from the object you're viewing. A small number places you close to the center of the 3D world. For example, if an object were rotating around the center point of the 3D world, it might appear to exit the screen. If you are farther away from the center of the world, you'll see the complete rotation. `MovieClip.center_x` and `MovieClip.center_y` define where the center of the Stage is.

You need to account for the fact that Flash uses the upper-left corner of the movie as it's registration (0,0) point. You can shift that by adding a value to both X and Y—half the screen height and width would do nicely to position yourself in the middle of the screen. So you'll add half of the screen width to your X value and half of your screen height to your Y value. In a 550×400 pixel movie, you would set `MovieClip.center_x` to 275 and `MovieClip.center_y` to 200.

Listing 14.2   The Second Section of the 3D Engine Code

```
// setting the 3D x
MovieClip.prototype._setX = function(val){
      this.__x = val;
      this._render();
}

// getting the 3D y
MovieClip.prototype._getX = function(){
      return this.__x;
}

// combining the getter/setter into the x_pos property
MovieClip.prototype.addProperty("x_pos", MovieClip.prototype._getX,
➥MovieClip.prototype._setX);

// setting the 3D y
MovieClip.prototype._setY = function(val){
      this.__y = val;
      this._render();
}

// getting the 3D y
MovieClip.prototype._getY = function(){
      return this.__y;
}

// combining the getter/setter into the y_pos property
MovieClip.prototype.addProperty("y_pos", MovieClip.prototype._getY,
➥MovieClip.prototype._setY);

// setting the 3D z
MovieClip.prototype._setZ = function(val){
      this.__z = val;
      this._render();
}
```

continues ▶

Listing 14.2   Continued

```
// getting the 3D z
MovieClip.prototype._getZ = function(){
      return this.__z;
}

// combining the getter/setter into the z_pos property
MovieClip.prototype.addProperty("z_pos", MovieClip.prototype._getZ,
➡MovieClip.prototype._setZ);
```

The code in Listing 14.2 creates new special properties for movie clips in 3D space. Specifically, it adds special functions that mimic the _x and _y properties of a regular movie clip, except that you're working in 3D space to both get and set the X, Y, and Z positions of the movie clip. You use the addProperty method to add the "setter" and "getter" to a special property (x_pos, y_pos, z_pos). Now the setter and getter functions are essentially hidden in x_pos, y_pos, or z_pos, and you can use those properties to get or set values in 3D space.

Listing 14.3   The Third Section of the 3D Engine Code

```
// handle the drawing of the MCs
MovieClip.prototype._render = function(){

        // the z "factor"
        var factor = (MovieClip.fov) / (MovieClip.fov - this.__z);

        // adjusting for perspective place the movieclip in 2D space
        this._x = (this.__x - MovieClip.origin_x) * factor +
        ➡MovieClip.center_x;
        this._y = (this.__y - MovieClip.origin_y) * factor +
        ➡MovieClip.center_y;

        // adjust scale and alpha of MC for perspective
        this._xscale = 100 * factor;
        this._yscale = this._xscale;
        this._alpha = this._xscale;
}

// rearrange the depths of all sub-movieclips based on Z depth
MovieClip.prototype.fixDepths = function(){

        // collect all sub MCs into an array
        var mcs = new Array();
        for (var i in this){
                if (typeof(this[i]) == "movieclip"){
                        mcs.push(this[i]);
                }
        }
        // sort that array based on the z_pos property
        mcs.sort(function(a, b){
                var val1 = a.z_pos;
                var val2 = b.z_pos;
```

```
        if (val1 < val2){
              return -1;
        }else if (val1 > val2){
              return 1;
        }else{
              return 0;
        }
    });

    // loop through the MCs and place on new depth
    var max = mcs.length;
    for (var i=0; i<max; ++i){
          mcs[i].swapDepths(i);

    }
}
```

The code in Listing 14.3 acts to position the movie clip in 3D space. There are two functions here—render() and fixDepths(). The render() function takes care of placing the object in 2D space as it would appear in 3D space. Think about what happens when you look into a cardboard box. You see the bottom of the box and part of the sides. If you flatten that view into 2D space, it looks something like Figure 14.27. To move an object realistically in this view, you have to calculate where it is in 3D space and project that into 2D space. This function also takes care of changing the Alpha and Brightness as the object moves forward and backward along the Z-axis.

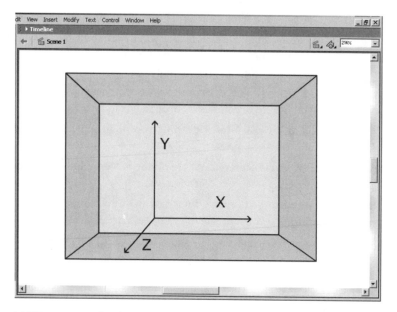

Figure 14.27   A 2D overhead view of a box. To move things realistically in 2D space, you have to account for the differences in 2D and 3D positioning.

The `fixDepth()` function loops through all the movie clips beneath a given instance and sets the depth of the movie clip according to its relative position.

To see the full code, open 3d.as from the Examples/Chapter14 folder on the CD in a text editor. Are you still here? Good. In the next exercise, you'll implement this engine in a movie.

Exercise 14.11   Adding the 3D Event Engine to Your File

In this exercise, you'll add the 3D event engine to your file and set up its required properties.

1. Copy 3d.as from the Examples/Chapter14 folder on the companion CD and save it to your hard drive.

2. Open 3d_basic.fla from the Examples/Chapter14 folder on the companion CD and save it to your hard drive in the same directory that you saved 3d.as.

   This movie currently contains three layers: Actions, Crosshairs, and Ball.

3. Select the Ball movie clip on the Stage and use the Properties Inspector to give it an instance name of **ball_mc**.

4. Select frame 1 of the main Timeline and open the Actions panel (F2).

5. The first thing you need to do is include the 3D event engine (3d.as). Enter the following code in the Actions panel:

   ```
   #include "3d.as"
   ```

   Make sure you do *not* put a semicolon at the end of that line or it won't work.

   Now it's time to put the engine to use. Before you do anything else, you'll need to define the "world" that your 3D object will exist in. To define your world, you need to give Flash three pieces of information:

   • **Where X and Y sit in 3D space.** In other words, you need to tell Flash where the vanishing point for your movie is (`origin_x` and `origin_y`).

   • **What the Field of View is.** How wide or narrow of an angle are you viewing this from (`fov`)?

   • **Where the 3D world is centered.** Where on the Stage should the center of your 3D world be (`center_x` and `center_y`)?

     These values need to be available for all of the movie clips you'll eventually attach to the Stage, so you'll define the values as part of the `MovieClip` object.

6. Enter the following code in the Actions panel after the `include` statement:

   ```
   MovieClip.origin_x = 0;
   MovieClip.origin_y = 0;
   MovieClip.fov = 300;
   MovieClip.center_x = 275;
   MovieClip.center_y = 200;
   ```

Now that you've defined the most basic parameters of your 3D world, it's time to position ball_mc on the Stage and start moving it.

7. Use ActionScript to place the ball in the center of your 3D world by positioning it so that it's centered where X, Y, and Z all equal 0. Remember, x_pos, y_pos, and z_pos are set up in the 3D event engine. To do so, enter the following code:

```
ball_mc.x_pos = 0;
ball_mc.y_pos = 0;
ball_mc.z_pos = 0;
```

8. Go ahead and save and test your movie. The ball_mc instance should reposition itself in the center of the Stage (see Figure 14.28). You won't be able to tell just yet, but it's also in the center of your 3D world.

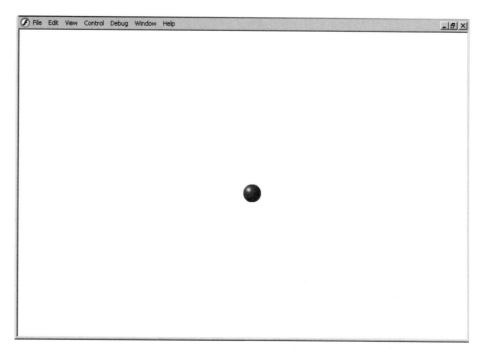

Figure 14.28 By setting x_pos, y_pos, and z_pos, you position the movie clip in the center of your 3D world.

In Exercise 14.12, you'll begin working with the event engine to add some motion to your file. You'll be building up the complexity of the motion slowly so that you can understand how the event engine is controlling the movement of your movie clip.

Exercise 14.12   Adding Some Motion to Your File

To see how the event engine handles movement, begin by adding in basic movement control using the arrow keys. First, you'll program movement in the left, right, up, and down directions using the isDown method of the Key object and the onEnterFrame event handler.

1. Start with moving the ball to the left (a negative direction). When you use the onEnterFrame event handler, you have to pass it a function that tells it what to do. After the last line of code you entered in the previous exercise, enter this:

```
onEnterFrame = function(){
        if (Key.isDown(Key.LEFT)){
                ball_mc.x_pos -= 2;
        }
}
```

2. Save and test your movie. Press the Left Arrow key and the ball should move to the left on the Stage.

3. You'll need to enter three more if statements inside of the onEnterFrame event handler to control the other directions. Modify your code so that the event handler looks like this:

```
onEnterFrame = function(){
        if (Key.isDown(Key.LEFT)){
                ball_mc.x_pos -= 2;
        }
        if (Key.isDown(Key.RIGHT)){
                ball_mc.x_pos += 2;
        }
        if (Key.isDown(Key.UP)){
                ball_mc.y_pos -= 2;
        }
        if (Key.isDown(Key.DOWN)){
                ball_mc.y_pos += 2;
        }
}
```

4. Save and test your movie. You can move the ball up, down, right, and left. But you're not seeing the real effect of the 3D engine yet. To see that, you'll need to reposition the ball on the Z-axis.

You've run out of arrow keys, so you'll need to pick some different keys to control the movement toward and away from you. If you're going to do that, you need to know the ASCII key code values that Flash recognizes so that you can reference the key in ActionScript. To keep this simple and to allow you to customize the script to suit your preferences, Table 14.1 shows the subset of ASCII key codes for the keyboard keys that can be used in Flash.

Table 14.1   The ASCII Key Codes

Key	ASCII Code	Key	ASCII Code
A or a	65	1 or !	49
B or b	66	2 or @	50
C or c	67	3 or #	51
D or d	68	4 or $	52
E or e	69	5 or %	53
F or f	70	6 or ^	54
G or g	71	7 or &	55
H or h	72	8 or *	56
I or I	73	9 or (	57
J or j	74	0 or)	48
K or k	75		
L or l	76		
M or m	77		
N or n	78		
O or o	79		
P or p	80		
Q or q	81		
R or r	82		
S or s	83		
T or t	84		
U or u	85		
V or v	86		
W or w	87		
X or x	88		
Y or y	89		
Z or z	90		

5. Setting the Z position of the ball is no different from setting the X and Y. You just set the special property (z_pos) that is set up in the event engine. In the code below the key A (65) is used to increase the z_pos and Z (90) is used to decrease it. Make sure you're still inside the onFrameEvent handler and enter the following code:

```
if (Key.isDown(65)){
    ball_mc.z_pos += 2;
}
if (Key.isDown(90)){
    ball_mc.z_pos -= 2;
}
```

6. Save and test your movie. Note what happens as you move the ball forward and back in Z space. The ball appears to move faster the closer it is to you. The farther away from you the ball is, the more faded it appears. Try pressing the arrow and A and Z keys at the same time to see the 3D movement. It's very realistic.

In case you need a little assistance, your completed code should look like Listing 14.4.

Listing 14.4   Keyboard Motion Control in 3D Space

```
#include "3d.as"

// set the properties of the 3D space
MovieClip.origin_x = 0;
MovieClip.origin_y = 0;
MovieClip.fov = 300;
MovieClip.center_x = 275;
MovieClip.center_y = 200;

ball_mc.x_pos = 0;
ball_mc.y_pos = 0;
ball_mc.z_pos = 0;

onEnterFrame = function(){
        if (Key.isDown(Key.LEFT)){
                ball_mc.x_pos -= 2;
        }
        if (Key.isDown(Key.RIGHT)){
                ball_mc.x_pos += 2;
        }
        if (Key.isDown(Key.UP)){
                ball_mc.y_pos -= 2;
        }
        if (Key.isDown(Key.DOWN)){
                ball_mc.y_pos += 2;
        }
        if (Key.isDown(65)){
                ball_mc.z_pos += 2;
        }
        if (Key.isDown(90)){
                ball_mc.z_pos -= 2;
        }
}
```

That was a fairly simple demonstration.

Controlling Movement with Advanced ActionScript

You can also add multiple balls to the Stage and control their actions with ActionScript alone—no key presses needed. In fact, you can easily set up a fairly complex tweening action that would be extremely difficult to create by hand by utilizing the existing 3D engine.

Let's examine this. Open 3d_advanced.fla from the Examples/Chapter14 folder on the companion CD and save it to your hard drive in the same directory as the 3d.as file.

To see the existing code, select frame 1 of the Actions layer and open the Actions panel. The code looks like this:

```
#include "3d.as"

// set the properties of the 3D space
MovieClip.origin_x = 0;
MovieClip.origin_y = 0;
MovieClip.fov = 300;
MovieClip.center_x = 275;
MovieClip.center_y = 200;
```

This is exactly what you had set up in the previous file, minus the keyboard controls.

The only other difference in this file is that the ball_mc movie clip has an instance name of ball0_mc. You'll see why a little later when you dynamically add additional balls to the Stage.

So that you can understand how this code works, start with just the one ball. After the code gets sorted out, you'll see how to add additional balls to the Stage for more fun.

You want the ball to move across the Stage. You could just keep incrementing the value of the ball, but that would be boring. To move the ball, you are going to use a variable as an incremented—a value that will be continually increased.

You will need some knowledge of trigonometry to understand the next section. But even if you come up empty-handed (or headed), cut and paste will still make the code work!

To keep things uncluttered, you'll use "a" as the variable name. The a variable gets initialized to the original X position of the ball, which is 0. Instead of worrying about where the ball is at any given point, just take the *sine* of a, use that value to position the ball, increment a, and do it all over again. Think about what would happen. If a is 0, taking the sine of 0 gives you 0. As a is incremented, the sine of a will continue to increase until a reaches a value of 90. When a is 90, the sine of a is 1. Then the sine of a will decrease again. By using the sine of a to set your X position, you can get the ball to move back and forth across the Stage. And as an added bonus, you'll get built-in easing. If you're scratching your head in confusion, just take a look at Table 14.2. The value of a is on the left, and the sine of that value is on the right.

Table 14.2   The Value and Sine of *a*

a	sin(a)	cos(a)	tan(a)
0	0.00	1.00	0.00
30	0.50	0.87	0.58
60	0.87	0.50	1.73
90	1.00	0.00	invalid
120	0.87	0.50	-1.73
150	0.50	0.87	-0.577
180	0.00	1.00	0.00
210	0.50	0.87	
240	0.87	0.50	
270	1.00	0.00	
300	0.87	0.50	
330	0.50	0.87	
360	0.00	1.00	

Having the X position oscillate between 0 and 1 would be, well, boring. But you can multiply the value to exaggerate it. The higher the number you multiply by, the larger the oscillation. Exercise 14.13 puts this into practice.

Exercise 14.13   Making the Ball Oscillate

First, get the oscillation going along the X-axis. To keep things simple, you'll use a as the variable to increment. Initialize your variable, and then set up the onEnterFrame event handler.

1. You should still be in 3d_advanced.fla. After the last line of code in frame 1 of the Actions layer, enter the following code:

```
a=0;
onEnterFrame = function () {
        ball0_mc.x_pos = Math.sin(a)*200;
        a += .1;
}
```

2. Save and test your movie. You should have one ball oscillating from left to right on the Stage.

3. You already know that you can control not only the X position, but also the Y and Z positions. Change your code to add the following two lines after the line where you set the x_pos:

```
ball0_mc.y_pos = Math.sin(a)*200;
ball0_mc.z_pos = Math.sin(a)*200;
```

4. Save and test your movie.

5. Why not change the depth, but use the cosine of variable *a* this time? The sine and cosine behave in opposite ways. If you decrease your Z position while X is increasing, you get much more interesting movement. Change the following line:

```
ball0_mc.z_pos = Math.sin(a)*200;
```

to this:

```
ball0_mc.z_pos = Math.cos(a)*200;
```

6. Save and test your movie. Now you've got something interesting happening. That one small change—reversing the values for the Z position—makes the ball move on an elliptical path.

So what happens if you throw a few more balls into the mix? Check out Exercise 14.14.

Exercise 14.14   Adding a Few Extra Balls

This time, you'll use duplicateMovieClip to place nine more instances of ball_mc on the Stage. All you need to do is set up a simple for loop.

1. Still in 3d_advanced.fla, add the following loop before the onEnterFrame handler you've been working with:

```
// create 9 copies of the ball
for (var i=1; i<10; ++i){
      ball0_mc.duplicateMovieClip("ball"+i+"_mc", i);
}
```

All you are doing is initializing the variable i to 1, setting up the condition for the loop (i < 10), and then incrementing i by one on each pass through the loop. On each pass through the loop, you duplicate the ball0_mc movie clip on the Stage and assign it a new instance name and level. On the first pass through the loop, you'll be creating ball1_mc on level 1. On the second pass, you'll get ball2_mc on level 2, and so on.

2. Save and test your movie. It doesn't look like much happened, does it?

That's just because the balls, except for ball0_mc, are all stacked one on top of the other in the middle of the Stage. If you choose Debug > List Objects in the test window, you'll see that you have 10 instances of the ball movie clip—ball0_mc through ball9_mc. If you're really observant, you'll notice that the ball that is looping on the Stage continually stays behind the balls it's looping around. Oops. There's a little depth problem there.

Obviously, the next thing to do is get the rest of those balls moving around the Stage so you can actually see them.

To get all of the balls moving, you need to do two things —you need to offset their positions from one another, and you need to set each ball's position. That's all going to happen inside another loop.

3. Add a new line right after the opening curly brace of your onEnterFrame event handler, and set up another for loop that will loop through the numbers 0 through 9:

```
for (var i=0; i<10; ++i) {
```

4. The question becomes where to close this loop. You want to close it after you set the Z position, but before you increment a. Add your closing curly brace now.

Your complete code at this stage for the onEnterFrame event handler should look like this:

```
onEnterFrame = function(){
        for (var i=0; i<10; ++i){
                ball0_mc.x_pos = Math.sin(a)*200;
                ball0_mc.y_pos = Math.sin(a)*200;
                ball0_mc.z_pos = Math.cos(a)*200;
        }

        a += .1;
}
```

You still need to do the following things to this bit of code:

- Make the instance name of the movie clip being updated dynamic.

- Set the offset.

- Replace variable a with your new offset.

5. To make the instance name dynamic, change each reference of ball0_mc to this:

```
this["ball"+i+"_mc"]
```

Your code should now look like this:

```
this["ball"+i+"_mc"].x_pos = Math.sin(a)*200;
this["ball"+i+"_mc"].y_pos = Math.sin(a*4)*30;
this["ball"+i+"_mc"].z_pos = Math.cos(a)*200;
```

Each time you pass through the loop, the instance name gets updated: ball0_mc, ball1_mc, ball2_mc, and so on.

6. Just above this block of code, but still inside the for loop, you need to add the code that will offset these balls from one another. Enter the following code:

```
offset = a - i/4;
```

Why is it i divided by 4? It's completely arbitrary. But to my eye, the results look good. Feel free to experiment with that number.

7. Next, replace the occurrences of a in this bit of code with offset.

8. Save and test your code.

   If you watch closely, you still have a positioning problem. Fortunately the fix for that is built into the 3D engine—all you have to do is call the fixDepths() function.

9. Just above the line where you increment a (outside of the for loop where you set your positioning), add the following line:

   ```
   this.fixDepths();
   ```

10. Save and test your movie. Try setting that up by hand! (See Figure 14.29.)

Figure 14.29 By using a 3D engine and a little trigonometry, you can set up complex tween-like motions that would be extremely difficult to produce any other way.

Your completed code should look like Listing 14.5.

Listing 14.5   Multiple mcs on a 3D Roll

```
#include "3d.as"

// set the properties of the 3D space
MovieClip.origin_x = 0;
MovieClip.origin_y = 0;
MovieClip.fov = 300;
MovieClip.center_x = 275;
MovieClip.center_y = 200;

// create 9 copies of the ball
for (var i=1; i<10; ++i){
      ball0_mc.duplicateMovieClip("ball"+i+"_mc", i);
}


a = 0;
this.onEnterFrame = function(){
      for (var i=0; i<10; ++i) {
      offset = a - i/4;
      // make the x oscillate
//
      this["ball"+i+"_mc"].x_pos = Math.sin(offset)*200;
      this["ball"+i+"_mc"].y_pos = Math.sin(offset*4)*30;
      this["ball"+i+"_mc"].z_pos = Math.cos(offset)*200;
      }
      this.fixDepths();
      // increment to the next position
      a += .1;
}
```

Don't stop there, play around with the numbers—reset the field of view, change how many humps you get on the Y-axis, change the value you increment variable a by, change the amount of the offset. By playing with these values, you'll get a much better handle on how they affect the file.

Summary

Now that you've taken a look at a couple of different ways to approach incorporating 3D in your Flash movies, you should be ready to start adding 3D to your own projects. You can develop your effects yourself in Flash, either by hand or by using ActionScript, or you can use third-party tools such as Swift 3D or Vecta3D to help you quickly create much more complex images.

Where do you go from here? If you're interested in working with 3D models but are unable to invest in a package such as 3ds max, LightWave 3D, or SOFTIMAGE|3D, you can find a large number of wireframe 3D models on the Internet that you can import into either Swift 3D or Vecta3D and then alter to fit your needs. A couple of sites that you can check are `www.3dcafe.com/asp/meshes.asp` and `www.digitalproducer.com/aHTM/HomeSet.htm`.

If you're interesting in expanding your ActionScript 3D capabilities, you're going to need to invest some time and study a little math. You can actually create some very interesting motion by just playing around with some simple mathematical formulas.

Chapter 15

Introduction to Object-Oriented Programming

If you're a designer who's never done any serious programming, your first tendency when you reach this chapter might be to panic. If you're a designer, why do you have to know anything about programming?

You don't have to become a brilliant programmer, but the more you know about how programming inside Flash works, the better prepared you'll be to take advantage of the power of ActionScript in your projects. You'll also be able to understand what those crazy programmers are talking about. Think about it: With a little effort on your part, you'll be able to drive the programmers nuts without using multiple masks and layers! Okay, it's time to talk about ActionScript and object-oriented programming.

In this chapter, you will learn about these topics:

- **Using object-orientated programming (OOP).** What is it? How should you think about this when developing your Flash movies? This section introduces you to some of the basics of programming and how to integrate it with MX.

- **Using MX OOP.** Programming in MX is not exactly like programming with C++, but it is getting closer. Learn a little about how it is different and where to go in MX to write code.

- **Writing OOP in MX: ActionScript coding.** This section helps you create objects and learn how to check syntax, how to output results, how (or why) to comment your code, and how to use a very powerful method of writing code called array syntax.

- **Prototyping: extending objects with ActionScript to do more.** This is not rocket science, but it includes some challenges. Learning how to make MX do more (modularly) is a good thing!

- **Event programming in MX.** This is not a new concept to MX—you might have used it in Flash 5, as in `onClipEvents`. However, MX goes to the next level. Learn how to handle events with MX, and get an introduction to using listeners.

- **Debugging your code.** This is the worst part of programming; if we could only write perfect code all the time. That's not going to happen, but MX does provide some stellar tools to make the debugging process less painful. Take a look at the improved Debug panel, and see how you can interact with your code line by line.

Programming Fundamentals

ActionScript is a type of object-oriented programming language. Object-oriented programming, or OOP, for short, is one of those terms you hear hard-core code geeks throwing around all the time. Consequently, to noncoders it sounds as though OOP is some scary, complicated topic beyond their comprehension. That couldn't be further from the truth! OOP is what is known as a programming methodology, which basically means that it's a way to think about and design solutions for programming-based problems.

Programming Methodologies

It turns out that there are two main programming methodologies: *procedural* programming and *object-oriented* programming. Most of the "classic" programming languages such as FORTRAN, Pascal, and C are based on the procedural method. This means that those languages attack problems in a step-by-step manner: First do task A, then task B, and finally task C. In procedural languages, if you use a certain bit of code a lot, you can place that bit of code into something that is known as a *function*. Functions are just small packets of reusable code. Functions don't actually do anything until you call them. When you call a function, you can pass information or values into it by using parameters or arguments. A function accepts certain parameters and then spits out a result based on those parameters.

Although procedural languages, such as C, are still used a lot, they suffer from a few distinct problems. First, although the functions in procedural programming are somewhat reusable, it's simply not possible to reuse the vast majority of procedural code. Why? Because procedural code is written to attack very specific problems. Therefore, most of the code is extremely specialized.

This specialization creates problems. Unless you are the original creator of a piece of code, it can take a long time to really comprehend what a particular piece of code does. The problem is that you must understand almost every single line of code to understand the code as a whole.

This leads to the final problem with procedural code: the fact that it is so focused on procedure. Why is this a problem? In programming, the data or information is as important as the code. There are distinct relationships between data and code that procedural languages simply ignore.

To address these issues and more, object-oriented programming was created. Many newer languages, such as Java, C++, JavaScript, and ActionScript, are object-oriented languages. Each of these languages implements OOP in a different way, but the one thing they all have in common is that they are based on objects.

Objects, Properties, and Methods

What, then, is an object? An *object* is simply a collection of related data and code. Sections of code within an object are known as *methods*, and pieces of data or information within an object are known as *properties*. That doesn't really explain the power of OOP, though—for that you'll need to look at an example.

Say that you want to build a car-racing game. In a procedural language, you would have to keep track of a lot of data: each car's speed, color, make, model, and so on. You would also need a large number of functions to handle things for each car, such as steering, turning headlights on or off, accelerating, and braking.

In an OOP language, you simply deal with a collection of car objects. You can easily create multiple car objects, with each car object being an abstract representation, or copy, of a single car object that acts as a "blueprint." The blueprint contains all the data about that car and all the code needed to manipulate the car. When you create new car objects, the blueprint relays all this information to the new objects. For example, each car object could have the same properties:

- color
- speed
- make
- model

Note

An abstraction of a car might sound a little bizarre. Whether you realize it or not, though, you think in abstractions all the time. A picture of a chair is not a chair. But you recognize the picture as *representing* a chair. That's an abstraction. That's all objects are, abstractions of ideas.

Each car object could also have the same methods:

- accelerate
- brake
- turn
- toggleHeadlights

The properties describe the object; the methods make the object do something. Although each one of your car objects is created from the same blueprint, the actual information inside each car object is unique and is not related to any of the other car objects (unless you made it that way). This means that although all car objects have the same properties, one car might be blue and another might be red. So, after you define a blueprint for how your car object works, you can very easily stamp out a bunch of car objects based on that blueprint, similar to the way an assembly line creates mass quantities of a product based on a single product design.

Class- versus Prototype-Based OOP Languages

It turns out that different languages handle that blueprint idea differently. The first camp, which includes Java and C++, uses the idea of a class. A *class* is just a standalone section of code that fully describes how to build a particular type of object. Class-based languages are, in general, the more robust of the two types of OOP languages.

The other camp, which includes JavaScript and ActionScript, is prototype-based. In these languages, you must create a *prototype object* that acts as your blueprint. Prototype objects are just like any other object, except that they have extra information in them that describes exactly how to build copies of them. Prototype-based languages incur less overhead than class-based ones, which is why Macromedia chose to make ActionScript a prototype-based language. In Flash, the smaller the file is, the better.

Creating and Using Objects

Flash MX uses a number of built-in objects. These include everything from the most basic object of all, the `Object` object, to the `XMLSocket` object, which handles the transfer of XML data over a TCP/IP socket.

When you want to create your own object based on one of the built-in objects in Flash, you use the keyword new. So, if you want to create a new array based on the `Array` object, all you have to do is launch the Actions panel (see Figure 15.1) and type this:

```
myObject = new Array();
```

You'll notice that after new, you specify the pre-existing object that you want your new object to be based on. Something else interesting happens here. Not only are you specifying the name of the object that you want, but you're also calling a function to create that object. How can you tell? Any time you see parentheses following an item in ActionScript, it's a pretty good indicator that you're dealing with a function or method. The parentheses indicate that you can pass a parameter or argument to the function.

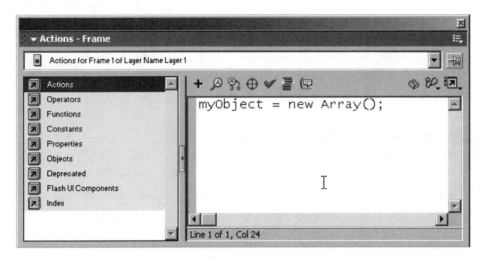

Figure 15.1   Use the Actions panel to create a new object.

 Tip

Notice the semicolon at the end of the line of code in Figure 15.1. Semicolons in ActionScript are like periods at the end of a sentence: They end a statement. Theoretically, you can sometimes get away without using semicolons, but don't go there. As your code becomes increasingly complex, you'll find yourself in a world of hurt if you don't follow the syntax rules.

When you create a new object, you are actually calling the prototype object's constructor method. A *constructor method* is just a special function that initializes your new object for you. Remember what a constructor method does—you'll be creating your own later!

Exercise 15.1   Creating a Shopping List Object

Let's say that you want to create a new array object to hold a shopping list. You can think of an array as rows of "holes" that hold variables, kind of like a row of mailboxes. Each mailbox has an identifier (the person who owns it) and can potentially hold some data in it (some mail). Arrays are the same. Each "slot" in an array has a unique identifier called its index, and each slot can hold a variable.

The first step is to create your array; then you have to populate it. The Array object also happens to have a built-in property called length, which contains the number of elements in the array.

1. Create a new file.
2. Select frame 1 in Layer 1, and launch the Actions panel.

Even if you've never used ActionScript, this exercise will be easiest to do using Expert mode. From the Options menu in the Actions panel, select Expert (see Figure 15.2).

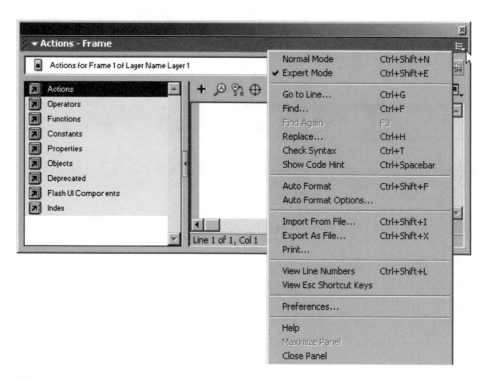

Figure 15.2   Use the Options menu to switch the Actions panel to Expert mode.

3. Now you're ready to create your first object. Type the following in the Actions list:

```
ShoppingList = new Array();
```

4. You've just created a new instance of the Array object (okay, you really haven't created it yet, but you will as soon as you test your movie), but right now the array is empty. So, let's put some data into a few of the arrays' "slots." When you want to directly address an element in array, you give the name of the array and then, immediately following it, specify the element in the array that you want to talk to in square brackets, like this: foo[0] (Arrays always start at 0).

```
ShoppingList[0] = "bread";
ShoppingList[1] = "milk";
ShoppingList[2] = "toilet paper";
```

5. To actually see the values of the elements in the ShoppingList array, you'll need to write a couple of lines of code that will print the contents of your array in the Output window. For this you'll use a trace action (see Figure 15.3). Under the last item that you added to the ShoppingList, add the following lines:

```
trace(ShoppingList.length);
for (i=0; i < ShoppingList.length; i++) {
    trace (ShoppingList[i]);
}
```

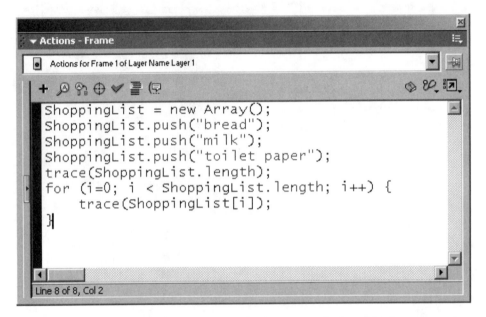

Figure 15.3 Create a new Array object and use the push method to add information to it. Use the trace action to display the information that you just added to the object in the Output window.

Note

If you want to display the properties in dynamic text fields rather than in the Output window, you must pass the values of the properties into variables and use the variables in the text fields. You can't directly access a property, even using dot syntax, from a text field.

The first line just prints the number of elements in the ShoppingList array; it's just a check for you.

Tip

Whenever you are working with blocks of code, you should add the closing curly brace as soon as you insert the opening curly brace. This will save you from syntax errors.

6. Before you test your new code, you should check for any syntax errors. Either click the blue checkmark just above the Actions list or press Ctrl+T (Windows) or Cmd+T (Macintosh).

Warning

Be forewarned that the Ctrl+T and Cmd+T shortcuts work this way only when you are in the Actions panel. Outside the Actions panel, they launch the Transform panel.

7. If you get the message "This Script Contains No Errors," proceed to Step 10 (see Figure 15.4). Otherwise, check the Output window and start debugging. Check the code in Listing 15.1 if you are having problems.

Figure 15.4   The Output window shows the result of the `trace` action that you set up for the `ShoppingList` object.

Tip

When you're working with ActionScript, both spelling and case count! If you're having problems, triple-check both.

Tip

The `trace` action is incredibly useful when you are testing and debugging ActionScript in Flash. You can use it to output strings of information, expressions, or both.

8. Save your file as shoppinglist.fla, and test your movie.

Your shopping list pops up in the Output window. If it doesn't, go back and check your code. It should be exactly the same as the code shown in Listing 15.1, minus the comments.

Listing 15.1   The Completed ActionScript for Creating and Displaying the Items in the *ShoppingList* Array Object, with Added Comments

```
// Create a new instance of the Array object
//
ShoppingList = new Array();
//
// Add new items to the ShoppingList array
//
trace (ShoppingList.length);
ShoppingList.push("bread");
ShoppingList.push("milk");
ShoppingList.push("toilet paper");
//
// List the items in the array in the Output window
//
for (i=0; i < ShoppingList.length; i++) {
    trace (ShoppingList[i]);
}
```

Note

Comments in Flash ActionScript (and C, C++, JavaScript, and Java, for that matter) are preceded by two forward slashes. Anything on the line after the slashes is not interpreted by Flash. If you want to comment multiple lines at one time, all you have to do is enclose the entire comment block, like this: `/* your comments here */`.

Tip

Adding comments to your code not only improves readability, but it also helps you document your thought process as you develop. You might have heard the phrase "Real coders don't comment." Real coders who don't comment should be slapped. Wading through year-old code trying to remember why you did something is a real pain in the backside. Make life easier on yourself and those who come after you: Comment your code.

If you've been working in Flash for a while, you've noticed that this same dot syntax is used to set and retrieve properties and variables of movie clips. This is because—you guessed it—movie clips *are* objects. The only difference between movie clip objects and other objects in Flash 5 is that instances of movie clip objects can't be created by using the new action. Instead, new movie clip objects are created by using the `attachMovie` or `duplicateMovie` actions. Also, movie clip objects can't be removed like normal objects; they are destroyed with the `removeMovieClip` method.

Static Objects

Not all of the built-in objects are used to create new objects. Some of them, including Key, Math, Mouse, and Selection, you can just use directly. These are known as *static* objects. For example, say that you want to use the Math object's sqrt method to get a number's square root. All you would have to type is this:

```
Answer = Math.sqrt(9);
trace(Answer);
```

Of course, you need the trace action only if you want to check your results in the Output window.

Array Syntax

As you can tell, creating objects is pretty easy. When you get used to it, using dot syntax is easy, too. As it happens, there's a second way to access the methods and properties of an object. This is frequently referred to as *array syntax* because it's based on the same method that you use to access the elements of an array.

Each element in an array has a unique number associated with it, as with lines on a piece of paper. The numbers start with 0 for the first element and simply increment by 1 from there. If you want to access the first element of your array, you use the array access operator [ ], like this:

```
first = ShoppingList[0];
trace (first);
```

The result that you see in the Output window is bread.

When you use array syntax to access an object's methods or properties, you don't reference them by number; you use the actual name of the method or property. This is sometimes referred to as an *associative array*. So, if you want to get the length property of your ShoppingList object using array syntax, you would type this:

```
size = ShoppingList["length"];
trace (size);
```

The result is exactly the same as accessing the length property with dot syntax. It's just a different approach.

Calling methods using array syntax is very similar; you just need to have the parentheses after the access operator:

```
ShoppingList["push"]("juice");
```

Note

You can use array syntax and dot syntax together when accessing a property of an object. For example, suppose that `ShoppingList` was a property of a larger object called `Groceries`. You could access the same length property of `ShoppingList` with these lines:

```
size = Groceries.ShoppingList["length"];
trace (size);
```

This code would result in the same output, despite using both dot syntax and array syntax in the same statement. Again, it's just another approach.

Notice that you are passing strings, not expressions, into these operators. Because it is just a string that you are passing into the array access operators, you can do all sorts of interesting and useful things. For example, the next two examples do exactly what the previous one does, just in a slightly different way. In the first example, you pass the name of the method into a variable. You then use the variable in place of the method name:

```
action = "push";
ShoppingList[action]("juice");
```

Note

Strings versus expressions: Strings in Flash are a series of characters, numbers, or punctuation marks enclosed in double or single quotation marks. Strings are interpreted literally. Expressions are variables or numbers that are evaluated to produce a value. The value can either be numeric or character—for example:

```
x = "one";
y = "two";
combo = (x + " and " + y);
trace (combo);
```

The strings "one" and "two" are passed into the variables x and y. The variables x and y are evaluated in the expression being passed into the variable combo. The result is the string one and two in the Output window (see Figure 15.5).

Figure 15.5 The Output window shows the result of concatenation of (x + " and " + y).

Look at another example of code that does something very similar. The code that follows is attached to a button. When you press the button, you dynamically generate 10 randomly placed instances of the shoppingBag movie clip on the Stage.

```
on(release) {
    for (i=0; i < 10; i++) {
        _root.attachMovie("shoppingBag", "mybag" + i, i);
        _root["mybag" + i]._x = Math.floor(550*Math.random()+10);
        _root["mybag" + i]._y = Math.floor(300*Math.random()+20);
        _root["mybag" + i].myinstance = "mybag"+i;
    }
}
```

You can actually see this snippet of code in action. Open shoppingBag.swf from the Examples/Chapter15 folder. The blue button in the lower-left corner has this snippet of code attached to it. Press the button, and you can see the dynamically generated instances of the shoppingBag. Notice that each instance of the shoppingBag has its own unique name—mybag followed by a number. The shopping bag is actually draggable, so if you can't see all the instances of the shopping bag, feel free to drag the bags around.

Array syntax is useful because movie clips are objects themselves (this includes the main Timeline). The variables that are held in a movie clip are actually properties of that object. By using the special keyword this (which just means "the object I am currently in"), you can easily access *any* variable dynamically by using array syntax. Consider this example:

```
dairy = "milk";
vegetable = "beans";
fruit = "mango";
myFood = fruit;
trace(this[myFood]);
```

You guessed it! This code prints mango in the Output window.

Extending Objects

With ActionScript, you can add your own methods and properties to an object any time you want. If you want to add a new property called type to your ShoppingList object, you would simply use this line:

```
ShoppingList.type = "Grocery list";
```

Adding new methods to an object isn't quite as straightforward, but it is still fairly simple. The idea is that you assign a new property to your object that is actually a function (hence, you have a method):

```
ShoppingList.oddSize = function(){
    return (this.length%2);
}
```

Note

The percent symbol (%) in the oddSize function is known as the *modulo operator*. The modulo operator divides the value of the expression on the left by the value of the expression on the right and returns the remainder.

You use the this keyword to reference the object that this method will be placed inside. This method returns 1 if there are an odd number of elements in this array; it returns 0 otherwise.

Note

You could also directly assign the function like this:

```
function oddSize (){
       return (this.length%2);
}
shoppingList.oddSize = oddSize;
```

Both ways work, but the technique shown here for adding methods is discouraged because you end up having copies of functions in places where they don't belong (in this case, the location where you created the oddSize function).

That's all there is to it! You can also use this technique to override the built-in method for an object. For example, the Array object has a built-in method called reverse that is used to reverse all the elements currently in the array. If you want to replace the Array object's reverse method with your own, all you have to do is create a function and then attach it to the Array object. You will learn later in this chapter why attaching the method in this manner overrides the built-in method. This function can be used to reverse an array:

```
list = new Array();
list.reverse = function(){
     for (var i=0;i<(this.length/2);++i){
          temp = this[i];
          this[i] = this[this.length-1-i];
          this[this.length-1-i] = temp;
     }
}
```

All of this is fine and good for individual objects, but sometimes you want to extend *every* object of a particular type. For example, you might want to add a new method to every Array object in your movie.

Note

Not a programmer and curious about what the code in the `list_reverse` function is actually doing? This is one of those `for` loops that was discussed earlier in Chapter 6, "Introduction to ActionScripting." The variable `i` is initialized to 0. As long as `i` is less than the length of the array you are using (divided by 2), the statements in the loop are executed. Every time you pass through the loop, `i` gets incremented by 1. For an array with a length of 4, here are the values on each pass:

i	this.length/2	temp	this[i]	this[this.length-1-i]
0	2	0	4 − 1 − 0 = 3	this[3]=0
1	2	1	4 − 1 − 1 = 2	this[2]=1
2	2	2	4 − 1 − 2 = 1	this[1]=2
3	2	3	4 − 1 − 3 = 0	this[0]=3

Here's another thing of note about this particular piece of code: Notice that you can't just swap the numbers one for the other. First you have to hand them off to an intermediary called `temp`. Think of it this way: If I am holding a box and you are holding a box (these are heavy boxes, with two hands required), we can't exchange boxes without one of us handing our box to someone else. It's the same way with variables: The value of `i` must be passed to a temporary holder while the values are being updated.

Extending Prototype Objects

To understand how you can extend prototype objects, you need to understand how Flash "finds" the methods and properties of an object.

So, if you were to type this line, Flash would first look to see if `oddsize` is attached to `ShoppingList`:

```
ShoppingList.oddsize();
```

Flash doesn't give up if it isn't! It then looks in a special (and not particularly obvious) place: The prototype object inside this object's prototype object.

Say what? Look at it this way: The prototype object `Array` already exists. The `Array` object contains another object named `prototype`. Any properties or methods that are inside the `prototype` object automatically are available to any objects that are created based on the `Array` object.

Here's how Flash plays "Hunt the Property (or Method)":

1. It check the object itself.

2. It checks the object named `prototype` within the object's prototype object.

Take a look at an example. If you want to add a new property called `priority` to every single array object in your whole movie, you would do this:

```
Array.prototype.priority = "urgent";
```

The really neat thing about this is that it affects *all* `Array` objects, even the ones that were created *before* you entered this code. That's power.

Finally, to round out this section on extending objects, you cannot add properties just to an object's prototype—you can also add methods! It looks a little strange syntax-wise because, to do so, you have to use an alternative way of defining functions. That way involves stating the name of the function and then setting it equal to a function definition. For example, say that you want to add a method to all your `Array` objects that will tell you whether your arrays have 15 or fewer items in them (so that you can go through the express line):

```
Array.prototype.expressLine = function(){
        return(this.length<=15);
}
```

Now every single array in your movie will have a method to check to see if there are fewer than 15 items in the array.

Passing by Value versus Passing by Reference

You need to understand one more important concept about using objects before you get into creating your own prototype objects. You need to understand the difference between passing by *value* and passing by *reference*. When you use a variable to send a value to a function like the one here, what happens?

```
function square(x){
        x = x *x;
        return (x);
}
a = 10;
b = square(a);
trace(b)
```

The variable a gets passed to the function by value. In other words, the value of the variable is sent into the function, and the actual variable isn't touched. The variable a is never modified because the multiplication inside the function is happening to a *copy* of the variable. The value of the variable a remains 10. The value of the variable b is modified because that's the variable that the function returns the value to. Variable b is 100 after this function is called.

Although all normal variables are passed by value in this manner, objects are not. Objects are passed by reference. This means that rather than making a copy of the object, Flash passes a reference to the original object into the function, not a copy. So, take a look at this code:

```
function addBread(list){
    list.push("bread");
}
ShoppingList = new Array();
addBread(ShoppingList);
```

In this case, ShoppingList is being passed to the addBread function by reference, so the push action inside the function actually adds to ShoppingList object! After this function is called, the ShoppingList object has the value bread as the first and only item in the array. So, any time you have to pass an object to a function, make sure that you don't modify the object unless you want the original to be modified.

Creating Custom Prototype Objects

For the majority of projects, using Flash's built-in objects is more than sufficient. Occasionally, though, especially with larger projects, you might need to create custom prototype objects. Why would you need to do this? You might be working with information that lends itself very nicely to being treated as an object. For example, say that you need to develop a check-in, check-out system for your local library. What does a library have lots of? Books, of course. You could create a Book object—Flash doesn't have one of those. Each book has properties, such as a title, an author, a year of publication, and so on. But what about methods? What kind of methods would a book have? Well, if you need to check a book in or out, you would need a method to handle that. Any time you are dealing with a collection of related information, you should be thinking about how that information could be grouped in an object.

Unlike with class-based OOP languages, in ActionScript there is no command that explicitly says, "The code beneath me defines a blueprint." In ActionScript, you simply build the various parts of the object and then tie them together at the end.

What parts do you need to build? First, you need to decide what properties your object should have. Remember, properties are used just to describe an object. Next you have to figure out what your object is actually going to do—you need to create methods to control your object's behavior.

In the next exercises, you go through the creation process for a custom book prototype object. Each Book object will be capable of holding all the information about a book, including being able to check the book out, check the book in, and retire the book.

Exercise 15.2 Initializing the Basic Properties

The first method that you need to create is a constructor method that will actually initialize a new Book object. In this case, when you initialize a new Book object, you need to set up a few variables. Notice that the constructor method has the same name as the type of object you're creating. You give the constructor method and the object that you want to create the same name so that you know what type of object the constructor is actually creating. It wouldn't make any sense to give your constructor a name of Dog if it's going to be used to create Book objects—unless, of course, you're really trying to drive someone nuts.

1. Create a new file. Save it as book.fla.

2. Select frame 1 and launch the Actions panel.

3. To initialize the new Book object, enter the following code:

```
// Book Object
//--------------------------------------
// Initialize the Book Object
function Book(author, title, available){
        this.author = author;
        this.title = title;
        this.available = available;
        this.retired = false;
}
```

4. Save your file.

That wasn't so bad—it initialized the basic properties of the Book object for you. Now you need to create the other methods for this object.

Exercise 15.3 Creating the *checkOut* Method

The next method checks the book out for you. If the book is available for checkout, the method returns a Boolean true; otherwise, it returns a Boolean false. Notice that the name of this function is the name of the class, an underscore, and then the name of the method. This naming scheme is not necessary, but it is used so that the code is easier to understand.

1. Position your cursor after the last curly brace in the Actions list, and press Return or Enter to add a new line.

2. Beginning on the new line, add the following code:

```
// Check the book out
Book.prototype.checkout = function(){
    if (this.available == true && !this.retired){
        trace("You checked out " + this.title);
        this.available = false;
        return(true);
    }else{
        trace("I'm sorry, you can't check out " + this.title + ".
        ➥It's already checked out.");
        return (false);
    }
}
```

3. Check your syntax and save your file. Save early, save often. It's a good thing.

What does this code do for you? You're planning to check out a book. The first thing the code does is check to see if the book is available. For a book to be available, it must not be checked out (`available = false`), and it can't be retired (`retired = true`).

> **Note**
>
> The ==, &&, !, and + operators get used in this block of code. These might be new to you. The equality operator (==) tests two expressions for equality; it does not make any value assignments. If the two expressions are equal, it returns a value of `true`. If the expressions are not equal, it returns a value of `false`. The && operator is known as the "short-circuit and": It tests the expression on the left side first. If that expression is true, && tests the expression on the right side. If both expressions are true, a value of `true` is returned. If either expression is false, a value of `false` is returned. The !, or logical NOT, operator inverts the value of an expression. So, if a book has been retired, `this.retired` would have a value of `true`. Inverting the value sets it to `false`, so you get kicked out of the `if` statement. That's a little funky, yes, but think through it a couple of times. The + is easy—it's used to concatenate strings of information. If the book you are checking out is *The Hunt for Red October*, the `trace` action prints "You checked out *The Hunt for Red October*" in the Output window.

If the value of `available` is equivalent to `true` and `retired` is not `true`, you can check out the book. If you check out the book, you need to change the value of `available` to `false`. Finally, if the book is available for checkout, the function returns a value of `true`. Otherwise, it returns a value of `false`.

You'll notice that there are a couple of `trace` actions in this function as well. These give you visual confirmation in the Output window that your code is working as expected.

Exercise 15.4   Creating the checkIn Method

Next you need to define the checkIn method for your object. Not surprisingly, this looks very similar to the checkOut method.

1. Position your cursor after the last curly brace in the Actions list, and press Return or Enter to add a new line.

2. Beginning on the new line, add the following code:

```
// Check the book in
Book.prototype.checkIn = function(){
    if (this.available == false){
        trace("Thank you for returning " + this.title);
        this.available = true;
        return(true);
    }else{
        trace("You can't check " + this.title + "in. It hasn't
        ↝been checked out yet.");
        return (false);
    }
}
```

3. Check your syntax and save your file.

This time, you are planning to return a book that you previously checked out. The first thing the code does is check to see if the book has actually been checked out. If the value of available is equivalent to false, you can check the book back in. You don't have to worry about whether the book has been retired; a book can't be retired until it has been checked back in. If you check the book in, you need to change the value of available to true so that someone else can check it out. If the book is available for checkout, the function returns a value of true. Otherwise, it returns a value of false.

Exercise 15.5   Creating the retire Method

Next you'll set up a method to enable you to retire a book. This doesn't delete the Book object; it just makes the book unavailable for checkout.

1. Position your cursor after the last curly brace in the Actions list, and press Return or Enter to add a new line.

2. Beginning on the new line, add the following code:

```
// Retire the book
Book.prototype.retire = function(){
    if (this.available){
        this.retired = true;
        trace("You have retired " + this.title);
        return(true);
    }else{
        trace("You can't retire " + this.title + ".    It is
        ↝currently checked out.");
```

```
                return (false);
        }
    }
```

3. Save your file.

Now you can retire a book so that it can't be checked out again.

It seems like the only thing you're missing is a method to delete a Book object. Naturally, Flash deletes an object from memory when it is no longer in use, but sometimes you want to explicitly remove an object. An operator built into ActionScript can take care of this for you. You just can't build it into your prototype object. Why? An object isn't allowed to delete itself. To delete an object, you use the `delete` operator (don't add this to your file right now).

```
delete(myBook);
```

The `delete` operator completely removes an instance of the Book object. It's the same as throwing the book into the incinerator.

Now you have a full custom prototype object. Your complete code should look like the code in Listing 15.2.

Listing 15.2   The Completed Code for the *Book* Object

```
// Book Object
//-------------------------------------
// Initialize the Book Object
function Book(author, title, available) {
    this.author = author;
    this.title = title;
    this.available = available;
    this.retired = false;
}
// Check the book out
Book.prototype.checkout = function(){
    if (this.available == true && !this.retired) {
        trace("You checked out: " + this.title);
        this.available = false;
        return(true);
    }else{
        trace("I'm sorry, you can't check out " + this.title + ".  It's
        ➥already checked out.");
        return(false);
    }
}
// Check the book in
Book.prototype.checkIn = function(){
    if (this.available == false) {
```

continues ▶

Listing 15.2   Continued

```
            trace("Thank you for returning " + this.title);
            this.available = true;
            return(true);
      }else{
            trace("You can't check " + this.title + "in.   It hasn't been
            ➥checked out yet.");
            return(false);
      }
}
// Retire the book
Book.prototype.retire = function() {
      if (this.available){
            this.retired = true;
            trace("You have retired " + this.title);
            return (true);
      }else{
            trace("You can't retire " + this.title + ".   It is currently
            ➥checked out.");
            return (false);
      }
}
```

Now you can start to use the methods that you just built into your Book object to create some books and then manipulate them.

Exercise 15.6   Creating New Instances of the *Book* Object

Creating your new objects is a straightforward process. You just use the Book constructor and pass it the parameters that it needs to initialize the individual book properties.

1. Position your cursor after the last curly brace in the Actions list, and press Return or Enter to add a new line.

2. Create three new Book objects: myBook, yourBook, and hisBook.

   ```
   myBook = new Book("Clancy, Tom", "The Hunt for Red October", true);
   yourBook = new Book("Jordan, Robert", "Lord of Chaos", true);
   hisBook = new Book("Stephenson, Neil", "The Diamond Age", true);
   ```

   This gives you three instances of the Book object in your current movie.

3. You probably want to prove to yourself that those objects are actually there (see Figure 15.6). All you need to do is throw in a few trace actions:

   ```
   // Display the contents of the Book objects
   trace(myBook.title + " by " + myBook.author + ".   Available:   " +
   ➥myBook.available);
   trace(yourBook.title + " by " + yourBook.author + ".   Available:   "
   ➥+ yourBook.available);
   trace(hisBook.title + " by " + hisBook.author + ".   Available:   " +
   ➥hisBook.available);
   ```

4. Check your syntax. Save and test your file.

If all went well, you should see all the properties for the three Book objects displayed in the Output window. If not, go back and check your code. Remember, spelling and capitalization count!

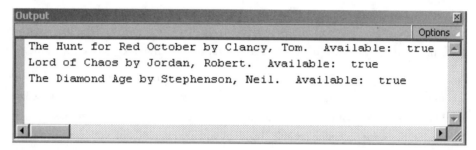

Figure 15.6   After you have created your new objects, you can set up a trace action to display their contents in the Output window.

Exercise 15.7   Using the Methods to Manipulate the *Book* Objects

Now that you can see the properties of your Book objects, it's time to manipulate them.

1. Position your cursor after the last curly brace in the Actions list, and press Return or Enter to add a new line.

2. Now it's playtime. Try adding the following lines:

```
myBook.checkOut();
myBook.retire();
myBook.checkIn();
myBook.retire();
yourBook.checkIn();
yourBook.checkOut();
hisBook.retire();
```

3. Save and test your file.

You can monitor what is happening to your Book objects in the Output window. If your Output window doesn't match Figure 15.7, go back and check your code for errors.

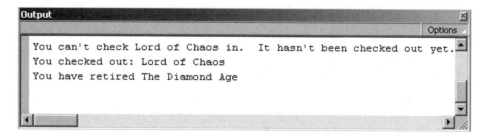

Figure 15.7   Now that your objects have been created, you can use their methods to manipulate them. The values of the trace actions displayed in the Output window let you know what's going on. If your output doesn't match this, you need to do some debugging.

First, you check out myBook (*The Hunt for Red October*). Then you try to retire it, but you can't because it's currently checked out. So, you check myBook (*The Hunt for Red October*) back in and then retire it. Next you try to check in yourBook (*Lord of Chaos*). But yourBook (*Lord of Chaos*) hasn't been checked out yet, so you can't. Instead, you check out yourBook (*Lord of Chaos*) and then retire hisBook (*The Diamond Age*). Play around with this until you are satisfied that you understand how these methods are working.

So, how did you create your new Book objects? You called the constructor just like you would for any other object. You don't always call the constructor function this way. For example, if you are trying to create an object and that object's prototype hasn't been declared in the same Timeline (movie clip) that you are currently in, you must explicitly reference the Timeline in which the prototype was declared. If you are working in a movie clip inside of the main Timeline and you want to create a new Book object inside the movie clip, you have to reference the constructor on the main Timeline:

```
MyBook = new _root.Book("Suess, Dr.", "Hop on Pop", 1);
```

Just as an added note, objects are good candidates for external libraries in Flash because they are fully self-contained. This lets you easily use the same library file for multiple projects. You could place your entire Book object (minus the code from Exercises 15.6 and 15.7) into a text file called Book.as. After you do this, all you have to do to be able to use the code that you just wrote is load it into your current file using an include statement. The only line in your Actions list would be this:

```
#include "Book.as"
```

Be very careful *not* to include a semicolon at the end of the include statement. If you do, your code won't run.

You can then add any additional statements that you want to use to work with the Book object.

Designing Objects for Flash

Now you know technically how to create your own custom prototype objects in ActionScript. What you might not know, especially if ActionScript is your first foray into the world of OOP, is how to design your objects.

Literally dozens of books cover object design. In fact, good object design is seen as less of a science and more of an art. However, you should stick to a few basic principles.

First, make sure that your object encapsulates a single abstract idea. This keeps your object focused and allows for a better chance of reuse because the object isn't overly specialized.

When you are designing the methods (the code that makes the object do something) for an object, try to avoid having to directly manipulate a property of the object. Instead, design functions to manipulate internal variables as needed. By creating code in this manner, you can modify the code internal to an object without ever having to change any of the code that actually uses the object (because the method calls won't change).

Finally, try to keep the actual usage of an object as simple as possible. The object itself can have horribly complex code inside it, but that should be transparent to the end user. The real art of coding is making something complex appear to be simple.

Events

Now that you know all about objects, it's time to take a foray into a new subject: *events*. Events and basic event-based programming existed in Flash 5, but they've grown significantly in both complexity and power in Flash MX.

So, what are events? An event is just when something happens in your movie. When Flash jumps to a frame, that's an event. When you click with the mouse, that's an event as well. An event can occur at any time. What it comes down to, though, is that events themselves aren't all that interesting. It's how you capture and handle those events that is both interesting and very powerful. Two different methods exist for handling events in Flash MX: overwriting and using listeners.

Event Handling via Overwriting

Overwriting was created back in Flash 5 and is the simpler event-handling method.

The idea behind overwriting is that Flash automatically attempts to call a particular method in an object when an event occurs. Usually, the method that is being called doesn't actually exist at first—or, if it does exist, it just performs a basic default action. So, to do what you want when the event occurs, you need to overwrite the method in question.

For example, the XML object contains a method called onLoad that is called any time new XML has been loaded and parsed. This is important because such operations take time, and often you will want your movie to pause while the XML is being worked on. Overwriting the onLoad method looks like this:

```
myXML = new XML();
myXML.onLoad = function(){
```

```
    trace("Got some XML!");
}
```

Now, when XML is loaded, you'll see "Got some XML!" printed in the Output window. Usually you would want to do something more significant, such as tell a particular movie clip to play, but this shows the concept.

It's very important to note that because the onLoad method is part of the myXML object, any reference to this inside onLoad will refer to myXML. Forgetting the scope of event handler code is a very common error; make sure that you always check that this means what you are expecting it to.

The use of overwriting for handling events was limited in Flash 5, but in Flash MX it's used all the time. For example, you can now handle the events for buttons and movie clips in this manner:

```
// handle a button's onPress event
MyButton.onPress = function(){
     this._parent.gotoAndStop("done");
}
```

Here, a particular button named myButton is getting its onPress method overwritten. This means that each time this button is pressed, the gotoAndStop method will be called.

```
// handle a MCs onEnterFrame event
myMC.onEnterFrame = function(){
     this._x += 2;
}
```

In this example, a movie clip's onEnterFrame method is being overwritten. The enterFrame event is fired each time Flash could potentially display a new frame. (For example, in a movie set to 12fps, an enterFrame event will fire 12 times a second.) So, this code moves the myMC movie clip 2 pixels to the right each frame.

At any time you can "turn off" your overwritten method by simply setting it to be undefined, like this:

```
myMC.onEnterFrame = undefined;
```

Using Listeners

Handling events via overwriting works well when an event always will be handled by a particular object. However, it tends not to work as cleanly when the event is more global in nature. For example, if you want to capture key presses using overwriting, you might try to do something like this (where myMC is a movie clip):

```
myMC.onKeyDown = function(){
     if (Key.isDown(Key.UP)){
```

```
              trace("You pressed the up arrow!");
       }
}
```

This code will always work fine with Flash 5, but Flash MX introduces the concept of movie clip *focus*. That is, movie clips, just like buttons or text fields, can now have focus, although only one movie clip at a time can have focus. Unless a movie clip currently has focus, it won't receive key or mouse events. Movie clip focus was introduced to handle the more complex tabbing/key shortcuts that Flash MX's new components support and also because now there is a better way to handle Mouse and Key events: listeners.

A *listener* is just an object—any object, in fact—that has particular methods defined. Which methods are defined inside it are based on what events it will listen to. For example, if you look up the Mouse object (Objects > Movie > Mouse) in the Actions panel, you will see that it defines three listener methods: onMouseDown, onMouseUp, and onMouseMove. So, to handle the mouse being pressed, a listener object must have a method in it named onMouseDown. A listener object can define any or all of the listener methods for the object that it will be listening to. So, an object can listen for onMouseDown events but ignore onMouseMove events.

Just having a listener object defined doesn't do anything, though. For a listener to receive events, you have to subscribe it to an event source. An event source is the object that defined what listener methods you could use, which, in this case, is Mouse. You do this by using the addListener method—for example:

```
// first create an object you'll use as a listener
myListener = new Object();
myListener.onMouseDown = function(){
     trace("The mouse was pressed!");
}

// then subscribe the listener
Mouse.addListener(myListener);
```

Then at any time you can unsubscribe the listener like this:

```
Mouse.removeListener(myListener);
```

This functionality is included in a number of the built-in objects in Flash MX, namely these:

- Key
- Mouse
- Selection

- Stage
- TextField

You've been introduced to some of the core concepts of object-oriented programming. Now the next step is knowing how to debug your code when you start writing it.

Debugging

With all your newly found programming knowledge, you are probably tempted to just jump right in and start coding. The problem with that is that, for any nontrivial code, you tend to spend just as much, if not more, time debugging the code as you do actually writing the code in the first place!

Debugging is easily the most frustrating part of programming, but at least some of that frustration can be cured by learning Flash's debugging tools. In fact, Flash MX's debugging tools stand head and shoulders above the tools available in earlier versions!

trace

The most simple yet probably most used debugging tool available in Flash (since version 4, no less) is the trace function. The trace function simply accepts a single argument and spits out that argument to the Output window (Window > Output).

```
trace("value: "+value);
```

Typically, trace is used to see values of variables at given points in your code so that you can figure out what is going on. It's also useful to sprinkle a number of trace statements in your code so that you can trace the logical path through your code.

Keep in mind, though, that trace works only in a test movie and will not work in the browser. Also remember that before you export your final SWF for a project, you need to go to the Flash tab in Publish Settings (File > Publish Settings) and turn on Remove Trace Actions. This prevents the trace actions from actually going into your final SWF.

Make sure that you don't turn on the Remove Trace Actions option accidentally: It will prevent all traces in your movie from working, even in Test Movie mode.

The Debug Panel

The Debug panel was present in Flash 5, but it was cumbersome and, well, buggy. In MX, all that has changed; the new and improved Debug panel is a programmer's dream come true. Here's a rundown of what the Debug panel can do while your movie *is running*:

- View the full movie clip structure of a movie

- View and modify all variables in a movie

- Mark specific variables and track those in their own area

- Keep track of the current function that is running and what functions were called along the way (this is called the call stack)

- Create or remove breakpoints on any line of code in the movie so that you can stop code execution to view its state (variables, properties, and so on)

- Step into or out of user-defined functions, to either examine them more closely or stop doing so

- Skip the execution of user-defined functions

First, to be able to use the Debugger panel (see Figure 15.8), you need to test your movie by going to the Control menu and selecting Debugger Movie (Ctrl+Shift+Enter).

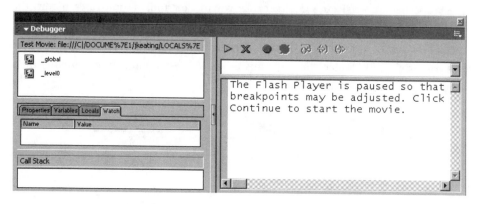

Figure 15.8   The Debug panel is divided into four panes.

Movie Clip Tree View

The movie clip Tree view displays a full, hierarchal tree of every movie clip in the movie. You can expand, collapse, and select movie clips in the tree. In addition, the tree is dynamic and updates as movie clips are added by ActionScript (see Figure 15.9).

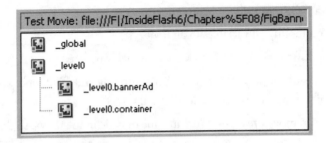

Figure 15.9   Tree view of a movie's movie clips in the Debug panel.

Objects/Properties/Variables

The next frame down enables you to view all the objects, properties, and variables within your movie. Both the Properties and Variables tabs are context-sensitive; they display the information about the movie clip that is currently selected in the Tree view frame above it.

The Properties tab (see Figure 15.10) enables you to view and, in some cases, modify the properties of the movie clips in your movie. Properties that you can only view but not modify are shown in a light gray in the interface; those that you can modify are shown in a darker gray. By double-clicking items in the Value column, you can modify their value (that is, if they are editable).

Properties	Variables	Locals	Watch

_level0

Name	Value
_alpha	100
_currentframe	2
_droptarget	
_focusrect	1
_framesloaded	3
_height	398
_highquality	1
_name	
_quality	HIGH
_rotation	0
_soundbuftime	5
_target	/
_totalframes	3
_url	file:///F|/API/APISiteShell/main.swf
_visible	true
_width	598
_x	0
_xmouse	35
_xscale	100

Figure 15.10   You can use the Properties tab to view all the properties of the selected movie clip.

The Variables tab (see Figure 15.11) is similar to the Properties tab, but instead of editing properties, you are editing actual variables in your movie. In addition to seeing just name/value pairs, you can dig down into your objects. You'll see a + sign next to any object that you can expand. Values in the Variables tab are editable in the same way as those in the Properties tab.

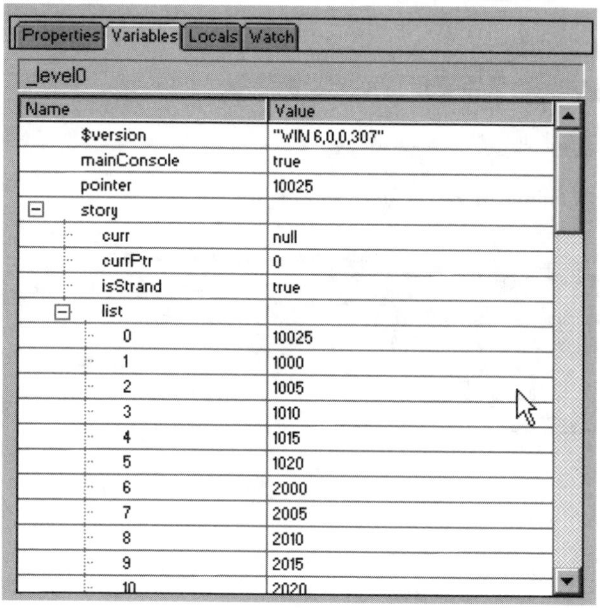

Properties	Variables	Locals	Watch

_level0

Name		Value
	$version	"WIN 6,0,0,307"
	mainConsole	true
	pointer	10025
⊟	story	
	curr	null
	currPtr	0
	isStrand	true
⊟	list	
	0	10025
	1	1000
	2	1005
	3	1010
	4	1015
	5	1020
	6	2000
	7	2005
	8	2010
	9	2015
	10	2020

Figure 15.11   The Variables tab enables you to take a look at all the variables in the movie.

The Locals tab (see Figure 15.12) is a special area where you can view variables local at the current point of execution in the program. For example, if you set a breakpoint inside a function (don't worry about what a breakpoint is for right now—we'll get to that in a minute, but for now just know that a breakpoint stops code execution), the Locals tab would display all the local variables inside that function.

Finally, the Watch tab (see Figure 15.13) enables you to view a subset of the variables and properties from the other tabs that you define. In all the other tabs, you can right-click (Control-click on the Mac) an item and select Watch. This adds the item to the Watch tab. If you do so a second time, it removes that item from the Watch tab. In addition, you can add or remove items directly from the Watch tab. However, you need to know the full path to an item to add it directly.

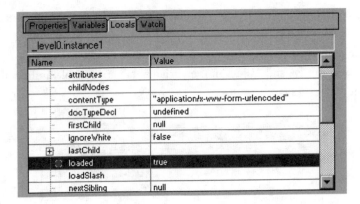

Figure 15.12   Examining the local function variables.

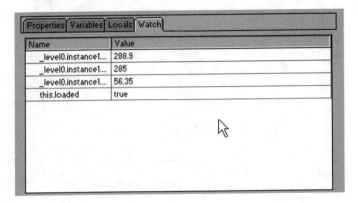

Figure 15.13   The Watch panel is used to track a few important variables.

Call Stack

The frame in the bottom-left area of the Debug panel displays the current call stack (see Figure 15.14). The call stack displays the functions that are currently being run and the function that started them. This enables you to more easily trace the path of execution in your program.

Breakpoints

The Debug panel gives you full access to all the code within your movie in its right frame. Not only can you simply view the code, but you also can interact with it by setting points in your code at which execution should halt so that you can examine the state of all the data and movie clips in your movie. These points are known as *breakpoints*.

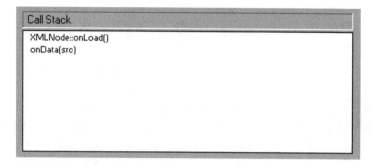

Figure 15.14   The current call stack of functions.

You can create a breakpoint at any time while debugging your movie by selecting the location of the code that you want from the drop-down menu and then selecting the line that you want to break at. Finally, you select the Toggle Breakpoint icon that is above the code pane (it looks like a stop sign—see Figure 15.15). You can later remove the breakpoint by pressing the Toggle Breakpoint icon a second time. If you want to start your code back up after it has stopped at a breakpoint, just press the Continue icon (green arrow).

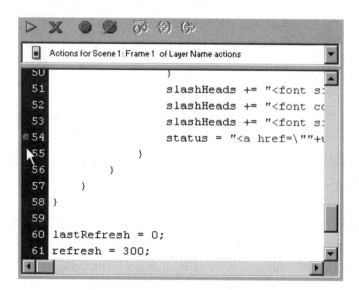

Figure 15.15   Breakpoints are shown with the stop sign icon next to them.

In addition to just starting and stopping your code, you can use the three other icons (Step Over, Step In, and Step Out—see Figure 15.16) located above the code pane for finer-grained control.

Figure 15.16   These three icons allow finer-grained control when using breakpoints to debug.

If your code is currently stopped, you can use Step Over to run that line of code but then immediately stop at the next line. This enables you to step line by line through code without having to set a lot of breakpoints. Keep in mind, though, that Step Over does *not* step into functions. It runs them but does not step through them line by line.

If your code is currently stopped on a line that contains a call to a custom function, you can use Step In to step into the function and examine it. This enables you to easily examine a function to make sure that it's doing what you think it should be.

Finally, Step Out enables you start execution of your program again but then stop as soon as the code exits from the current function it is inside. You can use this to quickly step out of a function that you were examining and get back to the code that called the function in the first place.

If you will be writing a lot of code, you will be spending a lot of time using trace and the Debug panel. If you use them and all of their abilities, you will find that your debugging effort will be much easier.

Summary

Wow, that's a lot to digest. So what key concepts should you understand before you try to move forward?

- **ActionScript in Flash MX is a full-blown object-oriented programming language.** It has prebuilt objects that you can use, or you can create your own custom objects.
- **Objects represent an abstract idea.** Objects have both properties and methods. Properties describe the object; methods describe how the object behaves.
- **You can add functionality to an existing object by attaching new methods to it.** You can also override an object's existing methods.
- **Events and event handling are key to programming complex applications in Flash.** Events can be handled either with the overwriting technique or with listeners.

- **Debugging your code is a lot easier if you use the tools that Flash MX provides you.** You still have the venerable `trace` action, but that has now been supplemented with a robust debugger that enables you to walk through, examine, and even add breakpoints to your code.

So, now you know not only what OOP is, but also how to actually use it with Flash MX. Using OOP in your Flash projects will make your code much more modular, easy to read, and easy to write!

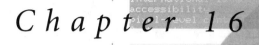

C h a p t e r 16

Inside the
Drawing API

The Drawing API (application program-

ming interface) is an exciting new feature

in Flash MX that enables you as a Flash

developer to draw vector primitives such as

lines and polygons on the fly with ActionScript. All aspects of the vectors (color, thickness, fill, and so on) are easily modified and relatively simple to use. The Drawing API is exciting because for the first time you can make your own code-driven vectors without having to resort to duplicating hundreds of movie clips or similar nasty hacks. With the API, it's now possible to draw all kinds of graphics on the fly, from graphs to simple vector 3D engines. The result: dynamic drawings that exist only as code.

In this chapter you learn how to do the following:

- Work with the virtual pen
- Change drawing styles
- Draw lines
- Draw curves
- Draw circles
- Handle fills
- Create gradients
- Draw and fill a dynamic working button

And you're going to do it all without ever touching a drawing tool!

The Drawing API's Methods

The Drawing API's methods are actually methods of the Movie Clip object. This means that you can create vector drawings in any movie clip, including the main Timeline and movie clips that you create dynamically. It's important to note, though, that because of the way the Drawing API works, any vectors that you create using it appear at the bottom of the content stack (as the bottom layer) inside the movie clip.

Before you start working with the Drawing API, you need to understand its methods:

- **moveTo.** Moves the virtual pen without drawing anything. This method takes two parameters, a value for X and a value for Y. These numbers indicate how many pixels in the X and Y directions the pen should be offset from the parent movie clip's registration point. An example of this method is moveTo(10,10).
- **lineStyle.** Sets the style of lines to be drawn. The lineStyle method can take three parameters: thickness, rgb, and alpha. The thickness of a line is in points and must be between 0 and 255. A thickness of 0 will give you a hairline (the smallest possible line that never gets wider, even when scaled). rgb is a hex

color value; the default is black: 0x000000. The alpha of the line can range from 0 to 100, with 0 being invisible and 100 being fully opaque. An example of this method is lineStyle(2,0x0000ff).

- **lineTo.** Moves the virtual pen and draws a line. This method takes two parameters, a value for X and a value for Y. It draws a line from the current pen position to the specified coordinates. An example of this method is lineTo(10,30).

- **curveTo.** Moves the virtual pen and draws a curve. The curveTo method requires four parameters—controlX, controlY, anchorX, and anchorY—that affect the bend in your line. An example of this method is curveTo(30,30,70,70).

- **clear.** Clears all code-created vectors from the current movie clip. Any drawings created with the standard Flash drawing tools are not affected. An example of this method is clear().

- **beginFill.** Starts a single-color fill. This method can take two parameters: rgb and alpha. rgb is required and must be a hex number. For example, a valid rgb for black would be 0x000000. alpha has valid values from 0 to 100. If no value is entered for alpha, Flash assumes a value of 100, or fully opaque. It goes before any lineTo or curveTo commands and requires an endFill() to finish it. An example of this method is beginFill(0xFF66FF,80).

- **beginGradientFill.** Starts a gradient fill. The beginGradientFill method must take five parameters: fillType, colors, alphas, ratios, and matrix. The fillType can be either linear or radial. colors is an array of hex colors to be used in the gradient. alpha is an array of alpha settings that corresponds to the color settings. ratios is an array of values between 0 and 255 that define the percentage of the width where the color is sampled at 100%. matrix is a bit trickier. For matrix, you can pass in a parameter that is an object that describes a 3 × 3 matrix. If you've had linear algebra, that will make sense. If you haven't, don't worry about it—just keep reading. An example of this method is beginGradientFill("linear", colors, alphas, ratios, matrix);.

- **endFill.** Ends a fill. An example of this method is endFill().

You'll notice the term *virtual pen* popping up a couple times. So what is the virtual pen? The virtual pen is the concept that the whole Drawing API is based upon: a set of coordinates that the next lineTo or curveTo call will draw from. The virtual pen defaults to the registration point of the parent movie clip. If you're working on the main Timeline, that's the upper-left corner (0,0). If you want to move the virtual pen without drawing, you use the moveTo method. The coordinate system that the virtual pen works in is just like the one used for movie clips; it's based on the relative position of the parent movie.

The best way to get used to working with the Drawing API is to dive right in and draw some basic shapes.

Drawing a Simple Square

So what do you need to do to draw a square? The first thing is to establish a line style. To draw a black square with a 2-point line at 50% alpha, the lineStyle is this:

```
this.lineStyle(2, 0x000000, 50);
```

The next step is to decide where your starting point should be. If you want the starting point, or upper-left corner, of your square to begin at the virtual pen's current location, you don't have to do anything. By default, the virtual pen right now is at the top left of the Stage. If you want to offset the virtual pen, use the moveTo() method.

Remember, the moveTo() method takes two parameters: a value for X and a value for Y. So, to move your virtual pen 10 pixels to the right and 10 pixels down, enter this:

```
this.moveTo(10, 10);
```

Okay, your line style is set and your pen is in position. Now you need to give the x and y coordinates for the corners of your square in sequential order. It's really not that hard. Just decide what you want the length of the sides to be, and use the lineTo() method to move your pen to that position. For your first horizontal line, your X position would be the current X position plus the length of the line that you want to draw. Your y position would remain 10. For the first vertical leg, your X position would remain at its new position, but you would add the length to current Y position, and so on. If the sides of your square were 20 pixels wide, your lineTo() calls would look like this:

```
this.lineTo(30,10);
this.lineTo(30,30);
this.lineTo(10,30);
this.lineTo(10,10)
```

Figure 16.1 shows you how this code would render on a grid.

That wasn't so hard. But don't take my word for it. Take a few moments and try the following exercise to get used to the basics of working with straight lines in the Drawing API.

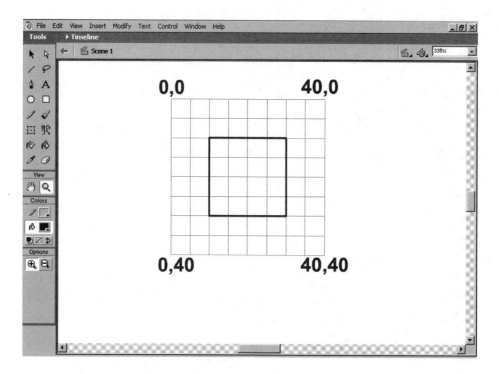

Figure 16.1   The example code would generate this in a grid space.

Exercise 16.1   Creating a Square Using the Drawing API

You've walked through the basics of using the Drawing API to create a square. Now create your own.

1. Open a new movie. Create a movie clip named **square**. Drag this empty movie clip onto the Stage, and give it an instance name of square as well.

2. Select frame 1 on the main Timeline and launch the Actions panel (F2).

3. Set your line style. For now, start with a 2-point black line at 100% alpha. Enter the following code:

```
square.lineStyle(2, 0x000000, 100);
```

4. Set the starting point for your square: an X position of 40 and a Y position 30. Add the following line of code to your Actions:

```
square.moveTo(40, 30);
```

5. Now the real fun starts. You can check your progress as you go. Make a square that has sides that are 50 pixels long. Start with the first horizontal line:

```
square.lineTo(90, 30);
```

6. Test your code. Your movie should now look like Figure 16.2.

   Now all you need to do is add the other three sides to your square. Remember, your virtual pen is currently at (90,30).

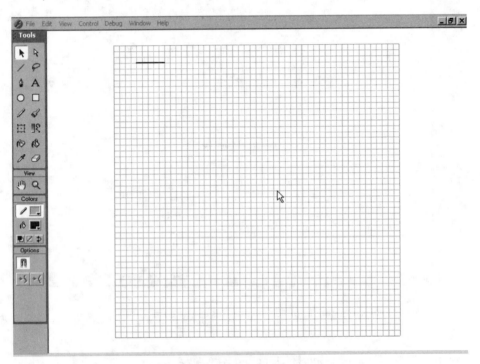

Figure 16.2   The code you've written so far draws a 2-point horizontal line that is 50 pixels long.

7. To draw the first vertical line of your square, leave the X position of the virtual pen in place and change the Y position by 50 pixels. Enter the following code:

```
square.lineTo(90, 80);
```

8. Save and test your movie again.

   Now think about what your next two moves should be. Go ahead and experiment. If you're having problems, look at Listing 16.1 for help. Your movie should look like Figure 16.3. Be sure to save it.

Listing 16.1   Completed Code for a Simple Square

```
square.lineStyle(2, 0x000000, 100);
square.moveTo(40, 30);
square.lineTo(90, 30);
square.lineTo(90, 80);
square.lineTo(40, 80);
square.lineTo(40, 30);
```

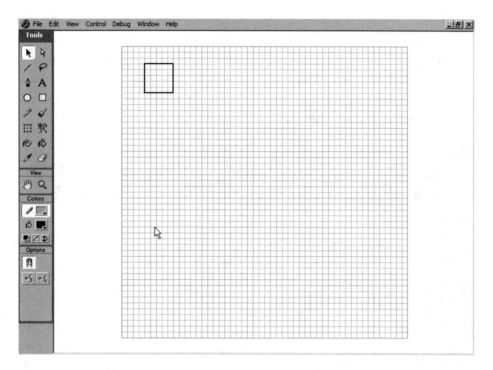

Figure 16.3 Using nothing but code, you can draw a square on the Stage.

Now just have some fun. Try changing the parameters to see how it affects your movie.

In addition to drawing lines, you can draw curves using the curveTo method. To understand how the Drawing API handles curves, you first need to know a bit about how Flash as a whole handles curves.

Drawing Curves with the Drawing API

Most vector-drawing programs, such as FreeHand and Illustrator, use a particular type of curve known as a *cubic Bezier curve*. Cubic Bezier curves use four points to define the curve: two anchors and two handles. The anchors define the endpoints of the curve, and the handles define the curve between those points. This type of curve is easy to use and powerful. A related curve, the *quadratic Bezier,* has its own set of properties that better match what Flash tries to offer.

Essentially, a quadratic Bezier curve is a cubic Bezier with its two handles fused to the same point. This means that quadratic Bezier curves can't create as many curves as a cubic Bezier, but quadratic Bezier curves require 25% less storage space for their descriptive information than cubic Beziers (see Figure 16.4). This space savings is why Flash stores all its curves as quadratic Beziers. It's also why the curveTo() method of the Drawing API uses quadratic Beziers.

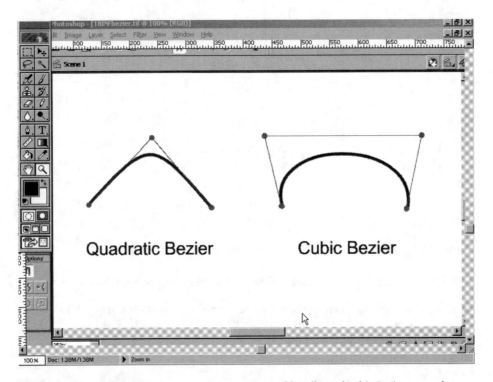

Figure 16.4   Quadratic Bezier curves have one control handle, and cubic Bezier curves have two control handles. Flash can work with a representation of a cubic Bezier curve, but it exports quadratic Beziers to save file size.

The actual syntax for the curveTo method is relatively simple; it takes only four arguments: the X and Y position of the handle and the X and Y position of the anchor:

```
curveTo(<handle x>, <handle y>, <anchor x>, <anchor y>);
```

The next exercise helps you get a visual idea of how such a code-created curve looks. You'll create a tool that lets you drag around both the anchors and handle for a quadratic Bezier curve—and you do it all with just ActionScript!

Exercise 16.2   Creating Curves Using the Drawing API

This exercise is a little more complex than the previous one, so go get your soda or coffee now.

1. Begin by creating a new, blank movie, and open the Actions panel.

2. Create three empty movie clips—one for each anchor and one for the handle—by typing this code into the Actions panel:

```
this.createEmptyMovieClip("anchor0_mc", 1);
this.createEmptyMovieClip("anchor1_mc", 2);
this.createEmptyMovieClip("handle_mc", 3);
```

Now you're going to use a neat little trick to create the content for these empty clips. You're going to define a lineStyle() for each clip with a line width of 10 pixels. Then you'll draw a 1-pixel line. What does this do for you? You end up creating a dot that's very close to a circle.

3. Beneath the code that you entered in the previous step, add the following (note that your anchors will be black and the handle will be blue):

```
anchor0_mc.lineStyle(10, 0x000000);
anchor1_mc.lineStyle(10, 0x000000);
handle_mc.lineStyle(10, 0x0000FF);

anchor0_mc.lineTo(1, 0);
anchor1_mc.lineTo(1, 0);
handle_mc.lineTo(1, 0);
```

If you test your movie now, all you'll see is a blue dot—that's because handle_mc is highest in the level stack and you haven't repositioned any of your movie clips yet.

4. Position all the movie clips:

```
handle_mc._x = 100;
handle_mc._y = 100;

anchor0_mc._x = 50;
anchor0_mc._y = 150;

anchor1_mc._x = 150;
anchor1_mc._y = 150;
```

5. Save and test your movie. Your movie should look like Figure 16.5.

Next you define a function that draws a curve on the main Timeline.

6. Beneath the code that you already entered, create an empty function called drawCurve():

```
function drawCurve(){
}
```

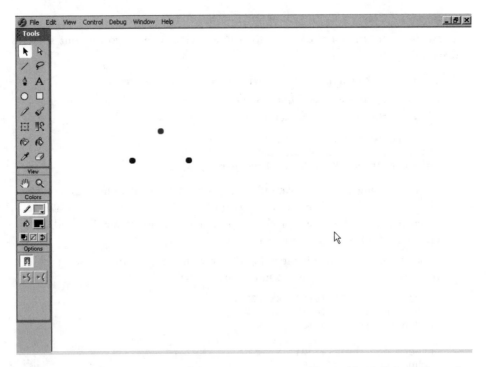

Figure 16.5 After you add the code to position the movie clips, the blue ball should be at the apex of the triangle, with the black anchors forming the base.

7. Clear out any old vectors that might exist on the root Timeline, and then set the lineStyle so that the line is hairline and red. Between the curly braces of the function, enter this:

```
_root.clear();
_root.lineStyle(0, 0xFF0000);
```

8. After the last line of code that you entered, add the following code:

```
_root.moveTo(_root.anchor0_mc._x, _root.anchor0_mc._y);
```

9. Next, draw your curve using the position of the handle movie clip and the other anchor movie clips. Finally, call updateAfterEvent() to force the Stage to redraw. Add the following code to your function:

```
_root.curveTo(_root.handle_mc._x, _root.handle_mc._y,
_root.anchor1_mc._x, _root.anchor1_mc._y);
updateAfterEvent();
```

You do this because when one of the anchors or the handle is being dragged, updateAfterEvent() is called. You want the action to be as smooth as possible, so you force the redraw. Your completed drawCurve() function should look like Listing 16.2.

Listing 16.2   The Completed *drawCurve()* Function

```
function drawCurve(){
    _root.clear();
    _root.lineStyle(0, 0xFF0000);
_root.moveTo(_root.anchor0_mc._x, _root.anchor0_mc._y);
    _root.curveTo(_root.handle_mc._x, _root.handle_mc._y,
_root.anchor1_mc._x, _root.anchor1_mc._y);
    updateAfterEvent();
}
```

10. You're not quite done yet. You still need to define the onPress method for the handler movie clip. When handle_mc is pressed, you want to start dragging it. And you want to set the onMouseMove() method of handle_mc equal to the drawCurve() method that you just defined. In other words, as long as the mouse is moving, you want to continually call your drawCurve() function. To do this, add the following code beneath the drawCurve() function:

```
handle_mc.onPress = function(){
    this.startDrag();
    this.onMouseMove = _root.drawCurve;
}
```

11. Go ahead and test your movie now. You can press the blue dot (handle) and start dragging it. As soon as you do, your curve will appear and be automatically updated (see Figure 16.6).

Of course, there's one minor issue: You can't let go of the handle. You'll fix that next. You need to define what happens when you release the mouse. In other words, you need to tell the onRelease method what it should do.

12. First you want to stop dragging the handle movie clip. Then you need to explicitly call the onMouseMove() method to update the curve. If you don't do this, you'll end up getting bizarre behavior in your curve when you whip the mouse around and then suddenly let it go. Finally, set the onMouseMove() method to undefined—you aren't actively modifying the curve if you aren't dragging the handle. If you don't set onMouseMove() to undefined, Flash will continue tracking the mouse movements—even when it's not necessary. That could potentially cause performance problems.

To accomplish these tasks, add the following code to your Actions list:

```
handle_mc.onRelease = function(){
    this.stopDrag();
    this.onMouseMove();
    this.onMouseMove = undefined;
}
```

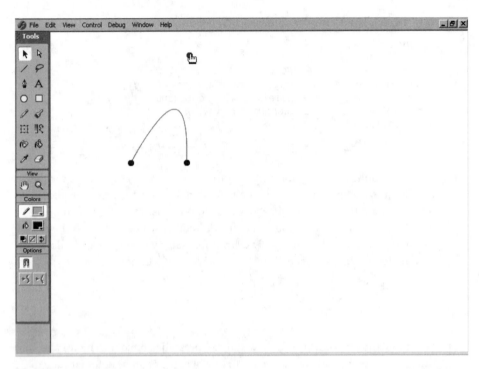

Figure 16.6   After you add the function to handle the `onPress` event, you can click the blue ball and see your Bezier curve.

13. In the bad old days, when mouse events could be associated only with buttons, developers got used to always checking for both `on(release)` and `on(releaseOutside)` events. You need to do that here, too. You want exactly the same things that happened during `onRelease` to happen during `onReleaseOutside`. The easiest way to do that is to set the `onReleaseOutside` method equal to the `onRelease` method by entering this:

    ```
    handle_mc.onReleaseOutside = handle_mc.onRelease;
    ```

14. Save and test your movie.

    You have a very cool little movie that very nicely demonstrates how a quadratic Bezier curve works. You could stop there, but that would be no fun. You can quickly and easily copy the methods you've already created and apply them to the anchors as well so that you can move all three endpoints.

15. Now you copy the methods so that they occur `onReleaseOutside` and also apply them to the anchors. Set the methods for the two anchors equal to the methods for the handle by adding the following code:

    ```
    anchor0_mc.onPress = anchor1_mc.onPress =
    handle_mc.onPress;
    ```

```
anchor0_mc.onRelease = anchor1_mc.onRelease =
handle_mc.onRelease;
anchor0_mc.onReleaseOutside = anchor1_mc.onReleaseOutside =
handle_mc.onRelease;
```

16. Make an initial call to `drawCurve()` so that the curve appears before you press either the handle or the anchors.

```
drawCurve();
```

17. Save and test your movie.

Now that's cool (see Figure 16.7). And you didn't draw a thing on the Stage using the traditional drawing tools. If you are having any difficulties, check your code against the code in Listing 16.3.

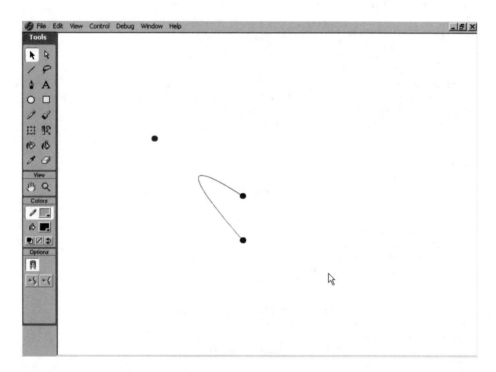

Figure 16.7   The results of the code for the quadratic Bezier curve.

Listing 16.3   The Full Code for Drawing Curves

```
this.createEmptyMovieClip("anchor0_mc", 1);
this.createEmptyMovieClip("anchor1_mc", 2);
this.createEmptyMovieClip("handle_mc", 3);

anchor0_mc.lineStyle(10, 0x000000);
anchor1_mc.lineStyle(10, 0x000000);
```

continues ▶

Listing 16.3   Continued

```
handle_mc.lineStyle(10, 0x0000FF);

anchor0_mc.lineTo(1, 0);
anchor1_mc.lineTo(1, 0);
handle_mc.lineTo(1, 0);

handle_mc._x = 100;
handle_mc._y = 100;

anchor0_mc._x = 50;
anchor0_mc._y = 150;

anchor1_mc._x = 150;
anchor1_mc._y = 150;

function drawCurve(){
     _root.clear();
     _root.lineStyle(0, 0xFF0000);
_root.moveTo(_root.anchor0_mc._x,
_root.anchor0_mc._y);
     _root.curveTo(_root.handle_mc._x, _root.handle_mc._y,
_root.anchor1_mc._x, _root.anchor1_mc._y);
     updateAfterEvent();
}

handle_mc.onPress = function(){
     this.startDrag();
     this.onMouseMove = _root.drawCurve;
}

handle_mc.onRelease = function(){
     this.stopDrag();
     this.onMouseMove();
     this.onMouseMove = undefined;
}

handle_mc.onReleaseOutside = handle_mc.onRelease;
anchor0_mc.onPress = anchor1_mc.onPress =
handle_mc.onPress;
anchor0_mc.onRelease = anchor1_mc.onRelease =
handle_mc.onRelease;
anchor0_mc.onReleaseOutside = anchor1_mc.onReleaseOutside =
handle_mc.onRelease;

drawCurve();
```

Now that you've got the curves thing down, how about tackling a circle? How hard can that be?

Drawing Circles with the Drawing API

One particular type of curve that's commonly needed is a circle. However, because there's no direct way of creating a circle with the Drawing API, it can be a bit difficult with Flash MX. Due to the nature of quadratic Beziers, in fact, it is impossible to draw a perfect circle. The good news is that you can come close enough that no one will notice! Actually, when you create a circle with Flash's drawing tools, Flash is doing something very similar to what you are about to do.

The math needed to create a circle is a bit of a bear; to make things easier, you're just going to define a function that you can use to draw any size of circle anywhere you want. By declaring this function as a member of movieClip.prototype, you'll be able to call this method from any movie clip in your entire movie.

For right now, what is important is that you use the moveTo() and curveTo() methods to draw your circle. The three parameters that the function will take are x, y, and r where the x and y are the coordinates that mark the center of the circle, and r is the radius of the circle.

The code that you need appears in Listing 16.4. You can either enter this code yourself or copy it from the circle.as file in the Examples/Chapter16 folder on the CD.

Listing 16.4   A Circle-Drawing Prototype

```
movieClip.prototype.drawCircle = function(x, y, r){
        var a = r * 0.414213562;
        var b = r * 0.707106781;
        this.moveTo(x+r, y);
        this.curveTo(x+r, y-a, x+b, y-b);
        this.curveTo(x+a, y-r, x, y-r);
        this.curveTo(x-a, y-r, x-b, y-b);
        this.curveTo(x-r, y-a, x-r, y);
        this.curveTo(x-r, y+a, x-b, y+b);
        this.curveTo(x-a, y+r, x, y+r);
        this.curveTo(x+a, y+r, x+b, y+b);
        this.curveTo(x+r, y+a, x+r, y);
}
```

Now all you have to do is define the lineStyle for the movie clip and call the drawCircle() function, passing in the values for x, y, and r.

Exercise 16.3   Creating Circles Using the Drawing API

Because the function that you need to draw a circle has already been defined, all you need to do is apply that function to a movie clip.

1. Open a new movie, and open the Actions panel.

2. Paste the circle prototype function in the first frame.

3. Create a new empty movie clip on the Stage by entering the following line code in the Actions list:

```
createEmptyMovieClip("circle_mc_1", 1);
```

4. Now all you need to do is set the line style and pass the X and Y coordinates and radius to the drawCircle() method. To create a circle with a 2-point black line centered on 50,50, with a radius of 20, enter the following code:

```
circle_mc_1.lineStyle(2, 0x000000);
circle_mc_1.drawCircle(50, 50, 20);
```

5. Save and test your movie. You should see something similar to Figure 16.8.

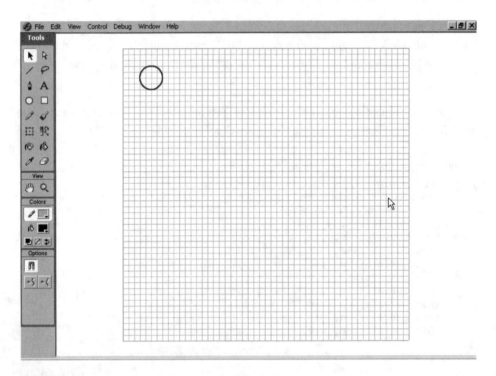

Figure 16.8 Your nearly perfect circle.

If you really want to have some fun, set up a few more circles. All you need to do for each circle is repeat Steps 3 and 4. For each circle, change the instance name of the clip (circle_mc_2, circle_mc_3, and so on), increment the _level value, change the parameters for lineStyle(), and use drawCircle() method as you wish. Hey, you've got 16,000 levels to work with—have a little fun!

In the next section, you take a look at working with fills using the Drawing API.

Creating Fills Using the Drawing API

After all that, fills should seem pretty simple—which is good because they are! You can create two types of fills: single-color fills and gradient fills. You start out learning how to create single-color fills and then learn the more complex gradient ones.

Single-Color Fills

To start a single-color fill, you use the `beginFill()` method:

```
beginFill(<color>, <alpha>);
```

Just as with the other Drawing API methods, the `color` parameter is an integer and the `alpha` parameter is an integer ranging from `0` to `100`. (As usual, `0` is fully transparent and `100` is fully opaque.)

To create a filled shape, move your virtual pen to where you want the shape to start. Then draw the shape using `lineTo()` or `curveTo()`, and finally run the `endFill()` method.

So why not give it a try?

Exercise 16.4   Creating a Single-Color Fill

This exercise will be extremely simple for you—you've seen almost all of the code before.

1. Open a new movie and save it as fill.fla to your hard drive.

2. To frame 1, add the code that you need to draw a square:

```
this.lineStyle(2, 0x000000, 100);
this.moveTo(10, 10);
this.lineTo(110, 10);
this.lineTo(110, 110);
this.lineTo(10, 110);
this.lineTo(10, 10);
```

3. To give the square a red fill, add one line of code after the `moveTo()` method and another at the very end. Add the code between the asterisks to the locations shown:

```
this.lineStyle(2, 0x000000, 100);
this.moveTo(10, 10);
//****************************
this.beginFill(0xFF0000);
//****************************
this.lineTo(110, 10);
this.lineTo(110, 110);
this.lineTo(10, 110);
this.lineTo(10, 10);
//****************************
this.endFill();
//****************************
```

4. Save and test your file (see Figure 16.9).

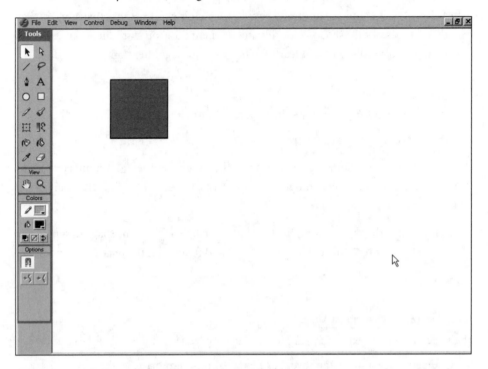

Figure 16.9 By adding two lines of code to what you've already learned, you can easily apply a single-color fill to a shape.

If you want a borderless red square, just remove the line that calls the lineStyle() method. That's really all there is to it.

Gradient Fills

Now that you know how fills work, it's time to take a look at the more complex gradient fills. Setting up a gradient fill requires the use of numerous arrays; if you aren't comfortable using arrays yet, be sure to check out Chapter 6, "Introduction to ActionScripting," before diving into this section.

The syntax of the startGradientFill method is as follows:

```
startGradientFill(<type>, <colors>, <alphas>, <ratios>, <matrix>);
```

All these parameters are required; if one is missing or malformed, you won't get any output.

The type parameter is a string and can be either linear or radial, depending on what type of fill you want. Linear gradients fade from color to color in a line, and radial gradients radiate in a circular fashion from a center point.

The colors, alphas, and ratios parameters are all arrays and must each have the same length. The colors array must be an array of integers representing the colors to be used in the gradient. The alphas array must be an array of integers from 0 to 100 that represent the alpha of the color at the same index in the colors array. The ratios array represents the position in the gradient where each color is centered, and its possible values can range from 0 (the left side or center of the gradient) to 255 (the right side or outer radius of the gradient).

So, for example, if you want to create a gradient that fades from red to white to blue, with all colors being evenly spaced apart and all 50% transparent, you would create arrays like this:

```
colors = [0xFF0000, 0xFFFFFF, 0x0000FF];
alphas = [50, 50, 50];
ratios = [0, 127, 255];
```

Now, the last parameter, matrix, is by far the most complex. In fact, matrix can take two forms: the "complex" form and the "simple" form. In the complex form, matrix needs to be an object with nine properties—a, b, c, d, e, f, h, i, and j—that represent a 3 × 3 transformation matrix. If you know linear algebra and know how transformation matrices work, you should have a good idea how the complex form works; otherwise, the simple form should do everything you need.

In the simple form, matrix is an object with six properties: matrixType, x, y, w, h, and r. The matrixType property must always be set to the string box. The x and y properties are used to represent where the upper-left corner of the gradient should be. The w and h arguments are used to specify the width and height of the gradient, respectively. Finally, the r property represents the rotation of the gradient, in radians.

Tip

To convert from degrees to radians, use the following equation:

r = (d × Math.PI)/170

Here, d is degrees and r is radians.

In the next exercise, you use the startGradientFill method to create sphere-like shading on a dynamically drawn circle.

Exercise 16.5   Creating a Gradient Fill

This exercise is only slightly more complex than the previous one—and only because you'll be working with a complex shape and arrays.

1. Open a new Flash movie and save it to your hard drive as **gradient.fla**.

2. Open the Actions panel, and import the circle.as code from the Examples/Chapter16 folder on the CD.

3. To give a good impression of a sphere, the gradient should be radial, should start out at white, should quickly fade to the color of the sphere, and then should get darker and finally a bit lighter to represent the reflection of light off the surface where the sphere is resting. How hard can that be?

   The colors you'll use are white (0xFFFFFF), medium blue (0x006699), and dark blue (0x003366). All alphas will be at 100%.

   Enter the following code:

   ```
   colors = [0xFFFFFF, 0x006699, 0x003366, 0x006699];
   alphas = [100, 100, 100, 100];

   ratios=[0,160,255,200];
   ```

4. The circle will have a radius of 50 pixels and will be centered at 100,100. To have the white highlight in the upper-left area of the circle, set the X and Y coordinates for the gradient to 50,50. The width and height of the gradient will be set to 70 so that the whole gradient will be seen inside the circle.

   Enter the following code:

   ```
   matrix = {matrixType:"box", x:50, y:50, w:70, h:70, r:0};
   ```

5. All that's left to do is start the fill, draw the circle, and end the fill. Add the following code:

   ```
   this.beginGradientFill("radial", colors, alphas, ratios,
   matrix);
   this.drawCircle(100, 100, 50);
   this.endFill();
   ```

When you save and test your movie, you should see a nicely shaded blue sphere (see Figure 16.10). If you are having problems, check the complete code in Listing 16.5.

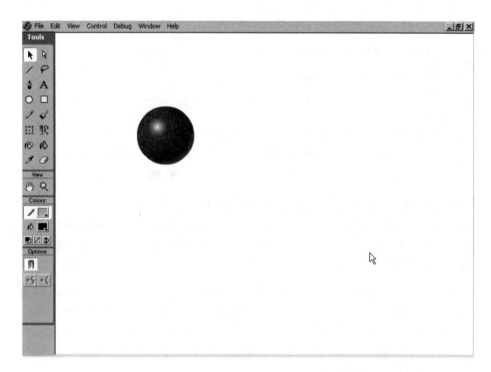

Figure 16.10   Sphere shading created with `startGradientFill`.

Listing 16.5   Completed Code for a Gradient Fill

```
movieClip.prototype.drawCircle = function(x, y, r){
    var a = r * 0.414213562;
    var b = r * 0.707106781;
    this.moveTo(x+r, y);
    this.curveTo(x+r, y-a, x+b, y-b);
    this.curveTo(x+a, y-r, x, y-r);
    this.curveTo(x-a, y-r, x-b, y-b);
    this.curveTo(x-r, y-a, x-r, y);
    this.curveTo(x-r, y+a, x-b, y+b);
    this.curveTo(x-a, y+r, x, y+r);
    this.curveTo(x+a, y+r, x+b, y+b);
    this.curveTo(x+r, y+a, x+r, y);
}


colors = [0xFFFFFF, 0x006699, 0x003366, 0x006699];
alphas = [100, 100, 100, 100];
```

continues ▶

Listing 16.5   Continued

```
ratios=[0,160,255,200];

matrix = {matrixType:"box", x:50, y:50, w:70, h:70, r:0};

this.beginGradientFill("radial", colors, alphas, ratios,
matrix);
this.drawCircle(100, 100, 50);
this.endFill();
```

You've looked at some general examples for using the Drawing API inside Flash. In the next section, you look at an example that is more suited for application development.

Using the Drawing API in the Real World

Why not finish off your tour of the Drawing API with a real-world example? Something that is often needed for prototyping designs is a simple way to quickly create "standard" system-like buttons—you know, the gray, 3D–ish kind we are all accustomed to.

If you're going to set up this wonderful button, what do you need to be able to do? Well, buttons usually have text, so you'll want to be able to specify text for your button. Each button will be its own movie clip, so you'll want to be able to give the button a name and a depth. You'll probably want your code to be accessible from any movie clip, so why not add it to movieClip.prototype?

That's plenty to get started with. It's time to start coding.

Exercise 16.6   Creating a Button Using the Drawing API

The very first thing to do is define the function that will create the button.

1. Create a new Flash file and save it as **button.fla** on your hard drive.

2. Open the Actions panel, and select the first frame of the main Timeline.

3. Now you need to define your function. Enter the following code:

   ```
   MovieClip.prototype.createButton = function(text, name, depth){
   ```

   As mentioned before, text, name, and depth will represent the text in the button, the name of the new movie clip, and the depth of the new movie clip, respectively.

4. Next, you need to create the actual movie clip. To do so, add the following code:

   ```
   this.createEmptyMovieClip(name, depth);
   var btn_mc = this[name];
   ```

Here you create the new movie clip at the proper depth and then create a shortcut to it, btn_mc.

5. The next logical step is to create the text field for the button. You'll use the shortcut that you just created to reference the button. Enter the following code after the last line you entered:

```
btn_mc.createTextField("btn_txt", 1, 0, 0, 1, 1);
btn_mc.btn_txt.autoSize = true;
btn_mc.btn_txt.selectable = false
btn_mc.btn_txt.text = text;
```

What does this do? First, it creates your text field inside btn_mc, names it btn_txt, sets its depth to 1, sets its position to 0,0, and sets its width and height to 1. Then the code specifies some of the properties of this field: autoSize, selectable, and text.

To make the field automatically resize to the text within it, autoSize is true. To ensure that the text in the buttons won't be selectable, the selectable property is false. Finally, the code sets the text of the field to be the text argument that was passed in.

6. Now you'll throw in a little text formatting. Add the following code to your list of Actions:

```
var btn_tf = new TextFormat();
btn_tf.font = "_sans";
btn_mc.btn_txt.setTextFormat(btn_tf);
```

This creates a textFormat object, btn_tf, and sets its font to be the built-in font _sans. Then the textFormat is applied to your textField.

7. Next you need to measure your text to determine what the size of the button should be. The two variables txtWidth and txtHeight will hold this information. Enter the following code:

```
btn_mc.txtWidth = btn_mc.btn_txt._width + 4;
btn_mc.txtHeight = btn_mc.btn_txt._height;
```

8. It's finally time to start drawing your button. The width of the button will be 4 pixels larger than the size of the button, just so that the text inside the button isn't crowded. Draw the up or unpressed state of the button:

```
btn_mc.drawUp = function(){
    this.btn_txt._x = 2;
    this.btn_txt._y = 1;
    this.clear();
    this.moveTo(this.txtWidth, 0);
    this.beginFill(0xCCCCCC);
    this.lineStyle(1, 0x000000);
    this.lineTo(this.txtWidth, this.txtHeight);
    this.lineTo(0, this.txtHeight);
    this.lineStyle(1, 0xFFFFFF);
    this.lineTo(0, 0);
```

```
        this.lineTo(this.txtWidth, 0);
        this.endFill();
    }
```

In this code, you start out by positioning the text field so that it's centered in the button. Then you clear all current drawings and draw the actual button according to the width and height previously measured. The lines on the left and top of the button are white, while those on the right and bottom are black, to give the impression of 3D. In addition, the button fill is set to a light gray, just like what you are accustomed to.

9. If your button will have an up state, you'll want to create a down state as well. The drawDown function is nearly identical to the drawUp function, except that the colors of the lines are flipped so that it appears that the button is indented now. Enter the following code:

```
btn_mc.drawDown = function(){
    this.btn_txt._x = 3;
    this.btn_txt._y = 2;
    this.clear();
    this.moveTo(this.txtWidth, 0);
    this.beginFill(0xCCCCCC);
    this.lineStyle(1, 0xFFFFFF);
    this.lineTo(this.txtWidth, this.txtHeight);
    this.lineTo(0, this.txtHeight);
    this.lineStyle(1, 0x000000);
    this.lineTo(0, 0);
    this.lineTo(this.txtWidth, 0);
    this.endFill();
}
```

10. Next you need to define the code that will make this code run when the button is pressed or released:

```
btn_mc.onPress = btn_mc.drawDown;
btn_mc.onRelease = function(){
    this.drawUp();
    this.onButton();
}
btn_mc.onReleaseOutside = btn_mc.drawUp;
```

Notice that, in addition to redrawing the button, the onRelease() method calls a method named onButton(). This is how you will be able to apply code to your buttons later.

11. Draw the initial state of your button and close the function:

```
        btn_mc.drawUp();
    }
```

12. To call your brand new function, add the following code outside the function:

```
this.createButton("My Button", "myButton_mc", 1);
```

If you want to trace something when the button is pressed, add this code:

```
myButton_mc.onButton = function(){
     trace("My button was pressed!");
}
```

It's time—save and test your movie. Your movie should look like Figure 16.11. That was a lot of code. If you don't get the results you expect, check your code against Listing 16.6.

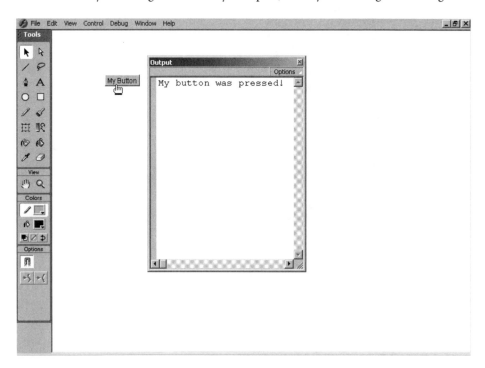

Figure 16.11   A 3-D button created entirely with code.

Listing 16.6   The Completed Button Code

```
MovieClip.prototype.createButton = function(text, name, depth){
     this.createEmptyMovieClip(name, depth);
     var btn_mc = this[name];

     btn_mc.createTextField("btn_txt", 1, 0, 0, 1, 1);
     btn_mc.btn_txt.autoSize = true;
     btn_mc.btn_txt.selectable = false
     btn_mc.btn_txt.text = text;

     var btn_tf = new TextFormat();
     btn_tf.font = "_sans";
     btn_mc.btn_txt.setTextFormat(btn_tf);
```

continues ▶

Listing 16.6   Continued

```
        btn_mc.txtWidth = btn_mc.btn_txt._width + 4;
        btn_mc.txtHeight = btn_mc.btn_txt._height;

        btn_mc.drawUp = function(){
            this.btn_txt._x = 2;
            this.btn_txt._y = 1;
            this.clear();
            this.moveTo(this.txtWidth, 0);
            this.beginFill(0xCCCCCC);
            this.lineStyle(1, 0x000000);
            this.lineTo(this.txtWidth, this.txtHeight);
            this.lineTo(0, this.txtHeight);
            this.lineStyle(1, 0xFFFFFF);
            this.lineTo(0, 0);
            this.lineTo(this.txtWidth, 0);
            this.endFill();
        }

        btn_mc.drawDown = function(){
            this.btn_txt._x = 3;
            this.btn_txt._y = 2;
            this.clear();
            this.moveTo(this.txtWidth, 0);
            this.beginFill(0xCCCCCC);
            this.lineStyle(1, 0xFFFFFF);
            this.lineTo(this.txtWidth, this.txtHeight);
            this.lineTo(0, this.txtHeight);
            this.lineStyle(1, 0x000000);
            this.lineTo(0, 0);
            this.lineTo(this.txtWidth, 0);
            this.endFill();
        }

        btn_mc.onPress = btn_mc.drawDown;
        btn_mc.onRelease = function(){
            this.drawUp();
            this.onButton();// calls a trace function below
        }
        btn_mc.onReleaseOutside = btn_mc.drawUp;

        btn_mc.drawUp();
}
this.createButton("My Button", "myButton_mc", 1);
myButton_mc.onButton = function(){
    trace("My button was pressed!");
}
```

Summary

If you've worked your way through this chapter, you should now be pretty comfortable with the new Drawing API in Flash MX. From lines to curves, fills, and gradients, you now have a very powerful tool on your belt that can assist you in innumerable ways.

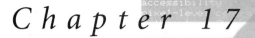

Chapter 17

Interface
Techniques

Flash MX makes it easy to create simple

interactivity. Buttons are the most obvious

example. Press a button and something

happens. However, if you want to add real

interactivity to your site, you need to get into ActionScript. In fact, what separates the Flash wannabes from the Flash gurus is a solid understanding of how to combine Actions to get the kind of interactivity they want. And this is even more true in Flash MX than it was in previous versions of Flash. Flash MX has a more solid object-oriented core than Flash 5 did—you have new and different ways of interacting with the objects on the Stage.

In this chapter, you get a solid introduction to some of the types of interactivity you can add to your Flash movies and the new ways you can apply that interactivity. The key here is everything, or nearly everything, is an object. You'll learn how to do the following:

- **Let your user move objects around inside your movie.** It used to be that you had to embed buttons in movie clips to create draggable objects. No more. Take a look at the basics of drag-and-drop interactivity from an object-oriented approach.

- **Make something happen when an object drops on a specific target.** Go beyond the simple dragging and take a look at the `_dropTarget` property.

- **Create a custom cursor.** You can use the Mouse object to create your very own cursor, and you can use ActionScript to control its state.

- **Create a reusable slider.** Create a slider that can be customized to suit your needs. You can probably find a whole host of sliders that have been created as Flash components, ready for you to use. But just in case, you should really know how to "roll your own."

- **Set up a scrolling text field.** Text fields can now be treated as objects! Finally, dynamic control over color, font, and size. Scrolling text fields are easy to set up. Using buttons to scroll through text boxes has become somewhat passé, and it's not terribly user-friendly. Try scrolling your text boxes with a scrolling bar component instead.

- **Create a dynamic preloader.** If you need a preloader for your movie, why not make it dynamic? Let your user see exactly how much of the movie has downloaded rather than leave them guessing.

Start by taking a look at how you can set up basic drag-and-drop-style interactivity with an object-oriented approach.

Basic Drag-and-Drop Interactivity

One of the fundamental types of interactivity you can add to a Flash movie is drag-and-drop. After you understand how to use drag-and-drop, a whole new world of possibilities opens up. With drag-and-drop, you can click on an object, drag it across the screen, and drop it in a new position. You can control what happens when the object is dropped. You can set it up so that the object can drop only on a specific area, or you can set it up so that the dragged movie changes when it's dropped on a specific area or target.

Drag-and-drop functionality, though simple, is an important and understandable user-interface element. Why do you think the visual operating systems, such as the Mac OS and Windows, won the operating system wars? It's because they enable users to pick up and drag their files and other screen elements around just like pieces of paper. It's a metaphor people understand.

In earlier releases of Flash, in order to create a draggable object, you had to embed a button inside of a movie clip–otherwise, you would end up dragging your Stage around. Buttons were the only Flash elements that could react to most mouse events. Not anymore. Now movie clips can also handle mouse events. The standard buttons are still useful–after all they already have their states set up–and they can be treated as objects as well. So you can use everything you already know; you'll just use it a little differently.

What do you need to do to a get a drag-and-drop interaction to work?

- You need something to drag.
- You need a draggable object that responds to a mouse event, so you'll either need to use a button or create a function to pass to the onPress event handler for your movie clip.
- You need any actions that you assign to a button to directly affect the Timeline in which the button exists. If you attach a Drag action to a button that exists on the main Timeline, you end up dragging the whole movie around. To get around this, you previously had to embed the button in a movie clip. Now you can use the onPress event handler and assign the actions to drag a button or a movie clip directly on a frame in the main Timeline.
- You need to assign a startDrag() action to the button or movie clip.
- You need to be able to drop the movie clip you're dragging (stopDrag())— either anywhere on the Stage or onto a specific target.

That's really all there is to it. Of course, there are a few other tricks you can use along the way, but those are the basics.

In Exercise 17.1, you use basic drag-and-drop functionality to pick up trash and throw it into a garbage can.

Exercise 17.1   Using Basic Drag-and-Drop Interactivity

The file for this exercise has already been started for you. It's a ruined city scene with three pieces of trash on the ground. You'll set up each piece of trash so that it can be picked up and dropped into the trashcan. And you're going to do it the new-fangled way using event handlers on the main Timeline.

1. Open trash.fla from the Examples/Chapter17 folder on the CD, and save it to your hard drive.

    The file has five layers: Sky, Background, Foreground, Garbage, and Trashcan. Your goal is to clean up the city and put all the trash in the trashcan.

2. Begin by selecting the dead fish movie clip on the Stage and use the Properties Inspector to assign it the instance name **deadFish_mc** (see Figure 17.1).

Figure 17.1 Use the Properties Inspector to give the dead fish an instance name so you can control it with ActionScript.

3. Now you can start adding actions. Add a new layer to your Timeline and name it **Actions**.

4. Select frame 1 of the Actions layer and open the Actions panel (F9).

5. You're going to set up an onPress event handler to control the dragging of deadFish_mc. With frame 1 selected, add the following code:

```
deadFish_mc.onPress = function () {
      this.startDrag();
}
```

6. Save and test your movie. You should be able to click on the dead fish and drag it around. If it's not working for you, make sure that you gave the dead fish an instance name of deadFish_mc.

    You can drag, but you can't drop just yet. As you may guess, that's just another event handler—you'll add that next.

7. You want the dead fish to drop on the Stage when you release the mouse button—to do that you'll use the onRelease event handler. In the Actions panel, add a new line after the last curly brace and enter the following code:

```
deadFish_mc.onRelease = function () {
      this.stopDrag();
}
```

8. Save and test your movie. You can now drag and drop the dead fish (see Figure 17.2).

Figure 17.2   With just a couple of actions, you can set up your movie clips so that you can both drag them and drop them on the Stage.

Next, you need to set up the same functionality for both paper_mc and sodaCan_mc. First, assign them instance names of **paper_mc** and **sodaCan_mc**, respectively. You could just repeat Steps 4 through 7, changing the movie clip instances as appropriate, but you don't really need to do that. You've already defined functions that tell the event handlers what to do—in essence, you created methods for the event handlers. So rather than repeat that code, you can just set the methods for the event handlers for the other two movie clips equal to the methods you just set up for deadFish_mc.

9. To set the methods for the event handlers for sodaCan_mc and paper_mc equal to the methods for deadFish_mc, just enter the following code:

```
sodaCan_mc.onPress = paper_mc.onPress = deadFish_mc.onPress;
sodaCan_mc.onRelease = paper_mc.onRelease = deadFish_mc.onRelease;
```

There's one more thing you really need to add before you test your movie. Any time you are working with an onRelease event, you really need to add in an onReleaseOutside event as well. Why? Because it's very possible for you to drag the mouse fast enough that you won't be over the movie clip when you release—and that can confuse Flash. You just need to apply the method you set up for the onRelease event handler to the onReleaseOutside handler.

10. To set the method for the onReleaseOutside handlers equal to the onRelease handlers, enter the following code:

```
sodaCan_mc.onReleaseOutside = paper_mc.onReleaseOutside =
deadFish_mc.onReleaseOutside = deadFish_mc.onRelease;
```

11. Save and test your movie. If you are having any problems, check Listing 17.1 for the complete code listing. Make sure you've assigned instance names to all of the movie clips.

Listing 17.1   All the Code You Need to Set Up a Workable Drag-and-Drop Interaction

```
deadFish_mc.onPress = function () {
    this.startDrag();
}
deadFish_mc.onRelease = function() {
    this.stopDrag();
}
sodaCan_mc.onPress = paper_mc.onPress = deadFish_mc.onPress;
sodaCan_mc.onRelease = paper_mc.onRelease = deadFish_mc.onRelease;
sodaCan_mc.onReleaseOutside = paper_mc.onReleaseOutside =
deadFish_mc.onReleaseOutside = deadFish_mc.onRelease;
```

Pretty straightforward, right? Although this works for just dragging and dropping the pieces of trash, it doesn't yet handle what happens if you drop your piece of garbage on the trashcan.

Drag-and-Drop with a Drop Target

For the garbage to be able to drop into the trashcan, the garbage needs to know where the trashcan is located. Right now, the trashcan is just a movie clip on the Stage; it needs an instance name so that you can talk to it: name it **trashcan_mc**.

After you've assigned an instance name to the trashcan movie clip, you can use the _droptarget property of the garbage movie clip you're dragging to control what happens next.

The _dropTarget property returns the full path to the instance of the object on which you drop something. Unfortunately, the path returned is in the deprecated slash syntax. You can get around that by using an eval() statement to convert the slash syntax to dot syntax. After you've done that, you can easily compare the instance name of the trashcan movie clip (_root.trashcan_mc) to the name of whatever you drop on. If it turns out that you have dropped it on top of the trashcan movie clip, you just need to make the current piece of trash invisible.

Now that you know what to do, give it a try in Exercise 17.2.

Exercise 17.2   Using _dropTarget

You already know that you need to assign the trashcan an instance name before you do anything else, so start there (if you haven't named it already).

1. Open the Instance panel (Window >Properties Inspector), select the trashcan on the Stage, and give it an instance name of **trashcan_mc**.

   The goal here is to make the garbage disappear if you drop it on the trashcan, so if you do drop one of the movie clips on the trashcan, you'll set the trashcan movie clip's _visible property to false. You'll need to set up a conditional statement to check and see if the _droptarget is the trashcan, but the question is where do you set that conditional statement? You're going to check for this condition when you release the piece of garbage, so the logical place to put the conditional is inside of the method you set up for the onRelease handler. The beauty of this is, when you set the statement up for the onRelease handler for deadFish_mc, it propagates through for all of the other movie clips as well—because you've already set the methods for the handlers to be equal.

2. To add the conditional statement to the existing code, add the following:

```
deadFish_mc.onRelease = function() {
     this.stopDrag();
//****************************************************
     if (eval(this._droptarget) == _root.trashcan_mc){
       this._visible = false;
     }
//****************************************************
}
```

3. Save and test your movie again. That one simple change made a big difference.

Any time you've entered some code, you can do a quick syntax check by pressing the
Check Syntax icon (blue checkmark) in the Actions panel (see Figure 17.3). This can help
you catch any errors before you test your movie.

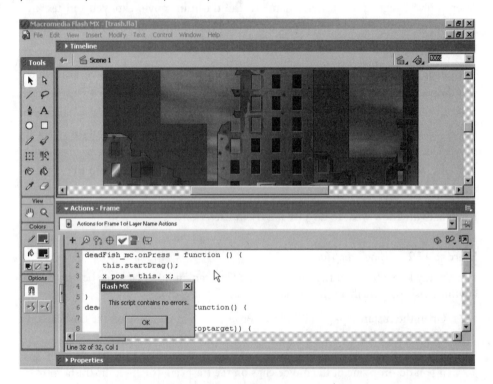

Figure 17.3   Use the Check Syntax icon to check your ActionScript syntax before you test
your movie. It'll save you lots of time.

You could stop here. But you can also add other functionality to this movie. For example, it doesn't make sense to be able to drop the trash in the sky or on top of buildings.
You can easily add a little bit of code that will snap the trash back to its original position
if it isn't dropped on either the ground or the trashcan. In fact, you can make use of a
feature that's new to Flash MX—the switch action.

The switch action allows you to set up a condition and then test for several possible out-
comes. The syntax for the switch action is as follows:

```
switch (condition) {
      case valueOne:
          code to execute here;
          break;
      case valueTwo:
          different code to execute here;
          break;
      default:
          code to execute if the other cases didn't match the
          ➥condition.
}
```

You can have as many case comparisons as you want to. If in this situation, valueOne
matches the *condition*, the code following the *case*, valueOne will execute. Notice that
break statement—you need that. Otherwise, the code in each of the case statements
will execute. So how does this help you solve your problem? You've already set up a
trashcan_mc drop target. You can set up another movie clip to be a drop target for the
ground. Then you can set up a switch action that checks to see what the drop target is.
In the first case statement, you can tell it what to do if the drop target evaluates to the
trashcan. In the second case statement, you can tell it what to do if the drop target evaluates to the ground. Finally, your default statement will handle what happens if the drop
target is neither the ground nor the trashcan.

Again, the place to add this new code is going to be inside of the function you set up for
the onRelease handler, as shown in Exercise 17.3.

Exercise 17.3   Using the switch Action to Make Decisions

This time, you'll make use of the switch action to determine what your actions will be.

1. Continue working in the movie from the previous exercise.

2. First, you need to set up the new drop target for the ground. Add a new layer
   between the Foreground and Trashcan layers, and name it **Ground**.

3. Select the Ground layer and use the Rectangle tool to draw a rectangle that covers the ground layer as illustrated in Figure 17.4.

4. Convert the rectangle you just drew to a movie clip named **ground_mc**.

5. In the Properties Inspector, give the ground_mc movie clip an instance name of
   ground_mc.

   Now you're ready to get back into the Actions panel and set up the switch action.

6. You will have to remove some code, because switch is going to replace your if
   statement.

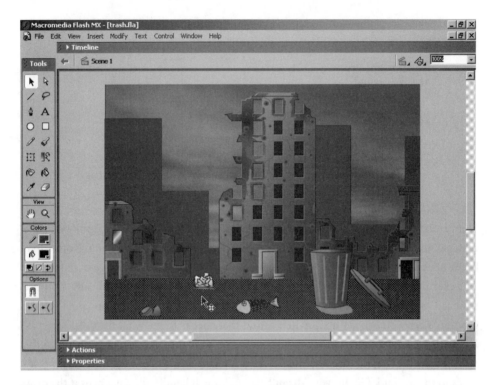

Figure 17.4   To set the ground as a target, you need to draw a shape that covers the ground area. Then you just need to convert the shape to a movie clip and give it an instance name.

Delete these two lines:

```
if(eval(this._dropTarget)==_root.trashcan_mc){
            this._visible=false;}
```

First you'll set up the switch action with trace statements to make sure it's working, then you can actually add code to the individual case statements. You should still be on frame 1 with the Actions panel open.

7. In the function for the onRelease handler, add the following code between the asterisks:

```
deadFish_mc.onRelease = function() {
      this.stopDrag();
//**************************************
      switch (eval(this._droptarget)) {
            case _root.trashcan_mc:
                  trace("trashcan");
                  break;
            case _root.ground_mc:
                  trace ("ground");
                  break;
            default:
```

```
            trace ("wrong");
        }
//**************************************
}
```

8. Save and test your movie. If you drag a piece of trash over the trashcan and drop it, the word "Trashcan" should open up in the Output window. "Ground" will appear if you drop the trash over the ground, and if you drop the trash anywhere but the trashcan or ground, you'll get the message "Wrong".

   If everything is working okay so far, it's time to add the rest of the code for the case statements. Here's what needs to happen:

   • If you drop the trash over the trashcan, it should disappear.

   • If you drop the trash over the ground, it can just drop.

   • If you drop the trash anywhere else, it should snap back to its original position.

9. To set up the trash to disappear when it's dropped on the trashcan, add the following line after the trace statement and before the break under case _root.trashcan_mc:

```
this._visible = false;
```

   It's the same line you used with your if statement earlier.

10. Save and test your movie. Try dragging any of the pieces of trash and dropping them on the trashcan. They should disappear.

    You don't need to do anything if the trash is dropped on the ground, so you can leave the case _root.ground_mc as is.

    To set up the trash to snap back into place if it isn't dropped on either the ground or the trashcan, you need to add code in a couple of places. First, you need to capture the original X and Y positions of the trash when you pick it up; then, you need to reset the X and Y positions when it's dropped.

11. To capture the original X and Y positions, you need to add a bit of code to the function you set up for the onPress handler. You should still be in frame 1 of the main Timeline with the Actions panel open. Add the code between the asterisks:

```
deadFish_mc.onPress = function () {
        this.startDrag();
//********************************
        x_pos = this._x;
        y_pos = this._y;
//********************************
}
```

    All you're doing is taking the current X and Y positions and saving the values to the variables x_pos and y_pos.

12. Now you need to add code in the case statement to force the trash to return to the values you just captured. Add the code between the asterisks:

```
default:
        trace ("wrong");
//**********************
        this._x = x_pos;
        this._y = y_pos;
//**********************
        break;
}
```

13. Save and test your movie. Now your completed code should look like Listing 17.2.

Listing 17.2   Complete ActionScript for Drag-and-Drop Using New MX features

```
deadFish_mc.onPress = function () {
        this.startDrag();
        x_pos = this._x;
        y_pos = this._y;
}
deadFish_mc.onRelease = function() {
        this.stopDrag();
        switch (eval(this._droptarget)) {
                case _root.trashcan_mc:
                        trace("trashcan");
                        this._visible = false;
                        break;
                case _root.ground_mc:
                        trace ("ground");
                        break;
                default:
                        trace ("wrong");
                        this._x = x_pos;
                        this._y = y_pos;
        }

}
sodaCan_mc.onPress = paper_mc.onPress = deadFish_mc.onPress;
sodaCan_mc.onRelease = paper_mc.onRelease = deadFish_mc.onRelease;
sodaCan_mc.onReleaseOutside = paper_mc.onReleaseOutside =
deadFish_mc.onReleaseOutside = deadFish_mc.onRelease;
```

Sure, you could stop here, but you're on a roll! Why not make the trashcan close once all the trash has been thrown away?

Because you already have a switch statement set up to handle what happens when you drop something in the trashcan, this is dead simple. You can use a variable *inCan* that you increment every time something is dropped in the trashcan. Then just set up a conditional statement that causes the canLid_mc movie clip to play (the animation for this movie clip is already set up).

14. Select the canLid_mc on the Stage and use the Properties Inspector to give it an instance name of **canLid_mc**.

15. You just need to add a few lines of code to the case `_root.trashcan_mc` statement. Add the following code between the asterisks:

```
case _root.trashcan_mc:
     trace("trashcan");
     this._visible = false;
//*******************************
     ++inCan;
     if (inCan == 3) {
          canLid_mc.play();
     }
//*******************************
     break;
}
```

16. Save and test your movie. Try dropping all three pieces of trash in the trashcan and see what happens (see Figure 17.5).You can compare your results with trash_final.fla in the Examples/Chapter17 folder on the companion CD.

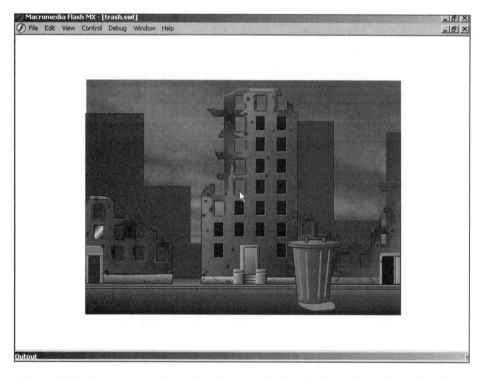

Figure 17.5   You can set up the code so that a movie clip that closes the trashcan plays when all the trash is in the can.

Next, you combine the drag-and-drop interaction you already know with creating a custom cursor.

Creating Custom Cursors

It's easy to create custom cursors. You can replace the existing boring arrow with just about anything you like. You also can set up the cursor to react to objects. You can control the cursor only while the user is inside the Flash movie; after they roll off the movie, the cursor returns to its default state. The steps for creating a custom cursor are fairly straight forward:

1. Hide the existing cursor.

2. Create a movie clip to replace the cursor.

3. Track the X and Y coordinates of the mouse so that you can control your cursor.

Hiding the existing cursor is easy. All you need to do is take advantage of the Mouse object's `hide()` and `show()` methods. The `hide()` method, big surprise here, hides the cursor. You probably can guess what the `show()` method does—it shows the cursor that's been hidden.

If you hide the cursor, you need to replace it with something. That something will be a movie clip that you create. Here's where the fun begins. Your new cursor can have as many different states as you want it to have. It can react differently to each and every object on the Stage, if you want it to.

You are going to track events on the Stage by using three of the Mouse listeners—`mouseUp`, `mouseDown`, and `mouseMove`. You can assign these listeners to one or more movie clips on the Stage, which will then listen for when these events occur. Then you can have your movie clips respond as appropriate. In the case of Exercise 17.4, your hit area is going to do all the listening and assign actions accordingly.

If you hide the default cursor, you still want your new cursor to follow your user's mouse movements. How do you do this? You assign the `hitArea_mc` to listen for `mouseMove`. Then you can use the `_xmouse` (current X position of the mouse) and `_ymouse` (current Y position of the mouse) properties to track the mouse position at any point in time.

In the next exercise, you create a movie that will have an irregular shape on the Stage. When the mouse pointer rolls over the shape, the pointer will change to an open hand. If you click the shape, the hand closes and you can drag the shape around. Here, you have a combination of actions—you're combining what you already know about drag-and-drop with cursor control and recognizing hit areas.

Exercise 17.4   Setting Up the Basic Movie

Before you can set up the actions to create a custom cursor, you need to get the basic movie elements in place on the Stage.

1. Open cursor.fla from the Examples/Chapter17 folder on the companion CD and save it to your hard drive.

2. You'll see two layers, Cursor and Hit Area. Select the Cursor layer You'll notice the cursor_mc movie clip has an instance name of—surprise—**cursor_mc**. If you double click on it, you will see the cursor_mc movie clip has two labeled frames, Open and Closed. The Open frame corresponds to the open hand, and the Closed frame corresponds to the closed hand. Return to the Main Stage.

3. Select the Hit Area layer. You will see the hitArea_mc movie clip has an instance name of **hitArea_mc** (see Figure 17.6).

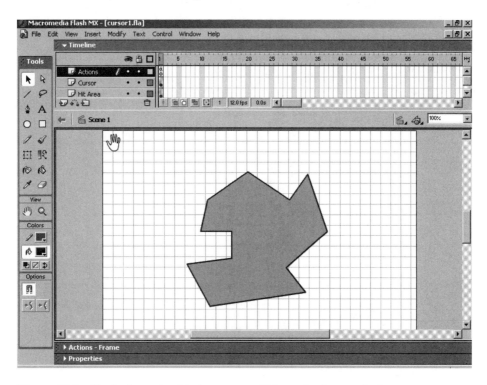

Figure 17.6   The basic movie with the cursor and hit area in place on the Stage.

When the movie first loads, you want the cursor_mc movie's clip default state to be invisible. You also want to track two variables—whether cursor_mc is over the shape on the Stage and whether the mouse button is down. You also want these two variables to default to false. Because you want to be able to access these variables from anywhere in the movie, make them global variables by prefacing the variable name with _global when you initially set them. After that, you can just refer to them as over and down and not worry about paths. Just be careful in more complex projects that your variable names are unique enough that you don't reuse them unintentionally.

4. Add a new layer and name it **Actions**. Select frame 1 of the Actions layer and add the following code:

```
cursor_mc._visible = false;
_global.over = false;
_global.down = false;
```

5. Save and test your movie. The default cursor should still be active and the cursor movie clip should be invisible.

   Now you have to decide what happens when the mouse is down, when the mouse is up, and when the mouse is over the hit area.

6. The first event you're going to code is the mouseDown event. This event fires any time the mouse is pressed, no matter where the cursor is on the Stage. You'll set up the code so that, if the mouse is pressesd over the hitArea_mc, it will start to drag that mc. First, you will check whether the mouse is currently over the hitArea_mc movie clip (don't worry about where this variable gets set to true—that comes later). If the mouse button is down and the variable over is true (meaning the cursor is over the hit area), you'll make the cursor switch to the closed hand. You'll reset the value of down to true. And then you will start your drag operation. After the last line of code you entered in Step 5, add the following:

```
hitArea_mc.onMouseDown = function () {
      if (over) {
            _root.cursor_mc.gotoAndStop("Closed");
            down = true;
            this.startDrag();
      }
}
```

7. The next event you have to script is mouseUp. This script should run only if down is set to true because you only care about the mouseUp event if the movie clip is currently being dragged around. If it is, you need to change the cursor_mc back to the open hand, set the down variable back to false, and stop dragging the hitArea_mc movie clip. To accomplish this, enter the following code after the last line of code you entered in Step 6:

```
hitArea_mc.onMouseUp = function () {
      if (down) {
            _root.cursor_mc.gotoAndStop("Open");
            down = false;
            this.stopDrag();    }
}
```

The final event you have to account for is the `mouseMove` event. This event fires every time the mouse is moved, so you need to keep your code as compact and efficient as possible. Because this code runs at every slight twitch of the mouse, long or inefficiently written code will slow down your movie.

8. Your first test is to see whether the mouse is currently over the hitArea_mc movie clip. To do this, you need to use the `hitTest()` method of the movie clip object. You pass three parameters to this method: the current X position of the mouse, the current Y position of the mouse, and whether you want to check for the actual shape of the movie clip (`true`) or just its bounding box (`false`). This is known as the Shape Flag option. To set up the shell for the `mouseMove()` event and the `hitTest()`, enter the following code:

```
hitArea_mc.onMouseMove = function () {
       if (this.hitTest(_root._xmouse, _root._ymouse, true)) {

       }
}
```

9. Think about what needs to happen if the cursor is over the hitArea_mc. Remember that you initialized the `over` variable to `false` when the movie loaded. Check to see whether that variable is still `false`; if it is, you want to change it to `true`—because now you *are* over the hitArea_mc. This is also when you'll hide the default cursor and change the visibility of the cursor_mc movie clip (which currently is set to the open hand) to `true`. Enter the following code between the asterisks:

```
hitArea_mc.onMouseMove = function () {
       if (this.hitTest(_root._xmouse, _root._ymouse, true)) {
//************************************************************
              if (!over) {
                     over = true;
                     Mouse.hide();
                     _root.cursor_mc._visible = true;
              }
//************************************************************
       }
}
```

10. Save your movie and test your file. You should be able to mouse over the shape on the Stage and watch the cursor change to the open hand. Even though you can change your cursor at this point, you won't be able to move it yet. You can click the hit area and drag it, but your custom cursor won't move. (See Figure 17.7.)

You don't need to do anything special if the `over` variable was already set to `true`, because that means nothing you're concerned about has changed. If you were over the hit area the last time the mouse moved and you're still over the hit area, nothing needs to be adjusted.

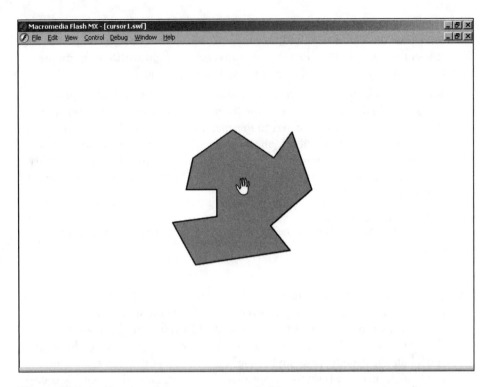

Figure 17.7 At this stage, when you mouse over the hit area, your mouse pointer disappears and is replaced by the open hand.

Now you need to set up an else statement to handle what will happen if you roll off the hitArea_mc movie clip. If you're no longer over the hitArea_mc, you need to check whether over is still set to true. You also need to check whether down is false. Why do you care if down is false? Well, if down is true, you're actually dragging the hitArea_mc; if you move your mouse quickly enough, the drag action might not keep up with you, but that doesn't count as rolling off the hitArea_mc. You basically need to reverse the process you set up when you rolled over the hitArea_mc: set over to false, show the mouse pointer, and hide the custom cursor.

11. Position your cursor and enter the following code between the asterisks:

```
hitArea_mc.onMouseMove = function () {
        if (this.hitTest(_root._xmouse, _root._ymouse, true)) {
            if (!over) {
                    over = true;
                    Mouse.hide();
                    _root.cursor_mc._visible = true;
            }
//************************************************************
    }else{
```

```
    if (over && !down){
        over = false;
        Mouse.show();
        _root.cursor_mc._visible = false;
    }
}
//*************************************************************
}
```

Note

The && operator first evaluates the left side of the expression and then returns a Boolean True or False. If the expression is True, Flash evaluates the right side of the expression. If both expressions are True, the final result is True. If either side of the expression evaluates to False, the final result is False. Using | |, Flash evaluates both sides of the expression. If either side of the expression is True, the final result is True. The operator ! inverts the value of an expression or variable and returns a Boolean True or False.

12. There's one more major issue you need to deal with. You need to be able to move the custom cursor around. When do you need to do this? You need to do this when you are either over or dragging the hitArea_mc movie clip. In either case, you need to update the position of the cursor_mc movie clip. All you need to do is set the X and Y positions of the cursor_mc movie clip equal to the X and Y positions of the mouse pointer. (See Figure 17.8.) The code you enter should go just after the close of the initial if statement. Enter the following code between the asterisks:

```
hitArea_mc.onMouseMove = function () {
    if (this.hitTest(_root._xmouse, _root._ymouse, true)) {
        if (!over) {
            over = true;
            Mouse.hide();
            _root.cursor_mc._visible = true;
        }
    }else{
        if (over && !down){
            over = false;
            Mouse.show();
            _root.cursor_mc._visible = false;
        }
    }
//*************************************************************
    if (over || down){
        _root.cursor_mc._x = _root._xmouse;
        _root.cursor_mc._y = _root._ymouse;
    }
//*************************************************************
}
```

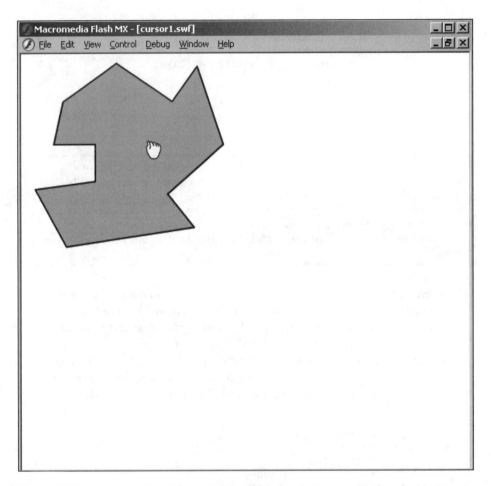

Figure 17.8   Now when the custom cursor is in the Closed state, you can drag the hit area while updating the position of the custom cursor at the same time.

13. All you have to do to finish your code is to add a special action to smooth out the dragging a little. This action is called `updateAfterEvent()`. It forces the movie clip to redraw anytime this event is fired—and it is completely independent of the movie's frame rate. Between the last two curly braces, enter the following code:

```
updateAfterEvent();
```

14. Click the Check Syntax icon in the Actions panel (blue checkmark) to make sure you don't have any syntax errors, and then save and test your movie. If you have any questions about the code, refer to Listing 17.3.

Listing 17.3   The Completed Actions for the Hit Area Movie Clip

```
cursor_mc._visible = false;
_global.over = false;
_global.down = false;


hitArea_mc.onMouseDown = function () {
     if (over) {
           _root.cursor_mc.gotoAndStop("closed");
           down = true;
           this.startDrag();
     }
}
hitArea_mc.onMouseUp = function () {
     if (down) {
           _root.cursor_mc.gotoAndStop("open");
           down = false;
           this.stopDrag(); }
}
hitArea_mc.onMouseMove = function () {
     if (this.hitTest(_root._xmouse, _root._ymouse, true)) {
           if (!over) {
                 over = true;
                 Mouse.hide();
                 _root.cursor_mc._visible = true;
           }

     }else{
           if (over && !down){
           over = false;
           Mouse.show();
           _root.cursor_mc._visible = false;
           }
     }

     if (over || down){
                 _root.cursor_mc._x = _root._xmouse;
                 _root.cursor_mc._y = _root._ymouse;
     }
     updateAfterEvent();
}
```

Now take a look at yet another way to use the drag-and-drop action.

Creating a Slide Control

One of the more common types of controls you see inside applications is a slide control.
The user can select a value within a given range by moving a slider that can move only
in a single dimension (left and right or up and down).

These slide controls are, in fact, just a slightly modified version of drag-and-drop. You might even find yourself using multiple slide controls in a single application. Instead of creating each control from scratch, why not create one self-contained slide control that you can reuse? You could save this as part of a custom Library and reuse it in any Flash movie. You'll also want to keep an eye on the Macromedia Flash Exchange for slider components—you can be sure you'll see some popping in there as developers learn how to create custom components in Flash MX.

So, what makes a slider control different from any other drag-and-drop interaction? For one thing, you need to constrain the movement of the object you're dragging to either a horizontal or vertical line. For another, sliders have a range.

When you are using a slider, the call you make to the `startDrag()` method is a little different from what you've used before. Just so you understand exactly how this special call to `startDrag()` is going to work, you need to understand the five arguments that you will pass to it.

- **lock.** A Boolean (True/False) that you use to lock the movie clip's center to the mouse pointer when you start dragging (True locks the pointer; False doesn't).
- **left.** Specifies the left limit of the drag area.
- **top.** Specifies the top limit of the drag area.
- **right.** Specifies the right limit of the drag area.
- **bottom.** Specifies the bottom limit of the drag area.

In Exercise 17.5, you begin building a reusable slider control.

Exercise 17.5   Setting Up the Graphics for the Slider

Before you can start adding code to your slider, you need to get the basic graphics set up on the Stage.

1. Open slider.fla from the Examples/Chapter17 folder on the CD.

   Open the Library. There are only two items: the sliderButton_mc and the slideGutter_mc movie clips. Notice spelling of slideGutter throughout to match up with the FLA.

2. The sliderButton_mc is what gets dragged, and the gutter is the visual object showing the extent of the range of the slider.

   Notice the Registration point for the slideGutter_mc. It's on the left side of the graphic and centered vertically. Why? It just makes the calculations easier—no negatives with which to deal.

3. You already decided that this is going to be a generalized slider, which you will reuse. That means it needs to be embedded in its own movie clip (you could also make it a custom Component, but that's another chapter). Create a new movie clip symbol (Insert > New Symbol) and name the new movie clip **slider_mc**.

4. Rename Layer 1 of the slider_mc movie clip **Gutter**, and drag a copy of the slideGutter_mc movie clip from the Library onto the Stage.

5. Center the slideGutter_mc so that its Registration point lines up with the Registration point of your new movie clip. (See Figure 17.9.)

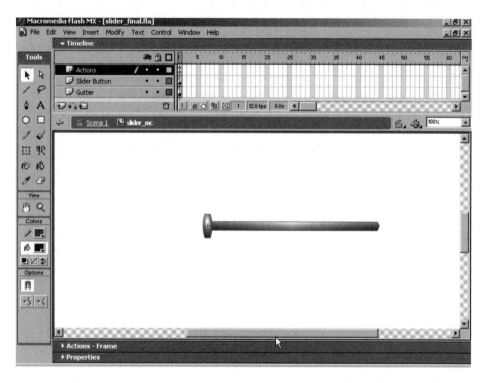

Figure 17.9   Align the slide gutter so that its Registration point aligns with the Registration point of your new movie clip.

6. With the slideGutter_mc movie clip selected, use the Properties Inspector to give it an instance name of **slideGutter_mc**.

7. Add a new layer to your movie and name it **Slider Button**.

8. With the Slider Button layer selected, drag a copy of the sliderButton_mc onto the Stage.

9. Align sliderButton_mc's registration point with the registration point of the movie clip.

10. Use the Properties Inspector to give the sliderButton_mc an instance name of **sliderButton_mc**.

Now it's time to add a little code to your movie! This is the code that will make the sliderButton_mc movie clip draggable. It's pretty standard code, a lot like the drag-and-drop exercises you did earlier, with one exception. This time you use the startDrag() method's constrain arguments to constrain the dragging to a given area, and that area will be defined by the size of the slideGutter_mc movie clip.

Exercise 17.6   Adding the Code for the Drag-and-Drop Interaction

You will lock the mouse to center, setting the left, top, and bottom limits to 0. You also will set the right limit by determining the width of the slideGutter_mc movie clip.

1. You should still be in the slider_mc movie clip. Add a new layer and name it **Actions**. You're putting all of your Actions inside the slider_mc movie clip, because you want to be able to have multiple versions of this slider on the Stage at the same time. You'll start by setting up the **startDrag** action for the sliderButton_mc. You'll also add a variable, down, to track whether or not the sliderButton_mc is being pressed.

2. Select frame 1 of the Actions layer and enter the following code:

```
sliderButton_mc.onPress = function () {
        this.startDrag(true, 0, 0, slideGutter_mc._width, 0);
        down = true;
}
```

   You're constraining the drag so that Y never changes, and you can only move on the X-axis between 0 and the width of the slideGutter_mc.

3. Go back to the main Timeline and drag a copy of slider_mc from the Library onto the Stage.

4. Save and test your movie.

   You should be able to drag sliderButton_mc onto the Stage, but its movement is constrained (see Figure 17.10). No big surprise here, you can't let go of the button—you'll need an onRelease event handler for that.

5. Double-click on the slider_mc movie clip to open it in Symbol-Editing mode.

6. Select frame 1 of the Actions layer and open the Actions panel if it is closed.

7. To add the onRelease event handler, just enter the following code after the onPress handler:

```
sliderButton_mc.onRelease = function () {
        this.stopDrag();
        down = false;
}
```

Figure 17.10   Now you can drag the sliderButton_mc, but its movement is constrained to the width of the slideGutter_mc movie clip.

Notice that you updated the value of the down variable. If you're no longer dragging the sliderButton_mc, down needs to be set to false.

8. As long as you're here, go ahead and pass the method you just set up for onRelease to onReleaseOutside. Enter the following code:

```
sliderButton_mc.onReleaseOutside = sliderButton_mc.onRelease;
```

You want to be able to capture information from your slider as it moves. Otherwise, what do you need a slider for? Every time the slider moves (onMouseMove), you'll capture its current X position. (Remember how you set the Registration point? The left side of the slider control has a value of 0.) If you divide the current X position by the total width of the sliderGutter_mc, you always get a value between 0 and 1 (inclusive). This way, your data isn't tied to any particular range of values.

You'll probably need different value ranges, depending on what you want to use your slider for. To accommodate that, you'll pass the value of onSlide as a parameter in a function call named slider—you'll be writing the function in just a moment.

9. After the last line of code you entered in Step 8, add the following code to capture the slider value:

```
sliderButton_mc.onMouseMove = function () {
        if (down){
                onSlide=this._x/slideGutter_mc._width;
                slider(onSlide);
        }
}
```

So, if the mouse moves and you happen to be dragging the slider, you'll update the onSlide variable with a value from 0–1. Believe it or not, that's all you have to do for your slider!

So now that you have a slider, what are you going to do with it? You know the `onSlide` variable always returns a value between 0 and 1. You'll probably find that you are in need of other ranges, such as 1 to 100 or −100 to 100. You'll take a look at how to deal with that in Exercise 17.7.

Exercise 17.7   Adding the Code to Use the Slider

You know you set up a function call inside the slider—you're going to attach a function to modify the `onSlide` variable next. In fact, you're going to do this with two different sliders on the Stage, so you can see how to modify the code as needed.

1. Go back to your main Timeline and drag another copy of the slider_mc movie clip onto the Stage.

2. Give each of the instances of the slider_mc its own instance name—use the instance names **sliderOne** and **sliderTwo**.

   You will write a simple function that outputs the value of `onSlide` for sliderOne, and a second function to modify that value for sliderTwo.

3. Add a new layer named **Actions** to the main Timeline and enter the following code in the Actions panel:

```
sliderOne.slider=function(onSlide){
        trace(onSlide);
}
```

   Notice that all you are doing is tracing the current value that is being passed into the function.

4. Save and test your movie. When you drag sliderOne, you should see values in your output window ranging from 0 to 1.

5. For sliderTwo, you want to output values from −100 to 100. And you want the numbers to be whole numbers. So now, onSlide can have 200 possible values. If you multiply onSlide by 200, you'll get numbers ranging from 0 to 200. To get the value range −100 to 100, you need to multiply by 200 and then subtract 100. You'll also use the round method of the Math object so you get nice even numbers. Beneath the code you entered on the main Timeline, enter the following code:

```
sliderTwo.slider=function(onSlide){
        val=Math.round(onSlide*200)-100;
        trace(val);
}
```

6. Save and test your movie—you can see your slider value in the Output window (see Figure 17.11).

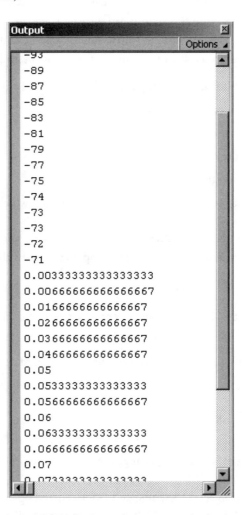

Figure 17.11   By setting up a function to catch the `onSlide` value in on the main Timeline, you can customize the output for each slider on the Stage.

By setting up functions for each of the sliders individually, you now have the power to modify the output value of the slider without ever having to go in and modify the code inside the slider itself.

In the next section, you take a look at another interface element that you can use with Flash—scrolling text.

Creating Scrolling Text

Another commonly used interactive element is a dynamic text field that has the capability to scroll if it contains more text than it can display. There are a couple of ways that you can approach creating a scrolling text field. You can take advantage of the ScrollBar component to get a field to scroll, or you can create your own scrolling buttons.

Setting up a scrolling text field is easy. If you're going to use the ScrollBar component, all you have to do is:

1. Create a dynamic text box.
2. Assign an identifier to the text field.
3. Load some text into the text field.
4. Drag the ScrollBar component onto the Stage and tell it which text field to scroll.

In Exercise 17.8, you'll use the ScrollBar component to create a scrolling text box. You'll find more information about the ScrollBar component (and other components) in Chapter 18, "Components."

Exercise 17.8   Using the ScrollBar Component to Create a Scrolling Text Field

Components are one of the best of the new MX features. A general favorite is the scrollbar.

1. Create a new file and save it as **textScroll.fla** on your hard drive.
2. Select the Text tool and use the Properties Inspector to change it to Dynamic Text.
3. Drag a text field onto the Stage.
4. In the Properties Inspector, give the text field an instance name of **myText**.
5. Still in the Properties Inspector, change the Line Type to Multiline and select Show Border Around Text.
6. Turn on Snap to Objects (View > Snap to Objects) and open the Components panel (Window > Components). Drag a copy of the ScrollBar component onto the Stage.
7. Okay—this part is way too cool—drag the component and drop it on the text field (see Figure 17.12). It will automatically snap to an edge and resize to fit the text field!

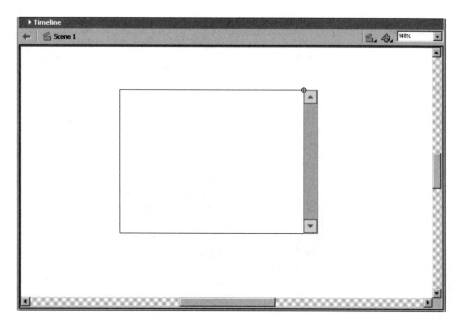

Figure 17.12   The ScrollBar component automatically resizes to fit the text field, as long as you have Snap to Objects turned on.

8. With the ScrollBar selected, look in the Properties Inspector. It should have set the Target TextField to myText (make sure the Parameters tab is selected).

9. Now all you need is some text to scroll. You could just assign a string of text to the text field, but you'll probably find that you most often load text from an external file, because you have a lot more flexibility that way. You can modify your text at any time without reopening the Flash file.

10. The trick to loading text from an external file is making sure that the text has loaded before you try to display it. You can use the onData event handler to make sure the text has loaded and then pass the text to the text field.

11. Copy the text.txt file from the Examples/Chapter17 folder and save it on your hard drive in the same directory as your Flash file.

12. Add a new layer to the Timeline and name it **Actions**.

13. Select frame 1 of the Actions layer and use loadVariables() to load the contents of the text.txt file into the main Timeline. Enter the following code:

```
this.loadVariables("text.txt");
```

Note

You can either load a simple, static text file or you can load a text file generated using middleware, such as Macromedia's ColdFusion, Microsoft's Active Server Pages (ASP), Perl, PHP, or any language that can generate a simple text file.

The format of the text file is important. The extension on the file is not. That means that as long as the text in the file is in the proper name/value pair format, the file can be created as a .txt, .asp, .cfm, .pl, .php, or whatever kind of file; it doesn't matter. The format for the name/value pair in the text file should look like this:

```
&text=This is some text.  Spaces are okay.&
```

Note that there are no quotes around the text string. If you put quotes around the text string, it's not going to work. If you do put quotes around the string and you've selected the HTML option on the Text panel, the only thing that is returned is <p align=left"> </p>. If the HTML option is not selected, a blank is returned. That being said, quotes inside the text string are usually acceptable. If you need to have a whole string appear in quotes, you need to URL encode the quotes (%22 in place of the quote mark). The URL encoding is just the % hexadecimal equivalent of a character. You'll find that certain other characters won't print out the way you want them to; you might have to URL encode them as well. You can find a URL encoding table at this location:

```
http://www.macromedia.com/support/flash/ts/documents/url_encoding.htm
```

14. Now you just need to load the text into your text field. The variable name in the text file is scrollText. When the main Timeline has received all of its data, you want to load the text into the myText text field. You can use the text property of the TextField object to pass in the data. Enter the following:

```
this.onData = function () {
       myText.text = scrollText;
}
```

15. Now save and test your movie (see Figure 17.13). That's a fairly painless way to add scrolling capabilities to a text field, don't you think?

If you decide not to use the ScrollBar component to scroll text, creating your own scrolling buttons isn't all that difficult. All you need to do is the following:

1. Create a dynamic text box.

2. Assign a variable name to the text box.

3. Assign some text to the variable.

4. Use the scroll and maxscroll properties with a couple of buttons (or a slider) to control the scrolling.

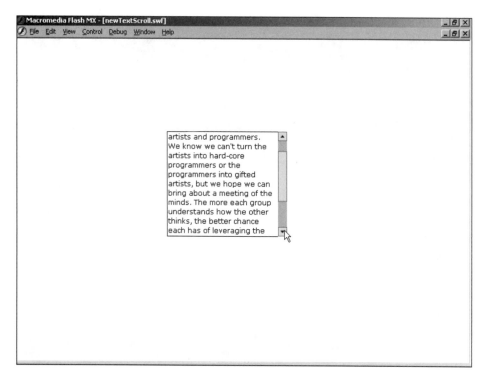

Figure 17.13   When you have your text loaded in from an external file, it scrolls very nicely.

That's really the gist of the whole process. Of course, you can make it as complex as you want. In fact, in Exercise 17.9, you make buttons visible and invisible depending on the values of `scroll` and `maxscroll`.

As you might have guessed, the key here is the scroll and maxscroll properties of the dynamic text boxes.

Exercise 17.9   Creating a Scrolling Text Field Using Buttons

Before you can start worrying about scrolling your text, you need to set up the dynamic text box on the Stage.

1. Open textScrollButtons.fla from the Examples/Chapter17 folder on the companion CD and save it to your hard drive.

   The text field (with an instance name of myText) and scrolling movie clips are already on the Stage (see Figure 17.14).

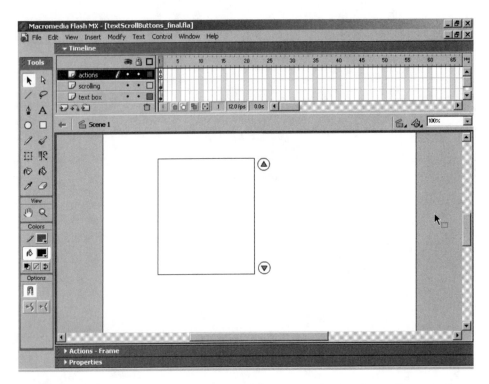

Figure 17.14   This time the text field has already been set up for you, along with movie clips that will behave as buttons.

2. If you haven't already done so, copy the text.txt file from the Examples/Chapter17 folder on the companion CD and save it to the same directory on your hard drive that you saved your Flash file.

3. Select frame 1 of the Actions layer—the text load has already been set up for you. It's exactly the same as in the previous exercise.

4. Go ahead and test your file. You have text, but no scrolling yet.

5. Select the upward-pointing movie clip and use the Instance panel to give it an instance name of **scrollUp**. Do the same thing for the downward-pointing movie clip, but change the instance name to **scrollDown**.

   Now you need to begin assigning the Actions that will control the scrolling for your text field. As you might guess, you'll be using the onPress, onRelease, and onEnterFrame event handlers to control what happens when the scrollUp and scrollDown movie clips are pressed.

6. Select frame 1 in the Actions layer and open the Actions panel. The first thing you'll do is set a variable, down, to true when the mouse button is pressed over a movie, and false when it is released. After the last line of code in the Actions panel, add the following:

```
scrollUp.onPress = function () {
      this.down = true;
}
scrollUp.onRelease = function () {
      this.down = false;
}
```

7. You want to do exactly the same thing for the scrollDown movie clip—but rather than repeat the code, just pass the methods you just set up for the scrollUp movie clip to the scrollDown movie clip. Enter the following code:

```
scrollDown.onPress = scrollUp.onPress;
scrollDown.onRelease = scrollUp.onRelease;
```

8. You also want to make sure you handle what happens onReleaseOutside, which is exactly the same as what happens onRelease. Modify the last line of code so that it looks like this:

```
scrollUp.onReleaseOutside = scrollDown.onReleaseOutside =
scrollDown.onRelease = scrollUp.onRelease;
```

So far, so good. But you still don't have any scrolling. All dynamic text fields have a built-in property called scroll. To make the text scroll, you simply increment or decrement this property of the text field. In this situation, you want to increment or decrement the scroll property of the text field while the variable down is true. To do this, you need to constantly monitor the state of the down variable. This is where the onEnterFrame event handler comes into play.

9. If the scrollUp movie clip is pressed, you want to decrement the scroll property. If the scrollDown movie clip is pressed, you want to increment the scroll property. To accomplish this, enter the following code at the end of your Actions list (you should still have frame 1 selected);

```
scrollUp.onEnterFrame = function () {
      if (this.down){
            --myText.scroll;
      }
}
scrollDown.onEnterFrame = function () {
      if (this.down){
            ++myText.scroll;
      }
}
```

10. Save and test your movie. You now have scrolling text.

There's one more small bit of functionality you can add to this movie—you can set it up so that the buttons are only visible when the text can be scrolled.

Wouldn't it be nice if you could set it up so that the movie clips with the scroll buttons were visible only when you needed them? When you're on the first line, you don't need the scrollUp movie clip. When you're at the bottom of the text, you don't need the scrollDown movie clip. It's not difficult at all to set up. You just need to change the condition in your existing if statement and add a second condition. Then you throw in an alternative if neither of the first two conditions are met:

- Instead of just checking whether down is true, add in a check to make sure the movie clip is visible as well. If both are true, scroll the text.

- If you've scrolled as far as possible in either direction, set the visibility of the movie clip to false.

- Otherwise, just set the visibility of the movie clip to true.

11. First, you just need to add the check for visibility to the existing if statements inside the onEnterFrame events:

```
scrollUp.onEnterFrame = function () {
        if (this._visible && this.down){
            --myText.scroll;
        }
}
scrollDown.onEnterFrame = function () {
        if (this._visible && this.down){
            ++myText.scroll;
        }
}
```

This doesn't really change much for you, since both of the movie clips are visible all the time—you're going to change that next.

12. Add an if else statement (between the asterisks) that checks whether scroll evaluates to 1—in other words, you're at the top of the text file. If scroll does evaluate to 1, make the scrollUp movie clip invisible; if not, make sure the visibility is set to true. For scrollUp, add the following code between the asterisks:

```
scrollUp.onEnterFrame = function () {
        if (this._visible && this.down){
            --myText.scroll;
        }
//***********************************************
        if (myText.scroll == 1){
            this._visible = false;
        }else{
            this._visible = true;
        }
//***********************************************
}
```

13. You just have one more bit of code to add for scrollDown. whether scroll and maxscroll are equal. If they are, mak movie clip invisible; if not, make sure the visibility is set t add the following code between the asterisks:

```
scrollDown.onEnterFrame = function () {
    if (this._visible && this.down){
        ++myText.scroll;
    }
//**********************************************
    if (myText.scroll == myText.maxscroll){
        this._visible = false;
    }else{
        this._visible = true;
    }
//**********************************************
}
```

14. That's it. Save and test your file. Now your buttons should appear and disappear as needed (see Figure 17.15).

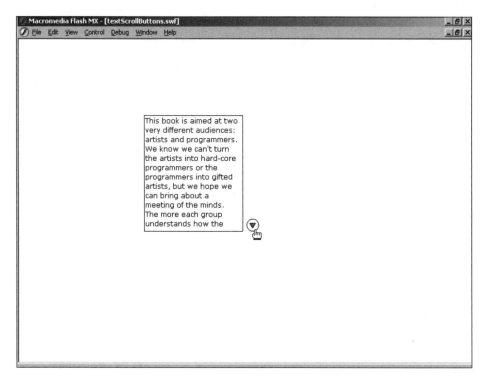

Figure 17.15 With the code you just entered, the scroll buttons are only visible when you can actually scroll in a particular direction.

modifying the text file and then launching the SWF file. Your text has changed, and you didn't need to reopen the FLA file or generate a new SWF file. That's a powerful new option for keeping content on your site fresh!

There's one final technique you'll take a look at in this chapter—creating a preloader.

Creating Preloaders

I don't know about you, but I don't like loading pages that don't give me any idea of how long I'm going to have to wait. I mean really, with some sites you have enough time to go out and wash the car before they complete their loading sequence. Wouldn't it be nice to know that up front so that you could do something worthwhile while you wait, instead of staring at the monitor and growing frustrated? Let your users know whether they have time to make a quick phone call or time to wash the car. Why not show the percent loaded to your user? A classic way to do this is to use a loading bar that scales according to the percentage of bytes loaded.

Adding a Percent Loading Bar

You can take advantage of a couple of methods to create a preloader, notably `getBytesLoaded()` and `getBytesTotal()`. With these methods, you can accurately determine how much of your movie has downloaded. If you're going to be building preloaders in Flash, you want to get to know these methods well:

- **getBytesLoaded().** The total number of bytes that have currently loaded. The syntax is `movieclip.getBytesLoaded()`.

- **getBytesTotal().** The total number of bytes for the entire movie, including all movie clips. The syntax is `movieclip.getBytesTotal()`.

You can use these two methods to set up some simple calculations that you can use to display the percentage of the movie that has currently loaded, both visually and as a calculated value.

So what do you need to get going here?

- A horizontal bar that you can scale

- A border around the bar that is constant so that you can see the load progress

Because you're going to be scaling the horizontal bar and not the border, the horizontal bar needs to be a separate movie clip. The way you set up the bar is important. You'll want the bar to load with the `_xscale` property set to 0. For that to work properly, without a lot of unnecessary code, you need to make sure that the Registration point for the bar is on the left side of the bar. If you decide to align the movie clips with the Registration points at the center, the loading bar still scales; however, it scales from the center outward.

In Exercise 17.10, you'll build your own dynamically scaling loading bar.

Exercise 17.10   Creating a Dynamically Scaling Loading Bar

1. Open a new file and save it to your hard drive as **preload.fla**.
2. To set up the visual portion of your preloader, the scaling bar, select the Rectangle tool and draw a rectangle with both a fill and stroke on the Stage as illustrated in Figure 17.16.

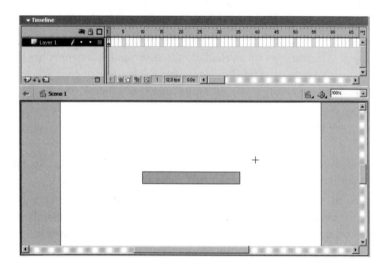

Figure 17.16   To begin creating your scaling loading bar, draw a rectangle that has both a stroke and fill.

3. Select the fill and convert it to a movie clip (F8) named **bar_mc**. Make sure you set the Registration point to be on the left side. Make sure you don't select the stroke when you do this.
4. With the bar_mc movie clip selected, use the Properties Inspector to assign it an instance name of **bar_mc**.
5. Next, you'll embed both the new movie clip and the stroke in another movie clip. Select both the bar_mc movie clip and the stroke and convert them into a new movie clip (F8) named **preload_mc**.

6. Select the preload_mc and use the Properties Inspector to give it an instance name of **preload_mc**.

7. On the main Timeline, add a new layer called **Actions**.

8. Select frame 1 of the Actions layer and open the Actions panel.

9. As you start to load your movie, you need to continually monitor its progress, so this a good time to set up an onEnterFrame event handler. You'll be controlling the preload_mc movie clip, so to get started add the following code to frame 1 of the main Timeline:

```
preload_mc.onEnterFrame = function () {

}
```

10. Next, you'll pass the values of the getBytesLoaded() and getBytesTotal() methods into variables. Why? Because it's more efficient to access a variable than to repeatedly call a method—and you'll be using these in several calculations. Add the following code between the curly braces:.

```
bytesLoaded = getBytesLoaded();
bytesTotal = getBytesTotal();
```

11. What needs to happen next? You need to make sure that something is actually loading. If it is, you'll set up a calculation to determine how much has loaded versus the total bytes that need to load. After the last line of code you entered, but before the final curly brace, enter the following code:

```
if (bytesTotal > -1) {
        percent = bytesLoaded/bytesTotal;
}
```

This will give you a value between 0 and 1. In order to convert this to a percent, which you'll need to do in the next step, just multiply by 100.

12. Based on the value of the variable percent (which will be between 0 and 1), you set the _xscale property for the bar_mc movie clip. Add a new blank line after the line where you set up the percent variable and add the following:

```
this.bar_mc._xscale = percent*100;
```

13. All you need to do now is add a conditional statement to check whether percent is equivalent to 1 (actually, it works better if you check for whether the percent is greater than .99). If it is, you want to make the preload_mc invisible and you want the main Timeline to advance to frame 2. After the last line you entered (but still inside the curly braces), add the following code:

```
if (percent > .99){
        this._visible = false;
        gotoAndPlay(2);
}
```

14. By adding just one more line of code, you can format the value for percent loaded and save it to a variable that can be displayed as part of the preloader. You can use the round method of the Math object to format the percent. Just add in the following code between the asterisks:.

```
if (bytesTotal > -1) {
        percent = bytesLoaded/bytesTotal;
        this.bar_mc._xscale = percent*100;
//*******************************************************
        preload_mc.percent_loaded = Math.round(percent*100)
//*******************************************************
        if (percent > .99){
                preload_mc._visible = false;
                gotoAndStop(2);
        }
}
```

Your complete code listing should look like Listing 17.4:

Listing 17.4   Complete Code for a Dynamic Preloader

```
preload_mc.onEnterFrame = function () {
     bytesLoaded = getBytesLoaded();
     bytesTotal = getBytesTotal();
//
     if (bytesTotal > -1) {
            percent = bytesLoaded/bytesTotal;
            this.bar_mc._xscale = percent*100;
            preload_mc.percentText = Math.round(percent*100)
            if (percent > .99){
                    preload_mc._visible = false;
                    gotoAndStop(2);
            }
     }
}
```

15. You still need to add a dynamic text box to the preloader so you can display the value you just calculated. Double-click on the preload_mc to open it in Symbol-Editing mode.

16. Beneath the bar_mc movie clip, add a line of static text that says **Percent Loaded:**. Next to the line you just added, add a dynamic text box with a variable name of **percentText**.

17. Before you save and test your movie, you need to load something bulky into frame 2. You can choose anything you like—if in doubt, try importing the bobAgain2.avi as an embedded movie clip—you can find that in the Examples/Chapter14 folder on the CD. Make sure you add a stop() action to frame 2 in the Actions layer.

Once you have something in frame 2, save and test your movie (see Figure 17.17). Either load your movie (and its HTML file) to a server or make sure you choose Show Streaming from View so that you can watch the preloading sequence.

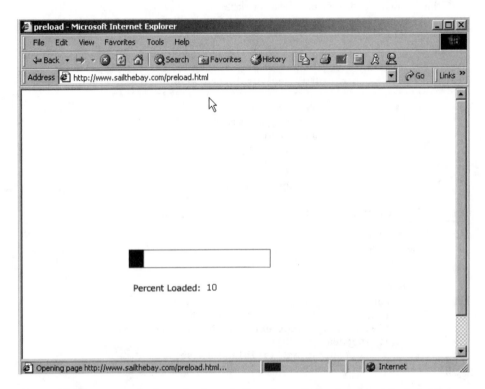

Figure 17.17   Your preloader scales dynamically and you display the percent loaded at the same time. No one will need to wonder how long they have to wait around to see your creation.

That's the basics for setting up a preloader. Obviously you can tailor this to suit your needs. You could set up the file to download a percentage of your file before playing rather than the entire file. It's entirely up to you.

Summary

You've now been introduced to different interface techniques that you can use in Flash: drag-and-drop, custom cursors, sliders, simple scrolling text, and preloaders. You've also had a chance to combine more than one type of interface interaction to create a single movie. Even with nothing but the elements introduced in this chapter, you should be able to come up with some brand new combinations of your own—you just need to put a little thought into it!

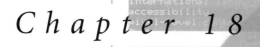

Chapter 18

Components

Components are an exciting new feature in

Flash MX. Finally, designers have access to

commonly used tools, such as Form

Objects, that can be dragged and dropped

into any Flash movie. Flash 5 and earlier required a considerable amount of ActionScript to perform what can be done easily with Components.

This chapter will be examine the current Components shipping with Flash MX, explain how these Components can be scripted together, and then explain how to get additional Components from the Internet.

Specifically, the chapter will cover the following:

- What Components are
- Using Components in Flash
- Extending Components with ActionScript
- Building your own Components

What Are Components?

If you have ever developed with tools such as Microsoft's Visual Basic or Java, you will be familiar with the term "Component." Essentially, a Component is a prebuilt section of code that can do a specific action. This one action can be something such as adding a scrollbar to a text field or adding an interactive button. The success of Components is that they are simple, small pieces of reusable code.

Flash 5 first introduced the concept of reusable objects with SmartClips. SmartClips were the predecessors to Components. SmartClips allowed you to drag reusable objects, such as form check boxes, onto the Stage easily. The benefit of SmartClips was that they allowed you to program precompiled check boxes onto the canvas. Once the boxes were on Stage, the Clip Parameter panel allowed you to modify predefined fields within the SmartClip. Components take this same idea and greatly extend it.

Flash MX Components, as shown in Figure 18.1, are much more versatile. To begin with, the entire architecture used to build a Component has been significantly over-hauled. Not only can you create more complex Components, but you can create Components that can be controlled more effectively with ActionScript. The connection to ActionScript allows you to achieve very complex and exciting solutions.

The construction of each Component is not too complex. Each Component is constructed from movie clips and ActionScript. That's it. Knowing this, you quickly see that any element of a Component can be modified. Later, you will be changing the visual appearance of a Component.

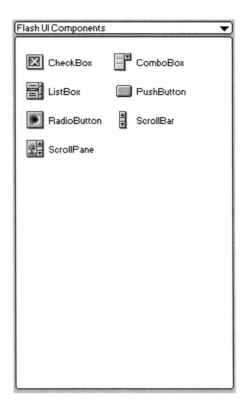

Figure 18.1   Flash MX comes with seven Components.

How Components Can Be Used

Out of the box, Flash comes with seven Components:

- ComboBox
- CheckBox
- ListBox
- PushButton
- RadioButton
- ScrollBar
- ScrollPane

A challenge placed on the shoulders of many Flash developers is how to move content from Flash forms into databases in much the same way as HTML forms. This initial collection of Components forms the foundation of what is needed to build Flash-based forms. Now you have the tools that will allow you to build forms that perform in the same way as HTML forms.

Why Use Components?

For developers, Components make sense. Why keep on rebuilding movie clips that you use all the time? With a Component, you can begin to build a library of tools that significantly enhance your projects. And you can use them over and over again.

Designers will find Components more accessible for the simple reason that they do not need to become experienced ActionScript developers. All designers need to know is how to set the parameters of the Component for it to work correctly.

Using Components

Okay, let's get down in the dirt with Components. The best way for you to see how easy Components are is to begin using them. Exercise 18.1 shows you how.

Exercise 18.1   Using the ScrollBar Component

In this exercise, you will use the ScrollBar Component. In many ways it is the simplest Component. However, simplicity is what makes it so useful. The ScrollBar Component allows you to easily add scrollbars to multiline text fields with text that rolls off the edge of the screen.

1. Create a new movie. Size the movie to 450 × 220, set it to 12fps, and give it a white background.
2. Add two layers. Name one layer **Scripts** and the second layer **Text**.
3. Select frame 1 of the Text layer. Choose the Text tool, and drag a text box onto the stage. In the Properties Inspector, set it to Dynamic Text. Give it an instance name of **body_txt**, and set the following:

   Show Border Around Text: **Selected**
   Multiline: **Selected**
   Width: **400**
   Height: **155**

4. Open the Component panel. Make sure View > Snap to Objects is checked. Click and drag the ScrollBar Component over to the far right side of the text field. The scrollbar will snap to the edge of the field. You can tell you've made a connection if the scrollbar becomes the same height as the text. If it does not snap immediately, select the top-left corner of the scrollbar (this is the registration point of the Component) to the top right of the text box. It will now snap into place.

5. The Properties panel changes to display a new set of options. These options are the Component Parameters. (See Figure 18.2.) Each Component comes with a set of parameters. It is these parameters that enable you to control how the Component itself works. The parameter that is most important right now is the Target Text Field parameter. This parameter controls which text field the scrollbar controls. You should see that the scrollbar has automatically picked up the name of the text field and entered the value body_txt. If it hasn't, your scrollbar may not have locked onto the text field, and you should try dragging it again.

Figure 18.2   The Component Parameters control how the Component will be implemented in the final movie. The ScrollBar Component only has two parameters. More complex Components have more parameters.

6. To test the text-scrolling features of the Component, you need some text in the text field. Select frame 1 of the Scripts layer. Open the Actions panel in Expert mode, and enter the following ActionScript:

```
body_txt.text = "IT WAS the best of times, it was the worst of
times, it was the age of wisdom, it was the age of foolishness,
it was the epoch of belief, it was the epoch of incredulity, it
was the season of Light, it was the season of Darkness, it was
the spring of hope, it was the winter of despair, we had
everything before us, we had nothing before us, we were all going
direct to Heaven, we were all going direct the other way - in
short, the period was so far like the present period, that some of
its noisiest authorities insisted on its being received, for good
or for evil, in the superlative degree of comparison only."
```

7. Press Ctrl + Enter to preview your work. The ScrollBar Component allows you to add vertical scrollbars without doing the complex coding that scrollbars traditionally required. (See Figure 18.3.) Save your file as Dickens.fla.

> IT WAS the best of times, it was the worst of times, it was the age of wisdom, it was the age of foolishness, it was the epoch of belief, it was the epoch of incredulity, it was the season of Light, it was the season of Darkness, it was the spring of hope, it was the winter of despair, we had everything before us, we had nothing before us, we were all going direct to Heaven, we were all going direct the other way- in short, the period was so far like the present period, that some of its noisiest authorities insisted on its being received, for good or for evil, in the

Figure 18.3   The ScrollBar makes it easy to see text that overflows in a text box.

As you can see, Components are incredibly easy to use. You can add them to a page and configure them to work with your files very quickly.

The ScrollBar is the most basic of Components. Now you are ready to work with more complex Components.

The Components That Come with Flash MX

There are six more Components that come with Flash MX. The focus of most of these Components is related to web forms. Forms are part of the standard for HTML. You don't need to do anything with JavaScript or images to create a web form. If you know HTML or have Dreamweaver (or a similar web page editor), you can easily create forms. Things are not so simple in Flash. Flash forms must be created with movie clips and ActionScript. Because the Form Components that come with Flash MX take care of the ActionScript for you, you can focus more on the development of the page content and worry less about form element construction.

Exercise 18.2   Using the Flash Form Components

In this exercise, you will learn how to use the most common Form Components.

1. Create a new movie. Add fives layers to the movie. Name the layers **Background**, **CheckBox**, **RadioBox**, **ComboBox**, and **PushButton**.

2. Select the Background layer and type the title **Build a house!**.

3. Select the RadioBox layer. On the stage type in **House Type**. From the Components panel, drag two RadioButton Components alongside the text. You will see in the Properties Inspector that you can modify the parameters of the RadioButton Components. The function of a radio button is to enable a user to choose one option from a number of choices. Here you have only two choices, but the end result is the same.

4. Select the first RadioButton Component. Name the button **Duplex**. The RadioButton Component has six parameters. The most important is Group Name. Collecting radio buttons under one name forces the software to allow only one radio button to be chosen. The name of each radio button is different. If you fail to give the button a group name, Flash will assign all radio buttons to radioGroup. It is this value that can be passed on when a choice is made.

5. Label the first RadioButton **Duplex**, as shown in Figure 18.4, and give it the Group Name **housetype**.

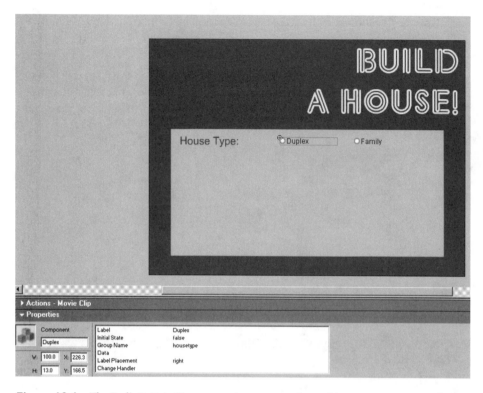

Figure 18.4   The RadioButton Component is more complex and has more parameters for a user to modify than the ScrollBar Component.

6.   Select the second RadioButton. Make this button's instance name and label both **Family**, and make the Group Name **housetype**.

7.   Preview the movie. You can only choose one radio button from the group. Don't worry about the other parameters—you will get to them later.

8.   Now add a CheckBox Component. Select the CheckBox layer. Add the text **Do you want a patio?**. Alongside the question mark, drag a CheckBox Component from the Components panel. Give the CheckBox an instance name of **patio** and delete the label. If you add additional CheckBox Components, you do not need to create a group name as with RadioButton Components.

9.   Preview the movie. You can select and deselect the check box. Of course, this is true of any check box, but you have done it all in Flash!

10.   Go back to the main movie. Select the ComboBox layer. Add the text **Where do you want to live?**, and drag a ComboBox Component from the Components panel to the right of the text. A ComboBox is very similar to the drop-down menu box so common in web forms.

11. Give the ComboBox an instance name of **city**. The ComboBox is one of more complicated Components. The two main parameters you need to focus on are Labels and Data.

12. Select the Labels Parameter. A magnifying glass appears on the far-right side. This symbol indicates that you can open the Values window to extend information entered in the parameter. (See Figure 18.5.) Select the magnifying glass and open the Labels parameter.

Figure 18.5 The Labels parameter is managed with the Values window.

13. You can insert new parameters by selecting the Plus symbol. A new row will automatically enter the value "default Value." Select this row and enter in **London**. Select the plus symbol two more times. Enter in the values **New York** and **Paris**. Click OK.

    The Label value is often different from the data you need from the ComboBox. For instance, you might have a list of states with their names fully spelled out in the Labels parameter, while the information to be passed back to the database might be just the two-letter abbreviations of the state names. The Data parameter allows you to effectively achieve this goal. In many ways, the parameter looks and operates in the same way as the Labels parameter.

14. Select the Data parameter to reveal a magnifying glass. Select this symbol to open a Values window that is identical to that of the Labels parameter. The information in the Data Values window must match up with the Labels parameter. Select the plus symbol three times and add **London**, **New York**, and **Paris**.

15. Preview the movie. You will be able to select the ComboBox and choose a city.

16. Return to the movie and select the ComboBox.

Up to this point, all of the features you have used have been identical to HTML forms. But this is Flash—you can customize everything to the *Nth* degree. This is demonstrated with two additional parameters for the ComboBox. The first parameter is the Editable parameter.

17. Select the Editable parameter. The parameter allows ComboBox to be either True or False. The default value is False. This means that you cannot edit any of the Label values when the movie is being played as a SWF file. Change the Value to True, and preview the movie. The ComboBox works in the same way as before in that you can choose from a drop-down list, but now you can type in your own city name if the option you are looking for is not there. Go ahead and type in **Washington DC**. The value is accepted.

18. The next Flash trick available with a ComboBox deals with the number of values present in a drop-down selection. Typically, when you choose a drop-down menu on a web page with a large number of choices, a scrollbar appears on the left side of the drop-down that enables you to scroll through the remaining options. Enter Flash ComboBoxes. The Row Count parameter enables you to programmatically limit the number of rows visible when the ComboBox is selected. If the number of rows exceeds this limit, a scrollbar will appear. Try doing that with HTML.

19. The final element you will add to the movie is a button to submit your form. From the Components panel, choose PushButton and drag it onto the Stage. Give the button an instance name of **submit**. There are only two parameters for the button. Choose the Label parameter from the Properties Inspector and label the button **Submit**.

20. Preview the form. You can use all of the objects on the stage. Save the file as House.fla.

Scripting Components

Now you have all of the tools needed to build a form, but nothing to do with your form. This section demonstrates how you can make forms elements interactive.

Activating Components with ActionScript

The logic within each Component is constructed with ActionScript, and the information within each parameter can be captured. Exercise 18.3 will demonstrate how you can do this with the Components you have used so far.

Built into each of the Components that come with Flash MX are a number of methods. These methods can be controlled programmatically. A list of the methods for each Component can be viewed by opening the Reference panel under Flash UI Components, as shown in Figure 18.6.

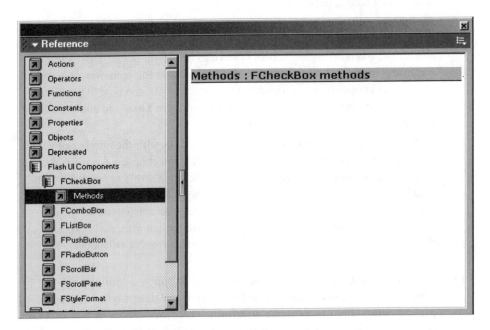

Figure 18.6   The Reference panel lists all of the methods that a Component has. This helps developers understand how the Components will work and expand their functionality.

Exercise 18.3   Passing Information from Components to Different Objects in the Movie

Now that you know Components can be programmed, you can do all sorts of interesting things with them.

1. Open House.fla. Add a new layer, and name that layer **Script**.

2. Select the Script and Background layers. Add a new key frame. Select frame 2 of the Background layer and draw two Dynamic text fields on the stage. Give the first one an instance name of **PatioText** and the second an instance name of **CityText**. Make both fields 400 pixels wide.

3. From the Components panel, drag a second PushButton Component onto the stage. Change the Label parameter of the button to **Reset** and give it an instance name of **Reset** as well.

   You want this to happen: As you select the Submit button, the information from the first screen is sent to the second screen. The Reset button then sends you back to the original screen and resets all of the values to their original settings.

4. Each PushButton has two parameters: Label and Click Handler. The Click Handler is the same as an Event in JavaScript. What you want to do is have the PushButton execute a script when you click the button. In the Click Handler parameter, write **onClick**.

5. Go back to frame 1. Add a new layer two frames long, and name it **Labels**. Add a keyframe for frames 1 and 2. Label the first frame **Start** and the second frame **Stop**.

6. Select the Submit PushButton and add **onClick** for the Click Handler in the Parameters section.

7. Now onto the fun part—the script! The first script you will write controls the movement from one screen to a second with the PushButtons. Select frame 1 of the Script layer and add the following script:

```
function onClick(btn) {
        if (btn == submit) {
                sethouse();
                gotoAndStop("stop");
        } else if (btn == reset) {
                gotoAndStop("start");
        }
}
```

Both buttons are scripted on the same page. The first line links the Click Handler, onClick, with the Submit and Reset buttons. The if/else statement is split between the two PushButtons. The first part of the statement dictates that users will be sent to the frame labeled "stop" when they press the Submit button. The else statement dictates users will be sent to the frame labeled "start" when they press the Reset button. These two buttons form your navigation.

The next step is to capture whether a user wants to have a Patio installed. This step requires a little more code. On the second screen, you want different events to happen if a user chooses to have a patio or not have a patio. To do this, you must first know the value of whether the check box is checked.

8. To determine whether the check box is checked, add the following code to frame 1 of the Scripts layer:

```
function setValues() {
        patio.setValue(patio);
}
```

Now that you know the value of the check box, you can do something with that knowledge. In this case, you are going to have one of two different messages presented.

9. Go to frame 2 of the Scripts layer, and add this if/else statement:

```
if (patio == true) {
        PatioText.text = "You want a house with a patio";
} else {
        PatioText.text = "You do not want a patio";
}
```

The PatioText field now has different text pasted into it, depending on the answer. Alternatively, you could have a movie on the stage that changes depending on which choice the user makes. Once you have the value of the check box, you can make that value be anything you like with ActionScript.

Capturing the value of the ComboBox is fairly easy in this exercise.

10. Select frame 2 two. In the Scripts layer, add the following script:

```
city_txt.text = "The city you would like to live in is "
+(city.getSelectedItem().data);+"."
```

Here you identify that text clip `city_text` will have text from the string/expression after the equals sign. The key to this is `city.getSelectedItem().data`. This section identifies the Component name city and allows you to select the information a user has chosen. The information captured is from the data parameter. This can be changed. For the code to work, you need to add two final lines of code to frame 1.

11. Move to the top of the code you have written and add the following line to the beginning of the script:

```
initValues();
```

This sets the following values as the initial values. This is important when you use the Reset button to return to a page.

12. Next, add a `stop();` command to the bottom of the script.

13. Preview the form. You can now make choices and, depending on your choices, the second screen will show your results.

Now that you have worked with three Components, see if you can capture the values of the RadioButtons and have them placed in a text file on the second screen.

Getting Information to and from a Database

So far you have tooled around with how to use Components to talk with each other. This is good for Components that are visual in appearance and merely add to the functionality of a movie, but what about those Form Components? Aren't you supposed to move the information you get from these to a database?

You will find that getting data to interact with Flash Form Components and a database is not that complicated.

There are two parts needed to pass data from Flash to the server: the connection and the database.

Note

A huge advantage Flash Forms have over normal HTML forms is the link between the web server and web client. HTML forms are intrinsically linked to the server. Server technologies, such as Microsoft's Active Server Pages (ASP) and Sun's Java, form a link from the web pages to a database. This forces the web forms and the server technology to be tied together.

With Flash, you have a separation of this link. Flash does not care what server language you are using. It can be ASP, .NET, ColdFusion, or any other language (you will find that in *Inside Flash MX* you used both Perl and PHP server languages). This separation of the user interface from the server makes the solution portable and, more importantly, when a new server technology change comes along, you can easily adapt by modifying a single line in your Flash movie. This radically increases the efficiency of your application development skills.

Typically, the connection will be through an Application Server Technology such as Microsoft's ASP. This technology enables Flash to connect to a database. The connection is called a RecordSet. Essentially, the RecordSet links the form fields in the Flash movie with table fields in a database. Leveraging technologies such as ODBC or JDBC, you can then connect the RecordSet with a specific database.

The following Application Servers work with Flash:

- Microsoft ASP and .NET
- Java
- PHP
- Perl
- JSP
- Macromedia ColdFusion

The second part to developing a dynamically driven web site is the database. There are many different types of databases available on the market. Being able to access a database to retrieve, review, and modify entries is critical for any web application. Some of the more common databases you will use Flash with are as follows:

- Microsoft Access
- Microsoft SQL Sever
- MySQL
- DB2

Each database comes with its own thrills and spills. It is a good idea to work with a database specialist to help configure the database to your specific needs.

> **Note**
> Macromedia has a site dedicated to web server database management. You can access the site at www.macromedia.com/desdev/topics/databases.html.

To pass information from Flash to a database, you need to set up a new variable. This variable controls what information is passed to the server and which server will be used to receive the information. Exercise 18.4 shows you how to accomplish this.

Exercise 18.4   Passing Data

Give passing data a try with the House.fla file from Exercise 18.3.

1. Select frame 1 of the scripts layer in House.fla, and at the end of the script add the following ActionScript:

```
function onSubmit() {
    formData = new LoadVars();
    formData.feature = "";
    formData.location = "";
    formData.building = "";
    formData.feature = patio.getValue();
    formData.building = house.getValue();
    formdata.location = city.getSelectedItem().data;
    }
    replyData.onLoad = handleReply;
    formData.sendAndLoad("http://yourwebsite/Submit.asp",
    ➥replyData);
    message_txt.text = "Order Submitted.";
}
```

   This script creates the new Variable, `formData`, which links the CheckBox (patio), Building type (house), and City ComboBox with data. The Method `SendAndLoad` passes that information to an ASP page. The ASP page contains a RecordSet that passes that content on to a database.

2. Add a new Dynamic text field to the stage. Give the text field an instance name of **message_txt** in frame 1.

   Now when you select the Submit button, a copy of your order will be sent to a database.

This section has not covered how to write the RecordSet because that is beyond the scope of this book. Tools such as Dreamweaver UltraDev and Dreamweaver MX will allow you to visually build RecordSets. The key is to remember that the field names in the Flash form must link with those in the RecordSet. Remember this and you cannot go wrong.

Modifying the Appearance of a Component

Not everything is what is seems. You are working hard on designing a Flash movie, and you want to add a Component. But the Component just doesn't work for the movie. It looks out of place. What are you going to do? You are going to act like a lizard and shed your skin…

Components are just movie clips and ActionScript. The element that you see is called a *skin*. The skin can be changed, as you will see in Exercise 18.5.

Exercise 18.5   Changing the Skin

In this exercise, you will change the appearance of a button on the Stage.

1. Open a new movie and drag an instance of the PushButton Component onto the Stage.

2. Open the Library, and expand the folder called Flash UI Components. Beneath this folder are two more folders and a graphic of the PushButton Component. The information you are interested in is within the Components Skin folder. Expand this, and expand the folder called FPushButton Skins.

   The FPushButton Skins folder contains four movie clips: fpb_disabled, fpb_down, fpb_over, and fpb_up. Each movie clip reflects the state of a button.

3. Right-click fpb_over and choose Edit. This opens the movie in Edit mode. You want to change the color of the center gray square to red. Double-click on the gray square. The graphic is in Inline Edit mode. Select the square, and change the color of the object to #FF0000.

4. Return to the main scene. Select Preview. Now, as you move over the PushButton, the button changes to red.

Without touching the code that constructs the button, you have changed the skin of the object. In addition to changing the color, you can change the total physical appearance of the button (which you will do in Exercise 18.6). This can be done with all Components. All Macromedia Components keep their skins in a folder called Component Skins.

Exercise 18.6   Scripting the Appearance of a Component

Changing the skin of a Component is great if you do not mind the changes being universal. Some Components, however, allow you to make scripted changes to individual Components on the stage.

1. Continue with the movie clip from Exercise 18.5. Now you have a PushButton on the stage that changes red as you move over it, but you need to add a second button that you want to be white. From the Library, drag a second instance of the PushButton Component onto the stage.

2. Give the second PushButton an instance name of **btn**.

3. In the Timeline, choose frame 1 of Layer 1. Add the following code:

```
btn.setStyleProperty("face", 0xffffff);
```

This script overrides the settings made in the Library. Using `setStyleProperty`, you can change the color of an instance within the Component. In this case, the Face of the button is now white.

4. Preview the button. You now have two PushButtons that perform the same, but look different.

Each Component can be modified however you want by changing the skin and programmatically changing the object.

Obtaining Components from Other Sources

Within the first week of Flash MX's release, it was very clear that Components were to be the next hot thing for Flash. Designers and developers, such as Branden Hall, busily set about supplying Components to the Flash community.

The number of Components you can download is increasing all the time. Some are neat little devices; others are just downright cool. Macromedia has a large number of Components available on its Macromedia Exchange web site. (Go to `http://exchange.macromedia.com` and choose the Flash Exchange.) To find the latest Components available for download, open the Answers panel and select the Update button—the top three Components will show up. Selecting one will send you to the Macromedia Exchange, where you can choose to download either a Mac or PC version of the file.

 Note

Components are inherently more complex than just a movie clip. The additional ActionScript enables you not only to customize the Component, but also to interact with it in a true object-oriented fashion. For this reason, you will find that a lot of companies are now selling Components instead of giving them away as was the custom in the past. This is a good move, because it provides Component developers with revenue to build better Components. This means you will have better tools that require you to spend less time building complex movies.

There are two key Component packages you can download that will significantly help you with your Flash work. They are the Flash Charting Components and the Flash UI Components Set 2. As you'll see in the following exercises, they are easy to use.

Exercise 18.7   Working with Flash Charting Components

When you have downloaded and installed the Flash Charting Components, you will be able to access the Components from the Component panel. As Figure 18.7 shows, there are three different charts: BarChart, LineChart, and PieChart. Each of the charts can be dragged onto the Stage and modified.

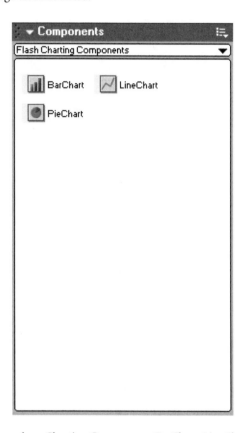

Figure 18.7   There are three Charting Components: BarChart, LineChart, and PieChart.

1. Create a new movie, and drag the BarChart Component onto the Stage.
2. The Properties panel changes to show the specific parameters of the BarChart. Select the Layout Parameters. The Value Window opens, as shown in Figure 18.8.
3. With Values window open, select Chart Title and change the title to **Sales: N.E. Region**.
4. Select YAxis Title, and change it to **Amount Sold**.
5. Select XAxis Title, and change it to **Sales Person**.
6. Click OK. The changes have been applied to the Stage.

Figure 18.8   The Layout Values define many of the visual elements on the stage.

7. Select the Category Labels parameter. Change the values to: **John**, **Anne**, **Jose**, **Khan**, and **Laurie**. Click OK.

8. Change the values in the Data Values field to reflect the sales of each person. Choose any number you like. If you choose large numbers, the numbers along the left side of the screen will automatically change to reflect the new number limit. Preview the final Movie. (See Figure 18.9.)

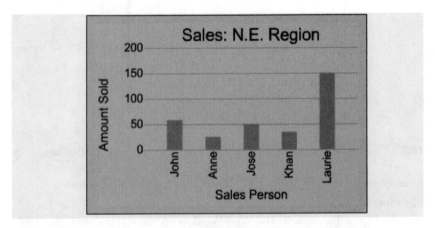

Figure 18.9   The bar chart dynamically changes to reflect the parameter changes.

As you can see, the BarChart Component is very flexible. In many ways, it is similar to Microsoft Excel charts. The difference here is that the entire Component is built in Flash—no need for an extra plug-in!

Exercise 18.8   Controlling a Line Chart

The LineChart Component is controlled in much the same way as the BarChart. You drag the chart onto the Stage and change the parameters of the chart.

1. Create a new movie and drag an instance of the LineChart Component onto the Stage.

2. From the Parameters, choose Layout Options. Change the values to the following:

   ChartTitle: **Sales Forecast**
   XAxisTitle: **Years**
   YAxisTitle: **Sales**
   LineColor: **0xFF0000**
   LineWeight: **3**

3. Click OK. The chart now has a red line, is thicker, and has different titles.

4. Select the Category Labels parameter and change the values to: **98, 99, 00, 01,** and **02.**

5. Keep the data values as they are. Preview the movie. The final movie shows the information you have added. Click on the year in the chart, and you will have a pop-up give you specific information. (See Figure 18.10.)

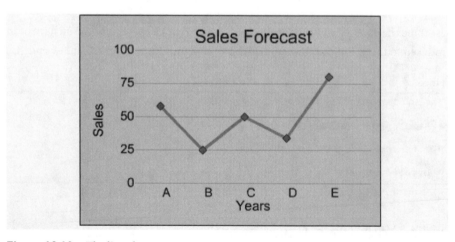

Figure 18.10   The line chart.

The final chart Component is PieChart. As with the two previous charts, you can easily add a PieChart Component to the Stage. The parameters allow you to easily modify the appearance of the content. Figure 18.11 shows you what the pie chart looks like on the stage.

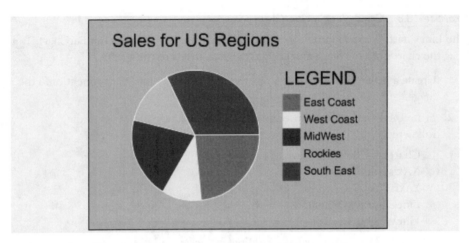

Figure 18.11   The pie chart.

Note

One interesting facet of the chart Components is the capability to link any chart with live data through the `setValueSource` method. This method can only be used successfully when a RecordSet has been loaded into Flash.

These three charts add rich functionality and ease of use to a presentation. You have been introduced to them, but their functionality can be significantly scripted and extended.

Note

You can download or buy additional Components at the following web sites:

- `http://exchange.macromedia.com`
- `http://www.flashcomponents.net`
- `http://www.were-here.com`

Building Your Own Component

As you can see from this chapter, Components are a superb addition to Flash. While there are a lot of Components you can buy and download, it is also easy to build your own Components.

Developing your own Components has a number of benefits. The initial benefit I have found is that developing a Component reduces the amount of time you spend redoing repetitive work. The second benefit is that you can package really good Components and sell them. (Hey, you can't blame me for being a capitalist.)

The first step to building your own Component is to decide what would work as a Component. Generally, you want to pick something that allows you to add variable data programmatically. For example, you fill in a form and then a presentation is built from that form.

In Exercise 18.9, you will build a basic Component. This will demonstrate how easy Components are to build.

Exercise 18.9   Building a Component

The Component you are going to build is a button. You will be able to change the text, the font, and the color of the text dynamically.

1. Begin by opening a new movie. Draw a 45-pixel oval on the stage. Convert this to a button, and name the button **PushButton**.

2. Add a new layer, and name the layer **Text**. With this layer selected, draw a Dynamic text box over the PushButton button. Label the text clip **LabelText**. Type **Submit** as the text. This text will be a placeholder for your script later.

3. Add a new layer and call it **Script**. Add the following code:

```
buttonLabel.textColor = labelColor;
myTextFormat = new TextFormat();
myTextFormat.font = labelFont;
buttonLabel.setTextFormat(myTextFormat);
```

4. Select both the text and PushButton on the stage and convert them into a movie clip. Name the movie clip **Component**.

5. Open the Library, right-click on the Component movie clip, and select the Component Definition option. This option enables you to convert the movie clip into a Component.

6. You will need to identify a number of variables you can control. Select the plus symbol (+) to add a new variable. Across the top you have to enter a name, variable, value, and type.

7. Enter **Button Label** for the first name, and give it the variable **label**. The Value should be **Submit** and the Type is **String**. Here you set up the link that enables you to make changes to the text.

8. Select the Submit (+) button two more times, and enter the following settings:

    Name: **Label Font**
    Variable: **labelFont**
    Value: **Times**
    Type: **Font Name**

9. For the third parameter, enter the following:

Name: **Label Color**
Variable: **labelColor**
Value: **#000000**
Type: **Color**

10. Click OK.

You will see that the icon for the Component has changed. You can now drag the Component onto the Stage. Parameters for the Component appear in the Properties panel. You can change the text, font, and color.

This is the simplest of Components. As you become more comfortable with programming, you should begin to extend and challenge yourself to create more complex Components. In the long run, they will save you a lot of time.

Summary

Component architecture is a significant step forward for Flash MX designers and developers. Now Flash movies can be built in the same mindset as Visual Basic and Java developers. Flash Components bring with them a big plus: All of the Components are built with Flash movie clips and ActionScript. This means that the Components can be added to a movie without requiring the end user to install a new plug-in. With this in mind, you can think of your Components as not simply standalone objects, but as tools that can be tightly integrated into your movie. If you need to extend the functionality of a Component, the only limitation is ActionScript and your knowledge of scripting. Component technology will radically reduce the amount of time you spend developing and allow you to spend more time creating.

Chapter 19

Emulating the Natural World: A Poet's Introduction to Physics

The world around you is controlled by laws

that enable you to predict the behavior of

objects under specific conditions. You

know that if you push a ball hard enough

on an even surface, it will start to roll, but that it will eventually come to a stop. A ball will roll downhill, gaining momentum as it progresses. A rubber ball has more bounce than a lead ball. If the ball hits a wall, it stops, breaks through the wall, or bounces off the wall in another direction. These are all things you know intuitively; you see them in action in your daily life. What you might not understand is why objects act this way.

If you understand a little bit about how these laws work in the real world, you can adapt them to control the behavior of objects in your Flash presentations. This lends a more realistic feel to your movie.

Although you can emulate the behavior of physical objects by using tweening and frame-by-frame animation, scripting the behavior is more effective. In this chapter, you learn how to do the following:

- **Control the speed and acceleration of objects on the Stage.** Moving objects around the Stage with ActionScript is not at all difficult. You'll see how you can give an object motion with button or key presses.

- **Throw objects.** You also can use ActionScript to let you pick up an object and throw it across the screen.

- **Mimic elastic behavior.** Elastic behavior also is fairly easy to do with Flash. You can make your objects snap back into place.

- **Detect collisions with walls and other objects.** After you have the basics covered, you're ready to move into detecting when objects collide and what to do with them when they do.

You start by getting acquainted with a few simple concepts, and you'll build from there.

Programming Simple Movement

There will come a time when you'll want to control how objects on the Stage are moved around, and you'll want more control than you get with simple tweening. You might be creating a game where the user controls an active object (like a ship), or you might be creating an application where you want to anticipate different movement possibilities. You're going to have to do this using ActionScript. However, before you begin madly coding, you need to understand a little bit about how objects behave in the real world. That means you're going to have to plunge into the world of physics. This shouldn't be a scary thing—most of it is just common sense with a dash of math. Where to start? A good place to start is with Isaac Newton's first law of motion. Newton's First Law of Motion says, in essence:

"Objects in motion tend to stay in motion and objects at rest tend to stay at rest unless they are acted upon by an outside force."

This is an easy concept to understand. A ball sitting in the middle of the floor, assuming the floor is level, is going to stay right where it is unless someone gives it a shove or kick. After that happens, the ball begins to move in a particular direction. For the moment, don't worry about the forces acting on the ball as it rolls. You'll learn about friction and gravity later.

The same thing applies to an object on the Stage in your Flash movie. If you have a movie clip sitting on the Stage, it's not going to move unless you apply a force in the form of a tween or by using actions.

After you apply a force to an object, it begins to move. This movement can be described in terms of speed or velocity. Although these two terms are similar, there is a significant difference between the two concepts:

- **Speed.** Also known as scalar, this is the rate of change in the position of an object.

- **Velocity.** Also known as vector, this measures the rate of change in position, but it also includes the direction the object is moving.

For the purposes of this chapter, you'll be dealing with speed. Determining the speed of an object is simple:

speed = (Original position – current position) ÷ time

The position is determined by the X and Y coordinates of the object. In a Flash movie, the X,Y grid that you are working with has its 0,0 point in the upper-left corner of the Stage. X values increase to the right and Y values increase toward the bottom of the Stage (see Figure 19.1). Flash is designed this way because Flash movies are destined for web sites where you never can be certain of the absolute middle, bottom, or right edges of a user's browser, but where you always know the location of the upper-left corner.

After you have speed, it's time to think about acceleration. Acceleration is computed like this:

acceleration = change in speed÷time

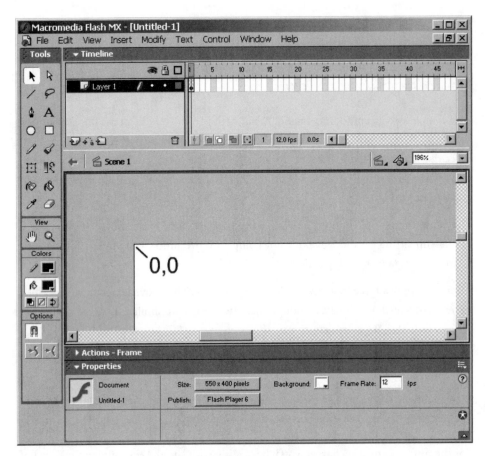

Figure 19.1   The coordinate system in Flash has its point of origin (0,0) in the upper-left corner of the Stage.

Another way to put that is like this:

acceleration = (final speed – beginning speed) ÷ time

When you think about acceleration, you need to be aware that acceleration includes both speeding up (positive acceleration) and slowing down (negative acceleration).

Say you decided to make a ball move around. In Flash 5 you would have to create a movie clip for the ball and then attach an `onClipEvent` action to it. In Flash MX, it's both easier and more flexible. All of the clip events (`load`, `unload`, `enterFrame`, `mouseDown`, `mouseUp`, `mouseMove`, `keyDown`, `keyUp`, and `data`) can instead be accessed via special event methods named by adding "on" to the event's name (`onLoad`, `onUnload`, and so on). For example, say you had a movie clip named ball_mc. The code you would place on the the main Timeline to cause the actions associated with ball_mc to run every frame would be this:

```
ball_mc.onEnterFrame = function{
      ...
}
```

The frame rate of the movie tells the SWF what its maximum frame rate is. This rate then dictates how often the onEnterFrame event occurs. Actions can, and do occur independently of enterFrame events, but the stage won't update until an onEnterFrame event occurs.

Button Control

To control your Ball movie clip, you need to change the speed of the ball in the X or Y direction, or in both directions.

You begin by giving the movie clip an instance name and initializing the speed variables to 0 when the movie clip first loads.

In Exercise 19.1, you'll practice controlling an object's speed and acceleration by using a combination of directional buttons in your movie and some ActionScript control.

Exercise 19.1   Controlling Movement with Button Presses

You have a series of options when it comes to controlling the movement of an object on the Stage. The object can move when one of the following occurs:

- A button is pressed
- A key is pressed
- Only while a button or key is pressed
- Continuously, after a button or key is pressed

You start by working with constant speed initiated by a button press.

1. Open movement.fla from the Examples/Chapter 19 folder. There are currently three layers: ball, buttons, and actions.

2. Select the Ball movie clip on the Stage and open the Properties Inspector (Window >Properties). Give the Ball movie clip an instance name of **ball_mc**. (See Figure 19.2.)

   You need to give the Ball movie clip an instance name so that you can control it using ActionScript.

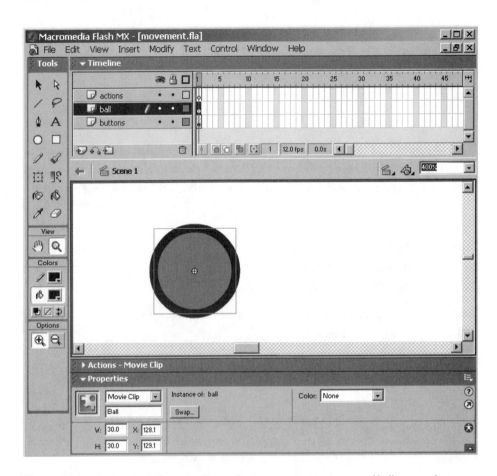

Figure 19.2 Assign the Ball movie clip on the Stage an instance name of ball_mc so that you can control it using ActionScript.

3. When the movie clip first loads, the speed of the ball on the Stage is 0. It's not moving. When you are writing code, it's always a good idea to initialize your variables, so do that first. With the first frame of the Actions layer selected, launch the Actions panel. Make sure you're working in Expert mode and enter the following code:

```
ball_mc.speedX = 0;
ball_mc.speedY = 0;
```

Now when the movie clip loads for the first time, your two variables for speed are set to 0. The ball isn't going anywhere.

Tip

Although it might feel a little awkward at first if you're a nonprogrammer, try getting accustomed to using Expert mode in Flash. It's a lot faster and a lot more flexible than Normal mode. If you ever find you need to see the parameters for a particular tag, you can quickly toggle back into Normal mode by using Ctrl+N (Windows) or Command+N (Macintosh). Use Ctrl+E (Windows) or Command+E (Macintosh) to return to Expert mode.

You want to track the speed of the Ball movie clip continuously. To do that, you need to assign ball_mc an onEnterFrame method.

In just a moment, you'll be adding some code to the directional buttons on the Stage that will let you change the speed of the ball. However, in the meantime, you need to let the ball know how fast it is moving; in other words, you will update its X and Y positions based on the current speed in both the X and Y directions.

4. You should still have the Actions panel open. Position your cursor after your current code and add a new line. Then, enter the following code:

```
ball_mc.onEnterFrame = function(){
        this._x += this.speedX;
        this._y += this.speedY;
}
```

this._x is the X position of this instance of the movie clip and this._y is the Y position. += is the addition assignment operator. This operator assigns this._x the current value of this._x plus the value of speedX.

Tip

The += operator, also known as the *addition assignment operator*, is used to add the current value of the expression on the left side of the operator to the value of the expression on the right side of the operator. It assigns the resulting value to the expression on the left. The two lines of code below are equivalent:

```
this._x += speedX;
this._x = this._x + speedX;
```

Think of this as a shortcut—just a little less code you have to write.

Note

What is this? It's a keyword that references the movie clip to which it's attached. When you need to refer to a property or variable of the movie clip instance that you currently are in, use this.

At this point, your ActionScript on frame 1 of the Actions layer should look like this:

```
ball_mc.speedX = 0;
ball_mc.speedY = 0;
ball_mc.onEnterFrame = function(){
        this._x += this.speedX;
        this._y += this.speedY;
}
```

Now it's time to add some actions to the buttons on the Stage so that you can tell the ball which direction to move and how fast to move. You begin with the button that increases the speed in the X direction (which makes the ball move right).

5. Select the button that points to the right. In Flash MX, you don't have to attach code directly to buttons anymore. Instead, the code will go in your Actions layer. But you'll need to give the button an instance name, **right_btn**. Then select your Actions layer and add the following code:

```
right_btn.onRelease = function(){

}
```

6. To increase the speed of the ball, all you need to do is increment its speed by 1. Use the increment operator (++) to increase the speed of the ball.

7. Create a new line between the curly brackets of the onRelease function and type the following:

```
++_root.ball_mc.speedX;
```

Tip

You don't actually have to use _root in this case to reference the ball because the ball and buttons are on the same Timeline. I'm a creature of habit, however.

Pre-incrementing the value in this fashion takes the current value of Ball.speedX and adds 1 to it.

Note

What is the difference in pre-incrementing and post-incrementing a variable? When you pre-increment a variable, you add 1 to the variable and return the new value. When you post-increment a variable, you add 1 to it, but not until after you return the value.

```
x = 1;
y = ++x;
```

After the second line of code has executed, both x and y are equal to 2.

```
x = 1;
y = x++
```

After the second line of code has executed, x = 2 and y = 1. The value of x wasn't incremented until after the current value of x was assigned to y.

Your code for this button, as illustrated in Figure 19.3, should look like this:

```
right_btn.onRelease = function(){
     ++_root.ball_mc.speedX;
}
```

Notice that this is going to increase the current speed in the X direction of the ball every time you press and release the button. That means you're adding acceleration into the equation as well.

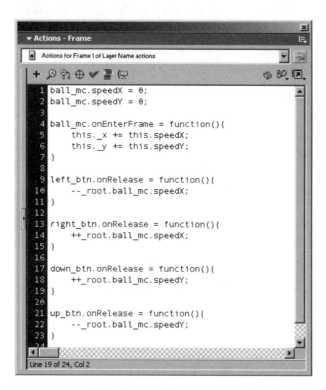

```
1 ball_mc.speedX = 0;
2 ball_mc.speedY = 0;
3
4 ball_mc.onEnterFrame = function(){
5      this._x += this.speedX;
6      this._y += this.speedY;
7 }
8
9 left_btn.onRelease = function(){
10      --_root.ball_mc.speedX;
11 }
12
13 right_btn.onRelease = function(){
14      ++_root.ball_mc.speedX;
15 }
16
17 down_btn.onRelease = function(){
18      ++_root.ball_mc.speedY;
19 }
20
21 up_btn.onRelease = function(){
22      --_root.ball_mc.speedY;
23 }
```

Figure 19.3   Add the code necessary to move the ball from left to right across the screen.

8. Test your movie. Every time you press and release the button that points to the right, the ball should pick up a little more speed until eventually it exits the movie.

9. For the button that decreases the speed in the X direction (which makes the ball go left), you use the same code, except that you change the increment (++) to a decrement (- -). Select the button that points to the left, give it its own instance name, **left_btn**, and then add the following code to your actions frame:

```
left_btn.onRelease = function(){
     --_root.ball_mc.speedX;
}
```

10. Test your movie. Notice that if you press the right button a couple of times to get the ball moving and then press the left button once, the ball doesn't reverse direction; it decreases its acceleration.

11. The code for changing speed in the Y direction will mirror the code that you just wrote. Remember that you'll need to change speedX to speedY. You'll decrement (- -) the value for the Up button and increment (++) the value for the Down button.

12. Select the button that points up, name it **up_btn**, and then add the following to your actions frame:

```
up_btn.onRelease = function(){
        --_root.ball_mc.speedY;
}
```

13. Select the button that points down, name it **down_btn**, and add the following to your actions frame:

```
right_btn.onRelease = function(){
        ++_root.ball_mc.speedY;
}
```

14. That's it. Save and test your movie.

If you want the ball to snap back onto the Stage after it escapes off of an edge, just set up the center button actions to set the speed in both directions to zero and the X and Y positions to a spot within the bounds of your movie.

If you're building a game, you might decide that you want to use the arrow keys instead of buttons to control your ball. That requires a few changes to your code.

Key Press Control

If you prefer to control the ball by using the arrow keys rather than the buttons, you need to make a few changes to the code in your existing movie.

In the previous exercise, the actions that caused the ball to move were in the four directional buttons. You need to transfer that functionality to the Up, Down, Left, and Right Arrow keys on your keyboard. The onEnterFrame method is where all the action takes place. Instead of capturing mouseEvents, you'll be capturing key presses. You do this using the Key object. The Key object is a top-level object. That means you don't actually have to create an instance of the object before you can use it.

What you're interested in is whether a key is being pressed. You'll use the _Key.isDown(keycode)_ method where the _keycode_ argument is the key code value assigned to a specific key. In this case, the key code values will be UP, DOWN, RIGHT, and LEFT. The method returns a value of true if the key specified in keycode is pressed.

In the previous exercise, the ball started moving and kept on going after you released the button. In Exercise 19.2, because you're testing for `Key.isDown()`, you'll have to add a little additional code to keep the ball on the move when you release the arrow key.

Exercise 19.2   Controlling Movement with the Arrow Keys

You start by setting up the actions for the Right Arrow key. If the Right Arrow key is being pressed, you want to move the ball on the Stage.

1. You still should be working in movement.fla, or you can open keymove.fla from the Examples/Chapter19 folder on the companion CD.

2. Select the Actions layer and add the following code to the `onEnterFrame` method you defined for the ball_mc (see Figure 19.4):

```
if (Key.isDown(Key.RIGHT)) {
        ++this.speedX;
}
```

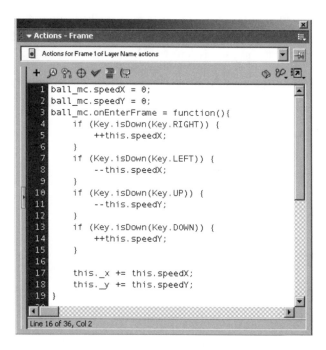

Figure 19.4   This time, you add all your actions to control the movement of the ball to the ball's `onEnterFrame`.

If the Right Arrow key is pressed, you increment the current speed in the X direction and you update the X position of the ball on the Stage. Your onEnterFrame code should now look like this:

```
ball_mc.onEnterFrame = function(){
        if (Key.isDown(Key.RIGHT)) {
                ++this.speedX;
        }
        this._x += speedX;
        this._y += speedY;
}
```

3. Test your movie to make sure you've entered the code correctly.

 Tip

It's always a good idea to check your syntax before you test your movie. When you're in the Actions panel, you can use Control+T (Windows) or Command+T (Macintosh) to do so.

4. Now you should be able to complete the rest of the if/else statements for the other three arrow keys. If you're not sure what you should do, check Listing 19.1. Remember that cut and paste is your friend.

Listing 19.1   The Completed ActionScript for Moving the Ball Around the Stage Using Key Presses

```
ball_mc.onEnterFrame = function(){
        if (Key.isDown(Key.RIGHT)) {
                ++this.speedX;
        }
        if (Key.isDown(Key.LEFT)) {
                --this.speedX;
        }
        if (Key.isDown(Key.UP)) {
                --this.speedY;
        }
        if (Key.isDown(Key.DOWN)) {
                ++this.speedY;
        }
        this._x += speedX;
        this._y += speedY;
}
```

5. Test your movie. Notice that the acceleration increases continuously if you hold down a directional key.

You know how to use button presses and key presses to move objects. Next take a look at how you can pick up an object and throw it.

Throwing Objects Around the Stage

Throwing an objects around the Stage is a little more complex than just moving the object with key or button presses. If you throw a baseball, it has a certain speed when it leaves your hand. However, as soon as it leaves your hand, it begins to slow down. Why? Friction: The baseball is in contact with the air around it, and as it moves through the air, the air impedes its forward motion. The baseball also is affected by gravity, but just worry about friction for the moment.

In this section, you create an object that you can "throw" around the stage with your mouse. You'll click and hold the object, move it to another location on the stage, and then let it go. This causes the object to continue in that direction. After you let go, you let friction take over.

Note

> Until you program floor, ceiling, or wall boundaries, it will be possible to "lose" the throwable object by flinging it past the boundaries of the Stage. If you want to, you can set up a button to snap it back to the screen. All you need to do is stop the ball's motion and give it new X and Y coordinates. To do so, just place a button on the Stage, give it an instance name of **reset_btn**, and then add the following code to your Timeline:
>
> ```
> reset_btn.onRelease = function(){
>         ball_mc.speedX = 0;
>         ball_mc.speedY = 0;
>         ball_mc._x = 100;
>         ball_mc._y = 100;
> }
> ```

Much of this will be familiar to you from the previous exercise. The variables that you need to track when you're throwing objects are a little different from the ones you used in the previous exercise. In Exercise 19.3, not only will you be initializing and keeping track of speed in both the X and Y directions, you'll also be initializing and tracking the following:

- **friction.** This decimal is the percentage of the speed that is used after friction is taken away. For example, if friction takes away 10% of the speed, this variable would be 1 − 0.10, or 0.90 (90%). You'll add friction as a constant when you initialize your variables. This variable does not change.

- **ratio.** This one is a little funky. This decimal number is just a percentage applied against an object's speed. You need only use a portion of the object's actual speed in your movie because the actual speed would cause the object to quickly fly off the screen. It's up to you to decide how much you want the action on the screen to slow down. In the early testing stages, you might want the number to be as much as 0.5, which removes half the object's speed. Later, as you're fine-tuning, you can nudge that number closer to 1 to speed things up.

- **oldX, oldY.** Where the object was when you started dragging it.
- **newX, newY.** Where the object is now.

In Flash MX it's easier to keep track of your code, because code for buttons and movie clips can all be in one place

Exercise 19.3   Creating a Throwable Movie Clip

First, you need to make your movie clip draggable. In Flash 5, this required embedded buttons, but now you can do it all with ActionScript.

1. Open throw.fla from the Examples/Chapter19 folder on the companion CD.
2. Select the ball movie clip located on the stage and set its instance name to **ball_mc**.

   The next thing you'll do is make the ball draggable.
3. Click on the first frame of the Actions layer and add the following code:

```
ball_mc.onPress = function(){
        this.startDrag();
}

ball_mc.onRelease = function(){
        this.stopDrag();
}

ball_mc.onReleaseOutside = ball_mc.onRelease;
```

> **Tip**
>
> Whenever you have code triggered by the release of a mouse, make sure that the code also will be triggered if you let go of the mouse when you've dragged the cursor off the movie clip or button. It's very easy to drag your cursor so fast that your symbol can't keep up.

The startDrag(target) action is used to make the movie clip draggable. In this case, you are specifying the target of the drag operation with this. Alternately, you could use startDrag(""). If there is nothing between the quotes, Flash assumes it's supposed to drag the object to which the action is attached.

When you release the button, you stop the Drag action using the stopDrag() action.

4. Test your movie to make sure the ball is draggable.

5. Return to the main Timeline and select the Actions layer.

6. When the movie loads for the first time, you need to initialize the variables you'll be using. Add the following actions:

```
ball_mc.friction = .9;
ball_mc.ratio = .5;
ball_mc.newX = ball_mc._x;
ball_mc.oldX = ball_mc._x;
ball_mc.newY = ball_mc._y;
ball_mc.oldY = ball_mc._y;
ball_mc.speedX = 0;
ball_mc.speedy = 0;
```

Now it's time to set up the actions for throwing the ball. You need to gather information about the ball's position as it is being dragged. If the ball is no longer being dragged, it's been thrown. This information needs to be collected continuously, so you'll use an onEnterFrame method for your ball, but different code when you are dragging or when the ball is just "gliding."

7. Move your cursor back into your onPress method and add the following code:

```
this.onEnterFrame = function(){
        this.oldX = this.newX;
        this.oldY = this.newY;
        this.newX = this._x;
        this.newY = this._y;
}
```

Now your code should look like this:

```
ball_mc.onPress = function(){
        this.startDrag();
        this.onEnterFrame = function(){
                this.oldX = this.newX;
                this.oldY = this.newY;
                this.newX = this._x;
                this.newY = this._y;
        }
}

ball_mc.onRelease = function(){
        this.stopDrag();
}

ball_mc.onReleaseOutside = ball_mc.onRelease;

ball_mc.friction = .9;
ball_mc.ratio = .5;
ball_mc.newX = ball_mc._x;
ball_mc.oldX = ball_mc._x;
ball_mc.newY = ball_mc._y;
```

```
ball_mc.oldY = ball_mc._y;
ball_mc.speedX = 0;
ball_mc.speedy = 0;
```

Tip

Notice that you're able to create your onEnterFrame method on the fly inside of your onPress method. This capability is new in Flash MX and gives you all sorts of new power. In particular, you can turn on or off any one of these event methods anytime you want.

While the ball is being dragged, you record the original position of the ball in the oldX and oldY variables. You record the new position, which is the place where the ball has moved to, in the newX and newY variables. You need to constantly update these variables when the object is moving so that you have an accurate record of the ball's distance traveled and speed. The greater the distance between the old position and the new position, the greater the speed.

Next you need to account for what is happening to the ball when it's no longer being dragged.

8. The speed in the X and Y directions will be the current speed multiplied by the value of the friction variable. The X and Y positions are the current positions plus the speed in the appropriate direction (see Figure 19.5). Inside of your onRelease method, add the following code:

```
this.speedX = (this.newX - this.oldX) * this.ratio;
this.speedY = (this.newY - this.oldY) * this.ratio;

this.onEnterFrame = function(){
        this.speedX *= this.friction;
        this.speedY *= this.friction;
        this._x += speedX;
        this._y += speedY;
}
```

If you test your movie now, you still won't be able to throw the ball. You need to add a few more actions to the onRelease method.

9. Locate your onRelease method, and under the stopDrag method add the following code:

```
this.speedX = (this.newX - this.oldX) * this.ratio;
this.speedY = (this.newY - this.oldY) * this.ratio;
```

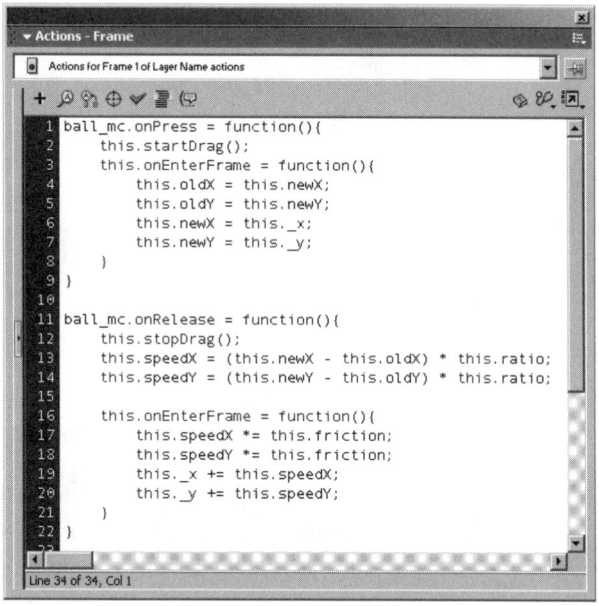

Figure 19.5   To throw the ball, you need to keep track not only of where it is now, but also where it just was. You use the variables newX, newY, oldX, and oldY to hold these values.

Your final code should look like Listing 19.2.

Listing 19.2   Complete ActionScript for Making a Ball Throwable

```
ball_mc.onPress = function(){
    this.startDrag();
    this.onEnterFrame = function(){
        this.oldX = this.newX;
        this.oldY = this.newY;
        this.newX = this._x;
        this.newY = this._y;
    }
}

ball_mc.onRelease = function(){
    this.stopDrag();
    this.speedX = (this.newX - this.oldX) * this.ratio;
    this.speedY = (this.newY - this.oldY) * this.ratio;


    this.onEnterFrame = function(){
        this.speedX *= this.friction;
        this.speedY *= this.friction;
        this._x += this.speedX;
```

continues ▶

Listing 19.2 Continued

```
                this._y += this.speedY;
        }
}

ball_mc.onReleaseOutside = ball_mc.onRelease;

ball_mc.friction = .9;
ball_mc.ratio = .5;
ball_mc.newX = ball_mc._x;
ball_mc.oldX = ball_mc._x;
ball_mc.newY = ball_mc._y;
ball_mc.oldY = ball_mc._y;
ball_mc.speedX = 0;
ball_mc.speedy = 0;
```

Get to know and love the equations for speed; you'll be seeing them a lot.

10. Save and test your movie. You should be able to grab the ball with your mouse and throw it across the Stage. And yes, you'll probably end up flinging it off the Stage.

How do you get the ball back after it's off the Stage? You could create a button to reset the X and Y positions of the ball. Alternately, you could define walls that your ball can't move past. Before you do that, however, take a look at another way to modify the throwing example that always pulls your ball back to a stable resting point.

Elastic Movement

You can create an object that will have a "gravitational pull" toward a fixed point when moved away from its point of origin. You'll be able to drag the object to any position and let it go, and then observe the object return to its origin in an elastic fashion. It will bounce back to the fixed point as if there were a rubber band attached between the ball and the fixed point.

In Exercise 19.4, the variable list that you'll be tracking to do this is very similar to the list of variables you tracked in the throwing example, with a couple exceptions. Instead of tracking the new and old positions of X and Y, you'll track the following:

- **baseX**. Holds the X position of the fixed point to which the ball will return elastically.

- **baseY**. Holds the Y position of the fixed point.

- **_x**. A movie clip property that returns the current X position of the ball.

- **_y**. A movie clip property that returns the current Y position of the ball.

Now take a look at how you use this new information to create elastic behavior.

Exercise 19.4   Creating Elastic Behavior

The first part of this exercise sets up the draggable code exactly as you did in the previous exercise. Those actions already are added for you here.

1. Open elastic.fla from the Examples/Chapter19 folder on the companion CD.

   Take a moment to think about what you are trying to accomplish. You want your ball to behave as if it were attached to an elastic band that is, in turn, attached to a fixed point. If you pull the ball away from the fixed point and let it go, you would expect the ball to not only attempt to return to the fixed point, but also to overshoot it and bounce back and forth until it ultimately comes to a stop.

   Notice that the ball movie clip that's on your stage is named **ball_mc**.

2. Now you need to add code to initialize your variables. On the main Timeline, select the first frame of the Actions layer and add the following:

   ```
   ball_mc.friction = .9;
   ball_mc.ratio = .3;
   ball_mc.speedX = 0;
   ball_mc.speedY = 0;
   ball_mc.baseX = ball_mc._x;
   ball_mc.baseY = ball_mc._y;
   ```

   Now that you have set up the variables, you need to set up the movie clip so that it is draggable.

3. Under the code you currently have in place on the main Timeline, add the following:

   ```
   ball_mc.onPress = function(){
        this.startDrag();
             this.onEnterFrame = undefined;
   }
   ```

4. Now you need to add the code that allows you to let go of the clip:

   ```
   ball_mc.onRelease = function(){
        this.stopDrag();
   }
   ```

   You are going to need to add further code to this onRelease method. In particular, you need to add the onEnterFrame code that will adjust the speed of the ball and adjust its position. Let's take a look at the math that's involved in this:

   - First, take the last value of speedX and decrease it by multiplying it by the amount of friction (speedX × friction).

   - Next, determine how far the ball has actually moved, which is the distance that the ball is from its original position. Add the reduced speed to the distance from the original position (baseX − this._x). You'll add that to the number calculated previously.

- Finally, multiply the number by the ratio to slow down the motion.

5. After the `stopDrag` action, add the framework of an `onEnterFrame` function:

```
this.onEnterFrame = function(){
}
```

6. Now, inside of the `onEnterFrame` method, add this code to handle the recalculation of the ball's speed:

```
this.speedX = (this.speedX * this.friction) + (this.baseX -
⮞this._x) * this.ratio;
this.speedY = (this.speedY * this.friction) + (this.baseY -
⮞this._y) * this.ratio;
```

Now all you have to do is use your new speed values to set the X and Y positions of the ball.

7. Add the following code after the equation for speedY:

```
this._x += this.speedX;
this._y += this.speedY;
```

So the new position is equal to the last position of the ball plus the current speed. (See Figure 19.6.) Your code now should look like Listing 19.3.

Listing 19.3   ActionScript for Drag with Elastic Behavior

```
ball_mc.friction = .9;
ball_mc.ratio = .3;
ball_mc.speedX = 0;
ball_mc.speedY = 0;
ball_mc.baseX = ball_mc._x;
ball_mc.baseY = ball_mc._y;

ball_mc.onPress = function(){
        this.startDrag();
        this.onEnterFrame = undefined;
}

ball_mc.onRelease = function(){
        this.stopDrag();
        this.onEnterFrame = function(){
                this.speedX = (this.speedX * this.friction) + (this.baseX
                ⮞- this._x) * this.ratio;
                this.speedY = (this.speedY * this.friction) + (this.baseY
                ⮞- this._y) * this.ratio;
                this._x += this.speedX;
                this._y += this.speedY;
        }
}
```

```
13 ball_mc.onRelease = function(){
14     this.stopDrag();
15     this.onEnterFrame = function(){
16         this.speedX = (this.speedX * this.friction) + (this.baseX - this._x) * this.ratio;
17         this.speedY = (this.speedY * this.friction) + (this.baseY - this._y) * this.ratio;
18         this._x += this.speedX;
19         this._y += this.speedY;
20     }
21 }
22
```

Figure 19.6   To add elasticity to the ball, you have to track its current position relative to its beginning position. The speed of the ball's return to its original point is based on how far away you moved it.

8. Save and test your movie. Drag your movie clip across the stage and let it go. It should spring back and forth elastically. You can play around with the values of friction and ratio to get the effect you want.

Next, you add in some additional complexity by determining when your object collides with something.

Detecting Collisions

How do you detect a collision between two objects? How do you decide what to do after a collision occurs?

There are two basic ways to detect collisions inside Flash. You can use the `MovieClip.hitTest()` method, which is useful in particular cases. As another option, you can rely on good old distance formulas, which are more flexible and not that hard to handle.

So, when do you use which method? With `hitTest`, you are testing either the intersection of a point with an object or the intersection of the bounding boxes of two movie clips. This is fine in a lot of cases, but what if you have two spheres that are colliding or a sphere colliding with the corner point of a box? Your collision detection won't be accurate using the `hitTest` method. In that case, you need to get down and dirty with some good old-fashioned calculations.

When do you use `hitTest`? It's great for simple collisions. It's also great for determining when your mouse is over a particular object. You actually used it already when you were setting up a custom cursor in Chapter 17, "Interface Techniques."

We start with exploring one way in which you can use the `hitTest()` method.

The *hitTest()* method

The `hitTest()` method enables you to quickly and simply determine when two objects have intersected or overlapped. You have the option of testing for just the bounding box of the target movie clip or you can test for the shape within the bounding box.

If you just want to test for the simple intersection of the bounding box of one object with another, you use this syntax:

```
myMovie.hitTest(theOtherMovie);
```

If the two objects intersect, the method returns a value of true. This is the method you can use to detect a simple collision.

If you want to get a little fancier and test for when you intersect an actual shape, you can specify the X and Y coordinates of the hit area on the Stage and set the `shapeFlag` to true. You'll probably use this method most often when you're trying to determine if the movie clip or the mouse pointer are within a certain area. The syntax is as follows:

```
myMovie.hitTest(x, y, shapeFlag);
```

You've already used the second method in Chapter 17 when you created a custom cursor. In Exercise 19.5, you'll use the first `hitTest()` method to determine when a futuristic speeder intersects with an immovable wall.

Exercise 19.5 Using *hitTest()* to Detect a Collision

The speeder in this exercise is controlled by key presses. Because you already know how to add those Actions, that part has been done for you.

1. Open hittest.fla from the Examples/Chapter19 folder on the companion CD.
2. First, click on the two movie clips on the stage. Speeder and Wall are named speeder_mc and wall_mc, respectively, so that you can access them with ActionScript (see Figure 19.7).
3. Select the first frame of the Actions layer and open the Actions panel. The code should look very familiar. It is the same code that you used to move the ball around the Stage with key presses in Exercise 19.1, with only the instance names changed.
4. You want to know when the movie clip you are in intersects with the Wall movie clip. After the last if statement, but before the curly brace that ends the onEnterFrame, enter the following code:

```
if(this.hittest(this._parent.wall_mc)){
     trace("I hit the wall.");
}
```

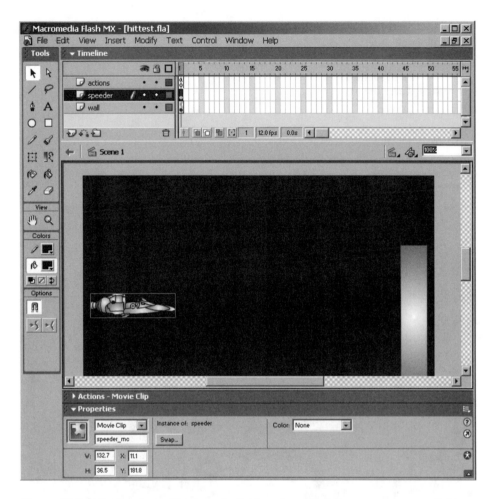

Figure 19.7   The Speeder and Wall movie clips have instance names so you can control them using ActionScript.

5. Test your movie. Make the speeder hit the wall by pressing the Right Arrow key.

   As soon as the speeder intersects with the wall, the Output window pops up with the message "I hit the wall." Because this is being called by onEnterFrame, you'll keep seeing that same message until the speeder and the wall are no longer overlapping.

6. Okay, that was fine, but what would you expect the speeder to do if it really hits the wall? Blow up, of course! As it happens, the speeder movie is a two-frame movie clip with an explosion in the second frame. This time, when the speeder hits the wall, stop it and blow it up. Figure 19.8 illustrates the speeder meeting its

unfortunate end. Remove the trace statement and alter your code to match the following code:

```
if(this.hitTest(this._parent.wall_mc)){
    this.speedX = 0;
    this.speedY = 0;
    this.gotoAndStop(2);
}
```

7. Test your movie. That was much more satisfactory, wasn't it? (See Figure 19.8.)

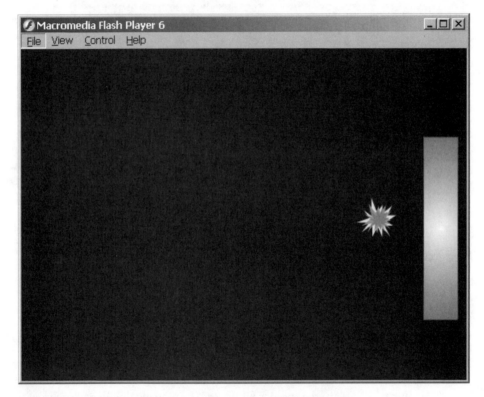

Figure 19.8   By stopping the speeder and blowing it up, you add a little more interest to the file.

That's one way to detect and react to a collision. However, what if you want to be able to bounce off of what you collide with? That's a little more complex.

Distance Calculations and Collisions

Another way to calculate collisions between objects is to do a little math. If you're not already familiar with the Pythagorean theorem, now is the time for a refresher course. Figure 19.9 shows a right triangle with its sides and two corner points labeled.

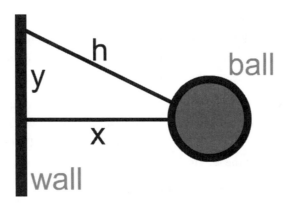

Figure 19.9   If you imagine a right triangle between the ball and the wall, with the hypotenuse being the distance between the two objects, you can start to set up some interesting calculations.

A and B are both sides of the triangle. C is the hypotenuse. Good old Pythagoras, a pre-Socratic Greek philosopher, came up with a theorem that states that $C^2 = A^2 + B^2$.

After you have this equation, you can start to rearrange it to get all kinds of interesting information. Let's say that you want to find the distance between point P and point Q. A would be equal to the X-axis value of Q (q.x) minus the X-axis value of P (p.x)—in other words:

$$A = (q.x - p.x)$$

If that's true, then the formula for B would be:

$$B = (q.y - p.y)$$

If you substitute those values into the first formula, you get this:

$$C^2 = (q.x - p.x)^2 + (q.y - p.y)^2$$

Or, as we first stated: $C^2 = A^2 + B^2$.

So to get C, which is the distance between P and Q, all you have to do is take the square root of both sides of the equation. So what? Think about it for a second. If Q and P are the center points of two objects on a collision course, in Flash, you can get those values from the _x and _y object properties. That means you can always figure out how far apart the two objects are. Now you're getting somewhere.

Take a look at the image on the right in Figure 19.9. You have a circle approaching a wall. The line between the wall and the circle represents the direction that the circle is moving (the wall is stationary). If you imagine a right triangle between these objects, you'd see something like the image on the left in Figure 19.9.

The formula that you've been looking at up to now gives you the distance between two points: in this case, the center points for the colliding objects. However, what you really want to know is when the edge of the circle impacts with the wall. That means that you'll have to take into account the radius (half the width) of the circle.

After the ball hits the wall, what happens? Assuming the ball isn't of sufficient mass to knock the wall down and that it is going fast enough not to be stopped by the wall, it's going to bounce. In fact, it's going to be reflected off the wall based on the angle of incidence, which is the angle at which it originally struck the wall. The Law of Reflection states that the angle of incidence is equal to the angle of reflection, as shown in Figure 19.10. Note that if the ball approaches the wall from the right and bounces, the sine of Y remains the same, but the sine of X reverses from negative to positive.

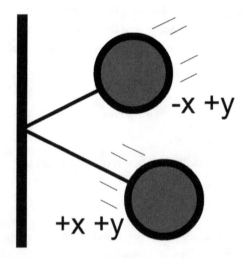

Figure 19.10   As the ball approaches from the right, the speed of X is negative and the speed of Y is positive. After the ball hits the wall, only the speed of X changes, and it becomes positive.

Those are the basics you need to know before you start writing your own code.

In the next exercise, you're going to approach the coding in a slightly different fashion. Because the code that you'll be developing will become moderately complex, it's a good idea to start thinking about how to make it as modular as possible.

You'll create a throwable ball again, but this time, you want to be able to bounce the ball off the sides of your movie. So, not only do you need to track information about the ball, but also you need to know something about the walls that are constraining it.

A Throwable Ball for Collisions

You've already set up a throwable ball. You know the basics for creating the ball and how to code it to make it draggable.

What needs to happen in the ball itself? Just like in the previous exercises, the ball needs to track the new and old X and Y positions and have code set up to react to whether it is being dragged. If the ball has been released, you need to update the X and Y positions based on the current speed.

But what about those walls? Before you start working on setting up the walls, get the throwable ball set up and working.

Locating Boundaries

If you're going to bounce the ball off of the walls, you need to know where the walls are, right? You'll need to provide Flash with the minimum and maximum X and Y values for the walls. These values are going to be constants; they won't change, so why not start by setting them up on the main Timeline?

Setting Up Your Constants

The logical place to start is to think about what constant values you'll need to track. Well, you need to know where the walls are, right? In Exercise 19.6, the first thing you'll do is set four variables that will contain the minimum and maximum X and Y values for the walls:

- **WALLLEFT.** The minimum X value.
- **WALLRIGHT.** The maximum X value.
- **WALLTOP.** The minimum Y value.
- **WALLBOTTOM.** The maximum Y value.

These values won't change, so a sensible place to initialize these variables would be on the first frame of the main Timeline.

Exercise 19.6   Setting Up Constants and the Function Call

For this exercise, the assumption is that you are working with the default movie size of 550 pixels × 400 pixels.

1. Open collision.fla from the Examples/Chapter19 folder on the companion CD.

   The Ball movie clip is already in a layer named Ball on the Stage and given the instance name of ball_mc.

2. Select the first frame of the Actions layer and open the Actions panel to see the code that makes it throwable. It's identical to what we saw in Listing 19.2.

   Now you'll just add a single line of code to the onEnterFrame event created when you release the ball, so that as the ball is gliding around, you constantly check to see if there has been a collision.

3. Select frame 1 of the main Timeline and after the line where you initialized ball_mc.speedY, enter the following in the Actions panel:

   ```
   _global.WALLLEFT = 0;
   _global.WALLRIGHT = 550;
   _global.WALLTOP = 0;
   _global.WALLBOTTOM = 400;
   ```

> **Tip**
>
> You might be wondering why the variable names in this case are in all capital letters. It's because they are constants, which are values that never change. Using a standard to denote constants makes them easier to find in your code so that you don't inadvertently change them. Constants should also be placed into _global so that they are accessible to all objects without having to deal with any paths to them.

   Now you'll just add a single line of code to the onEnterFrame event created when you release the ball, so that as the ball is gliding around, you constantly check to see if there has been a collision.

4. Locate the second to the last closing curly brace inside your onRelease method and there, inside the onEnterFrame method, add this line:

   ```
   this.checkWalls();
   ```

   You'll begin writing the checkWalls() function in the next exercise.

5. Before you start the next phase of the project, make sure your code works properly—that is you can fling the ball around. Save and test your movie. Right now checkWalls is getting called, but nothing is happening because it isn't defined yet!

Now that you've established where your walls are, it's time to start thinking about how to handle the collisions. Here's where all that nasty math stuff comes in. Actually, it's not all that bad.

Figuring Out the Distance Calculations

Now is the time to think about what information you know and what information you need. You're already collecting information about how fast, and in what direction, the ball is moving. You know how to determine the X and Y coordinates of the ball for any given time. In addition, you know where the walls are. You can start by working with the left wall.

You want to know when the ball intersects with the left wall, but you want to know when the edge of the ball, not the center, intersects with the wall. That means that you're going to need to account for half of the ball's width, or radius, in the equation. In fact, depending on whether you're moving in a positive or negative direction, you'll need to either add or subtract the value of the radius. Figure 19.11 illustrates this concept.

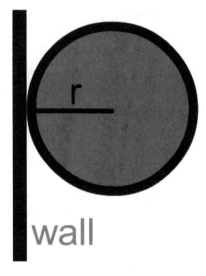

Figure 19.11   The combined position of the wall and the radius of the ball determine when a collision occurs.

So, you should see your conditional statement developing here: If this._x is less than the wall plus the radius, you need to do something.

What are you going to do? Well, for one thing, you need to change the direction that the ball is moving. If you remember the discussion earlier, the angle at which the ball hits the wall is known as its *angle of incidence*. The *angle of reflection*, the angle at which the ball leaves the wall, is the opposite of the angle of incidence. Don't panic; you don't have to start calculating angles. You just have to reverse either speedX or speedY, depending on which wall you're hitting.

You also can give the ball a little extra snap to its bounce by resetting its position before you reverse the direction. Why would you want to do this? While Flash is constantly updating the position of the ball, the ball still can get ahead of the calculations and go past the wall slightly. By immediately resetting the position of the ball so that its edge is on the proper side of the collision boundary, you keep the illusion of the bounce effect crisp and clean.

In Exercise 19.7, you'll set up the function with conditional statements to determine whether the ball has hit a wall, and then make it bounce.

Exercise 19.7   Bouncing Off the Wall

In this exercise, you'll create the checkWall() function that determines whether the ball has hit a wall and controls what happens to the ball when it does.

1. Back in frame 1 of the Actions layer on the main Timeline, open the Actions panel and declare your new function by entering the following code:

```
ball_mc.checkWalls = function() {

}
```

2. Start by setting up the left wall. Enter the following code between the asterisks:

```
ball_mc.checkWalls = function() {
//*********************************************************
        if (this._x < (WALLLEFT + this.radius)) {
                //reset the position of the ball inside the bounds
                this._x = ((WALLLEFT + this.radius) - this._x) +
                ➥WALLLEFT + this.radius;
                //Reverse the speed
                this.speedX *= -1;
        }
//*********************************************************
}
```

3. You're probably wondering where the value of the radius variable is coming from. The answer is that right now, it doesn't exist. You have to add that in. It's acceptable to add it after the function because this function is called after the variable is declared. The ball will never hit the wall before the radius has been

determined. If you're really worried about it, you can put the radius calculation before the function. It doesn't matter. After the last curly brace, enter the following code:

```
//determine the radius of the ball
ball_mc.radius = ball_mc._width/2;
```

4. Now is a good time to test your movie and make sure that you've entered the equations correctly. Try flinging the ball against the left wall. It should have a nice springy bounce.

5. Okay, now it's time to add the rest of the walls. Copy the first if statement and paste it just above the last curly brace, but still inside the function. Make the following changes:

- Subtract the radius instead of adding it (three occurrences).
- Change WALLLEFT to WALLRIGHT (three occurrences).
- Change the < (less than) to > (greater than).

Your code up to this point should look like Listing 19.4.

Listing 19.4   A Function to Check for Horizontal Collisions with Walls

```
ball_mc.checkWalls = function() {

        if (this._x < (WALLLEFT + this.radius)) {
                //reset the position of the ball inside the bounds
                this._x = ((WALLLEFT + this.radius) - this._x) + WALLLEFT
                ➥+ this.radius;
                //Reverse the speed
                this.speedX *= -1;
        }

        if (this._x > (WALLRIGHT - this.radius)) {
                //reset the position of the ball inside the bounds
                this._x = ((WALLRIGHT - this.radius) - this._x) +
                ➥WALLRIGHT - this.radius;
                //Reverse the speed
                this.speedX *= -1;
        }

}
//determine the radius of the ball
ball_mc.radius = ball_mc._width/2;
```

6. Next, you can copy both if statements and paste them just above the last curly brace. Make the following changes:

- Change each occurrence of x to y. (Don't make me say it—do it only for the last two if statements!)
- Change WALLLEFT to WALLTOP (three occurrences).
- Change WALLRIGHT to WALLBOTTOM (three occurrences).

Your completed checkWalls function code should look like Listing 19.5.

Listing 19.5   A Function to Make a Ball Bounce off Four Walls

```
ball_mc.checkWalls = function() {

        if (this._x < (WALLLEFT + this.radius)) {
                //reset the position of the ball inside the bounds
                this._x = ((WALLLEFT + this.radius) - this._x) + WALLLEFT
                ➥+ this.radius;
                //Reverse the speed
                this.speedX *= -1;
        }

        if (this._x > (WALLRIGHT - this.radius)) {
                //reset the position of the ball inside the bounds
                this._x = ((WALLRIGHT - this.radius) - this._x) +
                ➥WALLRIGHT - this.radius;
                //Reverse the speed
                this.speedX *= -1;
        }

        if (this._y < (WALLTOP + this.radius)) {
                //reset the position of the ball inside the bounds
                this._y = ((WALLTOP + this.radius) - this._y) + WALLTOP +
                ➥this.radius;
                //Reverse the speed
                this.speedY *= -1;
        }

        if (this._y > (WALLBOTTOM - this.radius)) {
                //reset the position of the ball inside the bounds
                this._y = ((WALLBOTTOM - this.radius) - this._y) +
                ➥WALLBOTTOM - this.radius;
                //Reverse the speed
                this.speedY *= -1;
        }
}
//determine the radius of the ball
ball_mc.radius = ball_mc._width/2;
```

7. Save and test your file. The ball should bounce, with believable angles, off all four walls.

Okay, that's pretty cool. However, what if you want obstacles inside the walls off of which the ball can bounce? That adds yet another layer of complexity.

Adding Obstacles into the Equation

Now the real fun starts. You're going to add some rectangular obstacles to the Stage for the ball to bounce off. However, you're not going to use your drawing tools to place them on the Stage. You're going to create a Box object that you can replicate as many times as you want.

Boxes aren't complex objects. The only parameters you need to keep track of are the left side, the right side, the top, and the bottom. How hard can that be? Well, you need to think about how you plan to get that box drawn on the Stage. The most obvious way to do this is to use `attachMovie()`. Thus, you'll need to create a Box movie clip in the Library and set its linkage.

Creating a Box

After your Box movie clip is ready to go, you're ready to write the function to create your object. In Exercise 19.8, you start by creating a Box movie clip.

Exercise 19.8   Creating the Box Movie Clip

You're going to create a simple box and set up its linkage properties.

1. You can continue working with the file from the last exercise or you can open collisionWithBox.fla in the Examples/Chapter19 folder.
2. From the main menu, select Insert > New Symbol. Make it a movie clip, give it a name of **Box**, and click OK.
3. Select the Rectangle tool and draw a rectangle on the Stage. You can choose to fill the rectangle; it doesn't matter.
4. Select the rectangle you just drew and use the Info panel (Window >Info) to resize it to 100 × 100 pixels. Use the Info panel to reposition the rectangle so that its upper-left corner is centered on the Registration point.
5. Open the Library and select the Box movie clip. Right- or Command-click the Box movie clip and select Linkage from the Options list. Change the following settings:

   Linkage: **Export for ActionScript**
   Identifier: **box**
6. Click OK.

In Exercise 19.9, you're going to create the function that creates the Box object. The Box object will take four parameters:

- `left.` The left wall (minimum X) of the box.
- `right.` The right wall (maximum X) of the box.

- **top.** The top (minimum Y) of the box.
- **bottom.** The bottom (maximum Y) of the box.

It will use these parameters and a variable named DEPTH to attach the new Box objects to the Stage and determine their width and height.

Exercise 19.9   Creating the Box Object

You're going to create the function that builds your Box object on the main Timeline.

1. Make sure you are on the main Timeline and select frame 1 in the Actions layer.

    As you are adding the code in this section, try to rearrange your code as you go along so that functions are all grouped together at the top of the code. It helps to keep your code organized and easier to check.

2. Add some blank lines before the first line of code and enter the following code to begin the function that builds the Box object:

    ```
    function Box (left, top, right, bottom) {

    }
    ```

    Next you need to do something with those parameters you're passing.

3. Pass the parameters into variables that are local to a single instance of the box. Add the following code between the curly braces of the function Box:

    ```
    this.left = left;
    this.top = top;
    this.right = right;
    this.bottom = bottom;
    ```

4. So far, so good. Now you need to set up the attachMovie method. Before the last curly brace, add the following code:

    ```
    this.attachMovie("box", "box"+depth, depth);
    this.mc = _root["box"+_depth];
    ++depth;
    ```

    Take a look at the second line of code you just entered. What's going on there? You are passing the movie clip you just created, by reference, into this.mc. Because these are attached movies, you need a way to reference their properties.

5. You need to size the box you're attaching to the Stage and set up the depth variable. To size the box, you have to tell it where its left side and top are. From there, you just need the width and the height. Add the following code before the final curly brace:

```
this.mc._x = this.left;
this.mc._y = this.top;
this.mc._width = this.right - this.left;
this.mc._height = this.bottom - this.top;
```

6. Just after the last curly brace, add this code:

```
_global.depth = 1;
```

7. You might be thinking you're done at this point, but you're not. You haven't actually created a box yet. You'll also want to make sure your ball isn't hidden under the box, so you'll change its depth too. After the very last line of code in the Actions panel, enter the following:

```
_global.BOXES = new Array();
BOXES[0] = new Box (300, 100, 200,300);
```

Add final line of code:

```
ball_mc.SwapDepth, (100);
```

The cool thing about this is you can add as many boxes to the Stage as you want, but you can get it working with just one first. Now your Box code should look like Listing 19.6. Note that the last three lines actually appear at the very bottom of your ActionScript.

Listing 19.6   ActionScript for Creating Box Obstacles

```
function Box (left, top, right, bottom) {
        this.left = left;
        this.top = top;
        this.right = right;
        this.bottom = bottom;
        _root.attachMovie("box", "box"+_root.depth, _root.depth);
        this.mc = _root["box"+_root.depth];
        ++_root.depth;
        this.mc._x = this.left;
        this.mc._y = this.top;
        this.mc._width = this.right - this.left;
        this.mc._height = this.bottom - this.top;
}
_global.depth = 1;
global.BOXES = new Array();
BOXES[0] = new Box (300, 100, 200,300);
```

8. Save and test your movie. (See Figure 19.12.) You should see a box as well as the throwable ball.

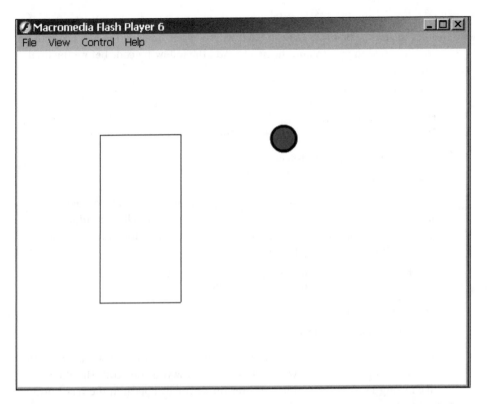

Figure 19.12   Your newly created Box object uses the `attachMovie()` method to attach the new instance of the Box movie clip to the movie.

Okay, your box is there, but it doesn't make for much of an obstacle. You guessed it. You have to write another function to check for box collisions.

Checking for Box Collisions

Checking for collisions with boxes on the Stage is a little more complex than checking for walls. You now have to keep track of where the ball was versus where it is now in different coordinate spaces. For example, the pseudocode to check for a ball approaching the box on the Stage from the left side of the screen would look something like this:

```
If the last x position was less than the left wall and the current x
position is greater than the left wall, and the current y position is
in between the top and bottom walls, you've had a collision with the
left wall—reset the x position of the ball and reverse the speed of X.
```

So what does that look like in reality? The actual conditional statement looks like this:

```
if (this._x - this.speedX < current.left this._x > current.left &&
this._y > current.top  && this._y < current.bottom){
      this._x = current.left - this._x + current.left;
      speedX *= -1;
}
```

This of course, assumes that current is an instance of the Box object. The code inside the if statement won't run unless all the conditions being tested are true.

Exercise 19.10   Creating the *checkBoxes()* Function

So now that you know the basics, it's time to start writing the function.

1. Launch the Actions panel and select frame 1 of the Actions layer.

2. Place your cursor after the last function.

3. Set up the shell for the function by entering the following code:

```
ball_mc.checkBoxes = function{

}
```

4. Even though you've only set up one box, you know that you can set up more than that. Thus, create a loop, and the appropriate variables, that will account for all the possible boxes. You can do this by entering the following code:

```
for (var i=0; i<_BOXES.length; ++i){
      var current = new Object();
      current.left = BOXES[i].left - this.radius;
      current.right =  BOXES[i].right + this.radius;
      current.top = BOXES[i].top - this.radius;
      current.bottom = BOXES[i].bottom + this.radius;
}
```

5. Set up the check for the collision with the left wall. After that one is working, it's all cut and paste and minor changes.

6. You've already had a look at the code you need to enter, so enter the following code between the curly braces of the checkBoxes() function:

```
if (this._x - this.speedX < current.left this._x > current.left &&
this._y > current.top  && this._y < current.bottom){
      this._x = current.left - this._x + current.left;
      this.speedX *= -1;
}
```

7. You're not ready to test your movie yet. You haven't called the function. Within your ball_mc.onRelease function, in the this.onEnterFrame function, add this code:

```
_this.checkBoxes();
```

8. Use the conditional (if) statement you just created as the template for the other three conditionals you'll need. You still need to check for the right wall, the top of the box, and the bottom of the box. Go ahead and try to create those on your own. If you need a cheat sheet, check Listing 19.7 below.

9. After you have your code set up, save and test your movie. Check your syntax before you test.

10. After you're satisfied with what you have, play around with setting up additional boxes on the Stage. The code is really bulletproof; you can have a lot of fun. (See Figure 19.13.) Here's a sample pattern of boxes you can play with:

```
BOXES[0] = new Box (80, 80, 160, 160);
BOXES[1] = new Box (240, 80, 320, 160);
BOXES[2] = new Box (400, 80, 480, 160);
BOXES[3] = new Box (160, 240, 240, 320);
BOXES[4] = new Box (320, 240, 400, 320);
```

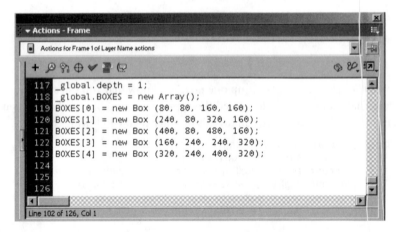

Figure 19.13   Because the box is an object, you can attach as many instances of it as you like to your movie by adding new Box objects to the Boxes array.

Listing 19.7   The ActionScript for the checkBoxes Function

```
ball_mc.checkBoxes = function(){
     for (var i=0; i<BOXES.length; ++i){
          var current = new Object();
          current.left = BOXES[i].left - this.radius;
          current.right = BOXES[i].right + this.radius;
          current.top = BOXES[i].top - this.radius;
          current.bottom = BOXES[i].bottom + this.radius;
          if (this._x - this.speedX < current.left && this._x >
          ➥current.left &&  this._y > current.top  && this._y <
          ➥current.bottom){
               this._x = current.left - this._x + current.left;
               this.speedX *= -1;
          }
```

```
          if (this._x - this.speedX > current.right && this._x <
          ↩current.right &&   this._y > current.top  && this._y <
          ↩current.bottom){
               this._x = current.right - this._x + current.right;
               this.speedX *= -1;
          }
          if (this._y - this.speedY < current.top && this._y >
          ↩current.top &&  this._x > current.left && this._x <
          ↩current.right){
               this._y = current.top - this._y + current.top;
               this.speedY *= -1;
          }
          if (this._y - this.speedY > current.bottom && this._y <
          ↩current.bottom &&  this._x > current.left  && this._x <
          ↩current.right){
               this._y = current.bottom - this._y + current.bottom;
               this.speedY *= -1;
          }
     }
}
```

And your fully compiled code should now look like Listing 19.8.

Listing 19.8   The Complete ActionScript for Detection of Walls and Obstacles with a Thrown Object

```
function Box (left, top, right, bottom) {
     this.left = left;
     this.top = top;
     this.right = right;
     this.bottom = bottom;
     _root.attachMovie("box", "box"+ depth, depth);
     this.mc = _root["box"+ depth];
     ++ depth;
     this.mc._x = this.left;
     this.mc._y = this.top;
     this.mc._width = this.right - this.left;
     this.mc._height = this.bottom - this.top;
}

ball_mc.onPress = function(){
     this.startDrag();
     this.onEnterFrame = function(){
          this.oldX = this.newX;
          this.oldY = this.newY;
          this.newX = this._x;
          this.newY = this._y;
     }
}

ball_mc.onRelease = function(){
     this.stopDrag();
```

continues ▶

Listing 19.8   Continued

```
        this.speedX = (this.newX - this.oldX) * this.ratio;
        this.speedY = (this.newY - this.oldY) * this.ratio;
        this.onEnterFrame = function(){
                this.speedX *= this.friction;
                this.speedY *= this.friction;
                this._x += this.speedX;
                this._y += this.speedY;
this.checkWalls()//except no values for walls!!
        }
}
ball_mc.onReleaseOutside = ball_mc.onRelease;
ball_mc.checkWalls = function() {

        if (this._x < (WALLLEFT + this.radius)) {
                //reset the position of the ball inside the bounds
                this._x = ((WALLLEFT + this.radius) - this._x) + WALLEFT
                ➥+ this.radius;
                //Reverse the speed
                this.speedX *= -1;
        }

        if (this._x > (WALLRIGHT - this.radius)) {
                //reset the position of the ball inside the bounds
                this._x = ((WALLRIGHT - this.radius) - this._x) +
                ➥WALLLRIGHT - this.radius;
                //Reverse the speed
                this.speedX *= -1;
        }

        if (this._y < (WALLTOP + this.radius)) {
                //reset the position of the ball inside the bounds
                this._y = ((WALLTOP + this.radius) - this._y) + WALLEFT +
                ➥this.radius;
                //Reverse the speed
                this.speedY *= -1;
        }

        if (this._y > (WALLBOTTOM - this.radius)) {
                //reset the position of the ball inside the bounds
                this._y = ((WALLBOTTOM - this.radius) - this._y) +
                ➥WALLLBOTTOM - this.radius;
                //Reverse the speed
                this.speedY *= -1;
        }
}




ball_mc.checkBoxes = function(){
```

```
for (var i=0; i<BOXES.length; ++i){
    var current = new Object();
    current.left = BOXES[i].left - this.radius;
    current.right = BOXES[i].right + this.radius;
    current.top = BOXES[i].top - this.radius;
    current.bottom = BOXES[i].bottom + this.radius;
    if (this._x - this.speedX < current.left && this._x >
    ➥current.left &&  this._y > current.top  && this._y <
    ➥current.bottom){
        this._x = current.left - this._x + current.left;
        this.speedX *= -1;
    }
    if (this._x - this.speedX > current.right && this._x <
    ➥current.right &&  this._y > current.top  && this._y <
    ➥current.bottom){
        this._x = current.right - this._x + current.right;
        this.speedX *= -1;
    }
    if (this._y - this.speedY < current.top && this._y >
    ➥current.top &&  this._x > current.left  && this._x <
    ➥current.right){
        this._y = current.top - this._y + current.top;
        this.speedY *= -1;
    }
    if (this._y - this.speedY > current.bottom && this._y <
    ➥current.bottom &&  this._x > current.left  && this._x <
    ➥current.right){
        this._y = current.bottom - this._y + current.bottom;
        this.speedY *= -1;
    }
    }
}
}


//determine the radius of the ball
ball_mc.radius = ball_mc._width/2;

_global.WALLLEFT = 0;
_global.WALLRIGHT = 550;
_global.WALLTOP = 0;
_global.WALLBOTTOM = 400;

ball_mc.friction = .9;
ball_mc.ratio = .5;
ball_mc.newX = ball_mc._x;
ball_mc.oldX = ball_mc._x;
ball_mc.newY = ball_mc._y;
ball_mc.oldY = ball_mc._y;
ball_mc.speedX = 0;
ball_mc.speedY = 0;
```

continues ▶

Listing 19.8   Continued

```
_global.depth = 1;
_global.BOXES = new Array();
BOXES[0] = new Box (300, 100, 200,300);
//add this code so the ball doesn't get stuck behind boxes
ball_mc.swapDepths(100);
```

Summary

Now, aren't you glad you didn't sleep through this chapter the way you slept through your physics class? Physics is fun, especially when you can see the results of your calculations. Not only can you have fun with physics, but also you can put it to work for you to give your Flash presentation an air of realism that would be hard to match in any other way.

So what have you learned to do in this chapter? You've learned how to control the position of a movie clip on the Stage using ActionScript and how to throw an object on the Screen. You've also learned how to create elastic behavior and how to work with collisions. That's not a bad start.

Whatever you do, don't stop here. It would be easy to write an entire book on Flash and physics, but we've had to cram just a little into one chapter. You've got a good base from which to work; it's up to you to take it to the next level. You can do that by looking at tutorials available on the web. You also can do it by cracking open a physics book. Why just imitate what everyone else is doing? Here are a couple links to get you started:

- Physics at the Interactive Learning Network at
  www.iln.net/html_p/c/72782/158557/404277/404287/404410_2079696.asp

- The Glenbrook South Physics Classroom at
  www.glenbrook.k12.il.us/gbssci/phys/Class/BBoard.html

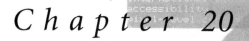

Chapter 20

Server-Side Communication

No single tool can do all things. Even Flash needs a little help. Connecting Flash with a remote server has never been easier or more robust. Faster XML and data processing, better variable management, and binary server communication enable fast and secure data transfers.

Flash can do more than you might think after you add the power of server-side technology. You will open the door to a new world and a completely new use for Flash. Combine server-side power with the Flash UI Component library and suddenly, Flash becomes your best choice for an ultimate user experience—not to mention the best choice for developing data management and control systems.

In this chapter, you get an overview of what makes server-side power operate and explore what is available to you both inside and outside Flash MX. You specifically will learn about the following:

- **The application server (middleware).** Examine how middleware languages extend the reach of Flash applications. Compare popular middleware languages and explore budgetary expense, learning curve, developer support, and server operating requirements.
- **Databases.** We review what a database is and how to set one up and make it available to the Flash Player through an application server.
- **Internal Flash MX features to communicate and interact with a server.** We review the Flash MX data engine used to load and process data using two different methods: LoadVars() and the improved XML engine.

There's a lot to cover in this chapter, but the best place to start is with middleware.

Middleware and the Application Server

You can think of middleware as the translator between the Flash Player and server applications. Server applications can access and manage databases that extend possible sources of data that a Flash movie can access. With this configuration, Flash can access data storage and relational database management systems (RDBMSs), file systems, email servers, Windows applications and components, Java components, and JavaBeans.

There are various middleware languages on the market. All perform at least the basic tasks necessary for delivering dynamic data to the web. These tasks include collecting form data, generating dynamic page content, and sending and receiving cookies. We won't look at all the application servers available today, but here is a small sample of the most commonly used languages:

- Macromedia ColdFusion
- Microsoft ASP.NET

- Sun Microsystems JSP
- The PHP Hypertext Processor

How does it work? When a web server receives a request for an application template, it sends the file to the application server for processing instead of returning it immediately to the browser that made the request. The application server then reads through the file and processes the instructions contained within. These instructions can connect the server with services or data provided by a database server, a mail server, or some other legacy server. The process is called a Just-In-Time (JIT) compiler.

The concept is simple. Develop a language that a lot of people can use to leverage extremely powerful application platforms. When the application server completes the process, the output is returned to the caller (usually a web browser) and formatted per the request (that is, in HTML, XML, text, or Flash ActionScript).

The client browser or Flash Player then decodes the document for display to the user. As mentioned, each platform has a different technique for scripting these instructions. They all fall into one of three categories. They are primarily based either on Sun Microsystem's standards-based Java 2 Enterprise Edition (J2EE) platform or a Microsoft proprietary-based ASP.NET platform. Groups such as the Apache Software Foundation offer programs of the third platform, which are open-source alternatives such as PHP, Mod_Perl, or Mason. (And you thought browser wars were something!) The .NET and J2EE platforms offer up very similar menus of functionality. J2EE and most open source environments are platform independent, where .NET is bound to Microsoft servers.

 Note

If you are interested in learning more about J2EE and .NET, check out some of these online resources:

- "Microsoft.NET vs. J2EE: How Do They Stack Up?"; by Jim Farley, August 2000, `http://java.oreilly.com/news/farley_0800_print.html`.
- "Picking a Winner: .NET vs. J2EE"; by Jim Farley, March 2001, `http://sdmagazine/com/print/documentID=11085`.
- "J2EE vs. Microsoft.NET, A Comparison of Building XML-Based Web Services"; by Sun Microsystems, Chad Vawter, and Ed Roman, June 2001, `www.theserverside.com/resources/pdf/J2EE-vs-DotNET.pdf`.

- "Java 2 Enterprise Edition (J2EE) Versus the .NET Platform. Two Visions for eBusiness"; by ObjectWatch and Roger Sessions, March 2001, `www.objectwatch.com/FinalJ2EEandDotNet.doc`.

- "Compare Microsoft .NET to J2EE Technology"; by Microsoft Corporation, `msdn.microsoft.com/net/compare/default.asp`.

- Additional papers can be found by searching for "J2EE vs .NET" on `www.google.com`.

Macromedia ColdFusion

Found at `www.macromedia.com/software/coldfusion/`, the complete ColdFusion package has two components: the application server and an integrated development environment. (See Figure 20.1.) The server can be acquired in four different versions, each varying either by cost or by feature set. The highest-end version is the ColdFusion Enterprise Edition. Dreamweaver MX is the Integrated Development Environment (IDE) that completes the set, although a developer is free to use any text-based editor to create the templates.

ColdFusion MX is equipped with advanced services that enable granular security implementations, remote development services, archived deployment, graphing, server clustering services, server monitoring, native database connections, Java Database Connectivity (JDBC) and Open Database Connectivity (ODBC) sockets, ColdFusion components, web services, XML support for native Flash gateway integration, and the ability to create and maintain indexes for searching using Verity.

Versions of the ColdFusion Server include the following:

- **ColdFusion Enterprise Edition.** A full-featured version of the server product.
- **ColdFusion Professional Edition.** A full-function version, but with limited tools. The pro version does not include archiving tools, clustering tools, or a variety of other tools.

There is no restriction in functionality between Enterprise and Professional.

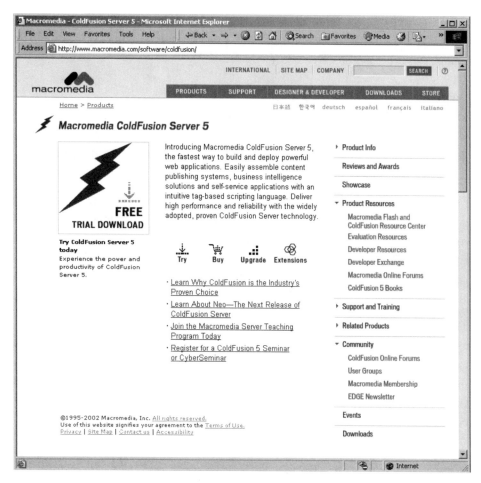

Figure 20.1   The Macromedia ColdFusion MX DevCenter contains articles on all aspects of the technology from Macromedia engineers and from the developer community. It also contains the Developer Exchange, which is an application that allows ColdFusion developers to share code bits and software built on or for ColdFusion.

What Stands Out

The most praised advantage of ColdFusion over other middleware systems is the low learning curve associated with ColdFusion Markup Language (CFML), the tag-based markup language ColdFusion Server uses to process programmer instructions. CFML instructions are abstracted into an HTML tag. Because instructions are abstracted into a tag-based syntax, a beginner can build a serviceable web application, access dynamic data, and display it in an HTML layout in a very short period of time. This enables developers who have no previous experience with programming to quickly grasp the logic, syntax, and structures of server-side manipulation.

Corporate and Community Support

Macromedia supports ColdFusion by providing forums and developer resources on its web site. These resources include articles, technical notes and documentation, and a developer gallery to which ColdFusion users can upload libraries of code to share their techniques with others.

Macromedia certified training facilities are widely available. They provide another avenue of corporate support. Macromedia's commitment to its ColdFusion developer community is shown through the over 180 ColdFusion user groups around the world. ColdFusion User Group (CFUG) meetings occur in various locations, giving developers an opportunity to meet and network face-to-face while sharing ColdFusion tips, tricks, and techniques.

There are many privately run web sites and tutorials. One useful source for Flash developers is `www.flashcfm.com`, which is a site that posts tutorials specifically targeted toward those who use ColdFusion with Flash. Another resource is a prolific ColdFusion mailing list, CF-Talk (`www.houseoffusion.com`). It receives dozens to hundreds of emails daily. In addition, you can access an online magazine at `www.sys-con.com/ColdFusion/`.

Note

You might want to choose ColdFusion as your middleware server if any of the following are true:

- You are not from a programming background.
- You prefer the use of a tag-based language, such as HTML.
- You are developing a site basic enough to use the free, reduced functionality version of ColdFusion Server.
- You need the advanced capabilities of the Professional or Enterprise editions.

ASP.NET (Microsoft .NET)

By itself, the phrase "Active Server Page (ASP)" could actually apply to any of the technologies in this section. An ASP is similar to ColdFusion in that ASP code is embedded into an HTML page. This code, like CFML, is processed on the server. The original HTML document and embedded code act as a template for the end product. Microsoft has incorporated ASP.NET (`http://msdn.microsoft.com/asp`) as the handle of its own implementation of an ASP.

ASP.NET development does not give a developer many out-of-the box resources. Development of more complicated modules is more of a do-it-yourself proposition. However, to that end, ASP.NET has excellent support for accessing Component Object Model (COM) objects. COM is a technology in which applications can share functionality by using reusable program building blocks. For example, when you are able to open a Microsoft Word document directly in a browser window, you are seeing COM at work. The browser was able to call a COM object that brought Word's functionality into the realm of the browser's operation (see Figure 20.2).

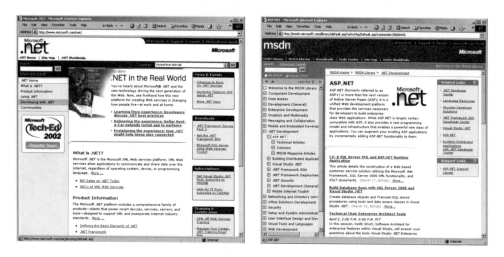

Figure 20.2   Microsoft's .NET web site and the ASP.NET web site.

What Stands Out

The biggest selling point for ASP.NET is that there is no sale involved. ASP.NET is distributed with all Windows platforms. The Microsoft web server (IIS) is set up to use ASP.NET from the start. It's free, it's available, and it's no trouble to find developers who already use it. However, this freedom comes with a price. As a Microsoft product on the .NET platform, adopting ASP.NET locks you in. Although any browser can request and display results from an ASP.NET application, only Microsoft operating systems and servers can work with ASP.NET applications. The code is not as transportable as servers on the J2EE platform.

Note

Sun Chili!Soft ASP (www.chilisoft.com) is a third-party ASP.NET clone that operates on Apache, iPlanet, and O'Reilley web servers. It differs from ASP.NET in that it provides support for Java, EJB, and CORBA objects.

Corporate and Community Support

As a direct result of ASP.NET's ubiquitous availability, you don't have to look hard to find a web application programmer who has worked in ASP.NET to join your team. You also don't need to spend a lot of effort looking for web sites, forums, or listservs. Although Microsoft does not provide support, it does host an enormous online developer network where many ASP.NET issues can be researched, including the following:

- ASP Lists at www.asplists.com

- 15 Seconds at www.15seconds.com

- ASP Index at www.aspin.com

- ASPWire at www.aspwire.com

Note

You might want to choose ASP.NET as your middleware server if any one of the following is true:

- You are deploying on IIS or Personal Web Server (PWS).

- You need a free application server.

- You have previous programming experience with VBScript.

- You want the ability to draw on a large network of developers.

- You will make extensive use of native Windows components.

Java Servlet/JSP (J2EE)

Found at http://java.sun.com/products/jsp/, JSP is a Java version of ASP. (See Figure 20.3.) Because JSP is based on Java, it inherits all the advantages of the language: object orientation, portability, and platform independence.

Java is easier to learn than C#, which is the language it was developed to resemble, and JSP makes working with Java easier with the use of a tag-based syntax. However, only a developer who is armed with previous Java programming experience will find JSP a quick language to learn. Of the four middleware technologies covered in this section, JSP has the highest learning curve because if you don't know Java, you won't easily understand JSP.

What Stands Out

Java, and its family of languages and methodologies, arguably holds the highest potential for powerful, scalable, and portable web development (see Figure 20.3). However, because seasoned Java developers are scarce and expensive to come by, you are not likely to see large Java applications developed cheaply.

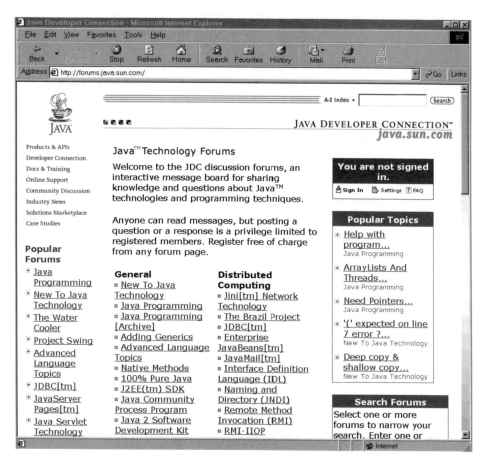

Figure 20.3   Sun Microsystem's JSP page.

Further emphasizing its platform independence, JSP templates can be distributed from more than one application server, unlike ColdFusion, PHP, and ASP.NET. Tomcat, the official servlet container and JSP implementation from Sun Microsystems, is open source and free.

Corporate and Community Support

JSP is receiving a lot of attention from the corporate sector. Its advantages entice large enterprise businesses to make it their choice. Macromedia is beginning to offer training courses that highlight JSP use on its JRun platform, and there are some JRun user groups and at least one useful online forum (`http://forums.java.sun.com`). However, it seems that in terms of an easily accessible and knowledgeable developer community, JSP is lagging behind the others.

Note

You might want to choose JSP as your middleware server if one of the following is true:

- You know Java.
- You have access to a pool of good Java developers.
- You want to deploy the application server on any platform, including Macintosh.

PHP: Hypertext Processor

Found at `www.php.net`, PHP is an open-source programming language that has recently gained prominence in the middleware marketplace. (See Figure 20.4.) Like the ColdFusion application server and ASP.NET, PHP was built to dynamically create HTML pages. It embeds the PHP syntax among the HTML to include dynamic elements and to serve the resulting page to the web. Since 1994, thousands of programmers with backgrounds in C, Perl, and Java have modified and extended the language.

The learning curve for PHP is on a par with ASP.NET. No one particular language will give you better preparation for PHP than another, but someone with prior programming knowledge will find it easier to learn PHP.

What Stands Out

PHP uses native database connections to manage data retrieval and does so very well, but this strength might also be its greatest weakness. Compared to ColdFusion especially, the problem becomes clear. ColdFusion database connections are abstracted so that all a developer must know is the tag syntax, which is very simple, and the Structured Query Language (SQL) statement.

If you plan to upsize your database, you would run into some problems in PHP. The ColdFusion tag that manages database connections would require one change among its attribute definitions. In a PHP version of the application, the entire code block that handled connecting to the database would need to be recoded using the proper connection terminology and syntax for the upsized database.

Figure 20.4   The PHP Group, a comprehensive PHP developer resource site.

An interesting PHP feature to note is its support for regular expressions (RegEx). Although the other options discussed in this section also parse RegEx, PHP is the only one to have developed two parsers. One is POSIX compliant, and the other works in a manner similar to Perl.

Corporate and Community Support

The corporate world has not really embraced PHP. Seeming to believe in the homily "You get what you pay for," many enterprise businesses shun the free, community-support model of PHP, preferring instead to use a commercial product, like ColdFusion, or a free product that has proper corporate infrastructure, like ASP.NET or JSP.

The portability difficulties associated with the way PHP accesses databases natively also add to this reluctance to view PHP as an enterprise technology solution. You can find some resources on the web, however. Check out `www.zend.com` (a partner web site) and `http://php.resourceindex.com` and `www.PHPBuilder.com` (PHP resource sites).

> **Note**
>
> You might want to choose PHP as your middleware server if one of the following is true:
>
> - You are deploying on UNIX, Win32, or OS X.
> - You need a free server product.
> - You are a proponent of open source software.
> - You have programming experience in at least one server language.

ColdFusion or PHP? ASP.NET or JSP?

Which one should you choose? Does one application server stand out above the others? The short answer is this: no.

When it comes down to the wire, in some cases, circumstances will make the decision of which server product is used. For instance, if an application will be hosted on several servers' varied operating systems and among them is one with a Macintosh operating system, JSP is the most likely choice. If easy access to the greatest number of trained developers is a must, ASP.NET might win over ColdFusion.

Other times, programmer preference or past experience might be the deciding factor. If it is important, for instance, that new programmers ramp up quickly, ColdFusion is best. For forward-thinkers who foresee a major RDBMS upgrade in years to come, PHP might lose in favor of a more portable option.

> **Note**
>
> ColdFusion and ASP.NET can take advantage of Macromedia's Flash Remoting service, which, to Flash developers, is a huge bonus in performance and development time.

Surely, however, one of these languages must perform better and serve pages faster, right? Well, with each language listed, a well-coded application running on an optimized installation of software and adhering to the best practices of the application program interface (API) will perform nearly identically in all scenarios.

Note

Differences in how fast an application server processes and returns its output, in fact, are not always attributable to the middleware itself, but to contributing factors inherent to the web server, the database server, coding practices, and even the operating system itself.

Server-Side Data Models

The concept of a database is very simple. It enables your application to manage, retrieve, and store data over indefinite periods of time. Understanding the basic concepts of a database is very important. As your ideas and intentions grow and as your systems get larger, understanding relational database concepts is critical for the scalability and expandability of your application.

There are two options accessible to Flash and to you:

- **The database.** A database is an application that collects and organizes data optimized for fast storage and retrieval. There are a wide variety of choices on the market—some are free and some are very expensive. Free databases, such as MySQL or PostgreSQL, are popular but are restricted in enterprise-level support and stability. Consumer-level databases, such as Microsoft Access or dBase, are available, and for most small-enterprise sites, they are suitable. When an application is expected to process a large number of database requests simultaneously, however, or when server up time is extremely important, server-grade database applications are required. Databases such as Microsoft SQL Server, Oracle, Sybase, and Informix are popular choices. Each database has its own list of pros and cons and should be evaluated to best suit the needs of your application.

- **XML.** Superficially, XML looks a lot like HTML, as it should—they both have roots from another markup language, Standard Generalized Markup Language (SGML). If you know HTML, you already know quite a bit about XML—tags, tag attributes, and so on. However, there is quite a difference between the two as well. For instance, XML is more strict than HTML. In addition, when working with XML, you have to be aware of some specific syntax rules.

Now, let's take a look at the database more closely.

The Database

A basic database for web usage is made up of four components. Assume, for this example (shown in Figure 20.5), that we want to store data in a database about a room full of people. The four necessary components are as follows:

- **Field.** Fields in a database are commonly referred to as database columns. They ask questions about your data. They might ask your first name, your last name, or similar types of questions. Consider a field to be like a variable. It has a name (firstName, lastName, emailAddress, and so on), and within that variable, we store values or data.

- **Record.** The record, commonly referred to as the row, represents the answers to the questions. As an example, each person whom we ask the same questions is stored in a record. Because we ask the same questions for each person, we could ask the database to return every record (or person) whose birthday is in March or whose last name ends in "Smith."

- **Table.** The database table contains a collection of records representing similar data. For example, you might have a table of users and another table of job titles. You could make a relationship between users and job titles and ask the database to return all users who drink too much coffee.

- **Query.** The query is the question that makes the relationship. Using a database query, you might tell the database to return a list of users living in Toronto or to combine the records of more then one table where certain fields are equal or similar. Database queries are controlled using SQL. This language is a standard across most database platforms (with a few different flavors for different systems), but, in spirit, they are identical.

An application server can send queries to databases using a variety of connection methods. ASP.NET uses the ADO.NET method, and Macromedia ColdFusion uses the CFQuery tag. In most cases and depending on your database, all platforms support the use of SQL or dynamic SQL. The application server stores the results from database queries in structured array variables. These variables can be processed to loop and output the rows (records) returned.

Databases must be mapped on a server to enable bidirectional communications with applications or services running. In the .NET environment, you will use a connecting bridge called ODBC. ODBC is a standard Windows service and is installed on all installations of Windows from Windows 3.1 forward.

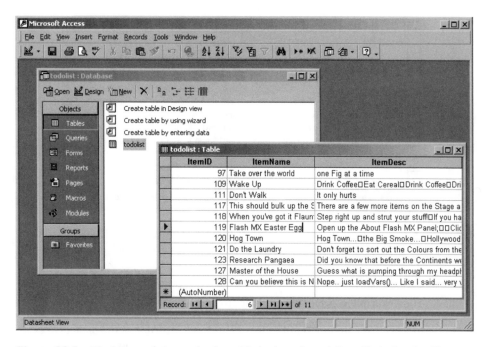

Figure 20.5   The Microsoft Access database. Notice how the todolist table looks a lot like a spreadsheet. Fields are called columns and records are called rows.

On a J2EE platform, the connecting bridge is JDBC. JDBC is an open source protocol. Most application servers have JDBC connectors for most popular database applications. This will be an issue to consider when choosing application server platforms. Macromedia and Merant are two leading companies producing native database connectors to widely used databases.

So, as you can see, there isn't much to getting started. Now let's review a sample database and connect it to an application server.

Exercise 20.1   Building Your Database

For this exercise, you will use Microsoft Access to review the sample database, todolist.mdb, which you'll find in the Examples/Chapter20 folder on the CD. You will have to connect this database with a server. For this exercise, we will walk through the connection steps on a Windows 2000 server and review the connection details through a ColdFusion server administrator (see Figure 20.6).

Figure 20.6 The todolist table inside Microsoft Access shows the columns (fields) and rows (records) of data in a spreadsheet format. You can edit the data directly inside these fields.

The todolist.mdb database is a simple, three-field Microsoft Access database with a single table. The fields in the database and their attributes are as follows:

- **ItemID.** This is a unique number that identifies a record. It is the database key field and is automatically generated every time a record is added to the database.

- **ItemName.** This is the actual item on your to-do list. It's a text field that allows up to 50 characters.

- **ItemDesc.** Use this field to describe your to-do list item more fully. This is a "text" field that allows up to 255 characters.

To allow your application to "talk" to your database, you need to set up what is known as a Data Source Name (DSN). This is an alias to your database that makes referring to your database a relatively simple process. Setting up a DSN is going to vary from operating system to operating system, but the general process is as follows:

1. Copy the todoList.mdb file from the CD-ROM's Examples/Chapter20 folder, and place it on a machine that will act as your server. Make sure you remove the "read only" property of the file after it has been copied.

2. Launch the ODBC Data Source Administrator for your system. (See Figure 20.7.)

3. You'll want to add a system DSN that will be accessible to all users on your machine, so select the System tab, and press Add.

4. Select the driver you'll need to set up your data source. For this example, the driver is Microsoft Access Driver (*.mdb).

5. Assign a data source name to your database. In this application, the data source name being used is toDoList.

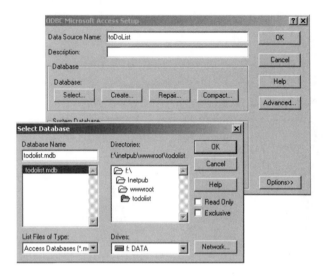

Figure 20.7   The ODBC Data Source Administrator.

6. Finally, select the directory where the database (todolist.mdb) resides, and then press OK. Now you can reference this database in your middleware application by using the DSN "toDoList" instead of typing a fully qualified path to the database.

7. If you plan to use this database in ColdFusion, you will need to map this DSN to ColdFusion through the ColdFusion Administrator's DataSource manager, as shown in Figure 20.8. Use the ODBC Bridge driver to make the connection.

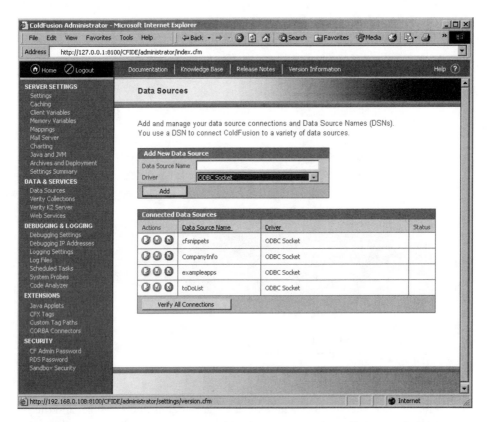

Figure 20.8   Map your ODBC DSN to ColdFusion MX using the ColdFusion Administrator. Select ODBC Socket.

If you are going to set up this file for testing on your own system, you must first set up a DSN. The name expected by the exercises to follow is "toDoList".

Now that you understand the basics of a database and have connected to your server using ODBC, let's do a call to it using ColdFusion. To do this example, you will need to have ColdFusion 5.0 or greater installed and running. There is a trial version located on the CD, or you can get a copy from the Macromedia web site.

You will also need a web server running. There is a free web server supplied with all Windows operating systems. Windows 95/98 use PWS, which is located on your operating system install disk. Windows 2000 uses Internet Information Server 5.0 (IIS 5.0). For more information on web servers for Windows, visit www.microsoft.com/iis/. Linux users can use Apache.

Accessing Your Data Using ColdFusion

In your favorite HTML editor, create a new file called SQLTest.cfm. Save it in a folder accessible by the ColdFusion server and the web server. You must be aware that running application server scripts (like this one) will not be processed unless they are accessed through the web server. The instructions in the file will not be parsed just by dragging the file into the browser or by double-clicking it. If you have ColdFusion installed on your local machine, there are three ways you can access the web root:

- http://localhost/folder/filename.cfm
- http://127.0.0.1/*folder*/*filename*.cfm
- http://*myComputersName*/*folder*/*filename*.cfm

Okay, so you've got your web server, your ColdFusion server, and your database file. You have created a new file on your server and have tested it through your web browser. Take a deep breath, and let's begin.

In the SQLTest.cfm file, you will need to run an SQL query on your database. This query will select all data and store it in a ColdFusion variable. You then will output the ResultSet to the requesting web browser as HTML. Let's look at the script:

```
<!DOCTYPE HTML PUBLIC "-//W3C//DTD HTML 4.0 Transitional//EN">

<html>
<head>
      <title>InsideFlash: Chapter 20: SQL Test</title>
</head>

<body>
<!--- :::: Query the Database, select all data, sort by ItemID,
Descending order --->
  <cfquery name="qGetAllItems" datasource="todolist">
    Select ItemID, ItemName, ItemDesc
    From ToDoList
    Order by ItemID DESC
  </cfquery>
```

Notice that the CFML is structured just like HTML. Review the lines starting with <CFQUERY>. The Select statement is our SQL query. It tells the database that we want all the records in the ToDoList table returned and sorted by ItemID, in descending order. Now let's output the Recordset to the browser as HTML:

```
<!--- Output the "qGetAllItems" Query --->
  <CFOUTPUT Query="qGetAllItems">
    #ItemID#: #ItemName#<br>
    #ItemDesc#<HR>
```

```
</CFOUTPUT>

</body>
</html>
```

SQL is a very simple language to understand. There are four main commands of which you should be aware:

- **SELECT.** SELECT tells the database to return records. Here is a simple SQL statement to select data, followed by the syntax for SELECT:

```
SELECT ItemID, ItemName, ItemDesc
FROM ToDoList
WHERE ItemID=4
ORDER BY ItemID DESC

SELECT [what fields]
FROM [what table]
WHERE [field] = [value]
ORDER BY [field] [order]
```

- **INSERT.** INSERT tells the database to put new records into the database. Here is a simple SQL statement to insert new data.

```
INSERT into ToDoList(ItemName, ItemDesc)
VALUES('This is the name of my item', 'this is the description')
```

String data must be wrapped in single quotations. Numbers do not need wrapping. The syntax for INSERT is simple:

```
INSERT into [what table]([list of fields])
VALUES([list of data, relative to the list of fields])
```

- **UPDATE.** UPDATE tells the database to change existing field values. Here is a simple SQL statement to UPDATE existing data:

```
UPDATE ToDoList
SET itemName='Kevin Towes',
    ItemDesc='ColdFusion Guy'
WHERE ItemID=5
```

The WHERE clause is important in the UPDATE command. If you forget it and execute the script, you run the risk of corrupting all your data. The SQL syntax for UPDATE is:

```
UPDATE [what table
SET [field] = [value]
WHERE [field] = [value]
```

- **DELETE.** DELETE will completely remove records from the table. DELETE is for-ever, with no undo, and should be used with great caution.

```
DELETE FROM Todo List
WHERE ItemID=5
```

The WHERE clause is even more important in the DELETE command. If you forget it and execute the script, you run the risk of erasing all your data, with no chance of undo, unless you have a backup. The SQL syntax for UPDATE is:

```
DELETE FROM [table name]
WHERE [field] = [value]
```

Now that you know the relative points of each middleware technology and have had a chance to review databases, it's time to explore how you invoke these servers from within Flash.

Connecting Flash with the Server

Before you explore the ActionScript objects and methods that will make communication possible, you should first understand what will happen and the relationship the Flash Player has with the server.

The Flash Player is a client that has loaded your Flash application (or movie) from a server. The player takes the role of the "caller," requesting data (and services) from a remote server. The server, depending on the type of file requested, always returns a response to the caller. This response could take many different forms and formats. Two principal file types, text (ASCII) or binary (Multipurpose Internet Mail Extensions [MIME]), can be received by the Flash Player. ASCII file types that can be processed by Flash include HTML, XML, ActionScript name and value pairs, and straight text.

Based on the services available to the server, these files might be generated "dynamically," based on a series of conditions transmitted from the caller to the server or based on the resources, such as a database, available to the server.

Let's explore different processes for calling the server.

Figures 20.9–20.13 illustrate the sequence of a data transfer between a Flash movie and an external middleware (ColdFusion MX) template.

Figure 20.9   End user requests an HTML file by clicking a hyperlink.

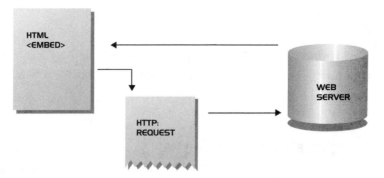

Figure 20.10   Server returns the file to the end user's browser. Browser processes client scripts, including the HTML <EMBED> tag. The <EMBED> tag sets up an HTTP request for a Flash file.

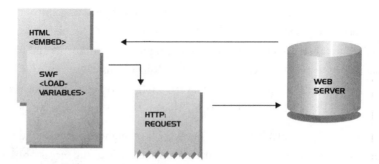

Figure 20.11   Server returns a SWF (Flash movie) to the end user's browser. A Flash plug-in processes ActionScript. A `loadVars()` action requests a ColdFusion template from the server.

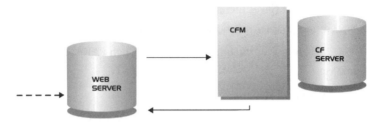

Figure 20.12   The server locates the ColdFusion template and forwards it to the ColdFusion application server for processing.

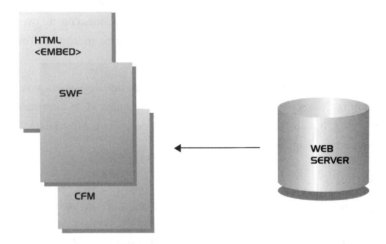

Figure 20.13   The processed ColdFusion file returns directly to the SWF. The SWF file uses strings ColdFusion prints out as Flash variables.

Now that you understand how the Flash Player communicates with a server, let's explore the various methods we discussed in the preceding section.

Flash MX Client Server Objects to Make the Connection

In this section, you explore a variety of options for connecting the Flash Player with the server. You will walk through an existing application step by step. The example was built using Flash MX and ColdFusion MX, but you should have no difficulty translating the ColdFusion language to the application server language of your choice.

Over previous versions, Flash MX offers a greater selection of connection methods with increased functionality. The exact flow will differ slightly depending on which method you use. The available methodologies are as follows:

- Using the loadVars() object (new in Flash MX)
- Using the loadVariables() action (for legacy Flash Players)

- Using the XML object (gives increased performance in Flash MX; see the "XML" section later in this chapter for more information)

- Passing URL variables over the query string or through PARAM attributes in the EMBED object

- Using the getURL() action

- Using Flash Remoting components (new in Flash MX; see Chapter 21, "Flash Remoting")

Macromedia has done an incredible job of addressing the server-side communication objects in Flash MX. The new loadVars() object gives you more control over your data transfer, including access to error information and progress indicators. You can even provide streaming data to the user during download!

The most exciting new method for Flash MX and server-side developers alike is the new Flash Remoting Components (FRC). This option is supplied as an after-market extension to Flash MX. It is also the fastest method to transfer and transform data. This option will be explored in Chapter 21.

loadVars()

If you are familiar with Flash 4 or 5, the loadVariables() action has been replaced with a much more efficient object, loadVars(). This option is available only to the movies played within the Flash 6 Player. If your Flash movie must be published for the Flash 4 or 5 Player, you are forced to use the traditional loadVariables() function to interact with the server.

The loadVars() object shares similar functionality to the XML object. It requests and receives data the same way. It also has a number of monitoring tools and an event handler (onLoad), just like the XML object. The primary difference between the two objects is the type of data they process. LoadVars() uses a unique ActionScript name and value pair to populate variables with data. LoadVars is missing all properties and methods associated with managing the XML DOM tree (more on XML later).

Let's take a look at how the ActionScript name and value pair is structured. It's not a difficult concept, really. The text file (or output) that the player calls will contain data that looks like this:

```
VariableName1=Value&VariableName2=Value
```

Every variable following the first variable is delimitated with the ampersand (&) and the value is set to everything following the equals (=) sign. There is no (documented) limit on the number of variables or the length of the string data that Flash will accept.

Now, you might ask this question: "What if the string data I want to send into Flash includes an ampersand?" Good question. The best way to send Flash a string value is to URL-encode it. What this means is that nonalphanumeric characters are encoded and will be decoded by the Flash Player. Here is an example.

This string:

```
"It's a lovely day today. We are going to Murray & Anne's wedding in
Canada!"
```

should be encoded as this:

```
"It%27s%20a%20lovely%20day%20today%2E%20%20We%20are%20going%20to%20Murra
y%20%26%20Anne%27s%20wedding%20in%20Canada%21"
```

All nonalphanumeric characters have been encoded. The apostrophe (') is represented by "%27" and spaces are encoded as "%20". How would you do this? There are a couple techniques. If you are using an application server such as Macromedia ColdFusion, there is a native function called URLEncodedFormat(). Wrap this string into this function, and ColdFusion will output a URL-encoded string. If you don't have an application server, place the string inside the Address bar of Internet Explorer, and then press Enter. The returned (error) page will encode the string for you!

The variable you set in this file will be accessible by Flash after it is loaded.

So, now that you know how to structure data for loadVars(), let's bring it into a Flash movie! You will do this by creating an instance of the loadVars object that is _global defined for the entire Flash move. Use the constructor new loadVars() to build an instance of the loadVars object.

```
_global.serverData= new loadVars();
```

After this object has been made an instance, you will access the range of methods available by referencing the instance name (in this case, serverData).

The primary methods you will need to make this work are .load and .loaded. To call the server, use the following:

```
ServerData.load("http://127.0.0.1:8100/insideFlash/myVars.txt")
stop();
```

This script calls the server for a text file called myVars.txt, which is located in the insideFlash folder on the server's web root. You have also stopped the playhead to wait for the data to be returned.

Now build a movieClip on a frame accessible by the playhead when it is stopped. This movieClip will act as a wait loop, and it will stop the playhead until the onLoad instance has completed. On the movieClip, create a clip event as follows:

```
onClipEvent (enterFrame) {
  IF (serverData.loaded) {
     _gotoAndPlay("someFrame");
      }
}
```

This script loops until the .load operation has completed. When the .load operation started, the .loaded property was automatically set to false. When the server completes its transfer, the .loaded property will become true. This will break us out of the loop you built and continue the movie.

You can use this same method to call an application server template, such as a ColdFusion template that might return data from a database or other data source. You don't need to do anything different, just ensure that you have the proper extension to call the ColdFusion template. We will look at building dynamic data sets using ColdFusion in the ToDoList exercise later in this chapter.

The loadVars() object can also send data from the Flash Player to the server. Why would you want to send data back to the server? You might be asking your user to enter a contest, and you need to save the entry form (that you built in Flash, of course) into a database. You need to send the Flash variables to a dynamic template on the server, which will process the files and insert them into a database table.

How you do it is simple. Just like before, you create an instance of the loadVars() object set to _global. Set or transfer your variables to this instance, and then run the loadVars.send method, as shown in the following code:

```
// set the loadVars instance, globally
_global.flashData= new loadVars();

// transfer _root variables into the instance "flashData"
flashData.usrName = _root.usrName;
flashData.usrEmail = _root.usrEmail;
flashData.usrPhone = _root.usrPhone;

// send the object and its variables to the server for processing
flashData.send("http://127.0.0.1:8100/insideFlash/CFProcess.cfm",this,"P
OST")
```

There are two additional attributes to the send method. The Target clip ("this") tells the Flash Player where to place server return objects (such as errors). The third attribute explains how to transfer the data to the server. Your options are GET and POST.

If your movie requires the server to respond back with variables, use the same method as was used during the load to build a wait clip, and instead of using the .send method, use .sendAndLoad, as shown in the following code:

```
// Send the object to the sever, expecting a return value
flashData.sendAndLoad("http://127.0.0.1:8100/insideFlash/CFProcess.cfm",
this,"POST")
```

That's it. loadVars() is a little more work then the old loadVariables() action, but you gain a lot more functionality.

loadVariables()

The loadVariables() action is an obsolete method with the introduction of the loadVars() object in Flash MX. However, it is the only option available if you have to publish using the Flash 4 or Flash 5 Player. It works exactly the same way as loadVars(), but requires some advanced ActionScripting to achieve the native functionality available in loadVars().

Here is a sample call to the server:

```
loadVariables("http://127.0.0.1:8100/insideFlash/CFProcess.cfm","_root",
➥"POST")
```

This example submits a form post to the server and returns any variables returned to the _root Timeline. To place the variables within an object, you can create an object and request that the server target that object to return the variables.

```
myServerVars = new object();
myServerVars.loadVariables("http://127.0.0.1:8100/insideFlash/CFProcess.
➥cfm",this,"POST")
```

loadVariables() will send variables only on the Timeline where it was called. In the first example, all variables present on the _root Timeline will be sent to the server (regardless of whether you want to use them). In the second example, only variables that exist in the myServerVars object will be sent. This practice is similar to the method used in loadVars(), and it provides more control over your inbound and outbound variables.

Passing Variables Through the URL

Passing URL variables is the absolute easiest way to populate variables outside Flash. A creative way to use it is to pass in session state information to the Flash Player.

Many application servers enable you to use a server "key" that uniquely identifies a user session. This is important for maintaining login states or shopping cart solutions. Because the Flash Player exists on the client's machine, it doesn't have access to browser cookies or the URL string. Both methods are used to identify a user to the server. For example, in ColdFusion, CFID and CFTOKEN are used to make this identification. Normally, these variables are stored in a client cookie; however, if your user has cookies disabled, developers commonly pass this information in the URL string.

```
<CFOUTPUT>
<OBJECT classid="clsid:D27CDB6E-AE6D-11cf-96B8-444553540000"
codebase="http://download.macromedia.com/pub/shockwave/cabs/flash/
➥swflash.cab##version=6,0,0,0"
WIDTH="550" HEIGHT="400" id="ToDoMX" ALIGN="">
 <PARAM NAME=movie VALUE="ToDoMX.swf?CFStateVars=#session.URLToken#">
 <PARAM NAME=quality VALUE=high>
 <PARAM NAME=bgcolor VALUE=##FFFFFF>
 <EMBED src="ToDoMX.swf?CFStateVars =#session.URLToken#"
        quality=high
        bgcolor=##FFFFFF
        WIDTH="550"
        HEIGHT="400"
        NAME="ToDoMX"
        ALIGN=""
        TYPE="application/x-shockwave-flash"
     PLUGINSPAGE="http://www.macromedia.com/go/getflashplayer"></EMBED>
</OBJECT>
</CFOUTPUT>
```

You can add more variables into this structure by separating them with the ampersand (&), as shown in the following code:

```
<PARAM NAME=movie
VALUE="ToDoMX.swf?CFStateVars=#session.URLToken#&MyVar=Value=MyOtherVar=
➥Another Value">
```

The line

```
<PARAM NAME=movie VALUE="ToDoMX.swf?CFStateVars=#session.URLToken#">
```

places the variable CFStateVars into the _root Timeline on _level0. In ColdFusion, the variable session.URLToken will output the required variables for state management. If you use the loadVars() object, you should copy this variable into loadVars() instances that you post to the server.

getURL()

getURL() and loadVariables() are very similar. One of the main differences, however, is that getURL() either results in an additional browser window when it is used to call an exterior template or it loads the external template in the same calling window. The latter result destroys the Flash movie.

`loadVars()` or `loadVariables()` are the best choices for sending a string of data from Flash into an external template behind the scenes because they both enable the Flash movie to retain control of the calling window. The external template then is able to manipulate the data as variables.

Building a ColdFusion/Flash MX Application Using *loadVars()*

Instead of having you build this application step by step, the text is going to walk you through the finished application. It's being presented this way because this application was built using both ColdFusion 5.0 and Flash MX, and you might not have access to a ColdFusion server. However, translating ColdFusion markup to your language of choice is a relatively painless process. What's important is that you understand how all the pieces are put together, the roles of the server and the client interface, and when to task each.

The application you'll be reviewing is a simple to-do list (see Figure 20.14). This to-do list lets you do several things. You can add new tasks to your list, along with a detailed description for each one. You can also delete tasks that have been completed. You can have as many tasks in your list as you like. All the information you enter, delete, and change in the list is captured in a database so that you can recall it at any time from anywhere.

For this example, you will need:

- A Flash MX authoring environment
- ColdFusion 5.0 or greater
- An ODBC connection to the toDoList.mdb file (see the section on databases earlier in this chapter)

You will start the exercise by examining the Flash file. Then you'll move to examining the ColdFusion template used to dynamically generate the ActionScript name and value list (as you saw earlier in this chapter). The list feeds the data to the Flash Player. Following that, we will walk through a ColdFusion template that will manage the data in the database. It will also delete, update, and insert new records.

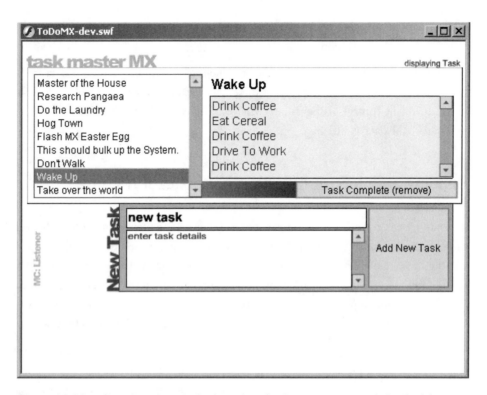

Figure 20.14   The task master MX displays a list of tasks. You can view task details, delete tasks, or add new tasks.

The Flash File (Task Master MX)

Open up the Task Master MX exercise file (todoListMX.fla) in Flash MX and the ColdFusion file in your favorite HTML editor (such as ColdFusion Studio, Homesite, or Dreamweaver). These files and trial versions of Flash MX and Dreamweaver MX are located on the CD.

There are three elements to this project:

- The Flash user interface (UI)
- Flash ActionScript
- ColdFusion (server-side) script and the database itself

Start by examining the Flash file in Flash MX. After you're familiar with the file, you can take a look at the ColdFusion file to see how each item is interacting with the others.

The Flash UI

The UI element is very simple. To keep it simple, there is no animation and design is very low. Building rich UIs in Flash MX has been made easier (when compared to earlier versions) with the introduction of the Flash UI components. Standard form controls, such as list and combo boxes, and scrollbars and radio buttons, make the job of building data management interfaces much easier (see Figure 20.15).

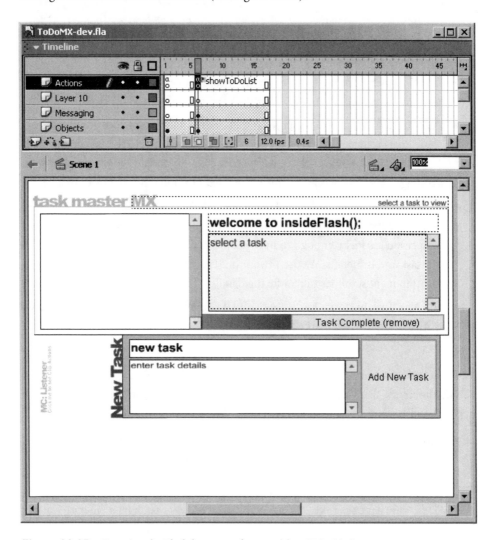

Figure 20.15   Examine the Flash layout on frame 6 (showToDoList).

In our Task Master MX example, you will see five main UI components:

- **Scrolling to-do list.** For this list, we used a Flash UI component (`FListBox`). This list box displays the tasks in your to-do list. You can have as many items as you want. Because you need to quickly see your task information, you have the option of clicking an item and displaying more information about it. Using the new Flash UI components eliminates a lot of work that was necessary in previous versions of Flash. When a user selects a task, the `changeHandler` (`showTask`) for the component runs a custom function built in the Actions layer of the _root Timeline. This function will be explained further on in this exercise.

- **Task Complete button.** Another Flash UI component (`FpushButton`) was used here. When pressed, the button calls the `removeTask` custom function.

- **Task display.** What good is a task list that doesn't allow you to see your tasks? There are two dynamic text boxes here. One displays the selected task name, and the second displays the task details. A Flash UI component (`FscrollBar`) adds scrolling to the details box. To control the text box, reference the text box's instance name by setting it in the `targetTextField` parameter of the scrollbar.

- **New task entry form.** Adding items to your to-do list is somewhat important (unless you are lucky enough to have people to do it for you). You can enter a new task and its details. We used two input text fields and added another Flash UI component scrollbar to handle the details.

- **Add New Task button.** One more Flash UI component (`FpushButton`) was used for this button. When pressed, the changeHandler calls the `addTask` function.

The Flash ActionScript

Behind the scenes, there are a series of ActionScript functions and objects that were built to handle events such as adding or removing tasks. Let's walk through the process:

- **Initial load.** This frame script calls the application server and requests a record-set containing the to-do tasks, the details, and a unique ID number (see Figure 20.16):

```
// set the Server name and the ColdFusion template location to
allow for simple install: Change this server to match yours
serverName = "http://127.0.0.1:8100/insideFlash/todolist/";

// (optional: uncomment the line below, to make this Flash file
look on your local server for the ColdFusion templates.
//serverName = "/insideFlash/todolist/";
```

```
// Instance the LoadVars to "serverData"
serverData = new LoadVars();

//Make the initial Call to the server
serverData.load(serverName+"todolist.cfm");

/* Stop the Playhead and wait for the server to respond
   See the MovieClip script on the OBJECTS Frame for the Wait loop
*/
stop();
```

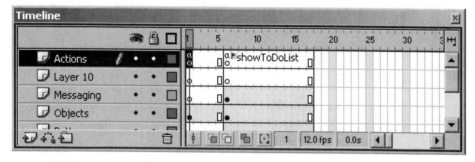

Figure 20.16   The Frame 1 initial load script is located on the Actions layer.

Tip

Making your server name dynamic allows you to move your application easily from one server to another. It also allows you to quickly change the folder where your templates might exist. This saves time because you won't need to look through all your code to find all the references to the server.

- **Wait for the server to respond.** After the .load command has been executed, we want to have the application wait for the data to load before displaying the interface. There is a movie clip on the Objects Layer in frame 1. This movie clip contains a clip event script that will move the playhead, revealing the interface, after the server has completed its transmission. Challenging the state of the .loaded property on the serverData object will let the movie pause until all data has been received in full. After it is loaded, the playhead will move to a frame where the processing script is waiting.

```
onClipEvent (enterFrame) {
  /* build the wait loop.  When the server has responded from the
  ➥.load operation
     tell the _root Timeline to goto the frame "showToDoList" */
  if (_root.serverData.loaded) {
    trace("server Responded");
    _root.gotoAndStop("showToDoList");
    }
```

```
/* Optional: this script displays the total bytes received of
➥the server file loaded
   dataLoaded is a Text object on the Timeline within this
   ➥MovieClip */
dataLoaded="loaded: <font color='#FF0000'><B>"+
_root.serverData.getBytesLoaded() +" </B></font><font
➥size='10'>BYTES<font>";

}
```

We do an extra step in this clip event. There has been a progress meter added. To demonstrate additional functionality for this exercise, we also added some HTML into the text and bolded in red the bytes that were loaded. Note that you cannot access the getTotalBytes() function when you call a dynamic template from the server. This function is available only for static files (.txt or .xml).

- **Initialize the returned recordset.** The Flash Player must process this data and store it in something that can be used efficiently and with the Flash UI components. There are a number of steps in this frame. First we will turn off the button that enables the user to remove a task. There is no mechanical reason for this, other than usability (see Figure 20.17).

```
// Turn off the remove button until there is a task shown.
removeButton._visible=false;
```

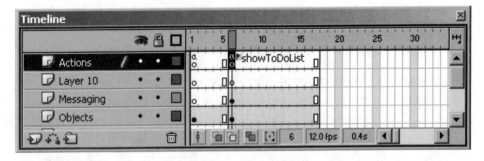

Figure 20.17   Frame 1: The following scripts are on frame 6 in the Actions layer.

- **Initialize the send data object.** The object used for sending data out to the server is initialized as flashVarsOUT. This structure will be used for all outgoing data sent to the server for processing.

```
// Prepare the flashVarsOUT object - used to send data to the
➥server
flashVarsOut = new LoadVars();
```

- **Initialize three arrays.** You will initialize one array for each field that will be transmitted from the server. These objects will store the column information returned and will give ActionScript an efficient way to access the data (using an index key or a row number).

```
// Set new Arrays for the Recordset
serverData.itemID = new Array();
serverData.itemName = new Array();
serverData.itemDesc = new Array();
```

- **Run the `initRecordset` function.** The function, which is defined in the following code, processes the returned data and stops the playhead.

```
initRecordSet();
stop();
```

- **Define the `initRecordSet()` function globally.** Defining a function globally is a new feature in Flash MX, and it is available from any Timeline or object. The principal role for this function is to transfer into an array structure the database column (field) data from the lists returned from the server. This is done so that ActionScript can relate the data by index or key. Index2 of the itemName array will be associated with index 2 of the itemDesc array. This is also required to populate the Flash UI component.

```
// :::: DEFINE THE FUNCTIONS USED TO PROCESS DATA

_global.initRecordSet = function() {
  // Split each Column Value List into an Array
  _root.serverData.itemID =
  ➥_root.serverData.col_itemID.split("¦¦");
  _root.serverData.itemName =
  ➥_root.serverData.col_itemName.split("¦¦");
  _root.serverData.itemDesc =
  ➥_root.serverData.col_itemDesc.split("¦¦");

  // Set the Flash MX Component (taskList) Dataprovider to the
  ➥ItemName
  _root.taskList.setDataProvider(_root.serverData.itemName);
}
```

- **Use the `.split` function.** In this exercise, the server returned three lists of data. Each list is delimited by a double pipe (II). A double pipe is used to separate the data because it is an obscure sting sequence that is very unlikely to be used in normal text. The `.split` function in Flash separates the list using this delimiter and then places it into the array. This process is done for each column returned. ActionScript will reference the data like this:

```
_root.serverData.itemDesc[2];
```

Finally, the function pushes the `serverData.itemDesc` array into the listBox component using the `.setDataProvider` method.

- **Show the task.** This function is invoked when a user clicks a task in the list. Displaying the task involves matching the task that was selected with its description and ID and then transferring the description and task name to the fields that will display it. This function also turns on the Remove Task button (setting it to `_visible`).

```
function showTask() {
  // this function is invoked when a user selects a Task from the
  ↩Component
  thisKey = _root.taskList.getSelectedIndex();
  /* Transfer the data from the column Arrays to the current
  ↩display, using the index */
  _root.itemDesc = _root.serverData.itemDesc[thisKey];
  _root.itemID = _root.serverData.itemID[thisKey];
  _root.itemName = _root.serverData.itemName[thisKey];
  // Turn on the remove Task Button
  _root.removeButton._visible=True;

  /* Update the system message (displayed in RED)*/
  _root.Message="displaying Task";
  trace(thisKey);
}
```

The variables `_root.itemDesc`, `_root.itemID`, and `_root.itemName` represent the current task being accessed. Each time a task is selected, we capture the index number of that task using the `.getSelectedIndex()` method of the listBox UI component. This index number is matched with the related data in the corresponding arrays. For example, if you click the second task name, the second task description (itemDesc) return the correct data.

Other actions include turning on the Remove Task button (in case it was hidden) and setting a message variable informing the user that something has happened. This is a useful technique for debugging.

- **Remove the task.** Invoked by the Remove Task button, this function calls the server again, telling it to remove the current task from the database. When it has completed, the task list is refreshed with the new list.

First, the function transfers only the current itemID (stored in the variable `_root.itemID`) into the `flashVarsOUT` object. You then set a variable, called serverAction, that the server will monitor. The action will be `deleteTask`. (This is explained further in the server-side script in the next section.) The

.sendAndLoad() method posts all variables stored in the flashVarsOUT structure to the server. The .sendAndLoad() method was used because the Flash Player needs to receive a response from the server with the updated data. This response triggers the listBox to be updated and removes the task from the list. Similar to the showTask function (as previously discussed), a message variable is set, informing the user of activity.

```
function removeTask() {
    // This function is invoked when the user clicks "remove Task"
    _root.flashVarsOUT.itemID = _root.itemID;
    _root.flashVarsOUT.serverAction = "deleteTask";
    _root.flashVarsOUT.sendAndLoad(serverName+"todolist.cfm",
    ➥_root.serverData, "POST");
    // Update the system message (displayed in RED)
    _root.Message="connecting with server...";
trace("removeTask");
}
```

- **Add a new task.** Invoked after the user has entered new data and pressed the Add Task button, the server is called to insert the new task into the database. Similar to the removeTask function, this task transfers data into the flashVarsOUT structure, and it is sent to the server using the sendAndLoad method, for exactly the same reason as the remove function was sent. Take note that the serverAction value is set to addTask. This tells the server to process this request differently. After all this, the form fields are cleared.

```
function addTask() {
    // This function is invoked when the user clicks "add Task"
    // Transfer the new information into the flashOUT object to send
    ➥to server
    _root.flashVarsOUT.new_itemName = _root.new_itemName;
    _root.flashVarsOUT.new_itemDesc = _root.new_itemDesc;

    // tell the server, to run the ADD Process
    _root.flashVarsOUT.serverAction = "addTask";

    // Connect to the server - sending the flashVarsOUT structure
    ➥through a POST method
    _root.flashVarsOUT.sendAndLoad(serverName+"todolist.cfm",
    ➥_root.serverData, "POST");

    // Clear the Form Fields
    _root.new_itemName ="";
    _root.new_itemDesc ="";

    _root.Message="connecting with server...";

    trace("addTask");
}
```

- **Wait for a server response.** There is a movie clip, named "listener," that monitors the .loaded property of the loadVars instance named "flashVarsOUT". This property becomes true when the server returns its results, and it will trigger a reinitialization of the recordset and the ToDo list. It also transfers the serverMessage variable set in the server-side template.

```
onClipEvent (enterFrame) {
if (_root.serverData.loaded) {
   _root.serverData.loaded=false;
   initRecordSet();
   _root.Message=__root.serverData.serverMessage;
   }
}
```

That's it for the Flash side of this equation. The full listings of these scripts can be found following the review of the ColdFusion template (which you will see later in this chapter).

The Server-Side ColdFusion Template

The ColdFusion file (todolist.cfm) handles the processing and transfer of data between the database and the Flash caller. On request, it will transfer data to the Flash caller, insert new tasks into the database, or delete tasks from the database.

Here are the primary functions in the ColdFusion template:

- **Delete tasks that have been completed.** This action is invoked when Flash sends the value deleteTask set in the serverAction variable. It runs a DELETE query on the Todo table, deleting the record that matches the itemID number sent.

  Using a condition <CFIF> statement, the script monitors the serverAction variable sent in from the Flash caller. The itemID variable, also sent from Flash, is used in the Delete command to ensure the proper record in the table is deleted. Remember that the itemID is a unique value in the table. No other record can have that value. This is why you should not try to match string values in the database.

```
<CFIF serverAction eq "deleteTask">
  <!--- ::::: REMOVE TASKS FROM THE DATABASE --->
  <cfquery name="deleteItems" datasource="todolist">
    Delete
    From ToDoList
    Where ItemID = #itemID#
  </cfquery>
```

- **Insert new tasks into the database.** This action is invoked when Flash sends the value addTask set in the serverAction variable. An INSERT query on the

ToDoList table is executed, inserting the values sent from Flash. The conditional statement <CFIF> is closed following this query using the </CFIF> tag. This script monitors for only two values in the serverAction variable.

```
<CFELSEIF serverAction eq "addTask">
  <!--- :::: ADD TASKS TO THE DATABASE --->
  <cfquery name="insertItems" datasource="todolist">
    Insert Into ToDoList (itemName,itemDesc)
    Values('#new_itemName#','#new_ItemDesc#')
  </cfquery>
</CFIF>
```

- **Select and return all tasks from the database.** This process is run each time the ColdFusion template is called. It performs a SELECT query on the ToDoList table in the ToDoList database. The query has no filters and sorts the data by itemID, which displays the most recent tasks at the bottom of the list.

```
<!--- :::: Pull all Table data and transform it for Flash
➥loadVars() methods --->
<!--- :::: Note this query is returned each time this file is run
➥--->
  <cfquery name="qGetAllItems" datasource="todolist">
    Select ItemID, ItemName, ItemDesc
    From ToDoList
    Order by ItemID
  </cfquery>
```

After the query has been run, you set up three ActionScript name and Value pairs to be returned to the Flash caller. The three variables represent the three columns returned from the SELECT query: itemID, itemDesc, and itemName.

```
  <CFSCRIPT>
FlashVar="&col_itemId="&URLEncodedFormat(valueList(qGetallItems.
➥itemID,"¦¦"));
    FlashVar=FlashVar& "&col_itemName=" &
    ➥URLEncodedFormat(valueList(qGetallItems.itemName,"¦¦"));
    FlashVar=FlashVar& "&col_ItemDesc=" &
    ➥URLEncodedFormat(valueList(qGetallItems.itemDesc,"¦¦"));
  </CFSCRIPT>
```

Using a special ColdFusion function (valueList), you can easily return a list of values with a delimiter of your choice. In this case, a double pipe ("||") was chosen as a unique separator. As previously discussed, this list will be transformed into a Flash array when Flash receives it after the ActionScript function initRecordSet() is invoked. Another ColdFusion function, URLEncodedFormat, was used to transform the entire list into a safe format for transport. It is decoded by the Flash Player.

The variable `FlashVar` was used to store all data. Each column is appended to the previous value of the `FlashVar` variable.

- **Output the data for Flash to read.** Because the data has been stored in a single variable, the output is quite simple:

```
<cfoutput>Begin=#FlashVar#</cfoutput>
```

As mentioned, there are no conditional statements wrapped around the select action in the ColdFusion template, so it will run every time the template is called. Note the position of the select action. It falls after both the insert and delete actions. This means that the data selected will be updated with all inserts and deletes that were previously executed (see Figure 20.18).

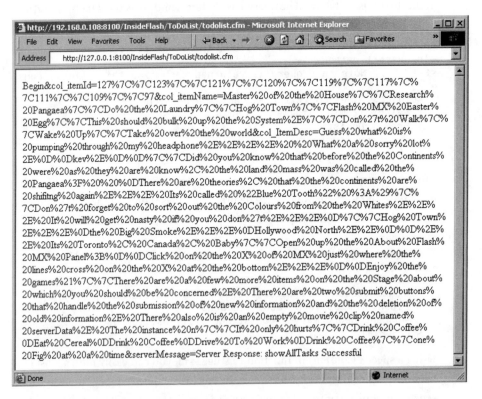

Figure 20.18 The output of the ActionScript name and value pairs as displayed in a web browser. This is what Flash will see.

That's it! You have now reviewed the basic process of using server-side processing inside Flash MX using `loadVars()`. As you can see, passing data back and forth between Flash and middleware applications can be very simple or quite complex. At the end of the day,

Flash doesn't really care what happens on the middleware side, as long as it gets its data back in a form—name/value pairs—it can understand. The full listing of each element is listed below, for your review.

The complete listing for the actions located on the Frame labeled showToDoList is lengthy, but not too daunting. See Listing 20.1.

Listing 20.1   The Complete Listing for the Actions Attached to the toDoList Movie Clip Instance

```
// Turn off the remove button until there is a task shown.
removeButton._visible=false;

// Prepare the flashVarsOUT object - used to send data to the server
flashVarsOut = new LoadVars();

// Set new Arrays for the Recordset
serverData.itemID = new Array();
serverData.itemName = new Array();
serverData.itemDesc = new Array();

initRecordSet();
stop();

// :::: DEFINE THE FUNCTIONS USED TO PROCESS DATA

_global.initRecordSet = function() {
  // Split each Column Value List into an Array
  _root.serverData.itemID = _root.serverData.col_itemID.split("¦¦");
  _root.serverData.itemName = _root.serverData.col_itemName.split("¦¦");
  _root.serverData.itemDesc = _root.serverData.col_itemDesc.split("¦¦");

  // Set the Flash MX Component (taskList) Dataprovider to the ItemName
  _root.taskList.setDataProvider(_root.serverData.itemName);
}

function showTask() {
  // this function is invoked when a user selects a Task from the
Component
  thisKey = _root.taskList.getSelectedIndex();
  /* Transfer the data from the column Arrays to the current display,
using the index */
  _root.itemDesc = _root.serverData.itemDesc[thisKey];
  _root.itemID = _root.serverData.itemID[thisKey];
  _root.itemName = _root.serverData.itemName[thisKey];
  // Turn on the remove Task Button
  _root.removeButton._visible=True;

  /* Update the system message (displayed in RED)*/
  _root.Message="displaying Task";
  trace(thisKey);
}
```

continues ▶

Listing 20.1   Continued

```
function removeTask() {
  // This function is invoked when the user clicks "remove Task"
  _root.flashVarsOUT.itemID = _root.itemID;
  _root.flashVarsOUT.serverAction = "deleteTask";
  _root.flashVarsOUT.sendAndLoad(serverName+"todolist.cfm",
➥_root.serverData, "POST");
  // Update the system message (displayed in RED)
  _root.Message="connecting with server...";
trace("removeTask");
}

function addTask() {
  // This function is invoked when the user clicks "add Task"
  // Transfer the new information into the flashOUT object to send to
➥server
  _root.flashVarsOUT.new_itemName = _root.new_itemName;
  _root.flashVarsOUT.new_itemDesc = _root.new_itemDesc;

  // tell the server, to run the ADD Process
  _root.flashVarsOUT.serverAction = "addTask";

  // Connect to the server - sending the flashVarsOUT structure through
➥a POST method
  _root.flashVarsOUT.sendAndLoad(serverName+"todolist.cfm",
➥_root.serverData, "POST");

  // Clear the Form Fields
  _root.new_itemName ="";
  _root.new_itemDesc ="";

  _root.Message="connecting with server...";
  trace("addTask");
}
```

Final ColdFusion Code Listing

So that you have a chance to see the whole ColdFusion file, rather than just chunks of it, the entire file is included in Listing 20.2. The only code you haven't seen so far is this:

```
<cfsetting enablecfoutputonly="Yes" showdebugoutput="No">
```

This code suppresses any white space, returns, or extraneous debugging data. Remember that Flash won't be happy with anything but name/value pairs. Additionally, at the beginning of the ColdFusion file, a series of variables gets initialized, as shown in Listing 20.2.

Listing 20.2   The Complete Listing for the ColdFusion File That Updates the Database and the Flash Movie

```
<cfsetting enablecfoutputonly="Yes" showdebugoutput="No">

<!--- :::: Initialize all Variables --->
  <CFPARAM NAME="serverAction" default="">


<CFIF serverAction eq "deleteTask">
  <!--- :::: REMOVE TASKS FROM THE DATABASE --->
  <cfquery name="deleteItems" datasource="todolist">
    Delete
    From ToDoList
    Where ItemID = #itemID#
  </cfquery>

<CFELSEIF serverAction eq "addTask">
  <!--- :::: ADD TASKS TO THE DATABASE --->
  <cfquery name="insertItems" datasource="todolist">
    Insert Into ToDoList (itemName,itemDesc)
    Values('#new_itemName#','#new_ItemDesc#')
  </cfquery>
</CFIF>


<!--- :::: Pull all Table data and transform it for Flash  loadVars()
➥methods --->
<!--- :::: Note this query is returned each time this file is run --->
  <cfquery name="qGetAllItems" datasource="todolist">
    Select ItemID, ItemName, ItemDesc
    From ToDoList
    Order by ItemID
  </cfquery>

  <CFSCRIPT>
    FlashVar="&col_itemId=" & URLEncodedFormat
    ➥(valueList(qGetallItems.itemID,"¦¦"));
    FlashVar=FlashVar& "&col_itemName=" & URLEncodedFormat
    ➥(valueList(qGetallItems.itemName,"¦¦"));
    FlashVar=FlashVar& "&col_ItemDesc=" & URLEncodedFormat
    ➥(valueList(qGetallItems.itemDesc,"¦¦"));
  </CFSCRIPT>
  <!--- :::: END DB CALL    ***                 --->

<!--- :::: Display for flash    ***             --->
<cfoutput>Begin=#FlashVar#</cfoutput>
```

Loading large amounts of data or complex variables using the LoadVars() method might prove limiting as you increase your demand for server-side data. XML is an alternative that enables your Flash application to consume larger and more complex data.

XML

XML was born out of one simple observation: Exchanging data between different computer programs is a difficult task. All the systems attempting to share data have to speak the same language. This starts getting really messy when different companies build the programs. Don't forget that there are lots of different types of data that might need to be exchanged and that data can look very different. Stock exchange information doesn't exactly look a lot like baseball scores or news stories, does it?

XML gets around these problems by presenting an architecture from which languages can be built. (This is why it's called extensible!)

- All XML tags must be enclosed in angle brackets (< and >).

- All XML tags must be closed.

- XML is case sensitive.

- All attributes must be enclosed in quotes.

Another important difference between HTML and XML is that there are no set tags in XML. `<flower></flower>` is just as legitimate as `<p></p>`. The XML document in Listing 20.3 clearly demonstrates both how similar and how different XML and HTML are. XML has tags, just like HTML, but the tags don't describe how the document will look; they describe just its data.

Listing 20.3   This Is a Simple XML Document

```
<plantList name="My List">
    <perennial>
        <variety>Rose</variety>
        <commonName>Zepherine Drouhin</commonName>
        <bloomColor>Deep Pink</bloomColor>
        <light>Part Shade</light>
    </perennial>
    <perennial>
        <variety>Delphineum</variety>
        <commonName>Delphineum Independence</commonName>
        <bloomColor>Deep Blue</bloomColor>
        <light>Sun</light>
    </perennial>
</plantList>
```

"But," I hear you arguing, "how does XML actually do anything if anything can be a tag?" Well, as mentioned earlier, XML doesn't actually define any language. That role is left to you as the developer.

DTDs and XML Schemas

As a developer, you can create what is known as a Document Type Definition (DTD) or XML schema. This scheme is a newer way of defining XML-based languages and was recently ratified by the World Wide Web Consortium (W3C), a web standards body. These documents define the actual tag set for a language. DTDs have their own special format. XML schemas actually use XML to define the tag set.

For example, there are a number of DTDs already in use for defining XML-based languages for news information, music, and DNA proteins. In fact, there is even a new version of HTML, XHTML, which is defined by an XML DTD. One of the biggest XML-based languages right now is the Simple Object Application Protocol (SOAP). SOAP is being defined by a number of major industry leaders and is being designed as a way different programs can share raw data and interoperate. It is also the cornerstone of Microsoft's .NET initiative.

Thus, any programming language that supports XML can easily exchange data with other languages. Both languages simply have to know which DTD or XML schema to use to parse the information. This is where you introduce Flash into the equation. Flash 5 introduced simple XML capabilities into ActionScript. This meant that Flash could be integrated into web applications in a variety of new exciting ways. Lots of web application languages, such as ASP.NET, ColdFusion, and PHP, already support XML. Integrating with these languages is simply a matter of making your Flash movies understand the XML that your server is outputting.

Flash and XML

You don't have to pay a lot of attention to DTDs and schemas. Flash's XML parser is known as nonvalidating, which means that Flash doesn't intrinsically work with actual DTD or XML schema documents. Instead, when Flash receives some XML, you must have code in place that will check the XML and use it appropriately.

XML performance in Flash MX has been dramatically improved. The XML object has become a native object in Flash MX. What does this mean? You will experience a dramatic improvement in performance from the Flash 6 Player when processing XML. With that said, caution should still be in the air. Flash was never meant to handle huge XML documents. There is no documented maximum limit to the size of an XML document that Flash can process safely. It is best practice to be very conservative with data—load only what you need to load. The actual document size that will make Flash choke varies, based on a number of factors, such as platform, CPU speed, how many tags are in the document, and how deeply those tags are nested. Deep documents that have many levels of tags inside each other are much slower to parse than flat documents that have few nested levels.

Now it's time to get into actually using XML with Flash!

Loading and Sending XML

All the XML functionality for Flash MX is encapsulated into two objects, XML and XMLSocket. The XML object is used to load and send XML through HTTP, exactly like you've seen in the `LoadVars()` object mentioned previously in this chapter. The object is also used to manipulate XML. The only difference is the special node processing methods that are required for parsing XML-encoded data. Two great new features in Flash MX are the `getBytesLoaded()` and `getTotalBytes()` functions. You can use these functions to monitor the loading of your file and (though not recommended) the streaming processing of it.

The XMLSocket object is used to send and receive XML over a direct socket connection with a special piece of server software. This is used for real-time two-way communication, but because there are only a few commercial server options for XMLSocket, its use isn't yet common.

Creating XML Objects

You create a new XML object exactly as you did with `LoadVars()`. The statement creates a new variable, myXML, and sets it equal to a blank XML object. All you have to do is type this:

```
myXML = new XML();
```

Acquiring XML into an XML object is done with the XML object's load method:

```
myXML.load("info.xml");
```

This loads a pre-existing XML document into your myXML object.

Loading XML Data

If you use XML much, you'll quickly discover that there are two main types of XML parsers out there: Simple API for XML (SAX) and DOM.

SAX parsers are event-based. This means that as the parser receives XML tags, it lets you know. DOM parsers wait until they have received a full XML document and then turn that document into an object-based data structure. As it happens, Flash's XML parser is

DOM-based, so it can't do anything with your XML until the entire XML document has finished loading. To deal with this, Flash's XML loading mechanisms are asynchronous. In other words, your movie will keep playing while Flash tries to fully load your XML document. After Flash loads the XML, it then parses it into a data structure. When the parsing is complete, the XML object automatically calls its own onLoad method.

Think about that for a minute. You have to wait for the XML to load and get parsed before you can do anything with it. That's latency, and latency is a fact of life when you're capturing data over the Internet. Get used to it, and be prepared to deal with it. You can't use the data that you're uploading until it's available. Consider building a loader animation to stall your application, or load your XML in advance of displaying.

Flash's internal onLoad method for the XML object doesn't actually do anything. That has a tendency to confuse people. The whole point is that you are supposed to override the onLoad event to make it do what you need it to do.

By overriding this method, you can make Flash let you know as soon as it's done loading and parsing an XML document. When Flash calls the onLoad method, it automatically sends as an argument a Boolean value stating whether the XML received was valid. The code to override the onLoad method would look like this:

```
// Create your object
myXML = new XML();
//Create your onLoad function
myXML.onLoad = function(valid){
    If (valid){
        trace("got good XML");
    }else{
        trace("got bad XML");
    }
}
//Load your XML
myXML.load("somexml.xml");
```

As soon as your somexml.xml document is fully loaded, you'll see either "Got good XML" or "Got bad XML" in the output window. That's not particularly useful, but at least you're getting some information.

Exercise 20.2   Overriding the XML Object *onLoad* Function

In this exercise, you'll set up a basic onLoad override. In later sections, you'll build on this, so make sure that you understand this part.

1. Create a new Flash file and save the file to your hard drive.
2. Copy the XML file that you're going to be loading (plantList.xml) to the same directory as your FLA file.

3. You need to create your new XML object now. Rename Layer 1 as **Actions**. Select frame 1, launch the Actions panel, and enter the following code:

```
// create your new XML object
   plantXML = new XML();
```

You can do one of two things now: You can load the XML, or you can write the function to override the internal onLoad event. It doesn't really matter which order you do these in. For this exercise, you start by creating the function that will get called when the XML loads.

4. Beneath the lines of code you just entered, add this:

```
// create your onLoad function
plantXML.onLoad = function(valid) {

      }
```

5. For what do you want to test? If the value of valid evaluates to true, you know that you've got good XML. Otherwise, you have a problem. Set up the appropriate if…else statement with traces so that you can see the outcome in the Output window. Between the curly braces, add the following code:

```
if (valid) {
        trace("Got good XML.");
      }else{
        trace("That's just not right.");
        }
```

6. Now it's time to load your XML. After the last curly brace, enter this:

```
// Load your XML
   plantXML.load("plantList.xml");
```

At this point, your code should look like this:

```
// create your new XML object
plantXML = new XML();
// create your onLoad function
plantXML.onLoad = function(valid) {
    if (valid) {
        trace("Got good XML.");
    }else{
        trace("That's just not right.");
    }
}
// Load your XML
   plantXML.load("plantListStructured.xml");
```

7. Save your work and test it.

If you've entered your code correctly and both the Flash file and the XML file are in the same directory, the Output window should pop up with the message "Got good XML."

So now you know that you're actually receiving XML data through the XML object. What about sending it?

Sending XML Data

To send XML to another application, you use the send or the sendAndLoad methods of the XML object. The only difference between the two is pretty obvious: sendAndLoad sends XML to a URL and expects a response back, while send is a "fire-and-forget" solution. Here's a quick example of send:

```
MyXML.send("/scripts/somescript.cfm");
```

The sticky bit with sending XML to the server comes with the server-side program to which you are sending the XML. This is an issue because the actual send is done through POST, and the MIME type of that POST data is application/x-www-form-urlencoded, which manages to confuse the heck out of many servers because, unlike most POSTs, the ones coming from Flash are not name/value pairs; instead, they are just raw XML. When you are developing the server-side program that will "catch" the XML, keep this in mind because it is the most common source of trouble by far.

At this point, you might be scratching your head. MIME types, POST, URL-encoded—what is all this stuff? Well, MIME is the content type or media type. These are codes that tell the server what to do with specific file types and what information about those file types to send back to the browser. The browser then uses that information to fire up the appropriate helper application.

Each MIME type has two parts: a type and a subtype. The type indicates a general category, such as application, audio, image, text, or video. The subtype further refines what is being sent. The type and subtype are always separated by a slash (/).

Additionally, there is the issue of sending information from Flash through POST, which is what the XML object does. There are two ways to send data back from web browsers to servers: GET and POST. GET sends the information through variables on the URL string. POST sends the variables in a separate HTTP header.

What does this have to do with XML? The original release of the Flash 5 Player always sent a MIME type of application/x-www-form-urlencoded. This is what you commonly use with CGI and ASP.NET scripts; it sends the data as name/value pairs separated by ampersands (&). However, with the XML object in Flash 5, the information returned by the POST isn't in name/value pairs; it's raw XML data. This caused problems with some XML servers.

The Flash 6 Player and the newer release of the Flash 5 Player have a new XML property called `contentType` that enables you to set the MIME type to whatever you need it to be (for example, application/xml). This property holds a string that will be used as the MIME type of any XML sent from that object. The format for the `contentType` property of the XML object looks like this:

```
MyXML.contentType = "application/xml";
```

Okay, let's get back to the loaded XML in your Flash application. If you're loading XML, you'd probably like to know how to use it.

Moving Around with XML

Remember that Flash uses a DOM-based system for working with XML. Under this system, after you have loaded and parsed some XML, you end up with a tree structure. The most common way to manipulate the XML is to walk through the XML tree to see what's there and to extract the relevant information.

Each node in an XML tree is actually an object. This is important! These objects can be either XML elements or text. For example, the structure listed in the following code snippet has five nodes. Three of those nodes are XML elements (`<person>`, `<firstName>`, and `<lastName>`). The remaining two nodes (John and Doe) are text nodes.

When you're stepping though a tree structure to extract information from the nodes, how are you going to know whether you're in an XML element or a text node? Actually, it's easy. The XML object has a property called nodeType. This read-only property can have a value of 1 or 3. A value of 1 tells you that you are inside an XML element (between the brackets). A value of 3 tells you that you're inside a text node.

```
<person>
    <firstName>
        John
    </firstName>
    <lastName>
        Doe
    </lastName>
</person>
```

Is nodeType the only XML property to which you have access? Of course not. However, this would be a good time to stop and take a look at some of the XML object properties that you have access to when you are working with nodes:

- **nodeType.** This read-only property can have a value of 1 or 3. A value of 1 tells you that you are inside an XML element (between the brackets). A value of 3 tells you that you're inside a text node.

- **nodeName.** If you are inside an XML element node, you can use this property to retrieve the element's name.

- **nodeValue.** If you're interested in retrieving the text inside a text node, you look for the nodeValue.

Remember these properties. They'll come in handy in a moment.

Now, picture the previous XML structure graphically represented as a tree. You might have noticed that your tree structure looks just like a family tree. In fact, Flash uses a lot of genealogy terminology, such as parent, child, and sibling, for moving around inside XML trees.

After Flash has loaded and parsed an XML document, the XML object that it was loaded into contains a single link to the new data structure, which is `firstChild`. This property of the XML object points to the root node of the tree. In the previous case, it would point to the <person> node. To find the firstChild for any XML object you have created, you just have to reference `this.firstChild`.

Summary

We've covered a lot in this chapter, but there is a lot to know! You now know enough about the main contenders of the middleware application server market to have an idea of which one might be the best choice for your needs. You also had a chance to review, in detail, two methods for communicating with the server. There is a lot going on—and in three different technologies!

As you understand and get familiar with the dance of exchanging data between Flash and other applications, you will develop your own techniques and best practices.

Developing an application methodology will become increasingly important and will save you time and money in the long term. Consider leveraging a larger development team. There is a clear division in skill sets between a Flash animator and a database administrator (DBA). As your Flash applications grow, it will become more and more important to employ the services of server-side and database developers who understand the idiosyncrasies of middleware technologies.

After you get accustomed to using middleware with Flash, you will have opened up a whole new world of interactive possibilities, including dynamic menuing systems and personalized sites. There's no limit to what you can do. We'll take it up a notch in Chapter 21 as we explore Flash remoting.

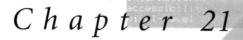

Chapter 21

Flash Remoting

Flash Remoting services provide Flash with
two things it has never had when accessing
external data: simplicity and power. The
Flash Remoting service secures the future
of Flash as a solid environment for web

application development. Combine this service with the Flash user interface (UI) components and form controls and you have a serious contender to HTML/DHTML/JavaScript for deploying highly responsive and rich user interfaces for data management and much more.

In Chapter 20, "Server-Side Communication," you explored two primary ways to import data from remote sources. In this chapter, you are introduced to a third (and probably the most important) way to receive both data and control from a server: the Flash Remoting service. Specifically, the chapter covers the following:

- **Getting started with Flash Remoting services.** Foundations and concepts describing two-way communication between the Flash 6 Player and the server.
- **ColdFusion Components (CFCs).** On the ColdFusion MX Server, CFCs can be consumed by Flash as a web service.
- **Server-side ActionScript.** A familiar language to Flash developers, it enables server-side processing of data, databases, and more.
- **Debugging tools.** Trace errors to their root using the Flash Remoting NetDebugger tools.
- **DataGlue.** Easily construct label and value pairs using returned server data to populate Flash UI components.

Get started with a general overview of the concepts and principles in use with Flash Remoting service. You will review, in detail, the server scripts and the Flash ActionScripts required to employ Flash Remoting service. The exercises walk you through building a simple authentication interface and a simple emailer.

The Flash Remoting Service

The Flash Remoting service is an elegant Flash application program interface (API) that enables server-side developers to connect ActionScript to remote server objects. What does that mean to you? It means that you now can use Flash to exchange data between objects such as recordset objects and Extensible Markup Language (XML) documents. In addition, you can do all this with high performance, security, speed, and reliability.

The Action Messaging Format (AMF) protocol feeds structured data from the application server to the client-side Flash 6 Player. Understanding this process saves you from transforming data into an XML document or into URL-encoded, named-value pairs.

There is a complete elimination of any server-side or Flash-side data transformation, which was required for use in the `loadVariables()` method, the `loadVars()` method, and in XML.

On the Flash side, there are simple methods for accessing data and recordsets generated by the application server. A network-connection debug utility (NetConnect Debugger) is included with the Flash Remoting components. It lets you monitor server-side errors and messaging. Server Side Action Script (SSAS) functionality enables you to use a flavor of ActionScript on the server to build dynamic functions and execute database calls.

Flash Remoting service connects Flash to a server gateway to invoke remote functions from your server or from public or pay-per-use services such as weather or stock services. Remote functions can be used to maintain a user's session state or to send an email message. Gateway services can even be populated into the Action panel in the Flash MX authoring environment.

Traditionally, importing complete data sets was required for efficient runtime results of the Flash Player. This caused a number of problems related to client memory, processor consumption, and download time. Using Flash Remoting services, the Flash Player can make more frequent and lighter-weight calls to the server. These calls request and store data in more efficient small packets, maintaining the integrity of the Flash application. Importing large amounts of data at one time is still an option, but you can also deliver incremental results back to the Flash Player so that you do not keep your customer waiting.

There are six areas covered in this section:

- Creating Flash Remoting services on the ColdFusion application server
- Interacting with Flash Remoting services in ActionScript
- Comparing SSAS with CFCs
- Understanding DataGlue
- Placing your service into the Flash MX ActionScript panel
- Debugging your connection gateway

A good place to start is to check out the available application servers.

Supported Application Servers

Macromedia Flash Remoting service requires three things: the Flash MX authoring environment, the Flash 6 Player, and an application server that supports the Flash Remoting services. Macromedia has created Flash Remoting components for four development platforms:

- Macromedia ColdFusion MX (native functionality)
- Microsoft ASP.NET (downloadable plug-in)
- Macromedia JRUN 4 (native functionality)
- IBM WebSphere (downloadable plug-in)

The functionality comes native in both Macromedia ColdFusion MX and JRUN 4—no additional installation is required. For Microsoft .NET and J2EE application servers, such as IBM WebSphere, implementations of Macromedia Flash Remoting are available from the Macromedia web site.

Flash Web Services

First of all, what is a web service? A web service enables different systems to communicate with each other using Internet protocols. Creating a Flash web service is easy. First, you need to determine the role of your web service and identify the input and output variables required. As an example, consider a web service that authenticates a user with a simple login/password challenge. This service can be consumed by the Flash Player or even by .NET or J2EE applications. This is the beauty and power of a true web service. Interoperability between devices and applications enables you to maintain a common code base for all your applications, regardless of whether they are compatible!

Before you begin to code, first define what's required to run your web service. Because this is an authentication process, you will require at least two variables:

- Login (string)
- Password (string)

When the client (Flash 6 Player) consumes the web service and the required variables are received, the service queries a database and checks whether the login/password combination exists. If the combination is there, the query returns a recordset with the user's data inside:

```
recordset: (FirstName, LastName, EmailAddress)
```

If the login/password combination is not entered correctly or doesn't exist, the query returns an empty recordset.

The client (Flash) can be developed to flow based on a simple recordset count value. For example, if no records were returned, client-side logic (ActionScript) can be used to prompt the user to re-enter the login/password combination again. If a record is returned (because the login/password combination is successful), you could have ActionScript in place that gives access to the secure area.

Flash Remoting Using CFCs

ColdFusion MX has a unique feature set that exposes the entire universe of functionality available to the traditional ColdFusion developer. In Chapter 20, you explored how to access databases and perform some simple server-side commands. The CFC (not to be confused with Flash MX components) enables you to define methods or functions that can be run (invoked) by any number of internal or remote services.

Components in ColdFusion enable developers to expose server-side objects that can be consumed as a Flash web service. Remember that the principal mandate of web services is interoperability. Thus, anything you develop in Exercise 21.1 can be consumed from another ColdFusion MX server, any Flash 6 Player, or any J2EE or .NET application that supports web services.

The CFC is a series of tags that define the component and its methods. `<CFCOMPONENT>` `</CFCOMPONENT>` describes the document as a CFC. Within the structure is a `<CFFUNCTION>` `</CFFUNCTION>` tag set. CFFUNCTION is the method, and it contains any ColdFusion scripts and tags available in the language. A single component can have a number of methods (functions) that can be called from Flash.

Tip

The name of a web service is defined by its filename, less its extension. On the ColdFusion server, you will save this script into a file called myComponent.cfc. It is referenced later in Flash as "myComponent".

Here is a sample of the CFC structure:

```
<CFCOMPONENT>
        <!--- Method 1 --->
        <CFFUNCTION NAME="method1" access="remote" returnType="query">


        </CFFUNCTION>
        <!--- Method 2 --->
        <CFFUNCTION NAME="method2" access="remote" returnType="query">
```

```
        </CFFUNCTION>
        <!--- Method 3 --->
        <CFFUNCTION NAME="method3" access="remote" returnType="query">


        </CFFUNCTION>
</CFCOMPONENT>
```

As you can see, the structure is simple. This example describes three functions, which are called methods inside Flash ActionScript. Each method returns a query result set to the Flash Player. ColdFusion Markup Language (CFML) is placed between the CFFUNCTION tags and is executed when that function is invoked.

Exercise 21.1   Build a Flash Authentication Application Using CFCs

In this exercise, you explore how to consume a CFC as a web service. You will build a simple login/password routine. Flash will interact with the ColdFusion server, which will challenge the login/password data against a database. There are a number of elements to this exercise; you should be familiar with basic ColdFusion and database techniques. (In Chapter 20, you can find more information on databases and ColdFusion database queries.)

For this exercise, you will need to set up a new database, or you can follow the steps for adding the login/password fields to the example Apps database that was installed during your ColdFusion MX install.

1. In your CFUSIONMX folder located where you installed ColdFusion MX, there is a folder called "db." Within that folder, open the Microsoft Access database called "cfexamples.mdb."

2. Right-click the tblEmployees table and choose Design View from the list.

3. At the bottom of the list of fields, you'll add two new fields. To add the first field, click in the first empty cell under the Field Name column and type **Login**.

   Tab to the Data Type field. By default, the data type will be Text. You don't need to change that.

   At the bottom of the window, you'll see a General tab with an entry for Allow Zero Length. Change the value there from No to Yes.

   Repeat your actions for the second field. The only difference will be the contents of the Field Name column, which will be Password.

4. Save and close your table.

5. Double-click the tblEmployees table. This will display all records in the table. Scroll all the way to the right and you'll see the two new fields you just added. Add a login/password to a couple of records. You'll need to remember any login/password combinations that you set so that you can use them later.

6. Close Microsoft Access, saving everything if prompted.

A revised version of this database (cfexamples-new.mdb) is available on the CD. If you would rather use that, copy it into the CFUSIONMX/DB folder, and make sure the file property is not set to read-only. You can check this by right-clicking the file and selecting Properties. If the read-only attribute is checked at the bottom of the dialog window, uncheck it.

Okay, now you are ready to begin constructing your first Flash web service.

Exercise 21.2   Building the Authentication Web Service

The authentication service will take login and password arguments and perform a lookup in the database. If a match is found, it returns the user's data. If no match is found, an empty structure or recordset is returned.

1. In your favorite ColdFusion authoring environment (ColdFusion Studio, Dreamweaver MX, UltraDev, or even BBEdit), set up the basic structure for your CFC with one function (method). Name your function **login**. This is how you will reference it using ActionScript. Set the access parameter to **remote**. This tells ColdFusion that this method will be accessed as a web service. Finally, set the returnType to **query**.

    Enter the following code:

    ```
    <CFCOMPONENT>
                        <!--- Authenticate User method --->
        <CFFUNCTION NAME="login" access="remote" returnType="query">

    <!--- Place the code from the following steps here --->


        </CFFUNCTION>
    </CFCOMPONENT>
    ```

2. Save the file in a folder in your web root called insideFlash. Name the file **myCoolService.cfc**.

3. Next, create the ColdFusion script to authenticate the user. Use a standard database lookup with two filters in your WHERE statement: Login and Password. The code after Step 4 will be placed between the CFFUNCTION tags you created previously.

4. Initialize the argument variables that will be passed from the Flash caller. Note that the CFARGUMENT tag is new to ColdFusion MX. Enter the following code between the opening and closing CFFUNCTION tags:

    ```
    <cfargument name="usrLogin" type="string">
    <cfargument name="usrPassword" type="string">
    ```

5. Build a database query using <CFQUERY> and filter the data using the login and password variables that will be passed from Flash. Wrapping the variables in a

TRIM function will remove any white space that might have been added in transit. Add the following code after the second `CFARGUMENT` tag:

```
<CFQUERY name="getLoginData" Datasource="MyDSN">
  SELECT *
  FROM myTable
  WHERE Login    = '#Trim(usrLogin)#'
         AND Password = '#Trim(usrPassword)#'
</CFQUERY>
```

This query will check all the records in the database and select any record where both the Login and Password match the values being passed in.

6. Use the `<CFRETURN>` tag to send the getLoginData query variable back to the caller (Flash). Enter the following line just after the last line of your query, but before the closing function tag:

```
<CFRETURN getLoginData>
```

7. Save your file. Run your new web service by browsing to it in a normal web browser such as Internet Explorer or Netscape. ColdFusion will generate full documentation on the component, describing its hierarchy, properties, and methods. You will receive full details on each method (function) you have built (see Figure 21.1).

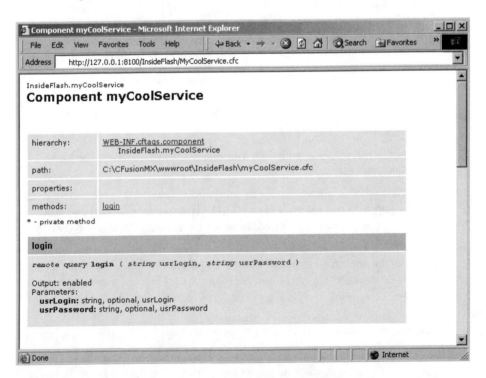

Figure 21.1   Call your CFC in a normal web browser, and ColdFusion will automatically build documentation for the service.

Congratulations, you are now ready to have your CFC consumed as a Flash web service. Keep in mind that while you are ultimately going to use this service for Flash, you can also use it in other ColdFusion MX applications—locally or remotely! Interoperability is the real beauty of the web service mandate.

Your final CFC should look like this:

```
<CFCOMPONENT>
  <!--- Authenticate User method --->
  <CFFUNCTION NAME="login" access="remote" returnType="query">
      <!--- Default Arguments for this method --->
      <cfargument name="usrLogin" type="string">
      <cfargument name="usrPassword" type="string">


      <!--- Do Database Lookup matching Login and Password --->
      <CFQUERY name="getLoginData" Datasource="exampleApps">
        SELECT *
        FROM tblEmployees
        WHERE Login = '#Trim(usrLogin)#'
          AND Password = '#Trim(usrPassword)#'
      </CFQUERY>

<!--- Return Query Set to Caller --->
      <CFRETURN getLoginData>
      </CFFUNCTION>
</CFCOMPONENT>
```

Exercise 21.3   The EMAIL Method

Now you can go one step further and add some additional functionality to your cool web service. This time, you will add a method that will open an email-send service. You'll add to the component you've already started (myCoolService.cfc).

1. First, define what parameters your email method will require to run. At a minimum, it will need these basic email fields:

    - TO (string)
    - FROM (string)
    - SUBJECT (string)
    - MESSAGE (string)

2. The only thing you need to send back to the caller (Flash) is a success or failure notification.

3. Set up a new <CFFUNCTION> just below your first one, but before the closing CFCOMPONENT tag. Give it the name **email**. The other attributes will be the same as you used in your first CFFUNCTION tag.

```
<CFFUNCTION NAME="email" access="remote" returnType="query">
<!--- Place the code from the following steps here --->
</CFFUNCTION>
```

4. Place the following code between the opening and closing CFFUNCTION tags you just created. Your email method will take four arguments, so set them up using the CFARGUMENT tag.

```
<cfargument name="TO" type="string">
<cfargument name="FROM" type="string">
<cfargument name="SUBJECT" type="string">
<cfargument name="MESSAGE" type="string">
```

5. You can use the <CFMAIL></CFMAIL> tag to run the mail command. Below your arguments, add the following:

```
<cfmail to="#TO#" from="#FROM#" subject="#SUBJECT#">
  #MESSAGE#
</cfmail>
```

6. This step is optional. If you skip this step, everything will work, but if you want to create a proper web service, you should trap errors. You can wrap your CFMAIL tag in an if statement to make sure that you don't send any bad email. In this if statement, you are going to do the following:

- Check that the TO, FROM, and MESSAGE fields have values assigned.

- Using a regular expression, you are going to check the TO and FROM email addresses to ensure that they are formatted properly (though not necessarily valid).

Wrap the CFMAIL tag you built in an IF statement. Also, set up two CFRETURN tags for the caller to use to determine success or failure. Use the following code:

```
<!--- Do Field Checks, do not process if failed --->
<CFIF REFindNoCase("[[:alnum:]_\.\-]+@([[:alnum:]_\.\-]+\.)
      ➥+[[:alpha:]]{2,4}",TO) AND
      REFindNoCase("[[:alnum:]_\.\-]+@([[:alnum:]_\.\-]+\.)
      ➥+[[:alpha:]]{2,4}",FROM) AND
      Message neq "">
  <!--- Do Mail Send: Return Success Code --->
  <cfmail to="#TO#" from="#FROM#" subject="#SUBJECT#">
    #MESSAGE#
  </cfmail>
  <CFReturn "SUCCESS">
<CFELSE>
  <!--- ERROR: Do NOT Send: Return Error Code --->
  <CFReturn "ERROR">
</CFIF>
```

7. Save your file.

Run your new web service again in a normal web browser such as Internet Explorer or Netscape. ColdFusion will generate full documentation on the component and you will notice that it is now showing methods and the parameters of those methods (see Figure 21.2).

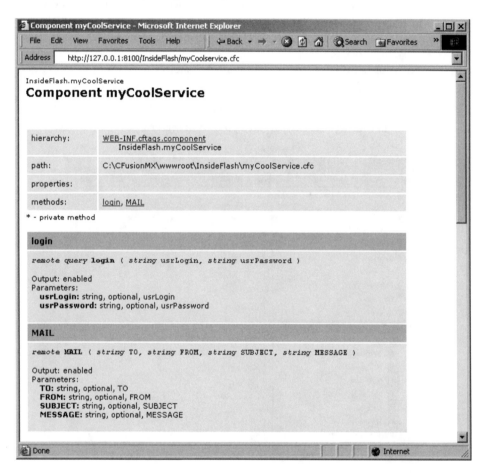

Figure 21.2   Call your CFC in a normal web browser. Notice that the second function is now documented within the same service.

Connecting Gateways in Flash MX

You have explored creating CFCs that are ready to be consumed by Flash as a web service. Now you need to access and interact with those services inside Flash MX. Before you can do this, you need to set up Flash MX with a new extension and become familiar with the new NetConnection commands required to access server objects and documents. The extension, Flash Remoting Components for the Flash MX Authoring Environment, can be found on the Macromedia web site at www.macromedia.com.

After the extension is installed, you will see the new Gateway ActionScript classes available in your ActionScript panel. This set of methods includes the NetServices, NetConnection, NetDebug, DataGlue, and Recordset classes. You will need these classes to begin accessing your web services on the application server (see Figure 21.3).

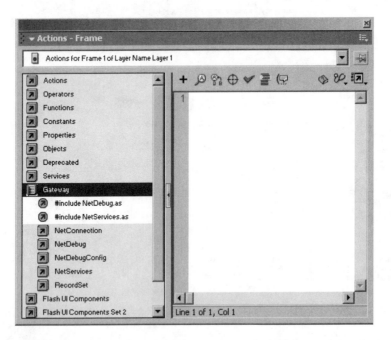

Figure 21.3   This is your Flash MX toolkit for data control and remote access.

- **NetServices.** The NetServices object is a collection of functions that helps you create and use connections to Flash Remoting services that you have created or have access to remotely. NetServices is required to engage the NetConnection objects used to run (invoke) a web service.

- **NetConnection.** The NetConnection object manages a bidirectional connection between the Flash Player and the Flash Remoting service provider. You use these methods to send data to and receive data from a web service.

- **NetDebug.** The NetDebug class enables you to monitor server messaging and data flow in and out of Flash. It is an invaluable addition to the Flash MX feature set.

- **Recordset.** The Recordset object is a client-side object that enables you to interact and manage recordsets returned from a Flash Remoting service provider. Methods are also available to create new recordsets within the Flash Player.

- **DataGlue.** This is a lightweight data binding utility that enables you to construct custom label and value pairs in Flash UI components. For example, you might want to display a person's name in a comboBox, but you also might want to access the person's ID number for database operations.

Making the Connection

Making the connection is easy. There are four steps in total, but the first two steps need to happen only once.

1. Include the Flash Remoting services class files.
2. Connect to the Flash Remoting service provider (your application server).
3. Create service functions and event handlers.
4. Set up your interface.

In Exercise 21.4, you create a Flash movie and include the necessary Flash Remoting services class files.

Exercise 21.4   Including the Flash Remoting Services Class Files

To access Flash Remoting in your movie, you must include a series of class files. These files enable the Flash Remoting components within your Flash movie. You must have these files to access any Flash Remoting function. There are quick references in your ActionScript panel under the Gateway folder.

1. Create a new movie in Flash MX.
2. Position your cursor in frame 1 of Layer 1 and open your ActionScript panel (Window > Actions).

3. Expand the Gateway category in the tool list and double-click once on each of the two include functions (`#include NetBug.as` and `#includeNetServices.as`) to add them to your Actions list (see Figure 21.4). Both files are required to perform any Flash Remoting services activities.

```
// Include the Required NetService class files
#include "NetDebug.as"
#include "NetServices.as"
```

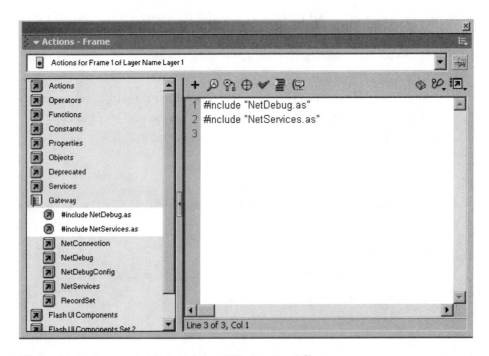

Figure 21.4   Include the NetDebug.as and NetServices.as files.

 Tip

When you are finished with your application, remove NetDebug.as. Including it adds unnecessary weight to the final Flash SWF movie.

If you are curious where these files exist, they were installed in the Install directory of Flash MX when you added the Flash Remoting extensions. When publishing a Flash movie, Flash MX first looks in the local directory of the FLA file, and then it looks in the Include directory located in the Install folder of Flash MX.

In Exercise 21.5, you connect your Flash movie to the ColdFusion application server.

Exercise 21.5   Connecting to the Flash Remoting Services Provider (Your Application Server)

Making the connection to your web service is easy. There are three things you need to do:

1. First, set up a conditional statement that will ensure that you connect to this service only once. While this is not a critical component, it is good coding practice. If this script for some reason finds itself in a loop, it might have a detrimental effect on your application server. To avoid having this happen, you can have your code check a variable for a null (empty) value. If there is nothing in the variable, you know that the connection has not been made and that your script will continue to make the connection and set the variable to true; thus, it won't be run again (by accident). If there is a value, your code skips the step. For this exercise, you use the variable isGatewayOpen. Below the two includes you added in Exercise 21.4, add the following code:

   ```
   if (isGatewayOpen == null) {
       // do this code only once
       isGatewayOpen = true;
         // Connection Code will go here
       }
   ```

2. Next, you must set the default connection to your web service provider and make the connection. This is done using two special methods from the NetServices class. The first is NetServices.setDefaultGatewayURL, which tells the Flash Player where the service is located. The second is NetServices.createGatewayConnection, which opens the connection to the server. Substitute the server name in the following code with your development server name. Enter the code after the isGatewayOpen = true line, but before the closing curly brace:

   ```
   NetServices.setDefaultGatewayUrl("http://127.0.0.1:8100/
   ➥flashservices/gateway");
   gatewayConnnection = NetServices.createGatewayConnection();
   ```

   It is important to note that the mapping "/flashservices/gateway" *is not* a folder located on the server. Referencing this structure *enables* the Flash Remoting services on the Application server. The /flashservices/gateway is mapped in most servers to the web root folder.

Tip

The default gatewayURL can also be set in a PARAM tag inside the embed tag within the HTML source on the host page, as shown in the following code:

```
<PARAM NAME=flashvars VALUE="gatewayURL=http://127.0.0.1:8100/
flashservices/gateway >
```

3. When your gateway has been set up and opened, you need to consume the Flash web service (in our example, this is your CFC). You do this by using the getService method. The method takes two parameters: the service name and the object that will receive it. The following code goes right beneath the code you just added and before the closing curly brace:

```
myCoolService= gatewayConnnection.getService
➥("insideFlash.myCoolService", this);
```

4. Create a folder called **insideFlash** on your web server root and save your Flash MX file as **flashConnection.fla**.

The Flash name you give the service connection will be what you will use to reference the functions or methods within the service. Using your previous example, you will call the myCoolService.cfc file that you created. This file is located in the folder insideFlash within the web root on the server. This file and its location are combined to form the name of the service. Your file structure now looks like this:

```
C:\ColdFusionMX\wwwroot\insideFlash\myCoolService.cfc
```

The web server root and the Flash gateway are mapped to C:\CFusionMX\ wwwroot\. Your service name is insideFlash.myCoolService.

You can connect to as many services as you need, but you should initialize them in one location to keep your code clean.

Your ActionScript in frame 1 of Layer 1 should now look like this:

```
// Include the Required NetService class files
#include "NetDebug.as"
#include "NetServices.as"

// connect to the Flash Remoting service provider
if (isGatewayOpen == null) {
 // do this code only once
 isGatewayOpen = true;

 NetServices.setDefaultGatewayUrl("http://127.0.0.1:8100/flashservices/
➥gateway");
 gatewayConnnection = NetServices.createGatewayConnection();

// connect to the Flash Remoting service providers
 myCoolService= gatewayConnnection.getService("insideFlash.
➥myCoolService ", this);
 }
```

So now you've got your connection set up. What needs to happen next? You need to call the functions you set up in your web service.

Creating Service Functions and Event Handlers

Your next step in this process is to call the functions (or methods) you have set up in your web service. These functions will be referred to as service functions from this point on.

Your web service has two functions that you are going to call, but you don't need to call them until the user has triggered them inside Flash. Thus, you need to build a Flash interface to facilitate the command. In Exercise 21.6, you'll continue working with the flashConnection.fla file that you created in Exercise 21.5.

Exercise 21.6   Building the Login Interface

1. Your first service function is an authentication method, so you need to build a login and password screen in Flash MX.

    In the flashConnection.fla file, add a new layer and drag it to the bottom of the layer stack. Name it **Input Fields**.

    Select the Text tool and in the Properties Inspector, change the Text type to Input Text.

    Draw two input text fields on the Stage using the Text tool. Set the property of each text field to Dynamic Text. Drag a PushButton component from the UI Components Library onto the Stage and place it beneath the input fields (see Figure 21.5).

2. Set the variable name of one input text box to **_root.usrLogin**, as shown in Figure 21.6.

3. Set the variable name of the second input box to **_root.usrPassword**.

4. In the properties of the Button component, change the Label name to **Continue** and change the Click Handler name to **authenticate**. You'll build the authenticate function in Flash in the next step. When the user clicks the Continue button, Flash runs the LOGIN service function, sending the login and password data.

    Now that you have an interface for your login function, you need to make the call to your server to run the user's login and password against the database. This is called "consuming a web service." As mentioned, you will be encapsulating this into a function called "authenticate" that is triggered when the user clicks the CONTINUE button on the interface.

5. Select frame 1 in Layer 1 and open the Actions panel. Place your cursor below the last line of code and begin to define your function. Create a new function called "authenticate". Enter the following code:

```
function Authenticate() {
    // This function will be run when the Continue button is
    ➡pressed

}
```

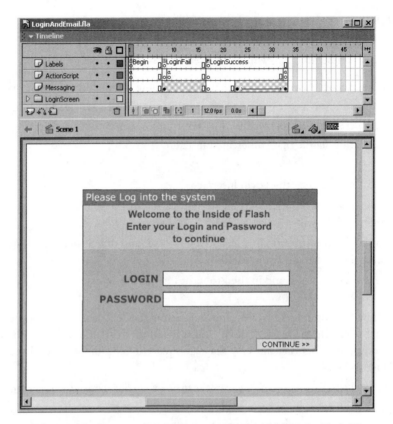

Figure 21.5   The login and password should contain two text fields and a Flash UI PushButton component.

Figure 21.6   Set the Var property of the text fields.

6. Within this function, you are going to run the "login" service function. Remember that this service takes two arguments (usrLogin and usrPassword). You will send those variables just as you would a normal function. The login and password data is stored in _root.usrLogin and _root.usrPassword, respectively.

```
myCoolService.Login(_root.usrLogin,_root.usrPassword);
```

7. The authenticate function should look like this when you are finished:

```
function Authenticate() {
   // This function will be invoked with the Continue button is
   pressed
   myCoolService.Login(_root.usrLogin,_root.usrPassword);
   }
```

The Default Responder for the Login Service Function

When the authenticate function is invoked, your server will be engaged, and it will begin processing the data you sent it. After it has finished processing, you can expect the server to return a query result set to Flash. If a record is returned, the user has logged in successfully. If the query result set is empty, you know that the login and password are in error, and you should prompt the user to try again. This challenge will be done within the Flash Player.

So how do you know when the server has completed its process? The server will automatically invoke an event handler when it has finished and returned the results. There are two event handlers that you need to set up in Flash: one object processes the results (onResult) and one traps any errors (onStatus). These are also referred to as default responders.

Your first event handler will set up the processes required when the server has completed. The tasks include the following:

- Determining if the login and password entered are correct
- Providing access to the private area of Flash
- Informing the user that his or her login and password are incorrect and to re-enter them

Building the *onResult* Event Handler

Service function event handler names have special naming requirements. To identify the onResult event handler for our login function, we will name it Login_result. Thus, our onStatus event handler will be called Login_status.

The syntax for these two handlers is the service function name followed by either _Result or _Status. If these functions do not exist, the server will not invoke them, and the data returned will be inaccessible.

A typical default responder will look like this:

```
function functionName_Result (result) {
   /*ActionScript to manage the data
      and control objects or the timeline. */
   }
```

Exercise 21.7   Building the Default Responder

In this exercise, you create a default responder that will be invoked to handle the returns from the service function, which is named Login. This function is responsible for determining if the user's login and password are correct. It takes one action if it is and a different action if it is not. It will perform the actions by interacting with the data object returned from ColdFusion.

1. Position the cursor below your authenticate function, and create the function that will wrap your process. Place a variable name (result) inside the function's brackets. The variable name can be anything; it doesn't need to be "result". This is simply the local function object to which the data will be returned. Access this object for the server's resultset. Add the following code:

```
function Login_Result (result) {
    /* This function will be invoked by the server when
       it has finished processing */
   }
```

2. Now you need to make the data in the resultset available for your Flash movie to use. You can do that by passing the result (which is an object) into another object on the main Timeline. Enter the following code between the curly braces of your function:

```
/* transfer the resultset into a _root-level object */
_root.userData = result;
```

3. Use a conditional statement (if) to challenge the returned data from the server to determine if the login/password combination was correct. If the server returns 0 records, the login/password combination is wrong. If it returns 1 record, the login/password combination is correct. Use standard movie controls to move the playhead to a LoginSuccess/LoginFail frame label. Add the following code beneath the last line you entered, but before the curly brace:

```
/* challange the rowCount to determine success/failure */
  if (result.getLength()== 1) {   //Success
    _root.gotoAndPlay("LoginSuccess");
    _root.cFirstName=result.items[0].FirstName;
    _root.cTitle=result.items[0].Title;
     }

  else{ // Fail
    _root.gotoAndPlay("LoginFail");
     }
```

The complete code for the login_Result function should look like this (see Figure 21.7):

```
function login_Result(result) {
  /* This function will be invoked by the
     server when it has finished processing */

  /* transfer the resultset into a _root-level object */
  _root.userData = result;

  /* challange the rowCount to determine success/failure */
  if (result.getLength()== 1) {   //Success
    _root.gotoAndPlay("LoginSuccess");
    _root.cFirstName=result.items[0].FirstName;
    _root.cTitle=result.items[0].Title;
      }

  else{ // Fail
    _root.gotoAndPlay("LoginFail");
      }
}
```

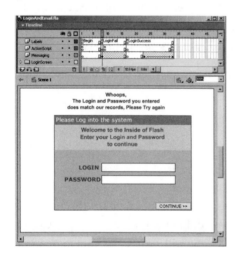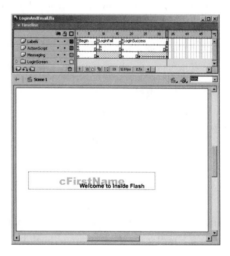

Figure 21.7   If the playhead lands on the frame "LoginFail" (left), it will look different then if it lands on "LoginSuccess" (right).

If the login/password combination entered was correct, you want to access the columns returned from the service function so that you can retrieve the user's first name and job title. This is one of the most important methods to understand, and it is extremely simple to use, as compared to traditional XML parsing.

You can access data *without* doing any transformation or parsing on it at all. In the previous example, you were able to access the values of the columns by directly accessing the column names. Here's how it worked:

```
_root.cFirstName=result.items[0].FirstName;
[local variable]=[resultset][row].[columnName];
```

Pretty simple, huh? Essentially, you are populating a variable outside the function with the results of (in this case) the first row returned (row 0). This process is very powerful, and it is much more reliable and less complex then the traditional ways to manage data within Flash.

By moving the resultset object out of the function, you can access the recordset whenever you like. In this case, you moved the data into an object called `_root.UserData`.

Building a Flash Mailer Using Web Services

Let's do one more example utilizing your email web service. You will create a simple email interface and send that data to the web service for execution. You will see how easy it is to leverage the powerful server-side functionality that is new to the Flash 6 Player.

In Flash MX, develop a simple email interface that includes the following input fields (see Figure 21.8):

- **TO.** _root.emailTO
- **FROM.** _root.emailFROM
- **SUBJECT.** _root.emailSUBJECT
- **MESSAGE.** _root.emailMESSAGE

Include a Flash MX component button, just as you did in the previous example. Create a click handler for the button and call it `emailSend`. You will create a function to respond to this handler (see Figure 21.9).

Figure 21.8   Your email form should look like this.

Figure 21.9   Add the click handler emailSend to the PushButton component.

Once again, set up two ActionScript functions. The first one will be used for the Send button to invoke your web service. The second function will be the event handler for the server when it has completed processing. This web service will not return a result set, just a success or fail notification that you will challenge with an if statement.

```
function emailSend() {
  Trace("sent");
  /* This function will be invoked when? the Continue button is pressed
  ➥*/
myCoolService.mail(_root.emailTO,_root.emailFROM,_root.emailSUBJECT,
➥_root.emailMESSAGE);
  }
```

```
function mail_Result(result) {
  trace("server response");
  /* This function will be invoked by the
     server when it has finished processing */

  if (result == "success") {   //Success
    _root.gotoAndPlay("EmailSuccess");
    }
  else { // Fail
    _root.gotoAndPlay("EmailFail");
    }
}
```

SSAS

For those of you who are not versed in ColdFusion, there is yet another way to leverage the power of an application server. Flash Remoting on ColdFusion MX has been extended with the ability to provide SSAS. SSAS is available only if you are using the ColdFusion MX application server.

What is SSAS? SSAS, in concept, is very similar to using CFCs, except it leverages a more familiar development language for Flash developers who don't know ColdFusion—that's right…ActionScript.

Note that you do not use any ColdFusion tags on the server side—not one, honest. SSAS includes two additional functions that are not available in Flash MX. The CF.query function enables you to access a ColdFusion data source and return results to Flash. The CF.http function executes an HTTP POST or GET operation on local or remote files. POST operations enable you to upload MIME file types to your server or post other data types (such as cookie, form field, URL, file, or CGI variables) directly to a server.

Take a moment to compare two code listings. Listing 21.1 is the authentication script you used previously. Listing 21.2 is the same functionality written using SSAS.

Listing 21.1   Server-Side Authentication Script Using CFCs

```
<CFCOMPONENT>
  <!--- Authenticate User method --->
  <CFFUNCTION NAME="login" access="remote" returnType="query">
      <!--- Default Arguments for this method --->
      <cfargument name="usrLogin" type="string">
      <cfargument name="usrPassword" type="string">


      <!--- Do Database Lookup matching Login and Password --->
      <CFQUERY name="getLoginData" Datasource="exampleApps">
        SELECT *
        FROM tblEmployees
        WHERE Login = '#Trim(usrLogin)#'
          AND Password = '#Trim(usrPassword)#'
      </CFQUERY>

<!--- Return Query Set to Caller --->
      <CFRETURN getLoginData>
      </CFFUNCTION>
</CFCOMPONENT>
```

Listing 21.2   Server-Side Authentication Script Using SSAS

```
function login(usrLogin,usrPassword) {
  theSQL="SELECT * FROM tblEmployees WHERE Login = '#Trim(usrLogin)#'
AND Password = '#Trim(usrPassword)#'";

  getLoginData=CF.query({datasource:"exampleApps", sql:theSQL});

  return getLoginData
}
```

This SSAS file exists on the ColdFusion MX server as login.asr. The .asr extension is a new extension in ColdFusion MX and will be parsed using the modified SSAS engine.

DataGlue

DataGlue is a Flash Remoting feature that enables you to *manually construct or format* the label and value data for Flash UI components such as ListBox or ComboBox. This is called "binding data" to a data consumer (the data consumer is the UI component that will receive and display the data).

As you know, both UI components are very similar to the HTML <SELECT> form control. Because Flash Remoting makes it easier to frequently interact with the server, you will want to transfer as little data as possible each time you connect. DataGlue helps ensure that your application server and Flash Player can run efficiently and quickly.

Consider this example: Let's say you have a database of employees. Your application server is responsible for controlling the database and storing and retrieving the data. Due to uncontrollable limitations of bandwidth, CPU, and security on the remote computer, you don't want to send every piece of data about every user into Flash unnecessarily. Your strategy should be to send the Flash Player only what it needs and no more. In this case, the first and last name of the person and a unique ID that will identify that person with a record in the database is all that is required.

You want your user to access the data by referencing a first and last name combination in a scrolling ListBox. When an employee's name is selected by the user, you want Flash to access and send that unique ID number to the ColdFusion server. ColdFusion will match the ID in the database very quickly and return the full record of the selected employee. To do this, you need to format the label of the ListBox to display "FirstName Lastname" and then to bind the data to the ListBox's label. The ID number will be stored in the Value property and that is what Flash will access when the user selects the associated label (Name).

This is different then just using the .setDataProvider(result) property because you have no control over what the user sees and what the script sees. Using DataGlue, you are given more control over the data in your UI component.

Let's look at some code:

```
// Include the Required NetService class files
#include "NetDebug.as"
#include "NetServices.as"
#include "DataGlue.as"
```

You will first need to include the DataGlue.as class file into your Flash movie. You insert it below the NetDebug.as and NetServices.as includes at the top of your script. If you do not plan to use the DataGlue feature, you should not include the class file because it will increase your Flash movie (SWF) file size.

This gives you access to two additional ActionScript methods:

- **DataGlue.bindFormatStrings()**. Manually format or construct the label and value pair for a list or combo box on the Flash Stage.
- **DataGlue.bindFormatFunction()**. Use a custom function to process your data before binding it to the label and value pair.

These two methods can be used in the default responder of your service function. For example, if you are calling a service in your CFC called "getData," you would include the DataGlue methods in the result function, as shown in the following code:

```
getData_result(result){actions to perform}
```

Let's assume that you have made your service call and that you have a recordset returned from your database. Let's take a closer look at both methods and how you would use them.

Binding Formatted Strings

You have to massage the data with which you want the user to interact. For our example, you have a recordset that contains three columns: FirstName, LastName, and EmployeeID. You want to display *both* the FirstName and the LastName in the UI component (data consumer). Using regular methods, you would normally do this using the .SetDataProvider() property of the component:

```
getData_result(result){
     myListBox.setDataProvider(result);
 }
```

The problem is that this will populate all three columns in both the Label and the Value of the component. So, the user would see something like this: Towes, Kevin, 28.

Although this is Okay, the EmployeeID "28" really has no relevance to the user. It would be better to display the data like this: "Towes, Kevin" or "Kevin Towes".

By using the .SetDataProvider, you are bound to the sequence of the columns returned from your service function. This is where DataGlue comes in. Using the DataGlue object, you can retain control over your data. Here is an example of the same default responder populating the data consumer (myListBox) using DataGlue binding:

```
getData_result(result){
        DataGlue.bindFormatStrings(myListBox,result,"#FirstName#
#LastName#","#EmployeeID#");
 }
```

What the script does is this:

1. Identify the data consumer. myListBox is a Flash ListBox UI component.

2. Identify the resultset returned from the service function. In this case, it is result.

3. Format the label of the ListBox. This is what the user will see. #FirstName# #LastName# will display the FirstName and LastName columns separated by a space. You can embed any characters within the quotations. A common use would be if you were displaying a list of products from your store, and you wanted to display the price of the product in the label. You would write this: #ProductName# price: $#price#.

4. Format the Value data as #EmployeeID#. This will not be seen by the user, but it is accessible through ActionScript by using the .getValue() function.

    MyListBox.getValue(); will contain the EmployeeID number of the selected label. The syntax for this function is this:

    ```
    DataGlue.bindFormatStrings([data consumer],[recordset],"[label
    ➥data]","[value data");
    ```

There is another way to achieve similar results, with even more control, using custom functions in place of formatting. To do this, you use binding Format Functions.

Binding Format Functions

Binding Format Functions give you additional flexibility to massage and format your data before binding it to the data consumer. A Format Function is a custom function (that you build) that takes a resultset as a parameter and returns an ActionScript object with two fields: the Label and the Value. Here's a sample:

```
getData_result(result){
        DataGlue.bindFormatFunction(myListBox,result,myFormatFunction);
 }
```

This script calls the custom function myFormatFunction and automatically sends the resultset stored in result as a parameter. Let's look at the myFormatFunction() custom function:

```
function myFormatFunction(result) {
/* make the firstname and lastname uppercase
   and combine them with a space separating them */
      myLabel= result.FirstName.toUpperCase(); + ' ' +
      ↳result.LastName.toUpperCase();

/* this simply transfers the employeeID data into the myData Var
   you can do any formatting you need to the value data */
      myData = result.EmployeeID;

// return the label and value pair to the caller
return {label: myLabel, data: myData};
}
```

DataGlue is a great feature of Flash Remoting, and it provides that extra control you need to build efficient and user-friendly form controls using the Flash UI components.

Putting Your Services in the Flash MX ActionScript Panel

Excited yet? It gets better. Flash Remoting enables you to place your web services directly in the Flash MX ActionScript panel (see Figure 21.10). You do this by using the Service Browser component installed when you added the Flash Remoting components to Flash MX.

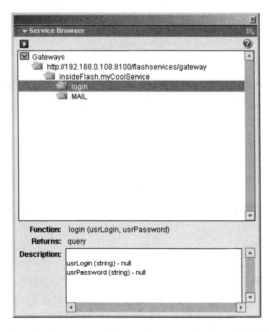

Figure 21.10   The Service Browser enables you to see methods available from ColdFusion.

You can add the methods exposed in the Flash web service to the Flash MX ActionScript panel. This feature also automatically adds the Code Hint so that your Flash developers know what input variables are required to invoke the service. This is useful if you practice code reuse or have large teams working on Flash applications. It enables you to take advantage of Flash web services easily and quickly. Here's how to go about it:

1. The Service Browser lets you connect and get descriptions for Flash web services. To open the Service Browser, select Window > Service Browser.

   First you have to add your service; then you add your service to the Actions panel.

2. In the Service Browser window, select the gateway and click the white triangle in the blue square in the upper-left corner of the Service Browser to get an Options menu.

3. Select Add Service. In the panel that opens, type the name of the folder you set up for your service on the web root, type a period, and then type the service name.

4. For the service that you just created, type the following:

   ```
   insideFlash.myCoolService
   ```

5. Click the Add Service button. If you entered the name of a valid service, you'll return to the main Service Browser page and you'll see the service and the methods you created in that service.

   If the service you entered doesn't exist, you'll get a message that says the following: "Service threw an Exception during method invocation: No service named *xxx* is known to the Gateway."

6. Click Done and remove the bogus service from the listing by selecting it and then choosing Remove Service from the menu. Go back to your web root and check the name of the folder and your Flash service again.

7. To actually add the service to the Actions panel, select the service in the Service Browser and select "Add Service to Actions Panel." Now open your Actions panel and check the Tool list.

There it is, in the Services category, right under the gateway. Now you can just double-click your email or login methods to use them in another Flash project.

The NetConnect Debugger

Debugging your Flash application when using Flash Remoting is made much easier with the NetConnect Debugger. This extension to Flash MX is available from the Window menu within Flash MX only after you have installed the Flash Remoting components. Its purpose? To make your life much easier. Each time the Flash Player calls the Flash gateway server, you can see what is happening. Watch variables and messages being passed between the Flash Player and the server.

You can monitor everything—the header, the time it takes, the arrays it returns, and where the call was coming from. All you have to do is ensure that you have the Debug class loaded and then this thing will light up! To be able to use the Debugger, you just have to make sure that you include the NetDebug.as file in your project (see Figure 21.11):

```
#include "NetDebug.as"
```

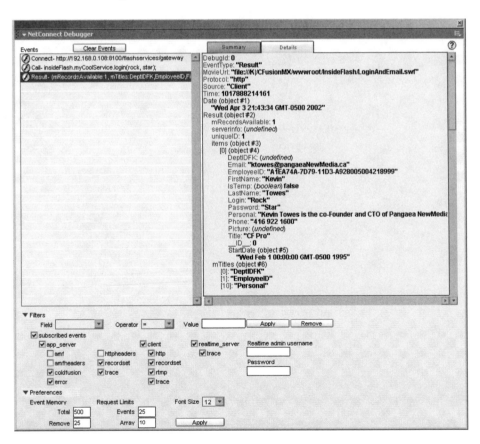

Figure 21.11   The NetConnect Debugger is available after you install the Flash Remoting components. It enables you to monitor the server communication for the Flash gateway only.

To open the Debugger, select Window > NetConnect Debugger. If you have the Debugger open when you test your movie, you'll see the events pop up as they occur. To get more information about an event, select it in the Events list. You'll see the name of the service that was called, along with other information, such as parameters, on the Summary tab. For more information, click the Detail tab.

This Debugger is a chapter unto itself, so we will leave our introduction as is.

Summary

So now you know one of the most powerful tools in Flash MX. There is a lot more you can do with Flash Remoting, perhaps enough for another book! You have just scratched the surface here. It is easy to say that you can expose any function of an application server to Flash with very little effort and with more reliability then ever before.

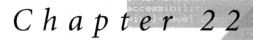

Chapter 22

Communicating with the Host Application

You've spent some time looking at how to

manipulate variables inside Flash. You've

even pulled information from outside

Flash, in the form of text files, into Flash to

help you control your movie. But what if

you want Flash to talk to your browser, or your browser to talk to Flash? What if you want to use JavaScript in the browser to control a Flash movie? Is it possible? Yes, it is. This chapter, along with Chapter 20, "Server-Side Communication," gives a solid background in how to communicate between Flash and other applications.

In this chapter, you'll look at these topics:

- **The `loadVariables()` action.** Use this to load variables from a text file or a server-side script behind the scenes.
- **The `getURL()` action.** Use this to load a new page and call JavaScript functions.
- **The `FSCommand()` action.** Use this to call functions and control the properties of the Standalone Player.
- **Flash methods of the `OBJECT` and `EMBED` tags.** Use these to let the browser communicate with Flash.
- **Macromedia JavaScript Integration Kit.** Use this with Flash and Dreamweaver.

Before getting into the specifics of *how* Flash communicates with other applications, however, take a moment to consider why you would want to communicate in the first place.

Using Flash Actions to Communicate with the Host Application

The first and most important question to ask is why you want Flash to communicate with another application—in this case, the browser. The answer is that if you can talk to the browser and the scripting languages supported by the browser, you can start to do some very cool things. For example, you can open and close additional windows and control the appearance of those windows. You can also set client-side cookies—so you can store information on your user's computer to help you remember them and then personalize your site for them. If you can talk to the browser, then you also have access to any JavaScript or VBScript functions on that page.

You can use three Flash actions to communicate with whatever application your Flash movie is embedded in. In fact, these actions work only in conjunction with an outside application:

- `loadVariables()`
- `getURL()`
- `FSCommand()`

The obvious host application for most Flash movies is the browser, but SWFs can also be played in a standalone player. Both of these possibilities will be explored in detail later. Additionally, the Flash plug-in has a number of special functions that can be called directly by JavaScript.

loadVariables()

You've already used `loadVariables()` several times to load variables from text files into Flash. You can also use `loadVariables()` to load variables from a variety of other sources, such as a CGI script, a ColdFusion (CFM) file, a JavaServer Pages (JSP) file, a PHP: Hypertext Preprocessor (PHP) file, or any other kind of server-side script. The only caveat with using `loadVariables()` to get external data is that the data must be provided in name/value pairs. That's what Flash understands, so you need to make sure that any script that is retrieving that information for you outputs it in the proper format.

Not only can Flash use `loadVariables()` to receive information, but it also can send information to these external applications.

The work of `loadVariables()` happens behind the scenes. You don't actually see anything happen until Flash or the receiving page processes the variables that were retrieved or sent. In the case of sending variables, you might not see anything happen in the Flash movie at all. Much of this is dealt with in Chapter 20.

getURL()

Similar to `loadVariables()`, you can use `getURL()` to pass variables to a server-side script, to load a new page, or open a new browser window, and even to call a scripted function inside the current HTML page. Calling a server-side script is covered in more detail in Chapter 20.

Using `getURL()` to load a new page is the simplest and most straightforward use of `getURL()`. The syntax for the `getURL()` action is as follows:

```
getURL("URL", "target", "send method");
```

Only the first argument, the URL that you are loading, is required. You can use the second argument to specify the location of the page to be loaded. You can use one of the standard reserved HTML frame target names (`_self`, `_blank`, `_parent`, and `_top`). Or, if you want to load to an existing HTML frame or window, you can specify its name. In addition to retrieving the new web page, you can send variables from your Flash movie to that page. The third option specifies how you would like to send those variables, with either GET or POST. When you do this, Flash simply harvests all the variables in the current Timeline (see Figure 22.1) and sends them—for example:

```
getURL ("http://www.figleaf.com", "_blank", "GET");
```

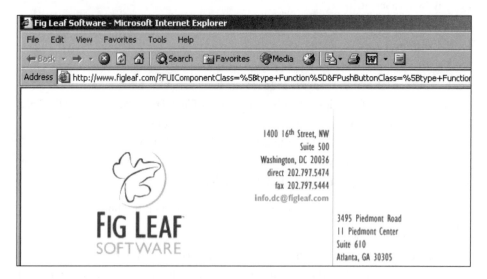

Figure 22.1   When you use the getURL() action with the method set to GET or POST, Flash harvests all the variables on the main Timeline and sends them to the page that you specify the URL for.

This code loads the Fig Leaf web site in a new window. Any variables in the current Timeline are sent to the Fig Leaf page via GET. Using the HTTP GET method will append all of the variables gathered from the movie's Timeline to the URL. This amendment to the URL will be visible in the address bar of the browser unless the address bar is hidden or the targeted frame is other than a top-level frame. Using the HTTP POST method will send the variables to the URL as part of a multi-part HTTP request and thus will not be visible.

Note

You cannot always do a POST to a web page. Most web servers will not allow you to POST to an HTML document and will throw an HTTP 405 error.

This is important to remember when you are allowing the web server to determine the default document as is the case in the getURL() snippet above. The default document might be an HTML document or an application server template like ColdFusion (as used to be the case for Fig Leaf). Simply changing the third argument, the method, in the snippet above will surface this error in the browser.

But wait—there's more. In the previous example, using getURL() doesn't give you any control over the window that you open. You can get around that by using getURL() to call a JavaScript function on the HTML page. But before you can go down that road, you need to understand a little bit about the Document Object Model (DOM) and how you can actually talk to the browser.

The Document Object Model

The Document Object Model (DOM) specifies the different objects in a web page and how those objects can be manipulated. Of course, in addition to the standardized DOM put forth by the W3C (www.w3.org/DOM/DOMTR), the DOM implementations for Internet Explorer and Netscape each made slight adjustments. Though, in all cases, the basic idea is that each page is composed of a series of objects. Each object has its own elements and attributes. For example, the browser window itself is considered an object that can have a predefined set of attributes that control its height, width, position, and so on. Forms are also objects.

Just as embedded Flash movie clips have a hierarchical structure, the DOM has a hierarchical structure. The root of the DOM is the window object, which you refer to using this line:

```
window
```

This is essentially equivalent to _root in a Flash movie. Beneath the window object in the hierarchy is the document object. The document object contains all the elements of the web page, including, but not limited to, the form, image, and link objects, as well as all of the objects that can be in a form. Just as you name movie clips in Flash, you can name different windows, forms, images, and so on. You also can refer to an element on a page by either its name or its index number (references to objects are held in the objects array). So, for example, if you have two forms on your page, FormA and FormB, to access FormA you can refer to either of these:

```
window.document.form[0]
```

```
window.document.formA
```

Also like the Flash objects, the different objects have methods that you can use to access attributes and properties.

Obviously, there is much more to the DOM than this brief description. As long as you understand the basics, though, you'll find it very easy to work with, especially if you're already accustomed to using dot and array syntax in Flash.

Now you'll take a look at how you can use Flash's getURL(), together with a call to a JavaScript function in the browser window.

Using *getURL()* to Call a JavaScript Function

Now that you've had a basic introduction to the concepts of the DOM, it's time to put that new information to use. One of the simplest JavaScript functions that you can set up is a function that will open and size a new window. The function to handle this must exist inside the HTML page, so you need to find a way for Flash to communicate with the browser page it's embedded in. You can do this with either the getURL() or FSCommand() actions. For now, you'll use getURL(); you'll explore the FSCommand() action later in this chapter.

To call a JavaScript function from Flash, you use this syntax:

```
getURL("javascript:functionName(variable1,variable2,variable3)");
```

Here, functionName() is the name of a function that is in the HTML page in which the Flash movie is embedded; the variables are the parameters that you pass into the function.

The window object has a method called open() that you can use to open the window and control its appearance. You have access to a number of attributes. All these attributes, with the exception of width and height, are Boolean values and default to True. The attributes that you'll use most often that are part of both the IE and Netscape DOMs are listed here:

- **toolbar.** The buttons at the top of the browser window (Back, Forward, Stop, and so on). Set to no to hide.

- **location.** The input field that displays the current URL. Set to no to hide.

- **status.** The bar at the bottom of the window that displays the status. Set to no to hide.

- **menubar.** The text menu bar at the top of the window. Note that you can't control this on a Mac because, on Macs, the menu bar isn't part of the browser window. Set to no to hide.

- **scrollbars.** Shows scrollbars if the document is larger than the window. Set to no to disable.

- **resizable.** Allows you to resize the window. Set to no to disable.

- **width.** Gives the width of the window, in pixels.

- **height.** Gives the height of the window, in pixels.

In Exercise 22.1, you'll use getURL() to call a JavaScript function and open a new browser window with specific dimensions.

Exercise 22.1   Opening New Browser Windows

You'll begin by creating a Flash movie and publishing it. Then you'll open the HTML page created and add the JavaScript function that you want to call to it.

1. Create a new Flash movie.

2. Drag a button from the Flash UI Components panel onto the Stage (Window > Components). Make the following changes to the button's properties on the Properties panel (Window > Properties):

   Instance Name: **launch_btn**
   Label: **Launch**
   Click Handler: **launch**

3. Select the Stage and launch the Actions panel. Create a function called launch to handle the mouse click event for the button:

```
function launch()
{

}
```

4. Next, you'll set up a series of variables that will hold the information that you want to pass to the JavaScript function on the HTML page. In this case, you'll be passing in the URL of the page to load, the name that you'll be assigning the window, and the settings that you want to control.

   You could just pass the values directly into the getURL() action that you'll be setting up, but passing the values into variables makes things a little more readable.

   Enter the following code between the curly braces:

```
url = "http://www.figleaf.com/";
windowName = "myWindow";
settings = "toolbar=no,location=no,status=no,menubar=no,
➥scrollbars=no,resizable=no,width=600,height=400";
```

   You'll be sending your visitor to the Fig Leaf web site, which will open in a 600 × 400 pixel window with no tool, menu, or status bars—and it won't be resizable.

5. To make the actual call to the function using getURL(), all you have to do is add this line of code before the last curly brace:

```
getURL("javascript:openWindow('"+url+"','"+windowName+"','"
➥+settings+"')");
```

Notice the formatting here. When you are calling JavaScript functions from Flash, you always must pass out literal values (because you are not *in* JavaScript, you can't just pass out variables—you have to send their values). So, you need to construct a string that JavaScript will understand. To do so, you need to wrap each argument that should be interpreted as a string in quotes. However, this string that you are building is already an argument of the getURL() function, so it already is surrounded by double quotes.

If you put more double quotes inside your JavaScript function call, it would confuse the getURL() function, so you need to do a little trickery. You can represent the quotes that you need for the JavaScript call with either single quotes or escaped quotes (\"). Single quotes, while a little unreadable, don't cause anywhere near as much confusion as \".

So, by escaping your double quotes with single quotes, the actual values that are received by the window.open() function in your JavaScript are properly quoted string literals.

Your completed function should look like this (see Figure 22.2):

```
function launch()
{
        url = "http://www.figleaf.com/";
        windowName = "myWindow";
        settings = "toolbar=no,location=no,status=no,menubar=no,
        ➥scrollbars=no,resizable=no,width=600,height=400";

        getURL("javascript:openWindow('"+url+"','"+windowName+"','"
        ➥+settings+"')");
}
```

6. Save your movie and publish both the HTML and SWF files.

7. Open Publish Settings and uncheck the HTML option on the Formats tab. You're going to add your own code to this page, and you don't want to overwrite it the next time you publish your movie. Save your file.

8. Open the HTML file that you created in your HTML editor of choice. Inside the <head></head>, tag you'll add your JavaScript function.

9. First, you need to set up your script block. Enter the following code:

```
<script language="JavaScript">
<!--

// -->
</script>
```

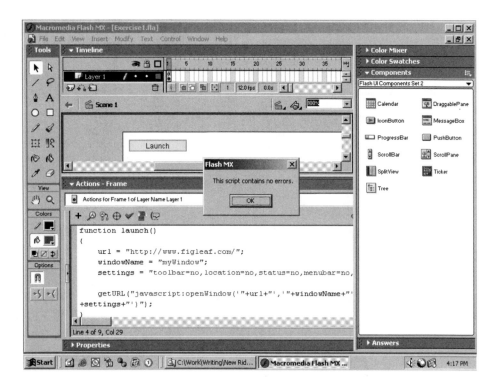

Figure 22.2 You can pass the values that you want to use into variables to simplify the getURL() code. It's always a good idea to check your syntax (Control+T or Command+T) before you proceed. Make certain the Action panel is selected when you use this shortcut key as it functions differently in different panels.

10. Next you'll create your function. You already know, from writing the ActionScript, that you'll be passing in three arguments, so add the shell for your new function to your existing code:

```
<script language="JavaScript">
<!--
function openWindow(url, windowName, settings)
{

}
// -->
</script>
```

11. All that's left to do is call the open() method of the window object. Enter the following line of code inside your new function:

```
window.open(url, windowname, settings);
```

Your completed code inside the <head> tag should look like this (see Figure
22.3):

```
<head>
<title>window1</title>
<script language="JavaScript">
<!--
function openWindow(url, windowName, settings)
{
    window.open(url, windowName, settings);
}
// -->
</script>
</head>
```

Figure 22.3 You add the JavaScript function that you want to call directly into the HTML
page. Your functions should all be between the <head></head> tags.

12. Save your HTML file and open it in a browser. Click your button. Assuming that
    you have an Internet connection open, you should launch the Fig Leaf web site
    in a new window.

Next, you'll take a look at how you can serve up some cookies using getURL() and
JavaScript.

Using *getURL()* to Set a Cookie

Depending on whom you talk to, cookies are either a wonderful thing or the work of the devil. So, what is a cookie? A *cookie* is just a small bit of data that is stored on your user's machine. What do you use cookies for?

- To maintain state between browser requests
- To remember information about your user, such as name, email, when he last visited your site, and so on

You can't go crazy and try and store huge amounts of information in your cookie. Remember, you and a bunch of other developers are storing information on your user's computer; you don't want to overload the storage space. Fortunately, you really can't; cookies are limited to 4K in size.

When you create a cookie, you need to give it some very specific information:

- **NAME=VALUE.** This is the name/value pair of the information that you want to store on your user's computer. You can pass more than one name/value pair in a single cookie.
- **expires=DATE.** If you want the cookie to be available the next time your user visits you, you need to set a date sometime in the future for the cookie to expire. If you don't set an expiration date, the cookie will expire as soon as the browser closes. The number that actually gets used here is based on UNIX epoch time, the number of milliseconds since midnight on January 1, 1970.
- **path=PATH.** You use this to set the subset of a domain that the cookie is valid for.
- **domain=DOMAIN_NAME.** This defaults to the domain name that generated the cookie.
- **secure.** If you mark a cookie as secure, it will be transmitted only across a secure channel (such as HTTPS).

So what does a cookie actually look like? Here's an example of some cookies from my cookie.txt (Netscape browser) file:

```
www.figleaf.com   FALSE   /   FALSE   2137622480 CFID    79246
www.figleaf.com   FALSE   /   FALSE   2137622480 CFTOKEN 99749128
```

The first part, www.figleaf.com, is the domain that the cookie was sent from. The second item indicates how the cookie was set—in this case, it's FALSE because the cookie was set by ColdFusion rather than through the HTTP header Set-cookie. The third item is the path. You might need a cookie to be retrieved for only a specific part of your site—you can set the path for which a cookie is returned. In this case, the cookie is returned no matter where you are on the site. The fourth field indicates whether the cookie should be returned only over a secure connection. The fifth field represents the expiration time. The last two fields are the name/value pair of the information that you want to store.

So how do you actually set a cookie from Flash? A cookie is a property of the document object, so setting a cookie using getURL() and JavaScript is fairly simple. Exercise 22.2 shows you how.

Exercise 22.2   Using *getURL()* to Set a Cookie

You'll start by creating a new movie and adding an input field and a button.

1. Create a new movie.

   You're going to set up an input field so that your user can enter his name and save it in a cookie.

2. Make sure the Properties panel is open (Window > Properties).

3. Select the Text Tool from the pallet and add a textbox to the Stage. Make the following changes in the Properties panel:

   Instance Name: **name_txt**
   Text Type: **Input Text**
   Line Type: **Single Line**
   Border: **Selected**

4. Drag a button from the Flash UI Components panel (Window > Components) onto the Stage (see Figure 22.4). Make the following changes on the Properties panel:

   Instance Name: **setcookie_btn**
   Label: **Set**
   Click Handler: **createCookie**

With the Stage selected, launch the Actions panel and add the button handler function createCookie:

```
function createCookie()
{

}
```

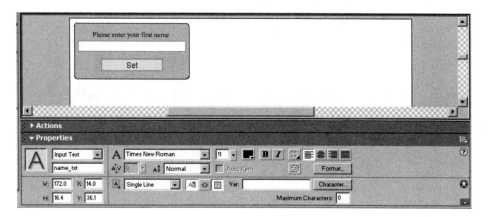

Figure 22.4   Set up an input field named `name_txt` to capture the value that you're going to save in your cookie. The `getURL()` action will be attached to the click handler of the button, setcookie_btn.

The `getURL()` call will be to a function called `setCookie`. `setCookie` will take six arguments:

- The cookie name (`myCookie`)
- The name entered in the input field (`_root.name_txt.text`)
- The number of days before the cookie expires (30 days)
- The path that the cookie should be returned for (/)
- The domain that the cookie is being sent from (leave this blank)
- Whether a secure connection is required (no—leave it blank)

5. Between the curly braces of the `createCookie()` button click handler, add the `getURL()` function (see Figure 22.5):

```
getURL("javascript:setCookie('myCookie','"+_root.name_txt.text+"',
'30','/','','');");
```

6. Save your file as **Cookie.fla**, and publish both the HTML and the SWF files.

7. Open the HTML file that you just created in your HTML editor of choice. Set up the shell for your new function along with all its arguments. Enter the following code between the `<head></head>` tags:

```
<script language="JavaScript">
<!--
function setCookie(name, value, days, path, domain, secure)
{

}
// -->
</script>
```

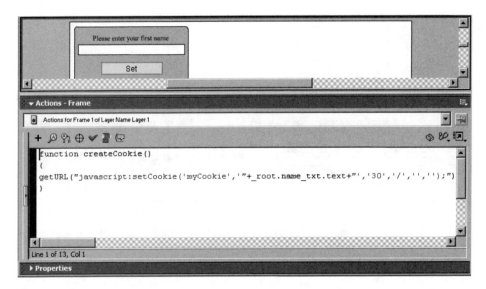

Figure 22.5   The getURL() call to the setCookie function passes six parameters to the browser.

8. Start by creating two new date objects: one is for today's date and the other for the expiration date you have to calculate.

```
<script language="JavaScript">
<!--
function setCookie(name, value, days, path, domain, secure)
{

    var expires = new Date();
    var today = new Date();

}
// -->
</script>
```

9. All the parameters that you need for this function are already being passed in the proper format, with the exception of the expiration date. What you're passing in so far is just the number 30, which stands for 30 days from now. You need to convert that to UNIX epoch time. Get the current UNIX epoch time and then convert the number of days until expiration to milliseconds and add that to the current UNIX epoch time. Sounds a little crazy, but it's actually pretty easy.

Now you're going to set up the calculation for the expiration date. You'll use today's date and add to it the number of days that you passed in, converted into milliseconds. All you have to do is add the following line:

```
expires.setTime(today.getTime() + (1000*60*60*24*parseInt(days)));
```

So far your code should look like this:

```
<script language="JavaScript">
<!--
function setCookie(name, value, days, path, domain, secure)
{
    var expires = new Date();
    var today = new Date();

    expires.setTime(today.getTime() +
    ➥(1000*60*60*24*parseInt(days)));
}
// -->
</script>
```

All you have left to do now is actually set your cookie.

10. Now `name`, `value`, and `expires` have values, so you can go ahead and reference them directly. You're going to be building a string to pass to `document.cookie`. The statement you're building is not complete with only those three values, so it is not terminated with a semicolon just yet.

```
<script language="JavaScript">
<!--
function setCookie(name, value, days, path, domain, secure)
{
        var expires = new Date();
        var_today = new Date();

        expires.setTime(today.getTime() +
        ➥(1000*60*60*24*parseInt(days)));

        document.cookie = name + "=" + value +  "; expires=" + expires +
}
// -->
</script>
```

Tip

The only values that you must pass into a cookie are the `name` and `value`, so you need to check the values that came in through the parameters to see whether they are blank. You can do that easily using the ternary operator (`?:`). The format is `expression_1 ? expression_2 : expression_3`, where `expression_1` is an expression that evaluates to True or False. If `expression_1` is true, the value of `expression_2` is returned. Otherwise, the value of `expression_3` is returned.

11. To complete the statement that actually creates the cookie, you'll start testing to see if the parameter being passed in has a value, and then you'll print the appropriate string. For example, if the path was left blank, you'll add `""` to the string; otherwise you'll add `"; path=" + path`. You'll do the same for `domain` and `secure`.

So far your code should look like this (see Figure 22.6):

```
<script language="JavaScript">
<!--
function setCookie(name,value,days,path,domain,secure)
{
        var expires = new Date();
        var today = new Date();

        expires.setTime(today.getTime() +
        ➥(1000*60*60*24*parseInt(days)));

        document.cookie = name + "=" + value +  "; expires=" +
        ➥expires +
                ((path == "") ? "" : ("; path=" + path)) +
                ((domain == "") ? "" : ("; domain=" + domain)) +
                ((secure == "secure") ? "; secure" : ""));
}
// -->
</script>
```

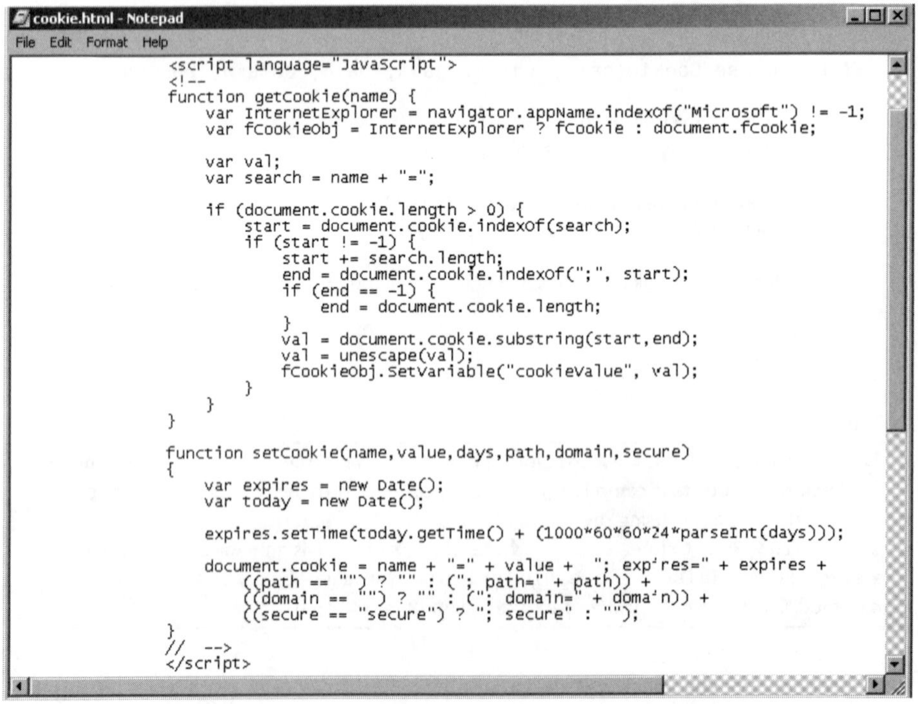

Figure 22.6 The completed `setCookie` function gets the UNIX epoch time and sets all the variables that you need for your cookie.

12. Save your file. Now open the HTML page in a browser. Enter your name into the text field, and press the button. Nothing happens. Or does it?

How are you going to tell whether your cookie was set? You could try to find the cookie on your hard drive. If you're using Netscape, it'll be in a file called cookies.txt. Under IE, you'll need to find the appropriate Cookies folder in your user profile. Rather than go through all that, how about trying to retrieve the cookie that you just set?

Setting the cookie is the hardest part. To retrieve a cookie, you just have to know its name. First you check to see whether there are any cookies by checking the length of the `document.cookie` object. If there are, then you need to check whether the cookie you were trying to set exists.

Exercise 22.3   Using *getURL()* to Retrieve a Cookie

Before you start writing the function to retrieve your cookie, you'll go back into your Flash movie and add a button that you can press to initiate the call to the new function.

1. If you closed the Flash movie from the previous exercise, Cookie.fla, open it now.
2. Before you do anything else, select Publish Settings and deselect HTML on the Format tab. You don't want to overwrite the JavaScript function that you've already written with a new HTML page.
3. Make sure the Properties panel is open (Window > Properties).
4. With your textbox selected, make the following changes in the Text Options panel:

   Instance Name: **value_txt**
   Var: **cookieValue**
   Text Type: **Input Text**
   Line Type: **Single Line**
   Border: **Selected**
5. Drag a button from the Flash UI Components panel (Window > Components) onto the Stage (see Figure 22.7). Make the following changes on the Properties panel:

   Instance Name: **getcookie_btn**
   Label: **Get**
   Click Handler: **retrieveCookie**

With the Stage selected, launch the Actions panel and add the button handler function `retrieveCookie`:

```
function retrieveCookie()
{

}
```

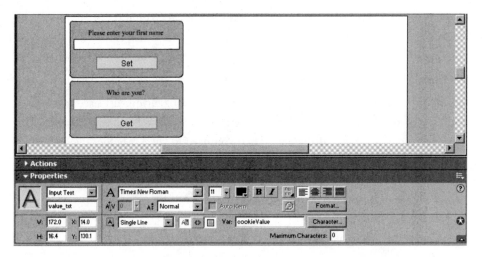

Figure 22.7   Set up an input field named value_txt to display the value that is stored in your cookie. As before, the getURL() action will be attached to the click handler of the button get-cookie_btn.

6. Inside the button handler function, add the following code to call the JavaScript function that you are going to build: getCookie. This function will take one argument: the name of the cookie to retrieve.

```
function retrieveCookie()
{
    getURL("javascript:getCookie('myCookie');");
}
```

7. Save and publish your file. Until you write the JavaScript for the getCookie function, the movie does not appear to function any better than it did before this exercise. In fact, an error will now be generated because you haven't written the getCookie function yet. Completing this will require a little more work and explanation.

So far, all of your communication has been in one direction—from Flash to the browser. Now you're going to do something a little different. You need to have the browser talk back to Flash. Fortunately, there is a way to do this. The plug-in and ActiveX control for both major browsers have built-in Flash methods that you can access with JavaScript. To get these methods to work, though, you have to make a few changes to your HTML file:

• The <object> tag must contain the ID attribute.
• The <embed> tag must contain the NAME attribute.
• The attribute swLiveConnect=true must be added to the <embed> tag.

The ID and NAME attributes identify your movie to JavaScript and must be the same for both tags. For now, you'll be working with only one of the Flash methods, SetVariable.

The other methods will be covered in the last part of this chapter. In the next part of this exercise, you'll add these new elements to your HTML file and set up the function to retrieve your cookie.

Note

The reason that the ID and NAME attributes of the <object> and the <embed> tag has to do with the differences between the Internet Explorer and Netscape DOMs.

Warning

At the time of this writing, there is a problem with the player on the Macintosh OS X platform. Current tests show JavaScript unable to invoke the player's externally script-able methods.

This next exercise relies upon just such a method, SetVariable, to pass the value of the cookie back into the movie. Until this is resolved, this exercise will not work for users on OS X.

8. You should still have your HTML page open in your favorite HTML editor.

9. Add the attribute ID="fCookie" to the <object> tag. Then add the attributes swLiveConnect="true" and NAME="fCookie" to the <embed> tag. In the end, your code block should look similar to this:

```
<object classid="clsid:D27CDB6E-AE6D-11cf-96B8-444553540000"

codebase="http://download.macromedia.com/pub/shockwave/cabs/flash/
➥swflash.cab#version=6,0,0,0"
                      width="550" height="400" id="fCookie">

               <PARAM NAME=movie VALUE="cookie.swf">
               <PARAM NAME=quality VALUE=high>
               <PARAM NAME=bgcolor VALUE=#FFFFFF>

               <embed src="cookie.swf"
                      width="550" height="400"
                      autostart="false" quality="high"
                      bgcolor="#FFFFFF" NAME="fCookie"
                      swLiveConnect="true" ALIGN=""
                      TYPE="application/x-shockwave-flash"

PLUGINSPAGE="http://www.macromedia.com/go/getflashplayer">
                      </EMBED>
               </object>
```

10. Now you're going to add a new function, getCookie(Name), between the
    <head></head> tags. The getCookie() function takes one parameter: name. Set
    up the declaration for function and add two lines inside to get the DOM object
    handle to the Flash movie so that you can access it directly (notice the use of the
    ternary operator here):

```
<script language="JavaScript">
<!--

function getCookie(name) {
        var InternetExplorer = navigator.appName.indexOf
        ➥("Microsoft") != -1;
        var fCookieObj = InternetExplorer ? fCookie :
        ➥document.fCookie;
}

function setCookie(name,value,days,path,domain,secure) {
        var expires = new Date();
        var_today = new Date();
        expires.setTime(today.getTime() +
        ➥(1000*60*60*24*parseInt(days)));
        document.cookie = name + "=" + value +  "; expires=" +
        ➥expires +
                ((path == "") ? "" : ("; path=" + path)) +
                ((domain == "") ? "" : ("; domain=" + domain)) +
                ((secure == "secure") ? "; secure" : ""));
}
// -->
</script>
```

11. You want to search the cookies based on the cookie name that you set earlier
    rather than just by the domain that set it. A single domain may set multiple
    cookies in your browser. If you look for a cookie set just by a specific domain,
    you'll get only the first cookie in that domain's list.

    You've already got the basic part of your function set up. This time, instead of
    adding the code line by line, I'll show you the whole function and then break it
    down with comments. The completed getCookie() function looks like this:

```
function getCookie(name) {
        var InternetExplorer =
        ➥navigator.appName.indexOf("Microsoft") != -1;
        var fCookieObj = InternetExplorer ? fCookie :
        ➥document.fCookie;

        var val;
        var search = name + "=";

        if (document.cookie.length > 0) {
                start = document.cookie.indexOf(search);
                if (start != -1) {
                        start += search.length;
```

```
        end = document.cookie.indexOf(";", start);
        if (end == -1) {
              end = document.cookie.length;
        }
        val = document.cookie.substring(start,end);
        val = unescape(val);
        fCookieObj.SetVariable("cookieValue", val);
      }
    }
}
```

So what does all this mean? Just read through the commented lines here, and you should get the idea:

```
function getCookie(Name) {
      var InternetExplorer = navigator.appName.indexOf
      ➥("Microsoft") != -1;
      var fCookieObj = InternetExplorer ? fCookie :
      ➥document.fCookie;

// Set up a new variable to hold the cookie value

      var val;

// Set up a new variable called search to hold the value of
// the parameter passed into the function plus =.  In this
// case, the value of search will be "myCookie="

      var search = name + "=";

// Check to see if there are any cookies set for the browser

      if (document.cookie.length > 0) {

// If the length of document.cookie is greater than 0, use the
// indexOf() property of the string to find and return the
// start position of the occurrence of "myCookie=".
// If "myCookie=" is not found, indexOf() returns a value
// of -1

            start = document.cookie.indexOf(search);

// If the index is not -1,  "myCookie=" was found

            if (start != -1) {
                  start += search.length;

// The end of the string is marked by a ;, so find the index of
// the semi-colon - begin the search at the index of start

                  end = document.cookie.indexOf(";", start);
                  if (end == -1) {
                        end = document.cookie.length;
                  }
```

```
            // Use the start and end variables to extract the substring you
            // want from the document.cookie string

                        val = document.cookie.substring(start, end);
                        val = unescape(val);

            // Use the Flash method, SetVariable, to send a name/value pair
            ➥back
            // to the main Timeline of your Flash movie.

                        fCookieObj.SetVariable("cookieValue", val);
                }
            }
        }
```

12. After you've entered the getCookie() function, save your HTML file and load it
    into a browser. You set your cookie in the previous exercise, and you should be
    able to immediately check for it—just click the second button. (See Figure 22.8.)

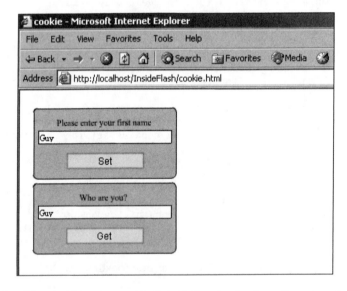

Figure 22.8   When you have your getCookie() function in place, all you have to do is click
on the button to retrieve your cookie.

Using getURL() isn't the only way to get Flash to talk to your browser. You can also use
the FSCommand() action.

FSCommand()

The FS commands have been part of Flash since its inception as Future Splash—and, in
fact, that's where the FS originally came from. The FSCommand() action enables you to

send two strings to whichever application is hosting your Flash movie. In a web browser, the FSCommand() action can be used to call either JavaScript or VBScript functions that exist in the HTML in much the same way that the getURL() action does.

The obvious question becomes, why would you choose one action over another? You'll probably find that you use getURL() much more frequently than you use FSCommand() when communicating with the browser, for the following reasons:

- getURL() enjoys wider browser support.

- getURL() is easier to implement than FSCommand().

So why would you ever use FSCommand()?

- You can get rid of the annoying click that you get whenever you call the getURL() action from Internet Explorer.

- FSCommand() is a fire-and-forget solution. In other words, it doesn't matter whether there is a script on the HTML page to catch it—it won't throw an error. While this can have certain advantages, it does make debugging problems with FSCommand() more challenging than calling JavaScript functions with getURL().

If you use the Flash with FSCommand template in Publish Settings, your life will be even easier because Flash will create an HTML page for you with all the hooks that you need to use the FSCommand(). It automatically adds the ID and NAME attributes, as well as the swLiveConnect attribute and the shell for the function that you can call.

With getURL(), you call a function based on its name, and you can have as many functions as you want. It's a little different with FSCommand(). The FSCommand() uses a router function. With Netscape, Flash automatically calls a JavaScript function named *moviename*_FSCommand(); with Internet Explorer, Flash calls a VBScript function named *movieid*_DoFSCommand(), where *moviename* and *movieid* are derived from the NAME and ID attributes of the <object> and <embed> tags. Fortunately, the Flash with FSCommand template includes the VBScript function, which, by default, simply calls the JavaScript function. This eliminates the need to actually write your code in both scripting languages. You've got to love that.

It is important to know which browsers don't support FSCommand(). The most notable browsers are Netscape 6 and 6.01 (all platforms), Netscape browsers of version 2 or earlier, and Internet Explorer on the Mac. FSCommand() doesn't work on those browsers because they both lack the code that is used to connect plug-ins with JavaScript. This is documented in the Flash TechNote 14625.

That being said, it's time to take a look at one of the ways you can use FSCommand(): to create alert messages. Try Exercise 22.4 in Internet Explorer, and listen for the click when you press your button—it won't be there.

> **Warning**
>
> At the time of this writing, there is a problem with the player on the Macintosh OS X platform. Current tests show problems with the FSCommand firing JavaScript methods.
>
> This next exercise relies upon this. Until this is resolved, this exercise will not work for users on OS X.

Exercise 22.4   Using *FSCommand()* with a Web Browser

For this example, you'll be making an interface for Flash to create JavaScript alert messages. This can come in very handy when you are trying to debug a movie outside the Flash authoring tool.

1. Create a new Flash movie.
2. Make sure the Properties panel is open (Window > Properties).
3. Select the Text tool from the pallet and draw a text box long enough to hold a short message on the Stage. Make the following changes in the Properties panel:

    Instance Name: **message_txt**
    Text Type: **Input Text**
    Line Type: **Single Line**
    Border: **Selected**

4. Drag a button from the Flash UI Components panel (Window > Components) onto the Stage and place it beneath the text field (see Figure 22.9). Make the following changes on the Properties panel:

    Instance Name: **alert_btn**
    Label: **Alert**
    Click Handler: **sendAlert**

5. With the Stage selected, launch the Actions panel, and add the following code for the button's click handler function:

```
function sendAlert()
{
        FSCommand("alert", _root.message_txt.text);
}
```

6. Save your file as **fsalert.fla**.
7. Now open the Publish Settings dialog box (File > Publish Settings) and make sure that both Flash and HTML are selected on the Formats tab. Select the HTML tab. For Template, choose Flash with FSCommand; then click Publish.

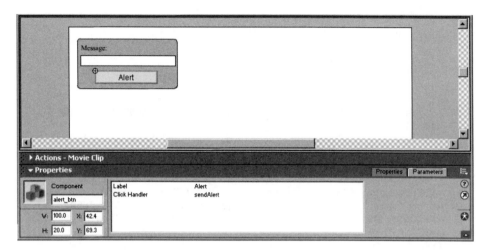

Figure 22.9   To capture a message to display for this exercise, you need to set up an input text field and a button.

8. In your HTML editor of choice, open your new fsalert.html file. It should look like this:

```
<HTML>
<HEAD>
<meta http-equiv=Content-Type content="text/html;  charset=ISO-
➥8859-1">
<TITLE>fsalert</TITLE>
</HEAD>
<BODY bgcolor="#FFFFFF">
<SCRIPT LANGUAGE=JavaScript>
<!--
var InternetExplorer = navigator.appName.indexOf("Microsoft") != -
➥1;
// Handle all the the FSCommand messages in a Flash movie
function fsalert_DoFSCommand(command, args) {
        var fsalertObj = InternetExplorer ? fsalert :
        ➥document.fsalert;
        //
        // Place your code here...
        //
}
// Hook for Internet Explorer
if (navigator.appName && navigator.appName.indexOf("Microsoft") !=
➥-1 &&
        navigator.userAgent.indexOf("Windows") != -1 &&
        ➥navigator.userAgent.indexOf("Windows 3.1") == -1) {
        document.write('<SCRIPT LANGUAGE=VBScript\> \n');
        document.write('on error resume next \n');
        document.write('Sub fsalert_FSCommand(ByVal command,
        ➥ByVal args)\n');
        document.write('  call fsalert_DoFSCommand(command, args)\n');
```

```
            document.write('end sub\n');
            document.write('</SCRIPT\> \n');
        }
    //-->
    </SCRIPT>
    <!-- URL's used in the movie-->
    <!-- text used in the movie-->
    <!--Message:--><OBJECT classid="clsid:D27CDB6E-AE6D-11cf-96B8-
    444553540000"
    codebase="http://download.macromedia.com/pub/shockwave/cabs/flash/
    ➥swflash.cab#version=6,0,0,0"
    ID="fsalert" WIDTH="550" HEIGHT="400" ALIGN="">
    <PARAM NAME=movie VALUE="fsalert.swf"> <PARAM NAME=quality
    ➥VALUE=high> <PARAM NAME=bgcolor VALUE=#FFFFFF> <EMBED
    ➥src="fsalert.swf" quality=high bgcolor=#FFFFFF  WIDTH="550"
    ➥HEIGHT="400" swLiveConnect=true ID="fsalert" NAME="fsalert"
    ➥ALIGN=""
    TYPE="application/x-shockwave-flash" PLUGINSPAGE="http://www.
    ➥macromedia.com/go/getflashplayer"></EMBED>
    </OBJECT>
    </BODY>
    </HTML>
```

Notice that Flash automatically added the NAME, ID, and swLiveConnect attributes to the <embed> and <object> tags. Flash also identifies to you where your JavaScript code will go, right where it says Place your code here!

9. Replace that entire line (including the comments) with the following code:

```
if (command == "alert"){
        alert(args);
}
```

10. Save your file, open it in your favorite browser, and give it a go.

Enter a message in the input box and click the button—instant pop-up message. (See Figure 22.10.)

Figure 22.10   If you enter a message and click the button, you get a pop-up message.

The Standalone Player

Although the previous example was very cool, FSCommand() is actually most often used in conjunction with the Standalone Player.

A special set of FSCommand() options exists for the Flash Standalone Player:

- **allowscale.** If set to false, the movie will not scale if the window size is changed.

- **exec.** Launches an external application, which can be referenced relative to the Standalone Player or specified as an absolute path. The path uses forward slashes (/) rather than backslashes (\).

- **fullscreen.** If set to true, the Standalone Player is maximized to fill the entire screen.

- **quit.** Exits the movie.

- **showmenu.** If set to true, the menu will not be displayed.

- **trapallkeys.** If set to true, all keystrokes are sent to the Flash movie.

Using getURL() in the Standalone Player will cause Internet Explorer to open a web page, even if Netscape is your default web browser. There is currently no workaround for this.

LoadVariables() can be used to send and receive variables from a text file or middleware on the server. The GET method will always be used when called by the Standalone Player, even if POST is specified.

Note

When publishing HTML, Flash does not insert the swLiveConnect=true argument in the <embed> tag unless you use the Flash with FSCommand template in Publish settings. If you publish a movie differently, be sure to add this argument manually, or the Flash methods will not work in Netscape.

JavaScript can be used to both get and set Flash variables, as well as to perform operations in Flash by using Macromedia's JavaScript methods for Flash objects. You'll look at these next.

JavaScript Methods for Flash Objects

The Flash plug-in and ActiveX control have built-in methods that can be accessed by JavaScript. For the Flash methods to work in JavaScript, the <object> must contain the ID attribute, and the <embed> tag must contain the NAME attribute. The values should be the same in both to avoid compatibility problems. It's important to note that with all the built-in capabilities of Flash MX, the average application will not need to make use of these capabilities. That doesn't mean that you won't ever use them, but most of these capabilities are more easily handled inside Flash.

After the Flash plug-in has loaded, the following partial list of standard methods are accessible to client-side JavaScript:

- **Back().** Steps the movie back a frame. Syntax:

  `window.document.yourMovie.Back();`

- **CurrentFrame().** Returns the current frame number. Syntax:

  `currentFrame = window.document.yourMovie.CurrentFrame();`

- **Drag(action).** Begins, ends, or cancels a drag operation of any object except: Line, Menu, Shape, or Timer. Syntax:

  `window.document.yourMovie.Drag(action);`

- **FlashVersion().** Returns the version of the Flash player. Syntax:

```
version = window.document.yourMovie.FlashVersion();
```

- **Forward().** Advances the movie to the next frame. Syntax:

```
window.document.yourMovie.Forward();.
```

- **FrameLoaded().** Returns true if the frame specified is loaded. Syntax:

```
isLoaded = window.document.yourMovie.FrameLoaded(frameNumber);
```

- **GetVariable("variableName").** Returns the value of the Flash variable variableName. Syntax:

```
flashVar = window.document.yourMovie.GetVariable("variableName");
```

- **GotoFrame(frameNumber).** Moves the playhead in the main Timeline to a specific frame. The values of frameNumber begin with 0, so to go to frame 2, the value would be 1. So that you don't request a frame that has not yet been loaded, you should use the PercentLoaded() method to make sure that the desired frame is available. Syntax:

```
window.document.yourMovie.GoToFrame(frameNumber);
```

- **IsPlaying().** Returns true if the movie is currently playing. Syntax:

```
isPlaying = window.document.yourMovie.IsPlaying();
```

- **LoadMovie(layerNumber,"url").** Causes Flash to load the movie specified by url to the layer specified by layerNumber. Syntax:

```
window.document.yourMovie.LoadMovie(layerNumber,
"http://www.yourURL.com/");
```

- **Move(left, top, width, height).** Causes movie to be repositioned. Only the first argument, left, is required; the rest (top, width, height) are optional. Syntax:

```
window.document.yourMovie.Move(10, 10);
```

- **Pan(x,y,mode).** Tells Flash to pan a movie if it is zoomed in. Negative x values cause the movie to pan to the left, and negative y values cause the movie to pan to the top. If the mode variable is set to 0, the x and y values are treated as pixels. If it is set to 1, the x and y values are treated as a percentage of the browser window size. Flash will not pan beyond the boundaries of the zoomed-in movie. Syntax:

```
window.document.yourMovie.Pan(x,y,mode);
```

- **PercentLoaded().** Returns the percent of the Flash movie that has downloaded to the web browser so far. The range is from 0 to 100. Syntax:

  ```
  loaded = window.document.yourMovie.PercentLoaded();
  ```

- **Play().** Starts playing the movie. Syntax:

  ```
  window.document.yourMovie.Play();
  ```

- **Rewind().** Moves the playhead to the first frame of the movie. Syntax:

  ```
  window.document.yourMovie.Rewind();
  ```

- **SetFocus().** Sets window focus on the movie in the Flash player. Syntax:

  ```
  window.document.yourMovie.SetFocus();
  ```

- **SetVariable("variableName","value").** Sets the Flash variable variableName to the value specified by the value variable. Syntax:

  ```
  window.document.yourMovie.SetVariable("VariableName", value);
  ```

- **SetZoomRect(left,top,right,bottom).** Zooms in on a rectangular area of the movie. The units for each variable are in *twips* (1/20 of a pixel). There are 1,440 units per inch, so, to calculate the coordinates from within Flash, set the ruler units to points and multiply the coordinates by 20. Syntax:

  ```
  window.document.yourMovie.SetZoomRect(left,top,right,bottom);
  ```

- **StopPlay().** Stops playing the movie. Syntax:

  ```
  window.document.yourMovie.StopPlay();
  ```

- **TotalFrames.** Returns the total number of frames in the movie. Syntax:

  ```
  totalFrames = window.document.yourMovie.TotalFrames;
  ```

- **Zoom(percent).** Zooms the movie using the percent variable as a relative scale factor. For example, Zoom(50) will double the size of the objects in the view, while Zoom(200) will cut in half the size of objects in the view. Zoom(0) will reset the view to 100%. It is not possible to zoom out any more than 100% (normal size). Syntax:

  ```
  window.document.yourMovie.Zoom(percent);
  ```

In addition to the standard methods, you have access to the Tell Target methods. The Tell Target methods let you control movie clips on the Timeline in Flash.

- **TCallFrame("movieClipInstance",frameNumber).** This executes the actions in the numbered frame of the movie clip instance. In call actions, the playhead does not move to the frame; just the actions are executed. Syntax:

```
window.document.yourMovie.TCallFrame("movieClipInstance",
➥frameNumber);
```

- **TCallLabel("movieClipInstance","label").** This executes the actions in the labeled frame of the movie clip instance. In call actions, the playhead does not move to the frame; just the actions are executed. Syntax:

```
window.document.yourMovie.TCallLabel("movieClipInstance",
➥frameLabel);
```

- **TCurrentFrame("movieClipInstance").** This returns the frame number where the playhead is located in the Timeline of the specified movie clip instance. It is zero-based, so if the playhead is on frame 1, the value 0 will be returned. Syntax:

```
currentFrame = window.document.yourMovie.TCurrentFrame
➥("movieClipInstance");
```

- **TCurrentLabel("movieClipInstance").** This returns the label name of the current frame of the Timeline of the specified movie clip instance. If that frame doesn't have a label, an empty string is returned. Syntax:

```
currentLabel = window.document.yourMovie.TCurrentLabel
➥("movieClipInstance");
```

- **TGotoFrame("movieClipInstance",frameNumber).** On the Timeline of the specified movie clip instance, the playhead is moved to the frame number specified by frameNumber. Syntax:

```
window.document.yourMovie.TCurrentFrame
➥("movieClipInstance", frameNumber);
```

- **TGotoLabel("movieClipInstance","label").** On the Timeline of the specified movie clip instance, the playhead is moved to the frame with the label specified by label. Syntax:

```
window.document.yourMovie.TGotoLabel("movieClipInstance",
➥"labelName");
```

- **TPlay("movieClipInstance").** This plays the Timeline of the specified movie clip instance. Syntax:

```
window.document.yourMovie.TPlay("movieClipInstance");
```

- **`TStopPlay("movieClipInstance")`.** This causes the Timeline of the specified movie clip instance to stop. Syntax:

```
window.document.yourMovie.TStopPlay("movieClipInstance");
```

- **`TGetProperty("movieClipInstance",property)`.** A string containing the requested property is returned from the Timeline of the specified movie clip instance. Syntax:

```
prop = window.document.yourMovie.TGetProperty("movieClipInstance",
➥property);
```

- **`TSetProperty("movieClipInstance",property,value)`.** Flash sets the value of the property on the Timeline specified by the movie clip instance. Syntax:

```
window.document.yourMovie.TSetProperty("movieClipInstance",
➥property,value);
```

If you plan to use any of the Flash methods, it's best to publish your HTML file using the Flash with FSCommand template because it will automatically set up everything you need. If you look in the HTML, you will see a variable created at one point that starts with the name of your FLA and ends with *Obj* (for example, `myFLAObj`). Just make sure that you copy and paste that line into any function that needs to use Flash methods. So, when you actually call the method, it will be like this:

```
myFLAObj.SetVariable("/foo", "bar");
```

Macromedia Dreamweaver JavaScript Integration Kit

If you also own Macromedia Dreamweaver, you can download Macromedia's JavaScript Integration Kit for Flash 5 at no cost. Yes, Flash 5—at the time of this writing, the Kit has not been upgraded for Flash MX, but almost everything (points made later) seems to run just the same. This kit contains a number of behaviors and scripts to make it easier to communicate between JavaScript and Flash. You can download it from `www.macromedia.com/software/dreamweaver/productinfo/extend/jik_flash5.html`.

After you have installed the kit with the Macromedia Extension Manager, you will have access to the following tools:

- **Browser Scripts for Flash.** These scripts provide JavaScript methods for Flash objects. Select Command > Browser Scripts for Flash to see a list of the JavaScript functions that can be inserted into your HTML file. These include functions to open new browser windows, set cookies, edit form lists, and control images.

- **Flash Deployment Kit.** The main component of the Flash Deployment Kit is the Flash Dispatcher behavior. This behavior uses a number of techniques for detecting Flash, depending on the user's browser and operating system. This is particularly helpful because there is no one foolproof method of detecting Flash. To use it, in the Behaviors panel, add the Macromedia Flash Dispatcher behavior. A dialog box will pop up that enables you to configure it for your needs.

> **Warning**
>
> Obviously the Deployment Kit in this version of the package will be unaware of MX. This will create problems until the overall Integration Kit is updated for MX.
>
> Since the code for these Dreamweaver Behaviors and Commands are accessible, it is possible to fix this problem as a stopgap until the update can be released. It is, however, beyond the scope of this text to cover the steps necessary.

- **Flash Player controls.** The Player controls make it easy to use Flash JavaScript methods to control the movie. These methods enable you to stop, play, fast-forward, rewind, go to a specific frame number, and even go to a specific frame based on a cookie. This feature can be used in conjunction with the Set_Cookie Browser Script for Flash to set cookies and control the playhead based on those cookies. The Player controls also allow you to zoom and pan the movie inside the embedded player. Finally, you can load a different movie into an embedded player, replacing it or overlapping it. To choose a control, create a link in the Behaviors panel; they are listed under MM Flash Player Controls.

- **Advanced Form Validations.** By setting up a hidden form field in your HTML page, you can use the Advanced Form Validations behaviors to send variables from Flash to JavaScript. These variables then can be tested to see if they match the correct formatting. Although these are useful for validating data in Flash forms, they can also be used to validate data in HTML forms.

Exercise 22.5 gives you a little demonstration of using the JavaScript Integration Kit with Flash.

Exercise 22.5   Validating Social Security and Credit Card Numbers

In this exercise, which requires Macromedia Dreamweaver and the JavaScript Integration Kit extension, you will create a Flash form that sends values to be validated by JavaScript. Follow these directions very carefully—it's easy to make a mistake and difficult to later figure out where that mistake might be.

1. Create a new Flash movie with the dimensions 250 × 100 pixels.

2. Make sure the Properties panel is open (Window > Properties).

3. Select the Text tool from the pallet and draw a text box at the top of the stage that takes up most of the width of the movie. Make the following changes in the Properties panel:

   Instance Name: **ssn_txt**
   Text Type: **Input Text**
   Line Type: **Single Line**
   Border: **Selected**

4. Duplicate the text box (Control+D or Command+D) and move it below the first. Make the following change in the Properties panel:

   Instance Name: **cc_txt**

5. Drag a button from the Flash UI Components panel (Window > Components) onto the Stage and place it beneath the two text boxes. Make the following changes in the Properties panel:

   Instance Name: **validate_btn**
   Label: **Validate**
   Click Handler: **validate**

6. With the Stage selected, launch the Actions panel and add the following code for the button's click handler function (see Figure 22.11):

```
function validate()
{
        getURL
("javascript:FDK_setFormText('myform','sshtml','"+_root.ssn_txt.text
⮕+"');FDK_setFormText('myform','cchtml','"+_root.cc_txt.text+"');");
        getURL("javascript:FDK_Validate('myform',false,true,'The Form
Could Not Be Submitted\\n\\n');");
}
```

7. Save your movie as **jikvalidation.fla**, and publish it.

8. In Macromedia Dreamweaver, open jikvalidation.html, which was just created by Flash.

9. Select the embedded movie. With the Properties Inspector, set both the name and the ID to **myMovie**. This allows the JavaScript Integration Kit behaviors to talk to your movie.

10. Insert a form below the movie (Insert > Form). In the Properties Inspector, name it **myForm**.

11. Click inside the form and insert hidden HTML form fields for both of the Flash form fields (Insert > Form Objects > Hidden Field).

12. Using the Properties Inspector, name the form fields **sshtml** and **cchtml**.

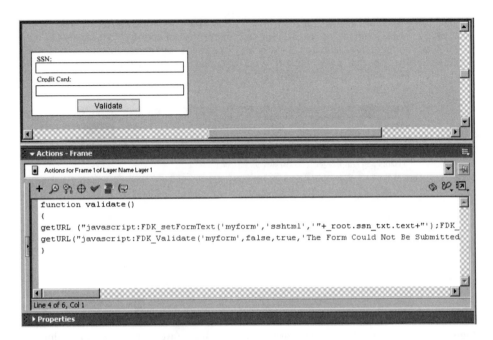

Figure 22.11   Multiple Flash form fields can be validated at once.

13. To insert the code that will handle the validation process, click the red form border; in the Behaviors Inspector, choose Advanced Validate Form. Select form
myform, and click OK. An onSubmit event is automatically placed in the <form>
tag that calls the FDK_Validate() function. You can instead use any event or
HTML link, however.

14. To insert the JavaScript function that will receive form field values from Flash,
select Commands > Browser Scripts for Flash. Then select FDK_setFormText and
click OK.

15. To insert the JavaScript that will actually validate the Social Security number in
the <head>, select the <body> tag (this is important) and, in the Behaviors
Inspector, select Advanced Form Validations > Social Security Number. Select
hidden sshtml in form myform, and click OK. An onLoad event is added to the
<body> tag:

```
onLoad="FDK_AddSSNValidation('myform','document.myform.sshtml',true,
➥false,'\'Please enter a valid social security number.\'')"
```

16. To insert the code that will validate the credit card number, select the <body> tag
(this is important) and, in the Behaviors Inspector, select Advanced Form
Validations > Credit Card Number. Select hidden cchtml in form myform, and
click OK. The onLoad event is updated to also include a call to the new function
(see Figure 22.12):

```
onLoad="FDK_AddSSNValidation('myform','document.myform.sshtml',true,
➥false,'\'Please enter a valid social security number.\'');
➥FDK_AddCreditCardValidation('myform','document.myform.cchtml',true,
➥false,'\'The credit card number you entered is not valid.\\nPlease
➥enter a new card and try again.\'')"
```

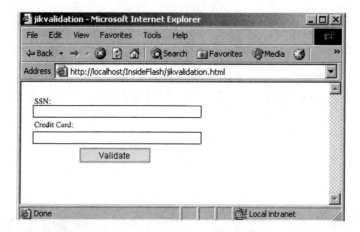

Figure 22.12   Being able to validate form fields in Flash can save a lot of time by avoiding multiple requests to the server.

17. If any of your form fields cannot be validated, a JavaScript window will pop up letting the user know which fields didn't validate. Be certain to complete the ACTION attribute of the form so it functions properly.

18. Save jikvalidation.html, and load it into your web browser.

19. First try submitting the form with no values. Then try with a valid Social Security number in the first field, and finally try with valid numbers in both fields.

As you can see, the Macromedia product line integrates very well. Now you can begin to see how you can use Flash and Dreamweaver together to harness the powers of each.

Summary

In this chapter, you've taken a look at how Flash and the browser can communicate with one another using loadVariables(), getURL(), and FSCommand(). In particular, you've learned how to make calls to functions that exist on the page in which the Flash movie is embedded with both getURL() and FSCommand(). You've also looked at how you can use the JavaScript methods of the <object> and <embed> tags to get the browser to communicate with Flash.

When communicating between the host application and Flash, just remember that there are always potential obstacles when depending on scripting languages in your browser. For example, there's a chance that your users will have scripting support turned off in their browsers. You also need to be mindful of which browsers support which level of communication. As long as you recognize the limitations, you can use these techniques to expand the scope of your Flash application.

Appendix A

ActionScript Objects Quick Reference

Flash MX has many new objects and a lot of

the older objects now have new uses. This

appendix lists all the objects and their con-

structor functions, methods, properties,

event handlers, and listeners. It also gives a brief description of their use. You might find this listing useful for when your copy of Flash MX isn't available. Note, however, that the reference material in Flash MX often has more detailed information. Each object lists the location of its full Help file in the Flash MX authoring environment.

Objects

- **Accessibility.** Object for creating accessible movies.
- **Arguments.** Object created every time a user-defined function is run. Arguments holds all the parameters passed to user-defined functions.
- **Array.** An Array object holds a list of data.
- **Boolean.** A Boolean object acts as an object wrapper to true/false values.
- **Button.** An object that represents button instances.
- **Capabilities.** An object containing information about the system's capabilities.
- **Color.** A Color object is used to modify the color of a movie clip with code.
- **CustomActions.** An object that manages custom actions.
- **Date.** A Date object holds and formats all types of date and time information.
- **Function.** An object, which represents a function.
- **Key.** The Key object is used to track keyboard presses.
- **LoadVars.** Object-oriented interface to `loadVariables()`.
- **Math.** The Math object acts as a library for complex math operators and functions.
- **Mouse.** The Mouse object is used to show or hide the mouse pointer.
- **MovieClip.** A MovieClip object points to an actual movie clip on the Stage.
- **Number.** A Number object acts as an object wrapper to normal numbers.
- **Object.** An Object object is the primitive ActionScript object type.
- **Selection.** The Selection object is used to set and get information about focus and selected areas of text fields.
- **Sound.** A Sound object controls the playback of a sound, including pan and volume.
- **Stage.** An object that controls the characteristics of the Flash movie Stage.
- **String.** A String object acts as an object wrapper to normal strings.
- **System.** An object containing system information.
- **TextField.** An object that represents text field instances.

- **TextFormat.** An object that controls text formatting in text fields.
- **XML.** An XML object that enables the loading, manipulation, and sending of XML data.
- **XMLSocket.** An XMLSocket object enables the sending and reception of XML data over a socket connection.

Terms

- **Constructor function.** When an object can be copied into an instance with ActionScript, this is done with a special function called a constructor. The constructor function usually starts with the keyword "new" and is followed by the name of the object you're calling. For example, the Human object could be instantiated with the syntax `"new Human();"`.

- **Method.** Methods make an object perform some kind of action or return a result. For example, the Human object might have methods for `grow()`, `run()`, and `eat()`.

- **Property.** Properties are the attributes of an object. For example, the Human object might have properties for hair color, height, and weight.

- **Event.** Some objects throw off events when they change or when other objects interact with them. For example, when the Human object has an empty stomach, it might throw off a hungry event. When objects have events, programmers can then use event handlers to react. When the `Human.hungry` event is detected, a feeding function might then be started.

- **Listener.** Listeners are new to Flash MX. A Listener is a function or another object that can "listen" for particular events to happen. When the event is detected, the function or object reacts. For example, we could subscribe the Human object with the instance name of "Mother" to listen for the `Human.hungry` event that is thrown by the Human object with the instance name of "Baby". When Mother detects `baby.hungry`, the Mother object responds with a particular Mother method, perhaps `mother.cookDinner()`.

- **Callback function.** When an event or listener uses a user-defined function, as described earlier in this bulleted list, this is known as a callback function.

Accessibility Object

Accessibility Object :: Reference > Objects > Movie

Accessibility Object Methods

Accessibility.**isActive()**

Indicates whether a screen reader program is currently active.

 Note

To learn more about the capabilities of your system, please see the "Capabilities" section of this appendix.

Arguments Object

Arguments Object :: Reference > Objects > Core

Arguments Object Properties

arguments.**callee**

Refers to the function that is currently being called.

arguments.**caller**

Refers to the Arguments object of the calling function.

arguments.**length**

The number of parameters actually passed to a function.

Array Object

Array Object :: Reference > Objects > Core

new Array()

new Array(length)

new Array(element0,...element*N*)

Constructor; lets you create an array. You can use the constructor to create different types of arrays: an empty array, an array with a specific length but whose elements have no values, or an array whose elements have specific values.

| **Length** | The number of elements in the array. |
| **element0...element *N*** | Individual elements passed into the array. |

Array Object Methods

myArray.**concat**(value0,...value*N*)

myArray.**concat**(*myArray2*)

Concatenates the elements specified in the parameters with the elements of myArray, and it then creates a new array.

value0,...valueN Elements to be concatenated in a new array.

myArray2 Array of elements to be concatenated in a new array.

myArray.**join**(separator)

Concatenates the converted string elements and inserts the separator between them.

separator Optional. Character or string used to separate each array element. By default, the separator is a comma (,).

myArray.**pop**()

Removes the last element from an array and returns the value of that element.

myArray.**push**(value0,...valueN)

Adds elements to the end of the array.

value0,...valueN One or more elements to be added to the array.

myArray.**reverse**()

Reverses the order of the array.

myArray.**shift**()

Removes the first element of the array and returns the value.

myArray.**slice**(start, end)

Extracts the values between the start and end parameters. The value at the start parameter is included in the result; the value at the end parameter is excluded. The values are returned in a new array.

start Number specifying the index position for the start of the slice.

end Number for the index position of the slice ending point.

myArray.**sort**(compareFunction)

Sorts the array without making a copy.

compareFunction Optional. A comparison function. If used, it determines how elements are sorted.

myArray.**sortOn**(fieldName)

Sorts the elements in an array based on a field in the array.

fieldName A string identifying a field in the array. The array sorts based on the values in this field.

myArray.**splice**(start, deleteCount, value0,...valueN)

Adds and removes elements in an array and modifies the array without making a copy.

start Beginning point to the insert/delete in the array.

deleteCount The number of elements to be deleted, including element specified in start parameter.

value0...valueN Optional. Elements to be inserted at the array index specified in the start parameter.

myArray.**toString**();

Returns the elements in the array as a string.

myArray.**unshift**(value0,...valueN);

Adds elements to the beginning of the array and returns the length of the array.

value0...valueN The elements to be inserted.

Array Object Properties

myArray.**length**

> Number of elements in the array.

Boolean

Boolean Object :: Reference > Objects > Core

new Boolean(x)

> Constructor; creates an instance of the Boolean object. If you omit the x parameter, the Boolean object is initialized with a value of false. If you specify a value for the x parameter, the method evaluates it and returns the result as a Boolean value.
>
> x   Optional. Any expression.

Boolean Object Methods

myBoolean.**toString**()

> Returns the string representation, true or false, of the Boolean object.

myBoolean.**valueOf**()

> Returns the primitive value type of the specified Boolean object.

Button

Button Object :: Reference > Objects > Movie

Button Object Methods

myButton.**getDepth()**

> Returns the depth of a button instance.

Button Object Properties

myButton.**enabled**

> Boolean. Specifies whether a button is enabled. The default value is true.

myButton.**tabEnabled**

> If the tabEnabled property is undefined or true, the object is included in automatic tab ordering. Might be set on an instance of the MovieClip, Button, or TextField objects. It is undefined by default.

myButton.**tabIndex**

> Lets you customize the tab ordering of objects in a movie. You can set the tabIndex property on a button, movie clip, or text field instance; it is undefined by default.

myButton.**trackAsMenu**

> Optional. Indicates whether other buttons or movie clips can receive mouse release events; enables the creation of menu systems.

myButton.**useHandCursor**

> Boolean. Indicates whether a hand cursor is displayed when a user rolls over a button.

Button Object Event Handlers

> A user-defined function must be defined to execute when the event is invoked.

myButton.**onDragOut** = function() {}

> Invoked when the mouse button is pressed over the button and the pointer then rolls outside the button.

myButton.**onDragOver** = function() {}

> Invoked when the user presses and drags the mouse button outside and then over the button.

myButton.**onKillFocus** = function(newFocus) {}

> An event that is invoked when a button loses keyboard focus.
>
> **newFocus**   The object that is receiving the focus.

myButton.**onRelease** = function() {}

> Invoked when a button is released.

myButton.**onReleaseOutside** = function() {}

> Invoked when the mouse is released while the pointer is outside the button after the button is pressed while the pointer is inside the button.

myButton.**onRollOut** = function() {}

> Invoked when the pointer rolls outside a button area.

myButton.**onRollOver** = function() {}

> Invoked when the pointer rolls over a button area.

myButton.**onSetFocus** = function(oldFocus) {}

> Invoked when a button receives keyboard focus.
>
> **oldFocus**   The object that loses the focus. For example, if the user presses the Tab key to move the input focus from a text field to a button, oldFocus contains the text field instance.

Capabilities

Capabilities Object :: Reference > Objects > Movie

Capabilities Object Properties

System.capabilities.**hasAccessibility**

> Boolean. Indicates whether the device supports communication between the Flash Player and accessibility aids. The default value is false. The server string is ACC.

System.capabilities.**hasAudio**

> Boolean. Indicates whether the player has audio capabilities. The default value is true. The server string is A.

System.capabilities.**hasAudioEncoder**

> An array of audio decoders. The server string is AE.

`System.capabilities.`**`hasMP3`**

Boolean. Indicates whether the player has an MP3 decoder. The default value is true. The server string is MP3.

`System.capabilities.`**`hasVideoEncoder`**

An array of video encoders. The server string is VE.

`System.capabilities.`**`pixelAspectRatio`**

Indicates the pixel aspect ratio of the screen. The default value is 1.0. The server string is PAR.

`System.capabilities.`**`screenColor`**

Indicates the color of the screen: color (color), gray (gray), or black and white (bw). The default value is color. The server string is SC.

`System.capabilities.`**`screenDPI`**

Indicates the dots per inch (dpi) of the screen, in pixels. The default value is 72. The server string is DPI.

`System.capabilities.`**`screenResolution`**

An integer that indicates the maximum horizontal resolution of the screen. The default value is 800 (pixels). The server string is SRX.

`System.capabilities.`**`screenResolution`**

An integer that indicates the maximum vertical resolution of the screen. The default value is 600 (pixels). The server string is SRY.

Color Object

Color Object :: Reference > Objects > Movie

`new Color (target)`

Constructor; creates an instance of the Color object for the movie clip specified by the target parameter. You can then use the methods of that Color object to change the color of the entire target movie clip.

`target`   The instance name of the movie clip that the color transformation will modify.

Color Object Methods

`myColor.`**`getRGB`**`()`

Returns the numeric values set by the last setRGB call.

`myColor.`**`getTransform`**`()`

Returns the transform value set by the last setTransform call.

`myColor.`**`setRGB`**`(0xRRGGBB)`

Specifies an RGB color for an instance of the Color object.

`0xRRGGBB`   The red, green, and blue color values in hexadecimal form.

myColor.**setTransform**(colorTransformObject)

Sets color transform information for an instance of the Color object.

    colorTransformObject   An object created with the new Object constructor. The parameters for a color transform object correspond to the settings in the Advanced Effect dialog box in the authoring environment.

CustomActions Object

CustomActions Object :: Reference > Objects > Authoring

CustomActions Object Methods

CustomActions.**get**(customActionsName)

Reads the content of the custom action XML definition file named customActionsName.

    customActionsName   The name of the custom action definition to retrieve.

CustomActions.**install**(customActionsName,customXMLDefinition)

Installs a new custom action XML definition file indicated by the customActionsName parameter.

    customActionsName   The name of the custom action definition to install.

    customXMLDefinition   The text of the XML definition to install.

CustomActions.**list**()

Returns an Array object containing the names of all the custom actions that are registered with the Flash authoring tool.

CustomActions.**uninstall**(customActionsName)

Removes the Custom Actions XML definition file named customActionsName.

    customActionsName   The name of the custom action definition to install.

Date Object

Date Object :: Reference > Objects > Core

new Date()

new Date(year, month, date, hour, min, sec, ms)

Constructor; creates a new Date object that holds the current date and time, or the date specified.

year	A value of 0–99 represents 1900–1999; four digits are needed for other years.
month	0 (January)–11 (December).
date	Optional. 1–31.
hour	Optional. 0 (midnight)–23 (11 p.m.).
min	Optional. 0–59.
sec	Optional. 0–59.
ms	Optional. 0–999.

Date Object Methods

`myDate.getDate()`

Returns the day of the month (1–31).

`myDate.getDay()`

Returns the day of the week (0–6).

`myDate.getFullYear()`

Returns the four-digit year.

`myDate.getHours()`

Returns the hour (0–23).

`myDate.getMilliseconds()`

Returns the milliseconds (0–999).

`myDate.getMinutes()`

Returns the minutes (0–59).

`myDate.getMonth()`

Returns the month (0–11).

`myDate.getSeconds()`

Returns the seconds (0–59).

`myDate.getTime()`

Returns the number of milliseconds that have elapsed since January 1, 1970, universal time.

`myDate.getTimezoneOffset()`

Returns the difference, in minutes, between universal time and local time.

`myDate.getUTCDate()`

Returns the day of the month (1–31) according to universal time.

`myDate.getUTCDay()`

Returns the day of the week (0–6) according to universal time.

`myDate.getUTCFullYear()`

Returns the four-digit year according to universal time.

`myDate.getUTCHours()`

Returns the hour (0–23) according to universal time.

`myDate.getUTCMilliseconds()`

Returns the milliseconds (0–999) according to universal time.

`myDate.getUTCMinutes()`

Returns the minutes (0–59) according to universal time.

`myDate.getUTCMonth()`

Returns the month (0–11) according to universal time.

`myDate.getUTCSeconds()`

Returns the seconds (0–59) according to universal time.

`myDate.getYear()`

Returns the year according to local time. The year is the full year minus 1900. For example, the year 2000 is represented as 100.

myDate.**setDate**(date)

> Sets the day of the month and returns the new time in milliseconds.
>
> **date**   1–31

myDate.**setFullYear**(year, month, date)

> Sets the year and returns the new time in milliseconds. If the month and date parameters are specified, they are also set.
>
> **year**   A four-digit number specifying a year. Two-digit numbers do not represent years; for example, 99 is not the year 1999, but the year 99.
>
> **month**   Optional. 0 (January)–11(December).
>
> **date**   Optional. 1–31.

myDate.**setHours**(hour, min, sec, ms)

> Sets the hours for the specified Date object in local time and returns the new time in milliseconds.
>
> **hour**   0 (midnight)–23 (11 p.m.).
>
> **min**   Optional. 0–59.
>
> **sec**   Optional. 0–59.
>
> **ms**   Optional. 0–999.

myDate.**setMilliseconds**(ms)

> Sets the milliseconds for the specified Date object in local time and returns the new time in milliseconds.
>
> **ms**   Optional. 0–999.

myDate.**setMinutes**(min, sec, ms)

> Sets the minutes for the specified Date object in local time and returns the new time in milliseconds.
>
> **min**   Optional. 0–59.
>
> **sec**   Optional. 0–59.
>
> **ms**   Optional. 0–999.

myDate.**setMonth**(month,date)

> Sets the month for the specified Date object in local time and returns the new time in milliseconds.
>
> **month**   0 (January)–11(December).
>
> **date**   Optional. 1–31.

myDate.**setSeconds**(seconds,ms)

> Sets the seconds for the specified Date object in local time and returns the new time in milliseconds.
>
> **sec**   Optional. 0–59.
>
> **ms**   Optional. 0–999.

myDate.**setTime**(value)

> Sets the date in milliseconds since midnight on January 1, 1970, and returns the new time in milliseconds.
>
> **value**   The elapsed time.

`myDate.`**`setUTCDate`**`(date)`

Sets the day of the month in universal time and returns the new time in milliseconds.

date   1–31.

`myDate.`**`setUTCFullYear`**`(year, month, date)`

Sets the year, month, and date in universal time and returns the new time in milliseconds.

year   A four-digit number specifying a year. Two-digit numbers do not represent years; for example, 99 is not the year 1999, but the year 99.

month   Optional. 0 (January)–11(December).

date   Optional. 1–31.

`myDate.`**`setUTCHours`**`(hour, min, sec, ms)`

Sets the hour, minute, second, and millisecond in universal time.

hour   0 (midnight)–23 (11 p.m.).

min   Optional. 0–59.

sec   Optional. 0–59.

ms   Optional. 0–999.

`myDate.`**`setUTCMilliseconds`**`(ms)`

Sets the milliseconds in universal time.

ms   Optional. 0–999.

`myDate.`**`setUTCMinutes`**`(minutes,seconds, ms)`

Sets the minute, second, and millisecond in universal time.

min   Optional. 0–59.

sec   Optional. 0–59.

ms   Optional. 0–999.

`myDate.`**`setUTCMonth`**`(month,date)`

Sets the month and date in universal time.

month   0 (January)–11 (December).

date   Optional. 1–31.

`myDate.`**`setUTCSeconds`**`(seconds,ms)`

Sets the seconds in universal time.

sec   Optional. 0–59.

ms   Optional. 0–999.

`myDate.`**`setYear`**`(year);`

Sets the year for the specified Date object in local time, and returns the new time in milliseconds.

year   If year is an integer 0–99, `setYear` sets the year at 1900+year; otherwise, the year is the value of the year parameter.

`myDate.`**`toString`**`();`

Returns a string of the date in a readable form.

myDate.**UTC**(year, month, date, hour, min, sec, ms)

Returns the number of milliseconds between midnight on January 1, 1970, universal time, and the time specified in the parameters. This method lets you create a Date object that assumes universal time instead of local time.

year   A four-digit number, for example, 2000.

month   0 (January)–11(December).

date   Optional. 1–31.

hour   0 (midnight)–23 (11 p.m.).

min   Optional. 0–59.

sec   Optional. 0–59.

ms   Optional. 0–999.

Function Object

Function Object ::   Reference > Objects > Core

Function Object Methods

myFunction.**apply**(thisObject, argumentsObject)

Specifies the value to be used within any function that ActionScript calls. This method also specifies the parameters to be passed to any called function.

thisObject   The object to which myFunction is applied.

argumentsObject   An array whose elements are passed to myFunction as parameters.

myFunction.**call**(thisObject, parameter1...parameterN)

Invokes the function represented by a Function object. Every function in ActionScript is represented by a Function object, so all functions support the call method. In almost all cases, the function call operator () might be used instead of the call method.

thisObject   Specifies the value of this within the function body.

parameter1,...parameterN The text of the XML definition to install.

Function Object Properties

myFunction.**prototype**

In a constructor function, the prototype property refers to an object that is the prototype of the constructed class. Each instance of the class that is created by the constructor function inherits all the properties and methods from the prototype object.

Key Object

Key Object :: Reference > Objects > Movie

Key Object Methods

Key.addListener(newListener)

Registers an object to receive onKeyDown and onKeyUp notification.

newListener   An object with methods onKeyDown and onKeyUp.

Key.getAscii()

Returns the ASCII code of the last key pressed or released. The ASCII values returned are English keyboard values.

Key.getCode()

Returns the key code value of the last key pressed.

Key.isDown(keycode)

Returns true if the key listed in keycode is depressed.

keycode   The key code value assigned to a specific key, or a Key object property associated with a specific key.

Key.isToggled(keycode)

Returns true if the Num Lock or Caps Key is activated.

keycode   The key code for Caps Lock (20) or Num Lock (144). On the Macintosh, the key code values for these keys are identical.

Key.removeListener(listener)

Removes an object previously registered with the addListener method. If the listener was successfully removed, the method returns true. If the listener was not successfully removed, the method returns false.

listener   An object.

Key Object Constants

Key.BACKSPACE

Keycode value for the Backspace key (8).

Key.CAPSLOCK

Keycode value for the Caps Lock key (20).

Key.CONTROL

Keycode for the Control key (17).

Key.DELETEKEY

Keycode for the Delete key (46).

Key.DOWN

Keycode for the Down Arrow key (40).

Key.END

Keycode for the End key (35).

Key.ENTER

Keycode for the Enter key (13).

Key.ESCAPE

Keycode for the Escape key (27).

Key.**HOME**

> Keycode for the Home key (36).

Key.**INSERT**

> Keycode for the Insert key (45).

Key.**LEFT**

> Keycode for the Left Arrow key (37).

Key.**PGDN**

> Keycode for the Page Down key (34).

Key.**PGUP**

> Keycode for the Page Up key (33).

Key.**RIGHT**

> Keycode for the Right Arrow key (39).

Key.**SHIFT**

> Keycode for the Shift Key (16).

Key.**SPACE**

> Keycode for the Space bar (32).

Key.**TAB**

> Keycode for the Tab key (9).

Key.**UP**

> Keycode for the Up Arrow key (38).

Key Object Listeners

To use listeners, you must create a Listener object. You then can define a function for a specific listener and use the `addListener` method to register the listener with the Key object. Listeners enable different pieces of code to cooperate because multiple listeners can receive notification about a single event.

The following syntax invokes listeners as well as the syntax listed:

```
someListener = new Object()
Key.addListener(someListener)
someListener.onKeyDown = function () {...}
```

> Notified when a key is pressed.

```
someListener.onKeyUp = function () {...}
```

> Notified when a key is released.

LoadVars Object

LoadVars Object :: Reference > Objects > Client/Server

`new LoadVars()`

> Constructor; creates an instance of the LoadVars object. You then can use the methods of that LoadVars object to send and load data.

LoadVars Object Methods

myLoadVars.**getBytesLoaded**()

Returns the number of bytes downloaded by a load or sendAndLoad method. The getBytesLoaded method returns as undefined if no load operation is in progress or if a load operation has not yet been initiated.

myLoadVars.**getBytesTotal**()

Returns the number of total bytes that are downloaded by a load or sendAndLoad operation. The getBytesTotal method returns as undefined if no load operation is in progress or if a load operation has not yet been initiated. The getBytesTotal method also returns as undefined if the number of total bytes can't be determined, as would be the case if the download was initiated but the server did not transmit an HTTP content-length.

myLoadVars.**load**("url")

Downloads variables from the specified url, parses the variable data, and places the resulting variables into myLoadVars.

url   The url from which to download the variables.

myLoadVarsObject.**send**("url",target,method)

Sends the variables in the myLoadVars object to the specified URL. All enumerable variables in the myLoadVars object are concatenated into a string in the application/x-www-urlform-encoded format by default, and the string is posted to the URL using the HTTP POST method.

url   The url to which to upload variables.

target   The browser frame window in which any response will be displayed.

method   The GET or POST method of the HTTP protocol.

myLoadVars.**sendAndLoad**("url", targetObject, method)

Posts variables in the myLoadVars object to the specified URL. The server response is downloaded, parsed as variable data, and the resulting variables are placed in the targetObject object.

url   The url to which to upload variables.

targetObject   The LoadVars object that receives the downloaded variables.

method   The GET or POST method of the HTTP protocol.

loadVarsObject.**toString**()

Returns a string containing all enumerable variables in the LoadVars object, in the MIME content encoding application/x-www-urlform-encoded.

LoadVars Object Properties

myLoadVars.**contentType**

The MIME type that is sent to the server when you call the LoadVars.send or LoadVars.sendAndLoad method. The default is application/x-www-urlform encoded.

myLoadVars.**loaded**

When a load or sendAndLoad operation is started, the loaded property is set to false. When the load or sendAndLoad operation completes, the loaded property is set to true. If the load operation has not yet completed or failed with an error, the loaded property remains set to false.

myLoadVars.**onLoad**(success)

> Invoked when a load or sendAndLoad operation has ended. If the operation was successful, the loadVarsObject is populated with variables downloaded by the load or sendAndLoad operation, and these variables are available when onLoad is invoked.
>
> **success**   Indicates whether the load operation ended in success (true) or failure (false).

Math Object

Math Object ::   Reference > Objects > Core

Math Object Methods

Math.**abs**(x)

> Returns the absolute value.
>
> **x**   Any number.

Math.**acos**(x)

> Returns the arc cosine of the number in radians.
>
> **x**   A number from –1.0–1.0.

Math.**asin**(x)

> Returns the arc sine of the number in radians.
>
> **x**   A number from –1.0–1.0.

Math.**atan**(x)

> Returns the arc tangent of the number in radians.
>
> **x**   Any number.

Math.**atan2**(y,x)

> Returns the arc tangent of y/x in radians.
>
> **y**   The y-axis point.
>
> **x**   The x-axis point.

Math.**ceil**(x)

> Returns the closest integer that is greater or equal to the number.
>
> **x**   Any number or expression.

Math.**cos**(x)

> Returns the cosine of the number in radians.
>
> **x**   An angle measured in radians.

Math.**exp**(x)

> Returns the value of the base of the natural algorithm.
>
> **x**   The exponent; a number or expression.

Math.**floor**(x)

> Returns the closest integer less than or equal to the number.
>
> **x**   A number or expression.

`Math.`**`log`**`(x)`

>   Returns the natural logarithm of the number.
>
>   **x**   A number or expression greater than 0.

`Math.`**`max`**`(x,y)`

>   Evaluates x and y and returns the larger number.
>
>   **x**   A number or expression.
>
>   **y**   A number or expression.

`Math.`**`min`**`(x, y)`

>   Evaluates x and y and returns the smaller number.
>
>   **x**   A number or expression.
>
>   **y**   A number or expression.

`Math.`**`pow`**`(base, exponent)`

>   Computes base to the power of exponent (base^{exponent}). For example,
>   `Math.pow(3,3);  // = 27 (3*3*3) or 3`^{3}
>
>   **base**   A number to be raised to a power.
>
>   **exponent**   The number to which the base is raised.

`Math.`**`random`**`()`

>   Returns a random number between 0 and 1.

`Math.`**`round`**`(x)`

>   Rounds the value to the nearest integer.
>
>   **x**   Any number.

`Math.`**`sin`**`(x)`

>   Returns the value of sine in radians.
>
>   **x**   An angle measured in radians.

`Math.`**`sqrt`**`(x)`

>   Returns the square root of the number.
>
>   **x**   A number or expression greater than 0.

`Math.`**`tan`**`(x)`

>   Returns the tangent of the number in radians.
>
>   **x**   An angle measured in radians.

Math Object Properties

`Math.`**`E`**

>   Euler's constant; the base of natural logarithms expressed as e.

`Math.`**`LN2`**

>   Natural log of 2.

`Math.`**`LN10`**

>   Natural log of 10.

`Math.`**`LOG2E`**

>   Base 2 of the log of e.

`Math.`**`LOG10E`**

>   Base 10 of the log of e.

Math.**PI**

> Value of pi with a value of 3.14159265358979.

Math.**SQRT1_2**

> Reciprocal of the square root of ?; has the approximate value of .707106781186.

Math.**SQRT2**

> Square root of 2 with the approximate value of 1.414213562373.

Mouse Object

Mouse Object ::   Reference > Objects > Movie

Mouse Object Methods

Mouse.**addListener**(newListener)

> Registers a Listener object to receive notifications of the onMouseDown, onMouseMove, and onMouseUp callback handlers.
>
> **newListener**   An object.

Mouse.**hide**()

> Hides the cursor in a movie.

Mouse.**removeListener**(listener)

> Removes a Listener object. Returns true if the Listener object is removed successfully. Otherwise, returns false.
>
> **listener**   An object.

Mouse.**show**()

> Displays the cursor in a movie.

Mouse Object Listeners

To use listeners, you must create a Listener object. You can then define a function for a specific listener and use the addListener method to register the listener with the Mouse object. Listeners make different pieces of code cooperate because multiple listeners can receive notification about a single event.

The following listeners respond to the subsequent syntax as well as what is shown:

```
someListener = new Object()
Mouse.addListener(someListener)
SomeListener.onMouseDown = function () {...}
```

> Notified when the mouse is pressed.

```
SomeListener.onMouseMove = function () {...}
```

> Notified when the mouse moves.

```
SomeListener.onMouseUp = function () {...}
```

> Notified when the mouse is released.

MovieClip Object

MovieClip Object :: Reference > Objects > Movie

MovieClip Object Methods

myMovieClip.**attachMovie**(idname, newname, depth, initObject)

Takes a symbol from the library and creates a new instance of the movie clip on the Stage.

idname	The name given in the Linkage dialog box in the library.
newname	A unique name for the instance of the movie clip being placed.
depth	The depth level of the movie clip.
initObject	Optional. An object containing properties with which to populate the newly attached movie clip.

myMovieClip.**createEmptyMovieClip**(instanceName, depth)

Creates an empty movie clip as a child of an existing movie clip.

instanceName	The instance name of the new text field.
depth	The depth level of the text field.
x	The x coordinate of the new text field.
y	The y coordinate of the new text field.
width	The width of the new text field.
height	The height of the new text field.

myMovieClip.**duplicateMovieClip**(newname, depth, initObject)

Creates a new instance of the specified movie clip while the movie is playing. Duplicated clips always begin playing at frame 1.

newname	A unique name for the instance of the duplicated movie clip.
depth	The depth level of the movie clip.
initObject	Optional. An object created with the Object constructor. Contains properties with which to populate the newly attached movie clip.

myMovieClip.**getBounds**(targetCoordinateSpace)

Returns an object with the properties xMin, xMax, yMin, and yMax.

targetCoordinateSpace	The target path of the Timeline whose coordinate system you want to use as a reference point.

myMovieClip.**getBytesLoaded**()

Returns the number of bytes loaded.

myMovieClip.**getBytesTotal**()

Returns the total number of bytes in a movie clip.

myMovieclip.**getDepth**()

Returns the depth of a movie clip instance.

myMovieClip.**getURL**("url", window, variables)

Loads a document specified in the url parameter into a window.

url	The URL of the target document.

window   Optional. Specifies the name, frame, or expression specifying the window or HTML frame into which the document is loaded. You can also use one of the following reserved target names: _self specifies the current frame in the current window, _blank specifies a new window, _parent specifies the parent of the current frame, and _top specifies the top-level frame in the current window.

variables   Optional. Specifies how any variables will be sent using a GET or POST method.

myMovieClip.**globalToLocal**(point)

Converts the point object from global (Stage) to local (movie clip) coordinates.

point   The name of an object specifying the x and y coordinates.

myMovieClip.**gotoAndPlay**(frame)

Starts playing a movie at the specified frame.

frame   The frame number to start playing.

myMovieClip.**gotoAndStop**(frame)

Goes to a specified frame in the movie and stops playing.

frame   The frame number to go to.

myMovieClip.**hitTest**(x, y, shapeFlag)

myMovieClip.**hitTest**(target)

Checks whether the movie clip overlaps with an area specified in the target or x and y parameters.

x   The x coordinate of the hit area.

y   The y coordinate of the hit area.

shapeFlag   A Boolean value to specify whether the bounding box (false) or entire shape (true) will be identified as the hit area.

target   The target path of the hit area.

myMovieClip.**loadMovie**("url", variables)

Loads additional Flash movies (SWF) or JPEG files without closing the current movie.

url   The absolute or relative URL of the SWF or JPEG to load.

variables   Optional. Specifies which method to use for sending and loading variables. Values are GET or POST.

myMovieClip.**loadVariables**("url", variables)

Reads data from an external text file into the myMovieClip movie and sets the values for variables in myMovieClip.

url   The absolute or relative URL for the external file that contains the variables to be loaded.

variables   Optional. Specifies which method to use for sending and loading variables. Values are GET or POST.

myMovieClip.**localToGlobal**(point)

Converts the point object from the local (movie clip) to global (movie) coordinates.

point   The name of an object specifying the x and y coordinates.

myMovieClip.**nextFrame**()

Advances to the next frame.

`myMovieClip.`**`play`**`()`

> Plays the movie clip.

`myMovieClip.`**`prevFrame`**`()`

> Sends the playhead back a frame.

`myMovieClip.`**`removeMovieClip`**`()`

> Removes a movie clip instance created with the `duplicateMovieClip` action.

`myMovieClip.`**`setMask`**`(maskMovieClip)`

> Makes the movie clip in the parameter `maskMovieClip` into a mask that reveals the movie clip specified by the `myMovieClip` parameter.

> **`maskMovieclip`**   The instance name of a movie clip that will be a mask.

`myMovieClip.`**`startDrag`**`(lock, left, top, right, bottom)`

> Enables the movie clip to be draggable.

> **`lock`**   A Boolean value; specifies if the movie clip will be locked to the center position of the mouse (true) or not (false).

> **`left`**, **`top`**, **`right`**, **`bottom`**   Optional. Values to constrain the drag of the movie clip.

`myMovieClip.`**`stop`**`()`

> Stops the movie clip.

`myMovieClip.`**`stopDrag`**`()`

> Ends the drag action of the movie clip.

`myMovieClip.`**`swapDepths`**`(depth)`

`myMovieClip.`**`swapDepths`**`(target)`

> Swaps the stacking order of the movie clips.

> **`depth`**   The depth level where the movie clip is to be placed.

> **`target`**   The movie clip instance whose depth is swapped by the instance specified in `myMovieClip`. Both instances must have the same parent movie clip.

`myMovieClip.`**`unloadMovie`**`()`

> Removes the movie clip loaded using the `loadMovie` or `attachMovie` methods.

Note that this event removes the contents of the movie without removing the instance properties or the handlers. To remove the entire movie clip, use `removeMovieClip()`.

MovieClip Object Drawing Methods

`myMovieClip.`**`beginFill`**`(rgb,alpha)`

> Indicates the beginning of a new drawing path.

> **`rgb`**   Optional. A hex color value (0xRRGGBB). If this parameter is not provided, no fill is used.

> **`alpha`**   Optional. 0–100. Specifies the alpha value of the fill. 100 is the default.

`myMovieClip.`**`beginGradientFill`**`(fillType, colors, alphas, ratios, matrix)`

> Indicates the beginning of a new drawing path.

> **`filltype`**   Either "linear" or "radial."

> **`colors`**   An array of RGB hexadecimal color (0xRRGGBB) values to be used in the gradient.

alphas   An array of alpha values, 0–100, for the corresponding colors in the colors array.

ratios   An array of color distribution ratios, 0–255.

matrix   An object that acts as a transformation matrix. The matrix object contains one of two possible sets of properties: a, b, c, d, e, f, g, h, i, which can be used to describe a 3 × 3 matrix; or `matrixType`, which is x, y, w, h, r.

myMovieClip.**clear**()

Removes all the drawing commands associated with a movie clip.

myMovieclip.**curveTo**(controlX,controlY,anchorX, anchorY)

Draws a curve using the current line style from the current drawing position to (anchorX, anchorY) using the control point specified by (controlX, controlY). The current drawing position is then set to (anchorX, anchorY).

controlX   Specifies a horizontal position relative to the registration point of the parent movie clip of the control point.

controlY   Specifies a vertical position relative to the registration point of the parent movie clip of the control point.

anchorX   Specifies a horizontal position relative to the registration point of the parent movie clip of the next anchor point.

anchorY   Specifies a vertical position relative to the registration point of the parent movie clip of the next anchor point.

myMovieClip.**endFill**()

Applies a fill to the lines and curves added since the last call to the `beginFill` or `beginGradientFill` method.

myMovieClip.**lineStyle**(thickness, rgb, alpha)

Specifies a line style that is used for subsequent calls to the `lineTo` and `curveTo` methods.

thickness   Optional. Indicates the thickness of the line in points, 0–255.

rgb   Optional. A hexadecimal color value (0xRRGGBB). If this parameter is not provided, black (0x000000) is used.

alpha   Optional. 0–100. Specifies the alpha value of the fill. 100 is the default.

myMovieclip.**lineTo**(x, y)

Draws a line using the current line style from the current drawing position to (x, y); the current drawing position is then set to (x, y).

x   The horizontal position relative to the registration point of the parent movie clip.

y   The vertical position relative to the registration point of the parent movie clip.

myMovieclip.**moveTo**(x, y)

Moves the current drawing position to (x, y).

x   The horizontal position relative to the registration point of the parent movie clip.

y   The vertical position relative to the registration point of the parent movie clip.

MovieClip Object Properties

myMovieClip.**enabled**

> Indicates whether a button movie clip in enabled. The default value is true.
> Boolean.

myMovieClip.**focusEnabled**

> If value is undefined or false, a movie clip cannot receive input focus unless it is a
> button movie clip.

myMovieclip.**hitArea**

> Designates another movie clip to serve as the hit area for a button movie clip.

myMovieclip.**tabChildren**

> If undefined or true, the children of a movie clip are included in automatic tab
> ordering. The default value is undefined.

myMovieclip.**tabEnabled**

> If undefined or true, the object is included in automatic tab ordering. Might be set
> on an instance of the MovieClip, Button, or TextField objects. It is undefined
> by default.

myMovieclip.**tabIndex**

> Lets you customize the tab ordering of objects in a movie. When used, automatic
> tab ordering is disabled, and the tab ordering is calculated from the tabIndex
> properties of objects in the movie.

myMovieClip.**trackAsMenu**

> Indicates whether other buttons or movie clips can receive mouse release events.
> Enables the creation of menu systems. Boolean.

myMovieclip.**useHandCursor**

> Indicates whether the hand cursor displays when a user rolls over a button movie
> clip. Boolean.

MovieClip Object Event Handlers

myMovieClip.**onData** = function () {...}

> Invoked when a movie clip receives data from a loadVariables or loadMovie
> call.

myMovieClip.**onDragOut** = function () {...}

> Invoked when the pointer is pressed and dragged outside and then over the movie
> clip.

myMovieClip.**onDragOver** = function () {...}

> Invoked when the pointer is pressed and dragged outside and then over the movie
> clip.

myMovieClip.**onEnterFrame** = function () {...}

> Invoked continually at the frame rate of the movie.

myMovieClip.**onKeyDown** = function () {...}

> Invoked when a movie clip has input focus and a key is pressed.

Note that the movie clip must have focusEnabled for this to work. Please see the
Selection object for setting the focus.

```
myMovieClip.onKeyUp = function () {...}
```
Invoked when a key is released.

Note that the movie clip must have focusEnabled for this to work. Please see the Selection object for setting the focus.

```
myMovieClip.onKillFocus = function (newFocus) {...}
```
Invoked when a movie clip loses keyboard focus. The onKillFocus method receives one parameter, newFocus, which is an object representing the new object receiving the focus.

newFocus   The object that is receiving the keyboard focus.

```
myMovieClip.onLoad = function () {...}
```
Invoked when the movie clip is instantiated and appears in the Timeline.

```
myMovieClip.onMouseDown = function () {...}
```
Invoked when the mouse button is pressed.

```
myMovieClip.onMouseMove = function () {...}
```
Invoked when the mouse moves.

```
myMovieClip.onMouseUp = function () {...}
```
Invoked when the mouse is released.

```
myMovieClip.onPress = function () {...}
```
Invoked when the mouse pointer is clicked on a movie clip.

```
myMovieClip.onRelease = function () {...}
```
Invoked when a button movie clip is released.

```
myMovieClip.onReleaseOutside = function () {...}
```
Invoked when the mouse is released while the pointer is outside the movie clip after the mouse button is pressed inside the movie clip.

```
myMovieClip.onRollOut = function () {...}
```
Invoked when the pointer rolls outside of a movie clip area.

```
myMovieClip.onRollOver = function () {...}
```
Invoked when the pointer rolls over a movie clip area.

```
myMovieClip.onSetFocus = function (oldFocus) {...}
```
Invoked when a movie clip receives keyboard focus. The oldFocus parameter is the object that loses the focus.

oldFocus   The object that loses the focus. For example, if the user presses the Tab key to move the input focus from a text field to a button, oldFocus contains the text field instance.

```
myMovieClip.onUnload
```
Invoked in the first frame after the movie clip is removed from the Timeline.

Number Object

Number Object :: Reference > Objects > Core

```
myNumber = new Number(value)
```

Constructor; creates a new Number object. You must use the Number constructor when using the `toString` and `valueOf` methods of the Number object. You do not use a constructor when using the properties of the Number object. The new Number constructor is primarily used as a placeholder. An instance of the Number object is not the same as the Number function that converts a parameter to a primitive value.

value   The numeric value of the Number object being created, or a value to be converted to a number.

Number Object Methods

```
myNumber.toString(radix)
```

Returns the string representation of the specified Number object (`myNumber`).

radix   Specifies the numeric base (2–36) to use for the number-to-string conversion. If you do not specify the radix parameter, the default value is 10.

`myNumber.valueOf()`   Returns the primitive value type of the specified Number object.

Number Object Constants

```
Number.MAX_VALUE
```

The largest representable number.

```
Number.MIN_VALUE
```

The smallest representable number.

```
Number.NaN
```

The IEEE-754 value representing Not A Number (NaN).

```
Number.NEGATIVE_INFINITY
```

Returns the IEEE-754 value representing negative infinity.

```
Number.POSITIVE_INFINITY
```

Returns the IEEE-754 value representing positive infinity. This value is the same as the global variable Infinity.

Object Object

Object Object :: Reference > Objects > Core

```
new Object(value)
```

Constructor; creates a new Object object.

value   Optional. A number, Boolean value, or string to be converted to an object.

Object Object Methods

myObject.**addProperty**(prop, getFunc, setFunc)

Creates a getter/setter property. When Flash reads a getter/setter property, it invokes the get function and the function's return value becomes a value of prop. When Flash writes a getter/setter property, it invokes the set function and passes it the new value as a parameter.

prop   The name of the object property to create.

getFunc   The function that is invoked to retrieve the value of the property; this parameter is a function object.

setFunc   The function that is invoked to set the value of the property; this parameter is a function object. If you pass the value null for this parameter, the property is read-only.

myObject.**registerClass**(symbolID, theClass)

Associates a movie clip symbol with an ActionScript object class. If a symbol doesn't exist, Flash creates an association between a string identifier and an object class.

symbolID   The linkage identifier of the movie clip symbol, or the string identifier for the ActionScript class.

theClass   A reference to the constructor function of the ActionScript class, or null to unregister the symbol.

myObject.**toString**()

Converts the specified object to a string and returns it.

myObject.**unwatch**(prop)

Removes a watchpoint that the Object.watch method created.

prop   The name of the object property that should no longer be watched, as a string.

myObject.**valueOf**()

Returns the primitive value of the specified object. If the object does not have a primitive value, the object itself is returned.

myObject.**watch**(prop, callback, userData)

Registers a callback function to be invoked when a specified property of an ActionScript object changes. When the property changes, the callback function is invoked with myObject as the containing object.

prop   A string indicating the name of the object property to watch.

callback   The function to invoke when the watched property changes. This parameter is a function object, not a function name as a string. The form of callback is callback (prop, oldval, newval, userData).

userData   Optional. An arbitrary piece of ActionScript data that is passed to the callback method. If the userData parameter is omitted, undefined is passed to the callback method.

Object Object Properties

myObject.**__proto__**

Refers to the prototype property of the constructor function that created myObject. The __proto__ property is automatically assigned to all objects when they are created. The ActionScript interpreter uses the __proto__ property to access the prototype property of the object's constructor function to find out what properties and methods the object inherits from its class.

Selection Object

Selection Object :: Reference > Objects > Movie

Selection Object Methods

Selection.**addListener**(newListener)

Registers an object to receive keyboard focus change notifications.

Selection.**getBeginIndex**()

Returns the index at the start of the selection.

Selection.**getCaretIndex**()

Returns the index of the blinking cursor position.

Selection.**getEndIndex**()

Returns the ending index of the current selection.

Selection.**getFocus**()

Returns variable name of the text field that has focus.

Selection.**removeListener**(listener)

Removes an object previously registered with addListener.

listener   The object that will no longer receive focus notifications.

Selection.**setFocus**("variablePath")

Focuses the editable text field associated with the variable specified by the variablePath.

variablePath   A string specifying the path to the name of a variable associated with a text field.

Selection.**setSelecton**(start, end);

Sets the selection in an editable text box.

start   The beginning index of the selection.

end   The ending index of the selection.

System Object

System Object :: Reference > Objects > Movie

System.capabilities

You can use the System.capabilites object to determine the abilities of the system and player hosting a Flash movie. This enables you to tailor content for different formats. For example, the screen of a cell phone (black and white, 100 square pixels) is different than the 1,000-square-pixel color PC screen. To provide appropriate content to as many users as possible, you can use the Capabilities object to determine the type of device a user has. You can then either specify to the server to send different SWFs based on the device capabilities, or you can tell the Flash movie to alter its presentation based on the capabilities of the device.

You can send capabilities information using a GET or POST HTTP method. The following is an example of a server string for a device that does not have MP3 support and that has a 400 × 200 pixel, 8 × 4 centimeter screen:

```
"A=t&MP3=f&AE=gsm&VE=h11&ACC=f&V=WIN%206%2C0%2C0%2C129&M=Macromedia
%WINDOWS&R=400x200&DP=72&COL=color&AR=1.0&OS=WINDOWS%2000&L=en-US"
```

The Capabilities object is available in Flash Player 6.

You must access all properties of the Capabilities object through the `System.capabilities` object.

`System.security.allowDomain`

> You can use `System.security.allowDomain` to share Flash movies from another domain. Using this method, you can identify domains where Flash can access other Flash movies.

`System.security.allowDomain( domain );`

`System.security.allowDomain("NewRiders.com");`

> Domains can be specified in the following three manners:

`NewRiders.com`, `http://NewRiders.com`, or `http://165.193.123.62`.

> Example: Movie1.swf resides on domain1.com
> (`http://domain1.com/Movie1.swf`).

> Movie2.swf resides on domain2.com
> (`http://domain2.com/Movie2.swf`).

> Movie1.swf loads Movie2.swf from domain2.com.

Movie1.swf contains this ActionScript:

`System.security.allowDomain("http://domain2.com");`

> For more information on this method, see the whitepaper on Macromedia Flash MX security by Mike Chambers (March 2002): `http://download.macromedia.com/pub/flash/whitepapers/security.pdf`.

Sound Object

Sound Object :: Reference > Objects > Movie

`New Sound(target);`

> Constructor; creates a new Sound object for a specified movie clip. If you do not specify a target instance, the Sound object controls all the sounds in the movie.

> **target**   The movie clip instance on which the Sound object operates. This parameter is optional.

Sound Object Methods

`mySound.`**`attachSound`**`("idName")`

> Attaches the sound from the library.

> **IdName**   The name set in the Linkage dialog box in the Library.

`mySound.`**`getBytesLoaded`**`()`

> Returns the number of bytes loaded (streamed) for the specified Sound object.

`mySound.`**`getBytesTotal`**`()`

> Returns the size, in bytes, of the specified Sound object.

mySound.**getPan**()

> Returns the pan level as an integer from –100–100.

mySound.**getTransform**()

> Returns the sound transform information set with the last setTransform call.

mySound.**getVolume()**

> Returns the volume level as an integer from 0–100.

mySound.**loadSound**("url", isStreaming)

> Loads an MP3 file into an instance of the Sound object.

> **url**   The absolute or relative URL for the external file that contains the sound file.

> **isStreaming**   Boolean. Indicates whether the sound is an event or a streaming sound.

mySound.**setPan**(pan)

> Determines how the sound is played in the left and right channels (speakers). For mono sounds, pan determines which speaker (left or right) the sound plays through.

> **pan**   A number from –100 (left)–100 (right).

mySound.**setTransform**(soundTransformObject)

> Sets the sound transform, or "balance" information, for a Sound object.

> **soundTransformObject**   An object holding sound transform parameters.

mySound.**setVolume**(volume)

> Sets the volume.

> **volume**   A number from 0 (no volume)–100 (highest volume).

mySound.**start**(secondsOffset, loop)

> Plays the attached sound.

> **secondsOffset**   The starting point of the sound.

> **Loop**   Optional. Specifies the number of times the sound should play consecutively.

mySound.**stop**("idName")

> Stops the sound.

> **idName**   Optional. Specifies a specific sound to stop playing.

Sound Object Properties

mySound.**duration**

> Read only. Returns the duration of a sound in milliseconds.

mySound.**position**

> Read only. Returns the number of milliseconds a sound has been playing.

Sound Object Event Handlers

mySoundObject.**onLoad** = callbackFunction

> Invoked automatically when a sound loads.

> **callbackFunction**   A function that executes when the onLoad event is invoked.

mySoundObject.**onSoundComplete** = callbackFunction

Invoked automatically when a sound finishes playing.

callbackFunction   A function that executes when the
                           onSoundComplete event is invoked.

Stage Object

Stage Object :: Reference > Objects > Movie

new Object(value)

Constructor; creates a new Object object.

value   Optional. A number, Boolean value, or string to be converted to an
                object.

Stage Object Methods

Stage.**addListener**(myListener)

Detects when a Flash movie is resized if **Stage.scaleMode** = "noScale". The
addListener method doesn't work with the default movie scaling setting
("showAll") or other scaling settings ("exactFit" and "noBorder").

myListener   An object that listens for a callback notification from the
                     onResize event.

Stage.**removeListener**(myListener)

Removes a Listener object created with addListener.

myListener   An object added to an object's callback list with the
                     addListener method.

Stage Object Properties

Stage.**align**

Indicates the current alignment of the Flash movie within the Stage.

Stage.**height**

Read only. Indicates the current height, in pixels, of the Flash movie Stage. When
the Stage.noScale property has a value of true, height represents the height of
the Flash Player. When the Stage.noScale value is false (movie scales when
player window resized), height represents the height of the Flash movie.

Stage.**scaleMode** = "value"

Indicates the current scaling of the Flash movie within the Stage. The scaleMode
property forces the movie into a specific scaling mode. By default, the movie uses
the HTML parameters set in the Publish Settings dialog box.

The scaleMode property can use the values "exactFit", "showAll", "noBorder",
and "noScale". Any other value sets the scaleMode property to the default
"showAll".

Stage.**showMenu**

No information.

`Stage.`**`width`**

Read only. Indicates the current width, in pixels, of the Flash movie Stage. When the value of `Stage.noScale` is true, the width property represents the width of the Player. When the value of `Stage.noScale` is false (movie scales when the Player window is resized), width represents the width of the Flash movie.

Stage Object Event Handlers

`Stage.`**`onResize`**`() = function() {...}`

Callback method; indicates that the Flash movie was resized. You can use this event to write a function that lays out the objects on the Stage when a movie is resized.

String Object

String Object :: Reference > Objects > Core

`new String(value)`

Constructor; creates a new String object.

`value`   The initial value of the new String object.

String Object Methods

`myString.`**`charAt`**`(index)`

Returns the character in the position specified by the parameter index.

`index`   The number of the character in the string to be returned.

`myString.`**`charCodeAt`**`(index)`

Returns a 16-bit integer from 0–65535 that represents the character specified by index.

`index`   Specifies the position of a character in the string.

`myString.`**`concat`**`(value1,...valueN)`

Combines the value of the String object with the parameters and returns a new string. Leaves the original string unchanged.

`value1,...valueN`   Zero or more values to be concatenated.

`myString.`**`fromCharCode`**`(c1, c2,...cN)`

Returns a string made up of the characters represented by the ASCII values in the parameters.

`c1,c2...cN`   Decimal integers that represent ASCII values.

`myString.`**`indexOf`**`(substring, startIndex)`

Searches the string and returns the position of the first occurrence of the specified substring. Returns –1 if the value is not found.

`substring`   The substring to be searched for within `myString`.

`startIndex`   Optional. The starting point in `myString` to search for substring.

myString.**lastIndexOf**(substring, startIndex)

Searches the string from right to left and returns the index of the last occurrence of substring.

substring   Specifies the string to be searched for.

startIndex   Optional. Specifies the starting point.

myString.**slice**(start, end)

Extracts a slice, or substring, of the specified String object; then returns it as a new string without modifying the original String object.

start   Specifies the index of the starting point for the slice. This character is included in the new string.

end   Specifies the index of the ending point for the slice. This character is not included in the new string.

myString.**split**("delimiter", limit)

Splits a String object into substrings by breaking it wherever the specified delimiter parameter occurs, and returns the substrings in an array.

delimiter   The character or string at which myString splits.

limit   Optional. The number of items to place into the array.

myString.**substr**(start, length)

Returns the characters in a string from the index specified in the start parameter through the number of characters specified in the length parameter. Returns a new string.

start   Indicates the position of the first character in myString to be used to create the substring.

length   Optional. The number of characters in the substring being created.

myString.**substring**(from, to)

Returns a string consisting of the characters between the points specified by the from and to parameters.

from   Indicates the position of the first character of myString used to create the substring.

to   Indicates 1+ the index of the last character in myString to be extracted.

myString.**toLowerCase**()

Returns a copy of the String object, with all the uppercase characters converted to lowercase. The original value is unchanged.

myString.**toUpperCase**()

Returns a copy of the String object, with all the lowercase characters converted to uppercase. The original value is unchanged.

String Object Properties

string.**length**

Returns the number of characters in the specified String object.

TextField Object

TextField Object :: Reference > Objects > Movie

TextField Object Methods

TextField.**addListener**(newListener)

Registers an object to receive event notifications. When the onChanged or onScroller event occurs, the TextField.onChanged and TextField.onScroller events are invoked, followed by the onChanged and onScroller methods of listening objects registered with addListener.

newListener   An object with the events onChanged and onScroller notifications.

TextField.**getDepth**()

Returns the depth of a text field.

TextField.**getFontList**()

Returns an Array object whose elements are the names of all fonts on the Flash Player host system, including fonts in the SWF file and any loaded asset SWF files. The names are of type string.

TextField.**getNewTextFormat**()

Returns a TextFormat object containing a copy of the text field's text format object. The text format object is the format that newly inserted text, such as text inserted with the replaceSel method or text entered by a user, receives. When getNewTextFormat is invoked, the TextFormat object returned has all its properties defined. No property is null.

TextField.**getTextFormat**()

TextField.**getTextFormat**(index)

TextField.**getTextFormat**(beginIndex, endIndex)

Usage 1: Returns a TextFormat object containing formatting information for all text in a text field. Only properties that are common to all text in the text field are set in the resulting TextFormat object. Any property that is mixed, meaning that it has different values at different points in the text, has its value set to null.

Usage 2: Returns a TextFormat object containing a copy of the text field's text format at index.

Usage 3: Returns a TextFormat object containing formatting information for the span of text from beginIndex to endIndex.

index   An integer that specifies a character in a string.

beginIndex   An integer that specifies the first character of the desired text span.

endIndex   An integer that specifies the first character after the desired text span.

Selection.**removeListener**(listener)

If the listener was successfully removed, the method returns a true value.

listener   The object that will no longer receive focus notifications.

TextField.**removeTextField**()

Removes the text field specified by TextField. This operation can be performed only on a text field that was created with the createTextField method of the MovieClip object.

`TextField.`**`replaceSel`**`(text)`

> Replaces the current selection with the contents of the text parameter.
>
> **`text`**   A string.

`TextField.`**`setNewTextFormat`**`(textFormat)`

> Sets a `TextFormat` object for newly inserted text, such as text inserted with the `replaceSel` method or text entered by a user in a text field. Each text field has a new text format. When text is inserted, the new text is assigned the new text format.
>
> **`textFormat`**   An instance of the `TextFormat` object.

`TextField.`**`setTextFormat`** `(textFormat)`

`TextField.`**`setTextFormat`** `(index, textFormat)`

`TextField.`**`setTextFormat`** `(beginIndex, endIndex, textFormat)`

> Sets a text format object for a specified range of text in a text field. You can assign each character in a text field a text format.
>
> Usage 1: Applies the properties of `textFormat` to all text in the text field.
>
> Usage 2: Applies the properties of `textFormat` to the character at position index.
>
> Usage 3: Applies the properties of the `textFormat` parameter to the span of text from the `beginIndex` parameter to the `endIndex` parameter.
>
> | | |
> |---|---|
> | **`textFormat`** | An instance of the `TextFormat` object. A `TextFormat` object contains character and paragraph formatting information. |
> | **`index`** | An integer. |
> | **`beginIndex`** | An integer that specifies the first character of the desired text span. |
> | **`endIndex`** | An integer that specifies the first character after the desired text span. |

TextFormat Object Properties

`TextField.`**`autoSize`**

> Controls automatic sizing and alignment of text fields.

`TextField.`**`background`**

> If true, the text field has a background fill. If false, the text field has no background fill.

`TextField.`**`backgroundColor`**

> The color of the text field background. `BackgroundColor` is visible only if the text field has a border. Default is 0xFFFFFF (white). This property can be retrieved or set, even if there currently is no background.

`TextField.`**`border`**

> If true, the text field has a border. If false, the text field has no border.

`TextField.`**`borderColor`**

> The color of the text field border. The default is 0x000000 (black). This property can be retrieved or set, even if there is currently no border.

`TextField.`**`bottomScroll`**

> Read only. An integer (1-based index) that indicates the bottom-most line that is currently visible in `TextField`.

TextField.**embedFonts**

> Boolean. When true, renders the text field using embedded font outlines. If false, it renders text field using device fonts.

TextField.**hscroll**

> Indicates the current horizontal scrolling position. If the hscroll property is **0**, the text is not horizontally scrolled.

TextField.**html**

> A flag that indicates whether the text field contains an HTML representation. If the html property is true, the text field is an HTML text field. If html is false, the text field is a non-HTML text field.

TextField.**htmlText**

> If the text field is an HTML text field, this property contains the HTML representation of the text field's contents. If the text field is not an HTML text field, it behaves identically to the text property. You can indicate that a text field is an HTML text field in the Properties Inspector, or by setting the text field's html property to true.

TextField.**length**

> Read only. Indicates the number of characters in a text field. This property returns the same value as text.length, but is faster. A character such as tab ("\t") counts as one character.

TextField.**maxChars**

> Indicates the maximum number of characters that the text field can contain. A script might insert more text than maxChars allows; the maxChars property indicates only how much text a user can enter. If the value of this property is null, there is no limit on the amount of text a user can enter.

TextField.**maxhscroll**

> Read only. Indicates the maximum value of TextField.hscroll.

TextField.**maxscroll**

> Read only. Indicates the maximum value of TextField.scroll.

TextField.**multilane**

> Indicates whether the text field is a multiline text field. If the value is true, the text field is multiline; if the value is false, the text field is a single-line text field.

TextField.**password**

> If the value of password is true, the text field is a password text field and hides the input characters. If false, the text field is not a password text field.

TextField.**restrict**

> Indicates the set of characters that a user might enter into the text field.

TextField.**scroll**

> Defines the vertical position of text in a text field.

TextField.**selectable**

> Boolean. Indicates whether the text field is selectable. The value true indicates that the text is selectable.

TextField.**tabEnabled**

> Might be set on an instance of the MovieClip, Button, or TextField objects. It is undefined by default.

TextField.**tabIndex**

> Lets you customize the tab ordering of objects in a movie. You can set the tabIndex property on a button, movie clip, or text field instance; it is undefined by default.

TextField.**text**

> Indicates the current text in the text field. Lines are separated by the carriage return character ('\r', ASCII 13). This property contains the normal, unformatted text in the text field, without HTML tags, even if the text field is HTML.

TextField.**textColor**

> Indicates the color of the text in a text field.

TextField.**textHeight**

> Indicates the height of the text.

TextField.**textWidth**

> Indicates the width of the text.

TextField.**type**

> Specifies the type of text field. There are two values: "dynamic", which specifies a dynamic text field and cannot be edited by the user, and "input", which specifies an input text field.

TextField.**_variable**

> The name of the variable with which the text field is associated. The type of this property is String.

TextField.**wordWrap**

> Boolean. Indicates if the text field has word wrap. If the value of wordWrap is true, the text field has word wrap; if the value is false, the text field does not have word wrap.

TextField Object Event Handlers

TextField.**onChanged**

> An event handler and a listener. Invoked when the content of a text field changes. By default, it is undefined; you can define it in a script.

TextField.**onKillFocus** = function (newFocus) {...}

> An event that is invoked when a text field loses keyboard focus.
>
> **newFocus**   The object that is receiving the focus.

TextField.**onScroller**

> An event handler and a listener. Invoked when one of the text field scroll properties changes.

TextField.**onSetFocus** = function(oldFocus){...}

> Invoked when a text field receives keyboard focus. The oldFocus parameter is the object that loses the focus. For example, if the user presses the Tab key to move the input focus from a button to a text field, oldFocus contains the text field instance.
>
> **oldFocus**   The object that loses the focus. For example, if the user presses the Tab key to move the input focus from a text field to a button, oldFocus contains the text field instance.

TextField Object Listeners

To use listeners, you must create a Listener object. You can then define a function for a specific listener and use the `addListener` method to register the listener with the `TextField` object. Listeners enable different pieces of code to cooperate because multiple listeners can receive notification about a single event.

The following listeners respond to the subsequent syntax as well as to what is shown:

```
someListener = new Object()
```

```
TextField.addListener(someListener)
```

```
TextField.onChanged = function() {...}
```

> An event handler and a listener. Invoked when the content of a text field changes. By default, it is undefined; you can define it in a script.

```
TextField.onScroller = function() {...}
```

> An event handler and a listener. Invoked when one of the text field scroll properties changes.

TextFormat Object

TextFormat Object :: Reference > Objects > Movie

```
new TextFormat(font, size, color, bold, italic, underline, url,
target, align, leftMargin, rightMargin, indent, leading)
```

> Constructor; creates an instance of the `TextFormat` object with the specified properties. You can then change the properties of the `TextFormat` object to change the formatting of text fields.
>
> Any parameter might be set to the value null to indicate that it is not defined. All the parameters are optional; any omitted parameters are treated as null.

font	Optional. The name of a font for text as a string.
size	Optional. An integer that indicates the point size.
color	Optional. The color of text using this text format. A number containing three. 8-bit RGB components; such as 0xFF0000 for red and 0x00FF00 for green.
bold	Optional. A Boolean value that indicates whether the text is boldface.
italic	Optional. A Boolean value that indicates whether the text is italicized.
underline	Optional. A Boolean value that indicates whether the text is underlined.
url	Optional. The URL to which the text in this text format hyperlinks. If url is an empty string, the text does not have a hyperlink.
target	Optional. The target window where the hyperlink is displayed. If the target window is an empty string, the text is displayed in the default target window, which is _self. If the `TextFormat.url` property is set to an empty string or to the value null, this property may be get or set but has no effect.

align	Optional. The alignment of the paragraph, represented as a string. If "left", the paragraph is left-aligned. If "center", the paragraph is centered. If "right", the paragraph is right-aligned.
leftMargin	Optional. Indicates the left margin of the paragraph, in points.
rightMargin	Optional. Indicates the right margin of the paragraph, in points.
indent	Optional. An integer that indicates the indentation from the left margin to the first character in the paragraph.
leading	Optional. A number that indicates the amount of leading vertical space between lines.

TextFormat Object Methods

TextFormat.getTextExtent (text)

Returns the size of the text string specified in the text parameter in this character format. The return value is an object of class Object with two properties, width, and height. The text is treated as plain text (not HTML). The text is a single line of text; carriage returns and line feeds are ignored, and no word wrap is applied.

Text   A string.

TextFormat Object Properties

TextFormat.align

Indicates the alignment of the paragraph, represented as a string.

TextFormat.blockIndent

A number that indicates the block indentation in points. Block indentation is applied to an entire block of text, that is, to all lines of the text.

TextFormat.bold

A Boolean value that indicates if the text is boldface.

TextFormat.bullet

A Boolean value that indicates that the text is part of a bulleted list.

TextFormat.color

Indicates the color of text. A number containing three, 8-bit RGB components, such as 0xFF0000 for red and 0x00FF00 for green.

TextFormat.font

The name of the font for text in this text format, as a string.

TextFormat.indent

An integer that indicates the indentation from the left margin to the first character in the paragraph.

TextFormat.italic

Boolean value that indicates whether text in this text format is italicized.

TextFormat.leading

The amount of leading vertical space between lines.

TextFormat.leftMargin

The left margin of the paragraph, in points.

TextFormat.rightMargin

The right margin of the paragraph, in points.

TextFormat.**size**

> The point size of text in this text format.

TextFormat.**tabStops**

> Specifies custom tab stops as an array of non-negative integers. Each tab stop is specified in points. If custom tab stops are not specified (null), the default tab stop is 4 (average character width).

TextFormat.**target**

> Indicates the target window where the hyperlink is displayed. If the target window is an empty string, the text is displayed in the default target window.

TextFormat.**underline**

> Boolean value that indicates if the text that uses this TextFormat is underlined.

TextFormat.**url**

> Indicates the URL to which text in this text format hyperlinks.

XML Object

XML Object :: Reference > Objects > Client/Server

new XML(source)

> Constructor; creates a new XML object. The constructor method must be used to create an instance of the XML object before calling any XML object method.
>
> **source**   Optional. The XML text parsed to create the new XML object.

XML Object Methods

myXML.**appendChild**(childNode)

> Appends the specified child node to the XML object's child list.
>
> **childNode**   The child node to be added to the specified XML object's child list.

myXML.**cloneNode**(deep)

> Constructs and returns a new XML node of the same type, name, value, and attributes as the specified XML object.
>
> **deep**   Boolean. Specifies whether the children of the XML object are recursively cloned.

myXML.**createElement**(name)

> Constructor; creates a new XML element with the name specified in the parameter. The new element initially has no parent, no children, and no siblings. The method returns a reference to the newly created XML object representing the element. This method and createTextNode are the constructor methods for creating nodes for an XML object.
>
> **name**   The tag name of the XML element being created.

myXML.**createTextNode**(text)

> Constructor; creates a new XML text node with the specified text. The new node initially has no parent, and text nodes cannot have children or siblings. This method returns a reference to the XML object representing the new text node. This method and createElement are the constructor methods for creating nodes for an XML object.

text   The text used to create the new text node.

XML.getBytesLoaded()

Returns the number of bytes loaded (streamed) for the XML document.

XML.getBytesTotal()

Returns the size, in bytes, of the XML document.

myXML.hasChildNodes()

Returns true if the specified XML object has child nodes; otherwise, returns false.

myXML.insertBefore(childNode, beforeNode)

Inserts a new child node into the XML object's child list, before the beforeNode node.

childNode   The node to be inserted.

beforeNode   The node before the insertion point for the childNode.

myXML.load(url)

Loads an XML document from the specified URL and replaces the contents of the specified XML object with the downloaded XML data.

url   The URL where the XML document to be loaded is located.

myXML.parseXML(source)

Parses the XML text specified in the source parameter and populates the specified XML object with the resulting XML tree.

source   The XML text to be parsed and passed to the specified XML object.

myXML.childNodes[1].removeNode()

Removes the specified XML object from its parent. All descendants of the node are also deleted.

myXML.send(url, window)

Encodes the specified XML object into an XML document and sends it to the specified URL using the POST method.

url   The destination URL for the specified XML object.

window   Optional.

myXML.sendAndLoad(url,targetXMLobject)

Encodes the specified XML object into an XML document, sends it to the specified URL using the POST method, downloads the server's response, and then loads it into the targetXMLobject specified in the parameters. The server response is loaded in the same manner used by the load method.

url   The destination URL for the specified XML object.

targetXMLobject   An XML object created with the XML constructor method that will receive the return information from the server.

myXML.toString()

Evaluates the specified XML object, constructs a textual representation of the XML structure including the node, children, and attributes, and returns the result as a string.

XML Object Properties

myXML.**attributes**

Collection. Read-write. Returns an associative array containing all attributes of the specified XML object.

myXML.**childNodes**

Collection. Read only. Returns an array of the specified XML object's children. Each element in the array is a reference to an XML object that represents a child node.

myXML.**contentType**

The MIME type that is sent to the server when you call the XML.send or XML.sendAndLoad method.

myXML.**XMLdocTypeDecl**

Sets and returns information about the XML document DOCTYPE declaration.

myXML.**firstChild**

Read only. Evaluates the specified XML object and references the first child in the parent node's children list.

myXML.**ignoreWhite**
XML.prototype.**ignoreWhite**

Boolean. Default setting is false. When set to true, text nodes that contain only white space are discarded during the parsing process. Text nodes with leading or trailing white space are unaffected.

myXML.**lastChild**

Read only. Evaluates the XML object and references the last child in the parent node's child list.

myXML.**loaded**

Boolean. Read only. Determines whether the document-loading process initiated by the XML.load() call has completed.

myXML.**nextSibling**

Read only. Evaluates the XML object and references the next sibling in the parent node's child list.

myXML.**nodeName**

Takes or returns the node name of the XML object.

myXML.**nodeType**

Read only. Takes or returns a nodeType value, where 1 is an XML element and 3 is a text node.

myXML.**nodeValue**

Returns the node value of the XML object. If the XML object is a text node, the nodeType is 3 and the nodeValue is the text of the node. If the XML object is an XML element (node type is 1), it has a nullnodeValue and is read only.

myXML.**parentNode**

Read only. References the parent node of the specified XML object or returns null if the node has no parent.

myXML.**previousSibling**

Read only. Returns a reference to the previous sibling in the parent node's child list.

myXML.**status**

Automatically sets and returns a numeric value indicating whether an XML document was successfully parsed into an XML object.

0   No error; parse was completed successfully.

-2   A CDATA section was not properly terminated.

-3   The XML declaration was not properly terminated.

-4   The DOCTYPE declaration was not properly terminated.

-5   A comment was not properly terminated.

-6   An XML element was malformed.

-7   Out of memory.

-8   An attribute value was not properly terminated.

-9   A start-tag was not matched with an end-tag.

-10   An end-tag was encountered without a matching start-tag.

myXML.**xmlDecl**

Sets and returns information about a document's XML declaration. After the XML document is parsed into an XML object, this property is set to the text of the document's XML declaration.

XML Object Event Handlers

myXML.**onData**()

Invoked when XML text has been completely downloaded from the server, or when an error occurs downloading XML text from a server. This handler is invoked before the XML is parsed and therefore can be used to call a custom parsing routine instead of using the Flash XML parser. The XML.onData method returns either the value undefined or a string that contains XML text downloaded from the server. If the returned value is undefined, an error occurred while downloading the XML from the server.

myXML.**onLoad**(success)

Invoked by the Flash Player when an XML document is received from the server.

success   Boolean. Indicates whether the XML object was successfully loaded with an XML.load or XML.sendAndLoad operation.

XMLSocket Object

XML Socket Object :: Reference > Objects > Client/Server

new XMLSocket();

Constructor; creates a new XMLSocket object. The XMLSocket object is not initially connected to any server.

XML Object Methods

myXMLSocket.**close**()

Closes the connection specified by XMLSocket object.

myXMLSocket.**connect**(host, port)

Establishes a connection to the specified Internet host using the specified TCP port (must be 1,024 or higher), and returns true or false depending on whether a connection is successfully established.

host   A fully qualified DNS domain name, or an IP address in the form *aaa.bbb.ccc.ddd*. Specify null to connect to the host server on which the movie resides.

port   The TCP port number on the host used to establish a connection. The port number must be 1,024 or higher.

myXMLSocket.**send**(object)

Converts the XML object or data specified in the object parameter to a string and transmits it to the server, followed by a zero byte. If object is an XML object, the string is the XML textual representation of the XML object.

object   An XML object or other data to transmit to the server.

XML Socket Object Event Handlers

myXMLSocket.**onClose**()

Method. A callback function that is invoked only when the server closes an open connection. The default implementation of this method performs no actions. To override the default implementation, you must assign a function containing your own actions.

myXMLSocket.**onConnect**(success)

Method. A callback function invoked by the Flash Player when a connection request initiated through the XMLSocket.connect method has succeeded or failed.

success   Boolean. Indicates whether a socket connection was successfully established.

XMLSocket.**onData**()

Invoked when an XML message has been downloaded from the server, terminated by a zero byte.

myXMLSocket.**onXML**(object)

Method. A callback function invoked by the Flash Player when the specified XML object containing an XML document arrives over an open XMLSocket connection. The default implementation of this method performs no actions. To override the default implementation, you must assign a function containing actions that you define.

object   An instance of the XML object containing a parsed XML document received from a server.

A p p e n d i x   B

ActionScript Quick Reference

This is a continuation of the Quick Reference from Appendix A. In this appendix, we now get into the Movie Control information.

Actions

Movie Control

Reference > Actions > Movie Control

gotoAndPlay(scene, frame)

Sends the playhead to the specified frame in a scene and plays from that frame. If no scene is specified, the playhead goes to the specified frame in the current scene.

scene   The scene name to which the playhead is sent.

frame   The frame number or label to which the playhead is sent.

gotoAndStop (scene, frame)

Sends the playhead to the specified frame in a scene and stops it. If no scene is specified, the playhead goes to the specified frame in the current scene.

scene   The scene name to which the playhead is sent.

frame   The frame number or label to which the playhead is sent.

nextFrame()

Sends the playhead to the next frame and stops it.

nextScene()

Sends the playhead to frame 1 of the next scene and stops it.

on()

Event handler; specifies the mouse event or keypress that trigger an action.

```
on(mouseEvent) {
        statement(s);
}
```

statement(s)   The instructions to execute when the mouseEvent takes place.

mouseEvent   A mouseEvent is a trigger called an "event." When the event takes place, the statements following it within curly brackets execute. Any of the following values can be specified for the mouseEvent parameter:

press	The mouse button is pressed while the pointer is over the button.
release	The mouse button is released while the pointer is over the button.
releaseOutside	The mouse button is released while the pointer is outside the button after the button is pressed while the pointer is inside the button.
rollOut	The pointer rolls outside the button area.
rollOver	The mouse pointer rolls over the button.
dragOut	While the pointer is over the button, the mouse button is pressed and then rolls outside the button area.

dragOver	While the pointer is over the button, the mouse button has been pressed, rolled outside the button, and then rolled back over the button.
keyPress ("key")	The specified key is pressed. The key portion of the parameter is specified using any of the key codes listed in Appendix C, "Keyboard Shortcut Quick Reference." This can use Flash or any of the key constants listed in the Property summary for the Key object.

play()

Moves the playhead forward in the timeline.

prevFrame()

Sends the playhead to the previous frame and stops it. If the current frame is 1, the playhead does not move.

prevScene()

Sends the playhead to frame 1 of the previous scene and stops it.

stop()

Stops the movie that is currently playing. The most common use of this action is to control movie clips with buttons.

stopAllSounds()

Stops all sounds currently playing in a movie without stopping the playhead. Sounds set to stream will resume playing as the playhead moves over the frames they are in.

Browser/Network

Reference > Actions > Browser/Network

fscommand("command", "parameters")

Enables the Flash movie to communicate with either the Flash Player or the program hosting the Flash Player, such as a web browser. You can also use the fscommand action to pass messages to Macromedia Director, Visual Basic, Visual C++, and other programs that can host ActiveX controls.

command	A string passed to the host application for any use or a command passed to the standalone Flash Player.
parameters	A string passed to the host application for any use or a value passed to the Flash Player.

getURL("url", window, "variables")

Loads a document from a specific URL into a window or passes variables to another application at a defined URL.

Note that this action acts like an HTML hyperlink, as in
`<a href="http://...."></a>`.

url	The URL from which to obtain the document.
window	Specifies the window or HTML frame into which the document should load. You can enter the name of a specific window or choose from the following reserved target names:

	_self	specifies the current frame in the current window.
	_blank	specifies a new window.
	_parent	specifies the parent of the current frame.
	_top	specifies the top-level frame in the current window.

Example:

getURL("getInfo.htm","_blank") opens a new browser window displaying the web page getInfo.htm.

getURL("getInfo.htm","_self") will display the web page getInfo.htm inside the current browser window, replacing the content.

variables	Optional. A GET or POST method for sending variables.

loadMovie("url", level/target, "variables")

Load a SWF or JPEG file into the Flash Player while the original movie is playing. The loadMovie action lets you display several movies at once and switch between movies without loading another HTML document. Without the loadMovie action, the Flash Player displays a single movie (SWF file) and then closes.

A movie or image loaded into a target inherits the position, rotation, and scale properties of the targeted movie clip. The upper-left corner of the loaded image or movie aligns with the registration point of the targeted movie clip. Alternatively, if the target is the _root timeline, the upper-left corner of the image or movie aligns with the upper-left corner of the Stage.

url	The URL from which to obtain the document.
level	An integer specifying the level into which the movie will be loaded.
target	A path to a target movie clip. The target movie clip will be replaced by the loaded movie or image. You must specify either a target movie clip or a level of a target movie; you can't specify both.
variables	Optional. A GET or POST method for sending variables.

loadMovieNum("url", level, "variables")

Loads a SWF or JPEG file into a level in the Flash Player while the originally loaded movie is playing. Normally, the Flash Player displays a single movie (SWF file) and then closes. The loadMovieNum action lets you display several movies at once and switch between movies without loading another HTML document.

The Flash Player has a stacking order of levels starting with level 0. These levels are like layers of acetate; they are transparent except for the objects on each level. When you use the loadMovieNum action, you must specify a level in the Flash Player into which the movie will load. After a movie is loaded into a level, you can use the _level*N* syntax, where *N* is the level number, to target the movie.

url	The URL from which to obtain the document.
level	An integer specifying the level in the Flash Player into which the movie will be loaded.
variables	Optional. A GET or POST method for sending variables.

loadVariables ("url", level/target, variables)

Reads data from an external file, such as a text file or text generated by a CGI script, Active Server Pages (ASP), or a Perl script, and sets the values for variables in a Flash Player level or a target movie clip. This action can also be used to update variables in the active movie with new values.

url	An absolute or relative URL where the variables are located.
level	An integer specifying the level in the Flash Player to receive the variables.
target	The target path to a movie clip that receives the loaded variables. You must specify either a target movie clip or a level (level) in the Flash Player; you can't specify both.
variables	Optional. Specifies an HTTP method for sending variables. The parameter must be the string GET or POST.

loadVariablesNum ("url", level, "variables")

Reads data from an external file, such as a text file or text generated by a CGI script, Active Server Pages (ASP), or a Perl script, and sets the values for variables in a Flash Player level. This action can also be used to update variables in the active movie with new values.

Note that this action is identical to LoadVariables except that this action targets the data to a level and not to a movie clip.

url	An absolute or relative URL where the variables are located.
level	An integer specifying the level in the Flash Player to receive the variables.
variables	Optional. Specifies an HTTP method for sending variables. The parameter must be the string GET or POST.

unloadMovie("target")

Removes a loaded movie clip from the Flash Player.

target	The target path of a movie clip.

unloadMovieNum(level)

Removes a loaded movie from the Flash Player.

level	Removes a loaded movie from the Flash Player.

MovieClip Control

Reference > Actions > MovieClip Control

duplicateMovieClip(target, newname, depth)

target	The target path of the movie clip to duplicate.
newname	A unique identifier for the duplicated movie clip.
depth	A unique depth level for the duplicated movie clip. The depth level is a stacking order for duplicated movie clips. This stacking order is much like the stacking order of layers in the Timeline; movie clips with a lower depth level are hidden under clips with a higher stacking order. You must assign each duplicated movie clip a unique depth level to prevent it from replacing movies on occupied depths.

onClipEvent

Event handler. Triggers actions defined for a specific instance of a movie clip.

movieEvent   A movieEvent is a trigger called an event. When the event takes place, the statements following it within curly brackets are executed. Any of the following values can be specified for the movieEvent parameter:

load   The action is initiated as soon as the movie clip is instantiated and appears in the timeline.

unload   The action is initiated in the first frame after the movie clip is removed from the timeline. The actions associated with the unload movie clip event are processed before any actions are attached to the affected frame.

enterFrame   The action is triggered continually at the frame rate of the movie. The actions associated with the enterFrame clip event are processed before any frame actions that are attached to the affected frames.

mouseMove   The action is initiated every time the mouse is moved. Use the _xmouse and _ymouse properties to determine the current mouse position.

mouseDown   The action is initiated when the left mouse button is pressed.

mouseUp   The action is initiated when the left mouse button is released.

keyDown   The action is initiated when a key is pressed. Use the Key.getCode method to retrieve information about the last key pressed.

keyUp   The action is initiated when a key is released. Use the Key.getCode method to retrieve information about the last key pressed.

data   The action is initiated when data is received in a loadVariables or loadMovie action. When specified with a loadVariables action, the data event occurs only once, when the last variable is loaded. When specified with a loadMovie action, the data event occurs repeatedly, as each section of data is retrieved.

statement(s)   The instructions to execute when the mouseEvent takes place.

removeMovieClip(target)

Deletes a movie clip instance that was created with the attachMovie or duplicateMovieClip methods of the MovieClip object, or with the duplicateMovieClip action.

target   The target path of a movie clip instance created with duplicateMovieClip, or the instance name of a movie clip created with the attachMovie or duplicateMovieClip methods of the MovieClip object.

setProperty("target", property, value/expression)

Changes a property value of a movie clip as the movie plays.

target	The path to the instance name of the movie clip whose property is to be set.
property	The property to be set.
value	The new literal value of the property.
expression	An equation that evaluates to the new value of the property.

startDrag(target, lock, left, top, right, bottom)

Makes the target movie clip draggable while the movie is playing. Only one movie clip can be dragged at a time. After a startDrag operation is executed, the movie clip remains draggable until explicitly stopped by a stopDrag action, or until a startDrag action for another movie clip is called.

target	The target path of the movie clip to drag.
lock	Optional. Boolean value specifying whether the draggable movie clip is locked to the center of the mouse position (true), or locked to the point where the user first clicked the movie clip (false).
left, **top**, **right**, **bottom**	Optional. Values relative to the coordinates of the movie clip's parent that specify a constraint rectangle for the movie clip.

stopDrag()

Stops the current drag operation.

updateAfterEvent()

Updates the display (independent of the frames per second set for the movie) when you call it within an onClipEvent handler or as part of a function or method that you pass to setInterval. Flash ignores calls to updateAfterEvent that are not within an onClipEvent handler or part of a function or method passed to setInterval.

Variables

Reference > Actions > Variables

delete (reference)

Operator. Destroys the object or variable specified by the reference parameter, and returns true if the object was successfully deleted; otherwise, returns a value of false. This operator is useful for freeing up memory used by scripts. Although delete is an operator, it is typically used as a statement.

The delete operator might fail and return false if the reference parameter does not exist, or it might not be deleted. Predefined objects and properties, and variables declared with var, cannot be deleted. You cannot use the delete operator to remove movie clips.

reference	The name of the variable or object to eliminate.

```
set(variable,expression)
```

Assigns a value to a variable. A variable is a container that holds data. The container itself is always the same, but the contents can change. By changing the value of a variable as the movie plays, you can record and save information about what the user has done, record values that change as the movie plays, or evaluate whether a condition is true or false.

Variables can hold any data type (for example, string, number, Boolean, object, or movie clip). The timeline of each movie and movie clip has its own set of variables, and each variable has its own value independent of variables on other timelines.

variable   An identifier to hold the value of the expression parameter.

expression   A value assigned to the variable.

```
var (variableName1 = value1)
```

Used to declare local variables. If you declare local variables inside a function, the variables are defined for the function and expire at the end of the function call. If variables are not declared inside a block ({}), but the action list was executed with a call action, the variables are local and expire at the end of the current list. If variables are not declared inside a block and the current action list was not executed with the call action, the variables are not local.

variableName   An identifier.

value   The value assigned to the variable.

```
with
```

Enables you to specify an object (such as a movie clip) with the `object` parameter and evaluate expressions and actions inside that object with the `statement(s)` parameter. This prevents you from having to repeatedly write the object's name or the path to the object.

```
with (object) {
    statement(s);
}
```

`with` is especially handy when repetition of long target names are being used:

```
with (_root.parentClip.childClip.babyClip) {
    statements (s);
}
```

object   An instance of an ActionScript object or movie clip.

statement(s)   An action or group of actions enclosed in curly brackets.

Conditions/Loops

Reference > Actions > Conditions/Loops

```
Break
```

Appears within a loop (for, for...in, do while, or while) or within a block of statements associated with a particular case within a switch action. Use the break action to break out of a series of nested loops.

case

Defines a condition for the switch action. The statements in the `statements` parameter execute if the `expression` parameter that follows the case keyword equals the expression parameter of the `switch` action using strict equality (===). The `case` statement must be used inside a switch statement.

`case expression: statements`

expression	Any expression.
statements	Any statements.

continue

Appears within several types of loop statements; it behaves differently in each type of loop.

while loop	Causes the Flash interpreter to skip the rest of the loop body and jump to the top of the loop, where the condition is tested.
do while loop	Causes the Flash interpreter to skip the rest of the loop body and jump to the bottom of the loop, where the condition is tested.
for loop	Causes the Flash interpreter to skip the rest of the loop body and jump to the evaluation of the for loop's post-expression.
for...in	Causes the Flash interpreter to skip the rest of the loop body and jump back to the top of the loop, where the next value in the enumeration is processed.

default

Defines the default case for a switch action. The statements execute if the Expression parameter of the switch action doesn't equal (using strict equality) any of the Expression parameters that follow the case keywords for a given switch action. A switch is not required to have a default case. A default case does not have to be last in the list.

`default: statements`

statement(s)	Any statements.

do while

Executes the statements and then evaluates the condition in a loop for as long as the condition is true.

```
do {
    statement(s)
} while (condition)
```

condition	The condition to evaluate.
statement(s)	The statement(s) to execute as long as the condition parameter evaluates to true.

else

Specifies the statements to run if the condition in the if statement returns false.

```
else statement
else {...statement(s)...}
```

condition	An expression that evaluates to true or false.
statement(s)	An alternative series of statements to run if the condition specified in the if statement is false.

else if

Evaluates a condition and specifies the statements to run if the condition in the initial if statement returns false. If the `else if` condition returns true, the Flash interpreter runs the statements that follow the condition inside curly brackets ({}). If the `else if` condition is false, Flash skips the statements inside the curly brackets and runs the statements following the curly brackets. Use the `else if` action to create branching logic in your scripts.

```
if (condition){
     statement(s);
} else if (condition){
     statement(s);
}
```

condition	An expression that evaluates to true or false.
statement(s)	An alternative series of statements to run if the condition specified in the `if` statement is false.

for

A loop construct that evaluates the init (initialize) expression once, and then begins a looping sequence by which, as long as the condition evaluates to true, the statement is executed and the next expression is evaluated.

```
for(init; condition; next) {
     statement(s);
}
```

init	An expression to evaluate before beginning the looping sequence, typically an assignment expression. A `var` statement is also permitted for this parameter.
condition	An expression that evaluates to true or false. The condition is evaluated before each loop iteration; the loop exits when the condition evaluates to false.
next	An expression to evaluate after each loop iteration; usually an assignment expression using the ++ (increment) or — (decrement) operators.
statement(s)	An instruction or instructions to execute within the body of the loop.

for...in

Loops through the properties of an object or element in an array, and executes the statement for each property of an object.

```
for(variableIterant in object){
     statement(s);
}
```

variableIterant	The name of a variable to act as the iterant, referencing each property of an object or element in an array.
object	The name of an object to be repeated.
statement(s)	An instruction to execute for each iteration.

if

Evaluates a condition to determine the next action in a movie. If the condition is true, Flash runs the statements that follow the condition inside curly brackets ({}). If the condition is false, Flash skips the statements inside the curly brackets and runs the statements following the curly brackets. Use the if action to create branching logic in your scripts.

```
if(condition) {
     statement(s);
}
```

condition	An expression that evaluates to true or false.
statement(s)	The instructions to execute if or when the condition evaluates to true.

switch

Creates a branching structure for ActionScript statements. Like the if action, the switch action tests a condition and executes statements if the condition returns a value of true.

```
switch (expression){
            caseClause:
      defaultClause:
}
```

expression	Any expression.
caseClause	A case keyword followed by an expression, a colon, and a group of statements to execute if the expression matches the switch expression parameter using strict equality (===).
defaultClause	A default keyword followed by statements to execute if none of the case expressions matches the switch expression parameter strict equality (===).

while

Tests an expression and runs a statement or series of statements repeatedly in a loop as long as the expression is true. Before the statement block is run, the condition is tested; if the test returns true, the statement block is run. If the condition is false, the statement block is skipped and the first statement after the while action's statement block is executed.

```
while(condition) {
     statement(s);
}
```

condition	The expression that is reevaluated each time the while action is executed. If the statement evaluates to true, the statement(s) is run.
statement(s)	The code to execute if the condition evaluates to true.

Printing

Reference > Actions > Printing

print

In normal mode in the Actions panel, choose As Vectors to print frames that do not contain bitmap images or use transparency (alpha) or color effects.

Prints the target movie clip according to the boundaries specified in the parameter (bmovie, bmax, or bframe). If you want to print specific frames in the target movie, attach a #P frame label to those frames. Although the print action results in higher quality prints than the printAsBitmap action, it cannot be used to print movies that use alpha transparencies or special color effects.

```
print ("target")
print ("target", "Bounding box")
```

target	The instance name of a movie clip to print. By default, all the frames in the target instance print. If you want to print specific frames in the movie clip, assign a #p frame label to those frames.
Bounding box	A modifier that sets the print area of the movie. This parameter is optional. You can choose one of the following:

	bmovie	Designates the bounding box of a specific frame in a movie as the print area for all printable frames in the movie. Assign a #b frame label to the frame whose bounding box you want to use as the print area.
	bmax	Designates a composite of all the bounding boxes of all the printable frames as the print area. Specify the bmax parameter when the printable frames in your movie vary in size.
	bframe	Designates that the bounding box of each printable frame be used as the print area for that frame. This changes the print area for each frame and scales the objects to fit the print area. Use bframe if you have objects of different sizes in each frame and want each object to fill the printed page.

printAsBitmap

Prints the target movie clip according to the boundaries specified in the parameter (bmovie, bmax, or bframe). If you want to print specific frames in the target movie, attach a #P frame label to those frames. Although the print action results in higher quality prints than the printAsBitmap action, it cannot be used to print movies that use alpha transparencies or special color effects.

```
printAsBitmap ("target")
printAsBitmap ("target", "Bounding box")
```

target	The instance name of movie clip to print. By default, all the frames in the movie are printed. If you want to print specific frames in the movie, attach a #P frame label to those frames.
Bounding box	A modifier that sets the print area of the movie. You can choose one of the following parameters:

	bmovie	Designates the bounding box of a specific frame in a movie as the print area for all printable frames in the movie. Assign a #b frame label to the frame whose bounding box you want to use as the print area.

bmax	Designates a composite of all the bounding boxes of all the printable frames as the print area. Specify the bmax parameter when the printable frames in your movie vary in size.
bframe	Designates that the bounding box of each printable frame be used as the print area for that frame. This changes the print area for each frame and scales the objects to fit the print area. Use bframe if you have objects of different sizes in each frame and want each object to fill the printed page.

printAsBitmapNum

Prints a level in the Flash Player as a bitmap. Use the printAsBitmapNum action to print movies that contain frames with objects that use transparency or color effects. The printAsBitmapNum action prints at the highest available resolution of the printer to maintain the highest possible definition and quality. To calculate the printable file size of a frame designated to print as a bitmap, multiply pixel width by pixel height by printer resolution.

```
printAsBitmapNum(level)
printAsBitmapNum(level, "Bounding box")
```

level	The level in the Flash Player to print. By default, all the frames in the level print. If you want to print specific frames in the level, assign a #p frame label to those frames.
Bounding box	A modifier that sets the print area of the movie. This parameter is optional. You can choose one of the following parameters:
bmovie	Designates the bounding box of a specific frame in a movie as the print area for all printable frames in the movie. Assign a #b frame label to the frame whose bounding box you want to use as the print area.
bmax	Designates a composite of all the bounding boxes of all the printable frames as the print area. Specify the bmax parameter when the printable frames in your movie vary in size.
bframe	Designates that the bounding box of each printable frame be used as the print area for that frame. This changes the print area for each frame and scales the objects to fit the print area. Use bframe if you have objects of different sizes in each frame and want each object to fill the printed page.

printNum

Prints the level in the Flash Player according to the boundaries specified in the Bounding box parameter (bmovie, bmax, bframe). If you want to print specific frames in the target movie, attach a #P frame label to those frames. Although using the printNum action results in higher quality prints than using the printAsBitmapNum action, you cannot use printNum to print movies with alpha transparencies or special color effects.

```
printNum (level)
printNum (level, "Bounding box")
```

level	The level in the Flash Player to print. By default, all the frames in the level print. If you want to print specific frames in the level, assign a #p frame label to those frames.
Bounding box	A modifier that sets the print area of the movie. You can choose one of the following parameters:

bmovie	Designates the bounding box of a specific frame in a movie as the print area for all printable frames in the movie. Assign a #b frame label to the frame whose bounding box you want to use as the print area.
bmax	Designates a composite of all the bounding boxes of all the printable frames as the print area. Specify the bmax parameter when the printable frames in your movie vary in size.
bframe	Designates that the bounding box of each printable frame be used as the print area for that frame. This changes the print area for each frame and scales the objects to fit the print area. Use bframe if you have objects of different sizes in each frame and want each object to fill the printed page.

User-Defined Functions

Reference > Actions > User-Defined Function

call

Executes the script in the called frame without moving the playhead to that frame. Local variables will not exist after the script is finished executing.

```
call(frame)
```

frame	The label or number of a frame in the timeline.

function

A set of statements that you define to perform a certain task. You can declare, or define, a function in one location and call, or invoke, it from different scripts in a movie. When you define a function, you can also specify parameters for the function. Parameters are placeholders for values on which the function operates. You can pass different parameters to a function each time you call it. This lets you reuse one function in many different situations.

```
function functionname (parameter0, ... parameterN){
     statement(s)
}
function (parameter0, ... parameterN){
     statement(s)
}
```

functionname	Optional. The name of the new function. Specifying a functionname allows you to reuse the function.
parameter0,...parameterN	Optional. An identifier that represents a parameter to pass to the function.
statement(s)	Any ActionScript instruction you have defined for the body of the function.

```
return
```
___
Specifies the value returned by a function. The `return` action evaluates an expression and returns the result as a value of the function in which it executes. The `return` action causes the function to stop running and replaces the function with the returned value. If the `return` statement is used alone, it returns null.

```
return expression
return
```

expression   A string, number, array, or object to evaluate and return as a value of the function.

Miscellaneous Actions

Reference > Actions > User-Defined Function
___
```
#endinitclip
```
___
Indicates the end of a block of component initialization actions.

```
#initclip
...component initialization actions go here...
#endinitclip
```

```
#include
```
___
Includes the contents of the file specified in the parameter when the movie is tested, published, or exported. The `#include` action is checked when a syntax check occurs.

```
#include "filename.as"
```

filename.as   The filename for the script to add to the Actions panel; .as is the recommended file extension.

```
#initclip
```
___
Indicates the start of a block of component initialization actions. When multiple clips are initialized at the same time, you can use the `order` parameter to specify which initialization occurs first. Component initialization actions execute when a movie clip symbol is defined. If the movie clip is an exported symbol, the component initialization actions execute before the actions on frame 1 of the SWF file. Otherwise, they execute immediately before the frame actions of the frame that contains the first instance of the associated movie clip symbol.

order   Optional. An integer that specifies the execution order of blocks of `#initclip` code.

```
clearInterval
```
___
Clears a call to the `setInterval` function.

```
clearInterval( intervalID )
```

intervalID   An object returned from a call to the `setInterval` function.

`// Comment Delimiter`

Indicates the beginning of a script comment. Any characters that appear between the comment delimiter `//` and the end-of-line character are interpreted as a comment and ignored by the ActionScript interpreter.

```
// comment
```

Note that this is the line-by-line format to comment; to comment out blocks of code, use `/*` at the beginning of the block and then `*/` at the end of the code block.

```
/*   comment open
*/   comment close
```

`setInterval`

Calls a function or a method or an object at periodic intervals while a movie plays. You can use an interval function to update variables from a database or update a time display.

```
setInterval(function, interval, arg1... argN )
setInterval(object, methodName, interval, arg1 ... argN )
```

function	A function name or a reference to an anonymous function.
object	An object derived from the Object object.
methodName	The name of the method to call on the `object` parameter.
interval	The time in milliseconds between calls to the function or `methodName` parameter.
arg1 ... argN	Optional parameters passed to the function or `methodName` parameter.

`trace`

Evaluates the expression and displays the result in the Output window in test mode.

```
trace(expression)
```

expression	An expression to evaluate. When a SWF file is opened in the Flash authoring tool (through the Test Movie command), the value of the expression parameter is displayed in the Output window.

Operators

Standard Operators

Reference > Operators

`" " String Delimiter`

When used before and after characters, quotes indicate that the characters have a literal value and are considered a string, not a variable, numerical value, or other ActionScript element.

```
"text"
```

() Parentheses

Performs a grouping operation on one or more parameters, or surrounds one or more parameters and passes them as parameters to a function outside the parentheses.

    (expression1, ... expressionN)

function(parameter1, ... parameterN)

expression1,...expression	Numbers, strings, variables, or text.
function	The function to be performed on the contents of the parentheses.
parameter1,...parameterN	A series of parameters to execute before the results are passed as parameters to the function outside the parentheses.

Arithmetic Operators

Reference > Operators > Arithmetic Operators

% Modulo

Calculates the remainder of expression1 divided by expression2.

expression1 % expression2

For example: 56 % 41; returns 15

expression1, expression2	Numbers or strings that convert to a numeric value.

* Multiplication

Multiplies two numerical expressions. If both expressions are integers, the product is an integer. If either or both expressions are floating-point numbers, the product is a floating-point number.

expression1 * expression2

expression1, expression2	Numbers.

+ Addition

Adds numeric expressions or concatenates (combines) strings. If one expression is a string, all other expressions are converted to strings and concatenated.

expression1 + expression2

expression1, expression2	Numbers or strings.

- Minus

When used for negating, it reverses the sign of the numerical expression. When used for negating, it reverses the sign of the numerical expression.

-expression
  expression1 - expression2

expression1, expression2	Numbers.

/ Division

Divides expression1 by expression2. The result of the division operation is a double-precision floating-point number.

```
expression1 / expression2
```

expression1, **expression2**   Numbers.

Assignment Operators

Reference > Operators > Assignment Operators

%= Modulo Assignment

Calculates the remainder of expression1 divided by expression2 and assigns the result to expression1.

```
expression1 %= expression2
```

For example:

```
x = 14;
y = 5;
x %= y; // x now equals 4
```

expression1, **expression2**   Numbers or strings that convert to a numeric value.

&= Bitwise AND Assignment

Assigns expression1 the value of expression1&expression2.

```
expression1 &= expression2
```

expression1, **expression2**   Numbers.

¦= Bitwise OR Assignment

Calculates the bitwise OR of expression1 and expression2 and assigns it to expression1.

```
expression1 ¦= expression2
```

expression1, **expression2**   Numbers.

*= Multiplication Assignment

When used for negating, it reverses the sign of the numerical expression. When used for negating, it reverses the sign of the numerical expression.

```
expression1 *= expression2
```

expression1, **expression2**   Numbers.

+= Addition Assignment

Adds or concatenates expression1 to expression2. The result of the division operation is a double-precision floating-point number. If the expressions are numbers, an addition operation happens; with strings, a concatenation operations is performed.

```
expression1 += expression2
```

expression1, **expression2**   Numbers or strings.

-= Subtraction Assignment

Subtracts expression2 from expression 1. The result of the subtraction operation is assigned to expression1. String expressions must be converted to numbers or NaN is returned.

```
expression1 -= expression2
```

> **expression1**, **expression2**   Numbers or strings that convert to a numeric value.

/= Division Assignment

Divides expression1 by expression2 and assigns the result to expression1.

```
expression1 / expression2
```

> **expression1**, **expression2**   Numbers.

<<= Bitwise Left Shift AND Assignment

Performs a bitwise left shift operation and stores the contents as a result in expression1.

```
expression1 <<= expression2
```

> **expression1**   A number or expression to be shifted left.
> **expression2**   A number or expression that converts to an integer from 0 to 31.

= Assignment

Assigns the type of expression2 (the parameter on the right) to the variable, array element, or property in expression1.

```
expression1 = expression2
```

> **expression1**   A variable, an element of an array, or a property of an object.
> **expression2**   A value of any type.

>>= Bitwise Right Shift AND Assignment

Performs a bitwise right-shift operation and stores the contents as a result in expression1.

```
expression1>>= expression2
```

> **expression1**   A number or expression to be shifted right.
> **expression2**   A number or expression that converts to an integer from 0 to 31.

>>>= Bitwise Unsigned Right Shift AND Assignment

Performs an unsigned bitwise right-shift operation and stores the contents as a result in expression1.

```
expression1 >>>= expression2
```

> **expression1**   A number or expression to be shifted right.
> **expression2**   A number or expression that converts to an integer from 0 to 31.

^= Bitwise XOR Assignment

Assigns expression1 the value of expression1^expression2.

```
expression1 ^= expression2
```

> **expression1**, **expression2**   Integers and variables.

Bitwise Operators

Reference > Operators > Bitwise Operators

& Bitwise AND

Converts expression1 and expression2 to 32-bit unsigned integers, and performs a Boolean AND operation on each bit of the integer parameters. The result is a new 32-bit unsigned integer.

expression1 & expression2

expression1, expression2   A number.

~ Bitwise NOT

Converts the expression to a 32-bit unsigned integer, and then inverts the bits. A bitwise NOT operation changes the sign of a number and subtracts 1.

~ expression

expression   A number.

¦ Bitwise OR

Converts expression1 and expression2 to 32-bit unsigned integers, and returns a 1 in each bit position where the corresponding bits of either expression1 or expression2 are 1.

expression1 ¦ expression2

expression1, expression2   A number.

<< Bitwise Left Shift

Converts expression1 and expression2 to 32-bit integers, and shifts all the bits in expression1 to the left by the number of places specified by the integer resulting from the conversion of expression2. The bit positions that are emptied as a result of this operation are filled in with 0. Shifting a value left by one position is the equivalent of multiplying it by 2.

expression1 << expression2

expression1   A number or expression to be shifted left.

expression2   A number or expression that converts to an integer from 0 to 31.

>> Bitwise Right Shift

Converts expression1 and expression2 to 32-bit integers, and shifts all the bits in expression1 to the right by the number of places specified by the integer resulting from the conversion of expression2. Bits that are shifted to the right are discarded. To preserve the sign of the original expression, the bits on the left are filled in with 0 if the most significant bit (the bit farthest to the left) of expression1 is 0, and filled in with 1 if the most significant bit is 1. Shifting a value right by one position is the equivalent of dividing by 2 and discarding the remainder.

expression1 >> expression2

expression1   A number or expression to be shifted right.

expression2   A number or expression that converts to an integer from 0 to 31.

>>> Bitwise Unsigned Right Shift

The same as the bitwise right shift (>>) operator except that it does not preserve the sign of the original expression because the bits on the left are always filled with 0.

```
expression1 >>> expression2
```

expression1   A number or expression to be shifted right.

expression2   A number or expression that converts to an integer from 0 to 31.

^ Bitwise XOR

Converts expression1 and expression2 to 32-bit unsigned integers, and returns a 1 in each bit position where the corresponding bits in expression1 or expression1, but not both, are 1.

```
expression1 ^ expression2
```

expression1, **expression2**   A number.

Comparison Operators

Reference > Operators > Comparison Operators

!= Inequality

Tests for the exact opposite of the == operator. Numbers, strings, and Boolean values are compared by value. Variables, objects, arrays, and functions are compared by reference.

```
expression1 != expression2
```

expression1, **expression2**   Number, string, Boolean, variable, object, array, or function.

!== Strict Inequality

Tests for the exact opposite of the === operator. The strict inequality operator performs the same as the inequality operator except that data types are not converted. Numbers, strings, and Boolean values are compared by value. Variables, objects, arrays, and functions are compared by reference.

```
expression1 !== expression2
```

expression1, **expression2**   Number, string, Boolean, variable, object, array or function.

< Less Than Comparison

Compares two expressions and determines whether expression1 is less than expression2. String expressions are evaluated using alphabetical order; all capital letters come before lowercase letters.

```
expression1 < expression2
```

expression1, **expression2**   A number or string.

<= Less Than Or Equal To Comparison

Compares two expressions and determines whether `expression1` is less than or equal to `expression2`. String expressions are evaluated using alphabetical order; all capital letters come before lowercase letters.

`expression1 <= expression2`

expression1, expression2   A number or string.

== Equality

Tests two expressions for equality. The result is true if the expressions are equal. Numbers and Boolean values are compared by value, and are considered equal if they have the same value. String expressions are equal if they have the same number of characters and the characters are identical. Variables, objects, arrays, and functions are compared by reference. Two variables are equal if they refer to the same object, array, or function. Two separate arrays are never considered equal, even if they have the same number of elements.

`expression1 == expression2`

expression1, expression2   Number, string, Boolean, variable, object, array, or function.

=== Strict Equality

Tests two expressions for equality; the strict equality operator performs just like the equality operator except that data types are not converted. The result is true if both expressions, including their data types, are equal.

`expression1 === expression2`

expression1, expression2   Number, string, Boolean, variable, object, array, or function.

> Greater Than Comparison

Compares two expressions and determines whether `expression1` is greater than `expression2`. String expressions are evaluated using alphabetical order; all capital letters come before lowercase letters.

`expression1 > expression2`

expression1, expression2   A number or string.

>= Greater Than Or Equal To Comparison

Compares two expressions and determines whether `expression1` is greater than or equal to `expression2`. String expressions are evaluated using alphabetical order; all capital letters come before lowercase letters.

`expression1 >= expression2`

expression1, expression2   A number or string.

Logical Operators

Reference > Operators > Logical Operators

! Logical NOT

Inverts the Boolean value of a variable or expression.

`!expression`

expression   A Boolean or a variable with the absolute or converted value of true or false.

&& Short-circuit AND

Performs a Boolean operation on the values of one or both of the expressions. Evaluates `expression1` (the expression on the left side of the operator) and returns false if the expression evaluates to false. If `expression1` evaluates to true, `expression2` (the expression on the right side of the operator) is evaluated. If `expression2` evaluates to true, the final result is true; otherwise, it is false.

`expression1 && expression2`

expression1, **expression2**   An expression that evaluates to a Boolean value, usually a comparison expression, such as `x < 5`.

¦¦ Logical OR

Evaluates `expression1` and `expression2`. The result is true if either or both expressions evaluate to true; the result is false only if both expressions evaluate to false. You can use the logical `OR` operator with any number of operands; if any operand evaluates to true, the result is true.

With non-Boolean expressions, the logical `OR` operator causes Flash to evaluate the expression on the left; if it can be converted to true, the result is true. Otherwise, it evaluates the expression on the right and the result is the value of that expression.

`expression1 ¦¦ expression2`

expression1, **expression2**   An expression that evaluates to a Boolean value, usually a comparison expression, such as `x < 5`.

Miscellanous Operators

++ Increment

A pre-increment and post-increment unary operator that adds 1 to an expression. The expression can be a variable, an element in an array, or a property of an object. The pre-increment form of the operator (++expression) adds 1 to expression and returns the result. The post-increment form of the operator (expression++) adds 1 to expression and returns the initial value of expression (the value prior to the addition).

`++expression`
`    expression++`

expression   A number.

— Decrement

A pre-decrement and post-decrement unary operator that subtracts 1 from the expression. The pre-decrement form of the operator (—expression) subtracts 1 from expression and returns the result. The post-decrement form of the operator (expression—) subtracts 1 from the expression and returns the initial value of expression (the value prior to the subtraction).

```
—expression
 expression—
```

expression   A number.

delete (reference)

Operator. Destroys the object or variable specified by the reference parameter, and returns true if the object was successfully deleted; otherwise, returns a value of false. This operator is useful for freeing up memory used by scripts. Although `delete` is an operator, it is typically used as a statement.

The `delete` operator might fail and return false if the `reference` parameter does not exist, or it might not be deleted. Predefined objects and properties, and variables declared with var, cannot be deleted. You cannot use the delete operator to remove movie clips.

reference   The name of the variable or object to eliminate.

?: Conditional

Instructs Flash to evaluate expression1, and if the value of expression1 is true, it returns the value of expression2; otherwise, it returns the value of expression3.

```
expression1 ? expression2: expression3
```

expression1	An expression that evaluates to a Boolean value, usually a comparison expression, such as x < 5.
expression2, **expression3**	Values of any type.

instanceof

Determines whether an object belongs to a specified class. Tests if object is an instance of class. An ActionScript object is said to be an instance of a class if the constructor function's prototype object is in the ActionScript object's prototype chain.

object	An ActionScript object.
class	A reference to an ActionScript constructor function, such as String or Date.

typeof

A unary operator placed before a single parameter. The typeof operator causes the Flash interpreter to evaluate expression; the result is a string specifying whether the expression is a string, a movie clip, an object, or a function.

```
typeof expression
```

expression   A string, a movie clip, a button, an object, or a function.

```
void
```

A unary operator that discards the expression value and returns an undefined value. The void operator is often used in comparisons using the == operator to test for undefined values.

```
void (expression)
```

Functions

Standard Functions

Reference > Functions

```
escape
```

Converts the parameter to a string and encodes it in a URL-encoded format, where all non-alphanumeric characters are escaped with % hexadecimal sequences.

```
escape(expression)
```

expression   The expression to convert into a string and encode in a URL-encoded format.

```
eval
```

Accesses variables, properties, objects, or movie clips by name. If the expression is a variable or a property, the value of the variable or property is returned. If the expression is an object or movie clip, a reference to the object or movie clip is returned. If the element named in the expression cannot be found, undefined is returned.

```
eval(expression)
```

expression   A string containing the name of a variable, property, object, or movie clip to retrieve.

```
getProperty
```

Returns the value of the specified property for the movie clip instance name.

```
getProperty(instancename , property)
```

instancename   The instance name of a movie clip for which the property is being retrieved.

property   A property of a movie clip.

```
getTimer
```

Returns the number of milliseconds that have elapsed since the movie started playing.

```
getTimer()
```

```
getVersion
```

Returns a string containing Flash Player version and platform information.

```
getVersion()
```

targetPath

Returns a string containing the target path of `movieClipObject`. The target path is returned in dot notation. To retrieve the target path in slash notation, use the _target property.

`targetpath(movieClipObject)`

> **movieClipObject**   Reference (for example, _root or _parent) to the movie clip for which the target path is being retrieved.

unescape

Evaluates the parameter x as a string, decodes the string from URL-encoded format (converting all hexadecimal sequences to ASCII characters), and returns the string.

`unescape(x)`

> **x**   A string with hexadecimal sequences to escape.

Conversion Functions

Reference > Functions > Conversion Functions

Array

No Info.

Boolean

Converts the parameter expression to a Boolean value and returns true or false.

`Boolean(expression)`

> **expression**   An expression to convert to a Boolean value.

Number

Converts the parameter expression to a number and returns the value of that number, 0 or false.

`Number(expression)`

> **expression**   An expression to convert to a number.

String

Returns a string representation of the specified parameter (true or false), or if the string can be converted to a number, a text representation of that number.

`String(expression)`

> **expression**   An expression to convert to a number.

Mathematical Functions

Reference > Functions > Mathematical Functions

`isFinite`

Evaluates the expression and returns true if it is a finite number, and false if it is infinity or negative infinity. The presence of infinity or negative infinity indicates a mathematical error condition such as division by 0.

`isFinite(expression)`

    expression   A Boolean, variable, or other expression to be evaluated.

`isNaN`

Evaluates the parameter and returns true if the value is not a number (NaN), indicating the presence of mathematical errors.

`isNaN(expression)`

    expression   A Boolean, variable, or other expression to be evaluated.

`parseFloat`

Converts a string to a floating-point number. The function reads, or "parses," and returns the numbers in a string until it reaches a character that is not a part of the initial number. If the string does not begin with a number that can be parsed, `parseFloat` returns NaN. White space preceding valid integers is ignored, as are trailing nonnumeric characters.

`parseFloat(string)`

    string   The string to read and convert to a floating-point number.

`parseInt`

Converts a string to an integer. If the specified string in the parameters cannot be converted to a number, the function returns NaN. Integers beginning with 0 or specifying a radix of 8 are interpreted as octal numbers. Strings beginning with 0x are interpreted as hexadecimal numbers. White space preceding valid integers is ignored, as are trailing nonnumeric characters.

`parseInt(expression, radix)`

    expression   A string to convert to an integer.

    radix   Optional. An integer representing the radix (base) of the number to parse. Legal values are from 2–36.

Constants

Reference > Constants

`false`

A unique Boolean value that represents the opposite of `true`.

newline

Inserts a carriage return character () that inserts a blank line into the ActionScript code. Use newline to make space for information that is retrieved by a function or action in your code.

null

A special value that can be assigned to variables, or returned by a function if no data was provided. You can use null to represent values that are missing or do not have a defined data type.

true

A unique Boolean value that represents the opposite of false.

undefined

A special value, usually used to indicate that a variable has not yet been assigned a value. A reference to an undefined value returns the special value undefined. The ActionScript code typeof(undefined) returns the string "undefined". The only value of type undefined is undefined.

When undefined is converted to a string, it converts to the empty string.

The value undefined is similar to the special value null. In fact, when null and undefined are compared with the equality operator, they compare as equal.

Properties

Movie Properties :: Reference > Properties

_alpha

Sets or retrieves the alpha transparency (value) of the movie clip specified by MovieClip. Valid values are 0 (fully transparent) to 100 (fully opaque). Objects in a movie clip with _alpha set to 0 are active, even though they are invisible. For example, you can still click a button in a movie clip with the _alpha property set to 0.

myMovieClip._alpha

_currentframe

Read only. Returns the number of the frame in which the playhead is located in the time-line specified by MovieClip.

myMovieClip._currentframe

_droptarget

Read only. Returns the absolute path in slash syntax notation of the movie clip instance on which the movie clip was dropped. The _droptarget property always returns a path that starts with a slash (/). To compare the _droptarget property of an instance to a reference, use the eval function to convert the returned value from slash syntax to a dot syntax reference.

myMovieClip._droptarget

_focusrect

A Boolean value that specifies whether a movie clip has a yellow rectangle around it when it has keyboard focus. This property can override the global _focusrect property.

```
myMovieClip._focusrect
```

_framesloaded

Read only. The number of frames that have been loaded from a streaming movie. This property is useful for determining whether the contents of a specific frame, and all the frames before it, have loaded and are available locally in the browser.

```
myMovieClip._framesloaded
```

_height

Sets and retrieves the height of the movie clip, in pixels.

```
myMovieClip._height
```

_name

Returns the instance name of the movie clip specified by MovieClip.

```
myMovieClip._name
```

_quality

Global. Sets or retrieves the rendering quality used for a movie. May be set to the following values: Low, Medium, High, or Best.

_rotation

Specifies the rotation of the movie clip in degrees.

```
myMovieClip._rotation
```

_soundbuftime

Global. Establishes the number of seconds of streaming sound to prebuffer. The default value is 5 seconds.

```
_soundbuftime = integer
```

   integer   The number of seconds before the movie starts to stream.

_target

Read only. Returns the target path of the movie clip instance specified in the MovieClip parameter.

```
myMovieClip._target
```

_totalframes

Read only. Returns the total number of frames in the movie clip instance specified in the MovieClip parameter.

```
myMovieClip._totalframes
```

_url

Read only. Retrieves the URL of the SWF file from which the movie clip was downloaded.

```
myMovieClip._url
```

_visible

Booloean value that indicates whether the movie specified by the MovieClip parameter is visible. Movie clips that are not visible (_visible property set to false) are disabled.

```
myMovieClip._visible
```

_width

Sets and retrieves the width of the movie clip, in pixels.

_x

An integer that sets the coordinate of a movie relative to the local coordinates of the parent movie clip. If a movie clip is in the main Timeline, its coordinate system refers to the upper-left corner of the Stage (0, 0). If the move clip is inside another movie clip that has transformations, the movie clip is in the local coordinate system of the enclosing movie clip.

```
myMovieClip._x
```

_xmouse

Read only. Returns the coordinate of the mouse position.

```
myMovieClip._xmouse
```

_xscale

Determines the horizontal scale (percentage) of the movie clip as applied from the registration point of the movie clip. The default registration point is 0,0.

```
myMovieClip._xscale
```

_y

Sets the coordinate of movie relative to the local coordinates of the parent movie clip. If a movie clip is in the main timeline, its coordinate system refers to the upper-left corner of the Stage (0, 0). If the move clip is inside another movie clip that has transformations, the movie clip is in the local coordinate system of the enclosing movie clip.

```
myMovieClip._y
```

_ymouse

Read only. Indicates the coordinate of the mouse position.

```
myMovieClip._ymouse
```

_yscale

Sets the vertical scale (percentage) of the movie clip as applied from the registration point of the movie clip. The default registration point is 0,0.

```
myMovieClip._yscale
```

Movie Properties : : Reference > Objects > Core

_global

Identifier. Creates global variables, objects, or classes. Unlike timeline-declared or locally-declared variables and functions, global variables and functions are visible to every time-line and scope in the Flash movie, provided they are not obscured by identifiers with the same names in inner scopes.

Movie Properties : : Reference > Objects > Movie

_level

A reference to the root movie timeline of _levelN. You must use the `loadMovieNum` action to load movies into the Flash Player before you use the `_level` property to target them. You can also use _levelN to target a loaded movie at the level assigned by N.

```
_levelN
```

_parent

Specifies or returns a reference to the movie clip or object that contains the current movie clip or object. The current object is the object containing the ActionScript code that references _parent. Use _parent to specify a relative path to movie clips or objects that are above the current movie clip or object.

```
_parent.property
_parent.method()
_parent._parent.property
_parent._parent.method()
```

    property   Any property of the `MovieClip` object.

    method   Any method of the `MovieClip` object.

_root

Specifies or returns a reference to the root movie timeline. If a movie has multiple levels, the root movie timeline is on the level containing the currently executing script.

```
_root.movieClip
_root.action
_root.property
```

    movieClip   The instance name of a movie clip.

    action   Any action or method of the `MovieClip` object.

    property   Any property of the `MovieClip` object.

UI Components

FCheckBox

Reference > Flash UI Components > FCheckBox

FCheckBox Component Methods

getEnabled

Indicates whether the check box instance is enabled or disabled.

`myCheckBox.getEnabled()`

getLabel

Retrieves the label of the check box.

`myCheckBox.getLabel()`

getValue

Indicates whether the check box is selected.

`myCheckBox.getValue()`

registerSkinElement

Registers a skin element to a style property. Use this method to register custom skin elements and properties to Flash UI or custom component skins by editing the code in the first frame of the Read Me layer of a skin in the Library.

`myCheckBox.registerSkinElement(element, styleProperty)`

element	A movie clip instance.
styleProperty	The name of an `FStyleFormat` property.

SetChangeHandler

Specifies a change handler to call when the value of the check box changes. You can specify the same change handler function for more than one component; the function always accepts the instance of the component that has changed as a parameter. Calling this method overrides the `ChangeHandler` parameter value specified in the authoring location.

`myCheckBox.setChangeHandler(functionName, location)`

functionName	A string specifying the name of the handler function to execute when the value of the check box changes. If the location parameter is not specified, this function must be in the same timeline as the component instance.
location	Optional. A path reference to a data object, movie clip, or timeline that contains the specified function. This parameter is optional and defaults to the parent.

setEnabled

Specifies whether the check box is enabled (true) or disabled (false). If a check box is disabled, it does not accept mouse or keyboard interaction from the user.

`myCheckBox.setEnabled(enable)`

> **Enable**   Boolean value specifying whether the check box is enabled (true) or disabled (false).

setLabel

Specifies the text label for the check box. By default, the label appears to the right of the check box. Calling this method overrides the label parameter specified in authoring.

`myCheckBox.setLabel(label)`

> **Label**   A string specifying the text label for the check box.

setLabelPlacement

Specifies whether the label appears to the left or right of the check box. Calling this method overrides the `LabelPlacement` parameter value set during authoring.

`myCheckBox.setLabelPlacement(labelPosition)`

> **labelPosition**   A text string; specify "left" or "right".

setSize

Specifies the width of the check box and redraws it. You cannot set the height of check box components. Calling this method overrides width scaling applied during authoring.

`myCheckBox.setSize(width)`

> **width**   An integer specifying the width of the check box, in pixels.

setStyleProperty

Sets an `FStyleFormat` property for an individual check box instance. Calling this method to specify a property overrides the setting for this property in the style format assigned to the component. Passing undefined as the value for a property removes all styles for that property.

`myCheckBox.setStyleProperty(styleProperty, value)`

> **styleProperty**   A string specifying a property of the `FStyleFormat` object.
>
> **value**   The value to set for the property.

setValue

Selects or deselects `myCheckBox` and triggers the change handler function specified (if any) at runtime. The default value is true.

`myCheckBox.setValue(select)`

> **select**   Boolean value specifying whether the check box is selected (true) or not (false).

FComboBox

Reference > Flash UI Components > FComboBox

FComboBox Methods

addItem

Adds a new item with the specified label and data to the end of the combo box list and updates the list. The data can be any Flash object, string, Boolean value, integer, object, or movie clip.

`myComboBox.addItem(label, data)`

> **label**   A text string to display in the combo box list.
>
> **data**   Optional. The value to associate with the list item.

addItemAt

Adds a new item with the specified label and optional associated data to the combo box list at the specified index position. The Data parameter can be any Flash object, string, Boolean value, integer, object, or movie clip. As each item is added, the list is updated and the scroll bar is resized.

`myComboBox.addItemAt(index, label, data)`

> **index**   An integer specifying the position at which to insert the item.
>
> **label**   A text string to display in the combo box list.
>
> **data**   Optional. The value to associate with the list item.

getEnabled

Indicates whether the combo box is enabled.

`myComboBox.getEnabled()`

getItemAt

Returns the item at the specified index as an object with the properties label and data.

`myComboBox.getItemAt(index)`

> **index**   An integer specifying the position of an item in the combo box.

getLength

Returns the number of items in the combo box list.

`myComboBox.getLength()`

getRowCount

Returns the number of rows visible in the combo box.

`myComboBox.getRowCount()`

getScrollPosition

Returns the index position of the item currently displayed at the top of the combo box list.

`myComboBox.getScrollPosition()`

getSelectedIndex

Returns the index of the item currently selected in the combo box, or returns undefined if no item is selected.

`myComboBox.getSelectedIndex()`

getSelectedItem

Returns the currently selected item as an object with the properties label and data, or returns undefined if no item is selected.

`myComboBox.getSelectedItem()`

getValue

Returns the text in the field at the top of the combo box, if the combo box is editable. If the combo box is static (not editable), this method returns the data associated with the selected item or the label of the item if no data is associated.

`myComboBox.getValue()`

registerSkinElement

Registers a skin element to a style property. Use this method to register custom skin elements and properties to Flash UI or custom component skins by editing the code in the first frame of the Read Me layer of a skin in the Library.

`myComboBox.registerSkinElement(element, styleProperty)`

> **element**   A movie clip instance.
>
> **styleProperty** The name of an `FStyleFormat` property.

removeAll

Removes all the items in the combo box list, updates it, and resizes the scroll bar. Combo boxes without items are displayed without a scroll bar. This method cannot be used if the combo box is disabled.

`myComboBox.removeAll()`

removeItemAt

Returns the item removed at the specified index and updates the list. When an item is removed from the list, the indexes of the subsequent items are updated to reflect their new positions in the list.

`myComboBox.removeItemAt(index)`

> **index**   An integer specifying the index of the item to remove.

replaceItemAt

Updates the item at the specified index with the specified label and data. If the item at the specified index has an associated data value and you do not specify a value for the `data` parameter, the data value of the list item is not changed.

`myComboBox.replaceItemAt(index, label, data)`

> **index**   An integer specifying the position of a list item.
>
> **label**   A string specifying a new label for the list item.
>
> **data**   The new value to associate with the list item. This parameter is optional; if you don't specify it, any data currently specified for the item remains in place.

setChangeHandler

Specifies a change handler to call when the selection in the combo box changes. You can specify the same change handler function for more than one component; the function always accepts the instance of the component that has changed as a parameter. Calling this method overrides the ChangeHandler parameter value specified in authoring.

myComboBox.setChangeHandler(functionName, location)

functionName	A string specifying the name of the handler function to execute when the selection in the combo box changes. If the location parameter is not specified, this function must be in the same timeline as the component instance.
location	Optional. A path reference to a data object, movie clip, or timeline that contains the specified function.

setDataProvider

Registers an outside object (dataProvider) as the data source for the combo box component. If dataProvider is an instance of the Array object, the object can specify label, data, or both, because object properties and the contents of the array can be copied to the combo box as labels, data, or both.

myComboBox.setDataProvider(dataProvider)

dataProvider	An array of text strings listing the items to add, an instance of the Array object specifying the items to add, or an instance of the DataProvider class.

setEditable

Determines whether the combo box is editable (true) or static (false). An editable combo box has a text field; when the user enters text, the combo box scrolls to the item with the same text. The text field can also be used to display text using FComboBox.setValue. Calling this method overrides the Editable parameter value set during authoring.

myComboBox.setEditable(editable)

editable	Boolean value specifying whether the combo box is editable (true) or static (false).

setEnabled

Determines whether the combo box is enabled (true) or disabled (false). If the combo box is disabled, it does not accept mouse or keyboard interaction from the user. If you omit the parameter, this method defaults to true.

myComboBox.setEnabled(enable)

enable	Boolean value specifying whether the combo box is enabled (true) or disabled (false).

setItemSymbol

Registers a graphic symbol to display the combo box list items. The default value is the FComboBoxItem symbol in the Library.

myComboBox.setItemSymbol(symbolID)

symbolID	The symbol linkage ID of a graphic symbol to display the contents of the combo box.

setRowCount

Sets the number of items that can be seen in the combo box's drop-down list without scrolling. Calling this method overrides the RowCount parameter value set during authoring.

`myComboBox.setRowCount(rows)`

rows   The maximum number of rows that the drop-down list can display without scrolling. The minimum value for the rows parameter is 3.

setSelectedndex

Selects the specified item and updates the combo box to show the item as selected. Calling this method does not affect the current open or closed state of the drop-down list. This method cannot be used if the combo box is disabled.

`myComboBox.setSelectedIndex(index)`

index   An integer specifying the index of the item to select.

setSize

Resizes the combo box to the specified width. The height cannot be set. Use this method to programmatically resize the combo box and update it at runtime.

`myComboBox.setSize(width)`

width   An integer specifying the width of the combo box, in pixels.

setStyleProperty

Sets an FStyleFormat property for an individual combo box instance. Calling this method to specify a property overrides the setting for this property in the style format assigned to the component. Passing undefined as the value for a property removes all styles for that property.

`myComboBox.setStyleProperty(styleProperty, value)`

styleProperty   A string specifying a property of the FStyleFormat object.

value   The value to set for the property.

setValue

Specifies the text displayed in the input field at the top of an editable combo box. If you call this method, the user can still input text in the field. This method can be used only with editable combo boxes.

`myComboBox.setValue(editableText)`

editableText   A string specifying the text to appear in the text field of an editable combo box.

sortItemsBy

Sorts the items in the combo box alphabetically or numerically, in the specified order, using the specified field name. If the fieldName items are a combination of text strings and integers, the integer items are listed first.

`myComboBox.sortItemsBy(fieldName, order)`

fieldName   A string specifying the name of the field used for sorting. This will normally be "label" or "data".

order   A string specifying whether to sort the items in ascending order ("ASC") or descending order ("DESC").

FListBox

Reference > Flash UI Components > FListBox

FListBox Methods

addItem

Adds a new item with the specified label and data to the end of the list box and updates the list. The data can be any Flash object, string, Boolean value, integer, object, or movie clip.

```
myListBox.addItem(label, data)
```

    label   A text string to display in the list box.

    data   Optional. The value to associate with the list item.

addItemAt

Adds a new item with the specified label and optional associated data to the list box at the specified index position. The Data parameter can be any Flash object, string, Boolean value, integer, object, or movie clip. As each item is added, the list is updated and the scroll bar is resized.

```
myListBox.addItemAt(index, label, data)
```

    index   An integer specifying the position at which to insert the item.

    label   A text string to display in the list box.

    data   Optional. The value to associate with the list item.

getEnabled

Indicates whether the list box is enabled.

```
myListBox.getEnabled()
```

getItemAt

Returns the item at the specified index as an object with the properties label and data.

```
myListBox.getItemAt(index)
```

    index   An integer specifying the position of an item in the list box.

getLength

Returns the number of items in the list box.

```
myListBox.getLength()
```

getRowCount

Returns the number of rows visible in the list box.

```
myListBox.getRowCount()
```

getScrollPosition

Returns the index position of the item currently displayed at the top of the list box.

```
myListBox.getScrollPosition()
```

getSelectedIndex

Returns the index of the item currently selected in the list box, or returns `undefined` if no item is selected.

`myListBox.getSelectedIndex()`

getSelectedIndices

Returns the index of the item currently selected in the list box, or returns `undefined` if no item is selected.

`myListBox.getSelectedIndices()`

getSelectedItem

Returns the currently selected item as an object with the properties label and data, or returns `undefined` if no item is selected.

`myListBox.getSelectedItem()`

getSelectedItems

Returns the currently selected items as an array of objects with the properties label and data, or returns `undefined` if no items are selected. This method can be used only to get the selected items in a multiple-selection list box.

`myListBox.getSelectedItems()`

getSelectMultiple

Indicates whether users can select multiple items (true) or only a single item (false) in the list box.

`myListBox.getSelectMultiple()`

getValue

Returns information about the item currently selected in the list box. If the item does not have specified data, this method returns the item's label; if the item has data associated, this method returns the data.

`myListBox.getValue()`

registerSkinElement

Registers a skin element to a style property. Use this method to register custom skin elements and properties to Flash UI or custom component skins by editing the code in the first frame of the Read Me layer of a skin in the Library.

`myListBox.registerSkinElement(element, styleProperty)`

element	A movie clip instance.
styleProperty	The name of an FStyleFormat property.

removeAll

Removes all the items in the list box, updates it, and resizes the scroll bar.

`myListBox.removeAll()`

removeItemAt

Removes the item at the specified index, updates the indexes of the list items following the removed item to reflect their new positions in the list, and then updates the list box and resizes the scroll bar. If no item exists at the specified index, this method returns undefined.

`myListBox.removeItemAt(index)`

> **index**   An integer specifying the index of the item to remove.

replaceItemAt

Updates the item at the specified index with the specified label and data. If the item at the specified index has an associated data value and you do not specify a value for the data parameter, the data value of the list item is not changed.

`myListBox.replaceItemAt(index, label, data)`

> **index**   An integer specifying the position of a list item.
>
> **label**   A string specifying a new label for the list item.
>
> **data**   Optional. The new value to associate with the list item. This parameter is optional; if you don't specify it, any data currently specified for the item remains in place.

setAutoHideScrollBar

Specifies whether the scroll bar is hidden when the number of items in the list box can be viewed without a scroll bar (true) or whether the scroll bar is always displayed (false). If this method is set to false and the number of items does not require a scroll bar, the scroll bar is displayed as disabled (dimmed).

`myListBox.setAutoHideScrollBar(hideScroll)`

> **hideScroll**   Boolean value specifying whether the scroll bar is hidden when not needed (true) or always displayed (false).

setChangeHandler

Specifies a change handler to call when the selection in the list box changes. You can specify the same change handler function for more than one component; the function always accepts the instance of the component that has changed as a parameter. Calling this method overrides the ChangeHandler parameter value specified in authoring.

`myListBox.setChangeHandler(functionName, location)`

> **functionName**   A string specifying the name of the handler function to execute when the selection in the list box changes. If the location parameter is not specified, this function must be in the same timeline as the component instance.
>
> **location**   Optional. A path reference to a data object, movie clip, or timeline that contains the specified function.

setDataProvider

Registers an outside object (dataProvider) as the data source for the list box component. If dataProvider is an instance of the Array object, the object can specify label, data, or both, because object properties and the contents of the array can be copied to the list box as labels, data, or both.

`myListBox.setDataProvider(dataProvider)`

dataProvider   An array of text strings listing the items to add, an instance of the Array object specifying the items to add, or an instance of the DataProvider class.

setEnabled

Determines whether the list box is enabled (true) or disabled (false). If the list box is disabled, it does not accept mouse or keyboard interaction from the user. If you omit the parameter, this method defaults to true.

`myListBox.setEnabled(enable)`

   enable   Boolean value specifying whether the list box is enabled (true) or disabled (false).

setItemSymbol

Registers a graphic symbol to display the list box items. The default value is the FComboBoxItem symbol in the Library.

`myListBox.setItemSymbol(symbolID)`

   symbolID   The symbol linkage ID of a graphic symbol to display the contents of the list box.

setRowCount

Sets the number of items that can be seen in the combo box's drop-down list without scrolling. Calling this method overrides the RowCount parameter value set during authoring.

`myListBox.setRowCount(rows)`

   rows   The maximum number of rows that the drop-down list can display without scrolling. The minimum value for the rows parameter is 3.

setScrollPosition

Causes the list box to scroll so that the specified item is displayed at the top.

`myListBox.setScrollPosition(index)`

   index   An integer specifying the index of the item to display at the top of the list box.

setSelectedIndex

Selects the specified item and updates the list box to show the item as selected.

`myListBox.setSelectedIndex(index)`

   index   An integer specifying the index of the item to select.

setSelectedIndices

Selects the items specified in the array of indexes and updates the list box.

`myListBox.setSelectedIndices(indexArray)`

   indexArray   An array of item indexes to select in the list box.

setSelectMultiple

Specifies whether users can select multiple items (true) or only single items (false) in the list box. The default setting is false. Calling this method overrides the `SelectMultiple` parameter value set during authoring.

`myListBox.setSelectMultiple(multipleSelect)`

multipleSelect	Value specifying multiple-selection mode (true) or single-selection mode (false).

setSize

Resizes the list box at runtime to the specified width and height. Calling this method overrides the `RowCount` parameter value set during authoring.

`myListBox.setSize(width)`

width	An integer specifying the width of the list box, in pixels.
height	An integer specifying the height of the list box, in pixels.

setStyleProperty

Sets an `FStyleFormat` property for an individual list box instance. Calling this method to specify a property overrides the setting for this property in the style format assigned to the component. Passing `undefined` as the value for a property removes all styles for that property.

`myListBox.setStyleProperty(styleProperty, value)`

styleProperty	A string specifying a property of the `FStyleFormat` object.
value	The value to set for the property.

setWidth

Specifies the width of the list box, in pixels.

`myListBox.setWidth(width)`

width	An integer specifying the width of the list box, in pixels.

sortItemsBy

Sorts the items in the list box alphabetically or numerically, in the specified order, using the specified field name. If the `fieldName` items are a combination of text strings and integers, the integer items are listed first.

`myListBox.sortItemsBy(fieldName, order)`

fieldName	A string specifying the name of the field used for sorting. This will normally be "`label`" or "`data`".
order	A string specifying whether to sort the items in ascending order ("`ASC`") or descending order ("`DESC`").

FPushButton

Reference > Flash UI Components > FPushButton

FPushButton Methods

getEnabled

Indicates whether the push button instance is enabled.

`myPushButton.getEnabled()`

getLabel

Returns the text label on the push button as a string.

`myPushButton.getLabel()`

registerSkinElement

Registers a skin element to a style property. Use this method to register custom skin elements and properties to Flash UI or custom component skins by editing the code in the first frame of the Read Me layer of a skin in the Library.

`myPushButton.registerSkinElement(element, styleProperty)`

element	A movie clip instance.
styleProperty	The name of an `FStyleFormat` property.

setClickHandler

Specifies a handler function to call when the user releases the push button. You can specify the same handler function for more than one component; the function always accepts the instance of the component that has changed as a parameter. Calling this method overrides the `ClickHandler` parameter value specified in authoring.

`myPushButton.setClickHandler(functionName, location)`

functionName	A string specifying the name of the handler function to execute when the user releases the push button. If the location parameter is not specified, this function must be in the same timeline as the component instance.
location	A path reference to a data object, movie clip, or timeline that contains the specified function. This parameter is optional and defaults to the parent timeline of the component.

setEnabled

Determines whether the push button is enabled (true) or disabled (false). If the push button is disabled, it does not accept mouse or keyboard interaction from the user. If you omit the parameter, this method defaults to true.

`myPushButton.setEnabled(enable)`

enable	Boolean value specifying whether the push button is enabled (true) or disabled (false).

setLabel

Applies a text label to the push button at runtime. Calling this method overrides the `label` parameter value specified in authoring.

`myPushButton.setLabel(label)`

> **label**   A string containing the text to appear on the push button.

setSize

Resizes the push button at runtime to the specified width and height. Calling this method overrides any sizing or scaling applied during authoring.

`myPushButton.setSize(width, height)`

> **width**   An integer specifying the width of the push button, in pixels.
>
> **height**   An integer specifying the height of the push button, in pixels.

setStyleProperty

Sets an `FStyleFormat` property for an individual push button instance. Calling this method to specify a property overrides the setting for this property in the style format assigned to the component. Passing undefined as the value for a property removes all styles for that property.

`myPushButton.setStyleProperty(styleProperty, value)`

> **styleProperty**   A string specifying a property of the `FStyleFormat` object.
>
> **value**   The value to set for the property.

FRadioButton

Reference > Flash UI Components > FRadioButton

FRadioButton Methods

getData

Returns the data associated with the specified radio button instance. Use `FRadioButton.getValue` to get the data associated with the selected radio button in a group of radio buttons.

`myRadioButton.getData()`

getGroupName

No Info.

getLabel

Returns the label of the specified radio button as a string. You cannot use this method to get the labels for a group of radio buttons.

`myRadioButton.getLabel()`

getState

Returns a Boolean value indicating whether myRadioButton is selected (true) or not (false).

`myRadioButton.getState()`

registerSkinElement

Registers a skin element to a style property. Use this method to register custom skin elements and properties to Flash UI or custom component skins by editing the code in the first frame of the Read Me layer of a skin in the Library.

`MyRadioButton.registerSkinElement(element, styleProperty)`

element	A movie clip instance.
styleProperty	The name of an FStyleFormat property.

setChangeHandler

Specifies a change handler to call when the selection in the list box changes. You can specify the same change handler function for more than one component; the function always accepts the instance of the component that has changed as a parameter. Calling this method overrides the ChangeHandler parameter value specified in authoring.

`myRadioButton.setChangeHandler(functionName, location)`

functionName	A string specifying the name of the handler function to execute when the selection in the radio button changes. If the location parameter is not specified, this function must be in the same timeline as the component instance.
location	Optional. A path reference to a data object, movie clip, or timeline that contains the specified function.

setData

Specifies the data to associate with the radio button instance. Calling this method overrides the Data parameter value set during authoring.

`myRadioButton.setData("data")`

data	The data to associate with the radio button instance.

setEnabled

Enables and disables radio buttons at runtime.

`myRadioButton.setEnabled(enable)`

enable	Boolean value specifying whether an individual radio button or all the buttons in a group are enabled (true) or disabled (false).

setGroupName

Applies a group name to a radio button instance or group of radio buttons at runtime. Calling this method overrides the GroupName parameter value set during authoring.

`myRadioButton.setGroupName(groupName)`

groupName	A string specifying the name of a radio button group.

setLabel

Applies a label to the radio button instance `myRadioButton` at runtime. Calling this method overrides the label parameter value specified in authoring. You cannot use this method to set labels for groups of radio buttons.

`myRadioButton.setLabel(label)`

    label   A text string specifying the label that appears to the right of the radio button.

setLabelPlacement

Specifies whether the label appears to the left or right of the radio button. Calling this method overrides the `LabelPlacement` parameter value set during authoring.

myRadioButton.setLabelPlacement(labelPosition)

    labelPosition   A text string; specify "`left`" or "`right`".

setSize

Specifies the width of the radio button in pixels and redraws the radio button. The height of radio button components cannot be set. Calling this method overrides width scaling applied during authoring.

`myRadioButton.setSize(width)`

    width   An integer specifying the size of the radio button, in pixels.

setState

Specifies whether `myRadioButton` is selected (true) or unselected (false). Only one radio button in a group (all having the same `GroupName` parameter) can have an initial state of true (selected). If more than one radio button has true specified for this parameter, the last radio button with an initial state parameter of true is selected.

`myRadioButton.setState("select")`

    select   Boolean value indicating whether the radio button is selected (true) or not (false).

setStyleProperty

Sets an `FStyleFormat` property for an individual list box instance. Calling this method to specify a property overrides the setting for this property in the style format assigned to the component. Passing undefined as the value for a property removes all styles for that property.

`myRadioButton.setStyleProperty(styleProperty, value)`

    styleProperty   A string specifying a property of the FStyleFormat object.

    value   The value to set for the property.

FRadioButtonGroup

Reference > Flash UI Components > FRadioButton >
FRadioButtonGroup

FRadioButtonGroup Methods

getEnabled

Indicates whether a radio button is enabled.

```
myRadioButtonGroup.getData()
```

getGroupName

No Info.

getValue

Returns the data associated with the selected radio button in `myRadioButtonGroup`, or
the label of the radio button if no data is specified. If no button is selected, the method
returns undefined.

```
myRadioButtonGroup.getValue()
```

registerSkinElement

Registers a skin element to a style property. Use this method to register custom skin elements and properties to Flash UI or custom component skins by editing the code in the
first frame of the Read Me layer of a skin in the Library.

```
myRadioButton.registerSkinElement(element, styleProperty)
```

element	A movie clip instance.
styleProperty	The name of an `FStyleFormat` property.

setChangeHandler

Specifies a change handler to call when the selection in the list box changes. You can specify the same change handler function for more than one component; the function always
accepts the instance of the component that has changed as a parameter. Calling this
method overrides the `ChangeHandler` parameter value specified in authoring.

```
myRadioButtonGroup.setChangeHandler(functionName, location)
```

functionName	A string specifying the name of the handler function to execute when the selection in the radio button changes. If the location parameter is not specified, this function must be in the same time-line as the component instance.
location	Optional. A path reference to a data object, movie clip, or timeline that contains the specified function.

setEnabled

Enables and disables radio buttons at runtime.

```
myRadioButtonGroup.setEnabled(enable)
```

enable	Boolean value specifying whether an individual radio button or all the buttons in a group are enabled (true) or disabled (false).

setGroupName

Applies a group name to a radio button instance or group of radio buttons at runtime. Calling this method overrides the GroupName parameter value set during authoring.

```
myRadioButtonGroup.setGroupName(groupName)
```

groupName   A string specifying the name of a radio button group.

setLabelPlacement

Specifies whether the label appears to the left or right of the radio button. Calling this method overrides the LabelPlacement parameter value set during authoring.

```
myRadioButtonGroup.setLabelPlacement(labelPosition)
```

labelPosition   A text string; specify "left" or "right".

setSize

Specifies the width of the radio button in pixels and redraws the radio button. The height of radio button components cannot be set. Calling this method overrides width scaling applied during authoring.

```
myRadioButtonGroup.setSize(width)
```

width   An integer specifying the size of the radio button, in pixels.

setStyleProperty

Sets an FStyleFormat property for an individual list box instance. Calling this method to specify a property overrides the setting for this property in the style format assigned to the component. Passing undefined as the value for a property removes all styles for that property.

```
myRadioButtonGroup.setStyleProperty(styleProperty, value)
```

styleProperty   A string specifying a property of the FStyleFormat object.

value   The value to set for the property.

setValue

Selects the radio button associated with the specified data and deselects any currently selected button in the same group. Calling this method overrides the Initial Value parameter value set during authoring.

```
myRadioButtonGroup.setValue("data")
```

data   The data associated with the radio button to select.

FScrollBar

Reference > Flash UI Components > FScrollBar

FScrollBar Methods

getEnabled

Indicates whether the scroll bar is enabled (true) or disabled (false).

```
myScrollBar.getEnabled()
```

getScrollPosition

Returns an integer specifying the position of the scroll box (thumb). The returned value is in the range defined by the `minPos` and `maxPos` properties that determine the scrolling boundaries of the scroll bar.

```
myScrollBar.getScrollPosition()
```

registerSkinElement

Registers a skin element to a style property. Use this method to register custom skin elements and properties to Flash UI or custom component skins by editing the code in the first frame of the Read Me layer of a skin in the Library.

```
myRadioButton.registerSkinElement(element, styleProperty)
```

element	A movie clip instance.
styleProperty	The name of an `FStyleFormat` property.

setChangeHandler

Specifies a change handler to call when the user moves the scroll bar's scroll box (thumb). You can specify the same change handler function for more than one component; the function always accepts the instance of the component that has changed as a parameter. Calling this method overrides the `ChangeHandler` parameter value specified in authoring.

```
myScrollBar.setChangeHandler(functionName, location)
```

functionName	A string specifying the name of the handler function to execute when the user moves the scroll box. If the location parameter is not specified, this function must be in the same timeline as the component instance.
location	Optional. A path reference to a data object, movie clip, or timeline that contains the specified function.

setEnabled

Boolean value specifying whether the scroll bar is enabled (true) or disabled (false).

```
myScrollBar.setEnabled(enable)
```

enable	Boolean value specifying whether an individual radio button or all the buttons in a group are enabled (true) or disabled (false).

setHorizontal

Specifies whether the scroll bar is applied to the target horizontally (true) or vertically (false). This method defaults to false.

```
myScrollBar.setHorizontal(horizontalScroll)
```

horizontalScroll	Boolean value specifying whether the scroll bar is horizontal (true) or vertical (false).

setLargeScroll

Sets the `largeScroll` property of the scroll bar instance at runtime. When the user clicks the scroll track once, the scroll box (thumb) moves the distance specified for one `largeScroll` position.

```
myScrollBar.setLargeScroll(largeScroll)
```

largeScroll   An integer specifying the number of positions to scroll when the user clicks the track once. The default value is the value set for pageSize with FScrollBar.setScrollProperties.

setScrollPosition

Specifies the position of the scroll box (thumb) on the scroll bar and executes the change handler function specified with FScrollBar.setChangeHandler.

myScrollBar.setScrollPosition(position)

position   An integer between the minPos and maxPos settings of the scroll bar.

setScrollProperties

Specifies the pageSize, minPos, and maxPos properties of the scroll bar and sets the scroll bar's scroll box (thumb) to the proper size.

myScrollBar.setScrollProperties(pageSize, minPos, maxPos)

pageSize   An integer representing the number of positions displayed in the page view.

minPos   An integer representing the minimum scrolled position.

maxPos   An integer representing the maximum scrolled position.

setScrollTarget

Specifies the text field instance to which the scroll bar applies. This instance must be defined in the same timeline and on the same level as the scroll bar. Calling this method overrides the TargetText Field parameter value set during authoring. Passing undefined for the target parameter disassociates the scroll bar from the text field.

myScrollBar.setScrollTarget(target)

target   A reference to the text field for the scroll bar.

setSize

Sets the length, in pixels, of the scroll bar at runtime. The width of scroll bar components cannot be set. Calling this method overrides any scaling and sizing applied during authoring.

myScrollBar.setSize(length)

length   An integer specifying the length of the scroll bar, in pixels.

setSmallScroll

Sets the smallScroll property of the scroll bar instance at runtime, if the text field has the focus. When the user clicks the scroll bar's arrows or an arrow key on the keyboard, the scroll box (thumb) moves the distance specified for one smallScroll position.

myScrollBar.setSmallScroll(smallScroll)

setStyleProperty

Sets an FStyleFormat property for an individual scroll bar instance. Calling this method to specify a property overrides the setting for this property in the style format assigned to the component. Passing undefined as the value for a property removes all styles for that property.

myScrollBar.setStyleProperty(styleProperty, value)

styleProperty   A string specifying a property of the FStyleFormat object.

value   The value to set for the property.

FScrollPane

Reference > Flash UI Components > FScrollPane

FScrollPane Methods

getPaneHeight

Returns the height of the scroll pane view. You can use this method only to get the height of a scroll pane that was sized with FScrollPane.setSize. This method works only if the scroll pane was sized with FScrollPane.setSize, not if you set the size using the _width and _height properties.

```
myScrollPane.getPaneHeight()
```

getPaneWidth

Returns the width of the scroll pane view. You can use this method only to get the width of a scroll pane that was sized with FScrollPane.setSize. This method works only if the scroll pane was sized with FScrollPane.setSize, not if you set the size using the _width and _height properties.

```
myScrollPane.getPaneWidth()
```

getScrollContent

Returns an instance of the content displayed in the scroll pane.

```
myScrollPane.getScrollContent()
```

getScrollPosition

Returns an object with the fields .x or .y specifying the current vertical or horizontal scroll position of the scroll pane view.

```
myScrollPane.getScrollPosition()
```

loadScrollContent

Specifies the URL of a SWF or JPEG file to display in the scroll pane.

```
myScrollPane.loadScrollContent("URL", funcName, location)
```

URL	A string specifying the URL of a SWF or JPEG file to load into the scroll pane.
funcName	Optional. A string specifying the name of the handler function to execute when the content of the scroll pane loads. If the location parameter is not specified, this function must be in the same timeline as the component instance.
location	Optional. A path reference to a data object, movie clip, or timeline that contains the specified function.

refreshPane

Resizes the scroll bars of the scroll pane when the content inside the scroll pane changes.

```
myScrollPane.refreshPane()
```

registerSkinElement

Registers a skin element to a style property. Use this method to register custom skin elements and properties to Flash UI or custom component skins by editing the code in the first frame of the Read Me layer of a skin in the Library.

```
myRadioButton.registerSkinElement(element, styleProperty)
```

element   A movie clip instance.

styleProperty   The name of an FStyleFormat property.

setDragContent

Specifies whether the user can change the scroll pane view by dragging its content in addition to using the scroll bars. Calling this method overrides the DragContent parameter value set during authoring.

```
myScrollPane.setDragContent(drag)
```

drag   Boolean value. True specifies that the user can change the view by dragging the content in the scroll pane; false specifies that the user can change the view only by using the scroll bars.

setHScroll

Determines whether a horizontal scroll bar is always displayed (true), never displayed (false), or only displayed when necessary ("auto").

```
myScrollPane.setHScroll(display)
```

display   Boolean value specifying whether the scroll bar is always displayed (true) or never displayed (false), or a string specifying that the scroll bar is displayed only when necessary ("auto").

setScrollContent

Specifies a movie clip to display in the scroll pane. Calling this method overrides the Scroll Content parameter value set in authoring.

```
myScrollPane.setScrollContent(target)
```

target   A text string specifying the symbol linkage ID of a movie clip in the Library or an instance of a movie clip.

setScrollPosition

Sets the scroll position to the specified x, y coordinate positions.

```
myScrollPane.setScrollPosition(x, y)
```

x   An integer specifying the number of pixels (from 0) to scroll to the right.

y   An integer specifying the number of pixels (from 0) to scroll down.

setSize

Sets the width and height, in pixels, of the scroll pane view at runtime. Calling this method overrides sizing applied during authoring.

```
myScrollPane.setSize(width, height)
```

width   An integer specifying the width of the scroll pane, in pixels.

height   An integer specifying the height of the scroll pane, in pixels.

setStyleProperty

Sets an `FStyleFormat` property for an individual scroll pane instance. Calling this method to specify a property overrides the setting for this property in the style format assigned to the component. Passing undefined as the value for a property removes all styles for that property.

`myScrollPane.setStyleProperty(styleProperty, value)`

styleProperty	A string specifying a property of the `FStyleFormat` object.
value	The value to set for the property.

setVScroll

Determines whether a vertical scroll bar is always displayed (true), never displayed (false), or only displayed when necessary ("auto").

`myScrollBar.setVScroll(display)`

display	Boolean value specifying whether a vertical scroll bar is always displayed (true) or never displayed (false), or a string specifying that the scroll bar is displayed only when necessary ("auto").

FStyleFormat

Reference > Flash UI Components > FStyleFormat

new FStyleFormat()

Constructor. Creates a new `FStyleFormat` object. You create new `FStyleFormat` objects to define text and color properties for custom style formats used with custom components or with the Flash UI components. All Flash UI components are assigned by default to `globalStyleFormat`, which is an instance of the `FStyleFormat` object.

globalStyleFormat

Object instance. An instance of the `FStyleFormat` object that defines the style format properties for Flash UI components. The `globalStyleFormat` instance is available after a Flash UI component is placed on the Stage. You set or change style format properites for Flash UI components by editing the properties in the `globalStyleFormat` object instance.

`globalStyleFormat.styleProperty`

styleProperty	A property of the `FStyleFormat` object.

FStyleFormat Methods

addListener

Registers the specified components to `myStyleFormat`. Use this method to register instances of Flash UI components or custom components to a custom style format.

`myStyleFormat.addListener(component1,...componentN)`

You can also use this method with the following syntax to register a custom component to the global style format used by all Flash UI components by default.

```
globalStyleFormat.addListener(customComponent)
```

| **component1,...componentN** | The component instances to register to myStyleFormat. |
| **customComponent** | The custom component to register to myStyleFormat. |

applyChanges

Updates the instance of the specified style format object and applies the changes to all the components assigned to the format. You must call this method when adding or removing listeners and setting or changing properties.

```
myStyleFormat.applyChanges(propertyName1,...propertyNameN)
```

The following syntax updates all the information in the style format (that is, assigned components and properties) regardless of whether they have changed.

```
myStyleFormat.applyChanges()
```

| **propertyName1,...propertyNameN** | A series of text strings specifying the properties to update for all components assigned to myStyleFormat. |

removeListener

Removes a component assigned to the style format.

```
myStyleFormat.removeListener(component)
```

| **component** | The component to remove from the style format. |

FStyleFormat Properties

arrow

The RGB color value for the arrow property used in scroll bars and drop-down lists in components such as scroll bars, list boxes, and combo boxes. The color value must be in the format 0xRRGGBB.

```
myStyleFormat.arrow
```

background

The RGB color value for the background portion of a component. For example, in a radio button or check box, the background portion is the space inside the selection area; in a list box or combo box, the background portion is the display area. The color value must be in the format 0xRRGGBB.

```
myStyleFormat.background
```

backgroundDisabled

The RGB color value for the background portion of a disabled component. The background color of disabled user interface elements is usually light gray. The color value must be in the format 0xRRGGBB.

```
myStyleFormat.backgroundDisabled
```

check

The RGB color value for the check mark in a selected check box. The color value must be in the format 0xRRGGBB.

`myStyleFormat.check`

darkshadow

The RGB color value for the inner border or darker shadow portion of a component, such as the inner edge of an unselected radio button circle or unselected check box. The color value must be in the format 0xRRGGBB.

`myStyleFormat.darkshadow`

embedFonts

No Info.

face

The RGB color value for the main color of a component, such as the gray used for the PushButton or ScrollBar component. The color value must be in the format 0xRRGGBB.

`myStyleFormat.face`

focusRectInner

No Info.

focusRectOuter

No Info.

foregroundDisabled

The RGB color value for the foreground of a disabled component. The foreground color of disabled user interface elements is usually medium gray. The color value must be in the format 0xRRGGBB.

`myStyleFormat.foregroundDisabled`

highlight

The RGB color value for the inner border or darker shadow portion of a component when it is selected, such as the inner edge of a radio button circle or check box. The color value must be in the format 0xRRGGBB.

`myStyleFormat.highlight`

highlight3D

The RGB color value for the outer border or light-shadow portion of a component when it is selected, such as the outer edge of a radio button circle or check box. The color value must be in the format 0xRRGGBB.

`myStyleFormat.highlight3D`

radioDot

The RGB color value for the selection dot in a radio button in a component. The color value must be in the format 0xRRGGBB.

`myStyleFormat.radioDot`

scrollTrack

The RGB color value for the track portion of a scroll bar. The ScrollBar component is used by the ScrollPane, ListBox, and ComboBox components, and changing the value of the scrollTrack property in the global style format changes the color of the scroll track in all components that use scroll bars. The color value must be in the format 0xRRGGBB.

```
myStyleFormat.scrollTrack
```

selection

The RGB color value for the bar used to highlight the selected item in a component's list. This property works with the FStyleFormat.textSelected property to display selected items, and you should coordinate the colors to make text easy to read. The color value must be in the format 0xRRGGBB.

```
myStyleFormat.selection
```

selectionDisabled

The RGB color value for the selection bar used to highlight a list item in a disabled component. The color value must be in the format 0xRRGGBB.

```
myStyleFormat.selectionDisabled
```

selectionUnfocused

The RGB color value for the selection bar (highlighting) in a component's list when the component doesn't have the keyboard focus. The color value must be in the format 0xRRGGBB.

```
myStyleFormat.selectionUnfocused
```

shadow

The RGB color value for the outer border or light shadow portion of a component, such as the outer edge of an unselected radio button circle or unselected check box. The color value must be in the format 0xRRGGBB.

```
myStyleFormat.shadow
```

textAlign

A text string specifying right, left, or center alignment for text displayed in all components assigned to the style format. The default setting is left.

```
myStyleFormat.textAlign
```

textBold

Boolean value specifying whether all text displayed in components using the style format is bold (true) or not (false). The default setting is false.

```
myStyleFormat.textBold
```

textColor

The RGB color value for the default text color in all components assigned to the style format. The color value must be in the format 0xRRGGBB.

```
myStyleFormat.textColor
```

textDisabled

The RGB color value for the default text color used to display text in disabled components assigned to the style format. The color value must be in the format 0xRRGGBB.

`myStyleFormat.textDisabled`

textFont

A text string specifying the font used to display text in all components assigned to the style format.

`myStyleFormat.textFont`

textIndent

An integer specifying the indentation, in pixels, from the left margin to the first text character for all text displayed using the style format.

`myStyleFormat.textIndent`

textItalic

Boolean value specifying whether all text displayed in components using the style format is italic (true) or not (false). The default setting is false.

`myStyleFormat.textItalic`

textLeftMargin

An integer specifying the left paragraph margin, in pixels, for all text displayed in components assigned to the style format.

`myStyleFormat.textLeftMargin`

textRightMargin

An integer specifying the right paragraph margin, in pixels, for all text displayed in components assigned to the style format.

`myStyleFormat.textRightMargin`

textSelected

An RGB color value specifying the color of selected text in components assigned to the style format. This property works with the `FStyleFormat.selection` property to display selected list items, and you should coordinate the colors to make the text easy to read. The color value must be in the format 0xRRGGBB.

`myStyleFormat.textSelected`

textSize

An integer specifying the point size of text displayed in components assigned to the style format. The default setting for this property is 12-point text.

`myStyleFormat.textSize`

textUnderline

Specifies whether text displayed in components using the specified style format is underlined (true) or not (false). The default setting is false.

`myStyleFormat.textUnderline`

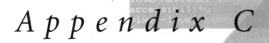

A p p e n d i x   C

Keyboard Shortcut
Quick Reference

Learning the keyboard shortcuts for any

program can be a terrific timesaver. It just

takes a little effort on your part. All the

drawing tools and almost any command

accessible from the main menu can be accessed using a keyboard shortcut. You can use the default Flash MX keyboard shortcuts, or you can use the keyboard shortcuts for Macromedia Fireworks 4, Macromedia FreeHand 10, Adobe Illustrator 10, or Adobe Photoshop 6. In addition, you can create your own.

Macromedia Standard Keyboard Shortcuts

Drawing Tools

The Drawing Tools shortcut commands are the same for both Windows and Macintosh platforms.

Tool	Windows and Macintosh
Arrow	V
Subselection	A
Line	N
Lasso	L
Pen	P
Text Tool	T
Oval	O
Rectangle	R
Pencil	Y
Paint Brush	B
Free Transform	Q
Fill Transform	F
Ink Bottle	S
Paint Bucket	K
Dropper	I
Eraser	E
Hand	H
Magnifier	M, Z

Drawing Menu Commands

File	Windows	Macintosh
New	Ctrl+N	Command+N
Open	Ctrl+O	Command+O
Open as Library	Ctrl+Shift+O	Command+Shift+O
Close	Ctrl+W	Command+W
Save	Ctrl+S	Command+S

File	Windows	Macintosh
Save As…	Ctrl+Shift+S	Command+Shift+S
Import…	Ctrl+R	Command+R
Export Movie…	Ctrl+Alt+Shift+S	Command+Option+Shift+S
Publish Settings…	Ctrl+Shift+F12	Command+Shift+F12
Publish Preview – Default	Ctrl+F12	Command+F12
Publish	Shift+F12	Shift+F12
Print…	Ctrl+P	Command+P
Exit	Ctrl+Q	Command+Q

Edit	Windows	Macintosh
Undo	Ctrl+Z	Command+Z
Redo	Ctrl+Y	Command+Y
Cut	Ctrl+X	Command+X
Copy	Ctrl+C	Command+C
Paste	Ctrl+V	Command+V
Paste in Place	Ctrl+Shift+V	Command+Shift+V
Clear	Backspace, Delete	Backspace, Delete
Duplicate	Ctrl+D	Command+D
Select All	Ctrl+A	Command+A
Deselect All	Ctrl+Shift+A	Command+Shift+A
Cut Frames	Ctrl+Alt+X	Command+Alt+X
Copy Frames	Ctrl+Alt+C	Command+Option+C
Paste Frames	Ctrl+Alt+V	Command+Option+V
Clear Frames	Alt+Backspace	Alt+Backspace
Select All Frames	Ctrl+Alt+A	Command+Option+A
Edit Symbols	Ctrl+E	Command+E
Edit Preferences	Ctrl+U	Command+U

If you are using Windows with Trillian as your messaging service, these commands will affect Trillian, but not Flash, if you have both applications open.

View	Windows	Macintosh
Go to First	Home	Home
Go to Previous	Page Up	Page Up
Go to Next	Page Down	Page Down
Go to Last	End	End
Zoom In	Ctrl+=	Command+=
Zoom Out	Ctrl+-	Command+-
100% Magnification	Ctrl+1	Command+1
Show Frame	Ctrl+2	Command+2

View	Windows	Macintosh
Show All	Ctrl+3	Command+3
Outlines	Ctrl+Alt+Shift+O	Command+Option+Shift+O
Fast	Ctrl+Alt+Shift+F	Command+Option+Shift+F
Antialias	Ctrl+Alt+Shift+A	Command+Option+Shift+A
Antialias Text (antialiases both text and shapes)	Ctrl+Alt+Shift+T	Command+Option+Shift+T
Toggle Timeline On/Off	Ctrl+Alt+T	Command+Option+T
Toggle Work Area Orientation	Ctrl+Shift+W	Command+Shift+W
Toggle Rulers On/Off	Ctrl+Alt+Shift+R	Command+Option+Shift+R
Show/Hide Grid	Ctrl+'	Command+'
Toggle Snap to Grid On/Off	Ctrl+Shift+'	Command+Shift+'
Edit Grid…	Ctrl+Alt+G	Command+Option+G
Toggle Show Guides On/Off	Ctrl+;	Command+;
Toggle Lock Guides On/Off	Ctrl+Alt+;	Command+Option+;
Toggle Snap to Guides On/Off	Ctrl+Shift+;	Command+Shift+;
Edit Guides…	Ctrl+Alt+Shift+G	Command+Option+Shift+G
Toggle Snap to Objects On/Off	Ctrl+Shift+/	Command+Shift+/
Toggle Show Shape Hints On/Off	Ctrl+Alt+H	Command+Option+H
Hide Edges (Selection Highlights)	Ctrl+H	Command+H
Hide/Show Panels	Tab or F4	Tab

Insert	Windows	Macintosh
Convert to Symbol	F8	F8
New Symbol…	Ctrl+F8	Command+F8
Frame	F5	F5
Remove Frames	Shift+F5	Shift+F5
Keyframe	F6	F6
Blank Keyframe	F7	F7
Clear Keyframe	Shift+F6	Shift+F6

Modify	Windows	Macintosh
Toggle Scene Panel On/Off	Shift+F2	Shift+F2
Open Document Properties	Ctrl+J	Command+J
Optimize Curves	Ctrl+Alt+Shift+C	Command+Option+Shift+C
Add Shape Hint	Ctrl+Shift+H	Command+Shift+H
Scale and Rotate	Ctrl+Alt+S	Command+Option+S

Remove Transform	Ctrl+Shift+Z	Command+Shift+Z
Bring to Front	Ctrl+Shift+Up Arrow	Command+Shift+Up Arrow
Bring Forward	Ctrl+Up Arrow	Command+Up Arrow
Send Backward	Ctrl+Down Arrow	Command+Down Arrow
Send to Back	Ctrl+Shift+Down Arrow	Command+Shift+Down Arrow
Lock	Ctrl+Alt+L	Command+Option+L
Unlock All	Ctrl+Alt+Shift+L	Command+Option+Shift+L
Group	Ctrl+G	Command+G
Ungroup	Ctrl+Shift+G	Command+Shift+G
Break Apart	Ctrl+B	Command+B
Distribute to Layers	Ctrl+Shift+D	Command+Shift+D

Text	Windows	Macintosh
Plain	Ctrl+Shift+P	Command+Shift+P
Bold	Ctrl+Shift+B	Command+Shift+B
Italic	Ctrl+Shift+I	Command+Shift+I
Align Left	Ctrl+Shift+L	Command+Shift+L
Align Center	Ctrl+Shift+C	Command+Shift+C
Align Right	Ctrl+Shift+R	Command+Shift+R
Justify	Ctrl+Shift+J	Command+Shift+J
Increase Tracking	Ctrl+Alt+Right Arrow	Command+Option+Right Arrow
Decrease Tracking	Ctrl+Alt+Left Arrow	Command+Option+Left Arrow
Reset Tracking	Ctrl+Alt+Up Arrow	Command+Option+Up Arrow

Control	Windows	Macintosh
Play	Enter	Enter
Rewind	Ctrl+Alt+R	Command+Option+R
Step Forward	.	.
Step Backward	,	,
Test Movie	Ctrl+Enter	Command+Enter
Debug Movie	Ctrl+Shift+Enter	Command+Shift+Enter
Test Scene	Ctrl+Alt+Enter	Command+Option+Enter
Enable/Disable Simple Buttons	Ctrl+Alt+B	Command+Option+B

Window	Windows	Macintosh
New Window	Ctrl+Alt+N	Command+Option+N
Timeline	Ctrl+Alt+T	Command+Option+T
Properties	Ctrl+F3	Command+F3
Align	Ctrl+K	Command+K
Color Mixer	Shift+F9	Shift+F9

continues ▶

Window	Windows	Macintosh
Color Swatches	Ctrl+F9	Command+F9
Info	Ctrl+I	Command+I
Scene	Shift+F2	Shift+F2
Transform	Ctrl+T	Command+T
Actions	F9	F9
Debugger	Shift+F4	Shift+F4
Movie Explorer	Alt+F3	Alt+F3
Reference	Shift+F1	Shift+F1
Output	F2	F2
Accessibility	Alt+F2	Alt+F2
Components	Ctrl+F7	Command+F7
Component Parameters	Alt+F7	Alt+F7
Library	Ctrl+L or F11	Command+L, F11

Help	Windows	Macintosh
Using Flash	F1	F1
		Command+Option

Test Movie Menu Commands

These are the commands that are available to you when you are in Test Movie mode. Note that there are other shortcuts listed when you are in Test Movie mode, but the ones listed here are the only ones that are particularly useful.

File	Windows	Macintosh
New	Ctrl+N	Command+N
Open	Ctrl+O	Command+0
Close	Ctrl+W	Command+W
Exit or Quit	Ctrl+Q	Command+Q

View	Windows	Macintosh
Zoom In	Ctrl+=	Command+=
Zoom Out	Ctrl+-	Command+-
100% Magnification	Ctrl+1	Command+1
Show Frame	Ctrl+2	Command+2
Show All	Ctrl+3	Command+3
Bandwidth Profiler	Ctrl+B	Command+B
Show Streaming	Ctrl+Enter	Command+Enter
Streaming Graph	Ctrl+G	Command+G
Frame by Frame Graph	Ctrl+F	Command+F

Control	Windows	Macintosh
Play	Enter	Enter
Rewind	Ctrl+Alt+R	Command+Option+R
Step Forward	.	.
Step Backward	,	,
Set/Remove Breakpoint	Ctrl+Shift+B	Command+Shift+B
Remove All Breakpoints	Ctrl+Shift+A	Command+Shift+A
Continue	F8	F8
Stop Debugging	F7	F7
Step In	F10	F10
Step Over	F9	F9
Step Out	F11	F11

Debug	Windows	Macintosh
List Objects	Ctrl+L	Command+L
List Variables	Ctrl+Alt+V	Command+Option+V

Window	Windows	Macintosh
Output	F2	F2
Debugger	Shift+F4	Shift+F4

Actions Panel Commands

Many of the Actions panel shortcuts are the same for both platforms. The general commands that are platform specific are listed first, followed by the Actions shortcuts that are the same for both platforms.

General Commands	Windows	Macintosh
Normal Mode	Ctrl+Shift+N	Command+Shift+N
Expert Mode	Ctrl+Shift+E	Command+Shift+E
Go to Line…	Ctrl+G	Command+G
Find…	Ctrl+F	Command+F
Find Again	F3	F3
Replace	Ctrl+H	Command+H
Check Syntax	Ctrl+T	Command+T
Show Code Hint	Ctrl+Spacebar	Command+Spacebar
Auto Format	Ctrl+Shift+F	Command+Shift+F
Import From File…	Ctrl+Shift+I	Command+Shift+I
Export As File…	Ctrl+Shift+X	Command+Shift+X
View Line Numbers	Ctrl+Shift+L	Command+Shift+L

Actions	Windows and Macintosh
break	Esc+br
call	Esc+ca
continue	Esc+co
do while	Esc+do
duplicateMovieClip	Esc+dm
else	Esc+el
elseif	Esc+ei
for	Esc+fr
for...in	Esc+fi
FSCommand	Esc+fs
function	Esc+fn
getURL	Esc+gu
gotoAndPlay	Esc+gp
gotoAndStop	Esc+gs
if	Esc+if
include	Esc+in
loadMovie	Esc+lm
loadMovieNum	Esc+ln
loadVariables	Esc+lv
loadVariablesNum	Esc+vn
nextFrame	Esc+nf
nextScene	Esc+ns
on	Esc+on
onClipEvent	Esc+oc
play	Esc+pl
prevFrame	Esc+pf
prevScene	Esc+ps
printAsBitmapNum	Esc+bn
printNum	Esc+pn
removeMovieClip	Esc+rm
return	Esc+rt
set	Esc+sv
setProperty	Esc+sp
startDrag	Esc+dr
stop	Esc+st
stopAllSounds	Esc+ss
stopDrag	Esc+sd
toggleHighQuality	Esc+tq
trace	Esc+tr
unloadMovie	Esc+um
unloadMoveNum	Esc+un
var	Esc+vr
while	Esc+wh
with	Esc+wt

Macromedia Flash 5 Keyboard Shortcuts

Yes, we know that you still love those old Flash 5 shortcuts. Fortunately, you can still use them. Here they are, in all of their former glory. Be aware that where there are entirely new commands in Flash MX, such as for the Free Transform tool, we've incorporated them into the Flash 5 shortcut set. The old shortcuts are not necessarily in the same order (that is, associated with the same menu item) as they were in Flash 5, but they're all there.

Drawing Tools

The Drawing Tools shortcut commands are the same for both the Windows and the Macintosh platforms.

Tool	Windows and Macintosh
Arrow	V
Subselection	A
Line	N
Lasso	L
Pen	P
Text Tool	T
Oval	O
Rectangle	R
Pencil	Y
Paint Brush	B
Free Transform	Q
Fill Transform	F
Ink Bottle	S
Paint Bucket	K
Dropper	I
Eraser	E
Hand	H
Magnifier	M, Z

Drawing Menu Commands

File	Windows	Macintosh
New	Ctrl+N	Command+N
Open	Ctrl+O	Command+O
Open as Library	Ctrl+Shift+O	Command+Shift+O
Close	Ctrl+W	Command+W
Save	Ctrl+S	Command+S
Save As...	Ctrl+Shift+S	Command+Shift+S

continues ▶

File	Windows	Macintosh
Import…	Ctrl+R	Command+R
Export Movie…	Ctrl+Alt+Shift+S	Command+Option+Shift+S
Publish Settings…	Ctrl+Shift+F12	Command+Shift+F12
Publish Preview – Default	Ctrl+F12, F12	Command+F12, F12
Publish	Shift+F12	Shift+F12
Print…	Ctrl+P	Command+P
Exit	Ctrl+Q	Command+Q

Edit	Windows	Macintosh
Undo	Ctrl+Z	Command+Z
Redo	Ctrl+Y	Command+Y
Cut	Ctrl+X	Command+X
Copy	Ctrl+C	Command+C
Paste	Ctrl+V	Command+V
Paste in Place	Ctrl+Shift+V	Command+Shift+V
Clear	Backspace, Delete	Backspace, Delete
Duplicate	Ctrl+D	Command+D
Select All	Ctrl+A	Command+A
Deselect All	Ctrl+Shift+A	Command+Shift+A
Cut Frames	Ctrl+Alt+X	Command+Option+X
Copy Frames	Ctrl+Alt+C	Command+Option+C
Paste Frames	Ctrl+Alt+V	Command+Option+V
Clear Frames	Alt+Backspace	Alt+Backspace
Edit Symbols	Ctrl+E	Command+E

View	Windows	Macintosh
Go to First	Home	Home
Go to Previous	Page Up	Page Up
Go to Next	Page Down	Page Down
Go to Last	End	End
Zoom In	Ctrl+=	Command+=
Zoom Out	Ctrl+-	Command+-
100% Magnification	Ctrl+1	Command+1
Show Frame	Ctrl+2	Command+2
Show All	Ctrl+3	Command+3
Outlines	Ctrl+Alt+Shift+O	Command+Option+Shift+O
Fast	Ctrl+Alt+Shift+F	Command+Option+Shift+F
Antialias	Ctrl+Alt+Shift+A	Command+Option+Shift+A
Antialias Text (antialiases both text and shapes)	Ctrl+Alt+Shift+T	Command+Option+Shift+T

View	Windows	Macintosh
Toggle Timeline On/Off	Ctrl+Alt+T	Command+Option+T
Toggle Work Area Orientation	Ctrl+Shift+W	Command+Shift+W
Toggle Rulers On/Off	Ctrl+Alt+Shift+R	Command+Option+Shift+R
Show/Hide Grid	Ctrl+'	Command+'
Toggle Snap to Grid On/Off	Ctrl+Shift+'	Command+Shift+'
Edit Grid…	Ctrl+Alt+G	Command+Option+G
Toggle Show Guides On/Off	Ctrl+;	Command+;
Toggle Lock Guides On/Off	Ctrl+Alt+;	Command+Option+;
Toggle Snap to Guides On/Off	Ctrl+Shift+;	Command+Shift+;
Edit Guides…	Ctrl+Alt+Shift+G	Command+Option+Shift+G
Toggle Snap to Objects On/Off	Ctrl+Shift+/	Command+Shift+/
Toggle Show Shape Hints On/Off	Ctrl+Alt+H	Command+Option+H
Hide Edges (Selection Highlights)	Ctrl+H	Command+H
Hide/Show Panels	Tab	Tab

Insert	Windows	Macintosh
Convert to Symbol	F8	F8
New Symbol…	Ctrl+F8	Command+F8
Frame	F5	F5
Remove Frames	Shift+F5	Shift+F5
Keyframe	F6	F6
Blank Keyframe	F7	F7
Clear Keyframe	Shift+F6	Shift+F6

Modify	Windows	Macintosh
Toggle Scene Panel On/Off	Ctrl+U	Command+U
Open Document Properties	Ctrl+M	Command+M
Optimize Curves	Ctrl+Alt+Shift+C	Command+Option+Shift+C
Add Shape Hint	Ctrl+Shift+H	Command+Shift+H
Scale and Rotate	Ctrl+Alt+S	Command+Option+S
Remove Transform	Ctrl+Shift+Z	Command+Shift+Z
Bring to Front	Ctrl+Shift+Up Arrow	Command+Shift+Up Arrow
Bring Forward	Ctrl+Up Arrow	Command+Up Arrow
Send Backward	Ctrl+Down Arrow	Command+Down Arrow
Send to Back	Ctrl+Shift+Down Arrow	Command+Shift+Down Arrow

continues ▶

Modify	Windows	Macintosh
Lock	Ctrl+Alt+L	Command+Option+L
Unlock All	Ctrl+Alt+Shift+L	Command+Option+Shift+L
Convert to Keyframes	F6	F6
Convert to Blank Keyframes	F7	F7
Group	Ctrl+G	Command+G
Ungroup	Ctrl+Shift+G	Command+Shift+G
Break Apart	Ctrl+B	Command+B
Distribute to Layers	Ctrl+Shift+D	Command+Shift+D

Text	Windows	Macintosh
Plain	Ctrl+Shift+P	Command+Shift+P
Bold	Ctrl+Shift+B	Command+Shift+B
Italic	Ctrl+Shift+I	Command+Shift+I
Align Left	Ctrl+Shift+L	Command+Shift+L
Align Center	Ctrl+Shift+C	Command+Shift+C
Align Right	Ctrl+Shift+R	Command+Shift+R
Justify	Ctrl+Shift+J	Command+Shift+J
Increase Tracking	Ctrl+Alt+Right Arrow	Command+Option+Right Arrow
Decrease Tracking	Ctrl+Alt+Left Arrow	Command+Option+Left Arrow
Reset Tracking	Ctrl+Alt+Up Arrow	Command+Option+Up Arrow

Control	Windows	Macintosh
Play	Enter	Enter
Rewind	Ctrl+Alt+R	Command+Option+R
Step Forward	.	.
Step Backward	,	,
Test Movie	Ctrl+Enter	Command+Enter
Debug Movie	Ctrl+Shift+Enter	Command+Shift+Enter
Test Scene	Ctrl+Alt+Enter	Command+Option+Enter
Enable/Disable Simple Buttons	Ctrl+Alt+B	Command+Option+B

Window	Windows	Macintosh
New Window	Ctrl+Alt+N	Command+Option+N
Timeline	Ctrl+Alt+T	Command+Option+T
Properties	Ctrl+F3	Command+F3
Align	Ctrl+K	Command+K
Color Mixer	Shift+F2	Shift+F2
Color Swatches	Shift+F3	Shift+F3
Info	Ctrl+I	Command+I

Window	Windows	Macintosh
Scene	Ctrl+U	Command+U
Transform	Ctrl+T	Command+T
Actions	Ctrl+Alt+A	Command+Option+A
Debugger	Shift+F4	Shift+F4
Movie Explorer	Ctrl+Alt+M	Command+Option+M
Reference	Shift+F1	Shift+F1
Output	Shift+F9	Shift+F9
Accessibility	F9	F9
Components	F11	F11
Component Parameters	Shift+F11	Shift+F11
Library	Ctrl+L	Command+L

Help	Windows	Macintosh
Using Flash	F1	F1

Test Movie Menu Commands

These are the commands that are available to you when you are in Test Movie mode. Note that there are other shortcuts listed when you are in Test Movie mode, but the ones listed here are the only ones that are actually useful.

File	Windows	Macintosh
New	Ctrl+N	Command+N
Open	Ctrl+O	Command+0
Close	Ctrl+W	Command+W
Exit or Quit	Ctrl+Q	Command+Q

View	Windows	Macintosh
Zoom In	Ctrl+=	Command+=
Zoom Out	Ctrl+-	Command+-
100% Magnification	Ctrl+1	Command+1
Show Frame	Ctrl+2	Command+2
Show All	Ctrl+3	Command+3
Bandwidth Profiler	Ctrl+B	Command+B
Show Streaming	Ctrl+Enter	Command+Enter
Streaming Graph	Ctrl+G	Command+G
Frame by Frame Graph	Ctrl+F	Command+F

Control	Windows	Macintosh
Play	Enter	Enter
Rewind	Ctrl+Alt+R	Command+Option+R
Step Forward	.	.
Step Backward	,	,
Set/Remove Breakpoint	Ctrl+Shift+B	Command+Shift+B
Remove All Breakpoints	Ctrl+Shift+A	Command+Shift+A
Continue	F8	F8
Stop Debugging	F7	F7
Step In	F10	F10
Step Over	F9	F9
Step Out	F11	F11

Debug	Windows	Macintosh
List Objects	Ctrl+L	Command+L
List Variables	Ctrl+Alt+V	Command+Option+V

Window	Windows	Macintosh
Output	F2	F2
Debugger	Shift+F4	Shift+F4

Actions Panel Commands

Many of the Actions panel shortcuts are the same for both platforms. The general commands that are platform-specific are listed first. They are followed by the Actions shortcuts that are the same for both platforms.

General Commands	Windows	Macintosh
Normal Mode	Ctrl+Shift+N	Command+Shift+N
Expert Mode	Ctrl+Shift+E	Command+Shift+E
Go to Line…	Ctrl+G	Command+G
Find…	Ctrl+F	Command+F
Find Again	F3	F3
Replace	Ctrl+H	Command+H
Check Syntax	Ctrl+T	Command+T
Show Code Hint	Ctrl+Spacebar	Command+Spacebar
Auto Format	Ctrl+Shift+F	Command+Shift+F
Import From File…	Ctrl+Shift+I	Command+Shift+I
Export As File…	Ctrl+Shift+X	Command+Shift+X
View Line Numbers	Ctrl+Shift+L	Command+Shift+L

Fireworks 44 Keyboard Shortcuts

People expect all the shortcuts from other applications to be applicable in Flash. Unfortunately, that just isn't the case. The alternate shortcut key sets are actually the Flash shortcuts, with some modifications to make them conform more closely to other applications with which you might be more comfortable. No matter which shortcut set you use, you'll find Flash-specific shortcuts sprinkled liberally throughout.

Drawing Tools

The Drawing Tools shortcut commands are the same for both Windows and Macintosh platforms.

Drawing Toolbar	Windows and Macintosh
Arrow	V
Subselect	A
Line	N
Lasso	L
Pen	P
Text	T
Oval	O
Rectangle	R
Pencil	Y
Paint Brush	B
Ink Bottle	S
Paint Bucket	K
Dropper	I
Eraser	E
Hand	H
Magnifier	Z

Drawing Menu Commands

File	Windows	Macintosh
New	Ctrl+N	Command+N
Open	Ctrl+O	Command+O
Open as Library	Ctrl+Shift+O	Command+Shift+O
Close	Ctrl+W	Command+W
Save	Ctrl+S	Command+S
Save As…	Ctrl+Shift+S	Command+Shift+S
Import	Ctrl+R	Command+R
Export Movie	Ctrl+Alt+Shift+S	Command+Option+Shift+S

continues ▶

File	Windows	Macintosh
Export Image	Ctrl+Shift+R	Command+Shift+R
Publish	Shift+F12	Shift+F12
Publish Settings	Ctrl+Shift+F12	Command+Shift+F12
Publish Preview > Default	F12	F12
Print	Ctrl+P	Command+P
Exit	Ctrl+Q	Command+Q

Edit	Windows	Macintosh
Undo	Ctrl+Z	Command+Z
Redo	Ctrl+Shift+Z	Command+Shift+Z
Cut	Ctrl+X	Command+X
Copy	Ctrl+C	Command+C
Paste	Ctrl+V	Command+V
Paste in Place	Ctrl+Shift+V	Command+Shift+V
Clear	Backspace, Delete	Backspace, Delete
Duplicate	Ctrl+Alt+D	Command+Option+D
Select All	Ctrl+A	Command+A
Deselect All	Ctrl+D	Command+D
Cut Frames	Ctrl+Alt+X	Command+Option+X
Copy Frames	Ctrl+Alt+C	Command+Option+C
Paste Frames	Ctrl+Alt+V	Command+Option+V
Edit Symbols	Ctrl+E	Command+E

View	Windows	Macintosh
Goto First	Home	Home
Goto Previous	Page Up	Page Up
Goto Next	Page Down	Page Down
Goto Last	End	End
Zoom In	Ctrl+=	Command+=
Zoom Out	Ctrl+-	Command+-
50% Magnification	Ctrl+5	Command+5
100% Magnification	Ctrl+1	Command+1
200% Magnification	Ctrl+2	Command+2
400% Magnification	Ctrl+4	Command+4
800% Magnification	Ctrl+8	Command+8
Show All	Ctrl+Shift+M	Command+Shift+M
Outlines	Ctrl+Alt+Shift+O	Command+Option+Shift+O
Fast	Ctrl+Alt+Shift+F	Command+Option+Shift+F
Antialias	Ctrl+Alt+Shift+A	Command+Option+Shift+A

Antialias Text	Ctrl+Alt+Shift+T	Command+Option+Shift+T
Work Area	Ctrl+Shift+W	Command+Shift+W
Rulers	Ctrl+Alt+R	Command+Option+R
Show Grid	Ctrl+'	Command+'
Snap to Grid	Ctrl+Shift+'	Command+Shift+'
Edit Grid	Ctrl+Alt+G	Command+Option+G
Show Guides	Ctrl+;	Command+;
Lock Guides	Ctrl+Alt+;	Command+Option+;
Snap to Guides	Ctrl+Shift+;	Command+Shift+;
Edit Guides	Ctrl+Alt+Shift+G	Command+Option+Shift+G
Snap to Objects	Ctrl+Shift+/	Command+Shift+/
Show Shape Hints	Ctrl+Alt+H	Command+Option+H
Hide Edges	Ctrl+H	Command+H
Hide Panels	Ctrl+Shift+H	Command+Shift+H

Insert	Windows	Macintosh
Convert to Symbol…	F8	F8
New Symbol…	Ctrl+F8	Command+F8
Frame	F5	F5
Remove Frames	Shift+F5	Shift+F5
Clear Keyframe	Shift+F6	Shift+F6

Modify	Windows	Macintosh
Layer	Ctrl+Alt+L	Command+Option+L
Document	Ctrl+M	Command+M
Scale and Rotate	Ctrl+Shift+T	Command+Shift+T
Rotate 90 CW	Ctrl+9	Command+9
Rotate 90 CCW	Ctrl+7	Command+7
Bring to Front	Ctrl+F	Command+F
Bring Forward	Ctrl+Shift+F	Command+Shift+F
Send Backward	Ctrl+Shift+B	Command+Shift+B
Send to Back	Ctrl+B	Command+B
Group	Ctrl+G	Command+G
Ungroup	Ctrl+U	Command+U
Break Apart	Ctrl+Shift+P	Command+Shift+P

Text	Windows	Macintosh
Plain	Ctrl+Alt+Shift+P	Command+Option+Shift+P
Bold	Ctrl+Alt+Shift+B	Command+Option+Shift+B
Italic	Ctrl+Alt+Shift+I	Command+Option+Shift+I
Align Left	Ctrl+Alt+Shift+L	Command+Option+Shift+L
Align Center	Ctrl+Alt+Shift+C	Command+Alt+Shift+C

Text	Windows	Macintosh
Align Right	Ctrl+Alt+Shift+R	Command+Alt+Shift+R
Justify	Ctrl+Alt+Shift+J	Command+Alt+Shift+J
Increase Tracking	Ctrl+Alt+Right Arrow	Command+Option+Right Arrow
Decrease Tracking	Ctrl+Alt+Left Arrow	Command+Option+Left Arrow
Reset Tracking	Ctrl+Alt+Up Arrow	Command+Option+Up Arrow

Control	Windows	Macintosh
Play	Enter	Enter
Step Forward	.	.
Step Backward	,	,
Test Movie	Ctrl+Enter	Command+Enter
Debug Movie	Ctrl+Shift+Enter	Command+Shift+Enter
Test Scene	Ctrl+Alt+Enter	Command+Option+Enter

Window	Windows	Macintosh
New Window	Ctrl+Alt+N	Command+Option+N
Tools	Ctrl+Alt+T	Command+Option+T
Align Panel	Ctrl+K	Command+K
Color Mixer	Ctrl+Alt+M	Command+Option+M
Color Swatches	Ctrl+Alt+S	Command+Option+S
Info Panel	Ctrl+Alt+I	Command+Option+I
Actions	Ctrl+Alt+A	Command+Option+A
Library	Ctrl+L	Command+Option+L

FreeHand 10 Keyboard Shortcuts

People expect all the shortcuts from other applications to be applicable in Flash. Unfortunately, that just isn't the case. The alternate shortcut key sets are actually the Flash shortcuts, with some modifications to make them conform more closely to other applications with which you might be more comfortable. No matter which shortcut set you use, you'll find Flash-specific shortcuts sprinkled liberally throughout.

Drawing Tools

Drawing Toolbar	Windows and Macintosh
Arrow	V
Line	N
Lasso	L
Pen	P
Text	A
Oval	E
Rectangle	R
Pencil	Y
Brush	B
Ink Bottle	S
Paint Bucket	K
Dropper	I
Hand	H
Magnifier	Z

Drawing Menu Commands

File	Windows	Macintosh
New	Ctrl+N	Command+N
Open	Ctrl+O	Command+O
Open as Library	Ctrl+Shift+O	Command+Shift+O
Close	Ctrl+W	Command+W
Save	Ctrl+S	Command+S
Save As…	Ctrl+Shift+S	Command+Shift+S
Import	Ctrl+R	Command+R
Export Movie	Ctrl+Alt+Shift+S	Command+Option+Shift+S
Export Image	Ctrl+Shift+R	Command+Shift+R
Publish Settings	Ctrl+Shift+F12	Command+Shift+F12
Publish Preview > Default	F12	F12
Publish	Shift+F12	Shift+F12
Print	Ctrl+P	Command+P
Exit	Ctrl+Q	Command+Q

Edit	Windows	Macintosh
Undo	Ctrl+Z	Command+Z
Redo	Ctrl+Y	Command+Y
Cut	Ctrl+X	Command+X
Copy	Ctrl+C	Command+C
Paste	Ctrl+V	Command+V
Paste in Place	Ctrl+Shift+V	Command+Shift+V
Clear	Backspace, Delete	Backspace, Delete
Duplicate	Ctrl+D	Command+D
Select All	Ctrl+A	Command+A
Deselect All	Ctrl+Shift+A	Command+Shift+A
Cut Frames	Ctrl+Alt+X	Command+Option+X
Copy Frames	Ctrl+Alt+C	Command+Option+C
Paste Frames	Ctrl+Alt+V	Command+Option+V
Edit Symbols	Ctrl+E	Command+E
Preferences	Ctrl+Shift+D	Command+Shift+D

View	Windows	Macintosh
Goto First	Home	Home
Goto Previous	Page Up	Page Up
Goto Next	Page Down	Page Down
Goto Last	End	End
Zoom In	Ctrl+=	Command+=
Zoom Out	Ctrl+ -	Command+ -
50% Magnification	Ctrl+5	Command+5
100% Magnification	Ctrl+1	Command+1
200% Magnification	Ctrl+2	Command+2
400% Magnification	Ctrl+4	Command+4
800% Magnification	Ctrl+8	Command+8
Show All	Ctrl+Alt+0	Command+Option+0
Outlines	Ctrl+K	Command+K
Fast	Ctrl+Shift+F	Command+Shift+F
Antialias	Ctrl+Alt+Shift+G	Command+Option+Shift+G
Antialias Text	Ctrl+Alt+Shift+T	Command+Option+Shift+T
Work Area	Ctrl+Shift+W	Command+Shift+W
Rulers	Ctrl+Alt+M	Command+Option+M
Show Grid	Ctrl+'	Command+'
Snap to Grid	Ctrl+Shift+'	Command+Shift+'
Show Guides	Ctrl+;	Command+;
Lock Guides	Ctrl+Alt+;	Command+Option+;
Snap to Guides	Ctrl+Alt+G	Command+Option+G
Hide Panels	Ctrl+Alt+H	Command+Option+H

Insert	Windows	Macintosh
Convert to Symbol	F8	F8
New Symbol	Ctrl+F8	Command+F8
Frame	F5	F5
Remove Frames	Shift+F5	Shift+F5
Keyframe	F6	F6
Blank Keyframe	F7	F7
Clear Keyframe	Shift+F6	Shift+F6

Modify	Windows	Macintosh
Layer	Ctrl+6	Command+6
Document	Ctrl+M	Command+M
Optimize	Ctrl+Alt+Shift+O	Command+Option+Shift+O
Add Shape Hint	Ctrl+Shift+H	Command+Shift+H
Scale	Ctrl+F10	Command+F10
Rotate and Skew	Ctrl+F2	Command+F2
Scale and Rotate	Ctrl+Alt+S	Command+Option+S
Flip Vertical	Ctrl+F9	Command+F9
Remove Transform	Ctrl+Shift+Z	Command+Shift+Z
Bring to Front	Ctrl+F	Command+F
Bring Forward	Ctrl+Alt+Shift+S	Command+Option+Shift+S
Send Backward	Ctrl+Alt+Shift+K	Command+Option+Shift+K
Send to Back	Ctrl+B	Command+B
Lock	Ctrl+L	Command+L
Group	Ctrl+G	Command+G
Ungroup	Ctrl+U	Command+U
Break Apart	Ctrl+Shift+P	Command+Shift+P

Text	Windows	Macintosh
Plain	Ctrl+Alt+Shift+P	Command+Option+Shift+P
Bold	Ctrl+Alt+B	Command+Option+B
Italic	Ctrl+Alt+I	Command+Option+I
Align Left	Ctrl+Alt+Shift+L	Command+Option+Shift+L
Align Center	Ctrl+Alt+Shift+M	Command+Option+Shift+M
Align Right	Ctrl+Alt+Shift+R	Command+Option+Shift+R
Justify	Ctrl+Alt+Shift+J	Command+Option+Shift+J
Increase Tracking	Ctrl+Alt+Right Arrow	Command+Option+Right Arrow
Decrease Tracking	Ctrl+Alt+Left Arrow	Command+Option+Left Arrow
Reset Tracking	Ctrl+Alt+Up Arrow	Command+Option+Up Arrow

Control	Windows	Macintosh
Play	Enter	Enter
Rewind	Ctrl+Alt+R	Command+Option+R
Step Forward	.	.
Step Backward	,	,
Test Movie	Ctrl+Enter	Command+Enter
Debug Movie	Ctrl+Shift+Enter	Command+Shift+Enter
Test Scene	Ctrl+Alt+Enter	Command+Option+Enter

Window	Windows	Macintosh
New Window	Ctrl+Alt+N	Command+Option+N
Main Toolbar	Ctrl+Alt+T	Command+Option+T
Tools	Ctrl+7	Command+7
Align Panel	Ctrl+Alt+A	Command+Option+A
Color Mixer	Ctrl+Shift+9	Command+Shift+9

Illustrator 10 Keyboard Shortcuts

People expect all the shortcuts from other applications to be applicable in Flash. Unfortunately, that just isn't the case. The alternate shortcut key sets are actually the Flash shortcuts, with some modifications to make them conform more closely to other applications with which you might be more comfortable. No matter which shortcut set you use, you'll find Flash-specific shortcuts sprinkled liberally throughout.

Drawing Tools

Drawing Toolbar	Windows and Macintosh
Arrow	V
Subselect Tool	A
Line	Shift+N
Lasso	Y
Pen	P
Text Tool	T
Oval	L
Rectangle	M
Pencil	N
Paint Brush	B
Ink Bottle	S
Paint Bucket	K
Dropper	I
Eraser	E
Hand	H
Magnifier	Z

Drawing Menu Commands

File	Windows	Macintosh
New	Ctrl+N	Command+N
Open	Ctrl+O	Command+O
Open as Library	Ctrl+Shift+O	Command+Shift+O
Close	Ctrl+W	Command+W
Save	Ctrl+S	Command+S
Save As…	Ctrl+Shift+S	Command+Shift+S
Export Movie	Ctrl+Alt+Shift+S	Command+Option+Shift+S
Publish Settings	Ctrl+Shift+F12	Command+Shift+F12
Publish Preview (Default)	F12	F12
Publish	Shift+F12	Shift+F12
Print	Ctrl+P	Command+P
Exit	Ctrl+Q	Command+Q

Edit	Windows	Macintosh
Undo	Ctrl+Z	Command+Z
Redo	Ctrl+Shift+Z	Command+Shift+Z
Cut	Ctrl+X	Command+X
Copy	Ctrl+C	Command+C
Paste	Ctrl+V	Command+V
Paste in Place	Ctrl+Shift+V	Command+Shift+V
Clear	Backspace, Delete	Backspace, Delete
Duplicate	Ctrl+D	Command+D
Select All	Ctrl+A	Command+A
Deselect All	Ctrl+Shift+A	Command+Shift+A
Cut Frames	Ctrl+Alt+X	Command+Option+X
Copy Frames	Ctrl+Alt+C	Command+Option+C
Paste Frames	Ctrl+Alt+V	Command+Option+V
Edit Symbols	Ctrl+E	Command+E
Preferences	Ctrl+K	Command+K
Keyboard Shortcuts	Ctrl+Alt+Shift+K	Command+Option+Shift+K

View	Windows	Macintosh
Goto First	Home	Home
Goto Previous	Page Up	Page Up
Goto Next	Page Down	Page Down
Goto Last	End	End
Zoom In	Ctrl+=	Command+=
Zoom Out	Ctrl+-	Command+-
100% Magnification	Ctrl+1	Command+1
Show All	Ctrl+3	Command+3
Outlines	Ctrl+Y	Command+Y
Fast	Ctrl+Alt+Shift+F	Command+Option+Shift+F
Antialias	Ctrl+Alt+Shift+A	Command+Option+Shift+A
Antialias Text	Ctrl+Alt+Shift+T	Command+Option+Shift+T
Timeline	Ctrl+Alt+T	Command+Option+T
Work Area	Ctrl+Shift+W	Command+Shift+W
Rulers	Ctrl+R	Command+R
Show Grid	Ctrl+'	Command+'
Snap to Grid	Ctrl+Shift+'	Command+Shift+'
Edit Grid	Ctrl+Alt+G	Command+Option+G
Show Guides	Ctrl+;	Command+;
Lock Guides	Ctrl+Alt+;	Command+Option+;
Snap to Guides	Ctrl+Shift+;	Command+Shift+;
Edit Guides	Ctrl+Alt+Shift+G	Command+Option+Shift+G

View	Windows	Macintosh
Snap to Objects	Ctrl+Shift+/	Command+Shift+/
Show Shape Hints	Ctrl+Alt+H	Command+Option+H
Hide Edges	Ctrl+H	Command+H
Hide Panels	Tab	Tab

Insert	Windows	Macintosh
Convert to Symbol	F8	F8
New Symbol	Ctrl+F8	Command+F8
Frame	F5	F5
Remove Frame	Shift+F5	Shift+F5
Keyframe	F6	F6
Blank Keyframe	F7	F7
Clear Keyframe	Shift+F6	Shift+F6

Modify	Windows	Macintosh
Optimize	Ctrl+Alt+Shift+C	Command+Option+Shift+C
Add Shape Hint	Ctrl+Shift+H	Command+Shift+H
Scale and Rotate	Ctrl+Alt+S	Command+Option+S
Bring to Front	Ctrl+Shift+]	Command+Shift+]
Bring Forward	Ctrl+]	Command+]
Send Backward	Ctrl+[	Command+[
Send to Back	Ctrl+Shift+[	Command+Shift+[
Lock	Ctrl+2	Command+2
Unlock All	Ctrl+Alt+2	Command+Option+2
Group	Ctrl+G	Command+G
Ungroup	Ctrl+Shift+G	Command+Shift+G
Break Apart	Ctrl+B	Command+B

Text	Windows	Macintosh
Plain	Ctrl+Shift+P	Command+Shift+P
Bold	Ctrl+Shift+B	Command+Shift+B
Italic	Ctrl+Shift+I	Command+Shift+I
Align Left	Ctrl+Shift+L	Command+Shift+L
Align Center	Ctrl+Shift+C	Command+Shift+C
Align Right	Ctrl+Shift+R	Command+Shift+R
Justify	Ctrl+Shift+J	Command+Shift+J
Increase Tracking	Ctrl+Alt+Right Arrow	Command+Option+Right Arrow
Decrease Tracking	Ctrl+Alt+Left Arrow	Command+Option+Left Arrow
Reset Tracking	Ctrl+Alt+Up Arrow	Command+Option+Up Arrow

Control	Windows	Macintosh
Play	Enter	Enter
Rewind	Ctrl+Alt+R	Command+Option+R
Step Forward	.	.
Step Backward	,	,
Test Movie	Ctrl+Enter	Command+Enter
Debug Movie	Ctrl+Shift+Enter	Command+Shift+Enter
Test Scene	Ctrl+Alt+Enter	Command+Option+Enter
Enable Simple Buttons	Ctrl+Alt+B	Command+Option+B

Window	Windows	Macintosh
New Window	Ctrl+Alt+N	Command+Option+N
Timeline	Ctrl+Alt+T	Command+Option+T
Info	Ctrl+Alt+I	Command+Option+I
Actions Panel	Ctrl+Alt+A	Command+Option+A
Movie Explorer	Ctrl+Alt+M	Command+Option+M
Library	Ctrl+L	Command+L

Photoshop 6 Keyboard Shortcuts

People expect all the shortcuts from other applications to be applicable in Flash. Unfortunately, that just isn't the case. The alternate shortcut key sets are actually the Flash shortcuts, with some modifications to make them conform more closely to other applications with which you might be more comfortable. No matter which shortcut set you use, you'll find Flash-specific shortcuts sprinkled liberally throughout.

Drawing Tools

Drawing Toolbar	Windows and Macintosh
Arrow	V
Subselect Tool	A
Line	Shift+N
Lasso	L
Pen	P
Text Tool	T
Oval	Shift+O
Rectangle	M
Pencil	N
Paint Brush	B
Free Transform	Ctrl+T/Command+T
Ink Bottle	S
Paint Bucket	K
Dropper	I
Eraser	E
Hand	H
Magnifier	Z

Drawing Menu Commands

File	Windows	Macintosh
New	Ctrl+N	Command+N
Open	Ctrl+O	Command+O
Open as Library	Ctrl+Shift+O	Command+Shift+O
Close	Ctrl+W	Command+W
Save	Ctrl+S	Command+S
Save As...	Ctrl+Shift+S	Command+Shift+S
Export Movie	Ctrl+Alt+Shift+S	Command+Option+Shift+S
Publish Settings	Ctrl+Shift+F12	Command+Shift+F12
Publish Preview (Default)	F12	F12

continues ▶

File	Windows	Macintosh
Publish	Shift+F12	Shift+F12
Page Setup	Ctrl+Shift+P	Command+Shift+P
Print	Ctrl+P	Command+P
Exit	Ctrl+Q	Command+Q

Edit	Windows	Macintosh
Undo	Ctrl+Z	Command+Z
Redo	Ctrl+Y	Command+Y
Cut	Ctrl+X	Command+X
Copy	Ctrl+C	Command+C
Paste	Ctrl+V	Command+V
Paste in Place	Ctrl+Shift+V	Command+Shift+V
Clear	Backspace, Delete	Backspace, Delete
Duplicate	Ctrl+D	Command+D
Select All	Ctrl+A	Command+A
Deselect All	Ctrl+Shift+A	Command+Shift+A
Cut Frames	Ctrl+Alt+X	Command+Option+X
Copy Frames	Ctrl+Alt+C	Command+Option+C
Paste Frames	Ctrl+Alt+V	Command+Option+V
Edit Symbols	Ctrl+E	Command+E
Preferences	Ctrl+K	Command+K

View	Windows	Macintosh
Goto First	Home	Home
Goto Previous	Page Up	Page Up
Goto Next	Page Down	Page Down
Goto Last	End	End
Zoom In	Ctrl+=	Command+=
Zoom Out	Ctrl+ -	Command+ -
100% Magnification	Ctrl+1	Command+1
Show Frame	Ctrl+2	Command+2
Show All	Ctrl+3	Command+3
Outlines	Ctrl+Alt+Shift+O	Command+Option+Shift+O
Fast	Ctrl+Alt+Shift+F	Command+Option+Shift+F
Antialias	Ctrl+Alt+Shift+A	Command+Option+Shift+A
Antialias Text	Ctrl+Alt+Shift+T	Command+Option+Shift+T
Timeline	Ctrl+Alt+T	Command+Option+T
Work Area	Ctrl+Shift+W	Command+Shift+W
Rulers	Ctrl+R	Command+R

View	Windows	Macintosh
Show Grid	Ctrl+'	Command+'
Snap to Grid	Ctrl+Shift+'	Command+Shift+'
Edit Grid	Ctrl+Alt+G	Command+Option+G
Show Guides	Ctrl+;	Command+;
Lock Guides	Ctrl+Alt+;	Command+Option+;
Snap to Guides	Ctrl+Shift+;	Command+Shift+;
Edit Guides	Ctrl+Alt+Shift+G	Command+Option+Shift+G
Snap to Objects	Ctrl+Shift+/	Command+Shift+/
Show Shape Hints	Ctrl+Alt+H	Command+Option+H
Hide Edges	Ctrl+H	Command+H
Hide Panels	Tab	Tab

Insert	Windows	Macintosh
Convert to Symbol	F8	F8
New Symbol	Ctrl+F8	Command+F8
Layer	Ctrl+Shift+N	Command+Shift+N
Frame	F5	F5
Remove Frame	Shift+F5	Shift+F5
Keyframe	F6	F6
Blank Keyframe	F7	F7
Clear Keyframe	Shift+F6	Shift+F6

Modify	Windows	Macintosh
Document	Ctrl+M	Command+M
Optimize	Ctrl+Alt+Shift+C	Command+Option+Shift+C
Add Shape Hint	Ctrl+Shift+H	Command+Shift+H
Scale and Rotate	Ctrl+Alt+S	Command+Option+S
Remove Transform	Ctrl+Shift+Z	Command+Shift+Z
Bring to Front	Ctrl+Shift+]	Command+Shift+]
Bring Forward	Ctrl+]	Command+]
Send Backward	Ctrl+[	Command+[
Send to Back	Ctrl+Shift+[	Command+Shift+[
Lock	Ctrl+Alt+L	Command+Option+L
Unlock All	Ctrl+Alt+Shift+L	Command+Option+Shift+L
Group	Ctrl+G	Command+G
Ungroup	Ctrl+Shift+G	Command+Shift+G
Break Apart	Ctrl+B	Command+B

Text	Windows	Macintosh
Bold	Ctrl+Shift+B	Command+Shift+B
Italic	Ctrl+Shift+I	Command+Shift+I
Align Left	Ctrl+Shift+L	Command+Shift+L
Align Center	Ctrl+Shift+C	Command+Shift+C
Align Right	Ctrl+Shift+R	Command+Shift+R
Justify	Ctrl+Shift+J	Command+Shift+J
Increase Tracking	Ctrl+Alt+Right Arrow	Command+Option+Right Arrow
Decrease Tracking	Ctrl+Alt+Left Arrow	Command+Option+Left Arrow
Reset Tracking	Ctrl+Alt+Up Arrow	Command+Option+Up Arrow

Control	Windows	Macintosh
Play	Enter	Enter
Rewind	Ctrl+Alt+R	Command+Option+R
Step Forward	.	.
Step Backward	,	,
Test Movie	Ctrl+Enter	Command+Enter
Debug Movie	Ctrl+Shift+Enter	Command+Shift+Enter
Test Scene	Ctrl+Alt+Enter	Command+Option+Enter
Enable Simple Buttons	Ctrl+Alt+B	Command+Option+B

Window	Windows	Macintosh
New Window	Ctrl+Alt+N	Command+Option+N
Timeline	Ctrl+Alt+T	Command+Option+T
Info	Ctrl+Alt+I	Command+Option+I
Actions Panel	Ctrl+Alt+A	Command+Option+A
Movie Explorer	Ctrl+Alt+M	Command+Option+M
Library	Ctrl+L	Command+L

A p p e n d i x   D

Flash Resources

A number of mailing lists, forums, web sites, and third-party software tools are available for you to use in conjunction with Flash. This is by no means a comprehensive listing, but it should give you a good sense of what is available.

Flash Mailing Lists

When all else fails and you just can't find the answer yourself, there is a large community of Flash developers out there willing to give you a hand. Some of these mailing lists have fairly high traffic.

If you subscribe to one or more of these lists and decide to unsubscribe later, you should note that, in all cases, the subscribe/unsubscribe information appears at the bottom of every email that is sent to you. Don't pester the already overworked list administrators with "unsubscribe" requests.

- **FlashCoders** (`chattyfig.figleaf.com`). A very high-traffic list specifically for Flash programmers. Some of the best in the business frequent this list.
- **Flasher** (`www.chinwag.com/flasher/info.shtml`). A great site for both designers and Flash techies.
- **FLASHmacromedia** (`groups.yahoo.com/group/FLASHmacromedia`). A moderated discussion group for all levels of Flash users.
- **FlashNewbie** (`chattyfig.figleaf.com`). A good site for anyone relatively new to Flash. Everybody has to start somewhere, and this is great for questions that you just aren't ready to ask the big boys yet.
- **FlashPro** (`muinar.com/flashpro`). A good site for professional (experienced) designers and programmers.

Web Sites

You might find that, with mailing lists, particularly the high-traffic ones, you become overwhelmed with email. A number of web sites also offer tutorials and FLA files that you can download and study. Many of the general-resource sites offer Flash-oriented forums as well. For those crisis days, there are also places where you can buy completed artwork.

General Sites

- **Flash Kit** (`www.flashkit.com`). A very large site and one of those one-stop-shopping kinds of places. You'll find tutorials, downloadable FLAs, forums—you name it, it's there.
- **Ultrashock** (`www.ultrashock.com`). Excellent tutorials and forums. Fig Leaf's Branden Hall is one of the moderators.
- **were-here.com** (`www.were-here.com`). Great tutorials and forums. You can also find games and even a career center.

ActionScripting Sites

- **FlashCoders archives (`chattyfig.figleaf.com`).** It's not just a mailing list—you also have access to the fully searchable archives of chattyfig.

- **moock.org (`www.moock.org/webdesign/flash`).** Colin Moock's site is one of the best out there for ActionScripting information. His site has tutorials and downloadable FLA files.

- **robertpenner.com (`www.robertpenner.com`).** Robert Penner's site is another excellent resource for high-level ActionScript.

- **levitated.net (`www.levitated.net`).** This one is a very cool experimental site with open source code available for you to download and experiment with.

- **flashcodehacks (`www.flashcodehacks.com/downloads/`).** For the ActionScripting geek in you, flashcodehacks offers links to a large number of resources, as well as files for download.

Magazine Sites

- **flashmagazine (`www.flashmagazine.com`).** Flashmagazine.com offers up articles, tutorials, and book reviews.

- **Flazoom.com (`www.flazoom.com`).** Flazoom.com is a great resource for articles about working with Flash. From usability to design principles, to what's going on in the world of Flash, this site is a must-read.

Sites for Purchasing Completed Graphics

- **graphicscene (`www.graphicscene.com`).** When you don't have the time to build it yourself, you can always purchase completed artwork from graphicscene.

Text Tools

Sometimes reinventing the wheel just isn't worth the effort. When you need a creative text effect, check out some of the companies that do this for a living. One thing to note about all these programs is that if the SWF file that you create contains movie clips, interactivity, or sound, you must use `loadMovie()` to add it to an existing Flash file. If you try to import the SWF file into Flash, the results might not be what you expect. For more on importing SWFs into Flash, see Chapter 4, "Importing, Using, and Optimizing Graphics." All these text-effect tools are standalone applications; you don't need Flash to use them. One note of caution: Overuse of text effects can be very annoying, as bad or worse than using the `<blink>` tag. So, if you're going to use them, use them judiciously.

- **SWfX (`www.wildform.com`).** Lets you quickly and easily create more than 300 different text effects that are output in the SWF format. SWfX currently creates 123 Flash 3 (nonhighlighted) effects that can be directly imported into your Flash. In addition, SWfX creates 180 Flash 4 effects that can be added to your Flash movie using the `loadMovie()` method. See Chapter 4 for more information about using externally generated SWFs with Flash. SWfX is available for both Windows and Macintosh platforms, and you can try out an online demo version.

- **FlaX (`www.flaxfx.com`).** Has 31 special-effects groups that also are very customizable. The program is very intuitive to use as well. You just punch a couple buttons and adjust some sliders. Another benefit is real-time display every time you change a setting. FlaX-generated SWF files can be imported directly into Flash, unless you've added and want to keep a link. You can also save your text animation as your default screen saver. It's available for Windows only, and you can try out a trial download.

- **Swish v2 (`www.swishzone.com`).** Although a little less intuitive than SWfx, Swishv2 offers the capability of adding sound and basic interactivity to your file. It also has 150 built-in effects. However, if you are planning to import the finished SWF file, remember that the sound and interactivity will not import. Again, `loadMovie()` is always an option. It's available for Windows and Macintosh, and you can sample a trial download.

3D Tools

These tools help you take Flash to that extra dimension—3D! Use these tools to create your 3D effects and export in SWF format for use in your Flash movies. All these tools are available in a standalone format; you don't need Flash to use them. Both Swift 3D and Vecta 3D are also available as plug-ins for 3ds max and other 3D programs.

- **Amorphium Pro (`www.amorphium.com`).** You can get really cool organic shapes that are tough to come up with any other way. It's completely unlike Swift 3D or Vecta 3D in that it uses a model much more akin to wax or clay modeling. It imports all major 3D formats. Amorphium Pro is available for Windows and Macintosh, and you can try it out as a trial download.

- **Swift 3D v2 (`www.swift3d.com`)** creates and exports 3D images and animations in SWF format. You can also import 3D formats created by such high-end 3D tools as 3ds max and SoftImage 3D. Swift 3D Standalone and the Swift 3D LW plug-in are available for Windows and Macintosh. Swift 3D MAX and Swift 3D X-SI plug-ins are available for Windows only. You can try out Swift as a trial download as well.

- **Vecta 3D (`www.vecta3d.com`)** can be purchased as a standalone version or as a plug-in for 3dsds max. It's available for Windows only and can be used as a trial download.

Cartoon Animation

Animation is obviously one of the things that Flash is great for. Achieving professional results is easy with a little plug-in help.

- **Toon Boom Studio (`www.toonboom.com`)**, created by USAnimation, lets you create movie-quality, two-dimensional animations for the web. What makes Toon Boom stand out as an animation tool is its 3-D stage—finally, camera angles in Flash. You saw in earlier chapters how time consuming it can be to lip sync your animation to a soundtrack—Toon Boom has built-in editing tools to help you do that. If you are working with character animation, you should definitely give this one a look. It's available for Windows and Macintosh.

Video Tools

Now that Flash MX has the capability to import video natively, having a third-party tool isn't quite as critical as it was before. But here are a couple of alternative tools:

- **Flix (`www.wildform.com`)** lets you encode a video file (ASF, AVI, MP3, MOV/QT, MPEG, WAV, WMA, WMV) into a SWF. This allows your viewers to see video without a media player; all they need is the Flash plug-in. Customizable presets for different bandwidths let you control your viewers' experience.

- **Turbine Video Encoder (`www.blue-pac.com`)** lets you create low-bit-rate streaming video for use in Flash. You can encode QuickTime, AVI, and MPEG video. Available for Windows only.

Tools to Create Screen Savers

One of the most frequently asked questions on mailing lists is how to create screen savers from Flash movies. All these packages help make screen-saver creation fast and easy:

- **Creator** (`www.flashjester.com`) can turn your projector file into a screen saver. It includes all the tools you need to create, package, and distribute screen savers in one program. It's available for Windows only, and you can download a trial version.

- **FlashForge** (`www.goldshell.com`) converts your Macromedia Flash files into a screen-saver and also offers an installer. It's available for Windows only, and you can sample it as a trial download.

- **SWF Studio** (`www.northcode.com`) creates both screen savers and standalone projectors. With the capability to play video and audio, get drive lists, read and write to the hard drive, and send emails, this is by far the most full-featured of the screen-saver packages. If only it were cross-platform; it's available for Windows only. You can sample a trial download.

- **Screenweaver v2.05** (`www.swifftools.com`) enables you to create screen savers from Flash or Director Projectors. It can also create screen savers from Astound and PowerPoint presentations. It's available for Windows only, and you can sample it as a trial download.

Other Tools

These tools don't fall into a single category; they are a collection of tools and utilities to help improve your Flash workflow:

- **Swift-Generator** (`www.swift-tools.com`) is an interesting—if not particularly easy to use—tool that allows you to manipulate the ID tags of Flash objects. You can use it to swap out text, fonts, sounds, images, and ActionScript parameters in frames and buttons. Basically, it lets you modify the parts of a movie that are already there. You can also use it to fill in Generator variables in Generator templates (Generator templates are not supported in Flash MX—to take advantage of templates, you must keep a copy of Flash 5). This one is for advanced users only.

- **Swift-MP3** (`www.swift-tools.com`) is a free utility that converts MP3 files into Flash files containing pure streaming audio data. You can use this to create your own Flash MP3 player. It's available for Windows, Linux, FreeBSD, MacOS X, and Solaris.

- **Ming** (`www.opaque.net/ming`) is a free utility used in conjunction with other programming languages (C++, Perl, PHP, and more) to produce SWF files by programming directly in another language. Ming is an output library for generating SWFs. This is for all you programmers out there who want to harness the power in Flash—but only on your own terms. It's available for Windows and UNIX.

- **ASP Flash Turbine 5.0** (`www.blue-pac.com`) enables you to create dynamic content Flash files from Active Server Page scripts. This is another one of interest for those of you who miss Generator support in Flash MX. By using common ASP scripting, any database content or XML can be included on generated Flash movies. Turbine also enables you to update your Flash movies to perform information changes with greater ease. It's available for Windows only, and you can sample it as a trial download.

- **PHP Flash Turbine** (`www.blue-pac.com`) is another Generator-like template-based solution that uses PHP rather than ASP.

- **Direct Flash Turbine** (`www.blue-pac.com`) is a template-oriented dynamic Flash processor. This software gives you easy media-integration capabilities for projects that demand fast Flash generation that will make an impact. It's available for Windows and Linux, and it also is available as a trial download.

- **Jugglor** (`www.flashjester.com`) modifies existing projector files by making the projector file full-screen. This, in turn, makes the Esc key the one used to exit the file, and it changes the icon for the file. In the final product, the right-click menu is disabled. Jugglor packages up your file again into an EXE and a DLL. It's available for Windows only, as a trial download.

- Each of the **JTools** (`www.flashjester.com`) is an executable that determines what web page to go to by reading its INI file. Each tool—JStart, JAvi, JPrintor, JSave, and JShapor—is sold separately. JTools is available for Windows only, and you can sample it as a trial download.

- **Woof** (`www.flashjester.com`) enables you to view Shockwave files in a larger scale and even open the Shockwave in the Flash Shockwave Player. It's available for Windows only, as a trial download.

Royalty-Free Sound Resources

Most Flash presentations contain at least some sound, and many have complete sound-tracks. When you need royalty-free loops, sound effects, or complete songs, these are some of the highest-quality and most reliable resources we've come across:

- **www.cssmusic.com.** Offers royalty-free loops, sound effects, and complete tracks. Includes the searchable Digital Audio WorldWide Network (DAWN) that enables you to purchase single tracks from CDs.
- **deusx.com/studio.html.** Offers some free sounds and has CDs of loops and sound effects available for purchase.
- **www.doremedia.com.** Offers a free loop of the week, sound families, songs, loops, and sound effects. Has CDs, individual songs, and loops available for purchase. Also offers custom services.
- **www.flash-sounds.com.** Is a subscription-based site that offers unlimited access to high-quality loops, chords, voices, and sound effects.
- **www.killersound.com.** Offers a royalty-free library of loops, SoundSets, and sound effects. Also offers custom audio and voiceovers.
- **www.loopfrog.com.** Offers royalty-free loops and some free sound effects.
- **www.sonicfoundry.** Created by the makers of Acid Pro, a very popular loop-based music creation package. Offers an extensive collection of loops in a wide range of genres made specifically for use with Acid Pro 3.0.
- **www.soundrangers.com.** Offers royalty-free loops, sound effects, sound packs, and CDs, as well as custom sounds.

Font Resources

Everyone is always on the lookout for that perfect font for a project. From itty-bitty screen fonts to flamboyant fonts, these sites should help you get moving:

- **www.mimiml.com.** This is a great resource for those itty-bitty screen fonts known as pixel fonts. The site has fonts that you can purchase as well as free fonts. When you need something legible at small sizes, this is the place to go. And, for Pete's sake, read the directions before you use them.
- **www.pcfonts.com and www.macfonts.com.** If you can't find something that you can use here, you're not looking hard enough. Here, you'll find links to hundreds of font sites, all rated.

- `www.chank.com`. Here's a whole collection of irreverent and funky fonts.

- `www.fontface.com`. You'll find hundreds of free fonts at this site.

3D Modeling Resources

If you're using one of the 3D modeling tools that can export in SWF format, you might find that you need complex models that were created in high-end packages such as 3ds max, LightWave, or SoftImage 3D. Fortunately, quite a few models are available for you to use on the web:

- `www.3dcafe.com/asp/meshes.asp.` Here you'll find lots of free models that you can use with Swift 3D or Vecta 3D—mostly 3ds files, with a few other formats as well.

- `http://www.virtinterior.com`. If you need models for interior design, Virtual Interiors has a nice selection of both free models and those available for purchase.

- `www.3dmodelworks.com`. This site has 3D models available for purchase.

- `www.3dlinks.com/objects_free.cfm`. Here's another good source for free models.

- `www.3dark.com`. This is a resource site for 3D modelers.

A p p e n d i x   E

What's on the CD-ROM

The accompanying CD-ROM is packed
with all sorts of exercise files and products
to help you work with this book and with
Macromedia Flash MX. The following sections contain detailed descriptions of the
CD's contents.

For more information about the use of this CD, review the ReadMe.txt file in the root directory. This file includes important disclaimer information as well as information about installation, system requirements, troubleshooting, and technical support.

 Technical Support Issues

If you have difficulties with this CD, you can access the web site at
www.newriders.com.

System Requirements

This CD-ROM was configured for use on systems running Windows NT Workstation, Windows 95, Windows 98, and Windows 2000, and for systems running on Macintoshes. Your machine will need to meet the following system requirements for this CD to operate properly:

- Memory (RAM): 32MB
- Monitor: VGA, 640 × 480 or higher, with 256 color or higher
- Storage space: 40MB
- Other: Mouse or compatible pointing device
- Optional: Internet connection and web browser

Loading the CD Files

To load the files from the CD, insert the disk into your CD-ROM drive. If autoplay is enabled on your machine, the CD-ROM setup program starts automatically the first time you insert the disk. You can copy the files to your hard drive or use them right off the disk; however, if you use them directly off the disk, you won't be able to save your changes because all the files on the CD are read-only. However, you can use File > Save As and save them to your hard drive. If you copy the files directly from the CD to your hard drive, you'll have the same "read-only" issue to deal with (at least, if you're on a Windows machine). To unlock read-only files, all you need to do is this:

- **Windows.** Right-click the file and select Properties. On the General tab, deselect Read-only under Attributes and click OK.
- **Macintosh.** If your files are locked (they shouldn't be), just select the file and press Cmd + I. If the Locked check box is selected, deselect it.

Note that this CD-ROM uses long and mixed-case filenames, requiring the use of a protected-mode CD-ROM driver.

Tip

If you have Macromedia Dreamweaver or Macromedia Dreamweaver UltraDev installed, you can copy all the files to your hard drive and unlock them all with just a couple of easy steps (you shouldn't need to do this on a Macintosh). First, copy all the example files from the CD to a directory on your hard drive. Now all you have to do is launch Dreamweaver/UltraDev, create a new site, and make the folder that you just set up your local root folder. Let Dreamweaver create a cache for you. In the Site window, select the top-level folder, right-click (Windows) or Control-click (Macintosh) it, and select Turn Off Read-Only from the Options menu.

Exercise Files

This CD contains all the files you'll need to complete the exercises in *Inside Flash MX*. These files can be found in the root directory and are arranged by chapter. The Examples folder has Chapter folders for each chapter in the book that contain both the starting Flash files, where appropriate, and the finished files for each exercise. This folder also contains any additional sound or image files that you need to complete the exercise. Several ActionScript files (.as) also are included with some of the exercises on the CD. To make it easier for you to locate those for reuse, you'll find a folder at the root level named ActionsLibrary (in particular, you'll find the WDDX Serializer/Deserializer there).

Tip

In Windows, you can easily associate your favorite text editor with .as files so that you can open the files by double-clicking them. All you need to do is this: Right-click on any .as file and select Properties from the Options menu. You'll notice a Change button to the right of Opens With. Click that and select your program from the list. Click OK.

Third-Party Programs

This CD also contains several third-party programs and demos from leading industry companies. These programs have been carefully selected to help you strengthen your professional skills in Macromedia's Flash MX.

In addition to the exercise files, the CD contains a number of third-party programs to help with your Flash projects.

Trial software includes the following items:

- **Macromedia Flash MX.** This is the standard for creating high-impact interactive vector-based web sites. Directory: Macromedia/FlashMX/.

- **Macromedia FreeHand 10.** FreeHand 10 is the perfect complement to Flash MX. Use it to storyboard or create art for your Flash movie.

- **SWfX and Swish.** These are also standalone packages. SWfX and Swish are text-animation tools for use in conjunction with Flash. Depending on the type of animation created, the SWF files that these create either can be imported directly into Flash or loaded as external movies.

- **Sonic Foundry ACID Pro 3 and Syntrillium Cool Edit Pro.** Sound is half the fun. These two packages are in widespread use and are easy and effective to use. We use both at Fig Leaf.

- **Toon Boom Studio.** If you're working with animation, particularly character animation, you really should give Toon Boom Studio a try. Toon Boom lets you animate two-dimensional characters in three-dimensional space. You have the option to control camera angles and lighting.

- **EditPlus 2.** The ActionScript panel is much improved in Flash MX, but for editing external .as files, you'll probably find it more convenient to use an external editor. We use EditPlus 2 at Fig Leaf.

- **Loopfrog.** Here, you'll get royalty-free sound files.

For trial software not available on the CD, check Appendix D, "Flash Resources," for links on the web where you can download trial samples.

Read This Before Opening the Software

By opening the CD package, you agree to be bound by the following agreement:

You may not copy or redistribute the entire CD-ROM as a whole. Copying and redistribution of individual software programs on the CD-ROM is governed by terms set by individual copyright holders.

The installer, code, images, and actions from the author(s) are copyrighted by the publisher and the authors.

This software is sold as is, without warranty of any kind, either expressed or implied, including, but not limited to, the implied warranties of merchantability and fitness for a particular purpose. Neither the publisher nor its dealers or distributors assumes any liability for any alleged or actual damages arising from the use of this program. (Some states do not allow for the exclusion of implied warranties, so the exclusion might not apply to you.)

Index

X-Z

VOICES THAT MATTER

HOW TO CONTACT US

VISIT OUR WEB SITE

WWW.NEWRIDERS.COM

On our web site, you'll find information about our other books, authors, tables of contents, and book errata. You will also find information about book registration and how to purchase our books, both domestically and internationally.

EMAIL US

Contact us at: **nrfeedback@newriders.com**

- If you have comments or questions about this book
- To report errors that you have found in this book
- If you have a book proposal to submit or are interested in writing for New Riders
- If you are an expert in a computer topic or technology and are interested in being a technical editor who reviews manuscripts for technical accuracy

Contact us at: **nreducation@newriders.com**

- If you are an instructor from an educational institution who wants to preview New Riders books for classroom use. Email should include your name, title, school, department, address, phone number, office days/hours, text in use, and enrollment, along with your request for desk/examination copies and/or additional information.

Contact us at: **nrmedia@newriders.com**

- If you are a member of the media who is interested in reviewing copies of New Riders books. Send your name, mailing address, and email address, along with the name of the publication or web site you work for.

BULK PURCHASES/CORPORATE SALES

The publisher offers discounts on this book when ordered in quantity for bulk purchases and special sales. For sales within the U.S., please contact: Corporate and Government Sales (800) 382-3419 or **corpsales@pearsontechgroup.com**. Outside of the U.S., please contact: International Sales (317) 581-3793 or **international@pearsontechgroup.com**.

WRITE TO US

New Riders Publishing
201 W. 103rd St.
Indianapolis, IN 46290-1097

CALL/FAX US

Toll-free (800) 571-5840
If outside U.S. (317) 581-3500
Ask for New Riders
FAX: (317) 581-4663

New Riders

Solutions from experts you know and trust.

www.informit.com

OPERATING SYSTEMS

WEB DEVELOPMENT

PROGRAMMING

NETWORKING

CERTIFICATION

AND MORE...

Expert Access.
Free Content.

New Riders has partnered with **InformIT.com** to bring technical information to your desktop. Drawing on New Riders authors and reviewers to provide additional information on topics you're interested in, **InformIT.com** has free, in-depth information you won't find anywhere else.

- **Master the skills you need, when you need them**

- **Call on resources from some of the best minds in the industry**

- **Get answers when you need them, using InformIT's comprehensive library or live experts online**

- **Go above and beyond what you find in New Riders books, extending your knowledge**

As an **InformIT** partner, **New Riders** has shared the wisdom and knowledge of our authors with you online. Visit **InformIT.com** to see what you're missing.

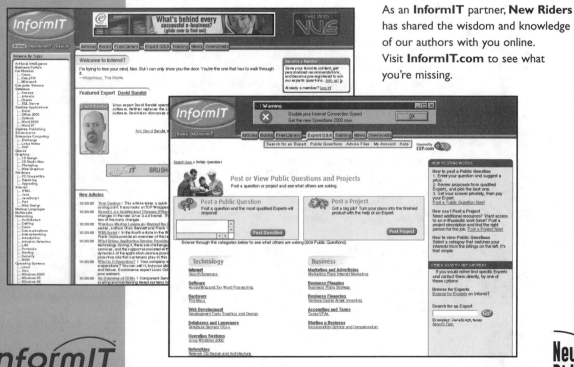

www.informit.com ▪ www.newriders.com

MACROMEDIA*

FLASH™ MX

**Flash Deconstruction:
The Process, Design, and
ActionScript of Juxt
Interactive**
Todd Purgason, Phil Scott
Bonnie Blake, Brian Drake
$45.00, 0735711496

**Flash ActionScript for
Designers: Drag, Slide, Fade**
Brendan Dawes
$45.00, 0735710473

Flash MX Magic
Matthew David, et al.
$45.00, 0735711607

Inside Flash MX
Jody Keating,
Fig Leaf Software
$49.99, 0735712549

**Object-Oriented
Programming
with ActionScript**
Branden Hall, Samuel Wan
$39.99, 0735711834

**Flash Enabled: Flash Design
and Development for Devices**
Phillip Torrone, Branden Hall,
Glenn Thomas, Mike Chambers,
et al.
$49.99, 0735711771

**Flash to the Core:
An Interactive Sketchbook
by Joshua Davis**
Joshua Davis
$45.00, 0735712883

**Skip Intro: Flash Usability &
Interface Design**
Duncan McAlester,
Michelangelo Capraro
$45.00, 073571178X

Flash MX Audio Magic
Brad Kozak, Eric Dolecki,
Craig Swann, Manuel Clement
$39.99, 0735711941

ActionScripting in Flash MX
Phillip Kerman
$39.99, 0735712956

**Flash MX Application Design
and Development**
Jessica Speigel
$45.00, 0735712425

The Flash Animator
Sandro Corsaro
$49.99, 0735712824

The Flash MX Project
Cheryl Brumbaugh-Duncan
$35.00, 0735712832

New
Riders

VOICES
THAT MATTER™

VIEW CART

search ⊙

‣ Registration already a member? Log in. ‣ Book Registration

Publishing
the Voices
that Matter

OUR AUTHORS

PRESS ROOM

| web development | design | photoshop | new media | 3-D | server technologies |

EDUCATORS

ABOUT US

CONTACT US

You already know that New Riders brings you the **Voices That Matter**.

But what does that mean? It means that New Riders brings you the

Voices that challenge your assumptions, take your talents to the next

level, or simply help you better understand the complex technical world

we're all navigating.

Visit **www.newriders.com** to find:

- ▶ *Discounts* on specific book purchases
- ▶ Never before published chapters
- ▶ Sample chapters and excerpts
- ▶ Author bios and interviews
- ▶ Contests and enter-to-wins
- ▶ Up-to-date industry event information
- ▶ Book reviews
- ▶ Special offers from our friends and partners
- ▶ Info on how to join our User Group program
- ▶ Ways to have your Voice heard

New
Riders

WWW.NEWRIDERS.COM

Colophon

Inside Flash MX was created and edited using many programs, including Macromedia Flash, Macromedia FreeHand, Adobe Photoshop, Adobe Illustrator, QuarkXPress, and Microsoft Word. The fonts used are Minion for body text, Gill Sans for headings, and MCPdigital for code. The book was printed on 50# Husky Offset Smooth paper at R.R. Donnelley & Sons in Crawfordsville, Indiana. Prepress consisted of PostScript computer-to-plate technology (filmless process). The cover was printed at Moore Langen Printing in Terre Haute, Indiana, on 12pt, coated on one side.

The *Inside Flash MX* CD

The CD that accompanies this book contains valuable resources for anyone using Macromedia Flash:

- **Project files.** All the example files provided by the authors enable you to work through the step-by-step projects.

- **Flash-related software.** Demos of Macromedia Flash MX and FreeHand 10, as well as third-party software such as SWfX, Swish, ACID Pro 3, and EditPlus2.

- **Royalty-free sounds.** Over two dozen cool, loop-ready sounds for use in your Flash creations.

- **Web resources.** An extensive list of Flash-related resources from across the web.

Accessing the Example Files from the CD

The majority of the exercises in this book use pre-built software files that contain pre-set parameters, artwork, audio, or other important information you need to work through and build the final project.

All the project files are conveniently located in the CD's Examples directory. To access the project files for Chapter 11, "Animation Techniques," for example, locate the following directory on the accompanying CD: Examples\Chapter11.

We recommend that you copy the project files to your hard drive, but this is not absolutely necessary if you don't intend to save the project files.

Note

For a complete list of the CD-ROM contents, please see Appendix E, "What's on the CD-ROM."